Carolyn A. Capallo

75-84544

646-0818

Date 1-23-80 SH

No. 09379

Price 12.80

RICHARD M. HODGETTS

Florida International University
Miami, Florida

1979

W. B. SAUNDERS COMPANY
Philadelphia   London   Toronto

SECOND EDITION

MANAGEMENT:
THEORY,
PROCESS,
AND
PRACTICE

W. B. Saunders Company: West Washington Square
Philadelphia, PA 19105

1 St. Anne's Road
Eastbourne, East Sussex BN21 3UN, England

1 Goldthorne Avenue
Toronto, M8Z 5T9, Canada

Library of Congress Cataloging in Publication Data

Hodgetts, Richard M.

Management: theory, process, and practice.

Includes bibliographies and indexes.

1. Management.   I. Title.

HD31.H556 1979   658.4   77–16976

ISBN 0–7216–4714–6

Management: Theory Process and Practice   ISBN   0-7216-4714-6

Last digit is the print number: 9   8   7   6   5   4   3   2   1

This book is dedicated to
Sally, Steven, and Jennifer.

PREFACE

Mankind's progress in this century may be characterized by technical and scientific prowess, but it is accounted for by managerial expertise. Without the ability to formulate objectives, to devise plans, and to coordinate men and materials in a synergistic fashion, Henry Ford would never have built his production line and Neil Armstrong would never have walked on the moon. In many undertakings, management, the process of getting things done through people, is the key to success or failure.

The purpose of this book is to familiarize the reader with basic modern management concepts and to acquaint him or her with the present status as well as the future of this growing field. It is assumed that the reader is either a newcomer or a practitioner with little formal training in management. As such, this book can be used effectively in the first management course in undergraduate or junior colleges. It can also be employed in professional training courses and is useful to the practicing executive who wishes to update his or her knowledge of the field.

DISTIN-GUISHING FEATURES

I have attempted to present the concepts of modern management in an interesting, easy-to-read style through the use of the following special features:

ORGANIZATION. This book is divided into three major parts. Part I covers the history of management thought and provides a basis for understanding the evolution of modern management. Part II examines modern management theory and practice, emphasizing and explaining many of the concepts important to the practicing manager. Part III reviews new developments on the management horizon, from the impact of industrial technology on people to the development of modern organization structures, and from business's social responsibility programs to the ways in which multinational corporations conduct their foreign operations.

EXHIBITS. Numerous tables, charts, and illustrations are employed in this text, both to highlight important concepts and to present them in a comprehensible manner.

HISTORICAL PICTURES AND BIOGRAPHICAL SKETCHES. In Part I, a number of important contributors to early management thought are discussed. In order to provide the reader with a better understanding of these individuals, a picture and a brief biographical sketch of many of them have been included.

SHORT CASES. Too often students learn theories without understanding their practical applications. For this reason, I have included four short cases at the end of each chapter, providing the reader with an opportunity to apply the principles, processes, and practices presented in the chapter, and thus reinforcing the major concepts introduced.

COMPREHENSIVE CASES.   There are four comprehensive cases in the book, each located at the end of a major section or part. The purpose of these cases is to provide the reader with an opportunity to integrate and apply many of the ideas contained in the preceding chapters to a realistic situation.

GLOSSARY OF TERMS.   At the end of the text the reader will find a glossary of terms that identifies or describes many of the concepts presented in the book. This glossary is more comprehensive than that contained in any other basic management text and should provide a definition or explanation of the most important topics contained herein.

SUPPLE-MENTS AND TEACHING AIDS

The following supplements and teaching aids have been designed to accompany this text:

Study Guide and Readings—contains readings, fill-in, true-false, and multiple choice questions, work projects for each chapter, and selected readings.

Teacher's Manual—contains a synopsis of the goals and material in each chapter. In addition, there are answers to the review and study questions at the end of each chapter, questions associated with the cases at the end of each chapter, and a large pool of true-false and multiple choice questions for testing purposes.

ACKNOWL-EDGMENTS

There are many individuals who have played a decisive role in helping me write this book, although I accept full responsibility for all errors of omission and commission. In particular, I would like to thank Dr. Fred Luthans, University of Nebraska, who provided me with many helpful suggestions and ideas which I have incorporated into the book. I would also like to thank those who have read, reviewed, and commented on portions of the text. In particular, Robert L. Taylor, United States Air Force Academy; W. Edward Stead, Western Illinois University; A. R. Marchione, George Mason University; Ronald G. Greenwood, University of Wisconsin at LaCrosse; Philip M. Van Auken, Western Kentucky University; Art Bethke, Northeast Louisiana University; J. T. Danak, Eastern Michigan University; Frank Engelhart, PfP Associates; Thomas J. Shelly, Community College of Philadelphia; Daniel R. Hoyt, Arkansas State University; Jesse M. Smith, Boise State University; John Cicero, Northern Virginia Community College; and James Gatza, Insurance Institute of America.

Special appreciation is expressed to my colleagues at Florida International University: Dean George Simmons of the School of Business, Dr. Steve Altman, and Dr. Karl Magnuson. I am also grateful to Dean Henry Albers of the University of Petroleum and Minerals in Dhaharan, Saudi Arabia. Sincerest thanks to Ken Atwood, Lorraine Battista, Diana Crawford, Jack Fox, Jill Goldman, Wayne Koch, George Laurie, Sharon Marshall, Jack Neifert, Tom O'Connor, Karen O'Keefe, Frank Polizzano, Evelyn Weiman, Joyce Williams, and Lonnie Zienkiewicz, all of the W. B. Saunders Company. Finally, thanks go to Ruth Chapman and Rebecca Braidman for their assistance in typing the manuscript.

RICHARD M. HODGETTS

CONTENTS

PART III: RECENT DEVELOP- MENTS IN MANAGE- MENT

PART I
THE DEVELOPMENT OF EARLY MANAGEMENT THOUGHT

The purpose of this book is to present a systematic approach to the study of modern management. There are three major parts in all. In this first part, an examination of early management thought will be undertaken for the purpose of providing the reader with the requisite background for understanding how modern management theory evolved. After all, how can one truly understand where the field of management is, or where it is going, without some knowledge of where it has been?

The initial part of Chapter 1 provides a historical view of management, beginning with the Sumerians and continuing through the Industrial Revolution. Many "modern" management principles and practices are merely different applications of the very same concepts employed by organizations in antiquity. Of course, today it is being analyzed more systematically than ever before, and there is greater emphasis on textbook education in contrast to simple trial and error. Yet, in short, management has been practiced effectively for thousands of years. The latter part of Chapter 1 provides an examination of the scientific management movement. The Industrial Revolution brought about the factory system, and with it came a tremendous interest in developing tools and techniques for increasing worker productivity. The individuals who, through the use of time and motion study, work analysis, and incentive wage payment plans, helped to attain these efficiency increases are known as scientific managers. Their basic ideas and contributions to management will also be reviewed in this chapter.

In Chapter 2 the focus is on the early management theorists and behaviorists. As worker productivity rose, organizations found they needed more managers to handle their operations. Scientific management helped to bring about an increase in the manager-worker ratio. This, in turn, led to interest in the role of the manager, eventually culminating in investigations of such questions as: What is management? What are the functions of a manager? What general administrative guidelines should an effective manager employ? The people who sought to answer these questions, and in so doing formulated the basis of modern management thought, are often known as early management theorists. Some of their major contributions are reviewed in the first part of Chapter 2. Then, in the latter part of the chapter, an examination is made of early human behavior research in the work place. The scientific managers and early management theorists were greatly interested in the management of work. It was inevitable, however, that attention would also be focused on the management of people. What are the norms and values to which workers subscribe? What makes people tick? How can this information be employed for the benefit of both workers and the organizations? Individuals who are known today as human relations researchers provided some important early insights in this entire area.

Finally, in Chapter 3, the contributions of these three groups — scientific managers, management theorists, and human relationists — to early management thought are examined in perspective. Many of these writers and researchers made valuable contributions to management. However, some of their work had very serious shortcomings. In order to evaluate their contributions and to place them in proper perspective, it is also necessary to examine their weaknesses.

Thus, the overriding goal of Part I is to familiarize the reader with some of the important management developments that occurred prior to modern times. Today the horizons of management are expanding, but virtually all of these new areas had their genesis somewhere in early management thought. To understand and appreciate recent developments in the field, a grasp of the past is necessary.

CHAPTER ONE

FROM ANTIQUITY TO INDUSTRIALISM

Management has been popularly defined as "getting things done through people," and for thousands of years this has been the key to success for individuals and civilizations alike. Effective management practices have helped to raise the United States to a position of world power in this century. Such practices have also played key roles in the success and development of giant corporations such as General Motors, American Telephone and Telegraph, and IBM. Today, as the free and communist countries seek détente, effective management will be needed to bring both sides together. Thus, whether one is examining the prerequisites for world prominence, corporate growth, or international peace, management must be considered.

GOALS OF THE CHAPTER

The concept of management is not new; it has been practiced for thousands of years. The Sumerians employed it. So, too, did the Romans and all other civilizations that ever rose to prominence and power. But one need not turn to antiquated ruins and ancient documents to verify this statement. The Roman Catholic Church has survived to this day, owing in no small part to its outstanding administrative abilities. The same can be said for many of our large businesses that have been in existence for over a century.

The primary goals of this chapter are to examine the history of management from antiquity to industrialism. In the first part of the chapter, illustrations of effective management practices in early organizations are presented. Then the focus changes to more recent times and to the emergence of the factory system and the accompanying scientific management movement. Particular attention is devoted to the work and philosophy of the scientific managers who, in large part, helped usher in the industrial era.

When you are finished reading this chapter you should be able to:

1. Discuss the management contributions of the Sumerians, Romans, and Roman Catholic Church.
2. Explain Machiavelli's four principles of leadership.
3. Relate the importance of the Industrial Revolution in the development of management thought.
4. Describe the role of scientific management in the emergence of industrialism.
5. Identify some of the key scientific managers and their contributions to the development of modern management practices.

SUMERIANS

One of the earliest civilizations known to man is that of the Sumerians, famous for their development of a written language. From 3000 B.C. onward, priests in the city of Ur kept business, legal, and historical records on clay tablets. Some of these tablets relate the management practices of Sumerian priests, the most influential class in the civilization.

One of the ways in which the priests attained their high position was by refashioning religious doctrine. For example, initially the gods demanded human sacrifice. However, over time this changed, and the priests announced to the people that the deities would also be willing to accept substitutes such as money, oxen, goats, chickens, butter, oil, and cakes. Enriched by this beneficence, the priests soon became the wealthiest and most powerful class in Sumer. They also collected taxes and managed revenues and estates, but they did not squander these riches. Instead, they wrote down all transactions so that an account of their stewardship could be made to the chief priest. In fact, it is highly likely that the Sumerians developed a written language in response to their need for a *managerial control process.* As historian Will Durant wrote: "For centuries writing was a tool of commerce, a matter of contracts and bills, of shipments and receipts; and secondarily, perhaps, it was an instrument of religious record, an attempt to preserve magic formulas, ceremonial procedures, sacred legends, prayers and hymns from alteration or decay."[1] Thus, some of the earliest writings in existence provide illustrations of managerial control, an area that is still of major concern to the modern manager.

Managerial control process was developed.

ROMANS

The Romans have also provided numerous illustrations of effective management. Perhaps the most famous is Diocletian's reorganization of the empire.

Assuming his position in A.D. 284, Diocletian soon realized that his empire was unmanageable in its present form. There were far too many people and matters of importance for the emperor to handle himself. He therefore abandoned the old organization in which the provincial governors reported directly to him and designed a new structure. First, he divided the empire into 100 provinces. Each of these was then grouped into one of 13 dioceses. In turn, the dioceses were grouped into four major geographical divisions. Three individuals were appointed to administer three of these divisions while Diocletian kept the last one for himself. By interposing two levels of management between himself and the province governors, the emperor increased his control over the empire, and the province as a unit of government was reduced in importance. Under this new organization it was extremely difficult for anyone to defy imperial authority. To further enhance his power the emperor delegated only civil governmental authority to the governors, and thus the military forces stationed in their provinces were no longer under their control. These basic concepts employed by Diocletian are still used today by organizations attempting to stabilize their centralized authority.

Empire structure was reorganized.

During the time of the Roman Empire another great organization was coming into existence. However, unlike the empire, the Roman Catholic Church has survived the test of time.

---

[1]Will Durant, *The Story of Civilization*, Part 1, *Our Oriental Heritage* (New York: Simon and Schuster, 1954), p. 131.

In terms of longevity, "the most effective formal organization in the history of Western civilization has been the Roman Catholic Church."[2] This institution has made some significant contributions to management theory in the areas of the hierarchy of authority, specialization of activities along functional lines, and the staff concept.

ROMAN CATHOLIC CHURCH

Long before the great corporations of modern times were faced with the challenge of managing their far-flung operations, the Catholic Church had solved similar problems. An organizational structure had been designed and a *scalar chain of command* established from the Pope, through the bishops, to the priests, to the laity. The Church had also employed *functionalism,* assigning certain tasks to specific individuals. For example, in distinguishing between the functions of the bishop, presbyter, and deacon in the second century, two management historians have noted that "the bishop was the pastor, the presbyters constituted his council, and the deacons had under their special supervision the care of the poor and the sick."[3]

Functionalism

Job descriptions were developed.

The use of the staff principle was also widely employed in the Catholic Church. Advisory services were performed by various individuals and committees. However, the Church also made use of what can be termed *compulsory staff service.*

Staff Principle

...Under this rule the abbot of a Benedictine monastery must consult the elder monks about him before rendering decisions, even on minor matters. On matters of more vital importance he must consult everyone, even the youngest. The subordinates are not merely free to express their opinions. These opinions must be sought and solicited. This rule in no way abridges the line authority of the abbot in making the final decision. He is simply prohibited from rendering *any* decision until the rule is complied with.[4]

In addition, the concept of *staff independence* was employed. For example, in the Jesuit order the head of the Society does not choose his own advisors, although he is required to listen to them. These advisors are chosen for him, thereby avoiding the "yes man" pitfall. Mooney and Reiley explain:

Use of advisors was encouraged.

...These councilors are chosen by the general congregation. They are not appointed by the general of the Society and they are not removable by him. They are literally imposed upon him. Here we have something more than compulsory staff service. We have another principle, if possible, even more significant—that of *staff independence.*[5]

Today, many subordinates feel that their boss does not listen to them. Others openly admit that the superior expects them to conform to the image of the organization man. Over a thousand years ago the Roman Catholic Church was developing management practices for sidestepping these very pitfalls. Simultaneously, contributions were being made by individuals.

---

[2]Harold Koontz and Cyril O'Donnell, *Management: A Systems and Contingency Analysis of Managerial Functions,* 6th edition (New York: McGraw-Hill Book Company, 1976), p. 30.
[3]James D. Mooney and Alan C. Reiley, *Onward Industry!* (New York: Harper & Brothers Publishers, 1931), p. 246.
[4]*Ibid.*, p. 266.
[5]*Ibid.*, p. 268.

One of the most important individual contributors to the development of early management thought was Niccolò Machiavelli. Born in 1469 in Florence, Machiavelli secured employment in the city-state at the age of 29, eventually serving as unofficial emissary to every important city-state in Italy as well as to several outside countries. However, in 1512 the Medici family returned to power and Machiavelli lost his job and was exiled. The remainder of his life was spent in a vain effort to be reinstated.

The Bettman Archive, Inc.

Niccolò Machiavelli

Machiavelli wrote extensively during his time in exile. Some of his best known works include *The Prince* and *The Discourses*.[6] Throughout the former work he presented several broad management principles to which he believed leaders should subscribe. First, he emphasized the importance of relying upon *mass consent*. Machiavelli felt that the prince or leader's authority emanated from the bottom. No one was a leader unless the followers agreed. Five hundred years later some management theorists would be treating this concept as newly discovered, failing to realize that Machiavelli had identified and described it long before. Second, the leader must strive for *cohesiveness* in the organization. He must reward his friends and maintain their allegiance. In addition, the people should know what they can expect of their leader and understand what he expects of them. This is essential for maintaining cohesiveness. Third, the prince must have a *will to survive* in order to remain alert and prepared. If an overthrow of his regime is attempted, he will then be in a position to respond quickly and forcefully. Machiavelli believed that in these cases the prince was justified in taking harsh steps. There need be no pretense of virtue or justice on his part. Fourth, the prince has to be a *leader*, capable of setting an example for the people. This calls for wisdom, kindness, and justice — traits which should be exercised at all times, except when his survival is placed in jeopardy.

Four principles of leadership.

Machiavelli made a systematic analysis of the prince's (manager's) job and from it derived *practical* principles that are as useful today as they were 500 years ago. No wonder a recent writer has concluded that Machiavelli's works are "bursting with urgent advice and acute observations for top management of the great private and public corporations all over the world."[7]

THE INDUSTRIAL REVOLUTION

Although early civilizations and the writings of select individuals provide illustrations of effective management practices, the technological innovations of the Industrial Revolution had a more dynamic impact on managerial thinking than anything that had occurred previously. This is

---

[6]Niccolò, Machiavelli, *The Prince* and *The Discourses* (New York: The Modern Library, Inc., 1940).
[7]Antony Jay, *Management and Machiavelli* (New York: Holt, Rinehart and Winston, Inc., 1967), p. 4.

clearly seen in Great Britain between the years 1700 and 1785, when major changes occurred in the basic organization of production. These changes, in chronological order, are commonly referred to as the domestic system, the putting-out system, and the factory system.

The *domestic system* was predominant during the early eighteenth century. A family having enough labor to provide for its own survival would begin to turn out a product for sale by specializing in some area. For example, a loom or a spinning wheel might be purchased; then the group would buy raw materials, fabricate the textiles, and sell them at the local fair for whatever they would bring. The system was very successful and remained in existence for quite some time for two basic reasons. First, it was easy to set up this kind of operation because a loom or spinning wheel was not very expensive; there was ease of entry into the field. Second, transportation systems were inefficient, and it was therefore impossible for outside competition to provide fabricated textiles to the local people. This domestic system was basically a family-operated enterprise with business being conducted at an informal, unsophisticated level. Little concern was given to the development of efficient management practices or skills.

Domestic System

Family entrepreneurship emerged.

The domestic system was doomed, however, because of its inefficiency. As one might have guessed, it was not long before enterprising individuals at these local fairs began underwriting the entire risk themselves, agreeing to take all the goods a family could manufacture at a fixed price. This transition continued further, to the point where the individuals became willing both to provide the family with the raw materials it needed and to pay them a fixed amount for each unit of output they provided. The domestic system thus came to an end and the *putting-out system* emerged. The family was no longer an entrepreneurial enterprise. Now its members who processed the material were merely workers operating on a piece-rate basis.

Putting-Out System

Workers operated on a piece-rate basis.

The new system had advantages for both sides. On the one hand, the workers no longer had to concern themselves with either the purchasing of raw materials or the selling of finished goods. On the other hand, the dealer who was trying to fill orders from many buyers was able to insure himself of many supply sources. In addition, there was an impetus toward the development of faster and more efficient production tools for insuring that the orders would be filled on time. One result was the invention of the spinning jenny; another was the power loom. Such technological innovations heralded the advent of power-driven machinery.

The invention of power-driven machinery drastically revised the entire production process. Unlike the spinning wheel, this new machinery was far too expensive for the average worker to purchase; capital costs and capital requirements were beyond his means. As a result, the *factory system* came into existence. Machines were placed under one roof and the employees now came to a central location to work. The putting-out system was dead.

Factory System

Management in the factory system was characterized by strict control of operations. The owners of the enterprises were most concerned with making the greatest possible profit from their investment. There was,

Management now controlled all operations.

therefore, a great deal of interest focused on streamlining operations, eliminating waste, and motivating (in the form of money) workers to increase their output. These developments led to the emergence of the scientific management movement.

THE SCIENTIFIC MANAGEMENT MOVEMENT

The factory system caused management to focus on developing the most scientific, rational principles for handling its men, machines, materials, and money. This challenge took two major forms: (a) how to increase productivity (output/input) by making the work easier to perform; and (b) how to motivate the workers to take advantage of these new methods and techniques. The individuals who developed approaches for meeting these challenges helped lay the foundation for what is known today as *scientific management*. Two of the earliest scientific managers were Matthew Boulton and James Watt.

The Boulton and Watt Foundry

Forecasts were conducted.

Time-and-motion study was employed.

In 1800 Boulton and Watt were in the process of building a new factory for manufacturing steam engines. Using a highly scientific approach, they first made a systematic analysis of demand for such engines. Then, based on their estimates, they finalized plans for their new factory. In this new building, operations were designed and laid out according to the flow of work. In addition, the speeds of each machine were studied in an attempt to determine the expected output. This was broken down further into a series of minor operations so that each worker's job could be systematically analyzed. These were the rudiments of modern time-and-motion study at Boulton and Watt's Soho factory.

Work standards were established.

Third, wage payment systems were devised for each job. A piece-rate approach was used on those tasks that were standardized and could be easily classified into groups. Then a standard or expected output was determined for each job. Anyone who produced more than the standard received a bonus for this production. Workers who did not have jobs that permitted a piece-rate payment plan were hired for a weekly wage. However, interestingly enough, Boulton & Watt paid the foreman of these workers on a piece-rate basis, the logic being that he should encourage his work group to increase its output. These payment plans, especially the piece-rate ones, were worked out in such great detail that one management historian has reported:

> With many piece rates at Soho it was found that the time it took to make different-size items varied more nearly in proportion to the diameter of the part than to any other factor. A formula was therefore developed to express this relationship and was used for setting standards and piece rates—an example of management's use of standard data a century ahead of other firms. Soho managers, however, took great pains to make the system simple and easily understood by the workers. In all, three wage scales were used: (1) a flat piece rate for each article, (2) a piece rate varying according to size or diameter, and (3) a piece rate varying with the horsepower of the engine for fitting working gears.[8]

Cost accounting was used.

Fourth, the company employed an elaborately detailed accounting system. Raw material costs, labor charges, and finished goods inventory were all recorded. In addition, indirect costs were kept. With these records

---

[8]Claude S. George, Jr., *The History of Management Thought*, 2nd edition (Englewood Cliffs, N.J.: Prentice-Hall, Inc., 1972), p. 61.

the management was able to pinpoint inefficiencies and waste, ascertain productivity changes and job costs, and determine new wage scales based on the results.

This scientific approach to the management of men and machines eventually spread to the United States. The individuals who made scientific management a household word in America were, for the most part, trained mechanical engineers. Their major emphasis was on the management of *work* and, to a large degree, the worker was seen as a mere adjunct of the machines. The most famous scientific manager in America was Frederick Winslow Taylor.

Frederick W. Taylor, often referred to as the Father of Scientific Management, is the best known of all the scientific managers. Born in Germantown, Pennsylvania, in 1856, many of his early years were spent attending school in Germany and France and traveling on the European continent. In 1872 he enrolled in Phillips Exeter Academy to prepare for Harvard College. However, although he passed the entrance exams with honors, poor eyesight prevented him from attending that institution. In late 1874 he entered the pattern making and machinist trades, finding work in a small company owned by family friends.

Historical Picture Service, Chicago

Frederick W. Taylor

In 1878, with employment in the machinist trade difficult to obtain, Taylor went to work at the Midvale Steel Company as a laborer. Within eight years, he rose from ordinary laborer to timekeeper and then on to machinist, gang boss, foreman, assistant engineer, and, finally, chief engineer of the works. Meanwhile, continuing his education through correspondence courses and home study, he managed to complete all requirements for a mechanical engineering degree at Stevens Institute.[9]

Work standards were determined via time-and-motion study.

Taylor's success at Midvale must be attributed in large part to his production record; he knew how to get the work out. Initially, however, as gang boss he encountered stiff opposition from the men because he used pressure to achieve this increased output. He then realized that such pressure could be eliminated if management would determine what a proper day's work was for every position in the shop. Lacking such information, management relied upon past performance; the men, realizing this, deliberately kept output low. Such "systematic soldiering" on their part was recognized by Taylor. When he became foreman he attempted to eliminate as much of it as possible by determining exactly how much could be done by each man in the shop. He started his systematic study in the area of lathe operations. Employing time-and-motion study, he attempted to identify the specific tasks involved in this work and to calculate the time required to complete each one. Such time-and-motion experimentation was to be characteristic of his work from this point on,

---

[9]Frederick Winslow Taylor, *Scientific Management* (New York: Harper & Brothers Publishers, 1911), p. ix (Foreword by Harlow S. Person).

although his most famous experiments were later conducted at Bethlehem Steel.

BETHLEHEM STEEL EXPERIMENTS.   In 1898 Taylor went to work for the Bethlehem Steel Company. While there, he conducted important studies in the areas of pig iron handling, shoveling, and metal cutting.

The first of these experiments, *pig iron handling,* involved a group of about 75 men who were loading ingots (or "pigs") of iron into an open railroad car. Their job entailed picking up the pig of iron, which weighed about 92 pounds, carrying it up an inclined plane, and dropping it into the railroad car. When Taylor arrived at Bethlehem Steel, each man was loading an average of 12½ long tons[10] a day. Taylor decided to experiment with the job to see if he could increase the output. His research showed that a worker ought to be able to load 47 long tons a day, working 42 per cent of the time and "free of load" for the other 58 per cent. In order to test the validity of his theory, Taylor chose one of the workers, to whom he gave the pseudonym Schmidt, and began supervising the man very closely. He was told when and how to work. This basic task concept was explained by Taylor himself:

Work instructions were provided.

> Perhaps the most prominent single element in modern scientific management is the task idea. The work of every workman is fully planned out by the management at least one day in advance, and each man receives in most cases complete written instructions, describing in detail the task which he is to accomplish, as well as the means to be used in doing the work. And the work planned in advance in this way constitutes a task which is to be solved . . . not by the workman alone, but in almost all cases by the joint effort of the workman and the management. This task specifies not only what is to be done but how it is to be done and the exact time allowed for doing it.[11]

By early evening of the first day, Schmidt had loaded 47½ long tons. Other men in the group were then gradually trained to load this amount.

The second of Taylor's Bethlehem Steel experiments was concerned with the *shoveling of iron ore and rice coal.* When Taylor arrived, each of the workers was bringing his own shovel. When they shoveled iron ore, the weight per scoop would be very great, for the ore was quite heavy. Conversely, when they shoveled rice coal, the weight per scoop would not be very great, for the coal was quite light. Taylor's experiments indicated that an average scoop load of 21 pounds would result in maximum output. Thus, for heavy coal there should be a shovel with a small scoop, whereas for light coal the shovel should have a large scoop. In order to implement this approach, Taylor did away with everyone's bringing his own shovel. Instead, the company built a tool room to stock shovels, all designed to carry

Work tools were provided.

a 21-pound load, for handling various types of material. The results of Taylor's study are presented in Table 1–1. He estimated the first year's saving with the new plan to be over $36,000, and during the next six months, when all the yard was on task work, the annual saving was estimated at $75,000 to $80,000.

---

[10] A long ton weighs 2240 pounds.
[11] Taylor, *op. cit., Principles of Scientific Management,* p. 39.

TABLE 1–1   Results of Shoveling Experiments

	Old Plan	New Plan Task Work
The number of yard laborers was reduced from between	400 and 600	140
Average number of tons per man per day	16	59
Average earnings per man per day	$1.15	$1.88
Average cost of handling a ton of 2240 pounds	$0.072	$0.033

Source: Frederick Winslow Taylor, *Principles of Scientific Management* (New York: Harper & Brothers Publishers, 1911), p. 71.

The third area in which Taylor conducted experiments at Bethlehem Steel was that of *metal-cutting*. Actually, this was a continuation of work he had begun at Midvale. Through these experiments, Taylor gathered a wealth of data about the proper speeds and feeds needed for various machines. One of the results was a patent for high-speed steel, with which machine shops were able to decrease the average cutting time to one third of what it had formerly been. The patent proved so valuable that Taylor and his partner sold the rights for its use in England for $100,000.

TAYLOR'S WRITINGS AND PHILOSOPHY.   In 1885 Taylor joined the American Society of Mechanical Engineers (ASME) and presented two papers before the membership. The first, presented in 1895, was entitled "A Piece Rate System." In this paper, Taylor expressed concern over some of the current incentive payment schemes being used in industry. As an alternative, Taylor recommended a *differential piece-rate system*. For each job in which it was to be employed, a time-and-motion study was first conducted. On the basis of the results, a standard (a fair day's work) would be ascertained. If the worker produced less than standard, he would receive a certain price for each piece produced. If standard were reached or surpassed, a higher per unit piece-rate would be paid. For example, if standard were 100 pieces a day, with the low rate being 1.1¢ per piece and the high rate being 1.8¢ per piece, an individual producing 90 pieces would receive 99¢, whereas a person turning out 102 pieces would receive $1.84.

> Salary was tied to output.

One of the bases of this plan was Taylor's belief that the workmen in nearly every trade could (and would) materially increase their present output if they were assured of a greater permanent return for their time. Yet although Taylor placed great importance on the value of money, he also stressed the need for a systematic approach on the part of management in conducting its business. This idea went unnoticed by his followers, who devoted their attention to the mechanics of his payment plan.

In 1903 Taylor presented a second paper, entitled "Shop Management." This time, emphasis was on his *philosophy of management*. Taylor pointed out the need to provide high wages and attain low per unit production costs. This, he felt, entailed the scientific selection and training of workers coupled with management-employee cooperation. As before, his managerial philosophy was not understood.

Once again, in 1911, he put forth his ideas, this time in a book entitled *Principles of Scientific Management*. In this book Taylor outlined four principles, the scope of which was greater than time-and-motion study. They represented a combination of mechanical, conceptual, and philosophical ideas:

First.   Develop a science for each element of a man's work, which replaces the old rule-of-thumb method.
Second.   Scientifically select and then train, teach, and develop the workman, whereas in the past he chose his own work and trained himself as best he could.
Third.   Heartily cooperate with the men so as to insure all of the work being done in accordance with the principles of the science which has been developed.
Fourth.   There is an almost equal division of the work and the responsibility between the management and the workmen. The management take over all work for which they are better fitted than the workmen, while in the past almost all of the work and the greater part of the responsibility were thrown upon the men.[12]

Although his papers and writings brought him acclaim, Taylor's fame and his title Father of Scientific Management were probably accounted for more by the publicity he received at a House Congressional hearing in 1912 than by anything he had previously done. Speaking before the United States committee that was investigating systems of shop management, he related what he felt scientific management was *not*, as well as what it was.

Scientific management is not an efficiency device, not a device of any kind for securing efficiency; nor is it a bunch or group of efficiency devices. It is not a new system of figuring costs; it is not a new scheme of paying men; it is not a piecework system; it is not a bonus system; it is not a premium system; . . . .
Now, in its essence, scientific management involved a complete mental revolution on the part of the working man engaged in a particular establishment or industry — a complete mental revolution on the part of these men as to their duties toward their work, toward their fellow men, and toward their employers. And it involves the equally complete mental revolution on the part of those on the management's side — the foremen, the superintendent, the owner of the business, the board of directors — a complete revolution on their part as to their duties toward their fellow workers in the management, toward their workmen, and toward all of their daily problems. And without this complete mental revolution on both sides scientific management does not exist.[13]

His fame spread as a result of these hearings. Scientific management and Frederick Taylor become synonymous terms. In some quarters, the system of shop management that he advocated became known as the Taylor system. However, as he stated in his testimony before the House, he was only one of many people instrumental in developing this system. Another, to whom he gave specific credit, was Frank Gilbreth.

Frank Gilbreth

Frank Gilbreth, born in 1868, passed the entrance exams for the Massachusetts Institute of Technology, but decided instead to go into the contracting business. Beginning as an apprentice bricklayer, his attention was quickly aroused by the different sets of motions that were used in training bricklayers. First, the man was taught how to lay bricks; then he was taught how to work at a slow pace; finally, he was trained to work at a fast pace. Gilbreth wondered which of these three sets of motions was best.

---

[12]*Ibid.*, pp. 36–37.
[13]*Ibid.*, Taylor's Testimony Before the Special House Committee, pp. 26–27.

As a result, Gilbreth began studying the motions used by bricklayers. Were there any extraneous motions that could be eliminated, thereby reducing the time and effort necessary to lay bricks? After much experimentation, he was able to reduce the number of hand motions required to lay exterior brick from 18 to 4½ and interior brick from 18 to 2. He also developed an adjustable stand to eliminate the need for stooping to pick up the bricks. Likewise, mortar of proper consistency was used to eliminate "tapping." Thus, he was able to increase the number of bricks a man could lay in an hour from 120 to 350.

The Gilbreths

Bricklaying techniques were developed.

In 1904 Gilbreth married Lillian Moller. With her background in management and psychology, the two combined their talents for the purpose of developing better work methods. One of their most famous techniques was the use of motion pictures. By filming the individual at work and then playing back the film, they could analyze the person's motions and determine which, if any, were extraneous. Since the cameras in those days were hand cranked, Gilbreth invented the microchronometer, a clock with a large sweeping hand that records time to 1/2000 of a minute, and placed it in the field of work being filmed. (Today, unless the camera contains constant-speed electric motors, the microchronometer is still used in photographing time-and-motion patterns.) In this way, he could analyze the individual's motions while determining precisely how long the work took. In addition, the Gilbreths went so far as to categorize all hand motions into 17 basic motions such as "grasp," "hold," and "position," which they called therbligs, Gilbreth spelled backwards with the "t" and "h" transposed. Having made such monumental contributions to the area, it is no wonder that Frank Gilbreth is known as the Father of Motion Study.

Standard hand motions were categorized.

Another famous scientific manager of this period was Henry L. Gantt. Both a contemporary and protégé of Frederick Taylor, Gantt worked with Taylor at the Midvale Steel Company in 1887 and was impressed with his concepts. Gantt, however, had a far better understanding of the human element in the work environment than did his teacher. This is seen in the task-and-bonus system that he developed. In contrast with Taylor's differential piece-rate plan, Gantt's system guaranteed each worker a day's wage. In addition, if the man accomplished the task assigned to him for that day, he received a bonus. Like Taylor, Gantt was also aware of the need for instruction of the workers by management. In a paper presented to the ASME in 1908, "Training Workmen in Habits of Industry and Cooperation," he put forth these ideas, but he was ahead of his time. It was to be years before management agreed that training workers was one of its responsibilities.

Historical Picture Service, Chicago

Henry L. Gantt

The contribution for which Gantt is most famous is the Gantt chart, developed in 1917, which will be examined in Chapter 7. Along the horizontal axis time, work scheduled and work completed are measured. The vertical axis identifies the individuals and machines assigned to these work schedules. Simple in nature, the chart provides an effective planning and control technique. By the late 1950's the concept was being employed by the United States Navy in its Polaris Missile Project. Although the Navy's application involved much greater sophistication than did the original chart designed by Gantt, the basic concept was the same in that it stressed efficiency, a topic made famous by another early scientific manager, Harrington Emerson.

The Gantt chart is a planning and controlling tool.

From *Human Life*, April 1911

Harrington Emerson

Harrington Emerson is best known for his appearance before the Interstate Commerce Commission in 1910. The railroads wanted a rate increase, while shippers opposed it. Speaking on the shippers' behalf, Emerson told the committee that if the railroads would adopt scientific management principles, they could save one million dollars a day! His major concepts were set forth in his book The Twelve Principles of Efficiency.[14]

Emerson's principles were the following:

Twelve principles of efficiency.

1. Clearly Defined Ideals.   By this Emerson meant that the organization should formulate objectives and familiarize everyone in the company with them.
2. Common Sense.   In employing common sense, the manager should adhere to ideals, survey problems at a distance so they can be seen in their entirety, and seek good advice.
3. Competent Counsel.   The manager should look for qualified counsel whenever and wherever it can be found. Of course, it will not all come from one man. However, by obtaining the best from each person, competent counsel, on a collective basis, can be obtained.
4. Discipline.   There must be strict adherence to rules. In Emerson's view, discipline brings about allegiance to the other eleven principles.
5. Fair Deal.   In essence, this requires three managerial qualities: sympathy, imagination, and, most of all, justice.
6. Reliable, Immediate, Adequate, and Permanent Records.   Records provide a basis upon which intelligent decisions can be made. Unfortunately, too many companies keep poor records for cost control while accumulating other reports that are of no value.
7. Despatching.   By this term Emerson meant that organizations should formulate effective production scheduling and control techniques.
8. Standards and Schedules.   There must be a method and a time schedule for performing tasks. This can be accomplished through the use of time-and-motion studies, the establishment of work standards, and the proper placement of each worker on the job.

[14]Harrington Emerson, *The Twelve Principles of Efficiency* (New York: The Engineering Magazine Company, 1924).

9. Standardized Conditions.   A standardization of conditions will reduce waste by conserving both effort and money. This standardization can be applied to both individuals and the work environment.
10. Standardized Operations.   A standardization of operations, whenever and wherever possible, will greatly enhance efficiency.
11. Written Standard-Practice Instructions.   Written, standardized instructions that are continually updated can result in rapid progress toward the objective.
12. Efficiency Reward.   Efficiency should be rewarded. Emerson noted that "Efficiency constitutes 9 out of the 18 elements of cost-efficiency of quality and quantity and overhead for materials, for labor and for fixed charges. It has been found exceedingly satisfactory and convenient to base efficiency rewards on the cost of efficiencies, the method being so flexible as to be applicable to an individual operation of a few minutes' duration, or to all the work of a man for a long period, or to all the work of department or plan."[15]

As a result of his work, Emerson became known as the High Priest of Efficiency. In placing him in historical perspective, one historian has credited him with "codifying a set of principles to guide management, and this attempt, along with the soundness of his principles, served to reemphasize the growing awareness of the distinct nature and universality of management."[16]

SUMMARY

Management is not a new concept. It has been employed for thousands of years, as seen in the practices of the Sumerians, Romans, and Roman Catholic Church, as well as in the writings of Machiavelli. However, the emergence of the factory system presented management with a new challenge. It now became necessary to develop rational, scientific principles for handling men, materials, money, and machinery. The scientific managers played a major role in helping attain this objective.

The primary goal of these managers was that of achieving the highest productivity possible by devising efficient work methods and encouraging employees to take advantage of these new techniques. Early illustrations of this scientific approach can be found in Boulton and Watt's Soho factory. Operations were designed and laid out according to work flow; wage payment systems were created for each job; and an elaborately detailed accounting system was employed for keeping track of raw materials costs, labor charges, and finished goods inventory.

In America, scientific management was made famous by people such as Frederick Taylor. His experiments at Bethlehem Steel illustrated the importance of time-and-motion study, while his differential piece-rate system provides insight into the types of wage incentive payment plans used during this period. Other important scientific managers of the day included Frank Gilbreth, world renowned for his work in time-and-motion study; Henry Gantt, famous for the chart he developed; and Harrington Emerson, best known for his work in the area of efficiency.

When one steps back and examines the work of the scientific managers in America, it becomes evident that they were most concerned with the *management of work*. Their emphasis was on the lower levels of the organizational hierarchy and dealt with increasing the worker's daily output. Gradually, however, interest developed in two other directions: (a) management at the middle and upper levels of the organizational hierarchy, and (b) the role and importance of organizational behavior.

---

[15]*Ibid.*, p. 365.
[16]George, *op. cit.*, p. 109.

The two groups that led the way in these areas will be the focus of attention in the next chapter.

---

1. What contributions did the Sumerians make to early management thought? Put them in your own words.

2. How did Diocletian reorganize the Roman Empire? Be specific.

3. What were some of the contributions made by the Roman Catholic Church that merit a place for it in the annals of management history?

4. Identify and describe the four broad principles to which Machiavelli felt all leaders should subscribe.

5. What was the domestic system? Putting-out system? Factory system? Explain.

6. Boulton and Watt's Soho Foundry provides an excellent illustration of the scientific approach to management. Explain this statement.

7. Why is Frederick Taylor known as the Father of Scientific Management?

8. What were Taylor's principles of scientific management?

9. Why is Frank Gilbreth known as the Father of Motion Study?

10. Henry Gantt was a humanistic-scientific manager. Explain this statement.

11. What was Harrington Emerson's contribution to management? Explain.

12. What contribution did the scientific managers make to management thought?

**SELECTED
REFERENCES**

Cook-Taylor, R. W. *Introduction to a History of the Factory System.* London: Richard Bentley and Sons, 1886.

Emerson, H. *The Twelve Principles of Efficiency.* New York: The Engineering Magazine Company, 1924.

Gantt, H. L. *Work, Wages, and Profits.* New York: The Engineering Magazine Company, 1910.

George, C. S., Jr. *The History of Management Thought.* 2nd edition. Englewood Cliffs, N.J.: Prentice-Hall, Inc., 1972.

Gilbreth, F. B. *Bricklaying System.* New York: The Myron C. Clark Publishing Company, 1909.

Gilbreth, F. B. *Motion Study.* New York: D. Van Nostrand Company, Inc., 1911.

Gilbreth, L. M. *The Psychology of Management.* New York: Sturgis and Walton Company, 1914.

Jay, A. *Management and Machiavelli.* New York: Holt, Rinehart and Winston, Inc., 1967.

Kakar, S. *Frederick Taylor: A Study in Personality and Innovation.* Cambridge, Mass.: MIT Press, 1971.

Machiavelli, N. *The Prince* and *The Discourses.* New York: The Modern Library Inc., 1940.

Mooney, J. D., and A. C. Reiley. *Onward Industry!* New York: Harper & Brothers, Publishers, 1931.

Sterba, R. L. A. "The Organization and Management of the Temple Corporations in Ancient Mesopotamia." *Academy of Management Review,* July 1976, pp. 16–26.

Taylor, F. W. *Scientific Management.* New York: Harper & Brothers, Publishers, 1911.

Wrege, C. D., and A. G. Perroni. "Taylor's Pig-Tale: A Historical Analysis of Frederick W. Taylor's Pig-Iron Experiments." *Academy of Management Journal.* March 1974, pp. 6–27.

Wren, D. A. *The Evolution of Management Thought,* 2nd edition. New York: The Ronald Press Company, 1979.

Wright, C. D. *Report on the Factory System of the United States.* Washington, D.C.: Government Printing Office, 1884.

CASE: A GIANT EDIFICE

The Egyptians built numerous funerary edifices, the most famous of which is the Great Pyramid. The dimensions of the tomb provide some indication of their engineering abilities. Almost perfectly square, the pyramid, when intact, covered an area slightly over 13 acres and was approximately 147 meters high. The sides rose at an angle of 51°52' and were accurately oriented to the four cardinal points. In all, approximately 2,300,000 blocks, each weighing an average of 2.5 tons, were used in the structure. Modern engineers have calculated that the inside of the pyramid is so vast that the Cathedral of Florence, the Cathedral of Milan, St. Paul's in London, Westminster Abbey, and St. Peter's in Rome could all be grouped within it.

The physical dimensions of the structure, however, should not be allowed to overshadow the managerial skill that was required to build it. Stones had to be cut at the quarries, transported down river, removed from the raft, carried to the construction site, and then put in place. In addition, Herodotus, the Greek historian, reports that it took the Egyptians ten years to build the road from the river to the construction site and twenty years to actually erect the edifice using a work force of 100,000 men.

Questions

1. How much management expertise would the Egyptians have needed in building this pyramid? Defend your answer.

2. Do modern construction firms use the same basic management concepts in building skyscrapers as the Egyptians used in erecting the Great Pyramid? Explain.

3. Could modern construction firms build the Great Pyramid with less men in a shorter span of time than the Egyptians did? Why or why not? What does your answer reveal about modern management methods?

CASE: WHITE COLLAR OUTPUT[17]

Quite a lot has been written about increasing productivity among blue collar workers. However, there is currently a push to improve the efficiency of white collar workers as well, and there may be a need for it. William G. O'Brien, president of Science Management Corporation, a consulting firm that specializes in work-measurement programs, certainly seems to think so. According to him, manpower utilization in most offices rarely exceeds 60 per cent. As a result, as much as $800 million a day is lost to the United States economy, half of this resulting from inefficiency in white collar and service jobs. Mr. O'Brien attempts to recoup part of these losses for companies through the use of work measurement.

[17]The data in this case can be found in James C. Hyatt, "Productivity Push," *Wall Street Journal,* April 25, 1972, pp. 1, 30.

While "work measurement" suggests platoons of stern-faced engineers standing around with stopwatches in hand, Science Management officials say such tactics aren't necessary. The firm's staff does observe the work flow but relies mainly on massive tables prepared over the years to calculate "target times" for performing clerical jobs. These studies cover everything from the time it takes to prepare a first-class mailing label (24 seconds) or make a phone call (slightly over 24 seconds to notify someone that a duplicating order is ready) to the time required for a telephone-company draftsman to draw up a street conduit system 1,220 feet long (one hour).

With such figures in hand, the firm's staff determines the amount of work to be done and the amount of time needed to do it.

Many companies in the white collar and service fields who have tried work measurement say that employees respond favorably to the system because it lets them know what is expected of them.

Questions

1. Is scientific management as applicable to white collar jobs as it is to blue collar jobs? Explain.

2. Is Mr. O'Brien a scientific manager? In what way is his approach similar to that of the scientific managers? How does it differ? Explain.

3. Why would employees favor work measurement? Why would they oppose it? Explain.

CASE: FIGHTING THE "BLAHS"[18]

In the early hours of the morning, giant presses set up a deafening roar as they print *The New York Times.* However, thanks to Muzak, Inc., a division of the TelePrompter Corporation, a number of the pressmen are completely oblivious to the noise. This is because they are wearing plastic earmuffs wired for sound that allow them to go about their work while listening to old and new tunes, including *Stranger in Paradise, The Magnificent Seven,* and many other hits.

Muzak's studies indicate that worker productivity usually reaches its low point in midmorning and midafternoon and picks up just before people go to lunch or leave for the day. To boost productivity when the "blahs" set in, Muzak pipes in music. Is this approach really beneficial to productivity? "Bing" Muscio, president of Muzak, seems to think so. He claims that music has definite physiological and psychological effects on people. "It affects," he said, "the heartbeat and blood pressure, and moderates tenseness and anxiety." And an AT&T division manager agrees, pointing out that telephone operators report they are more relaxed with music by Muzak than they were prior to its installation. There are many other companies using Muzak's services, including Black & Decker and American Machine & Foundry Inc., that support these findings. However, the company does not confine its

---

[18]The data in this case can be found in "Muzak's Earmuffs For Noisy Jobs," *Business Week,* January 13, 1973, p. 62c.

services exclusively to business; Muzak speakers are even installed in the White House.

Questions

1. Is not music by Muzak another variation of scientific management, i.e., a change in some environmental condition designed to bring about increased productivity? Explain.

2. Can music actually cause greater work efficiency? Give your reasoning.

3. How could this approach be made more "scientific"?

CASE: SAME OLD STUFF

As part of honors convocation week, Bill Whitling, vice president of a large computer firm, had been asked to talk to a group of graduating seniors in the College of Business at State University. Bill was delighted to do so. He decided to speak about the dynamic environment in which his firm operated and the challenges facing the managers. At one point in his talk, he said:

Today, our management people are being confronted with new problems and we have to come up with brand new solutions. Managers in our company find that while a business education is helpful, there's a tremendous adjustment that has to be made in moving from the halls of academia to those of industry. Quite frankly, we've never before faced a similar situation; the challenges and problems are brand new.

During the question and answer session that followed, one student asked Bill, "Aren't the basic problems confronting the modern manager the same ones that his counterpart in antiquity had to face? The way I see it, whether we're building the Great Pyramid or the Hoover Dam, the management problems are virtually the same. Oh sure, the problems or issues may be more complex, but our forebears in the Roman Empire or some other early civilization probably wrestled with similar problems."

Questions

1. Are modern managers facing totally new problems or are they confronting the same old ones? Explain.

2. How can a knowledge of management history be of value to the practicing manager? Explain.

3. What problems do today's universities create for managers? Have these problems changed with time? Explain.

CHAPTER TWO

EARLY THEORETICAL AND BEHAVIORAL CONTRIBUTIONS

GOALS OF THE CHAPTER

As seen in Chapter 1, the scientific managers concentrated on the operational level of the organization. Their scope of activities encompassed the workers and the foremen, but little else. It was inevitable, however, that attention would gradually be focused further up the hierarchy as the scientific management movement led to changes in the composition of the worker-manager ratio. Horace K. Hathaway, vice president of the Tabor Manufacturing Company, explained:

> At the Tabor Manufacturing Company we have succeeded through the application of the Taylor principles of Scientific Management in increasing our production to about three times what it formerly was, with the total cost approximately the same and approximately the same total of men; of course with a very much smaller proportion of men in the shop, and a very much increased proportion of men in the planning department, or on the management side.[1]

With more and more people entering the management ranks, it was not long before the study of management began to receive attention. Questions such as What is management? What are the principles of organization? How can the manager be more effective in his job? began to be raised. The people who devoted attention to answering these questions helped formulate the basis of modern *management theory*. Many of them worked independently of each other, unaware that elsewhere someone was raising similar questions and arriving at virtually the same conclusions.

At the same time there were individuals concerned with the *human element* in business. Some of these people were most interested in the individual, and others were more concerned with studying group behavior. Both helped formulate the basis of the modern *behavioral* approach to management. The goals of this chapter are to examine the work of some of the most important management theorists and behaviorists.

When you are finished reading this chapter you should be able to:

1. Explain why Henri Fayol is considered to be the Father of Modern Management Theory.
2. Describe the conceptual framework of management put forth by James Mooney and Alan Reiley.
3. Identify the impact of Hugo Münsterberg on the field of industrial psychology.
4. Relate the importance of Elton Mayo to the behavioral field.
5. Discuss the value of the Hawthorne studies for the behavioral approach to management.

---

[1]*First Tuck School Conference on Scientific Management*, October 12–14, 1911 (Hanover, N.H.: The Amos Tuck School of Administration and Finance, Dartmouth College, 1912), p. 339.

6. Explain why Chester Barnard is often regarded as one of the greatest behavioral contributors of all time.

The early classical theorists had two basic characteristics. First, they defined management in terms of the functions of a manager. Second, they gave minimum attention to the role of behavior in organizations. The most famous classical theorist was Henri Fayol.

EARLY THEORISTS

Henri Fayol is commonly referred to as the Father of Modern Management Theory. Receiving his degree from the National School of Mines at St. Etienne at the age of 19, he entered the employ of a mining combine known as the Commentry-Fourchambault. There he remained for his entire career, attaining the position of general manager in 1888 and holding it until 1918, when he became a director of the firm. Throughout these years, he proved himself an outstanding administrator, evidenced by the fact that when he assumed the position of general manager the firm was in critical condition — but by 1918 its financial stability was excellent.

Henri Fayol

In 1916 Fayol wrote a monograph entitled *Industrial and General Administration*,[2] in which he sought to synthesize his managerial experience and knowledge. His overall goal was to elevate the status of administration by providing an *analytical framework for management*. One of the most important sections of the book dealt with the definition and teaching of administration.

Definition and Teaching of Administration

Fayol wrote that in administration, all activities and business undertakings could be divided into six groups. These were:

1. Technical operations (production, manufacture)
2. Commercial operations (purchases, sales, and exchanges)
3. Financial operations (finding and controlling capital)
4. Security operations (protection of goods and persons)
5. Accounting operations (stocktaking, balance sheet, costing, statistics)
6. Administrative operations (planning, organization, command, coordination, and control)[3]

In addition, he analyzed these six operations, noting that the workman's chief characteristic is technical ability, but as one goes up the organizational hierarchy, the relative importance of this ability declines while that of administrative ability increases:

Managers need administrative ability.

Technical ability is the chief characteristic of the lower employees of a big undertaking and the heads of small industrial concerns; administrative ability is the chief characteristic of all the men in important positions. Technical ability is the most important quality at the bottom of the industrial ladder and administrative ability at the top.[4]

---

[2]Henri Fayol, *Industrial and General Administration* (Translated from the French edition by J. A. Coubrough, Geneva: International Management Institute, 1929).
[3]*Ibid.*, p. 8.
[4]*Ibid.*, p. 15.

In contrasting Fayol with Taylor, it is evident that the former was far less concerned with the operational level and much more interested in approaching the subject from a general management point of view. In so doing, he made one of his greatest contributions to management, namely, the identification of the administrator's activities or *functions*: planning, organizing, commanding, coordinating, and controlling. If a manager could carry out these functions properly, he would be effective. Yet Fayol believed that insufficient attention was given to these functions. Many people recognized them as important, but believed they could only be learned on the job, as technical skills are. With this he disagreed, pointing out that administration could be taught in a scholastic setting, if only a *theory of administration* could be formulated.

Management can be taught.

Principles of Administra- tion

In Part II of his book, Fayol discussed principles of administration. Noting that the administrative function was concerned only with the human part of an undertaking, he hastened to explain that he employed the word "principles" and not laws or rules because of the flexibility required in applying them to people. Since these principles are hardly ever used twice in the same way because of changing conditions, the administrator has to adapt them to his needs. The fourteen principles that Fayol felt he had occasion to use most frequently were:

1. *Division of Labor.* By employing the classic concept of specialization of labor, increases in efficiency can be achieved.
2. *Authority and Responsibility.* According to Fayol, authority and re- sponsibility went hand in hand. Authority was "the right to com- mand and the power to make oneself obeyed."[5] Responsibility was a reward or penalty accompanying the use of this power. In later years this principle would be called parity of authority and respon- sibility, indicating that the two should always be equal. Naturally, this is a utopian view, in light of the fact that many administrators seem to desire authority but shun responsibility. Fayol understood this, pointing out that as one moves up an organizational hierarchy, it becomes more difficult to establish an individual's degree of responsibility. Operations become more complex, and cause and effect are more widely separated. For this reason, he concluded that "The best safeguard against abuse of authority, and against weak- ness on the part of a leader, is personal character, and particularly, high moral character."[6]

   Of more importance, however, was the distinction he drew be- tween statutory and personal authority. *Statutory authority* comes with a position; anyone holding a specific job has some statutory authority. *Personal authority* derives from the individual's intelli- gence, knowledge, moral character, and ability to command, often- times called informal authority or power. A good leader must have both statutory and personal authority.
3. *Discipline.* The essence of discipline is "obedience, diligence, energy, correct attitude, and outward marks of respect, within the limits

Fayol's 14 princi- ples of adminis- tration.

---

[5]*Ibid.*, p. 20.
[6]*Ibid.*

fixed by the agreement between a concern and its employees."[7] This alone, however, will not guarantee good discipline. An organization must also have effective leaders who are capable of enforcing penalties in the case of insubordination. In Fayol's words, discipline is what leaders *produce*. When discipline is poor, people have a tendency to blame the rank and file. Actually, bad discipline usually comes from bad leadership.

4. *Unity of Command.* Everyone should have one and only one boss. Fayol believed so strongly in this guideline that he referred to it in his book as a rule and not as a principle. In support of this idea, he even went so far as to oppose Frederick Taylor's concept of functional foremanship — proving at the same time that he was aware of Taylor's work in America.

Functional foremanship was an organizational concept devised by Taylor. He proposed that there should be eight foremen supervising each worker. He arrived at this number by breaking down the foreman's job into its basic subfunctions. Four of these men (route clerk, instruction card clerk, cost and time clerk, and shop disciplinarian) would be in the planning room. The other four (speed boss, inspector, repair boss, and gang boss) would be out on the shop floor managing the actual production operations. Figure 2–1 presents a simplified illustration of the concept. Although Fayol praised Taylor's contributions to time-and-motion study, he disagreed with the concept of functional foremanship, contending that "it is dangerous to allow the idea to get about that the principle of unity of command is unimportant and can be violated with impunity. We ought to retain the old scheme of organization, in which unity of command is respected...."[8]

5. *Unity of Management.* Not to be confused with unity of command, this principle calls for one manager and one plan for all operations having the same objective.
6. *Subordination of Individual Interests to the Common Good.* The goals of

---

[7]*Ibid.*
[8]*Ibid.*, p. 52.

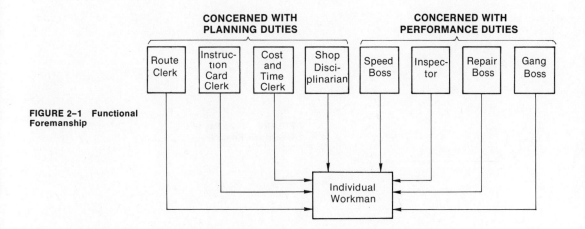

FIGURE 2–1 Functional Foremanship

the organization must take precedence over those of individuals or groups of employees.

7. *Remuneration of the Staff.* Fayol believed that a payment plan should: (a) insure fair remuneration; (b) encourage keenness by rewarding successful effort; and (c) not lead to rewards beyond a reasonable limit.

8. *Centralization.* In and of itself, centralization of authority is neither good nor bad, but it is always present to some degree. The challenge is to ascertain what degree is best for the organization.

9. *The Hierarchy.* The hierarchy, or *scalar chain* as it is often called, is the order of rank that runs through the organization from top to bottom. In order to preserve the integrity of the hierarchy and to insure unity of command, communications should follow this formal channel. However, Fayol was also cognizant of the red tape involved in a large organization and the inadvisability of always taking the long, formal route. In Figure 2–2, for example, to get a message from E to K it is necessary, if one is to follow the scalar chain, to go up the hierarchy to A and then down to K.

   To overcome this problem, Fayol prescribed his "gangplank principle." People at the same level of the hierarchy should be allowed to communicate directly, provided they have permission from their superiors to do so and they tell their respective chiefs afterwards what they have agreed to do. In this way, the integrity of the hierarchy is never threatened. Furthermore, Fayol remarked, if A made his subordinates B and H use the gangplank principle and they did likewise for their subordinates C and I, much greater efficiency would be introduced into the organization. Although it is an error to leave the hierarchical chain without a good reason, it would be a greater mistake to follow it when such a procedure would prove harmful to the undertaking.

10. *Order.* "A place for everything and everything in its place" was the way Fayol described this principle.

11. *Equity.* Equity results when friendliness is coupled with justice.

12. *Stability of Staff.* It takes time for an able employee to settle down to a job and perform satisfactorily. Thus, organizations should encourage the long-term commitment of their employees.

13. *Initiative.* Fayol defined initiative as the power to conceive and execute a plan of action.

14. *Esprit de Corps.* This spirit or morale depends upon harmony and unity among an organization's staff.

In conclusion, Fayol also pointed out that he had made no attempt to

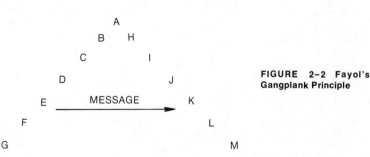

FIGURE 2–2 Fayol's Gangplank Principle

be exhaustive in his coverage of principles. He had merely described some of those he had used most often.

The second part of Fayol's book was devoted to a description of the five functions, or "elements" as he called them, of administration: planning, organizing, commanding, coordinating, and controlling. He elaborated upon each.

Elements of Administration

Planning requires a forecast of events and, based on the forecast, the construction of an operating program. These forecasts should extend as far into the future as the needs of the organization demand, although ten-year forecasts should be redrafted every five years.

Organizing entails the structuring of activities, materials, and personnel for accomplishing the assigned tasks. This calls for effective coordination of all the firm's resources.

Commanding encompasses the art of leadership coupled with the goal of putting the organization into motion. Setting a good example, making periodic examinations of the organization, eliminating incompetent personnel, and not getting bogged down with detail were some of the suggestions Fayol made for effectively carrying out this function.

Functions of management: planning, organizing, commanding, coordinating, and controlling.

Coordinating provides the requisite unity and harmony needed to attain organizational goals. One way of accomplishing this, Fayol believed, was through regular meetings of managers and subordinates. If this function were properly implemented, everything would flow smoothly.

Controlling entails seeing that everything is done in accord with the adopted plan. This function must be applied to all segments of an activity — men, materials, and operations alike.

Fayol's contribution to management theory cannot be overstated. First, he provided a conceptual framework for analyzing the management process. In the post-World War II era, when colleges of business in America began to flourish, it was Fayol's conceptual framework that provided the guidelines along which many management texts were written. Writers would identify a number of managerial functions and then describe each in depth. Some even went so far as to provide specific principles of management at the end of each section, e.g., principles of planning and principles of organizing. Known as the *management process school*, there is no doubt that the basic framework originated with Fayol.

Fayol's Contribution

Second, the attention Fayol focused on the need and possibility of teaching management via the development of a theory of administration put him in the forefront of classical management theoreticians. Much of what was to follow constituted an extension and development of his basic ideas. Two individuals who complemented his work were James D. Mooney and Alan C. Reiley.

James D. Mooney

James D. Mooney was a General Motors executive. Joining the firm in 1920, he worked his way up the organization ranks to become president of the General Motors Export Corporation. During the late 1930's, President Franklin Roosevelt selected Mooney as his personal secret emissary to Hitler in a vain attempt to end the war before America became involved. During World War II, Mooney helped convert General Motors to defense production and then left the firm to head the United States Navy Bureau of Aeronautics. After the war he became president and chairman of the board of Willys Overland Motors.[9] His cohort, Alan C. Reiley, was advertising manager of the Remington Company (currently the Remington Rand Division of the Sperry Rand Corporation) from 1900 to 1928. He was highly knowledgeable in the area of typewriters, authoring "The Story of the Typewriter" and serving as the contributor of the section on typewriters in the Encyclopaedia Britannica.[10]

James D. Mooney and Alan C. Reiley

In 1931, James D. Mooney and Alan C. Reiley authored a book entitled *Onward Industry!*,[11] later revised and called *Principles of Organization*.

The book complemented the work of Fayol while adding a new dimension via a rather complex conceptualized framework of management. The major thesis set forth in the text was that an efficient organization had to have formalism, which in turn had to be based on principles. To prove the thesis, the two men attempted to uncover, identify, define, and correlate the principles of organization.

For them, a principle applied to any fundamental truth that could be proven universal within its province. Using personal business experience and studies of military, government, church, and industry patterns, they constructed their model. Before examining their principles of organization, however, it should be noted that the framework for the analysis followed the order of the basic laws of logic employed by Lewis F. Anderson.[12] This logic postulates that every principle has a process and an effect; each process and effect, in turn, has its own principle, process, and effect. Mooney and Reiley's framework, shown in Table 2–1, was based on the following thesis:

1. The first principle of organization is *coordination*,[13] (which entails the orderly arrangement of group effort to provide unity of action in the pursuit of a common objective. This statement expresses the principles of organization in their entirety, and all other

---

[9]Daniel A. Wren, *The Evolution of Management Thought* (New York: The Ronald Press Company, 1972), p. 346.

[10]Henry H. Albers, *Principles of Management: A Modern Approach,* 3rd edition (New York: John Wiley & Sons, 1969), p. 46.

[11]James D. Mooney and Alan C. Reiley, *Onward Industry!* (New York: Harper & Brothers Publishers, 1931). The authors revised the book in 1939 and changed the title to *Principles of Organization.* In 1947, Mooney revised the book again and Reiley's name was dropped.

[12]Lewis F. Anderson, *Das Logische. Seine Gesetze und Kategorein* (Leipzig: Felix Meiner, 1929).

[13] Mooney and Reiley, *op. cit.,* p. 19.

TABLE 2–1   Logical Framework of the Principles of Organization

	Principle	Process	Effect
The Coordinating Principle	Authority or coordination *per se*	Processive coordination	Effective coordination
The Scalar Process	Leadership	Delegation	Functional definition
The Functional Effect	Determinative functionalism (legislative)	Applicative functionalism (executive)	Interpretative functionalism (judicial)

Source: James D. Mooney and Alan C. Reiley, *Onward Industry!* (New York: Harper & Brothers Publishers, 1931) p. 542. Reprinted with permission.

principles are subordinated to it. In turn, the principle is implemented by the *scalar process* — the chain of authority which runs from top to bottom in the organization. The result is the *functional effect*, which is the definition of the duties of each person in the scalar chain. Thus, the principle (coordination) has a process (scalar) and an effect (functional). And each of these three, in turn, has its own principle, process and effect, as seen in 2–4, which follow.

Mooney and Reiley's principle-process-effect thesis.

2. For completeness, coordination must have its own principle, process, and effect. The foundation of the coordinating principle is *authority* — the supreme coordinating power. This authority is put into process by *processive coordination*, which refers to all activities designed to bring about unity and direction of activity. The result is *effective coordination.*

3. The determining principle of the scalar process is *leadership*. This is put into process through *delegation* of authority to subordinates. The result is *functional definition*, or the assignment of the duties to be performed.

4. *Functional effect*, as seen in 1 above, is the end result of the coordinating principle and refers to the duties and responsibilities of individuals in the organization. The principle, process, and effect of *functional effect* are *determinative, applicative,* and *interpretative functionalism*. By determinative functionalism (principle) is meant the function of identifying broad objectives. Applicative functionalism (process) refers to the actual executing of the requisite activity. Interpretative functionalism (effect) deals with the analysis of what was accomplished in comparison to what was expected. Mooney and Reiley felt these three functions were similar to those carried out by the executive (determinative), legislative (applicative), and judicial (interpretative) branches of government.

Although their thesis is very difficult to follow unless read and reread several times, *Onward Industry!* was a major contribution to the development of early management theory. Mooney and Reiley attempted to show the causal relationships of fundamental organization principles. They also stressed the applicability of these principles to any activity or objective, refusing to be confined, as were other writers of the day, merely to industrial or production organizations. For them, the principles were universally applicable to all organized human effort.

Mooney and Reiley's Contribution

Although Mooney and Reiley arrived at their findings independently of Fayol, their work was similar to his in that it provided a basis from which to understand the management of organizations. This similarity was made clear through the writings of Lyndall F. Urwick.

Lyndall F. Urwick was educated at Oxford and served with distinction in the British Army during both world wars. From 1928 until 1933 he was Director of the International Management Institute in Geneva and Chairman of Urwick, Orr and Partners, Ltd., a management consulting firm in London, until his retirement.[14]

Lyndall F. Urwick

In 1943 Urwick wrote a book entitled *The Elements of Administration*,[15] in which he sought to integrate the theories of Taylor, Fayol, Mooney, Reiley, and other early management writers. While conceding that management was a social science that lacked the rigor and precision of the physical sciences, he also noted that there was a very large body of management knowledge available. It was his contention that if these ideas and concepts could be brought together in composite form, management would prove itself a much more scientific field of endeavor than it appeared to be.

A synthesis of current management knowledge was attempted.

In pursuing this goal, Urwick used Mooney and Reiley's principle-process-effect framework. By synthesizing the major ideas of the early classical theorists into this structure, Urwick discovered much agreement among these individuals regarding administrative principles. Commenting on the results of his work, he wrote:

> The main point . . . is that it focuses in a logical scheme various "Principles of Administration" formulated by different authorities. The fact that such "Principles"—worked out by persons of different nationalities, widely varying experience and, in the majority of cases, no knowledge of each other's work—were susceptible to such logical arrangement, is in itself highly significant.[16]

In retrospect, Urwick did not make an original contribution to management thought in terms of new output. However, he did synthesize the writings of many of the early theorists to accomplish his objective. Consequently, administration was proved to be far more scientific, better researched, and more clearly understood than had previously been believed.

BEHAVIORAL BEGINNINGS

At the time Urwick was conducting his analysis of management theory, interest was already being generated toward the behavioral side of management, marking the beginning of the human relations movement. Four of the earliest contributions to behavior and human relations in industry came from Hugo Münsterberg, Elton Mayo, the Hawthorne Studies, and Chester Barnard.

---

[14]Wren, *op. cit.*, p. 357.
[15]L. Urwick, *The Elements of Administration* (New York: Harper & Brothers, Publishers, 1943).
[16]*Ibid.*, p. 7.

Hugo Münsterberg was born in Danzig, Prussia, and educated in some of Europe's best schools. He received his Ph.D. from Leipzig in 1885, where he studied under Wilhelm Wundt, the Father of Modern Psychology, and his M.D. two years later from Heidelberg. In 1892 he came to Harvard as a visiting professor. Five years later he returned to direct that university's Psychological Laboratory.[17]

Although Münsterberg initially limited his work to laboratory experiments, he soon began expanding his psychological interests to include widely diverse fields such as law, sociology, medicine, and business. He became in his day the world's greatest authority on everything "from sex education to scientific management, from temperance to job training, from Emerson the essayist to Emerson the efficiency engineer, from table tipping to employee testing."[18] He also popularized psychology by showing how it could be of value to everyone.

In December 1916, while lecturing to a class of 60 Radcliffe girls on elementary psychology, he suddenly collapsed and died of a cerebral hemorrhage at the age of 53, cutting short a dynamic and fruitful career. His contributions have been of such great value to business that he is known as the Father of Industrial Psychology.

Historical Picture Service, Chicago

Hugo Münsterberg

One of Münsterberg's major objectives was to strengthen the bridge between scientific management and industrial efficiency by complementing the work of Taylor and his associates.[19] Münsterberg noted that the efficiency engineers placed great emphasis upon the physical skills of the worker but virtually overlooked psychological or mental skills. Commenting on the need to address the "psycho-technical problem," he wrote:

Scientific Management and Psychology

Mental skills are as important as physical skills.

> We have to analyze definite economic tasks with reference to the mental qualities which are necessary or desirable for them, and we have to find methods by which these mental qualities can be tested . . . the interests of commerce and industry can be helped only when both sides, the vocational demands and the personal function, are examined with equal scientific thoroughness.[20]

Münsterberg's interest in studying the man as well as the job led him into the area of vocational testing. His thesis was that tests should be designed that would help screen out unfit job applicants and workers. His most famous experiment was conducted among trolley car operators. However, he did not stop here, but expanded the concept by developing screening tests for other work groups, from ship's officers to telephone operators. Always the central objective was that of identifying whether or

Vocational Testing

[17]*Encyclopaedia Britannica*, 1973 edition, Vol. 15, p. 997.
[18]"Famous Firsts: Measuring Minds for the Job," *Business Week*, January 29, 1966, p. 60.
[19]Hugo Münsterberg, *Psychology and Industrial Efficiency* (Boston: Houghton Mifflin Company, 1913).
[20]*Ibid.*, p. 57.

not the person was psychologically fit for the job. Did he have the requisite mental skills? It was Münsterberg's belief that the key to industrial efficiency rested in the worker's ability to concentrate his attention only on elements directly concerned with good job performance. In the case of the trolley operators, a broad field of concentration was necessary if the individual was to identify and avoid possible accidents ahead of him. For other jobs, a narrower field of concentration might be more useful. In either case, psychological testing could be valuable in screening people at *all levels* of an organization:

Ability to concentrate is an important psychological factor.

> The results of experimental psychology will have to be introduced systematically into the study of the fitness of the personality from the lowest to the highest technical activity and from the simplest sensory function to the most complex mental achievement.[21]

Münsterberg's Contributions

Münsterberg made a number of important contributions to management. First, he popularized psychology by showing how it could be of value in many fields, thus heralding the advent of the psychologists into industry. However, it should not be inferred that because his work was popular it was unscientific, for he used his psychological laboratory at Harvard to develop many of the tools he employed in industry. He was a researcher and experimenter as well as a proponent of psychology.

Second, in addition to studying the psychological traits necessary to do a good job, he concerned himself with the psychological conditions under which the greatest amount of output could be attained. Included in this study were factors such as attention, fatigue, monotony, and the impact of social influences.

Third, he addressed himself to securing "the best possible effects," and in so doing combined some of the ideas of scientific management with those of psychology. For example, in advertising one wants people to read the ads quickly and accurately (scientific management), and to remember what was said and take appropriate action (psychology). Münsterberg carried this basic concept into the areas of buying, selling, and displaying. In each case, he showed how psychology could improve performance. By the time of his death, industrial psychology was well established as one of the important "new" areas of management.

Elton Mayo

Another field in which interest began to grow was that of sociology. One of the earliest and most significant contributors was Elton Mayo, an Australian who taught ethics, philosophy, and logic at the Queensland University and later studied medicine in Edinburgh, Scotland. While in Edinburgh, he became a research associate in the study of psychopathology. Then, under a grant from the Laura Spelman Rockefeller Fund, he came to America and joined the faculty of the Wharton School of Finance and Commerce of the University of Pennsylvania. In 1926, he joined the Harvard faculty as an associate professor of industrial research.[22]

[21]*Ibid.*, p. 96.
[22]Wren, *op. cit.*, pp. 277–278.

Mayo's most famous early experiment took place in a Philadelphia textile mill in 1923 to 1924. The purpose of the study was to identify the cause of high labor turnover in the mule spinning department. While turnover in the company's other departments was between five and six per cent a year, in the mule spinning department it was up to 250 per cent. Efficiency engineers had experimented with financial incentive schemes, but these had proved fruitless. The president then called in Mayo and his associates.

MAYO'S MULE SPINNING INQUIRY*

Mayo decided to make some changes in the work pattern to see if this would improve the situation. After securing management's permission, he introduced two ten-minute rest periods in the morning and two more in the afternoon for one of the groups in the department. During these periods the men were encouraged to lie down and, if possible, to sleep. The results were astounding. Morale improved, labor turnover ended, and production, despite the work breaks, remained the same. Soon the entire department was included in the rest-period experiment, and output increased tremendously. Monthly productivity, which had never been above 70 per cent, rose over the next five months to an overall average of 80 per cent, and with it came bonus pay.[23]

Rest Periods

With rest periods, productivity rose.

What led to the high morale, high productivity, and virtual elimination of labor turnover? Mayo felt it was the systematic introduction of the rest periods, which not only helped overcome physical fatigue but reduced "pessimistic revery."[24] There were thus two factors involved, fatigue and monotony. The first of these is physiological and quite easy to understand. The second is psychological and reflected Mayo's philosophy and training. For some time prior to this textile mill study, he had been writing about the importance of understanding the worker's *psychological* make-up. Everyone, Mayo felt, has mental eccentricities or minor irrationalities. Most people are capable of suppressing them to the degree that they are harmless. They do not lead to, for example, a nervous breakdown. However, Mayo believed that:

Analysis of the Results

Psychological factors are important.

What social and industrial research has not sufficiently realised as yet is that these minor irrationalities of the "average normal" person are cumulative in their effect. They may not cause "breakdown" in the individual but they do cause "breakdown" in the industry.[25]

There was, however, more here than Mayo and his associates realized. They had come up with some interesting physiological-psychological conclusions, but time and further research would be necessary before the experiment could be intelligently re-examined and additional, more substantial, findings obtained. The Hawthorne studies, which followed shortly thereafter, proved very useful in this regard.

---

*Mule: a type of spinning machine that makes thread or yarn from fibers; also called "mulejenny."
[23]Bonuses were paid on productivity over 75 per cent.
[24]By revery Mayo meant day-dreaming.
[25]Elton Mayo, "Irrationality and Revery," *Journal of Personnel Research*, March 1923, p. 482.

**HAWTHORNE
STUDIES**

The Hawthorne studies (1924–1932) had their roots in the logic of scientific management. The initial purpose of these experiments was to study the effect of illumination on output. The study, sponsored by the National Research Council, was begun in November 1924 at the Hawthorne Works of the Western Electric Company near Cicero, Illinois. Before it was all over, there would be four major phases: the illumination experiments, the relay assembly test room, the massive interviewing program, and the bank wiring observation room study.

**Illumination
Experiments**

The illumination phase of the Hawthorne studies lasted two and one-half years. During this period, three different experiments were conducted, and as the tests continued, the researchers improved their experimental design. They were, however, unable to ascertain the relationship that existed between illumination and output.

On the basis of their work, however, the researchers did reach two conclusions. First, lighting was only one factor affecting employee output and it was apparently a minor one at that. Second, attempts to measure the
*No direct rela-
tionship between
illumination and
productivity was
found.* effect of illumination on output were unsuccessful because there were many factors involved that were not controlled and any one of these could have influenced the outcome.

The company, however, did not feel that the experiments had been unsuccessful. On the contrary, they believed that they had gained invaluable experience in the technique of conducting research and were eager to push forward. The result was phase two, the Relay Assembly Test Room experiment. This stage of the program marked the entrance of Elton Mayo and a number of Harvard researchers.

**Relay
Assembly
Test Room**

In order to obtain more control over the factors affecting work performance, it was decided to isolate a small group of workers from the regular work force. Five female assemblers and a layout operator were placed in a room. In addition, the researchers put an observer in with them to record everything that happened and to maintain a friendly atmosphere. The girls were told that the experiment was not designed to boost production but merely to study various types of working conditions so that the most suitable environment could be ascertained. They were told to keep working at their regular pace.

For the first four months, some initial work changes were introduced into the room and the overall effect studied. Most of these changes were easily identified by the investigators. For example, in contrast to the regular department, the room was smaller and had better lighting and ventilation. The significance of some changes, however, was not fully grasped at the time. For example, the test room observer took over some of the supervision, but he was very lenient:

> The test room observer was chiefly concerned with creating a friendly relation with the operators which would ensure their co-operation. He was anxious to dispel any apprehensions they might have about the test and, in order to do this, he began to converse informally with them each day. Sometimes the topics he brought up pertained to their work,

sometimes to personal matters, and occasionally they took the form of a general inquiry as to the attitude of the operators toward the test.[26]

In addition, the girls were allowed to talk more freely among themselves and, because there were only a small number of them, they formed a much closer relationship than they had had in the regular department.

Once the impact of most of these new changes was noted, the researchers moved the experiment into its second stage. During this phase, rest pauses were introduced in order to see what effect they would have on output. The result was an increase in productivity, leading to the initial hypothesis that these pauses reduced fatigue and thereby improved output. Applying this theory further, the researchers introduced shorter work days and work weeks. Once again, output increased. However, these changes were later terminated, and when original conditions were reestablished, output still remained high, indicating that the change in conditions was not the only reason for the increase in output. Some of the investigators hypothesized that the increases were related not to the rest pauses or shorter working hours but to the improved outlook that the girls had toward their work. No one, however, seemed able to answer the question, To what can this improved outlook be related?

The girls had an improved outlook toward their work.

After rejecting various hypotheses, they concluded that the most likely cause was that changes in the social conditions and in the method of supervision brought about the improved attitude and increased output. In order to gather information on this, management decided to investigate employee attitudes and the factors to which they could be traced. The result was a massive interviewing program that started out simply as a plan for improving supervision, but actually marked the turning point in the research, overshadowing, for a time, all other aspects of the project.

Over 20,000 interviews were conducted in the third phase of the studies. The interviewers began by asking employees direct questions about supervision and the work environment in general. Although the interviewer made it clear that everything would be kept in strict confidence, the responses to questions were often guarded and stereotyped. The approach was therefore changed from direct to *nondirect* questioning. Now the employee was allowed to choose his own topic. The result was the gathering of a wealth of information about employee attitudes. The researchers realized that the individual's work performance, position, and status in the organization were determined not only by the person himself but by the group members as well. His peers had an effect on his performance. In order to study this more systematically, the research entered its fourth and final phase, that of the bank wiring observation room.

Massive Interviewing Program

A nondirective interviewing technique was employed.

In choosing a department to study, the investigators decided to concentrate on a small group engaged in one particular type of work rather than to encompass many groups with dissimilar jobs. The department

Bank Wiring Observation Room

---

[26]F. J. Roethlisberger and William J. Dickson, *Management and the Worker* (Cambridge, Mass.: Harvard University Press, 1939), p. 16.

chosen for the study was the bank wiring department. In this room there were three types of jobs: wireman, solderman, and inspector. The wireman set the pace for the rest by the number of bank terminals he wired. These were then soldered by the solderman and, finally, checked by the inspector. Since it took only one solderman to handle the work of three wiremen, the group consisted of nine wiremen, three soldermen, and two inspectors. For the next six months, the work and the behavior of this group were observed.

THE GROUP'S OUTPUT.   One significant finding was that most of the workers were restricting their output. The company norm (or standard) based on time-and-motion studies called for 7312 connections. The workers, however, completed only 6000 to 6600 connections, depending on the type of equipment being worked on. This informal standard had been formulated by the men, representing what they considered to be a proper day's work. There was no doubt that the men could have met the standard of 7312, but they did not do so. Why did the men restrict output? One told the interviewer that if they did too much work, the company would raise the expected amount. Another felt they might work themselves out of a job simply by working too hard and doing too much. Others felt that a slow pace protected the slower workers, preventing them from looking bad and getting bawled out by the management. In addition, it should be noted that management seemed to accept this informal rate as satisfactory, bringing pressure on the men only when they fell below this level.

Some men restricted their work output.

THE SUPERVISORY SITUATION.   Study of the supervisory situation in the room also provided human behavioral insights, for the manner in which the men treated their superiors differed. The hierarchy of supervisory titles is seen in Figure 2–3.

Most of the employees regarded the group chief as one of themselves. As a result, they thought nothing of disobeying him. The section chief fared a little better. Nevertheless, the men often argued with him and did not always obey his orders. The assistant foreman, on the other hand, received much different treatment. The men neither disobeyed him nor argued with his orders. This same pattern existed in the case of the foreman. In fact, when he was present, the men refrained from any activity that was not strictly in accord with the rules. Thus, as one pro-

The workers treated the managers differently.

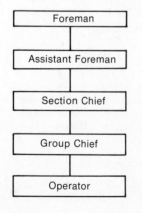

FIGURE 2–3 Partial Hierarchy of the Bank Wiring Observation Room

gressed up the organizational hierarchy, the degree of respect, or apprehensiveness, on the part of the men increased.

GROUP DYNAMICS.   Another aspect of the group that was closely observed was that of interpersonal relationships. Much knowledge about the informal organization that existed in the room was gained. For example, most of the men engaged in various games, including baseball pools, shooting craps, sharing candy, and "binging." The latter, a device used to control individual behavior, consisted of hitting a man as hard as possible on the upper arm. This person was then free to retaliate by striking back with a like blow. Although the overt reason was to see who could hit the hardest, the underlying cause was often one of punishment for those who were accomplishing either too much or too little.

> Interpersonal relations were studied.

Job trading and the helping of one another provided further bases for studying the group's behavior. Some individuals sought help while others gave it, although such action was in direct violation of company rules. This led to interest in the development of friendships and antagonisms. Who liked whom and who disliked whom?

SOCIAL CLIQUES.   By studying the types of games and other interactions of the participants, the investigators were able to divide the men into two groups, or cliques, A and B. Several conclusions were drawn from this finding. First, the men were not integrated on the basis of occupation. Clique A, for example, contained three wiremen, one solderman, and one inspector. Second, the location in the room influenced the formation of a clique. The A group was located in the front of the room, the B group in the rear. Third, some of the men were accepted by neither clique. Fourth, each clique regarded itself as superior to the other, based on either the things it did or the things it refrained from doing. For example, Clique A did not trade jobs, and did not engage in "binging" as often as did Clique B. Conversely, the members of Clique B did not argue among themselves as often or engage in games of chance, as did Clique A. Fifth, each clique had certain norms or sentiments to which one had to subscribe if he wished to be accepted as a member. Roethlisberger and Dickson identified these as being:

> The researchers were able to identify social cliques.

1. You should not turn out too much work. If you do, you are a "rate-buster."
2. You should not turn out too little work. If you do, you are a "chiseler."
3. You should not tell a superior anything that will react to the detriment of an associate. If you do, you are a "squealer."
4. You should not attempt to maintain social distance or act officious. If you are an inspector, for example, you should not act like one.[27]

> Norms of behavior were also identified.

To these, Homans later added:

5. You should not be noisy, self-assertive, and anxious for leadership.[28]

There is no doubt that the Hawthorne studies constituted the single most important foundation for the behavioral approach to management. The conclusions drawn were many and varied.

> **Findings and Implications of Hawthorne**

---

[27] *Ibid.*, p. 522.
[28] George C. Homans, *The Human Group* (New York: Harcourt, Brace & World, Inc., 1950), p. 79.

ELIMINATION OF MENTAL REVERY.   In Mayo's opinion, one of the major explanations of the results rested with the elimination of what he earlier called "pessimistic revery." However, based on the findings of the Hawthorne studies, he now realized that rest pauses or changes in the work environment did not, of themselves, overcome this problem. Rather, the key was to be found in the reorganization of the workers:

> ...What the company actually did for the group was to reconstruct entirely its whole industrial situation....The consequence was that there was a period during which the individual workers and the group had to re-adapt themselves to a new industrial milieu, a milieu in which their own self-determination and their social well-being ranked first and work was incidental....
>
> ...The Western Electric experiment was primarily directed not to the external condition but to the inner organization. By strengthening the "temperamental" inner equilibrium of the workers, the company enabled them to achieve a mental "steady state" which offered a high resistance to a variety of external conditions.[29]

The restructuring of the social network was more important than rest periods.

Thus Mayo realized that the results were caused not by scientific management practices (rest periods) but by socio-psychological phenomena (restructuring of social networks).

HAWTHORNE EFFECT.   A second finding, and probably the most widely cited, is that of the "Hawthorne effect." This means that novelty or interest in a new situation leads, at least initially, to positive results. Applying this concept to the increase in productivity in the relay room, many modern psychologists contend that it was not the changes in the rest pauses that led to increased output but the fact that the girls liked the new situation in which they were considered to be important. The attention lavished on them led them to increase their output. The Hawthorne effect seemed to lead to the decline in revery, but when investigated further, it appears not to have been the only factor involved.

The novelty of the situation was important.

SUPERVISORY CLIMATE.   Luthans[30] points out that not all groups in the study evidenced productivity increases. The girls in the relay assembly test room did more work than ever before, but the men in the bank wiring room restricted their output. Thus, there must be more than a mere Hawthorne effect and the resulting decline in pessimistic revery. In fact, when the girls were asked why they liked working in the test room better than the regular department, they gave the following reasons:

The style of supervision was another critical factor.

1. the small group
2. the type of supervision
3. earnings
4. novelty of the situation
5. interest in the experiment
6. attention shown by officials and investigators[31]

The last three of these reasons represent what might be called Hawthorne effect results; the first three do not.

What, then, accounted for the difference in output between the two rooms? Applying the first three responses of the girls to the relay and bank

---

[29]Elton Mayo, *The Human Problems of an Industrial Civilization* (New York: The Macmillan Co., 1933), pp. 70–72.
[30]Fred Luthans, *Organizational Behavior*, 2nd edition (New York: McGraw-Hill Book Company, 1977), p. 17.
[31]C. E. Turner, "Test Room Studies in Employee Effectiveness," *American Journal of Public Health*, June 1933, p. 583.

wiring room, it should be recalled that both were small, cohesive units working on an incentive basis. Thus, the major difference may well have been the *type of supervision*. In the relay room the observer took over some of the supervisory functions, but in a very lenient manner. In the bank wiring room, however, the regular supervisors were used to maintain order and control. The observer was relegated to a minor role, having none of the authority of his relay room counterpart.

This particular finding downplays the "Hawthorne effect," which has probably been overemphasized far too long. As C. E. Turner, a consultant to the studies, has stated:

> We at first thought that the *novelty* of test room conditions might be partly responsible for increased output but the continuing increase in production over a 4-year period suggests that it was not of great importance.[32]

This same basic finding was substantiated by Mayo himself, who, in his original analysis of supervision and productivity in the relay room, noted:

> ... getting closer supervision than ever before, the change is in the quality of the supervision. This—the change in quality of supervision—is by no means the whole change, but it is an important part of it.[33]

THE LIGHT FROM HAWTHORNE. The illumination experiment at Hawthorne served to "light the way" for the human relations research that was to follow. Mayo and his colleagues from Harvard, as well as representatives of the company who participated in the studies, deserve a great deal of credit. There were times when the results were so baffling that the average researcher would have thrown up his hands in disgust and walked away. There were other times, such as in the illumination and relay room experiments, when tests were reconducted because some independent variable had not been considered in the initial design. It was difficult for the original investigators of the human relations movement, but they persevered and two important milestones were reached as a result.

---

[32]*Ibid.*
[33]Mayo, *op. cit.*, p. 75.

Another individual who made a significant contribution to behavioral thought was Chester I. Barnard. Entering Harvard University in 1906, he studied economics and finished all the requirements in three years. However, he failed to receive his degree because he lacked a laboratory science. Since he passed the course with distinction, he felt it was pointless to take the lab section. Upon leaving the university, he joined the Statistical Department of the American Telephone and Telegraph system. In 1927 he became president of New Jersey Bell and remained in that capacity until his retirement. In addition, he worked with numerous other organizations, including the Rockefeller Foundation, of which he served as president for four years, and the United States Organization, of which he was president for three years.

Chester I. Barnard

First, important insights into individual and group behavior were uncovered. The researchers had no illusions about the amount of work to be done. There was still much more to do, but the groundwork had been laid. Second, attention was focused on the supervisory climate, providing an impetus for later research on leadership style.[34]

Barnard was interested in both making a logical analysis of organizational structure and applying sociological concepts to management, which he did in his book *The Functions of the Executive*.[35] His work has proved so influential to the study of management that one writer has credited him with having had "a more profound impact on the thinking about the complex subject matter of human organization than has any other contributor to the continuum of management thought."[36] Below are some of his ideas in condensed form.

Functions of the Executive

In his book, Barnard pointed out that although there may be universal characteristics of organizations, he knew of no theory that seemed to correspond to his experience or to the implicit understanding shared among leaders of an organization. Much of what had been written was just too descriptive and superficial. Furthermore, he felt some of the theses being espoused were based on incorrect logic. Using *executive experience* as his guide, Barnard sought to set forth both a theory of cooperation and a description of the organizational process.

He defined the formal organization as *a system of consciously coordinated activities or forces of two or more persons.*[37] Within this structure the executive is the most strategic factor; it is up to him to maintain a system of cooperative effort. The entire process is carried out through three essential executive functions: (a) providing a system of communication; (b) promoting the acquisition of essential effort; and (c) formulating and defining the purposes and objectives of the organization.

Establish and maintain a communication system.

The first of these functions, establishment and maintenance of a *communication* system, is the executive's *primary* job. It requires a coalescence of executive personnel and executive positions; it is accomplished through careful employee selection, the use of positive and negative sanctions, and the securing of the informal organization. This informal organization plays a key role in communication because it helps to reduce the necessity for formal decisions while minimizing what Barnard called "undesirable influences."

Promote acquisition of essential effort.

The second of the functions, to promote the acquisition of *essential effort* from organizational personnel, requires two main steps. First, the people have to be brought into a cooperative relationship with the organization; they have to be recruited in some way. Then, when this is accomplished, the organization must get them to identify with the firm. This requires the establishment of inducements and incentives.

The third executive function, formulating the *purpose and objectives* of the organization, requires the delegation of authority. Everyone is given a

---

[34]For example, there were the pioneering studies conducted by Ronald Lippett and Ralph K. White under Kurt Lewin at the University of Iowa. One of their most famous articles is "Patterns of Aggressive Behavior in Experimentally Created 'Social Climates,'" *The Journal of Social Psychology*, May 1939, pp. 271–276.

[35]Chester I. Barnard, *The Functions of the Executive* (Cambridge, Mass.: Harvard University Press, 1938).

[36]Claude S. George, Jr., *The History of Management Thought*, 2nd edition (Englewood Cliffs, N.J.: Prentice-Hall, Inc., 1972), p. 140.

[37]Barnard, *op. cit.*, p. 73.

piece of the overall master plan to implement. Then, by means of communication feedback, obstacles and difficulties can be identified and the plan changed appropriately. In light of such changes, new responsibilities can be assigned.

Formulate the purpose and objectives of the organization.

Throughout his book, Barnard emphasized the importance of *inducing* the subordinate to cooperate. Merely having the authority to give orders is insufficient, for the subordinate may refuse to obey. In fact, stated Barnard:

The Theory of Authority

> A person can and will accept a communication as authoritative only when four conditions simultaneously obtain: (a) he can and does understand the communication; (b) *at the time of his decision*, he believes it is not inconsistent with the purpose of the organization; (c) *at the time of his decision*, he believes it to be compatible with his personal interest, as a whole; and (d) he is able mentally and physically to comply with it.[38]

The result of this reasoning is what has become commonly known as the *acceptance theory of authority*.[39] Authority, or the right to command, depends upon whether or not the subordinates obey. Naturally, one could reason that it is possible for the executive to bring sanctions, but this will not necessarily ensure acceptance of the orders, for the employee may be willing to accept any fate dealt out by management.

Acceptance theory of authority.

The entire acceptance theory of authority would be quite threatening if this were all there was to it. Management might literally be at the mercy of the subordinates. However, Barnard realized that the consent and cooperation of subordinates are often easily obtained. First, the four conditions necessary for acceptance are generally present, so workers will regard a communication as authoritative. Second, each individual has a "zone of indifference." Orders falling within this zone are accepted without question. The others either fall on the neutral line or are conceived of as clearly unacceptable. The indifference zone tells the story, and it will be either wide or narrow, depending upon the inducements being accorded the individual and the sacrifices he is making on behalf of the organization. The effective executive assures that each individual feels he is receiving more from the organization than he is giving. When this occurs, the indifference zone is widened and the subordinates agreeably accept most orders. Third, one person's refusal to obey will affect the efficiency of the organization and threatens the other members. When this happens, fellow workers will often pressure the individual to comply. General stability within the organization results.

Zones of indifference are important.

Barnard made several important contributions to management theory. First, he described executive functions in analytic and dynamic terms, in contrast to the descriptive writers who had preceded him. Second, he

Barnard's Contribution

---

[38]*Ibid.*, p. 165.
[39]This basic concept was espoused earlier, when Machiavelli wrote about consent of the masses. See Chapter 1.

stimulated interest in topics such as communication, motivation, decision making, objectives, and organizational relationships. Third, he advanced the work of Fayol, Mooney, and Reiley. These individuals were concerned with management from the standpoint of principles and functions, but Barnard, drawing upon his interest in the psychological and sociological aspects of management, extended these ideas to include the interaction of people in the work force.

SUMMARY

The success of the scientific managers brought about changes in the worker-manager ratio and moved the focus of attention further up the hierarchy. The result was two distinct levels of inquiry about management. The first was related to management and sought to answer the question: What is management all about? The second was related to the conduct of people in organizations and sought to examine both individual and group behavior.

The most famous of the early management theorists was Henri Fayol. Fayol's outstanding contribution was the conceptual framework he provided for analyzing the management process. James D. Mooney and Alan C. Reiley complemented his work with their logical outline of the principles of organization and the conclusion that the first such principle is coordination. Lyndall Urwick, meanwhile, took the ideas of many of these early theorists and synthesized them in a manner proving that their work was susceptible to logical arrangement. A basic framework for the study of management was emerging.

In the behavioral area, Hugo Münsterberg examined the importance of psychology to industry, and Elton Mayo studied group behavior in organizations. The Hawthorne studies, however, made an even greater impact on the field, and they became the single most important foundation for the behavioral approach to management. Meanwhile, Chester Barnard, whose acceptance theory of authority is still regarded as a major landmark, made the most memorable contribution to early behavioral knowledge.

In the next chapter the material from these first two chapters will be placed in perspective. In this way, the stage will be set for a discussion of modern management theory and practice in Part II.

REVIEW AND STUDY QUESTIONS

1. Why is Henri Fayol known as the Father of Modern Management Theory?

2. What did Fayol mean by "Technical ability is the most important quality at the bottom of the industrial ladder and administrative ability at the top"?

3. Identify and describe Fayol's five management functions.

4. What is functional foremanship?

5. What did Fayol mean by "a principle of management"?

6. What contribution did James Mooney and Alan Reiley make to management theory?

7. Even though Lyndall Urwick made no original contribution in terms of input to management theory, he is a management scholar. Do you agree or disagree with this point of view?

8. Why is Hugo Münsterberg known as the Father of Industrial Psychology?

9. In what way can vocational testing be of value to the manager?

10. How important were rest pauses in Mayo's mule spinning inquiry? What other factors were significant?

11. Did the Hawthorne researchers find any relationship between illumination and output? Explain.

12. Why did the output of the women in the relay assembly test room increase? Give your reasoning.

13. Why did the men in the bank wiring room restrict their output? Explain.

14. What were the norms to which the workers in the bank wiring room subscribed? Identify and describe them.

15. Of what significance to management were the Hawthorne studies? Explain.

16. According to Chester Barnard, what are the three essential executive functions? Explain.

17. What is the acceptance theory of authority? Do you agree with it?

SELECTED REFERENCES

Barnard, C. I. *The Functions of the Executive.* Cambridge, Mass.: Harvard University Press, 1938.

Church, A. J. *The Making of an Executive.* New York: D. Appleton and Company, 1923.

Drever, J. *The Psychology of Industry.* London: Methuen & Co., Ltd., 1921.

Dutton, H. P. *Principles of Organization as Applied to Business.* New York: McGraw-Hill Book Company, 1931.

Edie, L. D. *Practical Psychology for Business Executives.* New York: H. W. Wilson Company, 1922.

Fayol, H. *General and Industrial Management.* London: Sir Isaac Pitman & Sons, Ltd., 1949.

Mee, J. F. *Management Thought in a Dynamic Economy.* New York: New York University Press, 1963.

Merrill, C. F., ed. *Classics in Management.* New York: American Management Association, 1960.

Mooney, J. D., and A. C. Reiley. *Onward Industry!* New York: Harper & Brothers, Publishers, 1931.

Münsterberg, H. *Business Psychology.* Chicago: LaSalle Extension University, 1915.

Münsterberg, H. *Psychology and Industrial Efficiency.* Boston: Houghton Mifflin Company, 1913.

Roethlisberger, F. J., and W. J. Dickson. *Management and the Worker.* Cambridge, Mass.: Harvard University Press, 1939.

Urwick, L. *The Elements of Administration.* New York: Harper & Brothers, Publishers, 1943.

Wren, D. A. *The Evolution of Management Thought.* New York: The Ronald Press Company, 1979.

CASE: TECHNICIANS AND MANAGERS

One day recently, a management consulting firm in New York City received a phone call from a local industrial machine manufacturer. The company's board of directors had just concluded its quarterly meeting and had decided that something had to be done to improve operations. For the sixth consecutive quarter, profits had declined. Sales were higher than ever, but costs were apparently out of control.

The consultants spent ten weeks examining the firm's operations. Everyone in the company was interviewed, from the chief executive officer to the janitor. When the team finished its analysis, it submitted a 212-page report to the board. One of its key findings was:

Since its inception, the company has had a policy of promoting from within. The prime criterion for these promotions appears to be technical competence. This is as true at the upper levels as at the lower ones. And it is not uncommon to find managers down on the machine floor examining and commenting on technical problems. Unfortunately, this leaves little time for managing. In fact, managerial functions such as planning, organizing and controlling are given almost no attention. What the company needs is an influx of outside management people who will place *less* attention on the technical side of the job and *more* on the management side.

Questions

1. How do these findings fit into Fayol's philosophy of management?

2. How common is it to find managers spending more time on the technical than on the managerial side of their job? Explain.

3. How can these problems be overcome?

CASE: A CALL FOR FORMAL TRAINING

College enrollments began to drop off in the mid-1970's, and private colleges and universities felt the effects most strongly. In an attempt to minimize the impact on his institution, William Smith, president of a large private university in the East, urged the faculty to do all it could to stimulate enrollments.

In response to the president's request, faculty in the College of Business decided to spend one day a week making scheduled appearances in local high schools to encourage graduating seniors to come to their university. If any of the students expressed interest, the faculty member would take down his or her name, address, and area of interest and turn the information over to the president's office. Depending upon the individual's desired major, a faculty member would then call on the student and his parents at home.

One of these students, Richard Makinaw, indicated an interest in business as a major, specifically management. As a result, Fred Quilting, a professor of management, arranged an appointment with Richard and his family for the purpose of explaining to them what the College of Business could offer. Richard seemed impressed, but his father did not. Part of the conversion was as follows:

Professor Quilting, I've got a very successful retail store and I want my son to come into the business with me. From what you say, your university could prepare him to take over some of my duties and, someday, run the entire operation himself. However, I'm not so sure that he can learn management from a book. I've been in the retail business for over twenty years, and most of what I've learned about management, I picked up the hard way.

Certainly, Mr. Mackinaw, we can't hope to give Richard all the experience and knowledge you have about management. But we can familiarize him with the basics of management and provide him with some important training.

I don't know. His mother and I are going to have to talk it over. My real concern is whether Richard would be better off joining me in the business

right after he graduates from high school or whether he should go on to college and study management formally.

Questions

1. Can management be studied in the classroom?

2. What are the advantages of studying management in college as opposed to learning about it on the job?

3. What recommendation would you make to Mr. Mackinaw? Explain.

CASE: THE FIREFIGHTER

A fire recently broke out on the third floor of a machine shop on Long Island. According to a spokesman for the fire department, workers on the floor had apparently been throwing oily rags in the corner for three or four days and they had not been picked up by the maintenance crew. As a result, when a careless worker flipped a lighted cigarette butt onto the rags, they immediately ignited.

As soon as they saw the blaze, most of the workers on the floor vacated the premises and gathered out in the parking lot. However, it was at least 15 minutes before anyone turned in an alarm. This was done by Pedro Rodriguez, a new employee who was delivering some equipment to one of the work stations when he suddenly saw the blaze. Acting quickly, Pedro pulled the fire alarm and then raced to the wall for a fire extinguisher. When the firemen arrived they found the new employee vigorously fighting the blaze. Thanks to his assistance, the fire was quickly brought under control. The first fireman on the scene told management, "Without that guy's quick thinking, you might have lost the whole building. He managed to confine the fire to one small area until we could get here and put it out." A thankful management gave Pedro a $10-a-week salary increase and a check for $500. Most of the workers, however, did not share the management's point of view. Some of their remarks included:

That guy Rodriguez is an idiot. He could have gotten his tail burned off. And for what? A crummy $500 and a small raise.

My job around here is running a drill press. They don't pay me to fight fires or even to report them. It's not in my job description.

Six months later, Pedro quit the company. When asked why, he said, "I don't like working with these guys. Somehow we just don't get on."

Questions

1. Based on the data in this case, what conclusions can you draw about the norms and values of the workers? Do they have a code of expected behavior? What is it?

2. If you were told that there was a union in this shop, would that help explain the comments made by the workers? Would it be possible to draw any conclusions about worker-management relations? Explain.

3. Why did Pedro quit? Give your reasoning.

CASE: WHO IS IN CHARGE HERE?

Webber Printing, a Midwest job printer, was founded in 1937. The firm prospered slowly for the first twenty years of its existence. However, in the late 1950's, thanks to a large investment in new machinery and equipment, the company expanded its operations and sales began to increase at an annual rate of 45 per cent. By 1964, Webber Printing had passed the $20 million mark. From then on, sales began to increase at a decreasing rate. Nevertheless, by 1978 the company topped the $100 million mark.

Success, however, had its price. In 1967, despite all attempts by the management to discourage such action, the workers voted to unionize. For years, Charles Webber, president and founder, had prided himself on having a nonunion shop. He had continually paid union scale and attempted to match all fringe benefits being provided by his unionized competitors. The men appreciated his efforts, but, as one of them put it, "After Mr. Webber dies, all of this could change. A union provides us assurance that we won't lose everything we've gotten over the years."

The union brought a new era to management-worker relations. Previously, everything had been done on a rather informal basis. Now the company organized into two armies: the management and the union. Over the next decade, at contract time both sides drove as hard a bargain as they could. However, the union had the upper hand because there was a shortage of qualified personnel in the area and a great demand for the company's printing services. Management capitulated to both salary and fringe benefit requests.

This turn of events angered Bob Handley, manager of one of the company's units. He felt the union was getting too big for its britches, and he refused to take any guff from the workers. He kept a close watch on his people and threatened to fire any of them who could not do "a fair day's work for a fair day's pay." In turn, the union complained that Bob was a troublemaker. His boss, Fred Wandott, called him in for a talk:

Bob, we've been getting some pressure from the union to ask you to loosen up and quit pushing the men so hard. Now, I know you have only the best interest of the firm in mind, but I think you'll get more work out of the men if you don't treat this union thing as a personal vendetta.

Mr. Wandott, I think those guys believe they're running this company. I'm the manager and they're the subordinates. They're supposed to obey my orders.

I realize that. But remember, you're only effective if they obey you. What good is a manager whose men refuse to comply with his orders? Now, you're going to have to ease up and realize that authority is a two-way street. There's the person who gives the orders and the individual who agrees to obey them.

Questions

1. What does Mr. Wandott mean by authority being a two-way street?

2. Does Bob believe in Barnard's acceptance theory of authority? Does Mr. Wandott? Explain.

3. How could Barnard's "zone of indifference" concept be of value to Bob in handling this problem? Explain.

CHAPTER THREE

EARLY MANAGEMENT
THOUGHT IN PERSPECTIVE

The scientific managers, early management theorists, and human relations researchers all made significant contributions to management, and all were complementary to one another. Taylor and his associates conducted important time- and motion-study research in the 1880 to 1920 era. Then along came the early theorists in the years between 1915 and 1945, providing important information about the administrative side of management. Finally, from 1912 to 1955, there were the human relations researchers, who added a new level of sophistication to management thought. The goal of this chapter is to place these three groups in perspective, first by examining some of the weaknesses and shortcomings of each, and then by reviewing the positive side of their contributions.

When you are finished reading this chapter you should:
1. Be aware of some shortcomings of the scientific managers.
2. Know some major deficiencies of the classical theorists.
3. Be cognizant of the inadequacies of the human relations approach.
4. Be able to put these three groups in perspective by comparing and contrasting their shortcomings with their positive accomplishments.

GOALS OF THE CHAPTER

Although the scientific managers made many important contributions to management, much of their work reflected a very limited understanding of the human element in the work place. For example, most of them seriously believed that money was the worker's *prime* motivation. This belief resulted in the development of various incentive payment plans such as Taylor's differential piece-rate; if the employees worked harder, they would earn more money. Such thinking led these traditionalists to view the worker as an "economic man."

SCIENTIFIC MANAGEMENT SHORTCOMINGS

The term "economic man" refers to a person who makes decisions that *maximize* his or her economic objectives. In the case of the worker, it is the individual willing to stay on the job from dawn until dusk in order to take home the greatest paycheck possible. Wage incentive plans are very important to the person because they provide this economic opportunity.

Lacking a solid understanding of human behavior, the scientific managers were unable to comprehend why all the employees did not take advantage of any chance to maximize their income. It never occurred to them that some people might be happy to earn a satisfactory amount of money, being "satisficers" rather than "maximizers." Simon has distinguished between these two types as follows:

Economic Man

45

Economic man
selects the best
available alterna-
tive.

> While economic man maximizes—selects the best alternative from among all those available to him; his cousin, whom we shall call administrative man, satisfices—looks for a course of action that is satisfactory or "good enough." Examples of satisficing criteria that are familiar enough to businessmen, if unfamiliar to most economists, are "share of market," "adequate profit," "fair price."[1]

**The Irration-
ality of
Rationalism**

Man is a com-
plex being.

A second shortcoming, complementary to the economic man theory, was their view of the worker as a totally rational human being who would weigh all alternatives and then choose the one that would give the greatest economic return. This thinking, of course, completely omitted any consideration of social factors. Furthermore, Blau notes, "To administer a social organization according to purely technical criteria of rationality is irrational, because it ignores the nonrational aspects of social conduct."[2] The term "complex" would have been much more appropriate than "economic," for there are many factors besides money that motivate the worker.

**The Black
Box**

The scientific managers could have overcome these problems if they had concerned themselves with what is called the "black box" concept. For example, if a company introduces a new incentive payment plan and productivity increases by ten per cent, this can be diagrammed in the following way:

FIGURE 3–1   Incentive Payment Plan Results

But *why* is there an increase in productivity? Is it brought about by the opportunity to earn more money? Is it caused by an increase in morale because the workers think management is interested in their well-being? Or is there a third, as yet undetermined, reason? As seen in Figure 3–2, the answer rests in the black box or *transformation process*, which takes place between the input and the output.

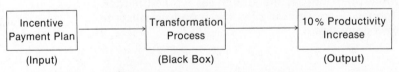

FIGURE 3–2   The Transformation Process

Understanding the human element requires an analysis of what goes on during this transformation process. The Hawthorne researchers attempted to study this process by ascertaining, for example, why output increased in the relay room but did not increase in the bank wiring room.

---

[1]Herbert A. Simon, *Administrative Behavior*, 2nd edition (New York: The Free Press, 1966), p. xxv.
[2]Peter M. Blau, *Bureaucracy in Modern Society* (New York: Random House Inc., 1956), p. 58.

The scientific managers, however, were unconcerned with this line of thinking. They knew that workers produce more while working individually as opposed to working in groups, and they used this information to guide them in organizing their work force. Their basic approach to the management of people was simplistic, and they pursued the matter no further.

The scientific managers did not analyze the transformation process.

The basic weakness of the classical theorists, especially Fayol, was that their writings on principles of management were often too general to be of much help to the practicing manager, as illustrated by the unity of command principle.

CLASSI- CAL MAN- AGEMENT DEFICIEN- CIES

Recall that the unity of command principle states that everyone should have one, and only one, boss. Gulick, another of the classical theorists, has indicated quite clearly the importance that early management theorists assigned to this principle:

Unity of Command

> The significance of this principle in the process of co-ordination and organization must not be lost sight of. In building a structure of co-ordination, it is often tempting to set up more than one boss for a man who is doing work which has more than one relationship. Even as great a philosopher of management as Taylor fell into this error in setting up separate foremen to deal with machinery, with materials, with speed, etc., each with the power of giving orders directly to the individual workman. The rigid adherence to the principle of unity of command may have its absurdities; these are, however, unimportant in comparison with the certainty of confusion, inefficiency, and irresponsibility which arise from the violation of the principle.[3]

However, this principle seems to be in conflict with the principle of specialization (or division of labor), which states that efficiency will be increased if one task is divided among members of a group. Simon notes:

> . . . if unity of command, in Gulick's sense, is observed, the decisions of a person at any point in the administrative hierarchy are subject to influence through only one channel of authority; and if his decisions are of a kind that requires expertise in more than one field of knowledge, then advisory and informational services must be relied upon to supply those premises which lie in a field not recognized by the mode of specialization in the organization. For example, if an accountant in a school department is subordinate to an educator, and if unity of command is observed, then the finance department cannot issue direct orders to him regarding the technical, accounting aspects of his work.[4]

If unity of command were to be as vigorously enforced as Gulick suggested, specialization would be impeded. Realistically, it is necessary to introduce some flexibility into the interpretation of the principle. In so doing, however, other problems arise, for now the principle lacks some of its previous "authority" and may be less effective in solving administrative problems. An analysis of the span of control principle makes this even more clear.

Unity of command is considered too inflexible a principle.

---

[3]Luther Gulick, "Notes on the Theory of Organization," as in Luther Gulick and L. Urwick, eds., *Papers on the Science of Administration* (New York: Institute of Public Administration, 1937), p. 9.
[4]Simon, *op. cit.*, pp. 23–24.

<table>
<tr><td>

Span of Control

</td><td>

Span of control refers to the number of individuals who report to a given superior. Specifically, the principle says that a superior can handle only a limited number of subordinates effectively. Although the number varied among classical theorists, most contended that the span should be no greater than nine.

</td></tr>
</table>

Span of Control

Span of control refers to the number of individuals who report to a given superior. Specifically, the principle says that a superior can handle only a limited number of subordinates effectively. Although the number varied among classical theorists, most contended that the span should be no greater than nine.

The span of control principle offers little operative assistance.

Although this is an interesting idea (its implications for organization will be discussed in a later chapter), it really provides little operative assistance to the manager. For example, in an organization with ten thousand people, if each manager has three subordinates, there will be nine levels in the hierarchy. Conversely, if each manager were to increase his or her span to ten, the number of levels could be reduced to five and the vertical flow of communication throughout the structure greatly enhanced. But which is best, a span of three or a span of ten? The principle as stated offers little assistance.

The Problem with Principles

The classical theorists who enumerated these lists of principles attempted to make management more of a science and less of an art. Although this was an admirable objective, in the process they forced a rigidity into some of the principles, such as unity of command; in the case of others, such as span of control, they employed a superficiality.

Close analysis of classical principles reflects many shortcomings. Overly mechanistic and nebulous, they dealt with authority, responsibility, and span of control as concepts. However, when managers attempted to apply these ideas to the organizational structure, the outcome was far from satisfactory.

INADEQUACY OF THE HUMAN RELATIONS APPROACH

The Hawthorne studies had a significant impact on management thought. For one thing, they complemented the work of the traditionalists. This is clearly seen in Figure 3–3, in which the contributions from Taylor, Fayol, and Mayo are applied to an organization chart. Taylor did the majority of his work at the foreman-worker level; Fayol's contribution came at the administrative management level; the Hawthorne studies cut across the entire spectrum, providing information that was valuable to management at all levels. However, there were a number of problems with the studies and the resulting human relations movement.

The Scientific Method and Hawthorne

One of the major criticisms of the human relations approach is directed at the very heart of the movement: some researchers claim that the Hawthorne studies were *not sufficiently scientific.* These critics contend that the researchers brought preconceived ideas and biases with them that affected their interpretation of the results. There are others who contend that the evidence which supported the conclusions was just plain flimsy. Landsberger, in *Hawthorne Revisited,*[5] criticized the studies further, challenging that the plant was not really typical because it was a thoroughly unpleasant place in which to work; that the researchers accepted management's objectives, viewing the worker as a mere means of attaining these goals; and that the researchers gave inadequate attention to the personal

The research procedure is criticized.

---

[5]Henry A. Landsberger, *Hawthorne Revisited* (Ithaca, N.Y.: Cornell University Press, 1958).

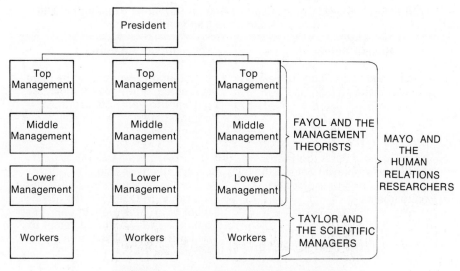

FIGURE 3–3 Contributions to Management Thought

attitudes people brought with them to the job, overlooking the effect of the unions and other extra-plant forces.

Another criticism of the human relations movement is directed at its very philosophy, which Megginson has summarized in the following way:

The Human Relations Philosophy

> This philosophy held that the business organization was a social system and that the employees were largely motivated and controlled by the human relationships in that system. Thus, the emphasis changed from an economic view of employees, in which the purpose of their productivity was to maximize the profit of the firm, to one of organizing and manipulating human relationships among personnel so that employees would receive the greatest personal satisfaction from their working environment.
>
> The basic assumption of the human relations approach was that the goal of human administration should be to provide the workers with job satisfaction. It was believed that employee participation should be obtained in order to produce job satisfaction and to improve employee morale. The assumption behind this belief was that greater job satisfaction would result in greater productivity. These cause and effect relationships—employee participation → job satisfaction, and job satisfaction → increased productivity—were the essence of the human relations philosophy.[6]

However, recent research challenges this concept that "happy workers are productive workers." Actually, job satisfaction is a multidimensional variable, impossible to explain in such simplistic terms. Output depends not only on a person's morale but also on his or her individual goals and motivation. In essence, the human relationists' philosophy was too simplistic, and by the late 1950's it was fading from the scene, to be replaced by what some individuals call a human resources philosophy, which contains a more viable interpretation of modern man (see Table 3–1).

Happy workers are not necessarily productive workers.

---

[6]Leon C. Megginson, *Personnel: A Behavioral Approach to Administration* (Homewood, Ill.: Richard D. Irwin, 1972), p. 7.

TABLE 3–1   Partial Comparison of Human Relations Philosophy with Human Resources Philosophy

Human Relations	Human Resources
1. People need to be liked, to be respected, and to belong.	1. In addition to wanting to be liked, respected, and needed, most people want to contribute to the accomplishment of worthwhile objectives.
2. The manager's basic job is to make each employee believe that he or she is part of the departmental team.	2. The manager's basic job is to create an environment in which subordinates can contribute their full range of talents to the attainment of organizational goals. In so doing, he or she must attempt to uncover and tap their creative resources.
3. The manager should be willing to explain his or her plans to the subordinates and discuss any objections they might have. On routine matters, he or she should encourage participation by them in the planning and decision-making process.	3. The manager should allow participation in important matters as well as routine ones. In fact, the more important the decision, the more vigorously he or she should attempt to involve the subordinates.
4. Within narrow limits, individuals and groups should be permitted to exercise self-direction and self-control in carrying out plans.	4. The manager should continually try to expand the subordinates' use of self-control and self-direction, especially as they develop and demonstrate increased insight and ability.
5. Involving subordinates in the communication and decision-making process will help them in satisfying their needs for belonging and individual recognition.	5. As the manager makes use of the subordinates' experiences, insights, and creative abilities, the overall quality of decision making and performance will improve.
6. High morale and reduced resistance to formal authority may lead to improved performance. They should at least reduce intradepartmental friction and make the manager's job easier.	6. Employee satisfaction is brought about by improved performance and the chance to contribute creatively to this improvement.

Adapted from Raymond E. Miles, "Human Relations or Human Resources?" *Harvard Business Review*, July–August 1965, p. 151.

THE POSITIVE SIDE OF THE PICTURE   Before concluding this chapter, it should be noted that only the shortcomings and deficiencies of the scientific managers, classical theorists, and human relationists have been mentioned here in an attempt to counterbalance the positive accomplishments outlined in Chapters 1 and 2. After all, if one is to see these groups in proper perspective, he or she must examine the weaknesses as well as the strengths.

Yet it would be unfair not to give credit to these three groups for their accomplishments. Certainly they made mistakes, but they were breaking new ground, and many of the facts known to us today remained mysteries to them. Still they persisted, gathering information that proved useful. The scientific management pioneers helped American industry reach new heights of efficiency. Contributions from the early management theorists have helped train executives in the principles of planning, organizing, and controlling. Human relations research provided important insights into human behavior in the work environment. It was noted, for example, that Mayo's early research in the textile mill resulted in some important physiological-psychological findings. By the mid-1940's, as more research was completed, however, he was able to reassess his earlier conclusions and formulate some new theories about the workers. One of these concerned the rabble hypothesis.

The *rabble hypothesis* holds that workers are a disorganized group of individuals, each acting in his own self-interest. Management's goal is to show each worker that this self-interest is best served when each conducts himself or herself in the manner desired by the company. This, of course, was the very approach subscribed to by Taylor.

Mayo's Philosophy Revisited

Mayo concluded that this hypothesis was invalid, because the individual does not operate independently. Rather, his or her actions are fashioned, at least in part, by the work group; the other members have a collective influence on him or her. That is one reason why, for example, technology and changing conditions are often viewed negatively by the workers. These conditions disturb the cohesiveness that exists among the members. The result is often a disequilibrium, manifested by complaints about supervision and working conditions. The individual becomes dissatisfied because the group's unity is under attack.

The rabble hypothesis is invalid.

When this occurs, Mayo noted, there are three basic responses an individual can make. First, there is the *logical* response, wherein the individual uses discrimination and individual judgment. Second, there is the *nonlogical* response, which is a result not of deliberation, but of social conditioning. It is adequate in handling the situation, but it is a direct result of training according to a social code of behavior. Third, there is the *irrational* response, often employed by groups that face a situation they are unable to handle. They cannot reason their way through the problem, so a logical solution is impossible. Their social training is inadequate to cope with the problem, so a nonlogical response is ineffective. This leaves only an irrational response, which is precisely the course of action they follow.[7] They have lost their capacity for disciplined cooperation.

An irrational response often occurs when an organization attempts to apply new knowledge to technical practice too quickly for general social adjustment. One of the most famous illustrations is found in the research study conducted by Trist and his associates, when they investigated the effects of changing technology on the nationalized coal mines in Great Britain.[8] Prior to World War I, the miners tended to work in small, independent teams. Each team was autonomous, and the individuals identified very strongly with their respective groups. New advances in

---

[7]Elton Mayo, *The Human Problems of An Industrial Civilization* (Cambridge, Mass.: Harvard University Press, 1946), pp. 157–158.
[8]E. L. Trist and K. W. Bamforth, "Some Social and Psychological Consequences of the Longwall Method of Coal-getting," *Human Relations*, February 1951, pp. 3–38.

Technology can impede group cohesiveness.

technology and equipment, however, led to changes in the composition of the work groups. Under the new system, 40 to 50 people were placed in each group and were spread over an area of about 200 yards. This change in the work pattern impeded close interpersonal relationships and group identifications. As a result, productivity suffered. In an effort to rectify the situation, the management restored many of the social and small group relationships. In turn, productivity, morale, and attendance improved substantially. Through this type of human relations study, the importance of factors such as group cohesiveness was recognized.

Improved Research Design

Another benefit stemming from the work of these human relations pioneers was improved research design. Some of the early Hawthorne experiments, for example, were redone because the researchers realized they were not controlling some of the causal variables. Their concern with formulating an adequate research procedure has carried over to the present day, as reflected in the high degree of importance currently assigned to the scientific method as a research tool. Although there is no universally accepted method, there is general agreement as to the basic steps involved. They are the following:

Steps in the scientific method.

1. *Identify the problem.* **Precisely what is the objective of the entire investigation?**
2. *Obtain preliminary information.* **Gather as much available data as possible about the problem area. Obtain background information.**
3. *Pose a tentative solution to the problem.* **State a hypothesis, which can be tested and proved to be either right or wrong, that is most likely to solve the problem.**
4. *Investigate the problem area.* **Using both available data and, if possible, information gathered through experimentation, examine the problem in its entirety.**
5. *Classify the information.* **Take all the data that have been gathered and put them in an order that expedites their use and helps establish a relationship with the hypothesis.**
6. *State a tentative answer to the problem.* **Draw a conclusion regarding the right answer to the problem.**
7. *Test the answer.* **Implement the solution. If it works, the problem is solved. If not, go back to step 3 and continue through the process again.**

This method is highly regarded by researchers. As Kerlinger notes:

> The scientific method has one characteristic that no other method of attaining knowledge has: self-correction. There are built-in checks all along the way to scientific knowledge. These checks are so conceived and used that they control and verify the scientist's activities and conclusions to the end of attaining dependable knowledge outside himself.[9]

The refinement of this procedure has played a key role in modern management.

SUMMARY

In perspective all three groups — the scientific managers, the classical theorists, and the human relationists — had shortcomings. Yet it must also be realized that they complemented each other, helping to form the basis for modern management theory and practice. The efficiency goals of the scientific managers and classical theorists led to the human relations philosophy of treating people well, which in turn has

---

[9]Fred N. Kerlinger, *Foundations of Behavioral Research*, 2nd edition (New York: Holt, Rinehart, and Winston, Inc., 1973), p. 6.

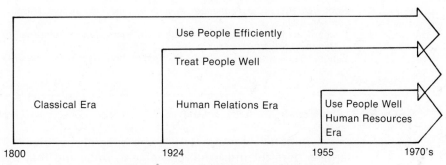

FIGURE 3–4 Changes in Managerial Philosophy

been replaced, as seen in Figure 3–4, by a human resources philosophy of using people well.

Part I of the book ends with this chapter. By now, the reader has been well grounded in the important historical management information he or she will need. The focus of attention will therefore be shifted to modern management theory and practice, answering questions such as: Where is management thought today? Whatever happened to the ideas espoused by Taylor? Are the concepts of Fayol still in vogue? What role are the behaviorists currently playing?

---

1. What is meant by the term "economic man"?

2. In understanding human behavior, what is meant by the term "irrationality of rationalism"?

3. How is the transformation process useful in understanding human behavior?

4. What is the major argument often raised against classical management principles? Be specific in your answer.

5. Did the Hawthorne researchers use the scientific method? Explain.

6. What is some of the criticism directed toward the Hawthorne studies?

7. Is a happy worker a productive worker? Explain.

8. How does the human relations philosophy differ from the human resources philosophy?

9. What was Mayo's rabble hypothesis? Was it an accurate hypothesis?

10. What is the scientific method? Outline the steps in the process.

REVIEW AND STUDY QUESTIONS

Anderson, B. F. *The Psychology Experiment: An Introduction to the Scientific Method.* Belmont, Calif.: Wadsworth Publishing, 1966.

Argyris, C. *Personality and Organization.* New York: Harper & Row Publishers, 1957.

Dubin, R. *Human Relations in Administration,* 2nd edition. Englewood Cliffs, N.J.: Prentice-Hall, Inc., 1961.

Landsberger, H. A. *Hawthorne Revisited.* Ithaca, N.Y.: State School of Industrial and Labor Relations, Cornell University, 1958.

Mayo, E. *The Human Problems of an Industrial Civilization.* Cambridge, Mass.: Harvard University Press, 1946.

SELECTED REFERENCES

Roethlisberger, F. J. *Management and Morale.* Cambridge, Mass.: Harvard University Press, 1941.

Shepard, J. M. "On Alex Carey's Radical Criticism of the Hawthorne Studies." *Academy of Management Journal.* March 1971, pp. 23–32.

Simon, H. A. *Administrative Behavior,* 3rd edition. New York: The Free Press, 1976.

CASE: FOR A FEW DOLLARS MORE

A national manufacturing firm recently received a number of large orders for industrial equipment. Realizing that they would be unable to fill the orders unless a dramatic increase in output could be achieved, the company instituted an incentive plan to supplement the current hourly wage. Under this new program, all increases in productivity would result in direct pay increases of similar magnitude. For example:

Old Hourly Salary	Productivity Increase	Productivity Bonus	New Hourly Wage
$4.50	10%	$ .45	$4.95
$4.50	20%	$ .90	$5.40
$4.50	30%	$1.35	$5.85
$4.50	40%	$1.80	$6.30
$4.50	50%	$2.25	$6.75

In addition, the company was willing to apply the same incentive scheme for Saturday work, which paid time and a half, and Sunday work, which paid double time. Top management indicated that it was shooting for a 40 per cent increase in productivity across the board.

Within sixty days, however, it became evident to management that the plan was not working. On the average, productivity was up only 17 per cent and, despite all management efforts to promote weekend work, only 23 per cent of the workers were willing to work on Saturday and 14 per cent on Sunday.

One manager, in giving his opinion of the situation said, "What more do the workers want? Under this new pay scheme they can increase their salaries way above what they would ordinarily earn. However, most of the men I talked to say they're not interested in the extra money. One of them told me he spent the whole weekend working in his garden. Another took his kids fishing for two days. I just don't understand these guys. I guess the Protestant Ethic is dead. These guys would rather loaf than work."

One of the workers, however, gave a different reason for the less-than-expected productivity increases. "Who cares about the extra money?" he asked. "I'm making more than enough now. What am I going to do with an extra $2,000? Better that I stay home and enjoy my family and watch television on Sunday. I'm not going to knock myself out for a few dollars more."

Questions

1. Why is the incentive scheme having so little effect?

2. How would Frederick Taylor interpret the results?

3. What suggestions would you make to the management? Explain, incorporating into your answer the black box concept.

CASE: MY BOSS DOESN'T UNDERSTAND ME

Today, many workers feel that their superiors do not really understand them. Managers are accused of having very set, erroneous ideas about how to handle their people. These include concepts such as people (a) dislike work; (b) have to be threatened with punishment to get them to attain organizational objectives; (c) lack ambition; (d) dislike responsibility; and (e) want to be told what to do. Does management really operate under these assumptions? Robert Townsend, former president of Avis Rent-a-Car, seems to think so. He summarizes the above five managerial assumptions like this:

1. **Office hours nine to five for everybody except the fattest cats at the top. Just a giant cheap time clock. (Are we buying brains or hours?)**
2. **Unilateral promotions. For more money and a bigger title I'm expected to jump at the chance of moving my family to New York City. I run away from the friends and a life style in Denver that have made me and my family happy and effective. (Organization comes first; individuals must sacrifice themselves to its demands.)**
3. **Hundreds of millions of dollars are spent annually "communicating" with employees. The message always boils down to: "Work hard, obey orders. We'll take care of you." (That message is obsolete by fifty years and wasn't very promising then.)**[10]

Questions

1. Did the scientific managers operate according to the above five managerial assumptions? Explain.

2. What have we learned from the Hawthorne research that shows that these assumptions are wrong? Explain.

3. What can management do to overcome these erroneous assumptions?

CASE: USE ME WELL

Not long ago, a New York based firm decided to open an office in Paris. Many of the firm's international customers were located in France, and the company felt it could provide better service to these people if it had a representative stationed nearby.

There were a number of people in the company who seemed to have both the desire and the necessary prerequisites to head up the office. One of these was Ben Milton, who had been with the company for ten years and had an excellent working knowledge of the firm's operations. In hopes of being appointed to the foreign office, Ben went in and talked to his superior, Dick Allen. However, Dick tried to discourage him from taking the job. "What do you want to go to Paris for?" he asked. "There's going to be plenty of work over there, and with the currency exchange problems you'd probably wind up mak-

---

[10]Robert Townsend, *Up the Organization* (Greenwood, Conn.: Fawcett Publications, Inc., 1971), p. 120.

ing less money than if you just stayed home. Believe me, it's going to be a thankless job. Besides, don't you like it here? Don't we treat you well?" Ben admitted that they did, but he was, nevertheless, interested in the overseas position and said he would appreciate any help Dick could give him.

A few weeks later the decision was announced. A younger man who had been with the firm for five years was given the job. Two weeks later, Dick went on vacation for a month. When he returned, much to his surprise, he found a letter of resignation on his desk. Ben Milton had left the company a week before. One part of his letter read, "I feel that I am not being used to the best of my ability. I have therefore decided to take a position where I can employ my talents to the fullest." Some time later Dick heard that Ben was managing an office in Brussels for one of the company's competitors.

Questions

1. What was Ben looking for in his job that he did not find?

2. Why was Dick surprised to learn that Ben had resigned?

3. What basic error did Dick make in handling Ben's request? How does it relate to the human resources philosophy?

CASE: MANAGEMENT CHALLENGES[11]

As management enters the 1980's it is going to find itself confronting six major challenges, according to Neil H. Jacoby, dean emeritus of the Graduate School of Management at U.C.L.A. The first of these is the challenge of high political turbulence and uncertainty. The United States will have to cope with unprecedented problems of inflation, unemployment, and energy supply, while simultaneously trying to reconcile conflicting claims on the national product by labor union members, stockholders, public employees, farmers, and other interest groups.

The second challenge is that of low economic growth. During the 1980's it is highly unlikely that this country will see real growth in the range of 5 to 7 per cent. Rather, national income will probably average around 3 per cent.

Third, capital and credit will become very expensive, making it more and more necessary for business firms to turn to outside sources of funding to support expansion and renovation of facilities. A New York Stock Exchange study projects private investment demand over the period from 1975 to 1985 at $4 trillion, leaving a $500 billion gap.

Fourth, industrial discipline will weaken. Business firms will find that owing to changing values, both workers and customers will have less loyalty to any one particular organization. Additionally, firms with authoritarian hierarchies will find that their structures are no longer viable in tomorrow's business world.

Fifth, business managers in the next decade will have to respond

---

[11]The data in this case can be found in: Neil H. Jacoby, "Six Challenges to Business Management," *Business Horizons,* August 1976, pp. 29–37.

to the burgeoning demands of the consumers, environmentalists, and civil rights advocates, and to the thickening networks of governmental regulation that these demands will produce.

Sixth, and most basic to American business people, will be the task of re-establishing in the public mind the conviction that profit-seeking enterprises competing in open markets are the most efficient means of satisfying consumer demand, and that economic freedoms are a bulwark to our own political liberties.

Questions

1. A careful analysis of these six challenges may leave the average manager feeling quite overwhelmed. With which of the six do you think scientific managers would feel most comfortable dealing? Least comfortable?

2. With which of these would the administrative theorists such as Fayol feel most comfortable? What about Barnard and the behavioral theorists?

3. Since none of the above-mentioned people or groups may feel comfortable with all of the above six challenges, what particular difficulty does this present to the modern manager? Explain.

PART II
MODERN MANAGEMENT THEORY AND PRACTICE

In this part of the book, modern management theory and practice will be examined. Part II is divided into five sections, A through E. The first, which encompasses Chapter 4, will outline the three schools of management thought that are currently the most popular. Then, having set the stage, the next three sections, Chapters 5 through 14, will review the basic ideas and concepts subscribed to by members of these schools. Finally, the last section, consisting of Chapter 15, will address itself to the current status and future direction of management theory. In particular, the issue of synthesizing the three schools into one will be examined.

The major goals of Part II are to acquaint the reader with modern management theory by providing a framework within which to analyze the area and to familiarize him or her with effective management practices. The ideas and concepts in this part of the book form the foundation of effective management. By the end of Chapter 15, the reader should have a good understanding both of how management has developed since the days of the early Hawthorne research and of where it is going. In addition, he or she should have gathered useful information on some of the most basic and current management tools and techniques.

THE DEVELOPMENT OF MODERN MANAGEMENT THEORY

In this section the development of modern management theory will be reviewed. Remember from Part I that there were many people who made contributions to early management thought. Some of these, such as Henri Fayol, attempted to put together a framework within which management could be analyzed. Others, such as Taylor and his associates, emphasized time and motion study. Still others were concerned with the socio-psychological side of the job, as seen in the case of Mayo and his associates. Whatever happened to these ideas? The answer is that they are still with us today, although in modified form. In Chapter 4 it will be seen that the concepts of these three groups have contributed to the formation of modern schools of management thought. The goal of Chapter 4 is to provide a basis from which the reader can understand these current developments.

CHAPTER FOUR

MODERN SCHOOLS OF MANAGEMENT THOUGHT

Since World War II, a great deal of management research has been conducted. The concepts of Taylor, Fayol, Mayo, and their associates have been expanded in an attempt to provide increased knowledge about the field of management. The result has been that, at least at the present time, management theory is in the "schools" phase, and any student who approaches the field without a basic understanding of these schools does so at a considerable disadvantage. **GOALS OF THE CHAPTER**

These schools represent viewpoints regarding what management is and how it should be studied. Of course, not everyone in management can be placed in a particular school; some defy such simple categorization. Nevertheless, the background and training of management theorists and practitioners is reflected in their beliefs about management and, in most cases, make them candidates for one of the three schools of thought that will be examined in this chapter. The first is the management process school; the second, the quantitative school; the third, the behavioral school.

Today, these three schools represent the most prominent trends in management thought, although they certainly are not universally accepted. For example, authors such as Koontz and O'Donnell list nine schools of thought: (1) management process, (2) empirical, (3) interpersonal behavior, (4) group behavior, (5) cooperative social systems, (6) sociotechnical systems, (7) decision theory, (8) communications center, and (9) mathematical.[1]

Others, such as Miner, opt for five: (1) classical, (2) human relations, (3) structuralist, (4) behavioral humanist, and (5) decision making.[2] Nevertheless, the three that will be discussed in this chapter encompass virtually all the ideas put forth by these and other authors, and provide a general picture of management theory as it currently exists.

The goal of this chapter is to examine each of these three schools in depth. When you have finished reading the chapter you should:
1. Know the basic beliefs and tenets of the management process school.
2. Be aware of the ideas to which advocates of the quantitative school subscribe.
3. Understand the philosophy and composition of the behavioral school.
4. Be familiar with the weaknesses present in each of the three schools.
5. Be able to discuss the possibility of synthesizing the three schools into a unified composite.

---

[1]Harold Koontz and Cyril O'Donnell, *Management: A Systems and Contingency Analysis of Managerial Functions*, 6th edition (New York: McGraw-Hill Book Company, 1976), p. 57.
[2]John B. Miner, *The Management Process*, 2nd edition (New York: Macmillan Publishing Co., 1978), pp. 88–90.

MANAGE-MENT PROCESS SCHOOL

The *management process,* or classical, school traces its ancestry to Fayol. The primary approach used by this school is to identify the managerial functions. It will be remembered that Fayol identified them as planning, organizing, commanding, coordinating, and controlling. Proponents of this school view these functions as a process that is carried out by the manager.

During the years immediately following World War II, this school grew and flourished. The major reason for its acceptance can be traced to the outline it provides for the systematic study of management. By identifying management functions and then examining each in detail, a student is provided with a wealth of information about the field. Although modern management scientists (quantitative theorists) and behaviorists might take issue with this statement, some of the most prominent books in the field have been based on a process framework. Table 4–1 presents Fayol's management process followed by those of seven other current textbook authors or co-authors. As seen in the table, there is agreement regarding the functions of planning, organizing, and controlling, whereas there appears to be disagreement about the others. However, many process school advocates place the blame on *semantics.* What one person calls directing, another includes in his definition of organizing. If the functions were spelled out in detail, everyone would have the same list of subfunctions or activities.

TABLE 4–1   The Management Process As Seen By Various Authors*

Functions	Fayol	Dessler	Haimann & Scott	Hampton	Koontz & O'Donnell	Sisk	Terry	Wren & Voich
Planning	X	X	X	X	X	X	X	X
Organizing	X	X	X	X	X	X	X	X
Commanding	X							
Staffing		X	X		X			
Directing					X			
Influencing			X					
Actuating							X	
Coordinating	X							
Leading		X		X		X		
Controlling	X	X	X	X	X	X	X	X

*Sources
1. Henri Fayol, *General and Industrial Management* (London: Sir Isaac Pitman and Sons, Ltd., 1949).
2. Gary Dessler, *Management Fundamentals: A Framework* (Reston, Va.: Reston Publishing Company, 1977).
3. Theo Haimann, William Scott, and Patrick E. Connor, 3rd edition, *Managing the Modern Organization* (Boston: Houghton Mifflin Company, 1978).
4. David R. Hampton, *Contemporary Management* (New York: McGraw-Hill Book Company, 1977).
5. Harold Koontz and Cyril O'Donnell, *Management: A Systems and Contingency Analysis of Managerial Functions,* 6th edition (New York: McGraw-Hill Book Company, 1976).
6. Henry L. Sisk, *Management and Organization,* 3rd edition (Chicago: South-Western Publishing Company, 1977).
7. George R. Terry, *Principles of Management,* 7th edition (Homewood, Ill.: Richard D. Irwin, Inc., 1977).
8. Daniel A. Wren and Dan Voich, Jr., *Principles of Management: Process and Behavior,* 2nd edition (New York: The Ronald Press, 1976).

A major tenet of the process school is that by analyzing management along functional lines, a framework can be constructed into which all new management concepts can be placed. A skeletal design emerges of, for example, planning, organizing, and controlling. Any new mathematical or behavioral technique that can improve managerial performance will fall into one of these three functional areas. The result is an enduring systematic design. Although this concept is under attack today, there is little doubt that the framework provided by the management process school has been the major reason for its acceptance by both students and practitioners.

An On-going Framework

Process approach provides a skeletal design.

Management process proponents see the manager's job as a process of interrelated functions. For example, in the case of planning, organizing, and controlling. Figure 4–1 does *not* represent management as a process because the functions follow in sequential order; there is only an *indirect* relationship between planning and controlling. Everything seems to be rigidly predetermined. Instead, Figure 4–2 is more accurate because it represents management as consisting of *interrelated* functions, which are neither totally random nor rigidly predetermined. They are, instead, dynamic functions, each one playing an integral role in a larger picture, which consists of the integration of all the functions. The total is seen as being more than the sum of its parts.

Management As a Process

Management is viewed as an interrelated functional process.

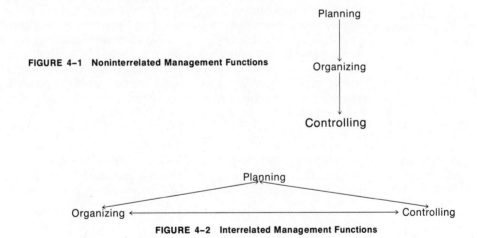

FIGURE 4–1   Noninterrelated Management Functions

FIGURE 4–2   Interrelated Management Functions

Another belief of process school advocates is that management principles can be derived from an intellectual analysis of the managerial functions. By dividing the manager's job into its functional components, principles based upon each function can be extracted. For example, there is the *primacy of planning* principle, which states that, at least initially, planning precedes all other managerial functions. A manager must plan before he or she can organize and control. *Absoluteness of responsibility*, a principle of organizing, states that a manager cannot escape responsibility for the activities of individual subordinates. The manager may delegate authority, but cannot delegate responsibility. If something goes wrong, the manager as well as the subordinate, is responsible. A principle of control is the *exception principle*, which holds

Management Principles

that managers should concern themselves with exceptional cases and not routine results. Significant deviations, such as very good or very bad profit performance, merit the manager's time far more than average or expected results.

These principles are designed to improve organizational efficiency. They must *not*, however, be looked upon as rules, since a rule is supposed to be inflexible. For example, "no smoking" is a rule because it demands a certain kind of action and allows no deviations. Conversely, a principle, as used here, is merely a useful guideline and does not require rigid adherence. Advocates of the management process school, therefore, view principles as *general* guidelines that must remain constant focal points for research. If a particular principle proves invalid or useless, it should be discarded, but it must not be assumed that a principle will be useful at all times or under all conditions, or that a violation constitutes invalidation. Since management is an art as well as a science, the manager remains the final arbiter in choosing and applying these principles.

Principles are used as general guidelines.

Universality of Management Functions

Advocates believe that management process is universal.

Process school advocates also believe that basic management functions are performed by all managers, regardless of enterprise, activity, or hierarchical level. The manager of a manufacturing plant, the administrator of a hospital, and the local chief of police all carry out the same managerial functions. This is also true for their subordinate managers all the way down the hierarchy, although the percentage of time devoted to each function will, of course, vary according to the level. For example, using planning, organizing, and controlling as illustrations, low-level managers, who are concerned with detailed and routine types of work, tend to do more controlling and less planning and organizing. However, as one progresses up the organizational chain, the work requires more creativity and administrative ability, resulting in an increase in the amount of time needed for planning and a decrease in that required for controlling (see Figure 4–3).

A Philosophy of Management

The process school also stresses the development of a management philosophy. This requires answering questions such as: Precisely what does a manager do? What kinds of values are important to manage-

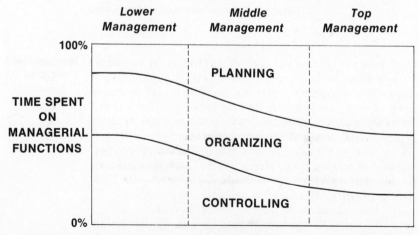

FIGURE 4–3 Functions Performed by Managers at Different Levels of the Hierarchy

ment? What values are important to the workers? The development of a management philosophy results in helping the manager mentally establish relationships between material things and human beings. Process school advocates believe that managers can accomplish this feat more easily by following the management process, because their activities revolve around certain functions, and in carrying them out, they employ the fundamental beliefs and attitudes to which they subscribe. The result is a *modus operandi* that links the management process with the fundamental ideals, basic concepts, and essential beliefs of the manager. The outcome is a philosophy that helps the manager win the support of the subordinates in achieving organizational objectives. It also provides the groundwork for future action.

A philosophy of management can be developed.

The process school has many advantages, the major one undoubtedly being the framework it offers for analyzing the field. Although viewed by many of its critics as static and too simplistic to be useful, it has been better received by practitioners and students than any of the other schools.

The *quantitative*, or management science, school consists of those theorists who see management as a body of quantitative tools and methodologies designed to aid today's manager in making complex operations/production-related decisions. Proponents of this school are concerned with decision making and, to a large degree, are modern-day adherents of Taylor's scientific management movement. A great deal of their attention is given to defining objectives and the problems that surround their achievement. This type of orderly, logical methodology is very helpful in constructing the kinds of models needed for solving complex problems. Moreover, the approach has been very effective, as will be seen later in the book, in dealing with inventory, materials, and production control problems.

QUANTITA-TIVE SCHOOL

In the post-World War II era, many management scientists emerged onto the business scene. Today, they go by various and sundry titles, from management analysts to operations researchers to systems analysts. However, they share a number of common characteristics, namely: (a) the application of scientific analysis to managerial problems; (b) the goal of improving the manager's decision-making ability; (c) a high regard for economic effectiveness criteria; (d) a reliance on mathematical models; and (e) the utilization of electronic computers. For purposes of this discussion, all individuals meeting these criteria shall be collectively placed in the quantitative school. Two topic areas that have been of major interest to these people are optimization and suboptimization.

Management scientists share some common characteristics.

In Chapter 3, it was noted that most people do not maximize their goals, they satisfice them. For example, the manager does not try to make all the possible profit, but does strive for a satisfactory level. There are times, however, when profit can be maximized through, for example, the *optimization* of production, i.e., the combining of all the resources in the right balance. This is a very difficult task, and to attain it an approach called *suboptimization* is often used. In a production setting consisting of materials being ordered, processed, and finished, for example, the firm would attempt to suboptimize each of these three components. Terry explains the process in this way:

Optimization and Suboptimization

Suppose our objective is to maximize production profits. To achieve this we consider the common portions of most enterprises to be (1) input, (2) process, and (3) output. Also, we optimize production, assuming all we can produce will be sold at a satisfactory market price. Since the totality—production—is to be optimized, its components of input, process, and output are optimized, as each relates to the totality. Common parlance for this is to suboptimize the components. Step No. 1: Input, or raw materials being received, are suboptimized. This will depend upon forecast demand, inventory carrying cost, and order processing cost. Likewise, Step No. 2: Process, or materials processed, are suboptimized by adequate consideration to production capacity, machine setup cost, and processing cost for each product. Last, Step No. 3: Suboptimization of output or products finished is obtained by considering product demand and transportation cost.[3]

Each step in the production process (ordering, processing, and finished goods) is affected by suboptimization factors (see Figure 4–4). The firm does not purchase all the raw materials it can; nor does it process or ship the total possible amount. Instead, it finds a balance that results in the ideal production level and the maximization of profit.

Mathematical Models

Optimization of resources is often achieved with the use of a mathematical model. The model can be a single equation or a series of equations, depending upon the number of factors involved and the complexity of the situation. In the construction of these models, management scientists have found calculus to be one of the most useful branches of mathematics because it allows them to measure the rate of change in a dependent variable in relation to changes in an independent variable. For example, if a company increases the size of its plant and cost per unit declines, the management might be very interested in learning the extent to which the production facilities can be expanded before the cost per unit will begin to increase. If the firm has a mathematical model constructed for this purpose, it merely has to determine at what point the cost per unit change moves from negative to either zero or positive, for at this point costs stop decreasing.

Problem solving via mathematical models is widely employed.

The same basic concept can also be used by, for example, an appliance store manager who wants to know how many different product

---

[3]George R. Terry, *Principles of Management*, 7th edition (Homewood, Illinois: Richard D. Irwin, Inc., 1977), p. 30.

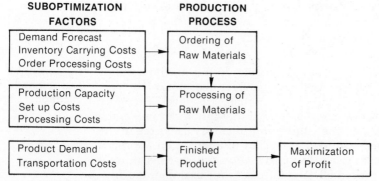

FIGURE 4–4   Optimization of Production and Maximization of Profit

lines he should carry. Assume that he formulates the following mathematical equation, which, to the best of his knowledge, is accurate:

$$Y = 16X - X^2$$

where Y is equal to maximum profit and X is equal to the number of product lines carried. The equation states that maximum profit is equal to sixteen times the number of product lines (16X) minus the number of product lines squared ($-X^2$). By increasing the value of X, the respective values of Y can be attained. For example:

$$\text{when } X = 0$$
$$Y = 16 \times 0 - 0^2$$
$$Y = 0$$
$$\text{when } X = 1$$
$$Y = 16 \times 1 - 1^2$$
$$Y = 15$$

By constructing the entire table up to the point where Y again equals zero, it is possible to identify the entire range of positive profit values.

X (product lines)	0	1	2	3	4	5	6	7	8	9	10	11	12	13	14	15	16
Y (profit)	0	15	28	39	48	55	60	63	64	63	60	55	48	39	28	15	0

Thus, the number of product lines that should be carried is eight, as this will result in a maximization of profit.

Overview and Contributions

Although highly simplified, the above mathematical model is representative of the ones employed by the management scientists. In fact, it is common to find adherents of this school relying strongly on mathematical tools and techniques such as linear programming, simulation, Monte Carlo theory, queuing theory, and game theory, topics that will be covered in Chapter 9. The quantitative school has gained many supporters in recent years. Increasing use of computers accompanied by the development of more sophisticated mathematical models for solving business problems has accounted for many of the advances made by this school. In addition, it has played an important role in the development of management thought by encouraging people to approach problem solving in an orderly fashion, looking more carefully at problem inputs and relationships (see Figure 4–5). This school has also promoted the need for goal formulation and the measurement of performance.

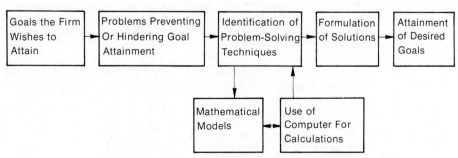

FIGURE 4–5 Problem Solving via a Quantitive Approach

BEHAVIORAL SCHOOL

The *behavioral* school grew out of the efforts of people such as Gantt and Münsterberg, who recognized the importance of the individual in the work place, and Mayo and Barnard, who were interested in group processes. Today, it is common to find individuals in this school with training in the social sciences, including psychology, sociology, anthropology, social psychology, and industrial psychology, applying their skills to business problems.

As one would expect, behavioral school proponents are largely concerned with human behavior. They contend that because management entails getting things done through people, the effective manager must understand the importance of factors such as needs, drives, motivation, leadership, personality, behavior, work groups, and the management of change; for these are going to have a direct effect on the manager's ability to manage. Although all members of the behavioral school share this philosophy, some place emphasis on the individual, others on the group. The behavioral school, therefore, consists of two "branches": the interpersonal behavior branch and the group behavior branch.

Interpersonal Behavior

Some behaviorists are very interested in interpersonal relations and are oriented toward individual and social psychology. They belong to the *interpersonal behavior branch* of the behavioral school:

Some focus primarily on individual behavior.

Their focus is the individual and his motivations as a socio-psychological being. Their emphasis varies from those who see psychology as a necessary part of the manager's job—a tool to help him understand and get the best from people by responding to their needs and motivation—to those who use the psychological behavior of individuals and groups as the core of management.[4]

Members of this branch believe that the individual, not just the work group, must be understood if the manager is to do an effective job.

Group Behavior

The other branch of the behavioral school, often confused with its interpersonal behavior cousins, consists of individuals who see management as a social system or collection of cultural interrelationships. Known collectively as the *group behavior branch*, they are highly sociological in nature, viewing human organizations as systems of interdependent groups, primary and secondary alike:

Others are highly sociological in their approach.

The recognition of the organized enterprise as a social organism—made up in turn of many social organisms within it, subject to all the attitudes, habits, pressures and conflicts of the cultural environment of people—has been helpful to both the theorist and the practicing manager. Among other helpful aspects are the awareness of the institutional foundations of organization authority, the influence of informal organization, and such social factors as those Wight Bakke has called "bonds of organization." Likewise, many of Barnard's insights . . . have brought the power of sociological understanding into the realm of management practice.[5]

Advocates of the group behavior branch see the manager as an individual who must interact and deal with groups. For this reason, they place

---

[4]Koontz and O'Donnell, *op. cit.*, p. 58.
[5]*Ibid.*, p. 59.

great emphasis on the need to understand both the formal and the informal organization.

Although the interpersonal behavior branch stresses the importance of understanding the individual (psychology) and the group behavior branch places prime importance on the knowledge of group behavior (sociology), the two are actually interdependent. The group is made up of individuals, but the whole is actually greater than the sum of its parts. Both psychology and sociology are important to the behaviorists regardless of the priorities assigned to each area.

Overview and Contributions

Although the behavioral school lacks the type of framework used by management process advocates, it certainly does not lack structure. For example, communication, motivation, and leadership, a few of the school's basic concerns, are areas of major analysis. However, instead of working from functions to activities and principles as do the management process advocates, the behaviorists work in the opposite direction; they start with human behavior research and build up to topics or functions. Thus, theirs is a much less rigid and more empirically based school of thought. Wortman and Luthans have enumerated several major contributions made to the field of management by these behaviorists including:

Behaviorists are highly empirical in their approach.

> ... **(1)** *conceptual,* **the formulation of concepts and explanations about individual and group behavior in the organization; (2)** *methodological,* **the empirical testing of these concepts in many different experimental and field settings; and (3)** *operations,* **the establishment of actual managerial policies and decisions based on these conceptual and methodological frameworks. Since behavioral approaches have become widely disseminated throughout the management literature, there has been an increasing acceptance of the behavioral approach by management.**[6]

Is there really a legitimate basis for these three schools of management thought or should a synthesis be immediately undertaken? Many writers in the field believe a coalescence of the differing viewpoints can be achieved, but one of the key obstacles, in their view, is that of *semantics*; everyone is really saying the same thing but is using different words. One group of authors believes that "As is so often true when intelligent men differ in their interpretations of problems, some of the trouble lies in key words."[7]

TOWARD A UNIFIED THEORY?

There is still much disagreement.

Another major barrier is identified as differing *definitions of management.* If the field were clearly defined in terms of fairly specific content, differences among the various schools of management might be reduced to the point where synthesis would be possible. Although the idea sounds plausible, the outlook at the present time is not good.[8] One of the reasons is the current lack of research:

> **The choice of a school or writer to follow presents a serious dilemma. . . . "I don't know" remains the appropriate answer. When sufficient research has been compiled, the schools will fade of their own accord. That they have not faded is good evidence that the quantity and quality of research to date is insufficient to render judgment.**

---

[6]Max S. Wortman, Jr., and Fred Luthans, eds., *Emerging Concepts in Management* (New York: Macmillan Publishing Co., 1975), p. 190.

[7]Koontz and O'Donnell, *op. cit.,* p. 66.

[8]W. Jack Duncan, "Transferring Management Theory To Practice," *Academy of Management Journal*, December 1974, pp. 724–738.

. . . No amount of argument between conflicting schools . . . is likely to achieve either consensus or truth.[9]

Advocates of each of the three schools believe strongly in their own point of view and resist attempts to be synthesized or integrated. For example, process school spokesmen have been vigorous in their attempts to bring the quantitative and behavioral people into their domain. However, the latter groups view their own contributions to management as much too significant to be relegated to the kind of secondary position being advocated for them by the process people. Nor are they necessarily wrong, for each of the three schools has its weaknesses as well as its strengths and, currently, no one of them possesses the characteristics necessary for a successful and meaningful integration of management theory.

THE WEAK-NESSES OF THE SCHOOLS

The process school, although the most widely accepted, at least for the teaching of basic management, is also subject to frequent attack.

Process School Weaknesses

A static approach?

One of the foremost arguments against the school is that it pays only lip service to the human element; actually, management is regarded as a very static and dehumanized process. Although its advocates argue that this is not the case at all, behaviorists in particular remain unswayed.

Many also attack the school's foundation, claiming that management principles are not universally applicable. They see them as being most appropriate in stable production-line situations, where unions are not very strong or where unemployment is quite high. However, when used in professional organizations, the principles often require modification, their application being contingent upon the specific situation. This is why Fayol and his associates, who operated under stable production-line situations, were able to use them effectively, whereas modern managers, operating under dynamic conditions, have trouble doing so.[10] In addition, there is a tendency among principle proponents to formulate generalizations as principles even though they have not been empirically validated.

Are management principles universally applicable?

A third argument, along the same lines, centers on the universality of the management process. Do all managers perform the same basic functions? There is considerable controversy on this point. Research has revealed that although similarities exist among various positions within firms, the same is not true among firms. When professional[11] (law firms, research and development laboratories, architectural firms, hospitals, universities) and administrative (manufacturing companies, retailing firms, insurance agencies, transportation companies) organizations are compared, studies have shown that the latter tend to be more bureaucratic, placing emphasis on rules, policies, procedures, and hierarchical authority. Conversely, in professional organizations, this power and authority tends to shift from the managerial jobs to those of the nonmanaging professions.[12]

Is management process universal?

---

[9]John B. Miner, *Management Theory* (New York: Macmillan Publishing Co., 1971), p. 150.
[10]*Ibid.*, pp. 139–140.
[11]As used here, professional organizations are those which: (a) are recognized by society as having professional status; (b) are encouraged and influenced by a professional association or society; and (c) have a set of specialized techniques supported by a body of theory. For further information on this point, the reader is directed to John B. Miner, *The Management Process: Theory, Research and Practice*, 2nd edition (New York: Macmillan Publishing Co., 1978), p. 324.
[12]See Richard H. Hall, "Some Organizational Considerations in the Professional-Organizational Relationship," *Administrative Science Quarterly*, December 1967, pp. 461–478; and Gerald D. Bell, "Predictability of Work Demands and Professionalization as Determinants of Workers' Discretion," *Academy of Management Journal*, March 1966, pp. 20–28.

For example, in hospitals doctors sometimes have as much freedom to make decisions as do top administrators. Nurses often have more freedom of action or discretion in carrying out their tasks than do certain middle managers. When Bell measured the amount of discretion employed by occupational groups in an eastern hospital in carrying out their work assignments, as seen in Table 4–2, he found that the higher the degree of professional training, the greater the amount of discretion the employees exercised.[13]

Results such as these have led Miner to conclude that "when decision-making authority is dispersed . . . some very sizeable changes in managerial functions must occur, relative to administrative organizations."[14] He continues by noting that:

> . . . analysis of professional versus administrative organizations once again leads to the conclusion that managerial functions are not universal. Not only do managerial jobs differ in their mix of functions depending on their level and the particular department involved, but they also differ from organization to organization. This interorganizational difference is particularly noticeable when administrative and professional types are compared.[15]

Quantitative School Weaknesses

The quantitative school is attacked on the grounds that it fails to see the complete picture. Is management a system of mathematical models and processes or is this too narrow a view? Critics opt for the latter, calling management science a tool and not a school. They note that mathematics is

---

[13]Bell, *op. cit.*, p. 23.
[14]John B. Miner, *Management Theory, op. cit.*, p. 88.
[15]*Ibid.*, p. 93.

TABLE 4–2   Occupations and Their Average Discretion Scores in a Professional Organization

Occupation	Average Discretion Score
Administrator	5.7
Doctor	5.6
Department head (nursing)	5.2
Department head (others)	5.4
Assistant department head (nursing)	4.9
Assistant department head (others)	5.0
Nurse (staff)	4.5
Dietary supervisor	3.7
Plumber, carpenter (semi-skilled worker)	3.2
Secretary	3.1
Pharmacist	3.0
Laboratory technician	3.0
Orderly	3.0
X-ray technician	2.3
Nurses' aide	2.2
Cook	2.0
Dietary helper	1.4
Housekeeper, launderer, etc.	1.3

Source: Gerald D. Bell, "Predictability of Work Demands and Professionalization as Determinants of Workers' Discretion," *Academy of Management Journal*, March 1966, p. 23. Reprinted with permission.

used in physics, engineering, chemistry, and medicine, but it has never emerged as a separate school in these disciplines. Why should it do so in the field of management? There is no doubt that the management sciences have supplied very useful tools for the manager to employ in solving complex problems. Inventory, material, and production control have all been facilitated thanks to these quantitative contributors. However, what about human behavior? How does one write an equation that solves "people" problems? Both the process and behavioral schools attack the quantitative theorists on this point and the latter appear hard pressed to refute the argument.

A tool or a school?

Behavioral School Weaknesses

The major argument lodged against the behaviorists is that they, like the management science people, do not see the complete picture. Psychology, sociology, and related areas are all important in the study of management, but there is more to the field than just human behavior; some forms of technical knowledge are also needed. The process school provides an important structural framework within which to study human behavior. The quantitative school offers an objective, quantifiable approach to decision making. Without these supplemental elements, managers cannot adequately apply their knowledge of behavior.

To be an effective manager, one must have more than a mere working knowledge of the human, dynamic model. True, the people in the work place constitute a continually changing social system, and an understanding of man's nonrational behavior is needed to supplement the assumptions of rationality often attributed to workers by their superiors. However, the critics argue that the behavioral school is only one segment, albeit an important one, of the total picture, and in and of itself is incomplete.

Failure to see the complete picture?

A CONCEPTUAL FRAMEWORK

As noted earlier, there is a need for further research if the three schools are ever to be synthesized. In addition, it should be realized that there are some who oppose any such action, contending that fundamental and inescapable differences exist among the various schools, making a unified theory of management impossible.

Whether or not the three schools will ever come together is a matter of current debate. However, the student of management is well advised to travel all three roads — process, quantitative, and behavioral — for each makes important contributions to the study of management.

SUMMARY

Modern management theory is currently in the "schools" phase. In this chapter the three schools of management thought were examined: management process, quantitative, and behavioral.

The management process, or classical school, traces its ancestry to Fayol. One of its major tenets is that by analyzing management along functional lines, a framework can be constructed into which all new management concepts can be placed. This framework consists of a process of interrelated functions such as planning, organizing, and controlling. Another belief of the process school is that management principles can be derived through an analysis of the managerial functions. A third tenet is that the basic management functions are performed by all managers, regardless of enterprise, activity, or hierarchical level. Additionally, the process school stresses the development of a management philosophy.

The quantitative, or management science, school consists of those theorists who see management as a system of mathematical models and processes. Relying heavily on the application of scientific analysis to managerial problems, economic effectiveness criteria, and the use of computers, adherents of this school have promoted the need for goal formulation and the measurement of performance.

The behavioral school consists of two branches: the interpersonal behavior branch and the group behavior branch. The former is heavily psychological in orientation; the latter is heavily sociological in emphasis. While this school lacks the type of framework used by management process advocates, it certainly does not lack structure. However, instead of working from functions to activities and principles as the management process advocates do, the behaviorists work in the opposite direction; they start with human behavior research and build up to topics or functions.

Today there is no unified theory of management. Several reasons can be cited including semantics, differing definitions of management, and lack of research. Advocates of each school claim that the others have serious flaws. The process school is seen as being too static; the quantitative school is seen as a series of useful tools but certainly not a school; the behaviorists are attacked as failing to see the total picture.

It is still unclear whether the three schools will ever by synthesized. For this reason, the student of management is well advised to travel all three roads. We will begin doing so in the next chapter, where the planning process is examined.

---

1. What are the basic beliefs of management process school advocates?

2. How important are management principles to process school advocates?

3. Precisely what is meant by the term "universality of management functions"?

4. What background or training do management scientists have?

5. What is meant by the term optimization? Suboptimization?

6. What are some of the contributions made to management theory by the management scientists?

7. Identify the two major branches of the behavioral school. Describe both.

8. What contributions have the behaviorists made to management?

9. In your own words, what are the primary weaknesses of the process school? The quantitative school? The behavioral school?

10. Will the three schools of management ever be merged or synthesized? Give your reasoning.

REVIEW AND STUDY QUESTIONS

Albers, H. H. *Principles of Management: A Modern Approach*, 4th edition. New York: John Wiley & Sons, Inc., 1974.
Fayol, H. *General and Industrial Management*, trans. Constance Starrs. London: Sir Isaac Pitman & Sons, Ltd., 1949.

SELECTED REFERENCES

Kelly, J. *Organizational Behaviour*, revised edition. Homewood, Ill.: Richard D. Irwin, Inc. and the Dorsey Press, 1974.

Koontz, H., ed. *Toward a Unified Theory of Management*. New York: McGraw-Hill Book Company, 1964.

Koontz, H. "The Management Theory Jungle." *Academy of Management Journal*. December 1961, pp. 174–188.

Koontz, H., and C. O'Donnell. *Management: A Systems and Contingency Analysis of Managerial Functions*, 6th edition. New York: McGraw-Hill Book Company, 1976.

Miner, J. B. *Management Theory.* New York: Macmillan Publishing Co., 1971.

Miner, J. B. *The Management Process: Theory, Research, and Practice.* New York: Macmillan Publishing Co., 1978.

Woolf, D. A. "The Management Theory Jungle Revisited." *Advanced Management Journal*. October 1965, pp. 6–15.

Wortman, M. S., Jr., and F. Luthans, eds. *Emerging Concepts in Management,* 2nd edition. New York: The Macmillan Company, 1975.

CASE: THE MANAGER'S JOB

In gathering data for her term paper "The Functions of the Manager," Jane Wadsworth, a junior at a large eastern business school, decided to interview five executives from different organizations. She asked the same question of each: "In your view, what are the functions of a manager?" Some of the executives explained their answers at great length, others merely listed a lot of managerial functions. In either event, at the end of the interview Jane would review their comments and then tell them how she was going to summarize their answers. All agreed with her summation. The result of the five interviews was as follows:

Functions	Manager 1	Manager 2	Manager 3	Manager 4	Manager 5
Planning	X	X	X	X	X
Organizing	X	X	X	X	X
Staffing			X		
Communicating		X			
Coordinating	X				
Motivating	X			X	
Directing			X		
Controlling	X	X	X	X	X

Questions

1. How do you account for the apparent discrepancies in the replies of the managers? Explain.

2. If you were told that one of these managers was from an insurance company and the others were from manufacturing firms, which of the above managers would you conclude to be the insurance man? Give your reasoning.

3. If you were told that one of the above five managers was a hospital administrator, which would you conclude to be the administrator? Give your reasoning.

CASE: THE ADVERTISING BUDGET

The importance of advertising was always something that Jay Hallen, owner of a large retail store, wondered about. In 1977 his store had an advertising budget of over $90,000, an increase of 17 per cent from the previous year, but Jay was really not sure how much of this money was being wisely spent. Nevertheless, he knew advertising was important, so he followed a simple guideline, spending 6 per cent of estimated sales for advertising.

In mid-1977 Jay received an announcement about a one-week management seminar being sponsored by a local university. Realizing that he had some middle-level managers who could profit from this training, he sent two of his up-and-coming people. When they returned, he learned that one of the speakers was a university professor who had talked about the need for constructing mathematical models for decision making purposes. One of the man's major points was that many companies spend more money on advertising than they should. However, unaware of where to draw the line, they spend more and more each year. In fact, he noted, a large percentage of firms tend to tie advertising to their sales forecast; i.e., if they estimate sales at $1 million, they spend $100,000; if they project sales at $2 million, they spend $200,000. "Actually," the speaker said, "this is a very simple, and generally erroneous, approach. The only way to really ascertain how much to spend on advertising is to measure previous expenditures and results."

Jay was unsure of exactly what the man meant but he liked the basic idea, so he called the university and asked the professor if he would consider undertaking a consulting assignment. The professor agreed, and for the next week he examined the company's past sales figures and advertising expenditures and conducted some computer analysis. At the end of that time he concluded that advertising effectiveness could be determined with the following formula:

$$Y = 10x - x^2 + 50,000$$
where:
   Y = total sales
   x = total advertising expenditures/$10,000

Questions

1. Using just the above formula, how much sales income will the store obtain with advertising expenditures (per $10,000) from $10,000 to $110,000?

2. Based on the above answers, how much advertising should this company do? Explain.

3. How useful are management scientists in the field of management? Explain.

CASE: A STATE OF CONFUSION

"Bill," said Jack Tuner, training director at Willowby Insurance, "how would you like to attend a training session in New York City this coming week?"

What's it going to be about?

Since when have you gotten so particular? Usually, when the company intends to send a few people to a training session, you jump at it. I can remember that winter you talked me into sending you to Miami Beach. You were sure interested in going to seminars then.

Yeah, but that was when I only had a little work to do. Now I've got work piled up on my desk and I don't want to run off to just any old training session.

I wouldn't ask you to go to just any training session. Besides, you know that I'm only asking you to repay a favor. Anyway, do you want to go or not?

Tell me what it's going to be about.

It's called "Understanding Today's Worker."

Yeah, well thanks, but I'm not interested.

Why not?

Because the last time you sent me to one of those behavioral seminars I came away more confused than before. Look, a lot of research being conducted in the behavioral sciences is great research, but it has no real applicability. I mean, there is just no way to take it back to the job and use it.

You mean those people never tell you how you can apply it?

Oh no, they do that. The problem is that the way they explain it and the way it really works are two different things. In short, I really think I'm a lot better off just doing things my own way and not messing around with all these new behavioral theories. They just leave me all confused.

Questions

1. Have the behaviorists really made any contribution to management? Explain.

2. How important is it to understand today's worker?

3. What does Bill mean by his statement that behavioral seminars leave him confused? Explain.

CASE: ONE OUT OF THREE

A midwestern insurance company recently had an opening in one of its lower-middle management positions. After evaluating a number of possible candidates, the selection committee narrowed its list to three people.

The first candidate was a newly hired management trainee who had only recently received a master's degree in business from a large eastern university. The man's major area of study at the undergraduate level had been general management, whereas at the graduate level he had a concentration in management theory and insurance. Although the company liked the individual's general management background and felt his insurance courses provided him with some of the technical training he would need in supervising company personnel, some of the committee members were afraid that the man's background was too general. "We need someone with a little more background and training in this business," said one of the members.

The second individual being considered for the position was a salesman who, for the past two years, had been the leading salesman in his regional office. He did not want to remain a salesman for the rest of his life, so when he learned that the company was looking for a lower level middle-manager, he immediately applied for the job. On the positive side, the committee liked his track record. "This man has illustrated that he can deliver in the field," said one member. "This has seasoned him for the management ranks. After all, isn't a manager a salesman selling management's point of view to the employees?" On the negative side, however, some of the committee members were afraid that the man might be too interested in personal selling and its behavioral aspects and fail to see "the complete picture." One of them put it this way: "There's more to managing than just getting along with people."

The third person being considered for the job worked in the firm's actuarial department. She did fine technical work, and one committee member who felt this woman would be ideal for the job remarked, "The backbone of an insurance company is its actuarial department. This woman knows the ins and outs of insurance. This technical competence will help her do a good job." There was, however, concern that the woman might be too used to working with numbers and not accustomed to managing people. "Technical skill is important," said one member, "but it's no substitute for handling people."

After discussing the three individuals for almost an hour, the chairman called for action. "Gentlemen, we have to make a decision on this matter today. We have a fair idea of the strong and weak points of each candidate. What do you say we choose one of the three and then adjourn for lunch?" Everyone agreed.

Questions

1. What characteristics of training would you look for in choosing from among the three candidates?

2. Which of the three candidates do you think would be most likely to be a management process advocate? A quantitative school supporter? A behavioral school advocate?

3. Based on your answer to the above question, which of the three would you choose for the job? Why?

SECTION B
THE MANAGEMENT PROCESS SCHOOL

The goal of this section is to examine the tenets of the management process school. It should be noted that the province of this school is determined by the managerial functions placed within its sphere. In this section, three functions will be examined: planning, organizing, and controlling. The reason for choosing these and no others is that virtually all management process advocates agree that the three are indeed within the realm of the process framework. Furthermore, many writers and researchers contend that the process school is less empirical and more philosophical than the quantitative or behavioral schools. This second criterion also favors the present choice.

Chapter 5 will be devoted exclusively to the planning process. In particular, attention will be focused on the need for comprehensive and strategic planning. Also, unavoidably crossing over into the behavioral school, the values of management in the planning process will be discussed. Short-run or operational planning will also be covered.

In Chapter 6, the organizing process will be reviewed. This chapter will present many of the "nuts-and-bolts ideas" involved in integrating the people with the structure. Some of the more important concepts will include the various forms of departmentalization available to the manager; organization by committee; types of authority; and the need for understanding the informal organization.

Finally, in Chapter 7, the control function will be examined and prime attention given to the need for effective feedback and evaluation. Some of the topics that will be reviewed include budgeting, break-even analysis, key area control, and management audits.

CHAPTER FIVE
THE PLANNING PROCESS

There is an adage in management, "If you don't know where you are going, any path will get you there." However, when one has objectives, as businesses should, planning is essential. The overall goals of this chapter are to examine the planning process, review what is meant by comprehensive, strategic, and operational planning, and discuss the advantages and limitations of planning.

When you are finished reading this chapter you should be able to:

1. Describe what is meant by the term *comprehensive planning*.
2. Define the term *strategic planning*.
3. Identify the three basic foundations of a strategic plan.
4. Relate some of the most common ways of conducting evaluations of both the external and internal environments.
5. Explain how a firm goes about developing a market niche.
6. Describe how a planning organization can help a business carry out comprehensive planning.
7. Outline some of the basic advantages of planning.
8. Explain why planning can help but is no panacea for dealing with the future.

GOALS OF THE CHAPTER

Modern businesses operate in a highly dynamic environment where change is a constant factor. As a result, it has become more and more necessary for companies to determine their objectives carefully, and then systematically to construct plans for attaining them. This has become a continuous process throughout every organization. Naturally, managers at the upper levels should be greatly concerned with long-range or strategic planning, whereas the attention of those managers at the lower levels ought to be focused mainly on operational planning. Yet research indicates that some top managers have not been devoting requisite attention to long-range planning. Rather, they tend to spend most of their time worrying about short-run goals and performance results. In fact, it is not uncommon to find some chief executive officers who believe that comprehensive planning is something that can be delegated to their subordinates. When the overall plan is completed, they breathe a sigh of relief, "Thank heavens that's over, now let's get back to work!"

Fortunately, however, there has been a marked trend in recent years toward *comprehensive planning,* a process in which *all* departments of the organization identify their objectives and determine how they will be attained. In this process, each department ties its objectives to those units above and below it in the hierarchy. An integrated plan results in which all groups are working toward the same basic objectives. Today comprehensive planning is being used not only by large organizations, but by medium and small ones as well. In fact, smaller companies are beginning to realize that, despite their limited resources, they have about the same fundamental planning requirements as larger

COMPRE-HENSIVE PLANNING

Comprehensive planning incorporates all levels of the organization.

companies.[1] This trend toward comprehensive planning on the part of large and small businesses alike is going to continue, and those firms that do not begin to take the requisite steps toward insuring overall, well-coordinated plans are going to find themselves unable to maintain the pace.

In this chapter, the specific aspects of the planning process will be examined. This process entails setting objectives and formulating the steps necessary to reach these goals. This requires both a long- and short-range perspective. Initial attention will be focused on strategic planning with high priority given to the area of forecasting. Then the topics of long- and intermediate-range objectives will be examined. Finally, operational planning will be discussed.

STRATEGIC PLANNING

Steiner has defined *strategic planning* as "the process of determining the major objectives of an organization and the policies and strategies that will govern the acquisition, use, and disposition of resources to achieve those objectives."[2] Strategic plans provide a firm with long-range direction and are an outgrowth of three basic foundations, the first of which is the fundamental *socio-economic purpose* of the organization: Why is the business in existence? However it is stated, a socio-economic purpose always entails a consideration of company survival (profits) and societal needs (social functions). The second fundamental foundation is the *values and philosophy of the top management*. This composite of values and ideals will influence the strategic plan because it helps dictate the manner in which management will treat its customers and employees. The third basic foundation is the assessment of the *organization's strengths and weaknesses* in light of the external and internal environment. These three basic foundations are interdependent, as seen in Figure 5–1.

---

[1]For an excellent discussion of this area see George A. Steiner, ed., *Managerial Long Range Planning* (New York: McGraw-Hill Book Company, 1963), p. 17.
[2]George Steiner, *Top Management Planning* (New York: The Macmillan Company, 1969), p. 34.

FIGURE 5–1 Basic Foundations of Strategic Plan

More and more business firms are beginning to re-evaluate their purpose for existence. For example, years ago, when Henry Ford entered the automobile business, he saw his basic mission as one of providing people with a basic necessity — a form of transportation. People needed cars for mobility and he could provide these vehicles. General Motors broadened this idea, viewing the automobile as a luxury as well as a necessity. As a result, the firm offered the customer more extras and a wider line, albeit at a higher price, and replaced Ford as the number one automobile manufacturer. The nation's railroads have done the same, restating their purpose for existence so that they are no longer in the passenger-carrying business, but in the transportation business. Today, almost all their profits are derived from the freight they carry. The movie industry has also redefined its basic mission and is no longer merely in the movie business; it is now in the business of informing as well as entertaining its audience.

Today, most businesses define their basic mission in very *broad* terms, since the purpose of this practice is to provide *general* direction. The following are some examples:
1. Volkswagen's mission is to provide an economic means of private transportation.
2. American Telephone and Telegraph's mission is to provide quick and efficient communication capabilities.
3. IBM's mission is to meet the problem-solving needs of businesses.
4. Shell Oil's mission is to meet the energy needs of mankind.
5. International Minerals and Chemical Corporation's mission is to increase agricultural productivity to feed the world's hungry.[3]

Unless an organization can define its socio-economic purpose, and redefine it as conditions change, it will lack a clear understanding of its basic mission and have great difficulty in constructing a strategic plan.

Basic Socio-economic Purpose

The basic purpose for existence must be identified.

In this decade, the idea of social responsibility has received a tremendous amount of attention. Equal opportunity, ecology, and consumerism have all become focal points for management consideration and action. Why did these issues rise to the fore? Part of the answer rests with external actions such as government legislation. However, even more significant (and generally overlooked) have been the social action programs proposed by businesses themselves. What led to such action? The answer rests in the values and beliefs of the top management.

All managers in an organization bring a certain set of values to the work place with them, and every generation tends to have differing values. The basic profile of the 1950 manager is different from that of the 1970 executive, and the manager of the 1980's will have still different values. In the late 1960's, General Electric's Business Environment Section conducted a study designed to explore the trends that would be taking place in the world during the upcoming decade. After interviewing educators in the social sciences and studying current writings of over fifty authors, the researchers constructed a profile of significant value systems changes that would occur between 1969 and 1980. The profile is seen in Figure 5–2. These changing values will have a direct impact on the philosophy of future managers as well as on the environ-

Management Values

Management values will influence the strategic plan.

---

[3]Philip Kotler, *Marketing Management: Analysis, Planning, and Control*, 3rd edition (Englewood Cliffs, N.J.: Prentice-Hall, Inc., 1976), pp. 52–53.

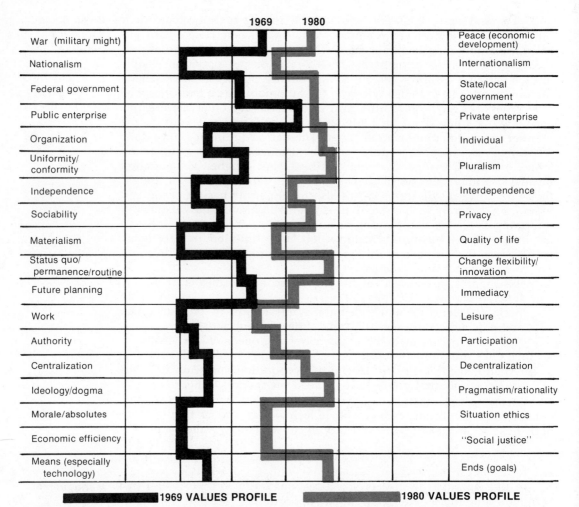

FIGURE 5–2   Profile of Significant Value-System Changes: 1969 to 1980, as Seen by General Electric's Business Environment Section (From Ian Wilson, "How Our Values Are Changing," *The Futurist*, February 1970, p. 9, published by the World Future Society, P.O. Box 30369, Bethesda Branch, Washington, D.C. 20014. Reprinted with permission.)

ment in which the organization operates. Because the manager lives in society, the individual will be influenced by its values.

Evaluation of the Environment

An evaluation of the external and internal environment assists the management in identifying organizational strengths and weaknesses. Based on these findings, objectives can be formulated. In evaluating the external environment, organizations rely most heavily on forecasting.

EXTERNAL ENVIRONMENTAL FORECASTING.   Forecasting the external environment can be done in a number of ways, depending on what the management would like to know. One thing, however, is clear. The environment is always changing, and the greater the change, the more important it is for the organization to gather data about it.

The dynamic environment of the business world can be seen through a sales comparison of the 20 largest industrials in the United States in 1966, when business conditions were very good, and in 1976, after the major recession of the early seventies. As shown in Table 5–1, nine of the top-ten firms in *Fortune's* 500 in 1966 had maintained their position in this elite group in 1976, the other one having fallen into the second-ten category. Of the second group of ten, however, only four were still in this category, one having moved up to the top ten and the other five having fallen further back. The table illustrates that no firm is ever standing still; it must be moving forward or it is falling behind. This is seen more dramatically in the case of the last ten industrials in *Fortune's* 500 in 1966 as compared with those in 1976 (See Table 5–2). If this dynamism is taking place among the large industrials, the nation's smaller business firms must be undergoing even more dramatic changes because they lack the size and financial strength of their giant counterparts. Thus, their need for forecasting change is even greater.

1. *Economic Forecasting.* The most common type of external forecasting is the *economic forecast.* If the economy is in an upswing, many businesses will find their positions improved; sales will rise and return on investments will increase. Conversely, a downturn will have a dampening effect. Much depends on the current state of the economy as reflected by gross national product (GNP), which is the value of goods and services produced in a year.

Various types of economic forecasts can be used to project developments in the external environment.

A. Extrapolation. The simplest form of economic forecast is that of *extrapolation.* This is nothing more than a projection of the current trend into the future. If a firm sold $100,000 worth of goods in 1976, $200,000 in 1977, and $300,000 in 1978, they might estimate continual $100,000 growth increments for the rest of the decade. Generally, of course, this is dangerous, because it fails to take into account changing environmental conditions as reflected in economic cycles. However, in cases such as population growth or life expectancy, a long-term forecast based on extrapolation can be fairly accurate.

**TABLE 5–1   Fortune's 20 Largest Industrials in 1966 and 1976
(On Basis of Sales)**

Rank in 1966	Rank in 1976
1. General Motors	1. Exxon (Standard Oil of N.J.)
2. Ford Motor	2. General Motors
3. Standard Oil (N.J.)	3. Ford Motor
4. General Electric	4. Texaco
5. Chrysler	5. Mobil Oil
6. Mobil Oil	6. Standard Oil of California
7. Texaco	7. Gulf Oil
8. U.S. Steel	8. International Business Machines
9. International Business Machines	9. General Electric
10. Gulf Oil	10. Chrysler
11. Western Electric	11. International Telephone and Telegraph
12. DuPont (E.I.) de Nemours	12. Standard Oil (Ind.)
13. Swift	13. Shell Oil
14. Shell Oil	14. U.S. Steel
15. Standard Oil (Ind.)	15. Atlantic Richfield
16. Standard Oil of California	16. DuPont (E.I.) de Nemours
17. Bethlehem Steel	17. Continental Oil
18. International Harvester	18. Western Electric
19. Westinghouse Electric	19. Proctor & Gamble
20. Radio Corporation of America	20. Tenneco

Source: *Fortune*, June 1967 and May 1977.

TABLE 5–2 Change in Selected Firms in Fortune's 500 Between 1966 and 1976 (On Basis of Sales)

Firm	Rank in 1966	Rank in 1976
Bangor Punta Alegre Sugar	491	–
Becton, Dickinson	492	367
Morton International	493	*
Maytag	494	–
Schering	495	*
B.V.D.	496	–
Mead Johnson	497	*
Parker-Hannifin	498	429
Signode	499	401
Curtis Publishing	500	–

– denotes that the firm was not anywhere in the top 500.
* denotes that the firm was merged or acquired by another.

Source: *Fortune*, June 1967 and May 1977.

B. Leads and Lags. The National Bureau of Economic Research (NBER) has discovered that when the economy turns up or down, there are some indicators that seem to precede the change, some that coincide with it, and still others that follow. There is thus a lead group, a coincident group, and a lag group.

Of greatest importance to forecasters are the lead indicators, for they tend to signal upcoming changes in the economic cycle. In all, there are twelve of them on the NBER's "short list," including average weekly hours worked, new business formations, new building permits, common stock prices, corporate profit after taxes, new orders for durable goods, and changes in consumer installment credit. Many forecasters place great value on these indicators, feeling they provide the best clues as to what is likely to happen.

Lag indicators are important in that they follow the economic cycle, making it possible to anticipate changes. The NBER has six indicators on its short list, including business expenditures for plant and equipment, unemployment rate, bank rates on short-term loans, manufacturers' inventories, and common and industrial loans outstanding. If the economy is beginning an upswing, banks can expect manufacturers to begin increasing their loans and investing money in plant and equipment. If the economy is beginning a downturn, there will be a reduction in business borrowing and plant and equipment expenditures, as well as a general increase in the unemployment rate.

Unfortunately, the lead and lag method is more than a matter of merely plugging various values into a mathematical equation. Qualitative judgments must also be made to determine the impact of the indicator. For example, if the number of residential building permits increases, orders for durable goods rise, and the average number of weekly hours worked goes up, then the GNP may start to rise. However, does this indicate that the company should float a new stock issue? Supposedly, the price of industrial stocks will begin to rise, but there is no certainty of this. In short, the lead and lag method helps the forecaster predict the future, but in so doing the individual is only making an educated guess. There is no guarantee that the guess is correct.

C. Econometrics. Another forecasting technique that is widely employed today is *econometrics*. This is a mathematical approach in which the main variables are brought together in a series of equations. GNP can then be forecast based on various assumptions arrived at through these equations. This technique provides the forecaster with a picture of what to expect under, for example, the most optimistic, most likely, and most pessimistic conditions.

The results can be further analyzed by applying them to the specific industry and company. For example, if General Motors estimates that there will be between 12 and 14 million automobiles sold (pessimistic and optimistic) and they will capture between 46 and 51 per cent of the market, sales will range from 5.52 to 7.14 million cars inclusive. This data can be used to construct initial income statements, illustrating profit and loss at various levels of sales. It is also possible to estimate production and marketing costs at these levels. Then, if the forecasters like, they can make changes in one area while leaving everything else the same. For example, what impact would a 15 per cent increase in advertising have on industry and company sales? The value of the econometric model is that it not only assists the company in forecasting the future, but also helps management predict results of various changes in strategy.

2. Governmental Action. Few companies escape the influence of governmental control. Most businesses face a host of laws designed to prevent monopoly, promote competition, and encourage ethical practices. In addition, there is the ever-present concern with monetary action, whereby the federal government can regulate credit through the federal reserve banks and open market operations. This spurs the economy forward or, in the case of runaway inflation, helps put on the brakes. Likewise, via fiscal action the federal government can pump money into the economy or draw it out either through higher taxes or a refusal to spend what has been currently collected. For these reasons, the government will have a direct impact on business strategy.

The effect of government action on aerospace provides a dynamic illustration. During the early 1960's, the federal government pumped billions of dollars into aerospace. The industry boomed as companies were awarded giant contracts and, in turn, subcontracted with smaller firms for some of the necessary hardware. Hundreds of thousands of jobs were created as America raced through Projects Mercury, Gemini, and Apollo. Once the moon was reached; however, the enthusiasm died. Public opinion polls showed that people no longer gave space research the high priority it once enjoyed. The war in Vietnam and inflation had become overriding issues, and governmental monetary and fiscal policy began to reflect these concerns. As a result, funds for aerospace were cut, and the stock of these firms plunged as layoffs occurred and cutbacks were made in an attempt to salvage what was left. By the early 1970's, some of the giants of the aerospace industry were only shells of what they had been.

3. Sales Forecasting. Businesses forecast the economy in general so as to set the stage for determining their own particular sales forecast. Some use an econometric approach, but not all businesses have the expertise for employing such a sophisticated technique. For them, the questions of how many goods (or services) we will sell, to whom, when, where, and how, in light of our economic projections, require a more down-to-earth sales forecast. In arriving at an answer, the first place to which a firm often turns is its own sales records. A survey of *current sales information* will indicate what products are selling best in which areas and to what kind of customers. Further sales forecast data

The impact of government control must be evaluated.

Sales forecasting can be conducted in a number of ways.

can often be obtained from the United States Bureau of the Census, the Department of Commerce, local trade associations, and the Chamber of Commerce.

Another, and often supplemental, method of gauging sales is the *jury of executive opinion.* In this approach, various executives in the organization are brought together for the purpose of constructing the sales forecast. Sometimes they work independently of each other; other times they form a joint opinion. In both cases, there is an input to the sales forecast based on what these executives believe will take place. Another version entails the review and modification of the forecast by the manager of marketing research. The value of the jury of executive opinion approach is that it allows input from executives who are in a position to make intelligent "guesstimates" about the future.

Another supplemental approach, often called the *grass-roots method,* entails a survey of the sales force. Since these people are in the field on a continuous basis, they should have some general ideas about what will and will not sell. These ideas are obtained by the sales manager, who compiles the results and sends them up the line. Here the composites from salespeople in all the districts and regions are aggregated and sent to central headquarters, where they are compared with the forecast constructed by a staff. Finally, changes are made based on management decisions regarding advertising, product line, price, and other such considerations. Then the forecast is reviewed and approved. The major advantage of the grass-roots method is that it obtains sales information from the people who are doing the actual selling.

A third supplemental approach is that of *user expectation.* How does the customer feel about the product? By going out and asking, the firm can obtain valuable information from the basic source, the consumer. Although some customers may say one thing and do another, if the firm obtains a large enough sample, it is possible to negate the impact of such responses.

INTERNAL ENVIRONMENTAL EVALUATION. A forecast of external environmental factors provides the organization with important planning infor-

THE WALL STREET JOURNAL

"Hold it, J.P.! This isn't the sales chart! It's the plans for our new staircase."

Reprinted by permission of the Wall Street Journal.

mation. However, this data must be supplemented with an evaluation of the internal environment, focusing particularly on the question, what are the company's internal strengths and weaknesses? In answering this question, there are two factors with which the manager need be concerned: material resources and personnel competence.

1. *Material Resources.*   The plant capacity plus the amount of cash, equipment, and inventory a company has on hand are important because they constitute the tools with which a strategic plan can be fashioned. Often these resources will help dictate a particular type of strategy. For example, a business with a large plant capacity will have a large fixed expense. However, if it can manufacture at capacity, the firm can spread these costs over many items, thereby reducing the cost per unit. This company will undoubtedly compete vigorously with a low price strategy. Conversely, a small manufacturer will not have so high a fixed expense but will also have fewer units among which to spread these costs. As a result, it is impossible to meet the big manufacturer head-to-head in a price war. Therefore, the small manufacturer will devise a strategy that the competition cannot or will not effectively combat, such as high price coupled with a great degree of personal selling.

Material resources such as cash, plant, and equipment must be evaluated.

A second reason for evaluating material resources is to ascertain the financial strength of the firm. If a company has $1 million in cash and $9 million in other assets, it can often maintain a strategic posture far longer than a firm with only one tenth of these assets. In turn this raises the question, how long should a firm remain with a particular strategic plan? The answer is, until it pays off or becomes evident that the results are not going to justify the costs. Unfortunately many firms adopt strategic plans that are not in accord with their material resources and as a result find themselves continually revising and modifying their plan. A strategic plan should always be tempered by the material resources available.

2. *Personnel Competence.*   The personnel in every organization will have a distinctive area of competence; there is something they do extremely well. For example, in a firm such as *The New York Times*, it is the ability with which the personnel can gather information from all over the world and compile it quickly, accurately, and in readable form. In contrast, many small papers use their people to gather local news happenings and rely upon AP and UPI sources to provide them with international news. Analogously, the "Big Three" auto manufacturers in America have the personnel needed to mass produce and market cars, whereas Rolls Royce is in the same basic business but concentrates its efforts less on marketing and more on production quality. Because a strategic plan must draw upon the company's strengths, personnel competence is an important consideration.

The competencies of the personnel must be identified.

DEVELOPING A PROPITIOUS NICHE

Based on the external and internal environmental analysis, the philosophy of the management, and the socio-economic mission of the organization, long-range objectives can be formulated. Before turning to that topic, however, it should be noted that every strategic plan must be designed so as to develop or take advantage of a particular niche. Every organization must find a thing(s) it does best and build a strategy around this forte or strength. For example, *The New York Times* has a specific market niche, selling its papers to thousands of people every day. It is not, however, the largest selling newspaper in New York City; this position is held by the *New York Daily News*. Anyone who has ever read the two papers knows that the *Daily News* is a picture newspaper written in a very easy-to-read style. It is much more appealing to the mass market than is *The New York Times*. Yet it would be foolish for *The Times* to copy the style of its competition. To do so would mean abandoning a niche in which its competencies are best employed. The basic mission, philosophy of management, and strength of *The Times* are all geared toward its current style of news coverage. This is what is known as *leading from strength*. Every well-formulated plan draws upon the organization's fortes in fashioning the most successful strategy possible.

Surprising as it may seem, many businesses do *not* lead from strength. Instead of utilizing their fortes, they tend to hold back and respond defensively to the environment. In fact, many managers spend an inordinate amount of time trying to straighten out little problem areas instead of boldly taking advantage of their strengths. They do not have a strategic or long-range plan. Most of their time is spent on day-to-day matters. They are like chess players who seize poisoned pawns because the immediate capture of any enemy is given priority over the long-range development of their own pieces.

> The firm must build a strategy that capitalizes on its strengths.

By identifying a niche in which its competencies can be effectively employed, an organization focuses on goals. However, in so doing, Drucker notes, the successful manager must never try to cover too much territory. Instead, he or she must "milk" a propitious niche for all it is worth, according to the following recommended guidelines:

1. Economic results require that managers concentrate their efforts on the smallest number of products, product lines, services, customers, markets, distribution channels, end uses, and so on which will produce the largest amount of revenue. Managers must minimize the attention devoted to products which produce primarily costs, because their value is too small or too splintered.
2. Economic results require also that staff efforts be concentrated on the very few activities that are capable of producing truly significant business results — with as little staff work and staff effort as possible spent on the others.
3. Effective cost control requires a similar concentration of work and efforts on those very few areas where improvement in cost performance will have significant impact on business performance and results — that is, on those areas where a relatively *minor* increase in efficiency will produce a *major* increase in economic effectiveness.
4. Managers must allocate resources, especially *high-grade human resources,* to activities which provide opportunities for high economic results.[4]

These basic ideas are employed by a number of firms, including General Electric, which handle their strategic business plan like an investment portfolio — pruning the losing lines and backing the successful ones through systematic analysis.[5] This process can be quite difficult, since, in the case of GE, it involves a review of over 40 distinct businesses. Each must be rated on quantitative factors such as sales, profit, and return on investment, as well as hard to quantify factors such as market share, technology needs, employee loyalty in the industry, competitive stance, and social need. In conducting its annual planning review, GE has developed a strategic business planning grid, presented in Figure 5–3. On this grid are two dimensions, industry attractiveness and business strengths. Depending on the combination of each (high, medium, or low) the firm will decide to: (a) invest and

---

[4]Peter F. Drucker, "Managing for Business Effectiveness," *Harvard Business Review*, May–June 1963, p. 56.

[5]"G.E.'s Jones Restructures His Top Team," *Business Week*, June 30, 1973, pp. 38–39.

A

INDUSTRY ATTRACTIVENESS

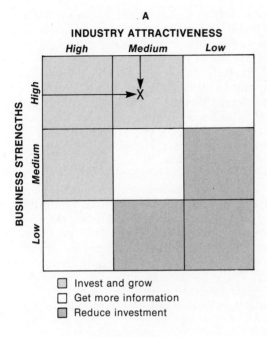

B

INDUSTRY ATTRACTIVENESS

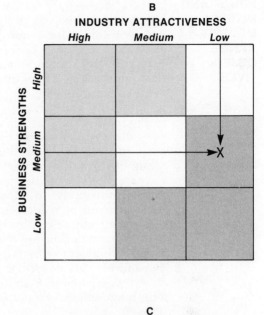

☐ Invest and grow
☐ Get more information
▨ Reduce investment

FIGURE 5–3 General Electric's Strategic Planning Grid

C

INDUSTRY ATTRACTIVENESS

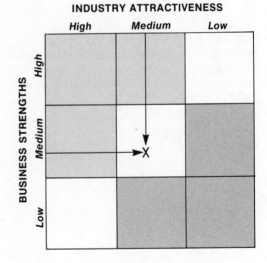

grow, (b) get further information because the business might go either way, or (c) reduce the investment.[6]

In Figure 5–3A industry attractiveness is medium and business strengths are high. In this case the company would opt to invest and grow. In Figure 5–3B industry attractiveness is low and business strengths are medium. In this situation the company would not invest further and would start to reduce or consolidate its holdings. Finally, in Figure 5–3C industry attractiveness and business strengths are both medium. As a result, the company would wait for further information before making a final decision.

[6]See "General Electric's 'Stoplight Strategy' for Planning," *Business Week*, April 28, 1975, p. 49.

LONG- AND INTER-MEDIATE-RANGE OBJEC-TIVES

From long-range goals, intermediate-range objectives can be formulated.

On the basis of the socio-economic purpose, values of the top managers, and an analysis of the external and internal environment, a business will formulate its long-range objectives. For a manufacturing firm, as seen in Figure 5–4, some of the more common goals will relate to manufacturing, finance, and marketing. However, in long-range perspective these goals are often nebulous. It is therefore helpful to reduce them to intermediate-range objectives, thereby increasing the amount of specificity and making the goals more action-oriented. For example, in Figure 5–4 there is a long-range objective of increasing sales by 15 per cent a year. How can this be attained? First, the intermediate-range goals need to be clearly defined — in this case, to win a contract currently up for bid to sell widgets to a large West Coast manufacturer; to increase the size of the plant; and to establish in-house management training programs. In addition, all the long-range objectives relate the basic mission of manufacturing and selling widgets. This mission, in turn, is directly related to the socio-economic purposes of the organization. The manufacturing and sale of widgets will result in profits as well as the fulfillment of certain social functions such as the satisfaction of demand for this particular good. There is thus an *interrelated hierarchy of objectives,* and the strategic plan assists the firm in identifying its long-range objectives and formulating the derivative intermediate-range goals.

OPERATIONAL PLANNING

The third and final type of planning is *operational* planning. Operational planning is short-range in contrast to strategic planning, and most low- and intermediate-level administrators spend a good deal of their time carrying out these short-range plans. Figure 5–5 shows the

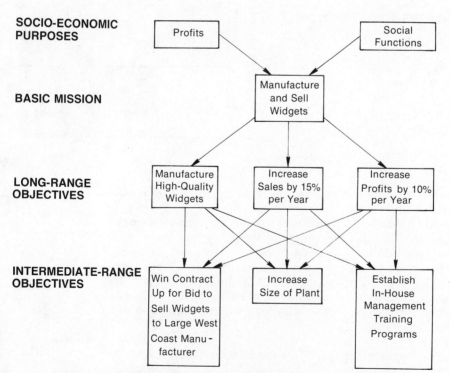

SOCIO-ECONOMIC PURPOSES

BASIC MISSION

LONG-RANGE OBJECTIVES

INTERMEDIATE-RANGE OBJECTIVES

FIGURE 5–4   Interrelationships of Long- and Intermediate-Range Objectives

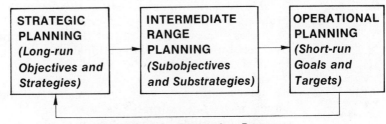

Feedback for Evaluation Purposes

FIGURE 5-5 A Planning Structure.

relationship between strategic and operational planning. Strategic planning can be viewed as the formulation of long-range objectives, whereas operational planning is the implementation of these decisions.

Operational planning is action-oriented.

The time-lapse between the formulation stage and the implementation stage may be as great as a decade, although it is most common to find firms opting for a five-year plan. For example, one survey of 420 companies revealed the following planning period distributions:[7]

No corporate plan	16%
Less than five years	6%
Five years only	53%
Five to ten years	8%
Ten years only	11%
More than ten years	6%

Most operational plans are divided into functional areas. In a manufacturing enterprise setting, for example, they would appear as in Figure 5–6. This plan is much more specific than its strategic counterpart, with goals and targets spelled out in great detail. As an operational plan comes down the chain of command, the level of abstraction decreases and the degree of specificity increases. Marketing plans, production plans, and financial plans are typical examples of operational planning.

[7]Reported in Steiner, *op. cit.*, p. 22.

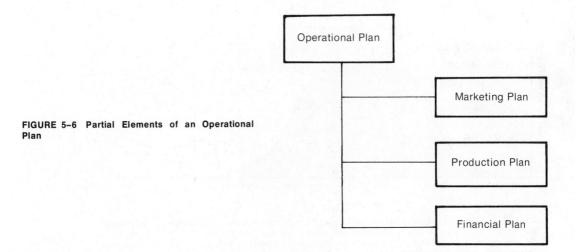

FIGURE 5-6 Partial Elements of an Operational Plan

**Marketing
Plan**

Selling current
products and de-
veloping new
ones are impor-
tant marketing
objectives.

Most marketing plans have two main objectives, selling current products and helping develop new ones. The former entails the setting of quotas and market shares for the various product lines. These objectives are translated into operational plans through advertising budgets, the maintenance of a sales force, the assignment of quotas, and the determination of product prices. Then at the end of the given period, i.e., six months or a year, performance will be evaluated and goals or targets revised accordingly.

Concurrently, the marketing plan will entail some consideration of new product development. Every business knows that each product has a limited life cycle (see Figure 5–7). Some goods will maintain their market position for years while others may never get off the ground, and today's big sellers may have no market demand five years from now. For these reasons, product planning is necessary, the basis of which is generating new product ideas. Sometimes these will come from the research and development lab; other times they may be the result of suggestions from top management, salesmen, customers, or consultants. No matter where they come from, however, only approximately two of every one hundred ideas will ever materialize in the form of profitable products. The rest will either be screened out for technical, economic, or market test reasons (95%) or will just plain fail to sell, despite all initial signs to the contrary (3%). An illustration of the latter is found in the case of Frost 8/80, a dry, white whisky introduced by the Brown-Forman Distillers Corporation. Despite an extensive market research program that pointed to widespread acceptance, production was halted after two years because sales were too low to justify further effort. The company lost a total of approximately $2 million.[8]

---

[8]Frederic C. Klein, "An Untimely End: How A New Product Was Brought to Market Only to Flop Miserably," *Wall Street Journal*, January 5, 1973, p. 1.

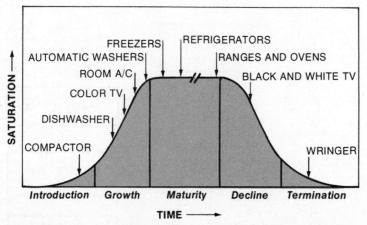

FIGURE 5–7 Life Cycle Stages of Various Products. Source: Adapted from John E. Smallwood, "The Product Life Cycle: A Key to Strategic Marketing Planning," *MSU Business Topics*, Winter 1973, p. 30. Reprinted by permission of the publisher, Division of Research, Graduate School of Business Administration, Michigan State University.

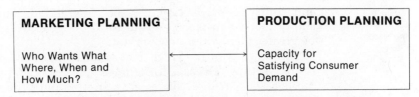

MARKETING PLANNING	**PRODUCTION PLANNING**
Who Wants What Where, When and How Much?	Capacity for Satisfying Consumer Demand

FIGURE 5–8   Interrelationship of Marketing and Production Planning

Production Plan

The production plan is designed to satisfy consumer demand by turning out the desired amount of goods. Sometimes production capability will be greater than estimated demand; other times it will be necessary for the manufacturing department to go to a second or third shift to meet this demand. Both instances illustrate that marketing and production planning are actually intertwined.

The basic objectives of a production plan will entail the purchase, coordination, and maintenance of factors of production — specifically machines, material, and people. How much will it cost to manufacture a particular good? The answer is going to depend on the costs associated with raw materials, merchandise, supplies, labor, and equipment. For this reason, the production plan will start with the desired number of units (the objective) and work backward, determining the amount of equipment and the number of people needed to attain these goals.

The main production objective is to satisfy consumer demand.

Financial Plan

The financial plan, as seen in Figure 5–9, also is interrelated with the marketing and production plans; each of the three influences the others. However, it should be noted that the financial plan is often given more importance than the other plans because it provides a quantitative basis for decision making and control. In an operational plan, managers want to know how well they are doing; financial data tell them. For example, in the production plan the vice president of production will follow cost per unit very closely; on the other hand, his marketing counterpart will be watching the sales curve. Both managers know that if things do not go well, the results will be reflected in the financial feedback.

The financial plan provides a quantitative basis for decision making and control.

Harmonizing Functional Plans

One way in which a firm will harmonize these three functional plans (marketing, production, finance) is through the use of the *budget*. Many managers believe the budget is a control technique, but it is a planning tool as well because it provides a basis for action. Expected results can be expressed in numerical terms; cash flows can be projected; man-hours to be worked in the current period can be calculated;

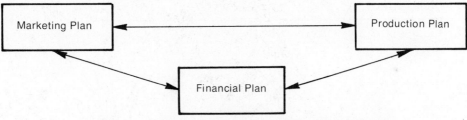

FIGURE 5–9   Interrelationships of Operational Planning Components

Budgets are useful in harmonizing plans.

and units of production can be determined. Furthermore, research shows that when plans are linked to budgets, overall accuracy tends to be greater than when they are not.[9]

Another way in which management harmonizes operational plans is by setting *financial objectives*, such as return on investment (profit/assets), market share, growth rate, and profit. In fact when marketing, production, and finance plans are harmonized, it is common to find the financial plan being the fulcrum upon which the other two are balanced. As seen in Figure 5–10, if the marketing or production plans are in disequilibrium, it will be reflected in the financial data and corrective action will be taken to re-establish the necessary balance.

USE OF A PLANNING ORGANIZATION

As noted previously, in many firms managers are most concerned with day-to-day problems. They do not have time to construct strategic plans; their interest rests in carrying out operational plans. For this reason, it is common to find departments drawing up their own budgets — with supporting justifications for any proposed capital expenditures — and forwarding these proposals to top management. Here departmental plans are combined into divisional plans, which in turn are reviewed, modified if necessary, and finally, approved by the top management.

However, the development of a comprehensive plan is never as simple as it might initially appear. There is always a tremendous amount of coordination required. For this reason many firms, especially corporations, have begun developing their own *planning organization*. It often takes from five to eight years before this structure is functioning smoothly (see Figure 5–11), yet there are two important advantages to be gleaned from it. First, some companies lack a complete appreciation for planning at the highest ranks of the organization. A planning organization can surmount this lack of complete commitment. Second, many managers throughout the structure have never really been taught the concept of planning. A planning organization helps overcome this deficiency.

A planning organization can help a firm design a comprehensive plan.

---

[9]Richard F. Vancil, "The Accuracy of Long-Range Planning," *Harvard Business Review*, September–October 1970, p. 100.

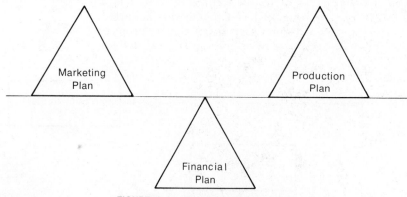

FIGURE 5–10 Functional Plan Fulcrum

PHASE	ACTION	TIME SPAN	TOTAL TIME ELAPSED
I	Establish executive planning committee	6–12 months	6–12 months
II	Select director of planning and provide *ad hoc* staff committee	About 12 months	18–24 months
III	Director develops permanent planning staff at corporate level; division planning committees added	12–36 months	30–60 months
IV	Appoint vice-president of planning and corporate development reporting to president and executive planning committee; select division planning coordinator	12–24 months	42–72 months
V	Specialize corporate development planning, and evaluation functions; provide division planning staffs reporting to division heads but with relationship to corporate development and planning department	12–36 months and beyond	60–108 months

FIGURE 5–11   Time Phases of a Planning Organization (From R. Hal Mason, "Developing A Planning Organization," *Business Horizons,* **August 1969, p. 62. Reprinted with permission.)**

Organizational Metamorphosis

Mason reports that a planning organization often begins at the top management level with the formation of a committee to identify and organize data on the firm and its industry position.[10] In Phase I attention is given to the development of a framework within which long-range planning can take place.

Phase II entails the formation of the first formal long-range plan. At best, it is often a rudimentary guide, lacking both depth and breadth. The plan is constructed by an executive planning staff at the upper divisions, which acts as consultant to the rest of the organization.

In Phase III, which occurs about three years after the plan's inception, the planning organization prepares its first comprehensive five-year plan. This is done through the coordination and integration of the plans prepared by the major operating units. It is a "bottom-up" approach; the departments within each division or unit create plans and send them up the line. Thus the division carries out the majority of the total planning effort. During this phase, divisional planning committees will be added to the operating units to assist both the unit and the planning organization. These committees will assess reporting procedures and information generated about products, customers, and competitors. For its part, the planning organization will assist the committee in the design of the information and reporting systems.

Planning organizations often go through five phases.

By the time the committee reaches Phase IV, the annual preparation of a long-range plan will have become routine. Operating divisions have usually become attuned to developing plans that are in harmony

---

[10]This five-phase metamorphosis comes from R. Hal Mason, "Developing a Planning Organization," *Business Horizons,* August 1969, pp. 61–69.

with each other. At this stage it is also common to find organizational planning taking on greater importance, and the head of the planning organization appointed to vice presidential rank (reporting directly to the president).

In Phase V, the final developmental step is reached. Mason describes the phase as follows:

> The activities of planning groups at all levels tend to shift their attention increasingly toward corporate development activities, which include the matching of opportunity to corporate capabilities and the development of those capabilities. The formal development of planning information has become routine in certain ways, and each division is aware of the types of data it must generate for planning purposes. An integrated set of plans is put together within a format, and corporate action is evaluated relative to plan. The machinery for developing plans and updating the corporate plan exists and is functioning. This frees the planning group so that it can devote a growing share of its total resources to searching the environment, evaluating corporate strengths and weaknesses, and identifying opportunities for corporate growth and profit improvement.[11]

This type of organization is being employed by an increasing number of firms which realize that intelligent planning requires a concerted effort on the part of the management.

Figure 5–12 illustrates the steps involved in the overall planning process for large, diversified firms. Note in the figure that everyone, from the chief executive officer down to the functional department manager, is involved in the process. As the organization goes through these formal planning cycles, the emphasis shifts from formulation of objectives (strategic planning) to implementation of the plan (operational planning) through budget approval.

ADVANTAGES OF PLANNING

A number of important advantages can be obtained by planning. First, it forces a firm to *forecast* the environment. No longer does the management assume a "wait and see" attitude. Instead, the company begins evaluating conditions and formulating its own response. Passivity gives way to activity.

Second, planning gives the company *direction* in the form of objectives. Once the organization knows what it can and cannot do over the next one to five years, it can begin setting goals. Day-to-day operational thinking gives way to more long-run designs.

Third, planning provides a basis for *teamwork*. Now that the goals are clearly defined, work assignments can be determined and everyone can begin to contribute to the fulfillment of these objectives. This often leads to high morale and also helps develop management talent. The manager can now delegate authority to subordinates and begin to evaluate performance. Without planning, this would be a haphazard dream; with planning, it is a reality.

Finally, planning helps management learn to *live with ambiguity*. This is especially true in long- and intermediate-range planning. Management must realize that there is virtue in vagueness. To demand clarity in all things leads to a refusal to do anything beyond operational planning.

---

[11]*Ibid.*, pp. 68–69.

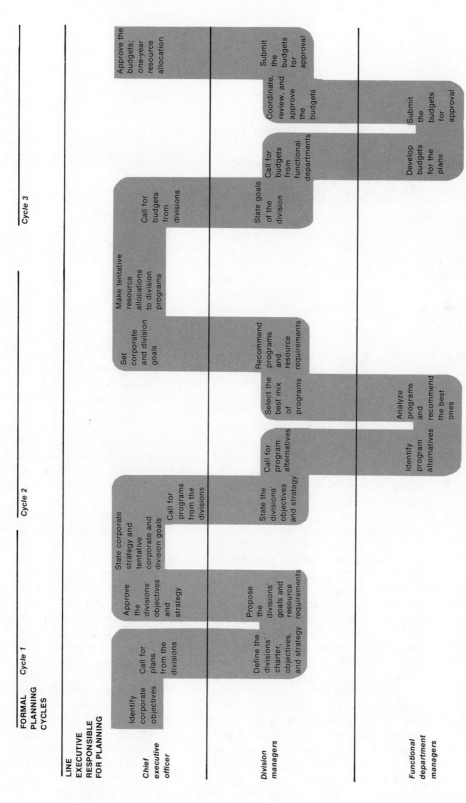

FIGURE 5–12 The Planning Process. Source: Adapted from Richard F. Vancil and Peter Lorange, "Strategic Planning in Diversified Companies," *Harvard Business Review*, January–February 1975, pp. 84–85.

"What really bugs me is to be outsmarted by a crummy little fox."

**PLANNING
IS NO
GUARAN-
TEE**

The development of the long-range plan and its integration with short-range plans are very useful. There is no guarantee, however, merely because a firm plans that it will be successful. Many things can go wrong, and they always relate back to the premises upon which the plan was formulated.

Sometimes, information coming in from the field is *erroneous*. Salespeople may give strong endorsement to a particular modification of a current product, but the modified good may not sell very well. What potential customers say they are going to do and what they end up doing may be two different things. This is a problem inherent in marketing research.

A second basic problem is the *economy*. A plan predicated on a rising economy will run into trouble if a downturn is encountered. For example, during the 1960's, the economy boomed and many organizational planners saw the future as more of the same. After all, it is far easier (and to many, more logical) to extrapolate the present than to answer the question, when will the bloom be off the rose? If a company has increased its sales by 25 per cent a year for the last five years, it is very difficult for management to estimate the following year's increase at 15 per cent. Psychologically, they are taking a 10 per cent cut. For this reason, many firms tend to extrapolate the economy during good times and estimate an upturn or leveling out during poor times. The economy is designed to fit the plan instead of vice versa.

A third problem can be the company's *financial position*. A plan may rely heavily on strong advertising and personal promotion, but if the company is unable to finance this kind of campaign, the plan could fall flat. In fact, a downward spiral may occur with reduced promotional expenses leading to the nonmaterialization of sales, which results in the cutback of any further promotional effort. The publishing industry often faces this problem because of its small profit margin. For example, a textbook will be given an estimated sales price of $15.95 and an annual market potential of 5000 copies. In addition, the advertising budget will be set at $10,000 for the first year and $5000 for the second. However, internal budgetary cuts may require changes in this plan; the price may be raised to $16.95 to help cover home office expenses. Yet such a move may result in a decline in demand to 3500 copies. Revenue has now dipped from an expected total of $79,750 to an actual total of $59,325. This, in turn, may lead the company to eliminate the follow-up advertising budget. Once the initial plan runs into trouble, everything goes awry because of the sequential cause-effect relationships. Every attempt to re-establish an equilibrium leads to further problems.

A fourth common problem is *lack of coordination*. The objectives are clear, but the functional departments do not synchronize their efforts. Sometimes this is caused by the staff's loss of enthusiasm for its own plan; more commonly, it results when the proposed plan is modified by higher authority. In either event, the human element comes into play and plans are not implemented according to a previously determined schedule.

In summary, planning is no panacea for dealing with the future. There are many things that can go wrong. Nevertheless, companies that do plan increase their chances for success, and it is for this reason that the planning process is important to management.

SUMMARY

In this chapter comprehensive planning, consisting of strategic, intermediate, and operational plans, has been examined. Prime attention was given to long-run considerations, and it was noted that most firms tend to be too short-run oriented. The roles played by the determination of the firm's basic socio-economic mission, values of the top management, and analysis of the organization's strengths and weaknesses in the formulation of the strategic plan were examined in detail. The latter requires accurate economic and sales forecasting coupled with a frank and honest evaluation of the company's material resources and personnel competencies. Only in this way can a niche be identified and long-range objectives formulated.

Although the long-range plan provides general direction, the intermediate and especially the operational plans are also important because they offer more specific direction. The operational plan often consists of derivative functional plans such as marketing, production, and finance plans, designed to attain short-run objectives while harmonizing with the previously determined long-range goals. Such short-range plans provide management with a method for gauging progress, serving as a basis from which to adapt or modify current plans and construct future ones.

Of course, no plan can be successfully implemented without a competent organization. There must be some process by which the work and the people come together. This organization will be the focus of attention in the next chapter.

---

1. Why has there been a marked trend toward comprehensive planning on the part of many business firms?

2. What is meant by "strategic planning"?

3. What are the three basic foundations of strategic planning? Describe each.

4. How do management values affect the planning process?

5. How does a firm conduct external environmental forecasting? Be specific.

6. How does a firm evaluate its internal environment?

7. What does "developing a niche" have to do with planning?

8. What is meant by operational planning?

9. How can a planning organization be useful to management?

10. What are some of the advantages of planning? Explain.

11. What are some of the disadvantages of planning? Explain.

12. What are some of the common problems that can cause a plan to go awry? Explain.

SELECTED REFERENCES

Angle, E. W. *Keys for Business Forecasting,* 4th edition. Richmond, Virginia: Federal Reserve Bank of Richmond, 1975.

Ansoff, H. I. "Managing Strategic Surprise By Response To Weak Signals." *California Management Review,* Winter 1975, pp. 21–33.

Banks, L. "The Mission Of Our Business Society." *Harvard Business Review,* May–June 1975, pp. 57–66.

Dessler, G. *Management Fundamentals: A Framework.* Reston, Va.: Reston Publishing Company, 1977.

Drucker, P. F. "Managing for Business Effectiveness." *Harvard Business Review,* May–June 1963, pp. 53–60.

Drucker, P. F. *Management: Tasks, Responsibilities, Practices.* New York: Harper & Row Publishers, 1974, Chapters 5–10.

Duncan, W. J. "Transferring Management Theory to Practice." *Academy of Management Journal,* December 1974, pp. 724–738.

Hobbs, J. M., and D. F. Heany. "Coupling Strategy To Operating Plans." *Harvard Business Review,* May–June 1977, pp. 119–126.

Hofer, C. W. "Toward A Contingency Theory of Business Strategy." *Academy of Management Journal,* December 1975, pp. 784–810.

Kalman, J. C., and R. M. Cyert. "Strategy: Formulation, Implementation and Monitoring." *Journal of Business,* July 1973, pp. 349–367.

Kinnunen, R. M. "Hypotheses Related To Strategy Formulation In Large Divisionalized Companies." *Academy of Management Review,* October 1976, pp. 7–14.

Koontz, H. "Making Strategic Planning Work." *Business Horizons,* April 1976, pp. 37–47.

Lebell, D., and O. J. Krasner. "Selecting Environmental Forecasting Techniques From Business Planning Requirements." *Academy of Management Review,* July 1977, pp. 373–383.

Linneman, R. E., and J. D. Kennell. "Shirt-Sleeve Approach to Long-Range Plans." *Harvard Business Review,* March–April 1977, pp. 141–150.

Lorange, P., and R. F. Vancil. "How to Design a Strategic Planning System." *Harvard Business Review,* September–October 1976, pp. 75–81.

McCaskey, M. B. "A Contingency Approach to Planning: Planning With Goals and Planning Without Goals." *Academy of Management Journal,* June 1974, pp. 281–291.

Mason, R. H. "Developing a Planning Organization." *Business Horizons,* August 1969, pp. 61–69.

Most, K. S. "Wanted: A Planning Model for the Firm." *Managerial Planning,* July–August 1973, pp. 1–6.

Pekar, P. P., Jr., and E. H. Burack. "Management Control of Strategic Plans Through Adaptive Techniques." *Academy of Management Journal.* March 1976, pp. 79–97.

Sisk, H. L. *Management and Organization,* 3rd edition. Chicago: SouthWestern Publishing Company, 1977.

Smallwood, J. E. "The Product Life Cycle: Key to Strategic Marketing Planning." *MSU Business Topics,* Winter 1973, pp. 29–35.

Steiner, G. A. *Top Management Planning.* New York: The Macmillan Company, 1969.

Terry, G. R. *Principles of Management,* 7th edition. Homewood, Ill.: Richard D. Irwin, Inc., 1977, Chapters 9–12.

Van Dam, A. "The Future of Global Business Forecasting." *Business Horizons,* August 1977, pp. 46–50.

Wheelright, S. C., and D. G. Clarke. "Corporate Forecasting: Promise and Reality." *Harvard Business Review,* November–December 1976, pp. 40–42.

Wilson, I. "How Our Values Are Changing." *The Futurist,* February 1970, pp. 5–9.

Woodward, H. N. "Management Strategies For Small Companies." *Harvard Business Review,* January–February 1976, pp. 113–121.

CASE: THE SUCCESSFUL RETREAT[12]

In the late 1960's Elliot and Ruth Handler, founders of Mattel, Inc., the world-famous toy manufacturer, got caught up in the general acquisition fever of the times. The firm began buying a wide assortment of companies ranging from the Audio Magnetic Electronic Corporation — a manufacturer of electronic tape — to Turco Manufacturing — a maker of playground equipment. These acquisitions helped Mattel raise its growth curve, and the stock became a Wall Street favorite.

However, hard times were just around the corner. In early 1971 a fire destroyed one of their toy plants, and a west coast strike kept virtually the entire toy line, which is manufactured in Taiwan and Hong Kong, sitting in the harbor until after the Christmas season. Then, in early 1974, the Securities & Exchange Commission and the company's stockholders charged that the firm had falsified financial reports.

Despite these problems, the toys kept selling. For example, the complete Barbie lines represented around $100 million in sales. However, Mattel needed to retreat and reorganize many diverse and unprofitable operations:

"One of the first things we did . . . was to pare the company down to a nucleus of areas where we have proven management expertise," says Spear, who had served as executive vice-president before the Handlers were forced out in 1975, catapulting him into the presidency. Now, the company has two main divisions: toys and a leisure and entertainment division, consisting of an aquarium manufacturer, a motion picture company, the Ringling Bros.-Barnum & Bailey touring circuses, and Circus World Park in Florida.

[12]The data in this case can be found in: "Mattel's Successful Retreat," *Business Week,* May 16, 1977, p. 43.

This retreat has proven to be successful, and the company now seems to be on its way back up.

Questions

1. What is the basic mission of the Mattel toy company? Put it in your own words.

2. What errors did Mattel make that resulted in its having to retreat and re-organize?

3. What does this case illustrate about the need for strategic planning?

CASE: A BETTER MOUSETRAP[13]

"If you build a better mousetrap," it is said, "the world will beat a path to your door." But will it really? The Woodstream Company had manufactured traps for catching all kinds of animals from elephants to grizzly bears. One day, the firm decided to design and manufacture a streamlined mousetrap.

A product designer was brought in to design a trap that would be modern enough for people to notice the change. The final product was made of plastic and looked like a sardine can with an arched doorway at floor level through which mice could enter. Any mouse coming through the doorway would trip a spring and be choked to death by a wire which, acting like an upside-down guillotine, would snap up from below.

The company called the new product "Little Champ" and priced it at 25¢, in contrast to the wooden ones, which sold at two for 15¢. Although the price was higher than average, the trap was easier to set, extremely efficient, and, perhaps best of all, could be cleaned and reused. It did not have to be thrown out with the mouse.

Looking forward to a booming demand, the company sent the traps out to hardware dealers across the nation. And there they sat on the shelf gathering dust. Despite the changes in the efficiency features, no one wanted them. Why? One individual explained the situation in this way:

"The company tried to develop a space-age mousetrap by researching the sleeping, eating and crawling habits of mice." . . . **"The little woman—who usually has to contend with the dead mouse—thought nothing of throwing away the old wooden snap-trap, mouse and all. But the new 25-cent trap was a different story—she didn't care for extracting the dead mouse and cleaning the trap."**

Whatever the reason, the venture failed. Mr. Woolworth, the company president, was unable to generate interest, although he cer-

---

[13]This case is adapted from Stephen J. Fansweet, "Dick Woolworth Builds a Better Mousetrap—and Falls on his Face," *Wall Street Journal,* September 24, 1970, p. 1.

tainly tried. For example, during the New York City garbage strike he wired Governor Rockefeller of New York, offering to ship a million rat traps for $144,000. But the governor was not even interested, and the Woodsteam Company finally gave up on the product.

Questions

1. What kind of planning should the Woodstream Company have done before manufacturing these traps?

2. Why was the company unable to sell the traps? Do you agree with the above analysis or are there other reasons? Explain.

3. Is there anything the company can now do with the traps or is the venture a total loss?

CASE: MILKING THE COW

Mark Anderson had been president of Anderson Printing for five years, having left a high-paying job as a salesman for an eastern publishing firm to return to the family business. "We were on the verge of selling out," he told Willy Chishilm, his management consultant. "My dad, who started the business, had died, and the other members of the family didn't want anything to do with it. That was when I began to look into the possibility of taking over the helm and seeing what I could do. Well, I don't have to tell you the story. You've been here for a week now looking over operations and examining our financial statements. You know better than anyone how well we've done over the last four years."

Willy moved his chair closer to the desk and placed some papers on top of it. "Mark, you look just great on paper. I have absolutely no arguments with your technical operations. Some of the new machinery you purchased is going to save you a lot of money in the long-run. And the morale of your staff is sky high. My management team has been talking to your people since Wednesday and there hasn't been one negative comment about anything."

"Surely this isn't your way of telling me that everything is perfect."

"No, it's merely my way of leading up to a plan of action that I would like to recommend to you. In a nutshell, you are just too short-run oriented. You have no real idea of where you are going. You've got a couple of banks that you are supplying with printed material and a lot of walk-in business and that's all."

"Say, don't forget that we have seventeen firms in town that send all their printing orders to us also."

"Okay, them too. However, that's all you've got. You are tied directly into the orders you are getting from these 'captive businesses' and anyone coming in off the streets and that's it."

"So what's so wrong with that? Look at our sales. In 1977 we did over $1 million of business. In 1978 we had sales of $1.25 million. This year we're anticipating $1.5 million, but at the rate we're going it's going to be closer to $1.7. It seems to me we're in great shape."

"Financially speaking, you are. However, have you any idea where Anderson Printing is going to be in 1983? Or how about 1993? What are your long-range plans?"

"Willy, I don't horse around with long-range planning. I don't need it. In this town there are two large banks and they send all their business to us. In addition, there are those other seventeen companies, most of them insurance firms, that need an awful lot of printing done. All I have to do is keep worrying about the next three months. That's my long-range plan, ninety days into the future. As long as I know I have enough financing at the bank and my collections are taking place on time, I have a good cash flow. What else is there to running a successful business?"

"Mark, do you think the banks you print for got to be as large as they are by planning ninety days into the future?"

"No, but then they are not in my situation. This business has a number of companies that rely upon it exclusively for their printing. There is no company in town that can match my price on any job because I've got the best equipment and can offer higher quality and lower prices than any of them. So why do I need to worry about long-range planning? My whole plan consists of keeping the machines in working order and not letting the competition get any technological jumps on me. That's the only way they can beat me out of a job, and it's just not going to happen. In a manner of speaking, I've carved a niche for myself. This niche is a very fat, profitable cow, and my job is to sit here and milk that cow for all it's worth. The last thing on my mind is long-range or, as you call it, strategic planning. Who needs it? When you've got a good thing going, enjoy it. What can long-range planning do for a business like mine?"

Questions

1. What are the advantages of long-range planning? Be specific.

2. What arguments should Willy raise in defense of his long-range planning proposal?

3. Can long-range planning really be of any value to Anderson Printing or is the firm better off remaining with its current short-range planning approach? Explain.

CASE: JUST LEAVE US ALONE

The Clayton Corporation was founded by Mr. Bud Clayton in 1956. The going was rough in the early years, but by 1965 things had started to improve, and in the late 60's, while the economy was dipping, Clayton's business was at its best. Sales and profits set new highs between 1973 and 1978, as seen by the following company data:

	Sales	Net Profit
1973	$2,600,000	$210,000
1974	2,900,000	245,000
1975	3,300,000	265,000
1976	4,000,000	300,000
1977	4,850,000	325,000
1978	6,000,000	395,000

The firm's record was so outstanding, in fact, that a number of large corporations made offers to buy it. Finally, after careful consideration, the offer from a large eastern conglomerate was accepted. In addition to a very lucrative financial settlement, the conglomerate agreed that Mr. Clayton and his management team would remain at the helm with business continuing as usual. The only major change was that all long-range plans and short-range performance goals (profitability, return on investment, sales, etc.) would have to be cleared with the planning organization at the conglomerate's headquarters so as to insure overall organizational coordination.

Initially everything went smoothly, but by the end of the first year it was apparent things were not going well at all. Mr. Clayton called a meeting of his top people to see if things could be ironed out. He also persuaded the vice president of corporate planning and his two staff assistants to fly in for the conference. Mr. Clayton sensed bad feelings between his people and the central planning group and believed it was time for both parties to air their gripes. The basic points of view presented by the two groups were as follows:

Clayton Group

Before we were purchased by the eastern conglomerate, we used to run our own show around here. After all, who knows more about how to manufacture and sell our product than we do? But now we're asked to coordinate our plans with those of seven other companies. And sometimes our suggested plans apparently don't fit in because they're rejected or modified by the corporate planning department. Well, we're fed up being told how to run our own end of the business. This concept of overall coordinated planning is having a drastic effect on the morale of our management team. Why don't you people just leave us alone?

Corporate Planning Group

We have eight major companies in our conglomerate. The only way we can make these eight work as one is to coordinate their long- and short-

range planning. Sure, no one likes to be told the way to do his job. And we don't mean to do that. But there has to be some harmony if we're to work as one big team. Now we can understand that managers don't like having their plans modified or revised, but this just can't be helped. And until the management of the Clayton Company realizes that they're part of a team, we're going to continue to have this problem. Big companies can't offer the personal touch that small ones can. When you become the member of a conglomerate you have to be willing to give up a little autonomy. Perhaps the Clayton management should try seeing things from our point of view.

Questions

1. Can a conglomerate operate as "one big team" without running into the kind of problems seen in this case?

2. Is the Clayton management right? Is the central planning organization indifferent to its problems?

3. How can this problem be solved? Present your solution.

CHAPTER SIX

THE ORGANIZING PROCESS

Organizing entails the assignment of duties and the coordination of efforts among all organizational personnel to ensure maximum efficiency in the attainment of predetermined objectives. The goals of this chapter are to examine the nature, purpose, and function of organizing.

When you have finished reading the chapter, you should be able to do the following:

1. Identify and describe the most commonly used forms of departmentalization.
2. Discuss the advantages and limitations of the committee form of organization.
3. Define the term *span of control* and relate its importance to effective organization design.
4. Describe the three types of authority used in organizational settings — line, staff, and functional — and relate their value in effective organizing.
5. Identify the determinants of decentralization and relate why some organizations are basically decentralized while others are basically centralized.
6. Describe the informal organization and discuss its importance to the modern manager.

GOALS OF THE CHAPTER

It has already been noted that the planning process encompasses strategic, intermediate, and operational plans. Our model can now be expanded, as seen in Figure 6–1, to include the organization structure, hence the often used phrase "from strategy to structure," which research has shown to be an accurate statement. Chandler, after conducting intensive studies of General Motors, Du Pont, Standard Oil of New Jersey, and Sears, Roebuck and Company, proved that strategy is indeed a prerequisite for structure.[1] If an organization does not know where it is going, there is no intelligent basis for organizing human effort and material resources. This chapter will be devoted to the various structures and concepts that can assist the manager in this process.

FROM STRATEGY TO STRUC-TURE

Strategy is a prerequisite for structure.

[1]Alfred D. Chandler, Jr., *Strategy and Structure* (Garden City, New York: Anchor Books, Doubleday & Company, Inc., 1966).

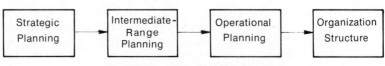

FIGURE 6–1 From Strategy to Structure

COMMON FORMS OF DEPART- MENTALI- ZATION

Perhaps the easiest way to grasp the function of organizing is to examine the mechanics of the process. By dividing the work and the personnel into group activities, departments can be formed for the purpose of specialization. The three most widely used types of departmentalization are functional, product, and territorial.

Functional Departmentalization

Functional departmentalization, the most widely used form of departmentalization, occurs when an enterprise organizes itself around the firm's major activities. In a manufacturing enterprise, in which these prime or *organic* functions are marketing, production, and finance, a typical functional organization chart would be that shown in Figure 6–2.

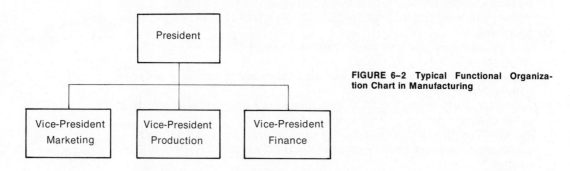

FIGURE 6–2 Typical Functional Organization Chart in Manufacturing

Functional departmentalization is the most widely used.

In nonmanufacturing firms these functions differ. For example, in a large bank they often include comptroller, operations, legal, and public relations. In an insurance company it would be common to find actuarial, underwriting, agency, and claim adjustment. In a public utility organic functions would include accounting, sales, engineering, and personnel. These are all illustrations of major functional departments, which, in turn, can have *derivative departments*. For example, expanding Figure 6–2 to include second-level functional departments might result in the following:

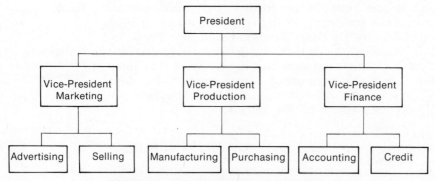

FIGURE 6–3 Derivative Functional Departments

Similar charts could be drawn for all functionally organized enterprises, but the structure need not stop at the second level. There may be third-, fourth-, and even fifth-level functional departments, depending on the size of the enterprise.

Perhaps the major reason why functional departmentalization is so widely employed is the emphasis it places on basic activities, providing a basis for specialization. However, there are drawbacks. This form of departmentalization can create "tunnel vision," whereby functional specialists see nothing but their own area of interest. Also, in some instances, firms will adopt functional departmentalization because they see other companies doing it, even though another form — departmentalization by product, for example — would actually be more beneficial.

Product departmentalization has been increasing in importance, especially among multi-line, large-scale enterprises. General Motors, Ford, Du Pont, RCA, and General Electric all employ it. Many firms using this form were originally organized functionally, but as they grew larger, a reorganization along product lines became necessary. A simplified illustration for a manufacturing firm appears in Figure 6–4.

Product Departmentalization

The organic functions of marketing, production, and finance can still be found in the structure, but prime attention is now given to the product lines. All activities related to a particular product are brought together.

Perhaps the main advantage of this form is its value in facilitating coordination and allowing for specialization. This can be especially beneficial if the firm is large. For example, today General Electric has nine major operating groups, each containing no less than five and, in some cases, as many as ten divisions. The consumer products and industrial groups are shown in Figure 6–5. If the company had opted for functional departmentalization, massive effective coordination would have proved impossible.

Product departmentalization is employed by many multi-line, large-scale companies.

This organizational form can also facilitate the measurement and control of operating performance. Since all revenues and costs can be differentiated and assigned to a particular product line, cost centers can be established, high profit areas can be cultivated, and unprofitable product lines can be dropped.

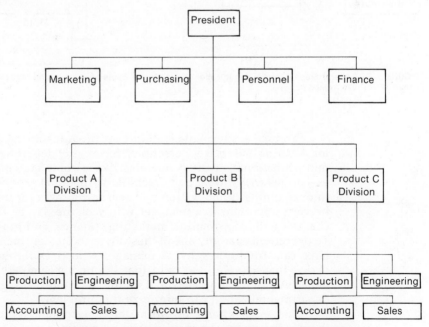

FIGURE 6–4   Product Organization Chart for a Manufacturing Firm

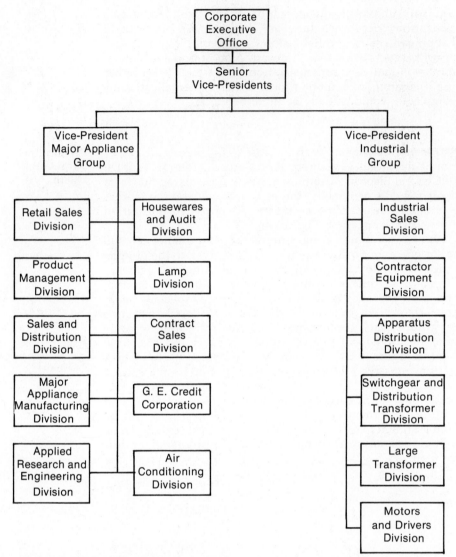

FIGURE 6–5 **General Electric Partial Organization Chart—Major Appliance Group and Industrial Group. (From 1976 Annual Report)**

Product departmentalization also provides an excellent opportunity for training executive personnel. Since the department or division is multi-functional, it often operates like a complete company, providing executives with a wealth of diversified functional experience that is useful in overcoming tunnel vision and seasoning them for the future. This can be very important to a manager who will one day be the chief executive charged with coordinating marketing, finance, and production activities. To overemphasize any one of these areas to the detriment of the others can have catastrophic results. A manager who rises through the marketing ranks, for example, may find that his or her sympathies rest with this department and might favor it in the decision-making process; product departmentalization can minimize this problem.

On the other hand, this form does have potential problem areas. First, the product divisions may try to become too autonomous, thereby presenting top management with a control problem. Second, because of its emphasis on semi-autonomism, product departmentalization works well only in those organizations that have a sufficient number of personnel with general management ability. Third, it is common to find product divisions duplicating some of the facilities found at the top levels of the structure, making it an expensive organizational form.

Territorial Departmenta- lization

When an enterprise is physically dispersed, as in the case of a large-scale organization, it is not uncommon to find *territorial departmentaliza-tion,* as seen in Figure 6–6. Contrasting this figure with that of product departmentalization (Figure 6–4) illustrates how similar the two forms really are.

The major advantage of a territorial organization is that of local operation. For example, by manufacturing close to the supply of raw materials a firm can produce its product at a lower cost per unit. Furthermore, by setting up a local sales department the personnel can get to know their customers and markets much better.

Geographically dispersed orga-nizations often employ territorial departmentaliza-tion.

The disadvantages are the same as those found in product departmentalization. It is often difficult for top management to control operations, and there is a tendency to duplicate services.

Other Types of Depart- mentalization

Functional, product, and geographic are only three types of departmentalization. There are numerous other forms, some of the most common being departmentalization by simple numbers, by time, by customer, and by equipment or process.

Departmentalization by *simple numbers* is used when the success of the undertaking depends exclusively upon manpower. In community chest drives, for example, each manager is given a number of volunteers and a section of the city to canvass. Success depends to a great extent on

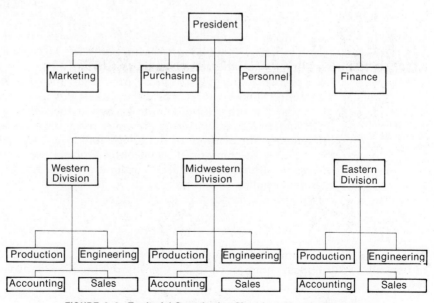

FIGURE 6–6 Territorial Organization Chart for a Manufacturing Firm

the number of people available to ring doorbells. Another illustration is the military, in which portions of the infantry are still organized on the basis of numbers of men. In a business setting, common labor crews are also organized this way.

Departmentalization by *time* is one of the oldest ways of grouping activities. It often consists of, for example, dividing the work force into three shifts: day, swing, and graveyard. Police departments all over the world still use this approach, as do industrial firms facing great demand for their goods.

Departmentalization by *customer* is used by organizations such as meat packers, retail stores, and container manufacturers. The meat packer will have major departments such as dairy, poultry, beef, lamb, veal, and by-products; the retail store will have major departments such as men's clothing, women's apparel, and children's wear; the container company will have major departments such as drug and chemical, closure and plastics, and beverage industries. Another example is educational institutions, which often offer both regular (day) courses and extension (night and off-campus) courses, catering to the needs of different groups of students. This form of departmentalization helps organizations meet the special and widely varying needs of their customers.

Equipment or process departmentalization is often used in manufacturing organizations, as in the establishment of an electronic data processing department. Similarly, in many plants it is common to find lathe presses or automatic screw machines arranged in one locale. The basic value of this organizational form is the economic advantages brought about by such groupings. By placing these machines together, greater efficiency can be obtained.

All the basic departmentalization patterns examined thus far represent common organizational forms. It should be noted, however, that every enterprise will employ its own particular variation. Most will have some form of *hybrid* design; for example, a *basically* functional organization chart with traces of product, equipment, process, customer, and/or territorial departmentalization. The chart is seldom what could be called *purely* functional or product or territorial.

COMMIT-TEE ORGA-NIZATIONS

Another common organizational form is that of the *committee*. Research indicates that committees are being increasingly employed in business. In general, there are two types. The most common is that appointed for a particular purpose *(ad hoc)*. After analyzing a problem situation or conducting some research, the committee gives its recommendations and disbands. The other type is often known as the *standing committee*, many of which are also advisory. If, however, they have the authority to order implementation of their recommendations, they are called *plural executives*. The most common illustration of a plural executive is the board of directors, although in a large corporation it is not uncommon to find high-level policy committees such as the executive committee or finance committee also serving in such a capacity.

Advantages of Commit-tees

Committees have some very important advantages to offer. Three of the most commonly cited are group deliberation, motivation, and coordination.

In addition, there are a number of other forms of departmentalization.

Another common organization form is the committee.

GROUP DELIBERATION.   A committee has more knowledge, experience, and judgment than any one individual alone. In short, two heads are better than one. When an organization focuses the attention of a committee on a particular problem, the result is often a solution superior to that which could be obtained from any one member working independently.

MOTIVATION.   Research has shown that when subordinates are permitted to participate in the decision-making process, enthusiasm for accepting and implementing the recommendations often increases. The personnel support the program because they had a hand in fashioning it. Committees can provide the basis for such action.

COORDINATION.   Committees are also useful in coordinating plans and transmitting information. In the implementation of a major program, for example, many departments may be involved, and a committee can help each to see where it fits in the overall plan. It can also obtain agreement on what each is going to do and when, thereby coordinating overall efforts.

Despite all their advantages, committees have become the butt of many jokes, such as "a camel is a horse designed by a committee," because the drawbacks to using this organizational design often outweigh the returns. Three of the most commonly cited disadvantages are waste of time, compromise, and lack of individual action.

Disadvantages of Committees

WASTE OF TIME.   The adage "time is money" can be well applied to committees. Many of them are far too large and spend an excessive amount of time discussing trivial matters. On the issue of size, Parkinson has noted that there is constant pressure to increase the number of people on a committee if for no other reason than to include more individuals with specialized knowledge.[2]

On the issue of time spent on trivial matters, he notes that complex issues often confound people and, because they are unwilling to admit their ignorance of the subject matter, lead them to adopt a policy of silence. The result is the dispatching of crucial decisions, such as allocating $1.2 billion for an atomic reactor, within a matter of minutes. However, on simple issues, understandable to all, such as the construction of a $2350 bicycle shed for use by the clerical staff, committee members come alive. Comprehending both the issue and expenses (and realizing they were lax in their participation in the atomic reactor topic), they spring into action with newfound vigor.[3] Parkinson attributes this phenomenon to the *law of triviality,* which states that "the time spent on any item of the agenda will be in inverse proportion to the sum involved."[4] If this is true, many committees may indeed not be worth the cost.

COMPROMISE.   Committees always pose the danger of compromise. After haggling over an issue for an extended period of time, the group may decide to mediate the matter. No one gets what he or she is after, but the ultimate decision is one everybody can live with. Unfortunately the result

---

[2]C. Northcote Parkinson, *Parkinson's Law* (Boston: Houghton Mifflin Company, 1957), Chapter 3.
[3]*Ibid.*
[4]*Ibid.*, p. 24.

is often a mediocre decision, representing the least common denominator.

LACK OF INDIVIDUAL ACTION.   There are some things that are better accomplished by individuals than by committees. For example, one very famous American Management Association report found that although committees were considered very useful in handling jurisdictional questions such as interdepartmental disputes, many executives regarded them as ineffective in carrying out functions such as decision making, organizing, executing, and leadership.[5] Instead, individual action was preferred. Thus, there are times when committees do not perform as well as the individual manager.

How to Use Committees Effectively

In light of the above drawbacks, there are several important guidelines to follow if committees are to be effectively employed. First, the objective of the group must be clearly stated. Second, participants must be carefully chosen, providing the expertise needed to attain the objective. Third, the size must be manageable, allowing for discussion and healthy disagreement without becoming too unwieldy in the process. Fourth, an agenda indicating the topics for discussion and analysis must be sent out beforehand so everyone will be prepared to begin immediately. Fifth, the chairman must be able to encourage participation while keeping the group headed toward the objective. Although these guidelines do not ensure success, they have been found to improve committee performance markedly because of their value in overcoming common pitfalls.

Five important guidelines for using committees effectively.

SPAN OF CONTROL

Another important organizing concept is *span of control,* which refers to the number of people reporting to a given superior. Many of the classical theorists believed the ideal span to be between three and six. Although this number is open to dispute, the span will certainly have a great deal of influence on the organizational design. For example, taking two companies with approximately the same number of personnel, Figure 6–7 illustrates how the structure would appear if a narrow span of control

---

[5]Ernest Dale, *Planning and Developing the Company Organization Structure,* Research Report No. 20 (New York: American Management Association, 1952), p. 92.

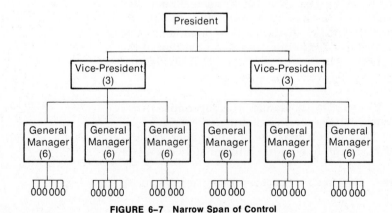

FIGURE 6–7   Narrow Span of Control

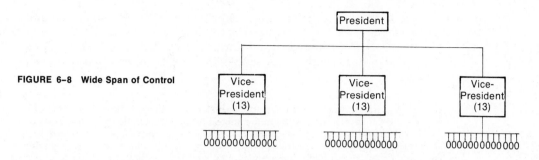

FIGURE 6–8 Wide Span of Control

were employed, while Figure 6–8 shows a company with a wide span of control.

A narrow span of control requires the organization to have more levels in the hierarchy. Thus, the structure looks very much like a pyramid. Conversely, the organization with the wide span of control has fewer levels and a very rectangular shape; it is not very deep, but very wide. The former organization chart is known as a *tall* structure and the latter as a *flat* structure.

Flat and Tall Structures

Classical or bureaucratic structures are typically very tall, characterized by narrow spans that allow the manager to exercise *tight control.* Having only a few subordinates, it is possible for the manager to be aware of everything the people are doing.

The most famous departure from the narrow span was made by Sears, Roebuck and Company and is often attributed to James C. Worthy, a management consultant and former vice president of the company.[6] After experimenting with both conventional and flat structures, Sears concluded that on the basis of sales volume, profit, morale, and management competence, the flat design was superior. Several factors accounted for the results. First, having a large number of subordinate managers, the superiors found they had to delegate important decisions; they did not have the time to do everything themselves. In turn, by being forced to manage, the subordinates became better at their jobs. This led to increased morale and higher quality performance. It also made store managers more selective in choosing subordinates, because they knew they would have to delegate considerable authority to them. In addition, by reducing the number of hierarchical levels, communication was improved. Such a structure helped overcome what Drucker, one of the best known and most highly regarded authorities on management today, calls the major malorganization symptom. He states it this way:

> The most common and most serious symptom of malorganization is multiplication of the number of management levels. A basic rule of organization is to build the *least possible* number of management levels and forge the shortest possible chain of command.[7]

This does not mean, however, that flat structures are *always* superior. Carzo and Yanouzas, for example, have conducted research that showed that groups operating under a basically tall structure had significantly better results than those operating under a flat structure.[8] Other re-

---

[6]James C. Worthy, "Organizational Structure and Employee Morale," *American Sociological Review*, April 1950, pp. 169–179; and "Factors Influencing Employee Morale," *Harvard Business Review*, January 1950, pp. 61–73.

[7]Peter F. Drucker, *Management: Tasks, Responsibilities, Practices* (New York: Harper & Row, Publishers, 1974), p. 546.

[8]Rocco Carzo, Jr., and John N. Yanouzas, "Effects of Flat and Tall Organization Structure," *Administrative Science Quarterly*, June 1969, pp. 178–191.

There are bene-
fits to both flat
and tall struc-
tures.
searchers have reached similar conclusions. Thus, there are arguments to be made for each side, indicating that the "right" span is a function of the situation; the manager, the subordinates, and the work itself must be considered. Perhaps House and Miner have summarized this entire area best:

> The implications for the span of control seem to be that (1) under most circumstances the optimal span is likely to be in the range 5 through 10; (2) the larger spans, say 8 through 10, are most often appropriate at the highest policy-making levels of an organization, where greater resources for diversified problem-solving appear to be needed (although diversified problem-solving without larger spans may well be possible); (3) the breadth of effective spans of first line supervisors is contingent on the technology of the organization; and (4) in prescribing the span of control for specific situations consideration must be given to a host of local factors such as the desirability of high group cohesiveness, the performance demands of the task, the degree of stress in the environment, task interdependencies, the need for member satisfaction, and the leadership skills available to the organization.[9]

In summary, the "right" span of management will vary from case to case.

AUTHORITY-RESPONSI-BILITY RELATION-SHIPS

Concurrent with the formation of an organization structure exists the need for assigning specific duties to the personnel. Often companies will construct *position descriptions*, outlining the functions each individual is to perform; the authority and responsibility associated with the position; and the inherent organizational relationships, *i.e.*, to whom does the person report, with whom will he or she be interacting, and to whom must he or she be responsible?

Sources of Authority

It has already been noted that authority is "the right to command." The *formal theory of authority*, which supports the organizational hierarchy, contends that authority comes from the top, as seen in Figure 6–9. Barnard, however, argued that authority actually comes from the bottom, because no one has authority unless subordinates accept directives, i.e., the famous *acceptance theory of authority*.

There are several other theories of authority. One is the *authority of the situation*. For example, if oily rags thrown into the corner of a machine shop suddenly start a fire, the alert machinist who calls the fire department is exercising authority of the situation. Although this authority is situational in nature, there is no doubt that the person has the right to command. Crisis situations, or those calling for instant action, often impel those present to assume authority whether or not it has been formally delegated to them.

Another theory of authority is known as the *authority of knowledge*. The person who knows the most about the situation may find himself or herself in charge of the operation. For example, the President of the United States is on his way to Paris for a summit conference. Twenty minutes out of Dulles International the plane encounters engine trouble. The pilot tells the President they are turning back. Although the Com-

---

[9]Robert J. House and John B. Miner, "Merging Management and Behavioral Theory: The Interaction Between Span of Control and Group Size," *Administrative Science Quarterly*, September 1969, pp. 461–462.

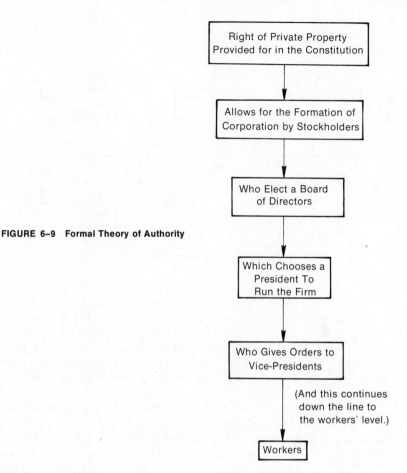

FIGURE 6–9   Formal Theory of Authority

mander in Chief has the authority to countermand this order, he does not, because he realizes the pilot knows far more about the situation than he does. Superior knowledge gives the pilot the requisite authority.

It is evident that there is more than one source of authority. The acceptance theory in particular illustrates that the concept is dynamic, pointing the way to consideration of such topics as power and the role of the informal organization. First, however, we must consider the three major types of authority: *line authority, staff authority,* and *functional authority.* Each is an essential part of the basic framework of an organization structure and although, like the forms of departmentalization just examined, they are always modified in practice, they are, and will continue to be, of central importance to the understanding of the organizing process.

There are three major types of authority.

LINE AUTHORITY   Line authority, the most fundamental type of authority, is often referred to as *direct authority* because it encompasses the right to give orders and to have decisions implemented. All superiors have line authority over their subordinates. The military provides a classic illustration. The general has line authority over the colonel, who has line authority over the major, and so on down the hierarchy. Analogously, the president of a company, as seen in Figure 6–10, has line authority over the vice

TYPES OF AUTHORITY

Line authority is direct authority.

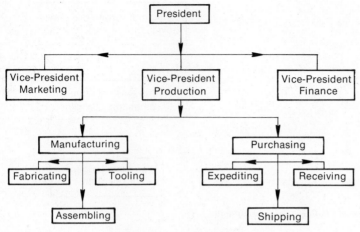

FIGURE 6–10   Line Authority

presidents. In turn, the vice president of production can give direct orders to his or her subordinates, the heads of manufacturing and purchasing, and they, in turn, have direct authority over their respective subordinates. Line authority results in a chain of command, often called the *scalar chain*, which runs from the top to the bottom of the organization and establishes an authority-responsibility relationship throughout.

STAFF AUTHORITY.   Staff authority is auxiliary authority. Its scope is limited in that it does not provide the right to command. Rather, the nature of the staff relationship is *supportive*. Individuals with staff authority assist, advise, recommend, and facilitate organizational activities. As an organization grows in size, executives face increasingly complex problems. Line authority alone is inadequate, and as a result, staff relationships are created.

Staff authority is auxiliary authority.

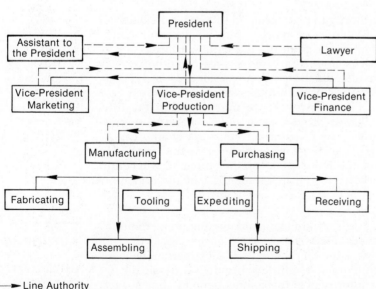

——▶ Line Authority
---▶ Staff Authority

FIGURE 6–11   Line-Staff Organization

One of the most common examples of staff authority is the subordinate manager who provides auxiliary services for his or her superior in the form of recommendations or advice. Another example is the appointment of an assistant to the president, whose job is to counsel the chief executive. A third illustration is the lawyer who is charged with providing legal advice to the president.

Many firms have found, to their dismay, that although staff authority can be advantageous, it can also lead to authority conflicts between the line and staff executives. One of the major causes rests in the attitudes of the two groups. For example, it is common to find that the line executive is the older person who came up the hard way. If he or she has a college degree, many of the hours may have been earned through correspondence study or night classes. Conversely, the staff counterpart is often a younger executive, perhaps with a master's degree in market research, who has many "bright ideas" about how to improve sales. The line executive sees the young person as lacking in practical experience. The staff executive sees the older person as unwilling to try new ideas.

Line-Staff Problems

A second problem arises from the fact that line executives have ultimate responsibility for the decisions they make. If they accept the staff recommendation and the results are poor, they cannot pass the buck. This makes them wary of staff advice. Conversely, staff people see hesitancy or refusal on the part of the line as indecisiveness and inability to recognize substantive recommendations. They feel the line should accept their expertise outright instead of having to be sold on the recommendations through diplomatic persuasion.

Some of the other common reasons for line-staff conflicts are brought about by the following attitudes and philosophies:

Line	Staff
1. Highly action-oriented.	1. Concerned with studying a problem in depth before making recommendations.
2. Highly intuitive in contrast to being analytical.	2. Highly analytical in contrast to being intuitive.
3. Often shortsighted.	3. Often too long-range oriented.
4. Often ask the wrong kinds of questions.	4. Have answers and therefore spend their time looking for questions.
5. Want simple, easy-to-use solutions.	5. Complicate the situation by providing esoteric data.
6. Accustomed to examining some of the available alternatives and choosing one of them.	6. Interested in examining all of the possible alternatives, weighing them, analyzing them, and then choosing the "best" one regardless of time or cost restraints.
7. Highly protective of the organization.	7. Highly critical of the organization.

Various causes of line-staff conflicts.

When these attitudes and philosophies are present, the organization will find it is not achieving maximum benefit from the staff. However, it is not necessary for these conditions to exist. There are various approaches that can be used to improve line-staff relations.

**Improving
Line-Staff
Relations**

There are a
number of steps
for improving
line-staff rela-
tions.

One of the most effective ways to facilitate line-staff cooperation is to get everyone to understand the nature of the authority relationships. If the line people realize that they are responsible for making operating decisions and staff people are there to assist them, the former may obtain a greater appreciation of the latter. Likewise, staff people must understand that theirs is only an auxiliary function; they must *sell* their ideas to line people. They cannot order implementation of their recommendations; they must persuade the line manager to adopt them.

A second approach is to encourage the line to *listen* to the staff. As seen in Chapter 1, the Catholic Church has used the concept of compulsory staff service for centuries, requiring the solicitation of staff advice. Although such a mandatory approach can have serious drawbacks in a business setting, line managers should at least be encouraged to listen to their staff. Many line executives have found that their proposals and plans are more readily accepted if they consult with the staff people before submitting them. Such an approach ensures a united front when top management asks the staff how they feel about the proposal.

A third method is that of keeping *staff specialists informed* about matters that fall within their province. No assistants can help line managers who fail to relate the kind of information they will need or to explain the types of decisions confronting them. When this is done, however, it paves the way for effective staff work.

Another useful method is that of *completed staff work.* This involves studying the problem and presenting a solution or recommendation in such a way that the line executive can either approve or disapprove the action. All details are worked out by the staff prior to presentation. Although the approach can involve a tremendous amount of time on the part of the staff people, it saves the line manager from being subjected to continual meetings and discussions on the matter. The entire project is assumed by the staff specialists, and the line people are not bothered with details until the entire issue is finally presented to them. This technique not only provides a basis for justifying the existence of staff, but also gives them an opportunity to sell their ideas to the line.

Functional au-
thority is the
right to give
orders in a de-
partment other
than one's own.

FUNCTIONAL AUTHORITY.   As an organization grows in size, specialization increases. In addition to the use of line and staff authority, many firms also employ functional authority, which can be defined as *authority in a department other than one's own.* This authority is delegated to an individual or department concerning a specified policy, practice, or process being carried out by individuals in other units, and it can be exercised by managers in both line and staff departments.[10] For example, in a product departmentalization structure, certain line managers (see Figure 6–12) may have functional authority over the product division managers. In such a case, the vice president of finance may be able to require the divisions to keep particular kinds of accounting records while the vice president of marketing may be able to request that weekly sales data be sent to him or her in tabular form. In a manner of speaking, the vice presidents have a slice of line authority in the divisions. It should be noted, however, that this is *limited* authority based on expertise and designed to improve organizational efficiency. For this reason, it is common to find functional authority limited to telling people *how* they are to

---

[10]Line departments carry out activities directly related to the accomplishment of the firm's major objectives, whereas staff departments carry out activities that are indirectly related to these objectives.

Autocad training of
Basic Commands

1.) Line — Copy
2.) Mirror —
3.) Move —
4.) rotate —
5.) ETC.
   Summary of
1 hr. to 1½ Course
training Course.

Proposal for manager
available position.
Randy Horton

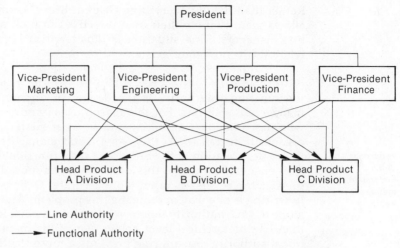

—— Line Authority

——► Functional Authority

FIGURE 6–12   Line Departments with Functional Authority

do something and *when* it should be done; it seldom involves where, what, or who, for this would seriously undermine the divisional manager's own line authority. Furthermore, the president will virtually always tell the division heads that functional authority is going to be delegated to the vice presidents of marketing, engineering, production, and finance, and ask the division heads' opinions. This way there is a minimum of power grabbing.

Functional authority can also be delegated to staff specialists. For example, the president may have many auxiliary personnel, including a public relations director and legal counsel. In a pure staff situation, each offers advice in his or her own area of expertise. However, the president may find it more efficient to delegate functional authority to these people.

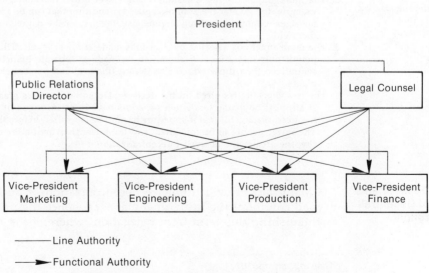

—— Line Authority

——► Functional Authority

FIGURE 6–13   Staff Departments With Functional Authority

Rather than having everything cleared through him or her, the president allows them to issue their own directives in their area of expertise to the line managers. This situation is illustrated in Figure 6–13. A pure staff relationship no longer exists.

PROBLEMS WITH FUNCTIONAL AUTHORITY.   The major problem in employing functional authority is the danger of undermining the integrity of managerial positions. For this reason, it is important to indicate precisely who has functional authority and in what matters. Unfortunately, many organizations fail to do this. As a result managers take wide latitude in their interpretation of the breadth of their functional authority, and confusion ensues. In theory, this authority is supposed to be limited, but in practice the reverse is often more accurate. Defining functional authority in writing is one way of reducing this problem. Another way is to limit the scope of such authority whenever possible, so that it does not extend more than one hierarchical level below that of the manager holding the functional authority. Such a rule prevents a top executive from undermining other managers in the structure by giving orders directly to their subordinates. In summary, although functional authority has advantages for the organization, it should be employed with prudence.

Functional authority can undermine a manager's authority.

DECENTRA-LIZATION OF AUTHORITY

For some time now many firms, especially large ones, have followed a policy of decentralizing authority. The term "decentralizing" should not be confused with that of delegating. Although the two are closely related, *decentralization* is much more encompassing in nature, reflecting a philosophy on the part of management regarding which decisions to send down the line and which to maintain near the top for purposes of organizational control. All organizations are characterized by some degree of decentralization, absolute centralization being virtually impossible. For this reason, decentralization must be viewed as a relative and not as an absolute concept. Dale has noted that the decentralization is greater:

1. The greater the number of decisions made lower down the management hierarchy.
2. The more important the decisions made lower down the management hierarchy. For example, the greater the sum of capital expenditure that can be approved by the plant manager without consulting anyone else, the greater the degree of decentralization in this field.
3. The more functions affected by decisions made at lower levels. Thus companies which permit only operational decisions to be made at separate branch plants are less decentralized than those which also permit financial and personnel decisions at branch plants.
4. The less checking required on the decision. Decentralization is greatest when no check at all must be made; less when superiors have to be informed of the decision after it has been made; still less if superiors have to be consulted before the decision is made. The fewer people to be consulted, and the lower they are on the management hierarchy, the greater the degree of decentralization.[11]

Decentralization is a relative concept.

Determinants of Decentralization

Many factors will influence decentralization of authority. Most are beyond control of the individual manager, hence the previous statement distinguishing this term from delegation, whereby the manager decides

[11]Dale, *op. cit.*, p. 107.

which duties to assign to a subordinate. The following represent some of the most important determinants of the degree of decentralization.

COST FACTORS.   As a rule of thumb, the greater the cost involved, the more likely it is that the decision will be made at the upper levels. It is not uncommon to find a firm with a policy permitting all expenditures of $500 or less to be approved by an operating department while all others have to be decided upon by a centralized purchasing or finance committee. In this way top management is able to control major expenditures, for example, for capital equipment. Many organizations, including General Motors, employ highly centralized controls in the financial area.

The degree of decentralization is dependent upon a number of factors.

UNIFORM POLICY.   A desire for uniform policies is another cause for centralization of authority. Standardization of quality, price, credit, and delivery can be beneficial because it ensures that everyone will be treated alike. Similarly, standardization of financial and accounting records makes it easier to compare the performance of various units and analyze their overall efficiency. When the firm wants everything done in a particular way, centralization of policy is desirable.

COMPANY SIZE.   As a firm gets larger, it is impossible to maintain the old degree of centralization; top management cannot continue to hold such a tight grip on the reins. It is common to find such firms reorganizing and assigning more authority to the various departments and operating units. In this way, the company reduces the expenses that often accompany growth. The units operate on a more autonomous basis, the top management concerning itself with tasks such as planning, financing, evaluating, and controlling the overall operations of the firm. Day-to-day activities are handled at the lower levels.

PHILOSOPHY OF TOP MANAGEMENT.   Many firms are highly centralized, whereas others are highly decentralized because of the character and philosophy of the top management. Henry Ford's firm was highly centralized because that was the way he wanted it; Ford decided matters for the entire company. Conversely, General Motors has been highly decentralized for years because in 1920 A.P. Sloan was able to get his reorganization plan accepted by the board of directors. In essence, it called for decentralization of operating authority to the divisions while maintaining centralized control at the top levels. Dale has described the two principles on which the recommendations rested as:

1. The responsibility attached to the chief executive of each operation shall in no way be limited. Each such organization headed by its chief executive shall be complete in every necessary function and enabled to exercise its full initiative in a logical development. (Decentralization of operations.)
2. Certain central organization functions are absolutely essential to the logical development and proper coordination of the Corporation's activities. (Centralized staff services to advise the line of specialized phases of the work, and central measurement of results to check the exercise of delegated responsibility.)[12]

PHILOSOPHY OF SUBORDINATE MANAGERS.   The philosophy of subordinate managers will affect decentralization in that it can either encourage or discourage such a policy. If subordinates want decentralization, top management may feel there is little to be gained by maintaining all important decision making at the upper levels. The desire by the subordinates for

---

[12]Ernest Dale, *The Great Organizers* (New York: McGraw-Hill Book Company, 1960), p. 87.

independence and the willingness to assume increased responsibility may convince them to become more decentralized. Conversely, if there is a shortage of managerial manpower, leaving the current group of subordinates with an excessive amount of work, the subordinates may encourage top management to maintain a more centralized approach.

FUNCTIONAL AREA.   Some functional areas of enterprise will be more decentralized than others. For example, in a manufacturing firm, production will often be highly decentralized. As the size of the facilities increases, authority will be decentralized so that it rests at the operating level. After all, who knows more about production operations than the people carrying them out? Sales also will often be decentralized for this same reason. Of course, in the case of budgets and controls there will still be a great deal of centralization, as there will be in the areas in which overall control is necessary such as pricing, advertising, and market research. Finance will be highly centralized in order to provide top management with an opportunity to maintain control over the entire organization. Although decisions on small expenditures may be made at the lower levels, those having a serious effect on the company's profit or financial stability will be made at the top.

THE ART OF DELE-GATION

Delegation is a process the manager uses in distributing work to the subordinates. The process encompasses three basic steps: the assigning of duties to the subordinates; the granting of authority to carry out these duties; and the creation of an obligation whereby the subordinate assumes responsibility to the superior to complete the task satisfactorily.[13]

Delegation, like decentralization, is often a matter of personal preference on the part of the manager. However, while some will delegate so much work to their subordinates that they will virtually abdicate their role as manager, it is far more common to find the reverse occurring. Many managers tend to hang on to everything, refusing to allow their subordinates to try their hands at anything. This unwillingness to let go is based on the assumption that the manager can do the job better than the subordinate, so why bother to delegate? Unfortunately, this attitude is often self-defeating, because it leads subordinates to the conclusion that they are not trusted by their superior. It also results in a failure to develop effective management talent. After all, how can a junior executive ever be expected to fill the boss's shoes if the young person never gets the opportunity to do so?

Steps to improved delegation.

These deficiencies can be overcome if the manager is willing to follow certain key steps. First, the manager must agree to try delegating authority and to do so in explicit terms. The subordinates must know exactly what they are to do and what kinds of results are going to be expected. Second, careful matching of the person with the job must be undertaken. Third, if there is a problem, the manager should have some form of "open-door" policy, whereby the subordinate can obtain assistance. Fourth, broad, not narrow, controls should be established so that the manager knows if things are going well; prime attention should be paid to significant deviations while minor problems are overlooked, at least initially. This way, the

---

[13]William H. Newman and E. Kirby Warren, *The Process of Management: Concepts, Behavior, and Practice,* 4th edition (Englewood Cliffs, N.J.: Prentice-Hall, 1977), pp. 39–42.

manager controls the situation without giving the impression of trying to monitor everything. After all, the subordinate should be expected to make some mistakes, regardless of his or her capabilities. Fifth, when the job is done, the manager should praise the subordinate's performance in the areas in which good results were obtained and express a willingness to work with the individual in improving the other areas. This can best be done by delegating more tasks to the subordinate, indicating that he or she still has the manager's trust and confidence.

Attention has thus far been focused exclusively on the formal organization as designed and implemented by management. No organization, however, actually operates in this manner. The individuals in the structure tend to remake it, changing things to meet their own needs. Although it is true that functional design theorists contend that an organization should initially be developed without regard for the human element, it is not long before this ideal structure gives way to a more practical one. Bakke termed this a *fusion process*, stating that:

THE INFORMAL ORGANIZA- TION

> When an individual and an organization come together in such a way that the individual is a participant in, and a member of, the organization and the two are mutually dependent on each other, both are reconstructed in the process. The organization to some degree remakes the individual and the individual to some degree remakes the organization.[14]

Consideration of this informal structure introduces a more dynamic view of the organization than is available from a mere analysis of the formal design. In obtaining a mental picture of the informal organization, it is helpful to regard it as a structure that is superimposed on the formal one.

The organization chart cannot show all the informal relationships that exist in the organization. To attempt to depict functional authority, for example, would lead to a mass of lines running all over the page. Likewise, it is virtually impossible to draw the informal organization. Not only are the relationships varied, but they are continually changing. Sometimes an informal organization consists of members of the same work group. Other times it involves intergroup membership as when formal lines are abandoned in the name of expediency and managers turn to unofficial channels in order to get things done. For example, the head of a production unit has a personal friend in the purchasing department whom he calls whenever it appears that some ordered raw materials will not arrive on time. His friend checks on the shipment and expedites it. A foreman on the assembly line has outstanding rapport with the union. When the labor contract comes up for re-negotiation, the industrial relations department calls in the foreman and asks him what to include in the new contract. The foreman is not a member of this department but he has an unofficial input into the contract. A production supervisor has a knack for developing new methods. As a result, she ends up with *de facto* jurisdiction over the methods department, even though this department is part of engineering.

The informal organization is not shown on the organization chart.

Informal relationships supplement formal authority. Realistically speaking, *real authority* consists of formal authority delegated by one's

Power and Authority

[14]E. Wight Bakke, *The Fusion Process* (New Haven: Labor and Management Center, Yale University, 1953), pp. 12–13.

superior (authority of the position) and personal power. Upon what does personal power depend? Numerous factors can be cited.

Sources of informal power.

Association with the right groups is helpful. The manager who belongs to the same country club as the company president may strike up a social friendship with the top executive. Once other members of the organization learn this, the manager may find individuals, including the immediate superior, much more willing to comply with his or her requests. The same is often true of the shop steward in a powerful union. The foreman may feel there is far more to be gained by keeping this person happy than by making demands on him or her. The last thing the foreman wants is a union-management rift, and the shop steward may be useful in preventing it.

Experience and *drive* are still other power factors. People who know their job and do it well find others willing to cooperate and assist them; interdepartmental doors are open to them. In addition, their superiors tend to rely on them and back them up if they run into a roadblock. No manager can afford to have productive subordinates stymied. Research shows that socio-psychological factors such as drive, decisiveness, and determination not only are positively viewed by others but often establish credibility about the person as someone who can be relied on. Real power increases as a result.

Education can also be helpful; some companies view it as a major criterion for promotion. When one group of researchers conducted a massive computer analysis of some 3202 individuals employed in the marketing department of a major petroleum corporation, they found education to be one of the most important variables in the promotion process.[15] In addition, their research revealed that not all the promotables were ranked very high on job performance, indicating that there is more than one route to securing power.[16]

Other power factors include *religion, politics, race,* and *national origin.* In some firms, especially at the upper levels, a Republican WASP may have more power than a Democratic Catholic because the people at the top belong to the former category. On the other hand, in Boston this same person may be at a decided disadvantage. Likewise, despite legislation to the contrary, race and national origin are still bases for the establishment of power relationships.

Formal and Informal Organizational Relationships

The informal organization can be very helpful to the company.

The informal organization is an inevitable product of human social processes. Unfortunately, too many organizations view it as a destructive element that must be weeded out. Actually, the informal organization has some very important advantages to offer. Primarily, it is a source of satisfaction for the members, often bringing about much higher morale than would otherwise be the case. This was clearly seen in the bank wiring room of the Hawthorne plant.

Early writings in the field pictured the informal organization as disruptive, the role of management being one of manipulating the group into accepting formal goals. Today, it is evident that such manipulation is seldom necessary. Oftentimes the goals of the formal and informal organizations are mutually reinforcing. Of course, this is not always true, but

---

[15]James W. Walker, Fred Luthans, and Richard M. Hodgetts, "Who Really Are the Promotables?" *Personnel Journal,* February 1970, pp. 123–127.
[16]Fred Luthans, James W. Walker, and Richard M. Hodgetts, "Evidence on the Validity of Management Education," *Academy of Management Journal,* December 1969, pp. 451–457.

until management is certain that the informal organization is in conflict with the formal, all attempts should be made to nurture the relationship. It does management no good to try to form a clear-cut distinction between the two. Actually, they are interrelated parts of a complex system. Management's job must be that of creating an organizational climate in which the goals and expectations of both groups can be attained.

In this chapter the nature, purpose, and function of organizing were examined. It was noted that organizing covers a very broad area and offers many alternatives to the manager. There are numerous forms of departmentalization including functional, product, territorial, simple numbers, time, customer, and equipment or process. Wide or narrow spans of control can be employed within each of these basic forms, and various types of authority can be delegated: line, staff, and functional.

Particular attention was also devoted to problem areas such as line-staff conflicts, by illustrating that organizing is certainly no mechanical function. There is a great deal of judgment involved in effectively coordinating all elements in the structure. This challenge was made even clearer with the introduction of the informal organization and the concept of personal power, for they bring a type of dynamism into the formal structure.

Although the organizing process brings the people and the work together, management still needs a basis for comparing the plan and the results. This activity, commonly referred to as the controlling process, will be the subject of the next chapter.

SUMMARY

REVIEW AND STUDY QUESTIONS

1. What is meant by "from strategy to structure"? Explain by including a discussion of the planning process in your answer.

2. What are the most widely used forms of departmentalization? List them.

3. How does functional departmentalization differ from product departmentalization? How does it differ from territorial departmentalization? What are the advantages associated with each?

4. What are the common advantages and disadvantages of committees?

5. How does a tall structure differ from a flat one?

6. What impact does the span of control have on the structure?

7. What is meant by the term "authority"? Where does authority come from?

8. What is line authority? Staff authority? Functional authority? Explain by using an illustration of each.

9. What are some common line-staff conflicts? What gives rise to them? How can they be prevented or overcome?

10. How does decentralization differ from delegation? Give an illustration of each.

11. What are some of the factors that influence the degree of delegation that

will take place in an organization? Differentiate between those that encourage it and those that discourage it.

12. What are some of the key steps to improving a manager's ability to delegate authority?

13. How does the formal organization differ from the informal? What role does personal power play? Explain in your own words.

14. Are the objectives of the formal and informal organization always in conflict? Defend your answer.

SELECTED REFERENCES

Chandler, A. D., Jr. *Strategy and Structure.* Garden City, New York: Anchor Books, Doubleday & Company, 1966.

Clark, P. A. *Organizational Design: Theory and Practice.* London: Tavistock Publishing, 1972.

Dale, E. *Planning and Developing the Company Organization Structure.* Research Report No. 20. New York: American Management Association, 1952.

Dale E. *The Great Organizers.* New York: McGraw-Hill Book Co., 1960.

Drucker, P. F. *Management: Tasks, Responsibilities, Practices.* New York: Harper & Row Publishers, 1974, Chapters 41–48.

House, R. J., and J. B. Miner. "Merging Management and Behavioral Theory: The Interaction Between Span of Control and Group Size." *Administrative Science Quarterly,* September 1969, pp. 451–464.

Parkinson, C. N. *Parkinson's Law.* Boston: Houghton Mifflin, 1957.

Urwick, Lt. Col. L. F. "V.A. Graicunas and The Span of Control." *Academy of Management Journal,* June 1974, pp. 349–353.

Urwick, L. F. "That Word 'Organization'." *Academy of Management Review,* January 1976, pp. 89–91.

Van Fleet, D. D., and A. G. Bedeian. "A History Of the Span Of Management." *Academy of Management Review,* July 1977, pp. 356–372.

CASE: A NEW SWITCH

Fun-For-All is a national manufacturing firm that produces and sells toys and games. Prior to 1968, the company specialized in children's toys, but in the late sixties adult games began to gain acceptance and Fun-For-All followed suit. The basic feature of the adult games is that they have no single, correct strategy and as a result require a great deal of thought on the part of the participant. For example, Monopoly, from Parker Brothers, has a basic strategy that often depends upon chance rather than skill. Players who are wise buy as much land as they can and start putting houses, and eventually hotels, on the property. However, true adult games such as chess are much more complex. There is no one right way to win a chess match; it all depends upon what one's opponent does and upon one's own skill. The same is true for backgammon.

In 1977 Fun-For-All decided to market an expensive ($100) backgammon set. The company was convinced that with the economy moving along well and people's outlook becoming more positive, demand for such a high-priced game would be sufficient to justify a 25 per cent return on investment.

By Christmas, thanks to timing and a strong advertising program, the firm had sold four times the number of sets it had initially forecast.

In 1978, because of growing sales, the management of Fun-For-All was considering reorganization. At the time, the firm was organized along functional lines (see Figure 6–14). However, the president thought the company might be wiser to change to product departmentalization, and some of the people in marketing also seemed to think that it would be a good idea. The production department, however, felt there was more to be gained from functional rather than product departmentalization. The finance people seemed indifferent about the matter, but indicated they would make an analysis of the two structures if the president desired.

The president's reorganization plan was to set up three product divisions: boy's toys, girl's toys, and adult games. The first two divisions accounted for over 75 per cent of the firm's sales, but the latter was growing rapidly and would, according to marketing estimates, account for over 50 per cent of all sales by 1982.

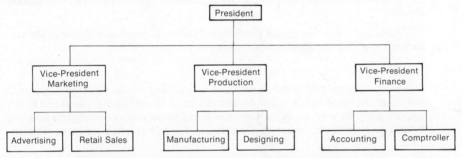

FIGURE 6–14   Fun-For-All, Inc. Organization Chart, September, 1978

Questions

1. Draw the proposed reorganization chart. Be as complete as possible.

2. What are the advantages of product departmentalization over functional departmentalization?

3. What recommendations would you make to the president before deciding to switch from functional to product departmentalization? Explain.

CASE: A MATTER OF OPINION

Abraham Liefeld had been a production manager for over thirty years, and there was virtually nothing he did not know about production. Mr. Liefeld's new assistant, Cathy Shackler, had great admiration for him. Cathy felt she had learned more about how to handle workers and obtain increased output in her first four weeks on the job than in her four years of undergraduate business school.

During this initial period, Cathy tried to keep her eyes and ears open; she was determined to learn as much about the job as possible. For example, she knew that Jack Charlton, another production manager, was a good friend of Mr. Liefeld's, and if Mr. Charlton ever called Mr. Liefeld for a favor and he was not in, Cathy should take care of it herself or see that it was done immediately. Gradually, she also began to learn the names and positions of other people with whom the production department came in contact on a rather regular basis. One of these was Fred Ackerman from the personnel department, who often visited Mr. Liefeld. Cathy knew Mr. Liefeld was interested in hiring some production supervisors and had asked Mr. Ackerman to take out some ads and to keep scouring the local colleges and universities when he went out recruiting.

About six months after Cathy had started, she knew her way around pretty well. At least she thought she did, until she inadvertently walked into Mr. Liefeld's office to find her boss and Mr. Ackerman in a shouting match. When they saw her their tempers immediately cooled. Cathy backed out the door. A few minutes later she noticed Mr. Ackerman leaving and she went back in:

I'm sorry, Mr. Liefeld. I didn't realize you had anyone in here with you.

That's okay, Cathy. Come on in. I think it's about time you realized that not everyone around here agrees with everyone else all of the time.

But what conflict can you be having with Mr. Ackerman? Isn't he in personnel

Yes, but he screens all incoming people. Remember those tests you took as part of your application process?

Sure.

Well, they're designed to find out something about your management potential. At least that's what Ackerman says. Supposedly, eight out of ten people who do well on them become good supervisory managers and the other two do not. Mr. Ackerman wants us to use that test as a screening device.

And you don't want to?

Let's put it this way. I want to see a man face-to-face and talk with him. I know what to look for in a good supervisor; I don't need any test to tell me how a man can handle himself. There's a young fellow who did poorly on the exam but I want to hire him. Mr. Ackerman disagrees.

Can he force you to use the test as a screening device?

No. His entire job is to evaluate the applicants and give me his recommendations. I decide who to hire in this department. That guy's getting a little too big for his britches. He's supposed to be advising me and he winds up giving me orders. Imagine, telling me that that young fellow I interviewed last week did poorly on the exam and I should forget about hiring him. Well, until the president decides that Ackerman has more savvy about how to run this department than I do, I'm going to make all the hiring decisions.

Questions

1. What kind of authority does Mr. Ackerman have? How do you know?

2. What kind of line-staff conflict is represented here? Explain.

3. How can these problems be prevented in the future? Be specific in your answer.

CASE: I DID IT MY WAY

Whenever one spoke of Shayling, Inc., one was speaking of Mr. Peter Shayling, founder, owner, president, and chairman of the board. Shayling, Inc., was one of the largest television retail and repair stores in the city, with gross sales of over $3 million. Mr. Shayling delighted in telling customers how he had started out in a small shop on the outskirts of town and gradually increased the size of his business to where he could afford to move into his current, modern, midtown facilities.

When the store was very small, Mr. Shayling and his wife did everything, including keeping the books. The only outside assistance they had was an accountant who came in every three months to balance the ledgers and compute the taxes. Gradually, as volume increased, Mr. Shayling began hiring help. First, he brought in a television repairman; then he hired a salesman. By mid-1978 there were fifteen people working for him, nine in the repair and delivery shop, six on the sales floor.

Although things appeared to be going well, Mr. Shayling admitted to his wife that he was disturbed by the large turnover of salesmen; on an average, he was losing one a month. He was also losing an average of one repairman every other month. About this time he received a call from a group of masters students in a nearby college of business who were taking an upper division management course that required them to analyze a local concern. They wanted to know if Mr. Shayling would let them write their paper on his company. Although initially skeptical, he was impressed by the fact that the team would put together a list of recommendations that would be turned over to him, so he agreed. "It's like getting free consulting," he told his wife.

Six weeks later the team sent him a copy of its paper. The analysis and recommendations were of great interest to Mr. Shayling. He felt the team had done an admirable job, and he intended to implement many of their suggested changes. However, there was one part of the paper with which he disagreed. It read as follows:

The high salesman turnover can be directly attributed to the owner's failure to delegate authority. No salesman is ever able to introduce a product to a customer or close a sale without Mr. Shayling getting into the act; he is everywhere. The result is a decline in morale brought about by the fact that the owner seems to lack faith in his own personnel. An analogous situation exists in the repair shop, although not to the same degree. In summary, Mr. Shayling should spend more time managing and less time looking over people's shoulders.

In defense of his actions, Mr. Shayling noted to his wife that the students undoubtedly lacked an understanding of the television repair business. "You've got to be on top of everything all the time," he said. "And far from getting in the way, I am really quite helpful to the salesmen. After all, who knows more about how to sell than me? I built this store from nothing and I did it my way. And there's no substitute for success. In fact, far from changing this habit, I think the salesmen would do an even better job if I spent more time helping them out."

Questions

1. Is failure to delegate a cause of poor morale? Explain.

2. How is Mr. Shayling's action typical of many owner-managers? Explain.

3. How can Mr. Shayling overcome his problem? Be specific in your recommendations.

4. Could the report have been worded differently so as to sell Mr. Shayling the recommendation? Explain.

CASE: RECENTRALIZATION[17]

The name Sears, Roebuck carries with it the connotation of decentralized authority. However, in recent years Sears has found that too much decentralization can be dangerous to overall profitability. Since 1976 the firm has been stripping its store managers of much of the authority they once had and has begun centralizing decision-making at its Chicago headquarters:

Sear's headquarters began to take more control in January 1976 . . . [and] by formally bringing the field forces into the highest reaches of corporate headquarters, has significantly narrowed a longstanding gap between headquarters and field operations. It also is the way that Sears chose to bring the field under closer control. With creation of the policy-setting body, store managers have lost much of their pricing authority, and nationwide retail promotions, once a rarity, have become a common maneuver.

"Local option has all but disappeared," one Sears man says. "The store managers don't have the right to turn down promotions now. If headquarters wants an item put on sale nationally during the first two weeks of August, it's put on sale the first two weeks in August. You don't find one guy doing it in July, another in September and another not at all."

Can this new strategy help Sears meet the challenges of the 1980's? Company officials seem to think so. In fact, during the first year of the new changes, Sears' monthly sales gain bettered those of the general-merchandise industry as a whole by three to ten percentage points. This is a remarkable performance for a company that has such a large sales base. During this period, Sears posted a profit increase of 4 per cent in the latest fiscal quarter, while J.C. Penney and K Mart's earnings were flat and F.W. Woolworth posted a 49 per cent decline.

Questions

1. What are the benefits of decentralization? What are the benefits of centralization?

2. In what way has recentralization of authority away from the store manager and back toward headquarters helped Sears improve its financial record?

3. Do you think the future will see a greater trend toward centralization by other retailers? Why or why not?

---

[17]The data in this case can be found in: David M. Elsner, "Sears, for Some Years in Disarray, Regains Its Former Momentum," *The Wall Street Journal,* August 9, 1977, pp. 1, 28.

CHAPTER SEVEN

THE CONTROLLING PROCESS

If an organization attains its objectives, more ambitious ones can be formulated. If it falls short of these goals, a revised plan is in order. In either case, an evaluation must be conducted, and this is where the controlling process comes in.

GOALS OF THE CHAPTER

The goals of this chapter are to examine the nature and process of control with prime focus on traditional, specialized, and overall control techniques. In this chapter you will note that there is a very strong link between planning and controlling, such that it is sometimes difficult to determine where one leaves off and the other begins.

When you are finished reading this chapter you should be able to:

1. Describe the three basic steps in the controlling process.
2. Discuss the requirements for an effective control system.
3. Relate how comprehensive and zero-base budgeting work.
4. Explain how the break-even point can be used for control purposes.
5. Present a brief description of the Gantt Chart, PERT, and milestone budgeting, noting how they can help an organization control its operations.
6. Describe some of the techniques often used for controlling an organization's overall performance.

As Fayol noted, "The control of an undertaking consists of seeing that everything is being carried out in accordance with the plan which has been adopted, the orders which have been given, and the principles which have been laid down. Its object is to point out mistakes in order that they may be rectified and prevented from occurring again."[1]

THE BASIC CONTROLLING PROCESS

The three basic steps in this controlling process are the establishment of standards, the comparison of performance against these standards, and the correction of deviations that have occurred. The latter two, of course, can only be attained through the establishment of effective feedback. This section will examine these three basic steps and the role of feedback in the controlling process.

Standards provide a basis against which performance can be measured. These standards are often a result of the goals the organization formulates during its planning phase. Sometimes they are very specific, being expressed in terms of costs, revenues, products, or man-hours worked. Other times they are more qualitative in nature such as a desire to

Establishing Standards

---

[1]Henri Fayol, *Industrial and General Administration* (Translated from the French edition by J. A. Coubrough, Geneva: International Management Institute, 1929), p. 77.

maintain high morale among the employees or to design a public relations program for gaining community goodwill.

**Comparing
Performance
With Standards**

Ideally, management should design a control system that permits it to identify major problems before they occur. For example, research shows that an individual's attitude toward the job declines before his or her productivity goes down. If management could identify this lead factor, it could begin taking steps to prevent the impending decline in output. However, since this is often more idealistic than practical, the next best step is to identify such deviations as early as possible. Most competent managers do so through use of the *exception principle*, which holds that attention should be focused on especially good or especially bad situations. In this way, the managers avoid spreading themselves too thin by trying to control every deviation.

**Some standards
are not easily
measured.**

The major problem most managers encounter is *how* to measure actual performance. Some standards are easily measurable, whereas others require custom-made appraisals. Still others seem to defy any form of accurate evaluation. For example, how does one really measure worker motivation, since motivation is an intervening variable? It is an internal, psychological process that is not directly observable and can only be judged by drawing inferences about a person. For example, if George appears interested in his work he is motivated, and vice versa. Yet this appraisal may well be inaccurate. Another common performance measurement dilemma occurs when a firm tries to evaluate a top-level manager such as the vice president of finance. Whatever criteria are used, they are often vague in nature. Management has found that as the work becomes less technical, standards are often difficult to develop and appraisals exceedingly hard to make. For this reason, in recent years there has been a trend toward evaluating personnel almost exclusively on objective bases. If the standard is not measurable, it is not employed. This approach is useful in that it greatly reduces subjective, biased evaluations while providing direction for the subordinates who now know the bases on which their performance will be judged.

**Correcting
Deviations**

The correction of deviations should begin with an investigation of *why* the error occurred. Sometimes a planning premise may have been wrong. Sales may have been lower than anticipated because of an overly optimistic forecast. Or a strike in the plant may have caused unexpected delays in production. The cause of the deviation will help determine the appropriate action. The key point to be noted here is that some problems are no one's fault. From time to time even the best market forecasts will be wrong. An example of this was illustrated in Chapter 5 in the case of Frost 8/80, the dry white whisky that, despite an extensive market research program, failed to achieve widespread acceptance. And in the case of a union strike, the walkout may be more a function of union demands than of management offers. For example, the company may be able to give a maximum offer of 15 per cent in salary and 4.2 per cent in fringe benefits over a two-year period. If the union refuses to settle for anything less than 20 per cent and 5.7 per cent respectively, a strike may be inevitable. In short, not all deviations are directly attributable to any one individual, and if management continually tries to assess blame for every error, employee attitudes toward work may suffer.

Of course, there are times when a manager will make an error in judgment or a worker will handle an order improperly. When this occurs, corrective action may require the replacement of the individual or the assignment of additional training. However, the action can only be determined after the specific causes of the deviation have been evaluated.

After the cause is identified, problem-solving measures can be enacted.

An ideal control system provides timely *feedback* that can be used to monitor and correct deviations. A basic illustration is provided by the human body. If something happens that causes the body to leave its "normal" state, basic control mechanisms will attempt to re-establish the status quo. This self-regulating or control property is known as *homeostasis*. For example, if a person cuts his finger, the body will begin working to coagulate the blood and close the wound. The feedback mechanism in the human system can perform phenomenal feats if conditions are not too severe, i.e., one suffers a massive heart attack or is hit by a Mack truck.

Establishing Effective Feedback

This same basic concept of feedback is present in the thermostat system of a home. The desired temperature is determined by setting an indicator, and this is communicated to the system that controls the furnace. If a family desires 68°F, the heating unit will maintain the temperature at this level, turning on and off as necessary.

An organization also requires a feedback system. With the information provided by such a system, the company can monitor activities by identifying those that are not in accord with plans and taking the necessary corrective action. The establishment of such a system results in the type of process depicted in Figure 7-1.

It should be noted, however, that organizational control systems differ from those found in the human body and the home thermostat in that the latter are often automatic and employ, at least in the short-run, only data from within the system. Organizational control, on the other hand, is seldom automatic. Usually, by the time feedback results are evaluated, other errors have occurred, and the organization is involved in a game of "catch-up." In addition, organizational control employs data from outside the system. This occurs in the corrective process when the manager decides how to handle deviations, thereby introducing new decisions or inputs into the process. For this reason, mechanical control systems are often known as *closed-loop* systems, whereas organizational control systems are often called *open-loop* systems. Naturally, the latter must be viewed on a spectrum. If most organizational decisions are handled via established policies or procedures, the system is more auto-

Organizations must develop effective feedback control systems.

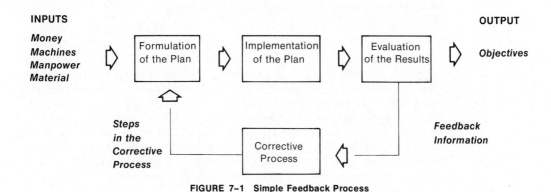

FIGURE 7-1 Simple Feedback Process

matic than one requiring managers to formulate their own action. Nevertheless, even with feedback, organizational control presents a challenge to the manager.

**REQUIRE-
MENTS
FOR AN
EFFECTIVE
CONTROL
SYSTEM**

The process of control is not an automatic phenomenon. If the organization wants an effective control system, it has to tailor one to its own specifications. In addition to the two previously mentioned requirements, namely, that controls be objective and the manager employ the exception principle, the following are some other prerequisites for an effective control system.

**Provide Useful,
Understandable
Information**

Control systems will differ from organization to organization and from manager to manager. Information that is valuable to one individual may be useless to another. The key question each must ask is, what information do I need to control the activities within my jurisdiction? This approach is valuable for two reasons. First, it forces the manager to decide what he or she needs to know and in what form. This is known as information design and results in useful, understandable data. Second, it provides a basis for screening out reports and information that the individual may be receiving which are of no value in the control process.

Timeliness

Controls should report deviations quickly. In addition, a well-designed system should be capable of identifying potential problem areas before they manifest themselves. For example, forecasting a cash flow for the next 90 days based on optimistic, most likely, and pessimistic conditions can provide management with a short-run financial picture. If it appears likely that the company will run out of cash, i.e., only under the most optimistic conditions will it remain in the black, there is still time to negotiate a loan with a local bank. In this way, controls become lead rather than lag factors.

Flexibility

Most plans will deviate from expectations and some will be outright failures. Unless a control system is flexible, it will be unable to maintain control of operations during these periods. The value of flexible control can be readily seen in the use of budgets that are increased or contracted based on the volume of business (flexible budgets). These techniques help management control operations regardless of economic conditions.

Economical

A control system must be worth the expense. However, it is often difficult to determine when the marginal costs associated with the system equal the marginal revenues obtained from it. Naturally, a small company cannot afford to install the expensive systems employed by a large corporation, but what about a minor expenditure such as a time clock? If a firm puts one in, will tardiness be reduced? Will work output increase? The answer to the first question may be "yes" while the answer to the second may be "no." People might show up on time and not leave early for home, but that does not mean they will do more work. They may just sit around waiting to clock out at 5 p.m. On the other hand, productivity may rise, and although a large firm may be able to absorb low productivity, a small one may not, so the system might prove useful to the latter. In either event, if a firm decides to put in the time clock, it must be willing to compare results both before and after the installation. Only in this way can it be sure that the control mechanism was economical. This guideline also applies to revenues and expenses associated with control systems that are much more difficult to evaluate. For example, what is the cost-benefit ratio attached to a new monthly progress report that must be submitted by all unit managers? This may be difficult to answer, requiring a highly subjective estimate. Nevertheless, some attempt must be made to do so.

An effective control system must lead to corrective action; merely uncovering deviations from plans is not enough. The system must also disclose where the problem areas are and who is responsible for them. From here management can evaluate the situation and decide upon the appropriate action. Figure 7–2 provides an illustration of the controlling process in action.

Lead to Corrective Action

There is a large number of control techniques that can be employed by management. Some of the more traditional ones include budgeting, break-even point analysis, and personal observation.

TRADI-TIONAL CONTROL TECH-NIQUES

When budgets were mentioned earlier in the book (Chapter 5), it was noted that organizations often use them to harmonize functional plans. As such, the budget is a type of plan specifying anticipated results in numerical terms. However, it is also a control device that provides a basis for feedback, evaluation, and follow-up.

Budgeting

COMPREHENSIVE BUDGETING. Many organizations use comprehensive budgeting when all phases of operations are covered by budgets. This often begins with the submission of budget proposals by subordinate managers. After discussion with the superiors, the proposals are adjusted, if necessary, and then forwarded to higher management. The result is a bottom-up approach, which ensures consideration of the needs and desires of, and participation by, lower management. However, the process does not stop here. At the top of the organization there is often a budget committee which reviews the entire program. In a manufacturing firm, for example, this committee may consist of the president and the vice presidents of finance, marketing, and production, who have line authority to make whatever final budget revisions are necessary. In other cases, the committee may be staffed by lower ranking personnel who have advisory authority only. In either case, the result is an integration of the individual budgets into a comprehensive one and the paring away of excessive requests. Thus, although everyone has an input into the budget, the top management maintains the authority to make necessary adjustments. This is very important once one realizes that some departments will request 130 per cent of what they need and hope to be cut back no more than 20 per cent. Of course, the challenge is knowing where to cut. An overall 30 per

A "from-the-bottom-up" approach is used.

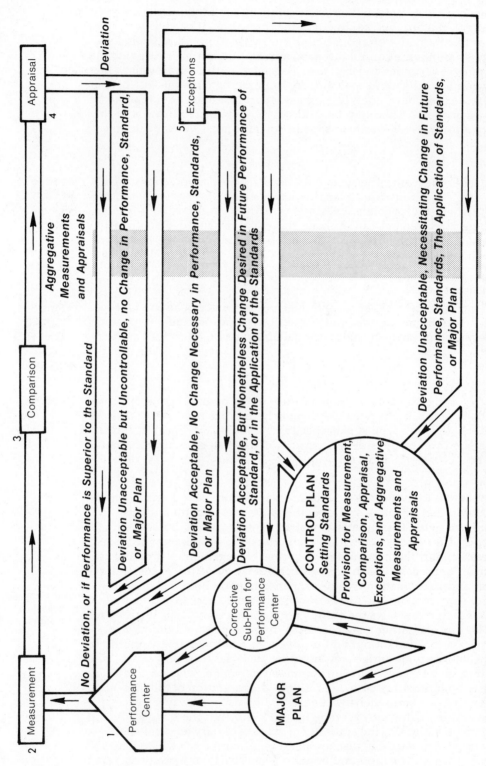

FIGURE 7–2 Controlling Process in Action (From Dale A. Henning, *Non-Financial Controls in Smaller Enterprises,* **University of Washington Bureau of Business Research, Seattle, 1964, p. 22. Reprinted with permission.)**

cent reduction in budget requests is harmful to those units that are not padding their estimates and helpful to those that are. For this reason, management must impress on its people the importance of submitting reasonable budgets.

ZERO-BASE BUDGETING. At the present time one of the most popular types of budgeting is *zero-base budgeting* (ZBB), which helps overcome the problems associated with submitting unreasonable budgets. In addition to its introduction to the federal bureaucracy by President Carter, ZBB is being currently used by a half-dozen states, a score of cities, and several hundred companies including Texas Instruments, Inc., Southern California Edison, Ford Motor, The Bank of Montreal, and Playboy Enterprises. The concept of ZBB, which is often applied to support services, is rather simple:

> Managers, starting at the lowest "cost centers" of an organization, must justify everything they do as if they were building their operation from scratch. Every manager isolates basic services and overhead items he controls—a typing pool, a computer, or a mailroom, for example—and then writes a brief outline of why each exists and how much it costs. This outline—or "decision package" in ZBB jargon—usually identifies a minimum expenditure level below the current outlay, plus an expanded service level if more money were available. It also examines alternative ways of performing a task, such as hiring temporary help or outside contractors. Finally, managers rank all their decision packages by priority and pass them on to their superiors, who go through the same exercise at a higher plane.[2]

When it comes to actual production areas such as product lines, however, ZBB is applied somewhat differently. In these cases the company decides how much profit it wants to make on its investment. Then each unit or division submits a budget requesting a given amount of money and relating the amount of profit that can be expected from this investment. By carefully reviewing each budget proposal and the expected return, the top management can prune the marginal lines and put its money behind the most promising winners.

Proponents of ZBB cite many advantages: (a) it focuses the budget process on a comprehensive analysis of objectives and needs; (b) it combines planning and budgeting into a single process; (c) it causes managers at every level to evaluate in detail the cost-effectiveness of their operations; and (d) it expands management participation in planning and budgeting at all levels of the organization.[3]

Opponents of ZBB, meanwhile, note that it requires a great deal more time, work, personnel, and money than more standard approaches to budgeting. Many business firms that have used ZBB, however, think that it saves more money than it costs. For example, Southern California Edison claims savings of over $300,000 annually thanks to ZBB; Westinghouse Electric saved $4.2 million in overhead costs in just one year with ZBB; and Ford Motor says that its savings run into "the millions."[4] In fact, ZBB is catching on so fast around the country that consulting companies are now beginning to hold ZBB seminars for business firms, and the major accounting firms are starting to advise their clients on zero-base budgeting.

---

[2]"What It Means to Build a Budget from Zero," *Business Week*, April 18, 1977, p. 160.
[3]"What Zero-Base Budgeting is and How Carter Wants to Use It," *U. S. News and World Report*, April 25, 1977, p. 92.
[4]*Business Week*, op. cit.

AVOIDING INFLEXIBILITY IN BUDGETING.   Budgets are useful planning and control tools, but they can prove cumbersome if overbudgeting occurs. Spelling out all expenses in detail deprives the manager of freedom of action. It can also lead to assigning higher priorities to the budget than to organizational objectives.

In order to avoid such inflexibility, there has been increasing interest given to the *variable expense budget*. This budget is used to complement the original one. With it, expenses and allowances are computed for different levels of activity. Then, after the budget period is over, calculations are made regarding what the expenses for each unit *should* have been. If activity was as expected, departments should be within their budgets. If, however, volume was much higher than expected there will be many who overspent. The company will then, based on a predetermined formula, compute what the expenses should have been and adjust departmental budgets accordingly. The variable budget, however, is not a substitute for a comprehensive budgetary program; rather, it is a supplement to it.

Some companies use a variation of the variable budget known as the *supplemental monthly budget*. Under this approach, a minimum operational budget is determined. Then, prior to the beginning of each month, a supplemental budget is drawn up that provides the units with additional funds based on volume expectations for the period. This approach differs from the variable budget in that adjustments are made before the period begins rather than after it is over.

Various forms of flexible budgets are being used.

Another version of the flexible budget is the *alternative budget*. Under this approach, the company establishes budgets for various levels of operations: high, medium, and low. Then, at the beginning of the particular period, managers are told under which budget they will be operating.

Approaches such as these all indicate the need for flexibility in the budgeting process; as sources of information feedback, they can provide a very useful function to the manager. However, one must be careful not to become too reliant on them. Budgets must be regarded only as tools for attaining organizational control.

Break-Even Point

Another common control technique is break-even analysis. At the end of any given period of operation, an organization hopes to make a profit. To do this, total revenue must be greater than total costs. For purposes of analysis, costs can be divided into two categories: fixed costs and variable costs. *Fixed costs* are those that will remain constant (at least in the short-run) regardless of operations. Examples include property insurance, property taxes, depreciation, and administrative salaries. *Variable costs* are those that will change in relation to output. In a manufacturing enterprise, labor salaries and cost of materials are typical examples.

Break-even point occurs when total fixed and variable expenses are covered.

In computing the break-even point (BEP), three cost-revenue components are of major importance to the manager: total fixed cost, selling price per unit, and variable cost per unit. By subtracting the variable cost associated with the unit from its selling price, a margin-above-cost is obtained. This margin can then be applied to the total fixed cost with the BEP occurring when the total of these margins equals total fixed cost. In simple mathematical terms:

$$BEP = \frac{TFC}{P - VC}$$

where: BEP = Break-even point in units
TFC = total fixed cost
P   = price per unit
VC = variable cost per unit

Consider the following example. Company A has conducted market research on a new product and determined that at $10 each it can sell 25,000 units. The firm's total fixed costs are $120,000 and its variable cost per unit is $4. Given this information, will the venture be profitable? The answer is going to depend on the BEP. Applying the relevant data to the formula results in the following:

$$BEP = \frac{\$120,000}{\$10 - 4}$$

$$= \frac{\$120,000}{6}$$

$$= 20,000 \text{ units}$$

The firm's BEP is 20,000 units. Figure 7–3 illustrates this solution graphically. Since sales are projected at 25,000 units, the venture should prove profitable. However, if market research showed a demand of anything less than 20,000 units, the company could not break even on the project.

BEP analysis is a useful control device because it emphasizes the marginal concept. In addition, it helps establish initial guidelines for control; i.e., fixed costs should remain at $120,000, variable cost per unit should be $4, and profits should occur after 20,000 units are sold. If costs or expected sales change, the management has a basis for evaluating the impact and taking the necessary corrective action.

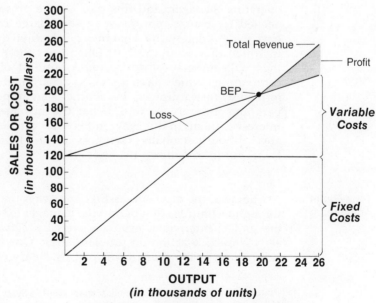

FIGURE 7–3 Break-Even Point Computation

Personal Observation

Another common control technique is *personal observation*. Although it is employed in virtually every organization, it is especially common in small and medium-sized firms. Non-profit organizations that are under little pressure to show results on a time-cost basis also make wide use of it.

A firsthand view can be useful.

Although personal observation alone is an incomplete form of control, it is an excellent supplement to budgets and break-even analysis. There are many things that a manager cannot discover from reporting forms that can be obtained with a casual stroll through the work place. There is no substitute for a firsthand view of operations, and personal observation provides just this.

SPECIALIZED CONTROL TECHNIQUES

In addition to traditional control techniques, management has developed many specialized tools to improve the quality of control. Space does not allow a discussion of all of them, but two will be examined: information design and time-event analyses.

Information Design

Information design is critical to an organization, especially in light of modern computers that can provide a wealth of data on virtually any area the manager would like to examine. Without some system for filtering out relevant from irrelevant information, managers can find themselves swamped with reports and numbers, most of which are meaningless to them. As Koontz and O'Donnell have pointed out:

> Managers who have experienced the impact of better and faster data processing are justly concerned with the danger of information indigestion. Their appetites for figures whetted, the data originators and processors are turning out material at an almost frightening rate. Managers are complaining of being buried under printouts, reports, projections, and forecasts which they do not have time to read or cannot understand, or which do not fill their particular needs.[5]

The result has been the development of specialized organizational systems and procedures designed to provide information useful to the operating manager; and this data can be presented in whatever form is needed for control purposes. In some large corporations, all managers have to do is determine what they need, when they need it, and the format in which they would like it. Oftentimes these are periodic reports that they will automatically receive. A spin-off of this concept is seen in corporations which have a service department that keeps executives informed by forwarding copies of articles and reports appearing in newspapers and journals on topics that the managers have indicated are of interest to them. In this way, individuals can keep up on their specialized area without personally having to spend a lot of time searching journals for useful information.

Time-Event Analyses

Some of the most successful approaches to control have been attained through techniques that permit the manager to see how all the segments of the project interrelate, evaluate overall progress, and identify and take early corrective action on problem areas. One of the earliest techniques, still in use, is the chart developed by Henry Gantt. The principles con-

---

[5]Harold Koontz and Cyril O'Donnell, *Management: A Systems and Contingency Analysis of Managerial Functions*, 6th edition (New York: McGraw-Hill Book Company, 1977), p. 677.

tained in it have served as the basis for both Program Evaluation and Review Technique (PERT) and milestone scheduling, which will be examined later in this section.

GANTT CHART.   The Gantt chart has proved to be a useful planning and control technique. The basic concept involves the graphic depiction of work progress over a period of time. An illustration is provided in Figure 7–4.

The Gantt chart is a control technique that is easy to read and understand.

An examination of the figure reveals that there are three orders being filled, each requiring certain operations to be performed. For the week illustrated in the chart, Order 1 is scheduled for manufacturing on Monday and Tuesday, assembling on Wednesday, painting on Thursday, and testing on Friday. Order 2 is scheduled for manufacturing on Monday, Tuesday, and Wednesday, assembling on Thursday, and painting on Friday. Order 3 is scheduled for manufacturing on Monday and Tuesday, assembling on Wednesday and Thursday, and painting on Friday. The solid vertical lines indicate the time required for each operation; the dotted horizontal lines denote progress; and the "V" after Thursday indicates that the chart reflects the situation as of the close of business on that day. Based on this information, it is evident that Order 1 is on time, Order 2 is a day ahead, and Order 3 is a day behind. With this information, the manager is in a position to control the situation by, for example, transferring those working on Order 2 to Order 3 and making up the lost day. This concept of identifying the work to be done and plotting it on a time axis has provided the foundation for PERT.

PROGRAM EVALUATION AND REVIEW TECHNIQUE.   PERT was developed by the Special Projects Office of the United States Navy and applied to the planning and control of the Polaris Weapon System in 1958. The technique has proved very useful in managing *complex* projects.

The manager receives only pertinent data.

PERT Network.   PERT employs what is called a time-event network. In building the network, events and activities are first identified. An *event* is a point in time when an activity is begun or finished and is generally represented in the network by a circle. An *activity* is an operation required to accomplish a particular goal and is represented in the network by an arrow. Figure 7–5 illustrates a simple PERT network that might be used to construct a house. The events are numbered for purposes of identification. Of course, an actual PERT network would not be used for such a simple project, but the basic concept is the same. It should be noted that the network not only identifies all the events but also establishes a relationship among them. For example, in Figure 7–5 event 3 cannot be

Relationships among the events are determined.

ORDER NUMBER	DAY				
	Monday	*Tuesday*	*Wednesday*	*Thursday*	*Friday*
1	Manufacture		Assemble	Paint	Test
2	Manufacture			Assemble	Paint
3	Manufacture		Assemble		Paint

FIGURE 7–4   Simplified Gantt Chart

completed before event 2, and event 8 must be finished before going on to event 10.

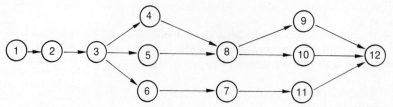

1. Begin House
2. Install Basement
3. Erect Frame
4. Put in Floors
5. Put on Roof
6. Put Brick Around Bottom of House
7. Finish Upper Outside Part of House
8. Wire Inside
9. Install Electric Heating Unit
10. Install Electric Kitchen Appliances
11. Put in Doors and Cabinets
12. Complete House

FIGURE 7–5 Simple PERT Network

Expected time can be calculated.

Once the network is constructed, attention is focused on time estimates. Quite often the people responsible for each activity assist in determining optimistic, most likely, and pessimistic time estimates for accomplishing their respective activities. These estimates are then used to compute the *expected time* for each activity. The equation for this is:

$$t_E = \frac{t_o + 4t_m + t_p}{6}$$

where: t_E = expected time
t_o = optimistic time
t_m = most likely time
t_p = pessimistic time

Figure 7–6 illustrates a PERT network with the three estimates for each activity and the expected time, expressed in weeks, directly below in parentheses. For example, the expected time between events 1 and 2 is:

$$t_E = \frac{8 + 4(10) + 12}{6}$$

$$t_E = 10 \text{ weeks}$$

The critical path is the longest path.

For control purposes, it is now possible to determine the *critical path*, which is that sequence of activities and events that is longer than any other. In Figure 7–6 there are only five possible paths through the network. Along with their expected times, they are:

Path	Expected Times	Total
1−2−3−6−11−14	10.0 + 5.0 + 6.0 + 13.8 + 12.0	46.8
1−2−3−7−11−14	10.0 + 5.0 + 5.2 + 14.8 + 12.0	47.0
1−2−4−8−12−14	10.0 + 2.0 + 15.0 + 8.0 + 6.0	41.0
1−2−4−9−12−14	10.0 + 2.0 + 10.3 + 7.0 + 6.0	35.3
1−2−5−10−13−14	10.0 + 2.2 + 18.0 + 10.0 + 4.0	44.2

Path 1−2−3−7−11−14 is the critical path, since it is longer than any other.

The final component that must be considered is slack. *Slack* is the time difference between scheduled completion and each of the paths. If, for example, the project in Figure 7–6 had to be completed within 52 weeks, all the paths would have slack. On the other hand, if the completion date was 40 weeks, four of the paths would have negative slack. In this case, they would have to be shortened if the schedule were to be met. There are a number of ways of doing this. Hopeman lists these as follows:

1. The expected time for particular activities may be reduced, if possible.
2. Men, machines, materials, and money can be transferred from slack paths to the critical path or near-critical paths.
3. Some activities may be eliminated from the project.
4. Additional men, machines, materials, and money may be allocated to the critical path or near-critical paths.
5. Some of the activities which are normally sequential may be done in parallel.[6]

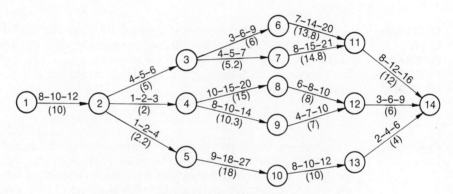

FIGURE 7–6   PERT Network With Time

Strengths and Limitations. Perhaps the major advantage of PERT is that it forces managers to plan. In addition, because of the times assigned to each activity, it provides a basis for identifying critical areas and correcting or monitoring them. On the other hand, PERT is only practical for non-recurring undertakings, and it must be possible to assign times to the events despite the fact that the entire project is new to the company. In addition, some managers have bemoaned PERT's emphasis on time without consideration to cost. As a result, in recent years there has been the development of PERT/COST, in which costs are applied to activities in the network.

MILESTONE SCHEDULING.   Although PERT is useful for sophisticated projects, it is often abandoned as the undertaking comes to a close and complexity declines. PERT can help integrate and simultaneously analyze thousands of activities, but as the project winds down, less complex control techniques can be more economically employed. One of these is milestone scheduling, an approach used by NASA in the management of the Apollo Program.[7]

A useful technique for less complex projects.

[6]Richard J. Hopeman, *Production: Concepts, Analysis Control*, 3rd edition (Columbus, Ohio: Charles E. Merrill Publishing Company, 1976), p. 343.

[7]*Program Scheduling and Review Handbook* (Washington, D.C.: National Aeronautics and Space Administration, NHB2330.1, October 1965).

This scheduling and control procedure employs bar charts, which are used to monitor progress. In this way, the manager can determine which segments of the undertaking are ahead of schedule, on time, or behind schedule. The technique is very similar to that of the Gantt chart, but instead of being used exclusively for production activities, it can be employed for virtually any undertaking.

In Figure 7–7 there are three milestones. The first was begun in January, is scheduled for completion at the end of August, and is on time. The second was begun in March, is scheduled for completion in October, and is currently a month ahead of expectations. The third was begun in April, is scheduled for completion in December, and is currently running a month behind expectations. Milestone scheduling allows the manager to see a program in its simpler parts, thereby providing more effective control than sophisticated techniques.

CONTROLLING OVERALL PERFORMANCE

Most of the techniques discussed thus far are useful in controlling specific activities, but they do not measure overall performance. In this section, some of the tools used for evaluating total accomplishments will be examined, including profit and loss, return on investment, key area control, and auditing.

Profit and Loss

Perhaps the most commonly employed overall control is the income statement, which shows all revenues and expenses for the particular period of operation and provides a basis for comparing actual and expected results. Of course, primary concern is going to be given to whether or not the firm finished in the black, but it is also possible to ascertain where the firm went wrong during the period, thereby establishing a basis for corrective action. In particular, the company can analyze the income statement in detail, noting how much each unit's operating expense has increased over the last year and determining whether each was justified or needs to be controlled during the next fiscal period. Additionally, it is possible to compare the profits (and losses) of operating divisions to see which was the most successful and why.

Return on Investment

Another widely used control technique is that of return on investment (ROI), which measures how well a firm is performing with the assets at its command. The method for computing ROI is presented in Figure 7–8.

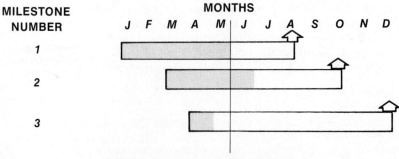

FIGURE 7–7 Simplified Milestone Schedule

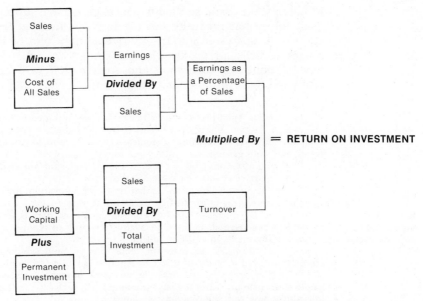

FIGURE 7–8   Computation of Return on Investment

The reason why ROI is favorably viewed by so many companies is that it answers the question, how well are we doing with what we have? After all, a firm with $4 million in profits is far ahead of one with $10,000 in profits. However, if the former company has a total investment of $10 billion but the latter has one of only $10,000, the smaller firm is doing far better than the larger in terms of overall performance. According to the ROI approach, profits are relative and efficiency is of major importance.

ROI measures a firm's ability to manage its assets.

The ROI concept need not be restricted to overall company results. It can be brought down to the divisional product level by way of measuring how well each division is doing. By comparing results with expectations, problem areas can be pinpointed for control purposes. The important thing to remember about ROI is that a good return will vary by industry, and results can only be judged in comparison with the competition. Also, exclusive reliance on this technique can lead to preoccupation with financial factors.[8] For this reason, it is advantageous to supplement profit and/or ROI with other overall control techniques such as key area control.

General Electric provides a good illustration of a firm employing key area control. For two decades now, the company has measured results in eight areas: profitability, market position, productivity, product leadership, personnel development, employee attitudes, public responsibility, and integration of short- and long-range goals. The firm has not been able to develop the desired measurements for all of these areas, but by concentrating attention on them it has been possible to obtain an appraisal of overall performance.

Key Area Control

It is interesting to note that GE prefers to use profitability rather than

---

[8]For example, for years Du Pont would not approve a new product program yielding less than a 20% ROI. As a result, they passed up xerography and the Land (Polaroid) camera. See "Lighting a Fire Under the Sleeping Giant," *Business Week*, September 12, 1970, pp. 40–41.

ROI. In recent years, some financial experts have supported this approach, concluding that regardless of the firm's efficiency, the final criterion of success is always profit. In any event, only one of the eight key areas relates directly to profit. The remainder are related to environmental factors (political, economic, and social) vital to overall control, as the following descriptions illustrate:

Profitability. **Total profits after all expenses, including cost of capital, are deducted.**

Market Position. **Share of the market is one of the key criteria here. In addition, the company attempts to measure customer satisfaction and to discover what the consumer wants but is not getting.**

Productivity. **Goods and services produced and sold are compared with the inputs necessary to arrive at some measure of productivity.**

Product Leadership. **Includes market position, innovation, and the ability to take advantage of new ideas in producing successful new products.**

Personnel Development. **The key criterion employed here is whether or not people are available when needed. Is there an adequate supply of manpower for meeting new and complex assignments in addition to filling vacancies?**

Employee Attitudes. **Absenteeism, labor turnover, and safety records are some of the criteria employed to evaluate attitudes. Another is the use of employee surveys.**

Public Responsibility. **Attention in this area is focused on many groups, including employees, customers, and the local community. In each case, indices have been developed to evaluate how well the company is doing.**

Integration of Short- and Long-Range Goals. **By encouraging formulation of long-range planning, the company ensures that short-run goals reflect these long-range objectives.**

Key control areas used by General Electric.

The GE approach is only one of many that can be employed for key area control. However, it highlights the importance of determining major criteria and monitoring performance in accord with the results obtained. No organization can maintain control of every aspect of operation. Instead, it must identify those that provide a basic picture of how well things are going and abide by the feedback obtained. Some organizations also rely upon various forms of auditing to help perform this function.

Auditing

When one hears the word audit, he or she may immediately think of a public accounting firm. However, there are three basic types of audits useful for overall control: external audits, internal audits, and management audits.

External audits are conducted by outside accounting people.

EXTERNAL AUDIT.   An external audit is conducted by outside accounting personnel and entails the examination and evaluation of the firm's financial transactions and accounts. This audit is generally performed by a certified public accounting firm, which expresses an opinion of the company's financial statements regarding their fairness, consistency, and conformity with the accepted principles of accounting. Usually this audit entails a detailed verification of all important balance sheet items with a view toward ascertaining whether the major assets, liability, and capital accounts are being accurately reported. The CPA firm does not delve into non-financial areas such as evaluating plans, policies, and procedures. However, when one realizes that the auditors will only certify accounts that are in order, it is evident that they provide an indirect control over all operations.

INTERNAL AUDIT. An internal audit is conducted by the organization's own staff specialists. In essence, the auditing team examines and evaluates the firm's operations, determining where things have gone well and where corrective action is needed. Generally, much of their work is restricted to the financial area, but this need not be the case. They can also be useful in evaluating non-quantitative areas. When this occurs, the internal audit goes further than its external counterpart and approaches what is commonly known as the management audit.

Internal audits are conducted by company personnel.

MANAGEMENT AUDIT. A management audit picks up where a financial audit leaves off. Sometimes this is conducted by the firm itself and is known as a *self-audit,* an approach first advocated by McKinsey back in the 1930's.[9]

Some management audits are carried out by the firm itself.

The purpose of the self-audit is to examine the company's position on a periodic basis, i.e., every two, three, or five years. By studying the market trends, technological changes, and political and social factors affecting the industry, the company can construct a forecast of the external environment.

Next, attention is turned to the firm itself. How well has it maintained its industry position? What is the competitive outlook? How do the customers feel about the firm's products? Answers to these questions help relate the company to its industry.

On the basis of the results, the firm can examine overall objectives and policies. From here, attention can be focused on programs, procedures, personnel, management, and financial positions. As the self-audit continues, attention moves from the macro- to the micro-level so that eventually all segments and activities of the company are analyzed. The problem with the self-audit, however, is that many firms do not find time to conduct one. Furthermore, for those who do, there are some very real dangers associated with using the company's own personnel, including bias and lack of competence.

One way of overcoming this problem is to employ an *external management audit* such as that conducted by the American Institute of Management. Founded a number of years ago by Jackson Martindell, the institute uses a list of 301 questions to rate companies in the area of fiscal policies, health of earnings, fairness to stockholders, research and development, sales vigor, economic function, directors, corporate structure, executive ability, and production efficiency.[10] Each of the ten areas is assigned a point value, with 3,500 of the 10,000 possible points allotted to managerial elements. To obtain a rating of "excellent," the company must receive 7,500 points.

Others are conducted by outside organizations.

Yet this is only one technique for conducting a management audit. Many others are available, from the approach recommended by Greenwood[11] for evaluating the overall firm to the one employed by the Defense Department in evaluating companies bidding on major defense contracts. It now appears that the future will see even greater interest in this area, for in the last decade management consulting and accounting audit firms have found management audits to be an attractive area for expansion.[12]

---

[9]Billy E. Goetz, *Management Planning and Control* (New York: McGraw-Hill Book Company, 1949), p. 167.

[10]Jackson Martindell, *The Scientific Appraisal of Management* (New York: Harper & Brothers, 1950) and *The Appraisal of Management* (New York: Harper & Brothers, 1962).

[11]W. T. Greenwood, *A Management Audit System*, revised edition (Carbondale, Ill.: School of Business, Southern Illinois University, 1967).

[12]See: "Should CPAs Be Management Consultants?" *Business Week*, April 18, 1977, pp. 70, 73.

After all, it is but a small step from their current activities to management auditing. Perhaps the future will see the development of a certified management audit analogous to the current independent certified accounting audit.

SUMMARY

In this chapter the controlling process has been examined. The three basic steps in this process are the establishment of standards, the comparison of performance with these standards, and correction of deviations. The key to the entire process rests on effective feedback.

In attaining this feedback, various control techniques are available to the manager. Some of the more traditional include budgeting, break-even point analysis, and personal observation. Some of the more specialized entail information design and time-event analyses such as PERT and milestone scheduling. These are not, however, designed to control overall performance. To do this, the manager must turn to other techniques such as profit and loss, return on investment, key area control, and auditing.

REVIEW AND STUDY QUESTIONS

1. What are the three basic steps in the controlling process? Describe each in your own words.

2. Why is feedback so important for effective control?

3. What are the requirements for an effective control system? List and explain some of them in your own words.

4. Of what value is budgeting in the controlling process? Does it lead to inflexibility? Explain.

5. How can the break-even point assist the manager in controlling operations? Explain, incorporating the following terms into your discussion: unit price, total fixed cost, and variable cost per unit.

6. What is meant by the term information design? How is it of value to the manager?

7. Why is PERT a useful control technique? Explain in your own words, incorporating into your discussion the following terms: events, activities, expected time, and the critical path.

8. Why is return on investment so widely used as an overall control technique? Is it better than a profit and loss approach? Explain.

9. What is meant by key area control? What are some of the areas used by General Electric in controlling its operations? Explain in your own words.

10. How useful are external audits in the control process? Internal audits? Management audits? Which is best, and why?

SELECTED REFERENCES

Barrett, M. E., and L. B. Fraser, III. "Conflicting Roles In Budgeting For Operations." *Harvard Business Review,* July–August 1977, pp. 137–146.

Buchele, R. B. "How to Evaluate a Firm." *California Management Review,* Fall 1962, pp. 5–17.

"Consultants Move to the Executive Suite." *Business Week,* November 7, 1977, pp. 76, 79.

Drucker, P. F. *Management: Tasks, Responsibilities, Practices.* New York: Harper & Row, Publishers, 1974, Chapter 39.

Farney, D. "Zero–Base Budgeting, A Pet Carter Project, Is Off to a Slow Start." *Wall Street Journal,* December 19, 1977, p. 16.

Gibbons, C. C. "The Psychology of Budgeting." *Business Horizons,* June 1972, pp. 47–58.

Giglioni, G. B., and A. G. Bedeian. "A Conspectus of Management Control Theory: 1900–1972." *Academy of Management Journal,* June 1974, pp. 292–305.

Koontz, H., and R. W. Bradspies. "Managing Through Feedforward Control." *Business Horizons,* June 1972, pp. 25–36.

Martindell, J. *The Appraisal of Management.* New York: Harper & Row, Publishers, 1962.

Schonberger, R. J. "Custom–Tailored PERT/CPM Systems." *Business Horizons,* December 1972, pp. 64–66.

Searby, F. W. "Return To Return On Investment." *Harvard Business Review,* March–April 1975, pp. 113–119.

"Should CPAs Be Management Consultants?" *Business Week,* April 18, 1977, pp. 70, 73.

Suver, J. D., and R. L. Brown. "Where Does Zero–Base Budgeting Work?" *Harvard Business Review,* November–December 1977, pp. 76–84.

Tannenbaum, A. S. *Control in Organizations.* New York: McGraw-Hill Book Company, 1968.

CASE: SAFETY MARGINS

Paula Wayland had been with the company for only a couple of months, but already she could tell that the job was to her liking. One of the things she enjoyed most was the increased responsibility. For example, she had been told to make up a departmental budget for the next fiscal year. After pouring over past budgetary requests and talking to her subordinates, she submitted her proposal. The next step in the process was to meet with her superior and defend the requests, and the proposal would then be sent up the line. Paula had been told by her subordinates that top management seldom cut back any requests. The key hurdle was getting one's superior to approve the recommended budget.

As a result, Paula spent most of the morning preparing herself for this meeting. She felt that everything in her request was essential, but she wanted to be able to defend each item. The meeting, however, did not quite go according to expectations:

Paula, I've examined your budget request and would like to talk to you about a few items. For example, under administrative expenses you estimate $47,612.

Yes sir. I can show you the worksheet I used, if you'd like.

Oh, that's not necessary. The only reason why the figure caught my eye was that it was such an odd amount. Look, let's round it off to $50,000.

Okay.

And there are a few other budget estimates I see here that are also in need of rounding, so I'll just change them also.

How much of an estimate does that make it?

It's exactly $210,000.

Well, that's a little bit higher than what I need. Are you sure its okay?

Sure, don't worry about it. You can never tell when something is going to cost a little bit more than you initially thought.

It's all right with me if it's all right with you.

Fine. And, oh, by the way, how did you arrive at these other estimates?

Well, I worked back from what I thought my department would be doing this fiscal year to how much it would cost to get this work done. There's a manual that was sent around to me, and I took my basic format from it.

That certainly is one way to get a handle on it, Paula. But let me suggest that you be sure to add some safety margins to each of your requests.

Safety margins?

Sure, you know. A little something extra just in case things go wrong. Besides, you never know when management is going to cut around here, and it always pays to have asked for a little more than you need when that happens. Do you know what I mean?

I think so.

Fine, well here's your budget back. Add in 10 per cent across the board and send it back in to me. I'll forward it from here.

Questions

1. Is Paula's superior right or wrong in suggesting that she change her budget requests? Explain.

2. How common do you think this kind of action is?

3. What are the dangers in overestimating budget requests? Be specific.

4. Why do you think this conversation occurred? Explain.

CASE: EFFICIENCY VS. PROFITABILITY

Fred Forsythe was a product division manager at Darby Inc., a midwestern manufacturing firm. In the late 1950's, the Darby management decided to abandon its profitability control guideline and begin evaluating product divisions on the basis of return on investment. It was felt that in this way overall efficiency could be measured.

The idea was fine with Fred, and for the next decade his division's ROI rose from 12.3 per cent to 15.7 per cent. However, during the late 60's the division began to encounter vigorous competition, and although the market for their product increased, Fred found himself spending more and more money on advertising and personal selling to maintain market share. The result was an eventual decline in ROI to 13.7 per cent by 1978. This in turn prompted comments from the top management, and Fred found himself being called into his boss's office.

Fred, the board of directors has been reviewing product division ROI's, and your's is the only one that has declined. Quite frankly, they're concerned.

Well, I am too, but if they think you can improve ROI in such a competitive industry, they're crazy. That's why we've been spending all that money on advertising and personal selling. I'd like to know one company that's making a greater ROI than we are. Or one competitive division that can match mine. There are none.

I'm sure that's true. But the question is, what are you going to do to improve your division's ROI?

I'd like to pose a different question. Why is the board evaluating my division on ROI? Don't they know when you get as large as we are, in as competitive an industry as this, that ROI slips? Why don't they evaluate me on profitability? My profits are up over last year, but I can't hold my ROI performance at an all-time high.

Do you want to write them a letter outlining your proposal?

No, but I do think it's time people stopped overrating ROI as a control technique.

Questions

1. What are the advantages of using ROI as an overall control technique? What are the disadvantages?

2. Should the board switch back from ROI to profits? Give your reasoning.

3. What action would you recommend for Fred? Explain.

CASE: DOING IT YOURSELF[13]

Management consultants can be very helpful in assisting an organization to control its operations. On the negative side, however, they can also be very expensive. As a result, many firms have turned to in-house consultants. Industry sources today estimate that 500 to 600 companies have some in-house consulting capability, up from about 100 five years ago. In addition to their cost-effectiveness, these internal consultants usually cost only about one third of what an outside consultant would run:

At California Federal Savings & Loan Association, the nation's fourth-largest S&L, a staff of seven internal consultants has two clear mandates: to cut operating costs and to make a profit on the service it offers—at least an 18 per cent investment. The group's projects have ranged from analyzing customer service and determining manpower needs to evaluating computer systems. In four years, the S&L has cut its 100 per cent dependence on outside consultants to 10 per cent.

At Southern New England Telephone Company, the consulting staff of nine works with staff and line managers to develop goals for their units, solve salary administration problems, rate subordinates for promotion, improve cooperation among workers, and a host of other projects. One three-year project, in which the organization, work flow, and distribution of work in the data processing group were examined, resulted in a saving of millions of dollars.

While most firms still use outside consultants for top management reorganizations or changes in corporate strategy, the insiders have some very important benefits to offer. Besides the cost saving, they are still around if their recommendations do not pan out. As one of them put it, "We're not a love-'em-and-leave-'em operation." Still another advantage is that these insiders often have a greater amount of familiarity with company operations and therefore know where to go for information and how to formulate their recommendations. Finally, advocates of this "do-it-yourself approach" point to the fact that insiders are often more credible than outsiders and so it is easier for them to get their recommendations accepted.

---

[13]The data in this case can be found in: "The Benefits of Doing Your Own Consulting," *Business Week*, May 16, 1977, pp. 62–64.

Questions

1. What are the advantages to be gained from a management audit? Explain.

2. In comparing and contrasting the value of inside and outside consultants, when would the former be of greatest value? When would the latter be preferable?

3. Do you think we will see greater use of inside consultants in the future? Why or why not?

CASE: THE DEAN'S DILEMMA

Things had certainly changed at State University. When Dean Williams had first come to the College of Business, it seemed that life was much simpler. However, as inflation spiraled upward, the taxpayers of the state gave every indication that they were through pouring money into the university. As a result, the administration announced that there would have to be a tightening up everywhere. Departmental lines would be cut and hiring determined on a need basis. And if this were not enough, legislators began raising the question of faculty evaluations. How do we know we are getting our money's worth, they asked, if there is no evaluation process?

In response to the question, the university administration announced that it was going to look into the matter. Thereupon, each dean was asked to poll his college and decide what form of evaluation process they felt was fair for judging performance. In the College of Business, two camps sprang up. The first wanted to evaluate teaching as the first prerequisite, with community affairs and research as secondary. The other group wanted to place research as primary and teaching and community affairs as secondary. The positions could be summarized as follows:

Teaching Is Primary

Position for: The university has been established by the people of this state to perform a specific service; namely, the dissemination of knowledge to the students. And this is the primary basis on which teachers should be evaluated. This process should take two paths: evaluations by the students in the classroom and evaluation by the departmental chairperson based on classroom observation.

Position against: Teaching is certainly important, but there is no way to judge truly effective performance. The students are going to be biased in their opinion, those receiving the highest grades being more positive in their comments about the instructors than those receiving the lowest grades. Thus the system encourages an easy grading policy. In addition, the chairperson is incapable of judging all the people because he or she is not an expert in every area. For example, how can a management chairperson, with an emphasis in organizational behavior, judge a colleague teaching mathematical decision making? Teaching is valuable, but because it cannot be quantified, it should be discarded as a basis for evaluation.

Research Is Primary

Position for: The only objective criterion available for judging teaching ability is research. A professor who conducts research is going to be better prepared than one who does not. In addition, the instructor has a responsibility to not only teach but to enhance the reputation of the university as well, and this can be done most effectively through research. In short, "publish or perish" is the only way to improve the quality of education, and it should be the basis for all evaluations.

Position against: To engage in a policy of "publish or perish" is to get into the numbers game. In addition, how is one to evaluate the contribution of each article? And in the case of books, is not remuneration in the form of royalties sufficient? Why should people be promoted or receive high evaluation when all they are doing is enhancing their own financial positions? Research is important, but it must not be allowed to occupy a primary position.

Questions

1. How should faculty performance be evaluated? Explain.

2. In light of your answer to the above question, what kinds of measuring tools should a dean employ to ensure that his faculty is doing a good job? Explain in detail.

COMPREHENSIVE CASE: A BUMPY ROAD TO SUCCESS[14]

Look up from a major football game and see a blimp in the sky and you immediately know it is a Goodyear blimp. See an advertisement for Goodrich tires and you know that "they're the other guys." Mention IRI, Inc., however, and no one will know what you are talking about — especially those not associated with the tire industry.

IRI, Inc. is the smallest tire manufacturer in the United States. Started in 1970, it is really a miracle that the company is still in operation. For example, in a business where the big competitors spend hundreds of millions of dollars on advertising each year to emblazon their logotypes on auto racing cars, garages, and golf tournaments, as well as on television, newspaper, and magazine advertising, IRI does not advertise. The firm simply cannot afford to. In addition to the huge expenditures commonly made for advertising, one must also consider the fact that the tire industry requires high capital investment, is dominated by militant labor unions, and attains a low return on investment.

From the very beginning, IRI's strategy has been to carve out a special little niche for itself alongside the big firms. Currently the company turns out only 600 radial auto tires daily. This constitutes only about one out of every 1250 tires being produced in the United States. Nevertheless, the president is happy because he sees this as a good start toward the firm's goal of 1 per cent of annual replacement-tire sales. Of course, at 1 per cent the company would still be very, very small when contrasted with, for example, Goodyear or Goodrich. Nevertheless, 1 per cent of the 1976 U.S. replacement-tire market would have meant $50 million in sales to IRI.

The company currently produces a steel-belted, whitewalled radial that has steel reinforcing wires not only in the tread but also in

---

[14]The data in this case can be found in: Bernard Wysocki, Jr., "Smallest Tire Company Overcomes its Errors, Survives Amid Giants,"*Wall Street Journal,* August 10, 1977, pp. 1, 31.

the sidewalls, in contrast to other American-made radial tires that have nylon, rayon, or polyester threads instead. The IRI radial carries a 50,000 mile warranty against tread wear and road hazards and sells for approximately $80. This is about $5 to $10 higher than most other radials, which typically carry a warranty for 40,000 miles or less.

The company president calls IRI's product the "Jack Daniel's of Tires" and continually boasts that the company's tire is the best passenger tire on the market worldwide. There are many people who agree with him, including one customer who recently noted that the people to whom his firm sold the tire were very pleased with its performance. Additionally, some cab companies report that their cabs have over 65,000 miles on their IRI tires and still have tread.

Stewart Smythe and George Edwards started IRI in 1964 as a maker of tire-retreading equipment. The company prospered briefly but then the federal government proposed tough standards for re-treaded tires and the two men decided it was time to diversify. In particular, they noticed that France's Michelin was making inroads in the American tire market with a steel-belted radial. They also saw that the giant tire manufacturers in Akron were slow to catch the trend toward both radials and steel. Throughout the 1960's, these tire companies were turning out largely bias-ply tires with glass-fabric belts.

In order to compete in this market Mr. Smythe, the president, managed to wheedle $700,000 in loans from the Small Business Administration and an insurance company, and persuaded investment bankers in Louisville and Baltimore to sell 12 per cent of the company to investors for $600,000. With this money IRI built a plant, hauled in machinery from seven countries, and in August, 1971, began rolling off 3,000 tires monthly.

The tires were not well made and all sorts of problems arose. Nevertheless, the company didn't fold, and things began to turn around:

IRI got a lucky break when a routine sales call by Bayer AG, the big German chemical concern, led to a useful technical agreement by which IRI got advanced rubber compounding know-how and the idea of putting steel in the sidewalls. More good news came when a Belgian concern developed a flexible 21-strand steel wire designed to smooth out the ride. And from Mr. Edwards and others came the novel idea of building tires on an assembly line rather than with the single work station setup common in the industry.

By mid-1974 the corporation was ready to take a second crack at the radial-tire market. Michelin tires were now well accepted in the market, and IRI set out to persuade Michelin dealers to carry IRI tires as well. Soon the firm had dozens of dealers, primarily in the South and West, but then a problem developed. The whitewalls of the IRI tire, which was full of chemicals to keep it from cracking, turned yellow and brown as the chemicals oozed out of the tire. While the oozing was intentional, Bayer never realized the effect it would have on whitewalls. In Europe, everyone ordered blackwall tires. The result was catastrophic for IRI. Sales dropped dramatically, the company began laying off personnel, and it stopped repaying its Small Business Administration loan.

Finally, things began to turn around once again. The oozing problem was solved and a whole new sales program was established:

The company began offering salesmen vacation trips as prizes for high sales. IRI executives put together a ten-minute sales film featuring Maxie, a

knight in armor, who explained the difference between IRI and other radials. The film was designed to sway the salesman, and was later used to help the salesman sway the consumer.

IRI didn't forget financial incentives. It encouraged the dealer to retail the tire for $12.50 above his Michelin retail price. Of the extra $12.50 profit, $10 goes to the dealer and $2.50 to the salesman.

The strategy began to pay off. Venture capitalists again began lending money to the firm. Today IRI has expanded its network to 80 dealers with 300 outlets. Production is straining the plant's 600-tire-a-day capacity and the firm is laying plans to expand to 1000 tires daily.

The company's president says that the firm would like to have three plants operating and a fourth under construction by 1980, as well as sales of $35 to $40 million annually. Of course, IRI is not out of the woods yet. Some industry analysts point to the fact that Michelin is now producing tires in the U.S. and some major manufacturers are beginning to push an aramid-fiber-belted tire as their premium quality product, boasting that the Du Pont-developed fiber is, pound for pound, stronger than steel. If this proves true it raises the possibility that IRI's tire will no longer be considered premium quality. Nevertheless, the *Wall Street Journal* reports:

Despite the problems, investors are taking a brighter view of the company these days, as the recent $4 million financing shows. And IRI is staffing itself with big things in mind. It has about a dozen executives, ranging from regional sales vice president up to chief executive. Their annual salaries total $450,000, which puts a drain on profits. But Mr. Smythe defends the practice. "This company is staffed to take us to the $50 million level;" he says, "if you staff a company to be a $3 million company, it stays a $3 million company."

Questions

1. How important is strategic planning to a firm like IRI, Inc.? Explain.

2. By which type of departmentalization (functional, product, geographical, etc.) would a firm like IRI, Inc. tend to be organized? Explain.

3. Which of the controlling tools discussed in Chapter 7 would be of most help to IRI, Inc.? Explain.

SECTION C
THE QUANTITATIVE SCHOOL

The goal of this section is to familiarize the reader with some of the basic ideas and concepts of the quantitative, or management science, school. As with the other two schools, there is no universal agreement regarding its domain. One can argue with all but the most quantitative subjects in this section simply by raising the question, does the material fit into one of the other schools? A good example is the topic of decision making. The process and behavioral schools would both claim that this area is within their domain. With this contention there is no argument, for decision making knows no bounds; it is an integral part of every manager's job. However, it will be discussed within this section because it offers an excellent opportunity to examine the entire area of modern quantitative decision making and is therefore of major importance to an understanding of the management sciences.

In Chapter 8 the decision-making process will be examined, and it will be noted that this process is certainly not a mechanical function. There are personal values involved in choosing from among alternatives, and to picture management scientists simply as cold, calculating mathematicians is erroneous. In Chapter 9 this concept of choosing from among alternatives will be extended through an examination of some of the important tools and techniques of operations research that are currently being employed by the modern manager.

Finally, in Chapter 10, information systems and decision making will be studied. Once information is analyzed, it must be transmitted to the appropriate manager for action. This requires a well designed information system, often complemented by the computer. We will examine how information systems and the computer are part of the quantitative school. We will also study the link between the quantitative school and the process school as well as the link between the quantitative school and the behavioral school. In fact, the last part of Chapter 10 will be dedicated to an analysis of some behavioral effects of information systems, thereby setting the stage for an analysis of this third school of management.

CHAPTER EIGHT

FUNDAMENTALS OF DECISION MAKING

The goal of this chapter is to examine the fundamentals of decision making. A review of the steps in the process will be first followed by an analysis of the impact of personal values on the decision-making process. Next, the types of decisions and the conditions under which they are made, i.e., certainty, risk, and uncertainty, will be scrutinized. Finally, two of the more common decision-making techniques, marginal and financial analysis, will be reviewed in detail.

GOALS OF THE CHAPTER

When you are finished reading this chapter you should be able to:

1. Define the steps in the decision-making process.
2. Discuss what is meant by the term *rationality* and relate its importance in understanding the decision-making process.
3. Explain how values affect decision making.
4. Outline a classification system for examining all decisions, including organizational and personal decisions, basic and routine decisions, and programmed and nonprogrammed decisions.
5. Relate the three basic conditions under which decisions are made.
6. Discuss the role of objective and subjective probability in decision making.
7. Describe the benefit of marginal analysis.
8. Explain the importance of financial analysis in decision making.

Decision making is commonly defined as *choosing from among alternatives.* Simon has identified the process as searching the environment for conditions calling for a decision; inventing, developing, and analyzing the available courses of action; and choosing one of the particular courses of action.[1] However, this three-step process, consisting of intelligence, design, and choice activities, is only one of many decision-making methods.

DECISION-MAKING PROCESS

Decision making involves choosing from among alternatives.

A second and more detailed method is the following:

1. **Identify the problem.**
2. **Diagnose the situation.**
3. **Collect and analyze data relevant to the issue.**
4. **Ascertain solutions that may be used in solving the problem.**
5. **Analyze these alternative solutions.**
6. **Select the approach that appears most likely to solve the problem.**
7. **Implement it.**

Regardless of the specific process employed by the manager, some formal diagnosis must be conducted, alternative solutions formulated and analyzed, and a decision made regarding the approach to take. This is as true in the development of strategic, intermediate, and operational plans as it is in solving simple job problems.

---

[1]Herbert A. Simon, *The New Science of Management Decision* (New York: Harper & Row, Publishers, Inc., 1960), p. 2.

One of the primary characteristics of this entire process is its dynamism, the steps being implemented within a time framework. The past is the time dimension in which the problem is identified and diagnosed. The present is the point at which the alternatives are formulated and a choice made regarding the plan of action. The future is the time period during which the decision will be implemented and an evaluation made regarding the outcome.

RATIONALITY AND THE MEANS-END HIERARCHY

There are degrees of rationality in decision making.

It is difficult to separate means from ends.

In Chapter 3, where Mayo's rabble hypothesis was examined, it was noted that not all decisions made by the workers are rational. Some are non-rational, others are irrational. The same is true at the managerial level. In addition, there are *degrees* of rationality. A man lost in the desert may wander in circles. Although this may be the wrong solution to the problem, is it not rational? After all, virtually everyone caught in this dilemma does it. This raises the question, precisely what is meant by the term *rational*? Some people assign the term to actions that attain a given end. In this case, the man in the desert is not acting rationally because his actions are not leading him out of his dilemma. Other individuals feel that rational refers to choosing the best alternative of those available. In this case, the man may be acting rationally because of the alternatives facing him. He may conclude that no one knows he is lost, so he cannot rely on a search party's finding him. His only salvation rests in saving himself by, for example, finding the nearest oasis. The only way to do this is to start walking and hope to locate one before too long.

Some decision theorists believe that rational decisions will be forthcoming if appropriate means for reaching desired goals are chosen. However, it is often difficult to separate means from ends, for every end is really just a means to another end. This is what is known as the *means-end hierarchy*. When the man in the desert finds the oasis he will remain there, using it as his base of operations (means) until he can establish contact with the outside world and have help sent to him (end). The plane that takes him out (means) will allow him to return to his old way of life (end).

In summary, rationality, as viewed within the decision-making framework, is a relative term — dependent upon the situation and the individuals involved. An objectively rational *organizational* decision designed to ensure the company a profitable year may be welcomed by the employees until they learn that it calls for the elimination of all Christmas bonuses; then it is seen as a non-rational or irrational decision. Likewise, *personally* rational decisions such as the establishment of 30-minute coffee breaks to eliminate excessive fatigue may be favorably viewed by the workers but seen by the management as disastrous to overall company efficiency. One reason, then, for this imprecision in decision making is the personal values of the people involved.

PERSONAL VALUES AND DECISION MAKING

Every manager has a certain set of values he or she brings to the work place. In Chapter 5, the General Electric changing-value profile for 1969 to 1980 was presented. These values can be further broken down and applied to managers on an individual basis. Spranger has identified six such values: theoretical, economic, aesthetic, social, political, and religious. The description of each is presented in Figure 8–1. When Guth and Tagiuri employed this classification scheme with high-

1. The *theoretical* man is primarily interested in the discovery of truth, in the systematic ordering of his knowledge. In pursuing this goal he typically takes a "cognitive" approach, looking for identities and differences, with relative disregard for the beauty or utility of objects, seeking only to observe and to reason. His interests are empirical, critical, and rational. He is an intellectual. Scientists or philosophers are often of this type (but they are not the only ones).

2. The *economic* man is primarily oriented toward what is useful. He is interested in the practical affairs of the business world; in the production, marketing, and consumption of goods; in the use of economic resources; and in the accumulation of tangible wealth. He is thoroughly "practical" and fits well the stereotype of the American businessman.

3. The *aesthetic* man finds his chief interest in the artistic aspects of life, although he need not be a creative artist. He values form and harmony. He views experience in terms of grace, symmetry, or harmony. Each single event is savored for its own sake.

4. The essential value for the *social* man is love of people—the altruistic or philanthropic aspect of love. The social man values people as ends, and tends to be kind, sympathetic, unselfish. He finds those who have strong theoretical, economic, and aesthetic orientations rather cold. Unlike the political type, the social man regards love as the most important component of human relationships. In its purest form the social orientation is selfless and approaches the religious attitude.

5. The *political* man is characteristically oriented toward power, not necessarily in politics, but in whatever area he functions. Most leaders have a high power orientation. Competition plays a large role in all life, and many writers have regarded power as the most universal motive. For some men, this motive is uppermost, driving them to seek personal power, influence, and recognition.

6. The *religious* man is one "whose mental structure is permanently directed to the creation of the highest and absolutely satisfying value experience." The dominant value for him is unity. He seeks to relate himself to the universe in a meaningful way and has a mystical orientation.

FIGURE 8–1   Spranger's Value Orientations (From William D. Guth and Renato Taguiri, "Personal Values and Corporate Strategy," *Harvard Business Review*, September–October 1965, Copyright 1965 by the President and Fellows of Harvard College; all rights reserved.)

level United States executives attending the Advanced Management Program of the Harvard Business School Seminar, they obtained the following average profile:[2]

Value	Score
Economic	45
Theoretical	44
Political	44
Religious	39
Aesthetic	35
Social	33
	240

The scores represent the importance of the values as seen by the average manager in the study.

[2]William D. Guth and Renato Tagiuri, "Personal Values and Corporate Strategy," *Harvard Business Review*, September–October, 1965, p. 126. The questionnaire was designed to yield 240 points distributed over the six values.

The economic, theoretical, and political scores seem justifiably high, for the top manager must be interested in efficiency and profit (economic), possess conceptual skills required for endeavors such as long-range planning (theoretical), and be able to get along with people and convince them to work together as a team (political). However, the researchers also found that the profiles varied considerably in regard to religious, aesthetic, and social values, indicating that one must not be too hasty in trying to construct a stereotype of the "typical" executive.

A manager's personal values will influence his or her decision making.

The personal values of each manager can have a significant effect on the decision-making process. This is one reason why social action programs, for example, internally generated and heavily funded by the company itself, have been undertaken by many business firms in recent years.[3] Managers are much more oriented toward social responsibility than they were a decade ago. However, this must not be construed to mean that the firm is going to expend all its energies on such programs. In fact, when researchers in one study asked chief executive officers to rank their responsibilities to society, stockholders, employees, customers and creditors, they received the results shown in Figure 8–2.

Businessmen were interested in fulfilling their social responsibility but were not going to put such programs ahead of their obligations to the stockholders. Again, personal values play an important role in the decision-making process.

TYPES OF DECISIONS

Organizational and Personal Decisions

Managers make many decisions, and in order to obtain a clear understanding of the decision-making process, a classification system is useful. Three such systems are available, each based on different types of decisions. They are organizational and personal decisions, basic and routine decisions, and programmed and nonprogrammed decisions.

Organizational decisions are those executives make in their official role as managers. The adoption of strategies, the setting of objectives, and the approval of plans constitute only a few of these. Such decisions are often delegated to others, requiring the support of many people throughout the organization if they are to be properly implemented.

Organizational decisions can be delegated to others.

Personal decisions are related to the manager as an individual, not as a member of the organization. Such decisions are not delegated to others because their implementation does not require the support of

Personal decisions are not delegated.

[3]See, for example: Fred Luthans and Richard M. Hodgetts, *Social Issues in Business: A Text With Current Readings and Cases,* 2nd edition (New York: Macmillan Publishing Co., Inc., 1976), Chapters 5, 7, and 9.

**Response by Top Company Executives to the Question:
To Whom Do You Owe Your Greatest Responsibility?**

Interest Group	Relative Ranking
Stockholders	1
Employees	2
Customers	3
Society	4
Creditors	5

FIGURE 8–2 (From Charles P. Edmonds, III and John H. Hand, "What Are The Real Long-Run Objectives of Business?" *Business Horizons,* December 1976, p. 77.)

organizational personnel. Deciding to retire, taking a job offer from a competitive firm, or slipping out and spending the afternoon on the golf course are all personal decisions.

Although it is possible to distinguish between organizational and personal decisions according to definition, in practice it is not. For example, when a company president who believes in equal opportunity decides to make a concerted effort to hire the hard-core unemployed, a personal decision is translated into an organizational one. Many decisions made by managers have both organizational and personal elements in them.

A second approach is to classify decisions into basic and routine categories. *Basic decisions* can be viewed as much more important than routine ones. They involve long-range commitments, large expenditures of funds, and such a degree of importance that a serious mistake might well jeopardize the well-being of the company. Selection of a product line, the choice of a new plant site, or a decision to integrate vertically by purchasing sources of raw materials to complement the current production facilities are all basic decisions.

Basic and Routine Decisions

Basic decisions can have major effects on the organization.

Routine decisions are often repetitive in nature, having only a minor impact on the firm. For this reason, most organizations have formulated a host of procedures to guide the manager in handling these matters. Since some individuals in the organization spend most of their time making routine decisions, these guidelines are very useful to them.

Routine decisions have only a minor impact on the firm.

At this point it may be helpful to define what is meant by procedures and policies. *Procedures* are guides to action. Often referred to as types of plans, they relate the chronological steps entailed in attaining some objective. Sometimes procedures are drawn up for use in a particular department. In a retail store, for example, there may be five steps involved in allowing a person to return faulty merchandise, from ascertaining that the goods were not damaged by the buyer to getting an "O.K." from the department manager. Other times procedures are organizational in nature, such as when there is a discrepancy in a paycheck: the employee must tell the payroll department to have the pay recalculated and, if there was an error, return the incorrect check for a revised one. Procedures are very useful in helping individuals with routine decisions because they break down the process into steps.

Procedures are guides to action and usually consist of a list of chronological steps entailed in attaining some objective.

Policies, often confused with procedures, are also types of plans, but they are guides to *thinking* as well as to action. As a result, they do not tell a manager how to do something; they merely channel the decision making along a particular line by delimiting the span of consideration. For example, a department may have a policy of hiring only those with a college education. However, how does one define a college education? If the manager is willing to accept one year of job experience and three years of formal college as the equivalent of a four-year diploma, it is evident that there is more than mere action involved; thinking is needed to determine the equivalency line. The manager knows he or she will accept no one without a college degree or its equivalent (action) and can confine all energies to evaluating the latter cases (thinking). In this case, a policy is helpful to the manager because it limits the number of people eligible for a job in his or her department. At the organizational level, policies are also useful. For example, a firm may have a policy of setting up new plants in cities with a population of at least 100,000. This is a guide to action because it limits the number of

Policies are guides to both thinking and action.

eligible cities. It is a guide to thinking because now the executive must decide in which particular city to build the new plant. Policies play an important role in handling basic decisions.

Programmed and Nonprogrammed Decisions

Programmed decisions are routine; unprogrammed decisions are novel and unstructured.

Simon, borrowing from computer technology, has proposed the classification of decisions into the areas of *programmed* and *nonprogrammed*. These two types can be viewed on a continuum, programmed being at one end and nonprogrammed at the other. Programmed decisions correspond roughly to the routine decisions, with procedures playing a key role. Nonprogrammed decisions are similar to the category of basic decisions, being highly novel, important, and unstructured in nature. Policies play an important role in making these decisions. The value of viewing decision making in this manner is that it permits a clearer understanding of the methods that accompany each type. Figure 8–3 presents Simon's traditional and modern decision-making scheme.

DECISION-MAKING CONDITIONS

There are three possible conditions under which decisions can be made: certainty, risk, and uncertainty.

Certainty

Certainty is present when the manager knows the outcome of each alternative.

Certainty is present when the manager knows exactly what will happen. Although conditions of certainty exist in but a small percentage of decisions made by the manager, they are present. For example, $1000 invested in a government note for one year at 6 per cent will return $60 in interest. Although it can be argued that there is a degree of risk in everything including government notes, for all practical purposes this investment can be labeled as "a sure thing."

Likewise, the allocation of resources to various product lines often constitutes decision making under conditions of certainty. The manager knows what physical resources are on hand and the amount of time it will take to process them into finished goods. If there are two or three processes available, the manager can conduct a cost-contribution study to determine which is most profitable (if profit is the decision guideline) or which will produce the good most quickly (if speed is of the essence). In dealing with fixed quantities such as raw materials and machines, the manager is often making decisions under certainty, the prime goal being that of determining the desired objective. Once this is accomplished, the manager can simply evaluate the alternatives and choose the best one.

Risk

Risk is present if the manager has only partial information for evaluating the outcome of each alternative.

Most of the manager's decisions are made under *risk conditions;* that is, some information is available but it is insufficient to answer all questions about the outcome. One method often used to assist the decision maker is that of probability estimates.

PROBABILITY ESTIMATES.   Although the manager may not know with a high degree of certainty the outcome of each decision, he or she may be able to estimate some level of probability for each of the possible alter-

DECISION-MAKING TECHNIQUES

TYPES OF DECISIONS	Traditional	Modern

Programmed:
 	
Routine, repetitive decisions
Organization develops specific processes for handling them
	1. Habit
	2. Clerical routine:
	   Standard operating procedures
	3. Organization structure:
	   Common expectations
	   A system of subgoals
	   Well-defined informational channels
		1. Operations Research:
		   Mathematical analysis
		   Models
		   Computer simulation
		2. Electronic data processing

Nonprogrammed: One-shot, ill-structured, novel, policy decisions Handled by general problem-solving processes	1. Judgment, intuition, and creativity 2. Rules of thumb 3. Selection and training of executives	Heuristic problem-solving techniques applied to: (a) training human decision makers (b) constructing heuristic computer programs

FIGURE 8–3 Traditional and Modern Techniques of Decision Making (From Herbert A. Simon, *The Shape of Automation,* Harper and Row, Publishers, Inc., New York, 1965, p. 62.)

"Is that all you have to say in your client's
defense? 'He's a nice guy and we'll all
miss him if he goes to prison'?"

Reprinted by permission of the Wall Street Journal.

natives. Such estimates are often based on *experience*. The manager
draws on past occurrences in determining the likelihood of particular
events. Naturally, no situation is ever identical to a previous one, but it
may be sufficiently similar to justify using experience as a guide. Probability assignments permit a determination of the expected values of all
events. For example, consider the case of the firm with four available
strategies: A, B, C, and D. Each has a *conditional value*, which is the
profit that will be returned to the firm if it is implemented and proves
successful; a *probability*, which is a likelihood of success; and an *expected value*, which is the result of the conditional value multiplied by the
probability. These data can be arranged as in Figure 8–4.

AVAILABLE STRATEGIES	CONDITIONAL VALUE	SUCCESS PROBABILITY	EXPECTED VALUE
A	$1,000,000	0.05	$50,000
B	800,000	0.10	80,000
C	750,000	0.20	150,000
D	400,000	0.65	260,000

FIGURE 8–4   Expected Values for Strategies A–D

The figure illustrates that the manager should opt for strategy D because it promises the greatest expected value. Although it has the lowest conditional value of all four, the probability of success is far higher.

If a probability can be determined on the basis of past experience, it is known as an *objective probability*. What is the probability of obtaining a head in the toss of a fair coin? It is 0.5. Over the long run, there will be just as many heads as tails. Likewise, many companies are able, on the basis of past experience, to assign objective probabilities to events such as predicting success on a particular psychological test. If a person ranks in the top 20 per cent, his or her success as a manager may be 0.8, indicating that eight out of every ten in this category have done well as managers.

Sometimes, however, it is not possible to determine a suitable objective probability estimate. The manager may not feel he or she has sufficient information to determine whether the success probability is 0.5 or 0.8. In this case, the individual must make a subjective estimate, employing what is commonly called "gut feel."

Although not as precise as an objective probability, *subjective probability* is nevertheless better than completely ignoring the probabilities of occurrence associated with the various alternatives. It also provides a basis for sharpening one's judgment in the case of future subjective probability assignments.

RISK PREFERENCE. The assignment of probabilities is never as simple as it might appear. The decision maker who finalizes the assignment is the ultimate arbiter, and different managers will assign varying estimates to identical alternatives for various reasons:

> . . . it can hardly be denied that the same top managers who make a decision involving risks of millions of dollars . . . in a given program with a chance of success of, say, 75 percent, would not be likely to do that with their own personal fortune, at least unless it were very large. Moreover, the same manager willing to opt for a 75 percent risk in one case might not do so in another. Furthermore, a top executive may go for a large advertising program where the chances of success are 70 percent, but might not decide in favor of an investment in plant and equipment unless the probabilities for success were higher. In other words, attitudes toward risk vary with events, as well as with people and position.
> While we do not know much about attitudes toward risk, we do know that some people are risk averters in some situations and gamblers in others, and that some people have by nature a high aversion to risk and others a low one.[4]

The risk preference of the manager will play a key role in determining his or her probability assignments. Figure 8–5 presents the preference curves of high-, average-, and low-risk takers. The S-curve illustrates the risk preferences of people in their personal lives. When the stakes are low, most individuals tend to be more willing to gamble than when they are high. For example, the author has asked businessmen if they would be willing to accept an outright gift of $5 or would prefer to take a chance on winning $15 or nothing against the correct call of the

---

[4]Harold Koontz and Cyril O'Donnell, *Management: A Systems and Contingency Analysis of Managerial Functions*, 6th edition (New York: McGraw-Hill Book Company, 1976), pp. 223–224.

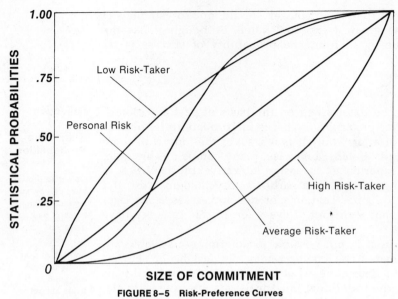

SIZE OF COMMITMENT

FIGURE 8–5   Risk-Preference Curves

flip of a fair coin. Most businessmen opt for the latter alternative, being willing to gamble for $15 or nothing. Conversely, when the stakes are raised to $50,000 and $150,000 respectively, most managers choose the certain $50,000 sum. Objectively speaking, they are unwise, for the expected value of the $150,000 is $75,000 ($150,000 × 0.5) since the odds are fifty-fifty that they will call the flip of the coin correctly. However, the managers prefer the guaranteed $50,000.

Uncertainty

Probability esti-
mates should be
developed even
if the manager is
making a deci-
sion under
uncertainty.

Uncertainty decisions are those for which managers feel they cannot develop probability estimates because they have no way of gauging the likelihood of the various alternatives. It is very difficult to say precisely when this occurs. Many individuals contend that experience and the ability to generalize from similar situations make uncertainty impossible; the manager can always assign some probability estimates to a decision matter. Yet there are times when executives may feel they are indeed dealing with uncertainty. Nevertheless, research shows that they are wise to construct conditional values for each alternative under each state of nature. For example, an airplane manufacturer is considering the production of a giant helicopter for the military and there are three basic design versions under serious consideration: A, B, and C. The first is the most sophisticated and expensive of the three, while the last is the least sophisticated and least expensive. The two basic states of nature are seen as being either a generation of peace or continual fighting of brush fire wars. Furthermore, the manufacturer has assigned conditional values to the respective strategies and states of nature as shown in Figure 8–6. Furthermore, if peace prevails, the military will buy the least expensive helicopter, but if brush fire wars continue, they will purchase the most expensive.

What decision should the manager make? If there is no reason for believing that one event is more likely to occur than any other, the

	STATES OF NATURE	
STRATEGIES	*Generation of Peace*	*Continual Brush Fire Wars*
Helicopter A	–$250,000	$5,000,000
Helicopter B	1,000,000	1,000,000
Helicopter C	4,500,000	500,000

FIGURE 8–6 Conditional Values Associated With Manufacturing Giant Helicopter

manager can employ what is called the *Laplace criterion,* which applies *equal probabilities* to all states of nature. If this approach is followed, the firm should manufacture Helicopter C, because it offers an expected value of $2,500,000 ($4,500,000 × 0.5 + $500,000 × 0.5), which is greater than that from either of the other strategies as seen in Figure 8–7. Helicopter A has an expected value of $2,375,000 (– $250,000 × 0.5 + $5,000,000 × 0.5). Helicopter B has an expected value of $1,000,000 ($1,000,000 × 0.5 + $1,000,000 × 0.5).

Equal probability can be applied to all events.

A second approach is the use of the pessimism criterion, or the *maximin* as it is often called, which holds that the manager should ascertain the worst conditions for each strategy, which as seen in Figure 8–6, are $250,000 $1,000,000 and $500,000 for A, B, and C respectively. Then the one that offers the *best* payoff under these conditions should be implemented. This would call for the manufacture of Helicopter B. By using this approach, the manager maximizes the minimum gain, hence the term maximin.

A pessimistic approach can be used.

A third approach is the use of the optimism criterion, commonly called *maximax.* Since the manager is unsure of the outcome, it is just as rational to be optimistic as pessimistic. He or she should therefore look on the bright side of things and assign a probability of, for example, 0.8 to the likelihood of the most favorable outcomes of each strategy and 0.2 to the least favorable outcomes of each. Then those best and worst conditional values associated with these three strategies can be multiplied by their respective probabilities to obtain weighted values as seen in Figure 8–8. Finally, these values can be added. In this instance, Helicopter A is the best choice. Using this approach, the manager maximizes the maximum gain.

An optimistic approach can be taken.

Dealing with decisions under uncertainty is no easy task. In the three approaches used here, a different strategy emerged as most favorable each time. The assumptions the manager makes regarding conditional values and probability estimates and the methods employed in evaluating the alternatives will all influence the outcome.

	STATES OF NATURE	
STRATEGIES	*Generation of Peace*	*Continual Brush Fire Wars*
Helicopter A	–$125,000	$2,500,000
Helicopter B	$500,000	$ 500,000
Helicopter C	$2,250,000	$ 250,000

FIGURE 8–7 Expected Values for Manufacturing Giant Helicopter Using Laplace Criterion (Equal Probability)

| | CONDITIONAL VALUES | | WEIGHTED VALUES | | SUM OF WEIGHTED VALUES |
| | *Best* | *Worst* | *Best* | *Worst* | |
STRATEGY	*Condition*	*Condition*	*Condition*	*Condition*	
Helicopter A	$5,000,000	−$250,000	$4,000,000	−$ 50,000	$3,950,000
Helicopter B	1,000,000	1,000,000	800,000	200,000	1,000,000
Helicopter C	4,500,000	500,000	3,600,000	100,000	3,700,000

FIGURE 8–8 Application of Optimism Criteria to Conditional Values for Helicopter Manufacture (0.8 Optimism and 0.2 Pessimism)

DECISION-MAKING TECHNIQUES

Thus far attention has been mainly focused on the environment in which the manager makes decisions, *i.e.*, certainty, risk, and uncertainty. However, it is also useful to examine some of the specific techniques that have proved valuable in the decision-making process, two of which are marginal analysis and financial analysis.

Marginal Analysis

For years, marginal analysis has been of interest to economists. Samuelson has explained the essence of the concept by the following description:

> The "marginal-product" of a productive factor is the extra product or output added by one extra unit of that factor, while other factors are being held constant. Labor's marginal-product is the extra output you get when you add one unit of labor, holding all other inputs constant. Similarly, land's marginal-product is the change in total product resulting from one additional unit of land with all other inputs held constant. . . .[5]

The manager can use the concept to answer questions such as how much more output will result if one more worker is hired? The answer, often called marginal physical product, provides a basis for determining whether or not one new man will bring about profitable additional output.

MARGINAL PHYSICAL PRODUCT.   Consider the case of the new shipping manager who has five men loading five trucks. After pondering the matter, the manager hires five new men so there are now two people loading each truck. The result, as seen in Figure 8–9, is that the total number of boxes loaded per day rises from 800 to 2000. The two men working as a team are able to do more than they could if working independently. With a third man on each team, the daily total rises to 2900.

By adding one worker, output may be increased.

Continuing on, as seen in the figure, the total mounts to 4000 and then drops off to 3700 when the number of workers per truck reaches seven. Why? Various causes can be cited. On the physical side, there may be just too many people involved and they are getting in each other's way. On the behavioral side, the seven men may be horseplaying more, or they may have agreed informally to hold down output. In either event, it is evident that seven workers per truck are too many.

If the manager's decision must rest solely on output, six is the ideal team size. However, it should be noted that there is a diminishing mar-

---

[5]Paul A. Samuelson, *Economics*, 10th edition (New York: McGraw-Hill Book Company, 1976), pp. 539–540.

NUMBER OF WORKERS PER TRUCK	TOTAL BOXES LOADED	MARGINAL PHYSICAL PRODUCT
0	0	800
1	800	1,200
2	2,000	900
3	2,900	600
4	3,500	400
5	3,900	100
6	4,000	(300)
7	3,700	

FIGURE 8–9 Units of Marginal Physical Product

ginal physical product after the second man is hired. The contributions from the third through the sixth increase the total but reduce the *average* from one thousand boxes when there are two workers to 967, 875, 780, and 667 respectively as the next four men are added. This rise in the total output with the accompanying decline in the marginal physical product is seen in Figures 8–10 and 8–11 respectively.

Profit Consideration

The decline in marginal output will limit the size of the work crew. More realistically, however, the manager will refine the decision further with a consideration of profit. How much money will the company make at each work crew size? Figure 8–12 shows total profits under the premise that there is a 10–cent profit for every box loaded if all costs except work crew salaries are considered. It is evident from the data that the company stands to make $240 a day if the work crew has five

However, profit is of more importance than mere physical output.

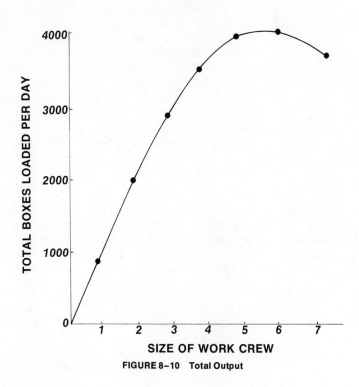

FIGURE 8–10 Total Output

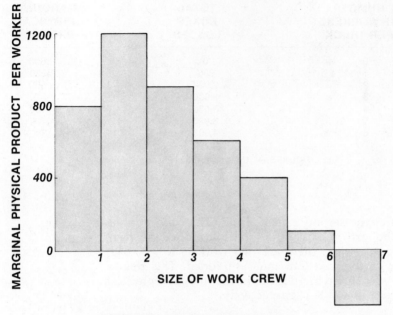

FIGURE 8-11 Bar graph of Physical Product

men. Any other size will result in a decline in this profit. In summary, the manager must consider profit as well as productivity in making his or her decision.

Earlier it was noted that most managers are satisficers (administrative people) and not maximizers (economic people). However, in some cases, especially production, the manager will often be far closer to the end of the spectrum represented by economic man than to that represented by administrative man. For example, consider the case of the aerospace firm that is pondering the acceptance of a subcontract to build communication satellite systems. The major contractor wants eight of them built and would like to know if the company is willing to undertake the contract. The purchase price of each system will be $18,000. In order to determine the profitability of the venture, the firm must first construct its cost and revenue data as seen in Figure 8-13. The information reveals that if the company manufactures all eight systems, it will lose $26,000. The ideal production is six, for at this point

Number of Workers	Salary Cost Per Day	Profit Per Box Before Loading Salaries	Boxes Loaded	Total Profit Before Loading Salaries	Total Profit
1	$ 30	$.10	800	$ 80	$ 50
2	60	.10	2000	200	140
3	90	.10	2900	290	200
4	120	.10	3500	350	230
5	150	.10	3900	390	240
6	180	.10	4000	400	220
7	210	.10	3700	370	160

FIGURE 8-12 Profit Per Truck

NUMBER MANUFACTURED	TOTAL REVENUE	TOTAL COST	TOTAL PROFIT	MARGINAL REVENUE	MARGINAL COST
1	$ 18,000	$ 30,000	($12,000)	$18,000	$30,000
2	36,000	35,000	1,000	18,000	5,000
3	54,000	40,000	14,000	18,000	5,000
4	72,000	50,000	22,000	18,000	10,000
5	90,000	60,000	30,000	18,000	10,000
6	108,000	76,000	32,000	18,000	16,000
7	126,000	110,000	16,000	18,000	34,000
8	144,000	170,000	(26,000)	18,000	60,000

FIGURE 8–13   Costs and Revenues Associated With Manufacture of Communications Systems

the firm will net $32,000. This is also seen in Figure 8–14, in which the data are presented graphically. The profit point at which the distance between total revenue and total cost is greatest is that corresponding to six units. The company should therefore refuse the contract.

The solution can be verified further if the *marginal revenue* and *marginal cost* data in Figure 8–13 are examined. For every unit manufactured, the company obtains marginal revenue of $18,000. However, it also has an accompanying marginal cost associated with the production. A scrutiny of this marginal revenue (MR) and marginal cost (MC) data shows that for the sixth unit the firm will increase overall profit by $2,000 ($18,000 − $16,000). At seven units, overall profits will decline by $16,000 because the marginal revenue is $18,000 but the marginal cost

Marginal revenue and marginal cost must be computed.

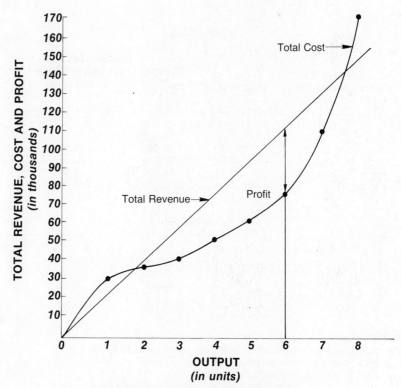

FIGURE 8–14   Maximum Profit Determination

associated with this unit is $34,000. The company should therefore agree to manufacture no more than six units. The profit maximization rule is to manufacture to the point where MC equals MR or, if they do not equalize, the last point where MR is larger than MC (as occurred in this case). Such an analysis can prove a useful decision-making technique for the manager because it not only helps identify the maximum profit point but also prevents undertaking of unprofitable ventures.

Financial Analysis

Although marginal analysis is useful to the manager, it is a specialized technique that considers situations one at a time. As such, it is not a particularly helpful long-range guide to action. To provide a dynamic view of the future, many managers have turned to financial analytical techniques, which can be used for functions such as estimating the profitability of an investment, calculating the payback period, and/or analyzing discounted cash inflows and outflows.

After-tax profitability is one guideline.

Consider the situation of the manager who is evaluating the purchase of two machines, A and B, on one basis only, *after-tax profitability*. Which machine will provide the most net profit for the firm? Machine A costs $150,000 and has an estimated useful life of five years. Machine B costs $200,000 and also has a five-year useful life. As seen in Figure 8–15, when depreciation and taxes are deducted, Machine A will return $55,000 in net income, whereas Machine B will net the firm $60,000. Therefore, on the basis of after-tax profitability, Machine B will be the manager's choice.

MACHINE A

Year	Added Income Before Taxes	Depreciation	Taxable Income	After-Tax Income (assuming 50 percent tax rate)
1	$30,000	$30,000	$ 0	$ 0
2	50,000	30,000	20,000	10,000
3	60,000	30,000	30,000	15,000
4	80,000	30,000	50,000	25,000
5	40,000	30,000	10,000	5,000
			$110,000	$55,000

MACHINE B

Year	Added Income Before Taxes	Depreciation	Taxable Income	After-Tax Income (assuming 50 percent tax rate)
1	$ 40,000	$40,000	$ 0	$ 0
2	60,000	40,000	20,000	10,000
3	80,000	40,000	40,000	20,000
4	100,000	40,000	60,000	30,000
5	40,000	40,000	0	0
			$120,000	$60,000

Notes:
1. Investment for Machine A is $150,000; Machine B, $200,000.
2. Both machines have an estimated life of 5 years.
3. Depreciation is on a straight-line basis.

FIGURE 8–15   Evaluating an Investment on the Basis of Net Profit

It should be noted, however, that although the B alternative is more profitable, it also entails an added investment of $50,000. This raises the question, has the manager made a wise choice by allowing net profit to be the sole guide? After all, should the company not expect to obtain more profit from the larger investment? Sometimes a manager is on sound ground when opting for the alternative returning the greatest net profit; other times, however, one may forego the consideration of profit and concentrate on the *payback period*, that is, how long it will take the company to recover its investment. Figure 8–16 presents the cumulative cash recovery period. Estimating weekly recovery as 1/52 of the annual total, it will require approximately 3 years, 33 weeks to recover the $150,000 invested for Machine A and 3 years, 37 weeks to recover the $200,000 invested for Machine B. On the basis of the payback period, the manager would opt for Machine A.

Payback period is another.

A third approach, even more useful than the previous two, is that of *net present value*. With this method the manager evaluates the expected return from each investment, using a *discounted dollar analysis* of cash inflows. Such an analysis presents *future* cash inflows in terms of *current* dollars. The longer the manager has to wait for the inflows, the less they are worth in current dollars. For purposes of illustration, assume that the manager chooses to discount the future inflows of funds by 10 per cent. In this case the annual cash flow recovery in Figure 8–17 has to be multiplied by the appropriate discount factor. For example, a dollar returned a year from today is worth 0.909 cents using a 10 per cent discount; while a dollar returned two years from today is worth 0.826 cents in current dollars. By multiplying the cash inflows by their respective discount factors, as seen in Figure 8–17, discounted dollars can be calculated for the five-year investment. Then, to obtain the net present value, the manager must merely subtract the initial investment from the discounted dollar total and opt for that alternative which returns the greatest amount. Machine A will return $22,035 ($172,035 minus $150,000), whereas Machine B will return $20,210 ($220,210 minus $200,000). Thus the manager should choose alternative A.

Discounted cash flow is a third.

MACHINE A

Year	After-Tax Income	Depreciation	Annual Cash Recovery	Cumulative Cash Recovery
1	$ 0	$30,000	$30,000	$ 30,000
2	10,000	30,000	40,000	70,000
3	15,000	30,000	45,000	115,000
4	25,000	30,000	55,000	170,000
5	5,000	30,000	35,000	205,000

MACHINE B

Year	After-Tax Income	Depreciation	Annual Cash Recovery	Cumulative Cash Recovery
1	$ 0	$40,000	$40,000	$ 40,000
2	10,000	40,000	50,000	90,000
3	20,000	40,000	60,000	150,000
4	30,000	40,000	70,000	220,000
5	0	40,000	40,000	260,000

FIGURE 8–16   Evaluating an Investment on the Basis of Payback Period

MACHINE A

Year	Outflows of Cash	Inflows of Cash	Discount Factor	Discounted Dollars
0	$150,000	$ 0	1.000	$150,000
1	0	30,000	0.909	27,270
2	0	40,000	0.826	33,040
3	0	45,000	0.751	33,795
4	0	55,000	0.683	37,565
5	0	35,000	0.621	21,735
Scrap Value (20%)		30,000	0.621	18,630
				$172,035

MACHINE B

Year	Outflows of Cash	Inflows of Cash	Discount Factor	Discounted Dollars
0	$200,000	$ 0	1.000	$200,000
1	0	40,000	0.909	36,360
2	0	50,000	0.826	41,300
3	0	60,000	0.751	45,060
4	0	70,000	0.683	47,810
5	0	40,000	0.621	24,840
Scrap Value (20%)		40,000	0.621	24,840
				$220,210

FIGURE 8–17   Discounted Cash Flows for Machines A and B

SUMMARY

In this chapter the fundamentals of decision making were examined. The decision-making process consists of: (a) identifying the problem; (b) diagnosing the situation; (c) collecting and analyzing data relevant to the issue; (d) ascertaining solutions that may be used in solving the problem; (e) analyzing these alternative solutions; (f) selecting the one that appears most likely to solve the problem; and (g) implementing it. Yet the decision-making process is more than a mere list of steps; there is a great deal of subjective as well as objective evaluation that must take place. For example, the personal values of the top manager will play a significant role in the assignment of risk and uncertainty probabilities. In many cases decision making may well be 75 per cent subjective, 25 per cent objective.

Nevertheless, the manager must be as rational as possible, drawing upon all techniques and guidelines available in choosing from among the various alternatives. Some of the techniques that are most useful in this process include the Laplace criterion, maximin criterion, maximax criterion, marginal analysis, and financial analysis. Yet these represent only a few of the techniques available to the modern manager. In the next chapter other commonly employed techniques will be examined.

REVIEW
AND STUDY
QUESTIONS

1. What is meant by the term decision making?

2. What are the steps in the decision-making process? Explain each.

3. What is meant by the term rationality? Are all decisions rational ones? Defend your answer.

4. How does value orientation affect the decision-making process? Give an illustration.

5. What are meant by organizational and personal decisions? Basic and routine decisions? Programmed and nonprogrammed decisions? Give an illustration of each.

6. How does a procedure differ from a policy?

7. What are the three basic conditions under which decisions are made? Explain each.

8. What roles do objective and subjective probability play in the decision-making process?

9. How does risk preference affect the decision-making process?

10. Of what benefit is marginal analysis to the manager in the decision-making process? Give an illustration.

11. Of what value is financial analysis to the manager in the decision-making process? Give an illustration.

SELECTED REFERENCES

Drucker, P. F. *Management: Tasks, Responsibilities, Practices.* New York: Harper & Row, Publishers, Inc., 1974, Chapter 37.

Greiner, L. E., D. P. Leitch, and L. B. Barnes. "Putting Judgment Back into Decisions." *Harvard Business Review,* March–April 1970, pp. 59–66.

Guth, W. D., and R. Tagiuri. "Personal Values and Corporate Strategy." *Harvard Business Review,* September–October 1965, pp. 123–132.

Ives, B. D. "Decisions Theory and the Practicing Manager." *Business Horizons,* June 1973, pp. 38–40.

Kabus, I. "You Can Bank On Uncertainty." *Harvard Business Review,* May–June 1976, pp. 95–105.

Sihler, W. W. "Framework for Financial Decisions." *Harvard Business Review,* March–April 1971, pp. 123–135.

Simon, H. *The New Science of Management Decision.* New York: Harper & Row, Publishers, Inc., 1960.

Williams, L. K. "Some Correlates of Risk Taking." *Personnel Psychology,* Autumn 1965, pp. 297–310.

CASE: FROM SKIS TO TENNIS RACKETS

When it comes to values and decision making, inventors provide interesting stories since many of them will invent a product, start a business, and then sell it. Howard Head, founder of the Head Ski Corporation, is an illustration.

Back in 1947 Howard Head had an idea that metal skis could be superior to wooden ones, provided they were engineered and built properly. Starting out with $6000 (mostly poker winnings), Head began to pursue his vision of a metal ski. Working with two assistants, who went unpaid for the first 18 months, Head went through forty versions of metal skis. The result was a product superior to anything on the market. So superior, in fact, that Head skis captured a large share of the high-priced ski market, and were internationally recognized as one of the finest skis available. Professional skiers bought them because of their high performance and reliability; amateurs purchased them because of their reputation and the status they carried.

During many of these early years, Howard Head required the retail dealers to use salespeople who skied to sell his product. On advertising he was just as strict, refusing to use endorsements by professional skiers; Head believed the performance of the skis was sufficient to induce sales, making professional endorsements unnecessary. Finally, like Henry Ford, he offered his product in one color only — black.

However, Howard Head was an inventor, not a manager. As the company moved from $10 million to $20 million in annual sales, it suffered acute growing pains. As a result, in 1971 Head sold the company and the name to AMF Inc. for $16 million.

Yet Howard Head is far from through. Very recently he broke back into the news with his famous Prince tennis racket. This racket is much larger than the average tennis racket. The string area is about 3.5 inches longer and 2 inches wider than the typical racket. Professionals are not overly enthusiastic but tennis buffs are claiming that it improves their game. In 1976 over 100,000 of these rackets were sold and in 1977 sales were 50 per cent higher.

Of course no one, including Howard Head, is claiming that he is a great manager. However, he does provide an excellent illustration of an inventor who knows when the product is sufficiently developed so that he can step aside and let the professional managers take over.

Questions

1. Using Spranger's values (theoretical, economic, aesthetic, social, political, religious) as your guide, which values are most important to Howard Head?

2. How much of a risk taker do you think Howard Head is?

3. Why did Howard Head sell his ski corporation? Why is he now trying to break back into the business world with a tennis racket? Are these decisions "rational"?

CASE: ONE, TWO, OR THREE

George Redin had fought the proposed increase in plant facilities. "It's a poor idea," he told the board of directors, "because there just isn't enough demand to sustain this increased supply. Four major firms have entered our industry in the last year and three more are knocking on the door; they know a profitable venture when they see one. The days of high prices and high profits are over. We are in for at least a decade of severe competition. Instead of increasing our capacity, we ought to be considering a new industry in which we can invest funds and maybe make a 15 per cent return on investment. Right now we have all our eggs in one basket and we are jeopardizing them by increasing our commitment with a 25 per cent increase in plant."

The board listened attentively but outvoted the president. Plant expansion was ordered and would be completed within eighteen months. George decided that the only way to salvage the company was to find some way of increasing demand for the product. After ten months of investigation and research, the president and his top executives agreed that there were three basic strategies available. First, they could increase the amount of advertising from $300,000 to $400,000. This would result in total sales of $30,000,000. Second, they could lower the price of the product by 20 per cent. Market research data indicated that this would lead to sales of $60,000,000. Finally, they could opt for a strong research and development program. If $1 million were invested in R & D, sales for the upcoming year would be $25 million. In terms of success probability, the executives estimated that the first of these strategies had a 60 per cent chance of succeeding, the second had a 20 per cent chance, whereas the third had a 70 per cent success probability. In addition, the tax rate associated with each of the three was 48, 50, and 46 per cent respectively.

Questions

1. Is this a case of decision making under certainty, risk, or uncertainty? Explain.

2. What are the expected values associated with each of the three strategies? Show all your calculations. In light of your work, which of the three strategies should the management choose?

3. Will the net profit margin before taxes associated with each of the three strategies have any bearing on the final decision? Explain why or why not.

CASE: THE PROFITABLE PEN

Jack Price, president of Wilten Manufacturing, and his staff of planning advisors had spent the morning discussing the manufacture of a new felt pen. The process for the pen had been discovered in their R & D lab. The company's plan was to blanket the New York City area with an advertising campaign announcing the new product. Although the pen would be priced higher than that of the competition, its estimated life was four times that of the average felt pen currently on the market.

Through the use of market research and all the information they could obtain about the success of competitive firms, the company compiled the following demand schedule and total cost figures for the first year of operations:

Price	Felt Pens Demanded	Total Cost
$1.20	Virtually zero	$ 80,000
1.10	100,000	90,000
1.00	115,000	100,000
.90	130,000	105,000
.80	140,000	115,000
.70	150,000	130,000
.60	155,000	145,000
.50	160,000	170,000

Realizing that this was probably the most accurate information they would be able to obtain, the president and his advisors decided to push ahead with the production and sale of the new pen if the figures indicated the venture would be profitable. Then, if they were successful in the New York City area, they would expand their market to the national level. However, if the current data indicated that the product could not be successfully marketed because of lack of demand and/or excessive costs, they would sell the process to one of their competitors. The president saw little problem with this latter alternative, since the company had applied for a patent on the process and company attorneys indicated that there would be no trouble getting one. Initial estimates placed the value of the felt pen process at $60,000.

Questions

1. Given the data in the case, do you think the pen can be manufactured and marketed successfully? Explain in detail.

2. Would the firm be better off marketing the pen or selling the process? Show your calculations.

CASE: THE CAR DEALER'S DILEMMA

A local car dealer has been making an estimate of the number of cars he will sell with each of three strategies under two different states of nature. His data reveal the following:

	States of Nature	
Strategies	*Average Growth of GNP*	*Dynamic Growth of GNP*
Low Price	1300 cars	1400 cars
Increased Advertising	1200 cars	1600 cars
Improved Service	1250 cars	1500 cars

Questions

1. Using the Laplace criterion, which applies equal probability to all states of nature, which of the above three strategies should the dealer implement? Give your reasoning.

2. If the dealer uses the maximin approach, which of the above three strategies should he implement? Explain.

3. If the dealer employs a maximax criterion and assigns a 0.8 probability to dynamic growth and a 0.2 probability to average growth, which of the above alternatives should he implement? Explain.

CHAPTER NINE
MODERN QUANTITATIVE DECISION-MAKING TOOLS AND PROCESSES

Mathematical decision making has been given increased emphasis in recent years. The goal of this chapter is to examine some of the mathematical tools and processes currently being employed by managers. Before doing so, however, it should be noted that a quantitative approach has both advantages and disadvantages. On the positive side, for example, it is possible to screen out many of the subjective processes that often cause a decision to go awry. Also, in solving complex problems, faster and more accurate solutions can sometimes be obtained by use of a mathematical approach. On the other hand, quantitative tools cannot guarantee effective decision making; they have numerous limitations. For example, if the mathematical expression or model does not properly represent reality, the answer will be wrong. If, for example, a manager estimates that Decision A will produce either $1 million or nothing and has a success probability of 10 per cent, whereas Decision B will produce either $200,000 or nothing and has a success probability of 90 per cent, it would be wiser to choose Decision B. The former has an expected payoff of only $100,000 [($1 million) (.10) + ($0) (.90)], but the latter has an expected pay-off of $180,000 [($200,000) (.90) + ($0) (.10)].

However, what if the manager is wrong in the estimates and Decision A's probability for success is really .90 while that of Decision B is only .10? Then, because of erroneous probability assignments, the manager has made a serious mistake. Decision A's expected payoff of $900,000 [($1 million) (.90) + ($0) (.10)] will be much larger than that of Decision B's $20,000 [($200,000) (.10) + ($0) (.90)]. Second, sometimes the costs associated with a quantitative solution do not justify the returns; i.e., a mathematical approach may be much more expensive than a nonmathematical one. Third, many times it is difficult to quantify all the necessary variables associated with a problem. In such cases, a quantitative approach may not be possible.

Nevertheless, many managers are finding mathematical tools and techniques very helpful in the decision-making process. These tools, for the most part, fall under the heading of *operations research* (OR), and this chapter will examine some of them. In certain cases, a mathematical explanation will be made, whereas in others, because of time and space limitations, only a qualitative description will be given.

When you are finished reading this chapter you should be able to:
1. Define the term *operations research.*
2. Discuss the value of linear programming in the decision-making process.
3. Relate the importance of the economic order quantity formula in solving inventory control problems.
4. Solve simple game theory problems.
5. Explain how both queuing theory and the Monte Carlo method can help the manager in decision making.

6. Describe the format of a decision tree and the value of such trees in handling both short- and long-run problems.
7. Provide some illustrations of the kinds of problems managers often solve with heuristic programming.

OPERA-TIONS RE-SEARCH

The application of quantitative methods to decision making began in earnest during World War II. The approach has been termed *operations research* or *management science*. Simon tersely summed up its history when he wrote:

> Operations research is a movement that, emerging out of the military needs of World War II, has brought the decision-making problems of management within the range of interests of large numbers of natural scientists and, particularly, of mathematicians and statisticians. The operations researchers soon joined forces with mathematical economists who had come into the same area—to the mutual benefit of both groups. And by now there has been widespread fraternization between these exponents of the "new" scientific management and . . . industrial engineering. No meaningful line can be drawn any more to demarcate operations research from scientific management or scientific management from management science.[1]

Since it is so difficult to identify specifically the domain of operations research, there has been considerable confusion over the use of the term. Some attach it to any new mathematical approach to decision making. Others (e.g., mathematicians, physicists, engineers) claim there must be an interdisciplinary approach involved. Still others contend that the process or technique must be sophisticated before it falls under the heading of OR. In an attempt to make the area understandable, Koontz and O'Donnell have identified the essential methods of OR as applied to decision making as follows:

The essential methods of OR.

1. An emphasis on models that symbolize the relationship among the variables that are involved.
2. An emphasis on goals and the development of techniques for measuring effectiveness.
3. The incorporation of at least the most important variables into the model.
4. The design of a mathematical model.
5. The quantification of all variables to the greatest degree possible.
6. The supplementation of quantifiable data with the use of probability.[2]

Using these basic essentials, a number of problem-solving tools and techniques have been developed, including linear programming, inventory control, game theory, queuing theory, and Monte Carlo simulation. These techniques will be examined in this chapter.

LINEAR PROGRAM-MING

One of the most widely used techniques of operations research is that of linear programming. It has been described as:

What is linear programming?

> . . . a technique for specifying how to use limited resources or capacities of a business to obtain a particular objective, such as least cost, highest margin, or least time, when those resources have alternative uses. It is a technique that systematizes for certain conditions the process of selecting the most desirable course of action from a number of avail-

---

[1]Herbert A. Simon, *The New Science of Management Decision* (New York: Harper & Row, Publishers, Inc., 1960), p. 15.
[2]Adapted from Harold Koontz and Cyril O'Donnell, *Management: A Systems and Contingency Analysis of Managerial Functions,* 6th edition (New York: McGraw-Hill Book Company, 1976), pp. 207–208.

able courses of action, thereby giving management information for making a more effective decision about the resources under its control.[3]

All linear programming problems must have two basic characteristics. First, two or more activities must be competing for limited resources. Second, all relationships in the problem must be linear. If these two conditions exist, the technique can be employed. One of the easiest ways to grasp the fundamentals of the approach is to use it in solving a particular problem. Following is a simple illustration of an allocation problem, using one of the most common linear programming approaches, the graphic method.

Characteristics of linear programming problems.

Company A wishes to maximize its profit by manufacturing two products: Model A and Model B. There is a wholesaler who has signed a contract promising to take all the goods the company can manufacture over the next 30 days off its hands at a predetermined price. The basic question, therefore, is how many units of each to manufacture. Analysis reveals the following information:

The Graphic Method

TABLE 9–1   Company A's Resources

Hours Required Per Unit

Product	Manufacture	Paint	Assembly	Test	Profit Per Unit
Model A	15.0	1.0	3.0	3.0	$400
Model B	10.0	1.0	2.0	–	$300
Hours Available During Next 30 Days	**21,000**	**1,200**	**3,000**	**2,400**	

How many Model A and Model B units should be manufactured? It is virtually impossible to say merely by looking at the data. However, certain conclusions can be drawn in regard to constraints. For example, no more than 21,000 hours of manufacturing time are available to produce the two models. The constraint can be written in this way:

Mathematical expression of the constraints.

$$15A + 10B \leq 21,000 \text{ hours}$$

Likewise, the other three constraints (painting, assembly, and test) can be expressed as follows:

$$1A + 1B \leq 1200 \text{ hours}$$
$$3A + 2B \leq 3000 \text{ hours}$$
$$3A \leq 2400 \text{ hours}$$

In addition, maximization of the profit objective can be expressed by the statement:

$$\text{Profit maximization} = \$400A + \$300B$$

---

[3]Robert O. Ferguson and Lauren F. Sargent, *Linear Programming* (New York: McGraw-Hill Book Company, 1958), p. 3.

subject, of course, to the initial four constraints and the fact that A and B cannot be negative, i.e., there is no such thing as negative production and so A $\geq$ 0 and B $\geq$ 0.

Having identified the constraints and the profit maximization function, the maximum number of units that can be manufactured can now be determined. That is:

$$15A + 10B \leq 21{,}000 \text{ hours}$$
$$\text{if:} \qquad B = 0$$
$$\text{then:} \ 15A \leq 21{,}000$$
$$A \leq 1400$$

Conversely:

$$\text{if:} \qquad A = 0$$
$$\text{then:} \ 10B \leq 21{,}000$$
$$B \leq 2100$$

Thus, if only one model is produced, the greatest number of Model A and Model B units that can be manufactured is 1400 and 2100 respectively. This can be graphed as shown in Figure 9–1.

The maximum number of units of A and B respectively that can be painted is:

$$1A + 1B \leq 1200 \text{ hours}$$
$$\text{if:} \qquad B = 0$$
$$\text{then:} \ 1A \leq 1200$$
$$A \leq 1200$$

Conversely:

$$\text{if:} \qquad A = 0$$
$$\text{then:} \ 1B \leq 1200$$
$$B \leq 1200$$

This can be graphed as shown in Figure 9–2.

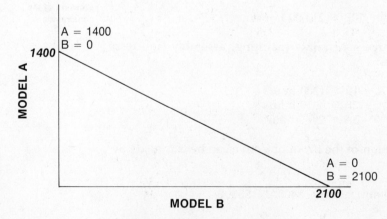

FIGURE 9–1 Manufacturing Constraints

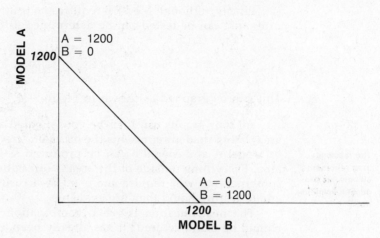

FIGURE 9-2 Painting Constraints

In terms of the assembly constraint, the number of Model A and Model B units that can be assembled can be determined as follows:

$$3A + 2B = 3000$$
$$\text{if:} \quad B = 0$$
$$\text{then:} \quad 3A = 3000$$
$$A = 1000$$

Conversely:

$$\text{if:} \quad A = 0$$
$$\text{then:} \quad 2B \leq 3000$$
$$B \leq 1500$$

This can be graphed as shown in Figure 9–3.

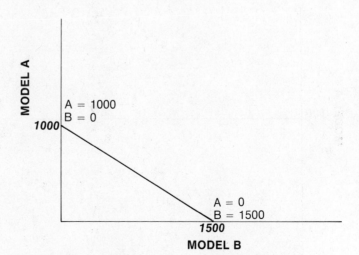

FIGURE 9-3 Assembly Constraints

Finally, although Model B requires no testing, the number of Model A units that can be tested can be determined as follows:

$$3A \leq 2400$$
$$A \leq 800$$

This can be graphed as shown in Figure 9–4.

All four graphs can then be consolidated as seen in Figure 9–5. The area that is shaded represents the *feasibility area;* that is, any combination of Model A and Model B can be produced as long as it falls within this area. Everything outside of the area is infeasible because those particular combinations will require more manufacturing, painting, assembling, and/or testing hours than are available.

The feasibility area represents all possible production combinations.

The next question is, what combination of those that are feasible should be manufactured? It has already been ascertained that:

$$\text{Profit maximization} = \$400A + \$300B$$

Therefore, for every three units of A or four units of B sold, the profit will be identical, namely, $1200. The ratio of A to B will be 3 to 4. If this ratio is maintained, starting as close to the origin as possible and gradually working outward, all combinations of feasible production can eventually be analyzed. Figure 9–6 shows this "isoprofit line" for $1200. If this line is continued out to its furthest point from the origin, it will either come to rest on one of the lines forming the feasibility boundary area or it will "nick" one of the four points labeled A, B, C, and D respectively in the figure. The slope of the isoprofit line shows that it will probably touch one of the four points before continuing out into the infeasible area, and this is precisely what happens. The isoprofit line will touch point C, and it is here that profit is maximized at 600 units of Model A and 600 units of Model B. This can be verified by examining all four points — A, B, C, and D.

Computation of the isoprofit line.

$$\text{Point A:} \quad \$400 \ (800) + \$300 \ (\ 0 \ \ ) = \$320{,}000$$
$$\text{Point B:} \quad \$400 \ (800) + \$300 \ (\ 300 \ ) = \$410{,}000$$
$$\text{Point C:} \quad \$400 \ (600) + \$300 \ (\ 600 \ ) = \$420{,}000$$
$$\text{Point D:} \quad \$400 \ (\ 0 \ \ ) + \$300 \ (1200) = \$360{,}000$$

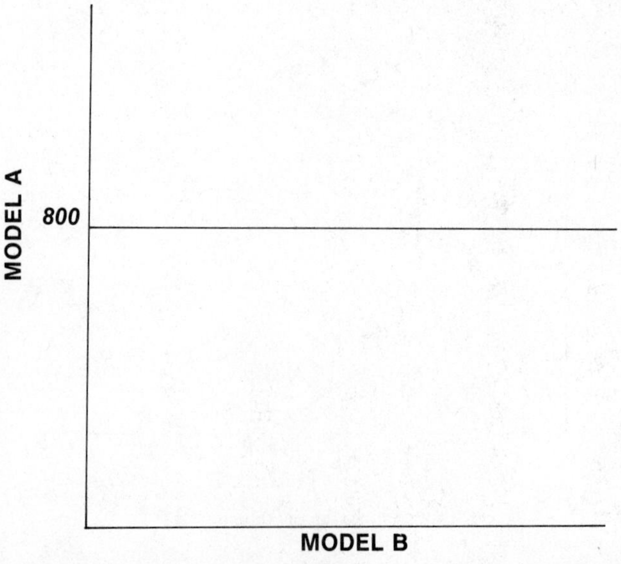

MODEL A

800

MODEL B

FIGURE 9–4   Testing Constraint

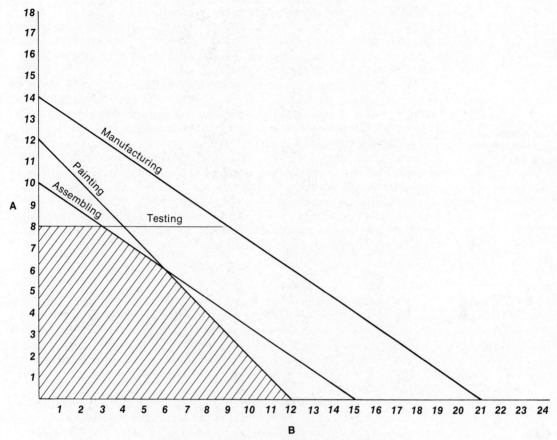

FIGURE 9–5   Feasibility Area (in hundreds of units)

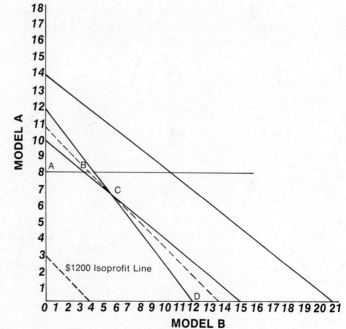

FIGURE 9–6 $1200 Isoprofit line (in hundreds of units)

No other combination will result in as much profit as that obtained at point C. If you wish, you can test this statement, as long as you remember to keep in mind the constraints that are present, e.g., one unit of A cannot be traded for one unit of B because it takes more time to manufacture a unit of A than to manufacture a unit of B.

Limitations of linear programming.

Linear programming can be used in the solution of many kinds of allocation decision problems, but its application is certainly limited. For example, to be employed effectively, the decision problem must be formulated in quantitative terms. In many instances, the costs associated with gathering these data outweigh the savings obtained from the use of the technique. Likewise, many allocation problems do not lend themselves to this approach because the relationship between the variables is not linear, although approximate solutions are sometimes possible. Finally, unless all variables are known with certainty, i.e., the model is deterministic, it is sometimes impossible to use the technique. Nevertheless, the approach has many advantages and its application in the area of business decision making is increasing.

INVENTORY CONTROL

Another common problem faced by managers is that of maintaining adequate inventories. On the one hand, no one wants to have too many units available because there are costs associated with carrying these goods. On the other hand, a store that runs out of inventory risks losing a customer's future business. In resolving this dilemma, it is necessary for the manager to analyze costs and formulate some assumptions about supply and demand.

There are two types of costs that merit the manager's consideration. The first are *clerical and administrative costs,* which are expenses associated with ordering inventory. Every time an order for more goods is placed, time and effort are expended. Naturally, if a firm wished to reduce these particular costs to their lowest possible level, it could place one order covering all the goods they would need for the entire year. However, this is unrealistic in light of the second type of costs, popularly known as *carrying costs.* Carrying costs refer to the amount of money invested in the inventory, as well as other sundry expenses covering storage space, taxes, and obsolesence. The greater the inventory the firm carries, the greater these expenses are going to be.

Solving the Problem

One way for the manager to solve the inventory problem is to make certain assumptions regarding future demand and then attempt a solution. Three of the most common assumptions made in determining optimal inventory size are: demand is known with certainty; the lead time necessary for reordering goods is also known with certainty; and the inventory will be depleted at a constant rate. These assumptions can be diagrammed as in Figure 9–7.

Assumptions made in determining optimal inventory size.

Naturally, these three assumptions are not realistic, but they do provide a basis from which the manager can make a decision. Now the manager has to decide if he or she wishes to use what can be labeled a trial-and-error approach, or if he wants to employ an OR tool known as the *economic order quantity* (EOQ) formula.

In order to illustrate the importance of the EOQ formula, the following problem will be solved using both approaches. Mr. Smith is the manager of an appliance department for a large eastern discount store. He has estimated annual demand for blenders for the upcoming year to be

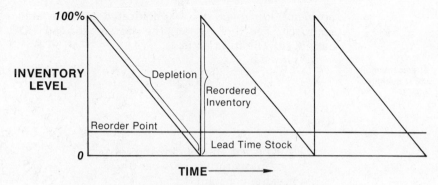

FIGURE 9–7   Constant Depletion Rate

5000. He has calculated the order costs (clerical and administrative) as $100 per order, and carrying costs have been broken down into component parts as follows: (a) value of a blender is $20; (b) insurance, taxes, storage, and other expenses are 5 per cent per year; and (c) average inventory carried at any one time is equal to total inventory divided by two.[4] It should be noted that carrying costs consist of the value of the inventory tied up at any one time and the costs associated with these particular goods.

In the first instance, if Mr. Smith takes the above data and constructs the total costs associated with each of a number of reorder levels the following will result:

TABLE 9–2   Trial-and-Error Approach

Number of Orders Placed	Size of Each Order	Order Cost	Carrying Cost $\left(\begin{array}{c} \text{Inventory}/2 \\ \times\ \$20\ \times\ 0.05 \end{array}\right)$	Total Cost
1	5000	$100	$2500.00	$2600.00
2	2500	200	1250.00	1450.00
3	1667	300	833.50	1133.50
6	833	600	416.50	1016.50
10	500	1000	250.00	1250.00
20	250	2000	125.00	2125.00

The above data indicate that the manager would be best off by placing six orders of 833 blenders each throughout the year. However, two points should be noted. First, Mr. Smith does not know that six is the ideal number of times to reorder. He merely knows that of the above alternatives, six is the best. However, what about the other reorder possibilities, namely, 4, 5, 7, 8, 9, and 11 to 19? Second, many inventory

---

[4]This is so because with a constant depletion rate, average inventory is *always* going to be equal to half of total inventory. For example, if a firm orders 1000 widgets and sells them at the rate of 20 per day for 50 days, there will be none left at the end of 10 weeks. However, if we take the amount on hand at the midpoint of each week, it will be: 950, 850, 750, 650, 550, 450, 350, 250, 150, and 50 units respectively. If you add all of these and divide by ten, you get 500. Thus in the EOQ formula the average inventory is determined to be: total inventory/2.

problems are much too sophisticated to be solved by such a simple approach. For this reason, the aforementioned EOQ formula is often employed. The formula is:

$$EOQ = \sqrt{\frac{2DA}{vr}}$$

where:

D = expected annual demand
A = administrative costs per order
v = value per item
r = estimate for taxes, insurance, and other expenses

When the data are placed in the formula, it appears as follows:

$$EOQ = \sqrt{\frac{2(5000)\ (\$100)}{(\$20) \times (0.05)}}$$

$$EOQ = \sqrt{\frac{\$1,000,000}{\$1.00}}$$

$$EOQ = \sqrt{1,000,000}$$

$$EOQ = 1000$$

This means that the manager's best decision would be to reorder in quantities of 1000. This will require the placement of five orders throughout the year, an alternative not pursued by Mr. Smith. The answer can be further verified through hand calculation. Five orders will result in total order costs of $500. The carrying costs will equal 1000 ÷ 2 × ($20 × 0.05), or $500 more. Thus, by ordering five times a year and not six, the manager can improve his total cost by $16.50 ($1016.50 − $1000). Figure 9–8 provides a graphic illustration of this solution.

This EOQ formula is used by many firms in solving inventory control problems. However, it is only one of many mathematical techniques that have been developed to help the manager make decisions. Another is game theory.

GAME THEORY

Game theory has not been widely used in solving business problems, but it has provided important insights into the elements of competition. The manager's job is to choose the best strategy available, taking into account his or her own actions and those of the competition. Thus, an understanding and appreciation of strategy can prove very useful.

Game theory involves what are termed "conflict of interest" situations. One individual (or organization) has goals that conflict with those of other individuals (or organizations). In addition, there are always two or more alternative courses of action available and the individual does not have full control over any of them. Commenting on the aspect of conflict, McDonald, in his book *Strategy in Poker, Business and War*, has written:

> The strategical situation in game theory lies in the interaction between two or more persons, each of whose actions is based on an expectation concerning the actions of others over whom he has no control. The outcome is dependent upon the personal moves of the participants. The policy followed in making these moves is strategy. Both the military

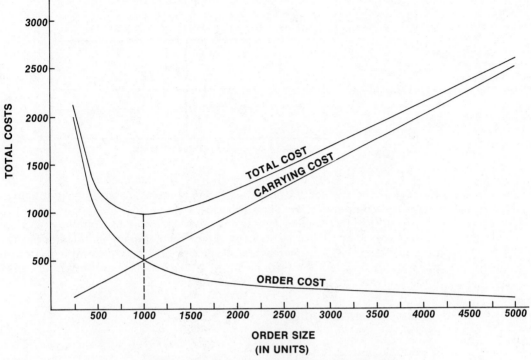

FIGURE 9–8 Order, Carrying, and Total Cost Relationships

strategist and the business man act continuously in this state of suspended animation. And regardless of the amount of information given them—short of the ideal of perfect information—they generally act in the final analysis on hunch; that is, they gamble without being able to calculate the risk.[5]

Most analysis conducted in the area of game theory has involved two-party *zero-sum* games. This means that there are two competitors and that one person's gain is the other person's loss. This concept can be seen more clearly if a payoff matrix is constructed, showing what each party stands to win or lose. Before doing so, however, it should be noted that a basic assumption of game theory is that no one side is any smarter than the other, so the payoffs in the matrix are known by *both* sides. The question is, in light of these payoffs, what should each side do?

Saddle Point Zero-Sum Games

In a zero-sum game, one party's gain is the other party's loss.

Consider, for example, two companies (Y and Z) with the following four alternative strategies:

Company Y
A = lower price
B = improve product quality

Company Z
C = increase advertising
D = hire more salesmen

[5]John McDonald, *Strategy in Poker, Business and War* (New York: W. W. North & Company, Inc., 1950), p. 16.

COMPANY Z STRATEGIES

	C	D
A	$3 Million	$3 Million
B	−$4 Million	+$5 Million

COMPANY Y STRATEGIES

FIGURE 9–9   Company Y Payoff Matrix

A 2 × 2 matrix illustration.

The payoff matrix for these respective strategies, in terms of gains and losses for Company Y, is seen in Figure 9–9.

In light of this, which strategy is most desirable to Company Y? The answer would appear to be strategy A, for the company stands to gain $3 million, regardless. Conversely, strategy C seems most desirable to Company Z, for they stand to lose no more than $3 million and might gain $4 million. Thus the best strategy appears to be A,C.

COMPANY Z STRATEGIES

COMPANY Y STRATEGIES		C	D	ROW MINIMA
	A	$3 Million	$4 Million	3 Million
	B	−$4 Million	$5 Million	−4 Million
COLUMN MAXIMA		3 Million	5 Million	

FIGURE 9–10   Determining if a Saddle Point Exists

Using the concepts of minimax and maximin, a saddle point or ideal strategy can be determined.

The logic can be verified by employing two of the most useful ideas developed in game theory. These are the concepts of minimax and maximin. *Minimax* involves minimizing the maximum loss, whereas *maximin* involves maximizing the minimum gain. Both of these concepts can be applied to the above payoff matrix to determine if there is a "saddle point" or ideal strategy. This is done by first determining the smallest number in each row (Row Minima) and then ascertaining the largest number in each column (Column Maxima). If the largest number in Row Minima equals the smallest number in Column Maxima, there is a *saddle point*.

Computation of the saddle point.

Since the largest number in Row Minima is indeed equal to the smallest number in Column Maxima, there is a saddle point or ideal strategy. This occurs at point A,C. Thus it was possible to identify the ideal strategy by means of a visual analysis.

The basic concept of game theory can be expanded into even larger matrices. For example, consider the effect of the following six strategies:

Company Y
A = lower price
B = improve product quality
C = increase advertising

Company Z
D = open more distribution centers
E = provide easier credit terms
F = hire more salesmen

When these six strategies are placed in a matrix, the following payoffs, from the standpoint of Company Y, result:

COMPANY Z STRATEGIES

	D	E	F
A	$2 Million	$6 Million	$12 Million
B	$14 Million	$8 Million	$10 Million
C	−$4 Million	$4 Million	−$6 Million

COMPANY Y STRATEGIES (rows A, B, C)

A 3 × 3 matrix illustration.

FIGURE 9–11   Company Y Payoff Matrix

A visual analysis of Figure 9–11 shows that strategy B is most favorable to Company Y. The least it will gain with this strategy is $8 million, and it can possibly gain $14 million. Conversely, strategy E appears most favorable to Company A, since the most it can lose is $8 million, in contrast to strategies D and F by which it can lose $14 million and $12 million respectively. However, because this matrix is a little more difficult to analyze than the previous one, it is desirable first to ascertain whether or not there is a saddle point. This can be done as follows:

COMPANY Z STRATEGIES

	D	E	F	ROW MINIMA
A	$2 Million	$6 Million	$12 Million	2 Million
B	$14 Million	$8 Million	$10 Million	8 Million
C	−$4 Million	$4 Million	−$6 Million	−6 Million
COLUMN MAXIMA	14 Million	8 Million	12 Million	

COMPANY Y STRATEGIES (rows A, B, C)

FIGURE 9–12   Saddle Point Calculation

There is a saddle point, the ideal strategy being B,E. Thus Company Y should initiate strategy B and Company Z should opt for strategy E. Remember, it pays neither side to opt for any other strategy if there is a saddle point. For example, according to the above matrix, if Company Y maintains strategy B, Company Z stands to lose much more than $8 million if it switches to either strategy D or F. Likewise, if Company Y changes to strategy A or C while Company Z stays with strategy E, Company Y will not gain as much as before.

Computation of the saddle point.

Non-Zero-Sum Mixed Strategy Games

The prior illustrations have all been examples of zero-sum games, but in realistic business settings zero-sum conditions rarely occur. Consider, for example, that profit per unit is $1, demand is 1000 units, and total profit in the market is $1000. Firms A and B both wish to obtain profits of $750 but, based on current information, this is impossible; the combined profits of the two cannot exceed $1000. Thus, only the firm capturing 75 per cent of the market will succeed. On the other hand, if the demand

Most situations
are non-zero-
sum in nature.

were to increase from 1000 to 2000 units, both companies could capture equal shares of the market and more than attain their respective goals. Because there are increases in demand, most businesses do not face the conditions characteristic of zero-sum games when dealing with sales volume. Most decisions are not made at the direct expense of the competition. They are thus *non-zero-sum* in nature.

Likewise, most strategy situations do not have saddle points. For example, consider the following matrix, a slight adaption of Figure 9–12, with its accompanying Row Minima and Column Maxima calculations:

		COMPANY Z STRATEGIES			**ROW MINIMA**
		D	*E*	*F*	
COMPANY Y STRATEGIES	**A**	$2 Million	$14 Million	$10 Million	2 Million
	B	$8 Million	$6 Million	$12 Million	6 Million
	C	−$4 Million	$16 Million	−$6 Million	−6 Million
COLUMN MAXIMA		8 Million	16 Million	12 Million	

FIGURE 9–13 Mixed Strategy

There is no saddle point, for the maxima of Row Minima is $6 million, whereas the minima of Column Maxima is $8 million. When there is no saddle point, it becomes necessary to design a *mixed* strategy. For example, if Company Y chose strategy B, Company Z would go to strategy E, choosing to lose $6 million. However, if Y knew what Z was going to do, it would opt for strategy C, thereby increasing its payoff from $6 million to $16 million. In turn, if Company Z knew this, it would choose strategy F, thereby gaining $6 million; and so on, each company second guessing the other. The only way to take advantage of the situation would be to determine some combination or mixed strategy. The method of calculating this will not be discussed here, but it should be noted that this mixed approach is far more realistic than the ideal or saddle-point strategy. If one firm found itself in an unfavorable saddle-point situation, it would alter its strategies drastically, thereby upsetting the old payoff matrix and establishing one more favorable to itself. Also, this examination of game theory has dealt with only two competitive sides. In a business setting, however, a firm is generally competing against many companies. Nevertheless, the concept of game theory has proved very useful in understanding the elements of competition. Its basic ideas have been experimentally expanded into bargaining and negotiating interactions and, for almost two decades now, have been employed in general management simulation games to train managers in strategy formulation and implementation.[6]

In most strategy
situations there
is not a saddle
point.

QUEUING THEORY

Another OR technique is that of queuing theory, often called *waiting-line theory*, which employs a mathematical technique for balancing waiting lines and service. These lines will occur whenever there is an irregular demand, and the manager must decide how to handle the situation. If the

---

[6]For example, see Richard M. Hodgetts, *Top Management Simulation* (Braintree, Mass.: D. H. Mark Publishing, 1970).

lines become too long and the waiting time proves excessive, customers will go elsewhere with their business. Conversely, if there is too much service, customers will be very happy but the costs will outrun the revenues. If, for example, one goes grocery shopping on Saturday morning, every cash register may be manned and the average waiting time may be fifteen minutes. Since these conditions exist all over town, the manager must be concerned only with keeping the registers manned. However, what should be done during slack periods such as Tuesday morning? If the manager assigns only two people to the registers, there may be a sudden influx of customers, creating long lines. On the other hand, if the manager keeps all the registers manned and there are only a few customers, most of the help will just be standing around doing nothing.

Naturally, the supermarket manager presents a very simple illustration because it takes little effort to move people from the stockroom to the cash register and back. As long as there is a sufficient number of employees on hand, they can be transferred around the store and waiting lines are not a serious problem. However, the same basic concept can be applied to a business firm faced with, for example, a problem of plant layout. How many loading docks and fork trucks will be needed to keep waiting time on the part of the company's delivery trucks at an acceptable level? If there are too many docks and fork trucks, there will be no waiting time for loading and unloading, but the expense associated with building the facilities will be quite great. Conversely, if there are too few docks and fork trucks, there will be a great deal of waiting time. Queuing theory can help provide an answer to this problem by means of mathematical equations. Sometimes, however, when arrival and service rates are not controllable, it becomes difficult to evaluate alternatives by means of equations alone. When this occurs, a Monte Carlo approach can often prove useful.

> Queuing theory helps the manager balance waiting lines and service.

MONTE CARLO TECHNIQUE

The Monte Carlo technique uses a *simulation* approach for the purpose of creating an artificial environment and then evaluating the effect of decisions within these surroundings. A simple illustration of a simulation is found in the case of aerodynamic testing conducted on model airplanes in a wind tunnel. By simulating the effect of air currents and gale winds on the craft, engineers can evaluate the proposed design and construction.

Monte Carlo is another type of simulation that attempts, via a random number generator or table, to simulate a particular environment and the effect of various decisions made within this artificial setting. An example can be found in the case of the plant manager who wants to determine the optimum number of trucks he should have in his delivery fleet. If there are too many, capital investment in the trucks coupled with excessive idle time will prove too high. The optimum number can be determined by using the Monte Carlo technique. First, the number of shipments arriving at the loading dock must be determined; next, the time it takes to make deliveries must be ascertained. Then the expenses of owning and operating the fleet have to be computed. Finally, the costs associated with being unable to make all deliveries on time must be calculated. Employing this basic information plus some other supplemental data and the use of random numbers, it is possible to simulate results based on different fleet sizes. This can be continued until the manager finds the optimum number of trucks. However, the technique is not restricted merely to ascertaining fleet sizes. It has been successfully used in many diverse activities from simulating machine breakdowns to determining arrivals and departures at airports.

> The Monte Carlo technique allows the manager to simulate various conditions and determine the best answer from the results.

DECISION TREES

Another OR tool is the decision tree. Many managers weigh alternatives based on their immediate or short-run results, but a decision-tree format permits a more dynamic approach because it makes some elements explicit that are generally implicit in other analyses. A decision tree is a graphic method that the manager can employ in identifying the alternative courses of action available to him in solving a problem; assigning probability estimates to events associated with these alternatives; and calculating the payoffs corresponding to each act-event combination.

For example, consider the case of a firm that has expansion funds and must decide what to do with them. After careful analysis, three alternatives are identified: (a) use the money to buy a new company; (b) expand the facilities of the current firm; or (c) put the money in a savings account and wait for better opportunities. In deciding which alternative is best, the company has gathered all the available information and constructed the decision tree in Figure 9–14.

Note in the figure that there are four important components. One is the *decision point*, represented by a *square*, which indicates where the decision maker must *choose a course of action*. A second is a *chance point*, represented by a *circle*, which indicates where a *chance event is expected* such as solid economic growth, stagnation, or high inflation. A third is a *branch*, represented by a *line* flowing from the chance points, which indicates an event and its likelihood such as 0.5 for solid growth, 0.3 for stagnation or 0.2 for high inflation. Finally, at the far right is *a payoff* associated with each branch. It is called a *conditional* payoff since its occurrence depends on certain conditions. For example, in Figure 9–14 the conditional ROI (return on investment) associated with buying a new firm and having solid economic growth is 15 per cent, but this return is conditional on the two preceding factors (buying the firm *and* having solid growth).

In building a decision tree, the company will start by identifying the three alternatives, the probabilities and events associated with each alternative, and the amount of return that can be expected from each. Having then constructed the tree, the firm will roll it back from right to left, analyzing as it goes.

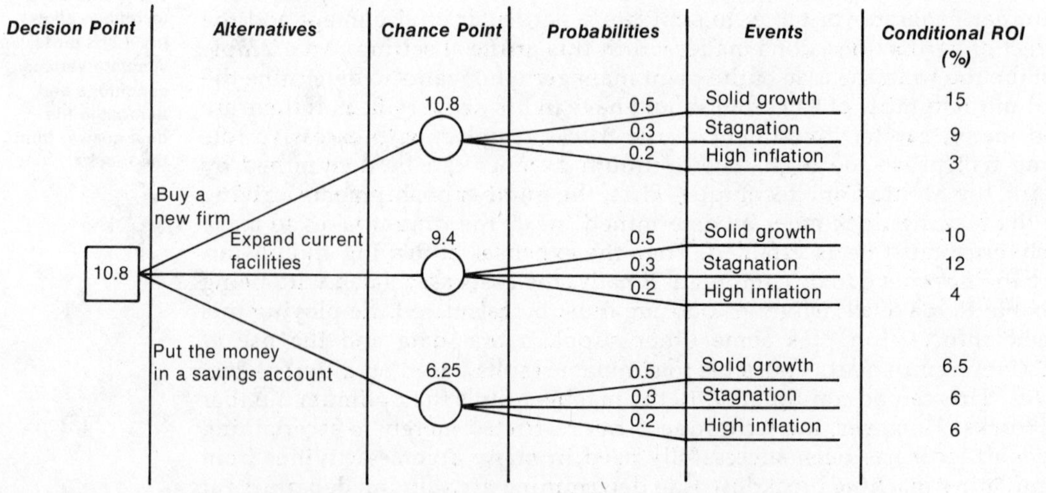

Decision Point	Alternatives	Chance Point	Probabilities	Events	Conditional ROI (%)
		10.8	0.5	Solid growth	15
			0.3	Stagnation	9
			0.2	High inflation	3
	Buy a new firm				
10.8	Expand current facilities	9.4	0.5	Solid growth	10
			0.3	Stagnation	12
			0.2	High inflation	4
	Put the money in a savings account	6.25	0.5	Solid growth	6.5
			0.3	Stagnation	6
			0.2	High inflation	6

FIGURE 9–14   Decision Tree for Investing Expansion Funds

This analysis is conducted, first, by taking the conditional ROIs at the far right of the tree and multiplying them by the probability of their occurrence. For example, if the company buys a new firm and there is solid growth in the economy, as seen in Figure 9–14, it will obtain a 15 per cent ROI. However, the probability of such an occurrence is .5. Likewise, the probabilities associated with stagnant growth, where the return will be 9 per cent, and high inflation, where the return will be 3 per cent, are .3 and .2 respectively. In order to determine the expected return associated with buying a new firm, each of the conditional ROIs is multiplied by its respective probability and the products are then totaled. For alternative one, buying the firm, the calculation is as follows:

Conditional ROI	Probability	Expected Return
15.0	.5	7.5
9.0	.3	2.7
3.0	.2	.6
		10.8

For alternative two, expanding current facilities, the calculation is:

Conditional ROI	Probability	Expected Return
10.0	.5	5.0
12.0	.3	3.6
4.0	.2	.8
		9.4

For alternative three, putting the money in a savings account, the calculation is:

Conditional ROI	Probability	Expected Return
6.5	.5	3.25
6.0	.3	1.80
6.0	.2	1.20
		6.25

These expected returns are often placed over the chance points on the decision tree. Remember, however, that they can be determined only *after* the tree has been drawn and the analysis of the branches has been conducted.

As can be seen, the first alternative is the best because it offers the greatest expected return. In evaluating alternatives, decision trees help the manager identify both what can happen and the likelihood of its occurrence. Note in *building* the tree that we moved from left to right but in *analyzing* it we moved from right to left.

In recent years many companies have begun using decision trees to handle situations that span two or more years. For example, consider the case of a company that must decide whether to buy a new machine or use overtime in handling current demand. The new machine will cost $30,000, whereas the overtime will cost $5,000. Whichever decision is made, the company will stay with it for one year and then make a follow-up decision. If it has installed a new machine in the first year, it may install a second machine, institute overtime, or use the existing facilities to the fullest. If it has opted for overtime in the first year, it may then install a new machine, install the machine *and* use overtime, or simply institute overtime.

Figure 9–15 illustrates the decision tree for this two-year period. The conditional profit is shown on the right side of the decision tree.

In order to determine which *initial* decision is the best — buy a new machine or use overtime — it is necessary to start rolling the tree back from the right. First, the conditional profits must be multiplied by their probabilities. For example, starting at the top of the tree, in determining the expected values of installing the second machine, the calculation is $120,000 \times 0.2 + 90,000 \times 0.7 + 75,000 \times 0.1 = \$94,500$. The same calculations for each of the other branches give expected values of $76,500, $60,000, $73,500, $60,000, and $58,500, respectively. Note that these numbers have all been entered over their respective chance points. Next, again starting at the top of the tree, the cost of installing a second machine must be compared with the cost of instituting overtime. When the costs of each are subtracted from their expected values of $94,500 and $76,500, the results are $64,500 and $71,500, respectively. Since the latter is greater, the firm will choose it. The next alternative down the tree calls for using existing facilities to the fullest extent. Since this has no additional costs associated with it, the $60,000 is carried back intact. Next is the cost of installing a new machine ($73,500 − $30,000 = $43,500) versus installing the machine and using overtime ($60,000 − $35,000 = $25,000). Since the former is less expensive, it is chosen. Then, on the lowest branch, there is the $58,500 expected value minus the $5,000 overtime, resulting in a new expected value of $53,500.

Now we are through the second year decisions and need merely roll the branches back one more year. Again starting at the top, there is a .7 probability associated with the $71,500 expected value and a .3 probability associated with the $60,000 expected value. From the sum of these answers we must subtract $30,000, the cost of buying a new machine. The calculation is:

$$
\begin{array}{rl}
\$71,500 \times .7 = & \$50,050 \\
\$60,000 \times .3 = & \underline{18,000} \\
& 68,050 \\
& \underline{-30,000} \quad \text{new machine cost} \\
& \$38,050
\end{array}
$$

This is the expected value of buying the new machine immediately. Meanwhile the expected value of using overtime in the first year is:

$$
\begin{array}{rl}
\$43,500 \times .7 = & \$30,450 \\
\$53,500 \times .3 = & \underline{16,050} \\
& 46,500 \\
& \underline{-5,000} \quad \text{use of overtime} \\
& 41,500
\end{array}
$$

Since the latter expected value of $41,500 is greater than the former $38,050, the company should opt for overtime rather than a new machine. Then *if sales rise* it should install a new machine the second year. If you look closely at Figure 9–14 you will see that if sales rise in year one the company is better off just installing a new machine rather than installing the machine *and* using overtime ($73,500 versus $60,000). Finally, *if sales fall* in year one the company should continue using overtime.

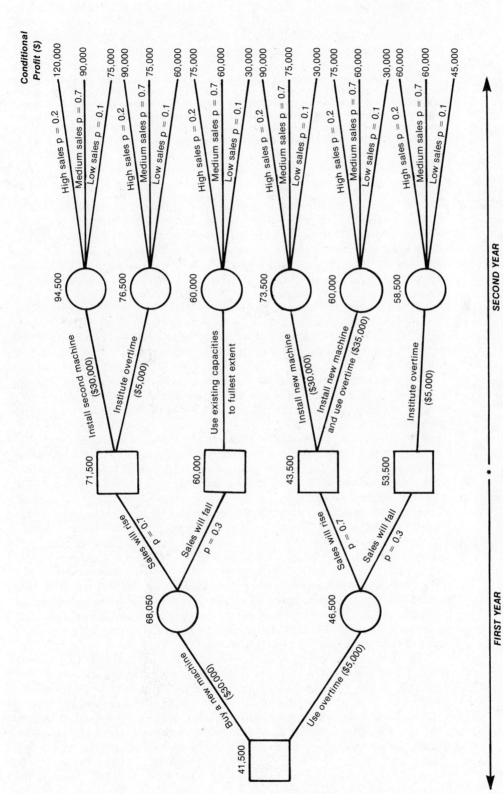

FIGURE 9-15 Decision Tree for a Two-Year Plan of Action (Adapted from: Efraim Turban and Jack R. Meredith, *Fundamentals of Management Science*, Dallas, Texas: Business Publications, Inc., 1977, p. 86.)

In the final analysis, the decision tree does not provide any definitive answers. However, it does allow the manager to weigh benefits against costs by assigning probabilities to specific events and then ascertaining the respective payoffs. As Turban and Meredith note:

> The unique feature of decision trees is that they allow management to *combine* a clear graphical presentation of the impact of various alternative courses of action with the analytical techniques of expected value. Using the decision tree, management can also examine the impact of a series of decisions (multiperiod decisions) on the objectives of the organization. The graphical presentation helps in understanding the interactions among alternative courses of action, uncertain events, and future consequences.[7]

HEURISTIC PROGRAMMING

Not all operations research approaches rely upon sophisticated mathematics. *Heuristic programming*, generally called heuristic problem-solving, is on the opposite end of the spectrum from the rigorous methodology used by some of the OR techniques already examined. Some problems are too large or too complex to be solved by a computer. Others are too unstructured, making a quantitative approach out of the question. In cases such as these, heuristic programming is often employed.

Heuristic means "serving to discover." Such an approach to problem-solving is subjective as well as objective in nature, relying upon experience, judgment, intuition, and the advice of associates. Two of the most common heuristic approaches to problem-solving are rules of thumb and trial and error.

Heuristic programming employs rules of thumb and the use of trial and error.

Problems are often nothing more than brain twisters that force the manager to think. Consider the following example. An epidemic has broken out in a city. All of the twelve local hospitals have called the nearby pharmaceutical manufacturer and asked to have a particular serum delivered immediately. It generally takes three weeks to manufacture this serum, but the pharmaceutical company just happens to have a quantity of it on hand. The serum is placed in vials, wrapped in twelve individual packages and rushed to the shipping dock. By this time, the crisis in the city has become so great that if each hospital does not have its allotted serum within the hour, patients will begin dying. Just as the manager of the shipping dock, Mr. Adams, rushes the packages to the waiting delivery truck, he receives a call from the man who wrapped the packages. One of them is missing a five-ounce vial of serum. The man is sending the vial down immediately, but in the interim, the manager's job is to ascertain which hospital has been shorted on its serum. Mr. Adams has only two minutes in which to determine this, and the only tool he has immediately available is a balance scale. How can the manager isolate the package that is missing the vial of serum? Before reading the next paragraph, you may wish to formulate your own solution.

There are a number of ways to solve the problem. One is to place six packages on each side of the scale. The side with the light package will not go down so far. Thus, the manager has reduced the number of possibilities to six. Then, by placing these on the scale, three to a side, he can reduce the number of possibilities to three. Now the problem becomes difficult. There is time for only one more weighing. How should it be done? The answer is to put one package on each side of the scale and if one

---

[7]Efraim Turban and Jack R. Meredith, *Fundamentals of Management Science* (Dallas, Texas: Business Publications, Inc., 1977), p. 89.

side drops, he has his answer. Conversely, if both sides balance, the light package must be the one remaining in his hand.[8]

As another illustration, consider the following case. Mary Anderson, a supervisor, is in the process of assigning work to one of her machinists. During this particular day, there are four jobs the machinist must do and Mary wants to keep setup time to a minimum. The individual's machine is currently "empty" and needs to be set up for the first of these jobs. The setup times from job to job are given in Table 9–3.

With the machine empty, as shown in Table 9–3, it will take 30 minutes to set up job 1, 40 minutes to set up job 2, 50 to set up job 3, and 60 to set up job 4. Once the first job is complete, the machinist can go on to the second. In order to read Figure 9–3, assume that Mary chooses to have job 3 done first. This will take 50 minutes to set up. By going down Table 9–3 to job 3 and reading across, you can see that the setup times for moving from job 3 to jobs 1, 2, and 4 are 10, 20, and 10 minutes, respectively. Let us now assume that Mary chooses job 2 as the second one. We can then go down Table 9–3 to job 2 and across to jobs 1 and 4 and see how long each of these will take. Let us say that Mary chooses job 4 as the third one; this will take 35 minutes. Finally, going down Figure 9–3 to job 4 and across to job 1 we see that this last job will take 25 minutes. Recapitulating the order and the times of the jobs shows the following:

Jobs	Setup Time
3	50
2	20
4	35
1	25
	130 minutes

It will take 130 minutes of setup time for the four jobs. Was this sequence of 3–2–4–1 the one with the lowest setup time? Before reading

---

[8]Adapted from Paul J. Gordon, "Heuristic Problem Solving: You Can Do It." *Business Horizons*, Spring 1962, pp. 43–53.

TABLE 9–3   Setup Time in Minutes

From Job \ To Job	1	2	3	4
Empty	30	40	50	60
1	0	35	15	25
2	45	0	40	35
3	10	20	0	10
4	25	40	30	0

TABLE 9–4   Enumeration Results

Sequence Job Numbers	Setup Times	Total Minutes
1–2–3–4	30 + 35 + 40 + 10	115
1–2–4–3	30 + 35 + 30 + 30	125
1–3–2–4	30 + 15 + 20 + 35	100
1–3–4–2	30 + 15 + 10 + 40	95 Minimum
1–4–2–3	30 + 25 + 40 + 40	135
1–4–3–2	30 + 25 + 30 + 20	105
2–1–3–4	40 + 45 + 15 + 10	120
2–1–4–3	40 + 45 + 25 + 30	140
2–3–1–2	40 + 40 + 10 + 35	125
2–3–2–1	40 + 40 + 20 + 45	145
2–4–2–3	35 + 30 + 40 + 40	145
2–4–3–2	35 + 30 + 30 + 20	115
3–1–2–4	50 + 10 + 35 + 35	130
3–1–4–2	50 + 10 + 25 + 40	125
3–2–1–4	50 + 20 + 45 + 25	140
3–2–4–1	50 + 20 + 35 + 25	130
3–4–1–2	50 + 40 + 25 + 35	150
3–4–2–1	50 + 40 + 40 + 45	135
4–1–2–3	60 + 25 + 35 + 40	160
4–1–3–2	60 + 25 + 15 + 20	120
4–2–1–3	60 + 40 + 45 + 15	160
4–2–3–1	60 + 40 + 40 + 10	150
4–3–2–1	60 + 30 + 20 + 45	155
4–3–1–2	60 + 30 + 10 + 35	135

on, analyze Table 9–3 yourself and determine the job sequence you would choose.

In Table 9–4 are the 24 different sequences for the four jobs. Note that the lowest time sequence is 1–3–4–2. Was this the sequence you chose? Most people do choose this one by following a simple rule. In moving from empty to the first job, they opt for the one with the lowest setup time and employ this same rule in moving from the first to the second job, second to the third, and third to the fourth. Depending on the setup times, such a heuristic rule can provide the best answer. However, keep in mind that a heuristic approach will not always give the best answer, but it can often help the manager arrive at good answers to work problems. For example, Mary's solution was better than twelve of the other sequences. However, by analyzing Table 9–4 more carefully, it is possible to reduce the total setup time by another 35 minutes.

These kinds of problems do not warrant sophisticated techniques, and they are far more common than those requiring linear programming and Monte Carlo simulation. Resource allocation, inventory control, plant layout, and job shop scheduling are all problems that can sometimes be solved through heuristic programming.

SUMMARY

In this chapter some of the modern quantitative decision-making tools and processes have been examined. Most of these fall under the heading of operations research and vary in complexity and mathematical rigor, yet all are valuable to the manager in the decision-making process.

Linear programming assists the manager in determining price-volume relationships for effectively utilizing the organization's resources. The example used in this chapter illustrated how the technique could be employed to allocate scarce resources while simultaneously maximizing profit. The second technique discussed, the economic order quantity formula, helps the decision maker decide at what point and in what quantities inventory should be replenished. The third technique discussed, game theory, is useful in providing the manager with important insights into the elements of competition. Sometimes this competition is best represented as a zero-sum game with a saddle point, but more often it is typified by a non-zero-sum game without a saddle point, in which case it is necessary to use a mixed strategy in solving the problem. A fourth quantitative technique is queuing or waiting line theory, which employs mathematical equations in balancing waiting lines and service. When it becomes difficult to evaluate alternatives by means of equations alone, many managers turn to the Monte Carlo technique, which uses a simulation approach and provides the decision maker with an opportunity to evaluate the effect of numerous decisions within this simulated environment. Then, based on the results, the manager is in a position to choose the one that best attains the objective.

Still another OR tool, and one that has been receiving increased attention in recent years, is the decision tree. This technique, which is less mathematical than those already mentioned, helps the manager weigh alternatives based on immediate and long-run results by encouraging the individual to: (a) identify the available courses of action; (b) assign probability estimates to the events associated with these alternatives; and (c) calculate the payoffs corresponding to each act-event combination. The last technique examined, heuristic programming, is the least mathematical of all, yet it is used far more often by the manager in every-day decision making (through rules of thumb and the use of trial and error) than any other OR tool.

Though quantitative analysis is important to the decision-making process, the analyzed data and results must be transmitted to the manager for appropriate action. To do so efficiently, the organization needs a well designed information system. The subjects of information systems and decision making will be the focus of attention in the next chapter.

---

1. What is meant by the term *operations research*?

2. In your own words, define linear programming. What are its advantages to the manager in the decision-making process? What are its drawbacks?

3. What is the graphic technique?

4. Of what value is game theory to the manager?

5. What are the variables involved in the economic order quantity formula? Of what value is the formula to the manager? Explain.

6. In game theory, what is meant by the term zero-sum game? Non-zero-sum game? Saddle point?

7. Most decisions made by the manager are non-zero-sum in nature. Explain this statement.

REVIEW AND STUDY QUESTIONS

8. What is meant by a mixed strategy?

9. What is meant by queuing theory?

10. Of what value is the Monte Carlo method to the manager in decision making? Explain.

11. How do decision trees help the manager in making long-run decisions? Short-run decisions?

12. What is heuristic programming?

13. Many of the daily problems faced by managers are solved by means of heuristic programming. Explain this statement.

SELECTED REFERENCES

Brown, R. V. "Do Managers Find Decision Theory Useful?" *Harvard Business Review,* May–June 1970, pp. 78–79.

Churchman, C. W., R. L. Ackoff, and E. L. Arnoff. *Introduction to Operations Research.* New York: John Wiley & Sons, 1957.

Ferguson, R. O., and L. F. Sargent. *Linear Programming.* New York: McGraw-Hill Book Company, 1968.

McDonald, J. *Strategy in Poker, Business and War.* New York: W. W. North & Company, 1950.

Magee, J. F. "Decision Trees for Decision Making." *Harvard Business Review,* July–August 1964, pp. 126–138.

Paranka, S. "Competitive Bidding Strategy." *Business Horizons,* June 1971, pp. 39–43.

Pollay, R. "The Structure of Executive Decisions and Decision Times." *Administrative Science Quarterly,* December 1970, pp. 459–471.

Simon, H. A. *The New Science of Management Decision.* New York: Harper & Row, Publishers, Inc., 1960.

Turban, E. N., and J. R. Meredith. *Fundamentals of Management Science.* Dallas, Texas: Business Publications, Inc., 1977, Chapters 4 and 14.

Vandell, R. F. "Management Evolution in the Quantitative World." *Harvard Business Review,* January–February 1970, pp. 83–92.

Virtis, J. R., and R. W. Garrett. "Weighing Risk in Capacity Expansion." *Harvard Business Review,* May–June 1970, pp. 132–140.

CASE: A LITTLE OF THIS AND A LITTLE OF THAT

The Willowby Corporation had lost quite a bit of money in the previous year. As a result its president, Fred Wilson, was determined to maximize profits as quickly as possible and show good first-quarter results. In attempting to carry out this objective, Harvey Landau, production manager at Willowby, found himself confronted with a resource allocation problem. The company was manufacturing two kinds of industrial machines, Type A and Type B. After examining the resources available to him, Harvey determined that he could solve the problem by means of the graphic method of linear programming. An analysis of the situation revealed that the following combinations and constraints for the two products were present:

Constraints	Type A	Type B
Assembly Time	120 machines	240 machines
Available Paint	150 machines	150 machines
Special Casing for Type A	100 machines	—
Special Casing for Type B	—	120 machines
Engines	180 machines	180 machines

After plotting these constraints on a graph, he determined that there were five points within the feasibility area, permitting the following combinations of Type A and Type B to be manufactured:

1. 100 A and   0 B
2. 100 A and 40 B
3. 90 A and 60 B
4. 30 A and 120 B
5.   0 A and 120 B

In addition, each unit of A would result in a $300 profit to the firm and each unit of B would bring in $200 in profit.

Questions

1. Verify the accuracy of the above five points by drawing a graphic representation of the constraints.

2. Which of the above five alternatives is most profitable to the firm? Show your work.

3. What other types of problems could Harvey solve by means of the graphic method? Give an illustration.

CASE: AN ECONOMIC APPROACH

Mr. Ed Sharp, local manager of a radio and television retail store, used to reorder merchandise on the basis of "gut feel." As he explained to one of his friends, "I don't know *exactly* when to reorder merchandise, I just use my best judgment." However, one day Roberta Sharp, his niece and a student in the Business College at State University, dropped by the store for a visit. When Roberta learned of her uncle's unscientific approach to reordering inventory she was shocked. "You should take a more refined approach to things, Uncle Ed," she said. There are lots of decision-making tools and techniques you could use. For example, there is the economic order quantity formula, which could pinpoint how many units you should order at any one time."

The uncle was impressed and decided to try his niece's suggestion. Together the two chose one of the most popular items in the store, a small AM-FM radio. After examining past sales records, they were able to obtain the following information: (a) the expected annual demand for the radio was 750 units; (b) the administrative costs associated with placing an order were $20; (c) the value of each radio was $30; and (d) the estimate for taxes, insurance, and other expenses was 10 per cent.

Questions

1. Using a trial-and-error approach, construct a table showing the size of each order, the order cost associated with this size, the carrying cost, and the total cost if the uncle reorders inventory 1, 2, 3, 4, 5, 10, and 20 times per year.

2. Using the EOQ formula in this chapter, determine the most economic reorder quantity.

3. How much money can the uncle save the store if he uses the EOQ formula rather than trial and error, assuming that he now reorders five times a year? Explain.

CASE: HALF AND HALF

A group of high school seniors were touring the facilities of a large bakery not long ago. Although the students were impressed with the mechanization of the operations, they were more interested in finding out how the firm decided how much bread or how many cakes to bake. When the tour was over, the students were taken to the cafeteria for coffee and pastries and asked if they had any questions. One of the seniors asked, "How do you know how many and what types of, for example, cookies to bake?" The tour guide smiled. "I'll tell you what," he said, "let me call one of our staff specialists in here and have him give you an answer to that." A few minutes later the man showed up with a portable blackboard and some papers containing production statistics.

I understand you're interested in finding out how we go about deciding how much of everything to bake. Actually, we use a mathematical approach whenever we can. There's a lot less guesswork in the business than there was twenty years ago. Let me explain, using baked cookies as an illustration.

Earlier in the day we took an inventory to see how much cookie mix, icing, labor, and oven space we had available for making both sugar and iced cookies, the only kinds we bake. Our calculations showed that we had enough cookie mix to bake, in dozens, either 2000 sugar or 1200 iced cookies. In addition, we had enough labor time to bake 1500 sugar or 1000 iced cookies, enough icing for 800 iced cookies, and enough oven space for 1200 sugar or iced cookies. Let me write those numbers on the blackboard for you along with the profit per dozen, which is 15 cents in the case of sugar cookies and 20 cents in the case of iced cookies.

The speaker then turned around and put the following data on the blackboard:

	Sugar Cookies	Iced Cookies
Cookie Mix	1200-dozen	1200-dozen
Labor	1500-dozen	1000-dozen
Icing	——	800-dozen
Oven Space	1200-dozen	1200-dozen
Profit	15¢ per dozen	20¢ per dozen

Now, given this information coupled with the fact that we know we can sell everything we make, how many of each type should we bake?

The students looked at the numbers but were confused. One individual pointed out that the firm could bake no more than 1200-dozen sugar and 800-dozen iced cookies, but no one seemed to know how to calculate the best combination of the two. After pondering the problem for five minutes, everyone admitted defeat. "Don't feel too bad," said the speaker. "Just by looking at the data it is impossible to say. However, by using a mathematical technique we can prove that the best combination to bake is 600-dozen sugar and 600-dozen iced. At this point profit is maximized."

The students were impressed. On the way out of the building one of them remarked, "I never realized baking was such a science. At my house it is still an art."

Questions

1. How much profit will the firm make if it bakes 600-dozen sugar and 600-dozen iced cookies? Show your calculations.

2. How is this company suboptimizing its resources? Optimizing its production? Maximizing its profit?

3. How important are mathematical tools and techniques to the modern manager?

CASE: THE BIG PAYOFF

Bill Hammer, science editor of a large publishing house, is about ready to release a new basic biology textbook. He is very interested in obtaining a large share of the basic biology text market. Although there are many competitors, there is one in particular who is also coming out with a new biology book. Therefore, Bill must formulate his strategy very carefully. For this reason, instead of just designing his own plan of action, he has decided to ask himself, what is the opposition going to do? He has come up with six basic strategies. The first three are those he intends to implement, the second three are those that he has heard will be employed by the competition. They are:

Bill's Strategy

1. Price the book lower than any other on the market.
2. Provide 10,000 complimentary copies to university professors.
3. Hire more salesmen to call on university professors and explain the strongpoints of the text.

Opposition's Strategy

4. Give large quantity discounts to the bookstores.
5. Increase the advertising budget substantially.
6. Print the text on extremely high quality paper so as to enhance its aesthetic value.

After giving the matter a greal deal of thought, Bill has concluded that the following payoff matrix represents the outcomes that will occur given each of the above strategies:

OPPOSITION

		D	E	F
	A	6	4	9
BILL	**B**	9	3	2
	C	7	1	5

Questions

1. After determining the numbers in Row Minima and Column Maxima, is there a saddle point? If so, what is your advice to Bill regarding strategy? If not, of what value is the above information to Bill?

2. If the competition is aware of the above payoff matrix and concludes it to be an accurate representation of reality, what will they do? Explain, bringing the concept of mixed strategy into your discussion.

CHAPTER TEN

INFORMATION SYSTEMS
AND DECISION MAKING

In addition to helping identify and evaluate alternative courses of action, quantitative school advocates are concerned with getting this information to those who need it. When this activity is added to those that have already been described in Chapters 8 and 9, it becomes obvious that, just like the process school, the quantitative school can be viewed as a *closed-loop* of interrelated activities. We have already seen in Figure 4–2 that the process school consists of planning, organizing, and controlling. The quantitative school can be diagrammed this way:

GOALS OF THE CHAPTER

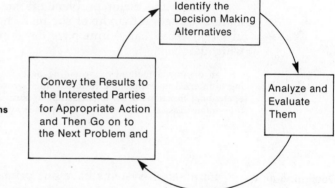

FIGURE 10–1   Quantitative School Functions

The part of Figure 10–1 which has not yet been examined is the one related to conveying the results. This is done through the use of information systems, which will be studied in this chapter. This will be our first goal. The second goal is to examine the role of computers in information systems. The third is to study the link that exists between the quantitative school and the process and behavioral schools.

When you have finished reading this chapter, you should be able to:
1. Explain how an information system can help improve a manager's decision making ability.
2. Describe how an information system is designed.
3. Relate some of the major uses of computers in modern organizations.
4. Discuss some of the shortcomings of computers.
5. Illustrate some of the behavioral impacts that information systems can have on the organizational personnel.
6. Discuss the link that exists between the quantitative and process schools and the quantitative and behavioral schools.

The manager has many functions. He or she is a strategist who must formulate objectives; a disseminator of information who must communicate these goals to other organizational members; and a company spokesperson who must provide information to outsiders. As such, the manager can be thought of as a nerve center responsible for obtaining external

INFORMATION SYSTEMS DESIGN

and internal information and passing it on to various groups. This information processing system can be depicted in the following way:

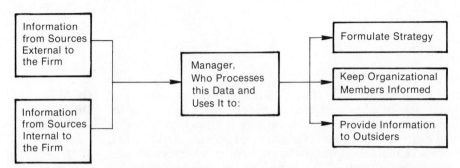

FIGURE 10–2   Manager as an Information Processor (Adapted from Henry Mintzberg, "The Myths of MIS," *California Management Review,* **Fall 1972, p. 93.)**

Perhaps the major problem the manager faces is that of receiving more information than he or she really needs. To deal with this problem, in recent years many firms have developed their own *information system* which is:

. . . an organized method of providing past, present, and projection information relating to internal operations and external intelligence. It supports the planning, control and operational functions of an organization by furnishing uniform information in the proper time-frame to assist the decision-making process.[1]

Designing an Information System

Major determinants.

Information systems have one primary goal: providing the manager with the necessary data for making intelligent decisions. Since there are three basic levels in the organization (upper, middle, and lower management), each with different interests and viewpoints, it is evident that much of this decision making information will have to be *tailor-made* to meet the needs of the respective level. The way in which this can be done becomes clear when one recognizes that there are two basic inputs necessary in any effective information system. The first can be called *major determinants*. These are factors that play a role in structuring the type of information management will be receiving. According to Zani, these consist of opportunities and risks, company strategy, company structure, management and decision-making processes, available technology, and available information sources.[2] The roles of these determinants will become more evident in the next section when an information system blueprint is examined.

The second input consists of *key success variables*. These are factors and tasks that determine success or failure. They will differ, of course, from company to company and from industry to industry:

For a consumer goods company manufacturing nondifferentiated products, the key success areas might be product promotion and understanding customer responses to product, marketing, and competitive changes.

---

[1]Walter J. Kennevan, "Mis Universe," *Data Management,* September 1970, p. 63.
[2]William M. Zani, "Blueprint for MIS," *Harvard Business Review,* November–December 1970, p. 96.

For a manufacturer of commodity products, manufacturing and distribution cost control and efficiency might be the major determinants of success.[3]

THE BLUEPRINT ITSELF.   The well-designed management information system blueprint brings together these determinants and key success variables, since all these factors are interrelated. For example, the general business environment (opportunities and risks) and the company resources (men, money, machines, material, and information) help establish overall strategy. In turn, this strategy serves as a basis for development of the organization structure. All four of these factors are related to the organization's key success variables. This interrelationship is schematically illustrated in Figure 10–3.

Blueprint brings key success variables together.

As just noted, the organization is structured to include three levels of managers, all of whom will be needing information vital for decision making. Those at the upper levels will be greatly interested in major developments in the external and internal arenas that will have an impact on the organization's strategic plan. Those at the middle level will need information that will help them coordinate the activities of upper and lower levels. Individuals at the lower levels will require data related to the production of goods and services. In designing the information-decision system for each level, primary attention must be focused on the relevance of the data to decision making.

The information required at the top levels will be very general in nature, forming the basis for strategic planning decisions. These include setting objectives, designing the organization structure, and choosing new product lines. At the intermediate levels the data will need to be somewhat more specific. It will include information useful for activities such as formulating budgets, planning working capital, and measuring, appraising, and improving management performance. At the lower levels the data will have to be very specific and might even be programmed through the use of mathematical models and techniques. It will include

---

[3]*Ibid.*, p. 98.

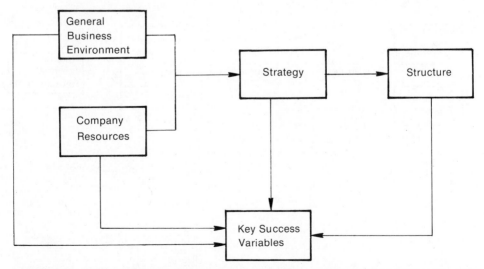

FIGURE 10–3 A Partial Information Systems Blueprint (Adapted from William M. Zani, "Blueprint for MIS," *Harvard Business Review*, November-December 1970, pp. 96–97.)

information on things such as production scheduling, inventory control, and the measurement, appraisal, and improvement of worker efficiency.

Working with these information requirements, the organization will develop an overall information system design, which will remain in operation for as long as it is useful. However, with new sources of information developing all the time, new information requirements springing up among the managers, and information technology continually changing, the system will have to be revamped periodically. Nevertheless, employing just the information in this section, it is possible to extend Figure 10–3 and develop a total information system blueprint as seen in Figure 10–4.

Decision-making information will differ by level.

It should be noted that the design not only gives primary emphasis to information system determinants and key success variables but also is structured with the needs of management in mind. It follows a "from the top down" philosophy. This is important, for as Zani notes:[4]

> If the design of management information systems begins on a high conceptual level and on a high managerial level as well, a company can avoid the unfortunate "bottom up" design phenomenon of recent history and begin to develop the real, and very great, potential of MIS as a tool for modern management.

In recent years many firms have begun employing management information systems. The benefits offered by such systems make them very valuable management tools.

INFORMATION SYSTEMS AND THE QUANTITATIVE SCHOOL

A cursory analysis of information systems might leave one wondering why the quantitative school advocates get involved in designing information systems. After all, up to now we have seen their interests as resting heavily in the area of mathematical formulas. In the last two decades, however, computers have begun to play a major role in organizational life. The initial interest of the quantitative theorists in the computer was for calculation purposes. Many of the tools discussed in the previous chapter are used in conjunction with the computer. By having prepackaged com-

---

[4]Zani, *op. cit.*, p. 100.

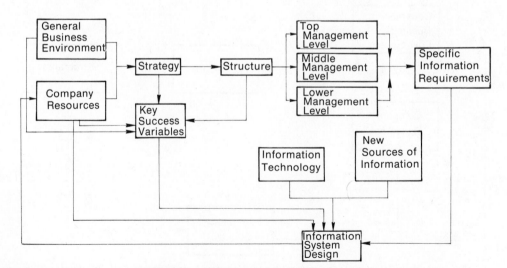

FIGURE 10–4 Total Information System Blueprint

puter programs for handling EOQ, linear programming, queuing theory, and Monte Carlo simulation problems, the quantitative theorists can often save themselves hundreds of hours of work time.

As computers became more commonplace in industry, individuals who were trained to program these machines and provide management with the output started to emerge. In addition to computer programmers, systems analysts also arrived on the scene. Although their emphasis is not as quantitative as is the mathematicians', these computer types share common characteristics with today's management scientists. These include: (a) the application of scientific analysis to managerial problems; (b) the goal of improving the manager's decision-making ability; (c) a high regard for economic effectiveness criteria; (d) a reliance on mathematical models; and (e) the use of electronic computers.

Computer and quantitative people have much in common.

Of course, the computer-oriented personnel are far less quantitative than their mathematical counterparts. In fact, in recent years some of them have contended that they are actually members of a fourth school of management — a systems school. The validity of their claims will be addressed in greater detail in Chapter 15. For the moment we want to take a closer look at what these systems people do. We already know that some of them help design information systems. Others work directly with the computer, an area we are now going to investigate. Before doing so, keep in mind that not all information systems are computerized, and the computer can do a lot more than merely solve mathematical equations and provide information for management decision making. However, as Boehm has so well noted:

> The uncertainties of these times have forced a shot-gun marriage between the executive decision maker and the systems analyst. This blending of human intuition, broad and nimble, with mathematical precision backed by the power of the computer, has brought the planning and conduct of business to a high plateau of rationality.
>
> Today more than half the companies in the *Fortune* "500" list have access to computer programs that model the national and world economies as integrated systems and that can be manipulated mathematically, thereby relating company policy and performance to many important economic factors. Many other companies, large and small, subscribe to such systems analysis models through their bankers or consultants.[5]

The past three decades have seen the entry of automation into business enterprises. Webster defines *automation* as "the technique of making an apparatus (as a calculating machine), a process (as of manufacturing) or a system (as of bookkeeping) operate automatically."[6] In broad terms, there have been four main areas of automation development: (1) automatic machinery; (2) integrated materials handling and processing equipment; (3) control mechanisms; and (4) electronic computers and data-processing machines. The fourth category, in particular computers, will be the center of focus here because of the role they are playing in the area of information systems.

INFORMATION SYSTEMS AND COMPUTERS

Modern computers are of two general types: *analog* and *digital*. The analog computer is a measuring machine used principally by engineers in

Modern Computers

---

[5]George A. W. Boehm, "Shaping Decisions With Systems Analysis," *Harvard Business Review*, September–October 1976, p. 91.
[6]*Webster's Third New International Dictionary*, volume 1 (Chicago: Encyclopedia Britannica, 1968), p. 148.

Computers are of
two types: ana-
log and digital.

solving job-related problems. The digital computer is a counting machine which, by electrical impulses, can perform arithmetic calculations at a speed far in excess of human capacity and for this reason is of great value to business firms.

The basic concept of the digital computer dates back hundreds of years. However, Charles Babbage, the English mathematician and mechanician, is regarded as the originator of the modern automatic computer. In 1834 he conceived the principle of the analytical engine, which was similar to the modern-day computer in that it would handle a large number of variables that could be fed into the machine on punched cards.

Today, of course, with the advent of the electronic computer, Babbage's concept has been developed in far greater depth than he ever imagined. Over the last thirty years, four generations of electronic computers have emerged and a fifth is on the horizon. The first relied on vacuum tubes and magnetic drums, the second on solid state devices and drum or magnetic cores, and the third on solid logic, technology, and monolithic integrated circuits. Fourth-generation computers, often referred to as "information handlers," are more versatile and powerful than any of their predecessors:

Computer power
has increased
dramatically.

> Perhaps the single most important overall achievement of fourth-generation computers is their ability to maintain a great volume of an organization's recorded information; thus the term "the information handlers." Company officials are now in a position to have direct access to authorized personnel resources, to schedule various production and inventory problems, and to perform information acquisition routines efficiently. Since all relevant information is available, any problems related to user inquiries can be handled on demand.
>
> The . . . reshuffling and maintenance of information have implications for management in general. For example, in the past it has been traditional that tactical decisions on unresolved critical issues be made at the company's headquarters or by executives using subjective judgment based on experience. Now the "information handler's" ability to provide any authorized manager at any time all the relevant information he needs is gradually increasing the managerial dependence on "live" information acquired directly on the spot for objective judgment and is resulting in more effective decision making.[7]

In addition, there has been the introduction of "time sharing," whereby a number of people can use the computer at the same time and encounter no delay in receiving results.

The future promises even more dramatic breakthroughs. For example, Awad reports that fifth generation computers "are expected to fully operationalize forecasting and other predictive models and make it possible for systems to interact among themselves for efficiency of data exchange."[8]

These computers will also be able to provide electronic funds transfer systems between banks and other financial institutions, so that money can be automatically removed from one bank and deposited in another.

Additionally, middle managers will find that they are able to use these computers in proceeding with planning and analysis of relevant problem areas without having to wait for clearance from the upper levels. Thus the computer holds great promise as a management decision-making tool.

---

[7]Elias M. Awad, *Introduction to Computers in Business*, (Englewood Cliffs, N.J.: Prentice-Hall, Inc., 1977), p. 76.
[8]*Ibid.*, p. 77.

Despite the development of new features, the fundamental elements of the computer have remained basically the same: input, processing, and output. First the data are fed into the computer. This generally takes the form of punched cards, magnetic tape, or some kind of printed document. Then the material is processed, with the computer coordinating material, making computations on data, or working out logical decisions. Finally, the material is translated into output. This often takes the form of printed material, punched cards, or a picture displayed on a screen. Since the computer can perform these operations in a fraction of the time it would take to complete them manually, it has become an important management tool. However, it is necessary to realize that a computer will only do what it is programmed to do.

The fundamental elements of the computer have remained the same.

Computer Programming

The computer program provides the machine with the step-by-step directions it is to follow. This program is usually fed into the computer on punched cards or, if it is going to be used over and over again, stored on tape or disk and called into action by the operator. Generally these programs are written in computer language. Two of the more common are FORTRAN (FORmula TRANslation), which is designed for scientific work, and COBOL (Common Business Oriented Language), which is used for business programs.

If the program is to be executed properly, it is often useful first to construct a flow chart of the operation. This chart can then be translated into computer language. Figure 10–5 illustrates the flow diagram used by an investor who is pondering the purchase of a new stock. The individual has certain prerequisites which all new stocks must meet. First, they must be listed on the New York Stock Exchange. Second, their price/earnings ratio must be under ten. Third, the current price must not be within 80 per cent of its annual high. If these three conditions are met and there are sufficient funds available in the bank or brokerage accounts, the investor will buy the stock. If not, the individual will evaluate the wisdom of taking a bank loan to buy the stock. Otherwise, the investor will compare the new stock with those in his or her present portfolio. If it appears to be a better buy than any of those currently there, the individual will sell these issues and purchase as many shares of the new stock as possible with the proceeds.

A flow diagram helps the programmer see the logic of the instructions. Anyone who has ever done any programming can attest to the fact that the machine operates like a moron; virtually nothing can be taken for granted (although the latest computers have a little flexibility along these lines). The computer will reject a program that lacks explicit instructions. Furthermore, a program deck that has run countless times will occasionally be rejected as erroneous because one of the cards is worn and cannot be read properly. This can result in hours of work and frustration as one searches for the error only to realize that a card merely has to be duplicated.

On the positive side, however, computer programming teaches logic. Since the computer has no mind of its own, the programmer must proceed slowly and accurately. When the machine rejects a program as illogical, the individual, despite all his or her work, knows that the flow diagram is erroneous; something has been omitted or one part of the diagram is nonsensical. There are times, of course, when the computer will miss a card, and if the program is fed in again, the desired output will be obtained. However, these are exceptional cases. When the machine rejects a program, it is almost always the programmer's error.

Computer programming teaches logic.

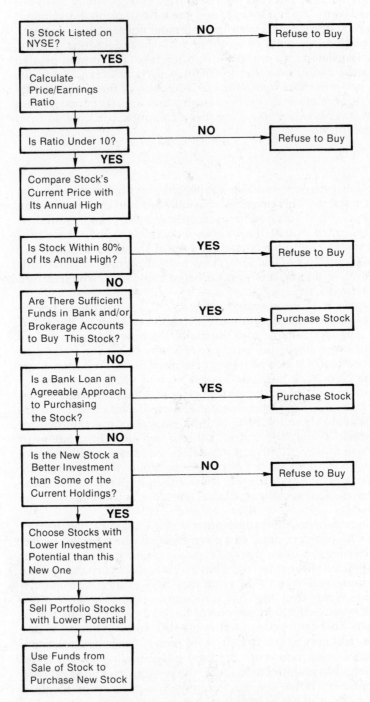

FIGURE 10–5   Stock Investor's Flow Diagram

The computer has many uses, from handling routine paperwork to providing information for top-level decision making. The most common uses are the routine ones. Most companies employ the computer to perform arithmetic and bookkeeping functions such as processing the payroll, computing customer account balances, or processing stockholder lists. During this decade it is highly likely that much of this routine paperwork still being handled by clerks will also be computerized.

Computer Uses

One type of paperwork seriously being considered for computerization is that of handling stock certificates. Today, the purchaser of stock is issued a certificate. When the person sells the security, the certificate must be turned over to the new buyer. However, since some stockholders will buy and sell a stock in the same day, it may be some time before the certificate ever gets to its rightful owner. Eliminating the use of certificates and putting all this information on a computer could result in far more accurate record keeping.

One of the widest uses of the computer is for *inventory control.* In retail stores, for example, it is common to find small coded tickets attached to all merchandise. When the items are sold, the tickets are torn off and sent to a central locale where the data are either placed on punched cards or read directly into the computer. In this way, the number of units on hand can be determined on a day to day basis and more inventory can be ordered at the appropriate time. Recently, some firms have automated their operations even further and, via machines on the sales floor, can report transactions directly to the computer for inventory purposes.

Inventory control.

Another major application of the computer is in making *airline reservations.* This is an illustration of what is known as "real time." The computer is relating what is going on as it is happening. In the case of reservations, the airline clerk feeds the information into a central computer via a console. The computer in turn scans its memory, reports whether there are any seats available on the desired flight, and automatically sends back a confirmation while simultaneously reducing the number of available seats.

Airline reservations.

Another approach that is gaining in popularity is that of the *data bank.* Information on a subject is fed into the computer memory, thereby creating a bank of data. In this way, individuals with questions on this subject can obtain ready answers. Airlines use this concept in regard to scheduled flights and departure times. For example, a man in San Francisco has business in Chicago on Friday. He then wants to go on to New York. What is the earliest flight he can catch after 6 P.M. on Friday that will take him to Kennedy International? The agent in San Francisco will probably not know since the person seldom handles Chicago to New York requests, but the airline will have this standard information in the computer so the agent can readily get it for the passenger. Some insurance companies use the data bank as a depository for all insurance policies. Agents seeking answers to policyholder questions can obtain, through telecommunications, up-to-date responses. Other firms feed personnel information into the data bank, including statistics such as salaries, work experience, educational background, and performance appraisals. In this way, they can obtain an immediate profile of an individual being considered for promotion or a list of personnel with a particular skill or training.[9] In the case of IBM, managers can obtain information on business activities in their own particular regions:

Data banks.

---

[9]See, for example, James W. Walker, Fred Luthans, and Richard M. Hodgetts, "Who Really Are the Promotables?" *Personnel Journal,* February 1970, pp. 123–127.

A marketing manager, for example, addresses the computer with a code number that identifies him and his responsibilities. When he inquires about the state of his business, the system displays on a screen a preanalyzed report on marketing activities in his particular region. Thus the user gets the information he needs but nothing more.[10]

Automatic bank tellers.

Another computer application that is gaining acceptance is the *automatic bank teller*. Today, in certain parts of the country, an individual can obtain money from a bank-teller machine after hours or on weekends by means of a special credit card. By placing this card in the machine, which is hooked up to a computer, and entering through a keyboard the personal identification code number and the amount he or she wishes to withdraw, the customer will automatically receive a packet of money and a coded receipt.[11] Furthermore, if the supply of funds allocated to the automatic teller begins to run low because of excessive withdrawals, the computer will alert a bank manager who can come down and make more money available. In addition, the computer-run machine is capable of receiving deposits, transferring funds from checking to savings (and vice versa), and accepting time-credit loan payments.

SIMULATION. In recent years, computers have also been employed to handle "what if" questions. By simulating a situation, the manager can plug in different decisions and evaluate the outcome of each:

If, say, the manager enters the price, the expected volume, and certain budgetary decisions, the computer will provide a pro forma profit and loss statement for that item. The judgment of the manager is used to suggest alternatives for consideration. The power of the computer is used to carry out the manager's understanding of the quantitative relationships between inputs and outputs—e.g., prices, volumes, and annual profits. The judgment of the manager is . . . called on to determine if the answer is acceptable or if further trials should be made to secure data or judgments which may produce a more acceptable output.[12]

Computer simulations.

The key to the successful use of the computer in this instance is determined by how well the company has been able to simulate actual conditions. If the model is accurate, the information being fed back to the manager is reliable; if not, the data upon which the individual is basing the decision is worthless.

A number of firms have been moving toward the use of computer simulation in helping managers make decisions. In addition to the effect of price on quantity, other typical "what if" questions include:

If a proposed new item of equipment is purchased or leased, what will be the effects on profits and cash flow of alternative financing methods?
If a wage increase is granted, what will be the effect on production rates, use of overtime, risk of seasonal inventory, and so on, for a production program?[13]

The questions, along with the assumptions made by the simulation designer and/or manager, are fed into the computer and evaluated according to the probability of their occurrence. The answer is then printed out in whatever form is desired, e.g., rate of return, cost analysis, balance sheet, income statement. Figure 10–6 provides a general illustration.

---

[10]Boehm, *op. cit.*, p. 96.
[11]Currently, in most places, withdrawals are limited to a maximum of $150 a day.
[12]Curtis H. Jones, "At Last: Real Computer Power for Decision Makers," *Harvard Business Review*, September–October 1970, p. 79.
[13]James B. Boulden and Elwood S. Buffa, "Corporate Models: On-Line, Real-Time Systems," *Harvard Business Review*, July–August 1970, p. 67.

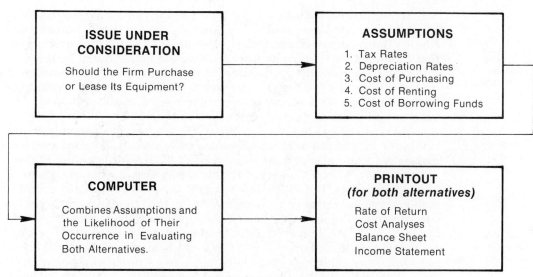

FIGURE 10–6   Simulation of a Purchase Vs. Lease Strategy

In addition, some firms have developed models that help them make decisions when some particular problem develops. Consider the following:

At 9:32 A.M., a blowout! A blast furnace breaks down in the steel plant. Cold iron will have to be heated to produce the molten iron normally supplied to the refining process from this furnace. Processing time will be almost doubled, reducing the shop's production capacity by 60%. The cost per ton of steel will certainly rise sharply as a result of the increased processing time. But how much will it rise?

Using a remote time-shared computer terminal in his office, a manager at Island Steel Company defines the new conditions resulting from the equipment failure and enters them in a set of models which simulate the steelmaking process and the costs involved. At 11:26 A.M.—less than two hours later, the same morning—he estimates the new cost figures and prepares a revised corporate profit projection . . . the computer has vastly enhanced his decision-making capability.[14]

Thus, the computer has proved to be a valuable tool for management decision making. However, there are some very important drawbacks which also merit consideration.

The most common argument raised against computers is that they are expensive investments which are never fully utilized. However, many managers, determined to have the latest, most sophisticated equipment, allow themselves to be sold more hardware than they really need. Zipf points out that, "We have seen over the past 12 years some incredible blunders. Twinkling lights, spinning tapes, and pastel cabinets seem to have a mesmerizing effect on some managers. In a pell-mell rush to be among the first to play with a new toy, enormous sums have been wasted."[15]

Drawbacks to Computers

Expensive play toys.

---

[14]*Ibid.*, p. 65.

[15]A. R. Zipf, "The Computer's Role in the 'Dividends or Disaster' Equation," *Computers and Management*, The 1967 Leatherbee Lectures (Boston: Harvard Business School, 1967) as found in "Retaining Mastery of the Computer," *Harvard Business Review*, September–October 1968, p. 70.

Second, managers have a habit of overrating computer results, failing to remember that the output is only as valid as the input. Luthans and Koester, for example, conducted an experiment in which they determined that individuals with no computer training are more willing to abide by information presented in computer printout form than in noncomputer printout form and vice versa. In short, people who lack a computer background are often awed by computer results and assign to them a validity and reliability that is not actually justified.[16]

Overrating computer information.

Third, managers tend to overrate the capabilities of the computer. In reality the limitations of the machine are quite severe, but many decision makers see these machines as characterized by HAL, the on-board computer in *2001: A Space Odyssey*.[17] Highly sophisticated, HAL is capable of phenomenal feats. In fact, he can virtually think like a human. Unfortunately, there is an error in his program but, being humanlike, he fights for survival and kills most of the crew before he is finally deprogrammed and rendered harmless. In reality, HAL is still very much a concept. As Dreyfus noted in his now-famous Rand Corporation memo, *Alchemy and Artificial Intelligence*, although there have been some promising beginnings, since then there has been no significant progress made by computers in areas such as translation, musical composition, theorem proving, and chess playing. In fact, digital computers cannot replicate fringe consciousness (an awareness of cues in the environment), conduct essence-accident discrimination (the ability to separate necessary from incidental characteristics), or handle ambiguity tolerance (a willingness to deal with variables that are not precisely defined but are useful to the problems at hand).[18] Although these attributes are essential to decision making, they continue to remain outside the realm of current computer capability.

Overrating computer capability.

In fact, many of the promises made about the computer, outside the sphere of computational work, have simply not materialized. Jones reports that, with the possible exception of logistics, the current trend is actually away from, not toward, computerized management decision making. Companies such as Western Electric, Hughes Aircraft, and Fairfield Manufacturing have all, to varying degrees, followed this retrenchment approach, shifting all or part of the decision-making functions from the computer to staff members. Of course, other companies are moving in the opposite direction, but the point is that the computer is only a management *tool* and not a replacement for the human decision maker. Alter has made the following observation along these lines:

> . . . My findings show what other researchers have reported: applications are being developed and used to *support* the manager responsible for making and implementing decisions, rather than to *replace* him. In other words, people in a growing number of organizations are using what are often called decision support systems to improve their managerial effectiveness.[19]

As long as managers are aware of what the computer cannot do, they are in a good position to evaluate its use in the decision-making process.

---

[16]Fred Luthans and Robert Koester, "The Impact of Computer Generated Information on the Choice Activities of Decision Makers," *Academy of Management Journal*, June 1976, pp. 328–332.

[17]Arthur C. Clarke, *2001: A Space Odyssey* (New York: The New American Library, Inc., 1968).

[18]Jones, *op. cit.*, p. 78.

[19]Steven L. Alter, "How Effective Managers Use Information Systems," *Harvard Business Review*, November–December 1976, p. 97.

A well designed information system can provide the manager with all of the information necessary to make effective decisions. However, since this decision process takes place at every level of the organization, it is inevitable that information systems will have an impact on the personnel. Before discussing the effects of such systems on organization members, it is important to note how the quantitative school overlaps that of the management process and behavioral areas. The quantitative people provide information useful in planning and controlling operations, two areas of key importance to the process school. Additionally, however, the quantitative people sometimes create behavioral problems among the personnel who feel threatened by new information systems and the introduction of computer facilities. The following sections examine the link between the quantitative and behavioral schools by studying the impact of change brought on by information systems.

INFORMATION SYSTEMS AND PEOPLE

Whenever change is introduced into an organization, there is a chance that it will result in dysfunctional behavior. Quite simply, change tends to frighten people, and the greater the change the more likely the personnel will resist or employ defense mechanisms of one form or another.

How is the introduction of a new information system received by organization personnel? Often it is seen as a more efficient information tool and is welcomed. However, because of the changes it brings, it is sometimes viewed by employees as a threat and can result in the development of frustration or anxiety. The response, of course, will depend on the situation. What one must realize is that like all other changes introduced into the system, information systems can cause behavioral problems.

INFORMATION SYSTEMS AND THE IMPACT OF CHANGE

FACTORS CAUSING DYSFUNCTIONAL BEHAVIOR.   Research indicates that when an information system is introduced into the organization five major factors can cause dysfunctional behavior.[20]

First, the new system often necessitates redefinition of departmental boundaries. Some people are going to be transferred to other departments; others end up staying in their present unit but are given new or expanded duties. In either case these changes, even though they may bring about greater operating efficiency, can cause employee resistance because they upset the status quo in the formal organization structure.

Second, there may be an accompanying effect on the informal structure. "An organization tends to develop a system of values, ethical codes, taboos, special working relations. . . . The impact of a new system on the informal structure can be as serious in terms of creating behavioral disturbances as the impact on the formal structure."[21]

Third, some people, especially older ones with many years of company service, often see the development as threatening. They believe the new system will replace them.

Fourth, in many organizations change is introduced without proper consideration of the opinions, fears, or anxieties of the personnel. When this happens, the management information system faces trouble from the very start.

Fifth, and closely related to the above factor, is the method of introducing change. McGregor has noted that, "A fair amount of research

New information systems can cause dysfunctional behavior.

---

[20]G. W. Dickson and John K. Simmons, "The Behavioral Side of MIS," *Business Horizons,* August 1970, pp. 59–71.
[21]*Ibid.,* p. 61.

has pointed up the fact that resistance to change is a reaction primarily to certain methods of instituting change rather than an inherent human characteristic."[22] Of course, these are not the only types of dysfunctional behavior. They are, however, the most common and can result in a host of frustration reactions.

FRUSTRATION REACTIONS. When one or more of the above factors is present, the personnel may encounter frustration. This frustration can manifest itself in many ways. The three general patterns most often associated with the introduction of a new information system are aggression, projection, and avoidance. To bring all of this together, consider the case of a company that installs a new system and, in the process, redefines departmental boundaries and breaks up an informal organization. How do the members of the informal group respond to the situation? Using a needs-satisfaction approach, Figure 10–7 provides an illustration.

Aggression is an attack (physical or nonphysical) against the object believed to be causing the problem. Sometimes this takes the form of sabotage. More commonly it occurs when people try to "beat the system." The following is an example:

> The setting was an information system in a complex organization designed to collect man-hours in different work stations on a daily basis. Workers were frequently rotating from one work station to another during the day, and were supposed to clock in and out each time they moved from one station to another. During the course of an interview, one worker indicated that there had been some "ganging up" on an unpopular foreman. Workers would not punch out of a particular area when leaving for another work station or would punch in at the unpopular foreman's area and then work in a different area.[23]

Marginal note: Common frustration reactions include aggression, projection, and avoidance.

---

[22]Douglas McGregor, "The Scanlon Plan Through a Psychologist's Eyes," in C. A. Walker, ed., *Technology, Industry and Man* (New York: McGraw-Hill Book Company, 1968), p. 124.
[23]Dickson and Simmons, *op. cit.,* p. 62.

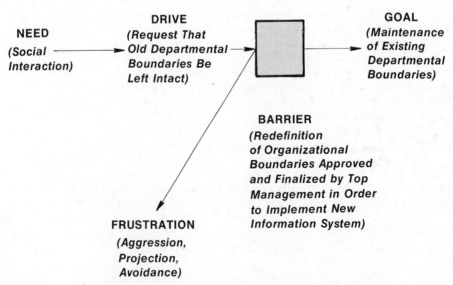

FIGURE 10–7   Frustration Created by a New Information System (Format adapted from Fred Luthans, *Organizational Behavior,* 2nd edition, New York, McGraw-Hill Book Company, 1977, p. 386.)

Projection occurs when people blame something (or someone) for their own shortcomings. For example, certain managers are incompetent, but claim that with the new information systems they are not receiving sufficient information for making effective decisions.

Avoidance takes place when people withdraw from a situation because it is too frustrating for them. This can occur in regard to an information system in which, for example, managers find they can receive the same information in less time from a different source, so they ignore the system's output.

THE ORGANIZATION AND INFORMATION SYSTEMS.   Thus far the negative aspects of information systems on the organization have been examined in general terms. In order to make a more specific analysis, however, it is necessary to consider the impact of such systems on four distinct subgroups in the hierarchy. These are operating personnel, operating management, technical staff, and top management.[24] Each will respond differently.

The *operating personnel* consists of two basic groups, nonclerical and clerical. The nonclerical people perform functions such as filling out forms or entering prepunched cards in a source recorder. When an organization computerizes and/or puts in a new information system, these people often feel threatened. Although some turn to minor sabotage such as "forgetting" to do certain things or making deliberate mistakes, most employ projection. The system is blamed for everything that goes wrong in the office.

Clerical workers are concerned principally with processing input and converting it into output, and they are considered part of the information system itself. Changes in their work patterns may entail moving them from a manual to an electronic data processing (EDP) system, for example. Although some people may be displaced, most are maintained on greatly upgraded jobs which require more education and formal training. Initially, however, these workers react negatively because they believe they are going to be replaced. Like their nonclerical counterparts, they adopt a projection type of behavior and start blaming the new system for any mistakes that occur.

Operating management consists of all management personnel from first line supervisors up to and including middle management. These individuals receive much of the output from information systems. However, these systems also tend to centralize decision making and increase control of higher-level managers over their subordinates. As a result, when these operating managers fight the system, they do so by providing inadequate support to it and by failing to use the decision-making information provided by it. In so doing, they employ aggression, avoidance, and projection.

The *technical staff*, consisting of programmers and systems designers, is most involved with the information system. For this reason, it exhibits none of the common dysfunctional behavior patterns. On the other hand, the technical staff does not get along well with the operating management people. There seems to be a natural clash between the system designers (technical staff) and the system users (operating managers).

Top management is little affected by new information systems. Research shows that many top executives just do not get involved in designing the corporate information system. Some may attend short computer

Organization subgroups respond differently.

---

[24]*Ibid.*, pp. 63–67.

TABLE 10–1   **Causes for Resistance to Information Systems (by working groups)**

	Operating (nonclerical)	Operating (clerical)	Operating Management	Top Management
Threats to economic security		X	X	
Threats to status or power		X	X*	
Increased job complexity	X		X	X
Uncertainty or unfamiliarity	X	X	X	X
Changed interpersonal relations or work patterns		X*	X	
Changed superior-sub-ordinate relationships		X*	X	
Increased rigidity or time pressure	X	X	X	
Role ambiguity		X	X*	X
Feelings of insecurity		X	X*	X*

X = The reason is possibly the cause of resistance to Information System development.
X* = The reason has a strong possibility of being the cause of resistance.

Source: G. W. Dickson and John K. Simmons, "The Behavioral Side of MIS," *Business Horizons*, August 1970, p. 68. Reprinted with permission.

courses in order to obtain background information in the area, and many pay lip service to the value of such systems in effective decision making. Most executives, however, are unconcerned with the area. The reasons for resistance (by work group) are explained in greater depth in Table 10–1.

However, it should be noted that while this section has examined the behavioral effects of information systems with primary emphasis on some of the dysfunctional aspects, this does *not* have to be the situation. Many of these frustration reactions can be prevented if management: (a) works closely with the affected units, training them to understand and accept the new system by pointing out the benefits to the company, while ensuring that any displaced personnel will be given jobs elsewhere in the organization; (b) designs the system with cogent inputs from all affected groups so that information from the system is both timely and useful; and (c) attains top management support from the very beginning. There are many advantages to be gained from a management information system and a firm can obtain them if it is aware of the potential problems and pitfalls associated with the establishment of such a system. More will be said about the behavior of individuals in organizations, starting in the next part of the book, when the behavioral school is examined.

SUMMARY   In this chapter two topics have been examined: information systems and the computer. Although many information systems are computerized, this is not universally true. Nevertheless, the two areas have one common characteristic: they help interrelate the departments and units of the organization into a harmonious system.

The primary goal of any information system is to provide decision-making information to the manager. For this reason, a well designed system must be planned with the needs of management in mind and must follow a "from the top down" philosophy. In addition, the system must discriminate by organization level, providing the right kinds of information to each. For example, top management will need general information from which they can formulate strategic plans. Middle management will need more specific data for drawing up budgets and measuring and appraising managerial performance. Lower-level management will need very specific data for use in areas such as production scheduling and inventory control.

The modern computer is often employed as part of an information system, providing necessary information to managers throughout the hierarchy. In addition to performing bookkeeping and arithmetic functions, it is also being used, for example, for inventory control and airline reservations. Another one of its latest applications is answering "what if" questions through simulation.

Despite their great value, computers have some important drawbacks of which management must be aware. First, many companies tend to buy a more complex computer than they need. Second, many managers place too much faith in computer printout results. Third, many managers tend to overrate the capabilities of the computer. There are a large number of things man still does much better than any machine and qualitative decision making is one of them.

The introduction of an information system can bring about dysfunctional behavior such as aggression, projection and avoidance. In order to overcome these problems, management must be willing to adopt a participative decision-making approach that introduces the new system, relates its advantages to the personnel, and assures that if any people are replaced because of it, employment will be secured for them elsewhere.

In this chapter we have done more than merely discuss information systems and the role of the computer. We have also noted how these systems help the managers do a better job of planning and controlling, thereby establishing the fact that there is a link between the quantitative and process schools. Likewise, we have noted that information systems can bring about dysfunctional behavior, illustrating in the process that any advocate of the quantitative school must also be aware of the behavioral side of enterprise. There is thus a link between quantitative and behavioral schools.

In the next chapter we will begin a more systematic analysis of this behavioral school and the ways in which its concepts can be used by the modern manager. We will start by studying the communication process.

---

1. What is a management information system? Explain.

2. Exactly what is the primary objective in the design of an effective information system?

3. What role should information system determinants and key success variables play in an information system design?

4. How does the modern computer differ from its early counterpart? What new technological changes have occurred? What new ones can be expected in the next decade?

REVIEW AND STUDY QUESTIONS

5. Why is the computer program so important to the processing of computerized data?

6. What are four common uses of the computer? Explain.

7. How is the computer being employed in answering "what if" questions? Give an illustration.

8. What are the basic drawbacks to the use of computers?

9. What are the three common dysfunctional forms of behavior often associated with the introduction of a new management information system? Explain each.

10. According to recent research, how do the operating personnel tend to oppose the introduction of an information system? The operating management? The technical staff? The top management?

11. In what ways do information systems provide a bridge between the quantitative school and the process school? The quantitative school and the behavioral school?

SELECTED REFERENCES

Alter, S. L. "How Effective Managers Use Information Systems," *Harvard Business Review,* November–December 1976, pp. 97–104.

Awad, E. M. *Introduction to Computers in Business.* Englewood Cliffs, N.J.: Prentice-Hall, Inc., 1977.

Boehm, G. A. W. "Shaping Decisions with Systems Analysis." *Harvard Business Review,* September–October 1976, pp. 91–99.

Boulden, J. B., and E. S. Buffa. "Corporate Models: On-Line, Real-Time Systems." *Harvard Business Review,* July–August 1970, pp. 65–83.

Burnett, G. J., and R. L. Nolan. "At Last, Major Roles for Minicomputers." *Harvard Business Review,* May–June 1970, pp. 148–156.

Clarke, A. C. *2001: A Space Odyssey.* New York: The New American Library, Inc., 1968.

Dickson, G. W., and J. K. Simmons. "The Behavioral Side of MIS." *Business Horizons,* August 1970, pp. 59–71.

Field, G. A. "Behavioral Aspects of the Computer." *MSU Business Topics,* Autumn 1970, pp. 27–33.

Gallagher, G. A. "Perceptions of the Value of a Management Information System." *Academy of Management Journal,* March 1974, pp. 46–55.

Hay, L. E. "What Is an Information System?" *Business Horizons,* February 1971, pp. 65–72.

Heenan, D. A., and R. B. Addleman. "Quantitative Techniques for Today's Decision Makers." *Harvard Business Review,* May–June 1976, pp. 32–33.

Jones, C. H. "At Last: Real Computer Power for Decision Makers." *Harvard Business Review,* September–October 1970, pp. 75–89.

Luthans, F., and R. Koester. "The Impact of Computer Generated Information on the Choice Activities of Decision Makers." *Academy of Management Journal,* June 1976, pp. 328–332.

Mintzberg, H. "The Myths of MIS." *California Management Review,* Fall 1972, pp. 92–97.

Zani, W. M. "Blueprint for MIS." *Harvard Business Review,* November–December 1970, pp. 95–100.

CASE: SOMEBODY GOOFED[25]

Computers often help organizations by processing information quickly — but unfortunately, not always efficiently. Sometimes the

---

[25]The information in this case can be found in: "When Computers Goof — Consumers Air Their Frustrations," *U.S. News and World Report,* May 2, 1977, pp. 61–62.

computer is programmed incorrectly or is not given the latest information. The result can be frustrating, as seen by the following incidents:

The Social Security Administration's computer notified a New Jersey man of his death and cut off his monthly benefits. It took four months for the man to persuade the local benefits office that he was still alive and that it was his wife who had died.

A woman in the Midwest received a credit card bill for $00.00. She ignored it and began receiving weekly notices about her "unpaid balance." She finally wrote the company a check for $00.00 and the notices stopped. However, she then received a charge for late payment of the bill.

A major hotel in Chicago sent a form letter to past customers thanking them for their patronage and telling them of the hotel's new modernization plan. Unfortunately, the computer programmer requested the wrong mailing list. As a result, hundreds of Chicago housewives opened letters thanking their husbands for patronizing the hotel. Calls then poured into the hotel from husbands demanding an explanation for their wives, who were threatening divorce.

In an effort to prevent such computer goofs, Shell Oil has set up a toll-free telephone line for customers who call about their computerized bills. Corning Glass Works has installed a computer to deal with complaints about the quality and durability of its products. The computer types an individualized letter in response to a consumer's gripe and, if necessary, also triggers an order to a warehouse for a replacement part. In light of such developments, most Americans admit that they never expect to return to an era when most business dealings are on a person to person basis, and believe they will have to live with computer-generated problems.

Questions

1. What are some of the advantages of using computers? Do they outweigh the disadvantages?

2. What does this case relate about the fallibility of computers and computer programmers?

3. Since computers are apparently here to stay, what steps can managers take to prevent incidents such as those described in this case?

CASE: THE OLD WAYS ARE BEST

When the Randler Corporation brought in an outside management consulting firm, it asked them to examine company operations from top to bottom. Return on investment had not been over 6 per cent in three years, and top management felt something had to be done. The company was relying on the consultants to tell them what this should be.

Six weeks later, the consultants submitted their list of recommendations. One of these called for the design of a new management information system. "Managers, at the present time, are relying too heavily on an outdated and ineffective reporting system," read part of the report. "This system should be scrapped and a new one designed from the top down, with major emphasis given to providing up-to-date, relevant data useful for decision making."

The idea sounded fine to the top staff and they ordered the EDP (electronic data processing) department to design a new information system. After talking to people at all levels of the hierarchy and evaluating the current reporting system, the EDP people submitted their proposal. The plan looked fine on paper, and the corporate president ordered it implemented.

Over the next twelve months, however, the company's return on investment failed to reflect any great changes in efficiency. As before, ROI stood below 6 per cent. When top management decided to find out why, one of the areas they examined was the new information system. In essence, they discovered that managers at all levels of the organization were still relying on their old reporting systems. Virtually no one was using any of the data being provided by the new system. When one of the managers was asked why he was not utilizing the new system, he replied, "Why should I? I have my own reporting system and it tells me all I need to know. If you ask me, this whole new information system design was just a waste of money."

Questions

1. What kinds of information should a manager receive from a well designed information system? Explain, incorporating "key success variables" into your answer.

2. What error did the company make in this case?

3. What recommendations are now in order? Explain.

CASE: WHAT IF?[26]

In October, 1969, Inland Steel bought a simulation program from On-Line Decisions, Inc., a computer software firm in Berkeley, California. With this model the steelmaker was able to simulate its annual profit and profit plan and make a five-year profit projection. In describing the usefulness of the program, Inland's comptroller explained, "You can test the effect of changing several variables at once. Calculating the effect of a change in scrap prices, for example, used to take as long as 12 manweeks. Now we can do it in minutes." In addition, the company was using the model to assist in top-level decision making in areas such as market research, budgeting, product profitability, cash flow, works accounting, facilities planning, corporate planning, and financial staff support.

In describing the model, James Boulden, president of On-Line and a developer of the simulation, said:

The model works best for manufacturing companies.... It's not well suited for use by a distribution organization with a huge inventory because of the large data storage costs... use of the broad based simulator wouldn't be economical.... "The model is also better for a large volume or

---

[26]The data in this case can be found in: "Pass the Simulation," *Industry Week*, March 23, 1970, pp. 47–48.

process type company rather than a job shop, but we could do it. It's also much better for planning purposes than process control. Clients typically work on annual, monthly, or even weekly projections. We want to get this down to daily use."

Commenting on its success in developing and selling these models, Mr. Boulden explained that the company currently had twenty clients, ranging in size from $500 million to $2 billion in sales. He predicted that "by the end of this year, one out of ten of the top 500 manufacturing companies will be our customers."

Questions

1. How valuable can these simulation models be in providing information for managerial decision making?

2. What are the drawbacks to this approach? Explain.

3. Do you think the future will see more or less of these computer simulation models? Why?

CASE: DON'T SAY IT'S IN THE MAIL[27]

Over the last twenty years banks have been relying more and more on computers to handle their back-room operations. Recently, however, bank customers have come in contact with these electronic devices. Today nearly 3000 banks are providing their customers with access to funds through more than 5000 automatic tellers. Additionally, the United States Treasury electronically deposits nearly six million checks monthly in the bank accounts of Social Security recipients and active and retired federal employees who get regular government payments.

Some people are predicting that this move toward electronic funds transfer (EFT) systems will eventually result in a "cashless society" since not only can deposits be made electronically but bills can be paid this way as well. The following is an example:

The scene: A typical American living room in the 1980's.

A working couple, whose pay has been deposited electronically in their bank account, sits down at the telephone with the monthly stack of bills.

They type "check" at a keyboard attached to the phone, dial a number, and their bill-paying chore is completed in a few minutes.

The couple then goes to the supermarket. They insert a bank card in a machine and, by electronic signal, their account is charged for the amount of the weekly grocery bill.

One of the big problems with this EFT system, however, is that from now on people will have to have money in their account. No longer will they be able to tell their creditor that their check is "in the mail."

[27]The data in this case can be found in: William J. Eaton, "We'll Have to Find a Different Alibi to Replace 'Check's in Mail' Routine," *The Miami Herald*, June 27, 1977, p. 15–A.

Questions

1. Is the computer really helpful to banking? After all, by making transactions easier, is it not encouraging individuals to spend more money than they would ordinarily? Explain.

2. Do you think this move toward EFT will result in unemployment? After all, will not the computer replace some of the bank tellers and other personnel?

3. What other areas do you think computers will revolutionize during the 1980's? Explain.

COMPREHENSIVE CASE: MINICOMPUTERS AND FRAUD[28]

We are now in the age of the computer. And for those organizations which find that giant computers offer too much and cost too much, it is possible that a minicomputer will prove ideal. In recent years the demand for minis has risen steadily, and sales of these small, relatively inexpensive computers have really taken off. International Data Corporation, a manufacturer of minis, estimates that by 1980 there will be over 500,000 of them in use.

While this is good news for computer makers, it is not good news for auditors, law enforcement agencies, and other groups concerned with computer crime. These people say that the rapid proliferation of minicomputers and their ease of operation by nonspecialist personnel, from a vice president to a secretary, is creating massive new potential for embezzlement and other fraud. Of course, most companies that use minis are trying to take steps to prevent such crimes. However, the number of horror stories that has surfaced in recent years is enough to lead one to conclude that stopping computer fraud is going to be a difficult, if not impossible, task.

For example, not long ago a salesman at a west coast manufacturing firm told a secretary, who operated a minicomputer as part of her duties, to make a seemingly innocuous change in the computer program. The secretary did so without question. What happened as a result of her action was that the computer began to accept orders for the company's goods at a price below a set minimum. The change ordered by the salesman lowered that minimum and allowed him to rack up big sales commissions selling at prices that undercut the competition. In the process, however, the salesman's company lost revenue of $75,000, the difference between the original minimum price and the new sales price. The company accidentally uncovered the lost revenue when the auditor stumbled across the computer program change while checking another transaction.

The above case of abuse is only one of many that have resulted from the widespread availability of minicomputers. Here are a few others:

---

[28]The data is this case can be found in: Hal Lancaster, "Rise of Minicomputers, Ease of Running Them, Facilitate New Frauds," *Wall Street Journal,* October 5, 1977, pp. 1, 35.

Consider, for example, the simple embezzlement arranged by a young junior accountant who ran the minicomputer system of an aerospace company. He was paying himself an extra $1000 a month by creating fictitious employees and having the computer issue checks to them; posing as the "employees," he simply cashed the checks himself. The fraud went undetected for two years, and was uncovered only after a company officer became curious when he noticed some unfamiliar names while glancing through a pile of cancelled checks.

It took a Southern California hospital a year to unearth the finaglings of another young accountant who used his access to its minicomputers in a tax scheme. He ordered the machine to transfer small sums, never more than $4 total per person, from the federal withholding tax accounts of his fellow employees to his own. At the end of the year his W–2 form showed a huge tax deduction that entitled him to a fat refund; his colleagues' forms showed deductions that were only a few dollars less than they should have been. This scheme was discovered only after a hospital janitor, for reasons unknown, added up the tax deductions on all his paychecks for the year and discovered the small discrepancy between that total and the one on his W–2 form.

Many of these computer frauds are discovered either by accident or because the participant starts to get a guilty conscience and decides to confess the crime. However, investigators are concerned about the many schemes that remain undetected because neither of these two events takes place. In fact, admits one investigator, the discovery of some computer crimes is a matter of the wildest luck. For example, a bank employee used a computer to steal over $2.5 million from his bank and went undetected by any bank officer or auditor. The scheme was discovered only when New York City police raided a gambling operation and found that one of the principal clients was the bank employee, who had been betting $30,000 a week on an $11,000 annual salary.

One of the main reasons why fraud is easier with the advent of minis is that lower level employees who are running the machines may be the only ones involved with its operating and functioning. Therefore, if the top executive asks for some information, it is up to the lower level employee to get it; the executive is not likely to take the time to learn how the machine operates. As a result, if the employee decides to start ripping off the company and the executive asks for some information that might expose the fraud, the employee will just tell the boss that "we can't get that type of information with this machine." If the boss accepts that explanation, the fraud may never be uncovered.

Additionally, when a fraud is discovered, many firms are reluctant to admit it, preferring to hush up the entire matter. For example, the salesman who had the secretary change the computer program so that it accepted low-cost bids received a reprimand from the company but was not fired because the firm judged him too valuable to lose. The aerospace concern's accountant was fired after making restitution. The hospital accountant was discharged, but received a favorable recommendation to avoid the possibility of a lawsuit in case he was unable to find another job.

Why do firms keep these frauds quiet? One reason is that they do not want the competition or the board of directors to know what has happened. A second reason is that if other employees find out about it, they just might try to rip off the company themselves. After all, if 500 people a year in a large organization are known to be stealing $10,000 each, there is a strong likelihood that other employees would like to get in on the action.

Some auditing firms are trying to reduce computer fraud by insisting that computer-using clients practice some minimum safeguards, and they may refuse to work for those who do not do so. At the very least, auditing firms advise their clients on the installation of controls. Major firms are also developing their own computer specialists to work with audit teams, and they themselves are making more use of computers in conducting such audits. Yet there is still much to be learned:

. . . Even the most up-to-date auditing and the most rigorous internal controls and security wouldn't stop fraud; no system is foolproof, industry sources maintain, and the real goal is to minimize losses. Says James Fosberg, senior vice president of Microdata Corporation, a minicomputer maker, "If the controller is going to rip off the company, he'll do it with or without a minicomputer. The mini is no different than a manual system or any other computer system. The people who have access to the information have the same ability to perpetrate fraud."

Questions

1. In what ways can minicomputers help organization managers make decisions? What types of decisions would these be? Use the information in Chapter 8 to formulate your answer.

2. With which of the quantitative tools discussed in Chapter 9 would minicomputers be helpful?

3. Why is there the chance of fraud when computers are used? What does your answer reveal about the future of computers in business? Explain.

SECTION D
THE BEHAVIORAL SCHOOL

The goal of this section is to familiarize the reader with some of the basic ideas and concepts of the behavioral school. Of course, to put all behavioral concepts into this school is erroneous, for the management process and management science people also value the importance of human behavior at work. Nevertheless, much of the latest, and most interesting, research conducted in management has been done by behaviorists.

In Chapter 11 the communication process will be examined with major attention given to both interpersonal and organizational communication. Unless managers can communicate with their people, they have no basis for either motivating or leading them. In particular, this chapter will focus on the communication process; some of the common barriers to effective communication; steps for overcoming these barriers; and the need to establish understanding between superiors and subordinates.

Then, in Chapter 12, the subject of motivation will be examined. Initial attention will be placed on the importance of understanding why people act as they do. In addition, some of the basic assumptions managers have about their employees will be reviewed. Then, current research findings designed to help the manager understand workers in general and individuals in particular will be presented.

Next, in Chapter 13, the area of leadership effectiveness will be examined. How does a manager prevail on the subordinates to devote their efforts to attaining organizational goals? In way of answering this question, one-, two- and three-dimensional leadership models will be reviewed. Emphasis will also be placed on the importance of contingency leadership styles.

Finally, in Chapter 14 the area of human resource development will be studied. It was noted earlier that the process school uses the control process to identify problems and take corrective action. The quantitative school uses information feedback systems for the same purpose: namely, identifying problems in the decision-making process and determining the types of information that will be needed to improve the process. Behaviorists, meanwhile, rely on human resource development programs to control the quality of the personnel. If there is faulty communication, poor motivation, or ineffective leadership, they will introduce behaviorally oriented programs tor overcoming these problems. In Chapter 14 some of these human resource programs will be examined.

CHAPTER ELEVEN

INTERPERSONAL AND ORGANIZATIONAL COMMUNICATION

GOALS OF THE CHAPTER

If management entails getting things done through people, communication is the essence of it, for without effective communication no one would know what he or she was supposed to be doing. Nor would there be any basis for answering questions, solving problems, obtaining feedback, or measuring results. The goals of this chapter are to examine interpersonal and organizational communication.

When you have finished reading this chapter you should be able to:

1. Describe the steps in the communication process.
2. Note some of the major barriers to effective communication.
3. Discuss why perception is considered to be the overriding cause of poor communication.
4. Identify the two basic types of communication channels available to the manager.
5. Relate the role of the grapevine in informal organizational communication.
6. Discuss the advantages and limitations of both written and oral communication.
7. Explain how managers can protect their credibility through the use of balance theory.
8. Note some of the major bad listening habits.
9. Illustrate how the ten commandments of good communication can result in more effective management practices.

INTERPERSONAL COMMUNICATION

One of the most important forms of communication is interpersonal communication, which entails the transmission of *meaning* from one person to another.

Communication Process

In the communication process, the sender constructs a message and passes it to the receiver. This individual interprets the message and takes action in a manner satisfactory to the sender.[1]

Many models have been developed to explain the communication process. One of these, formulated by Raymond Ross and presented in Figure 11–1, illustrates the process in complete yet understandable terms. The basic ideas contained in the figure will be developed throughout this chapter.

STEPS IN THE COMMUNICATION PROCESS. The important thing to note is that effective communication requires *both* information and understanding. Unfortunately, too many managers overlook the importance of

---

[1]For an excellent discussion of this topic see David K. Berlo, *The Process of Communication* (New York: Holt, Rinehart & Winston, Inc., 1960).

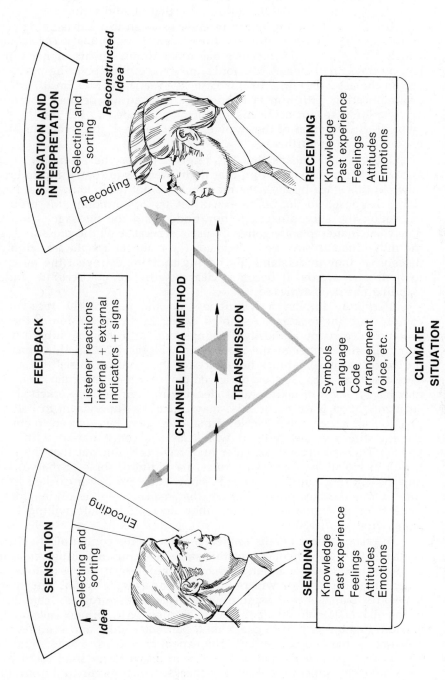

FIGURE 11-1 The Communication Process (From Raymond S. Ross, *Speech Communication: Fundamentals and Practice* © 1965. Reprinted with permission of Prentice-Hall, Inc., Englewood Cliffs, N.J.)

understanding and subscribe to what is known as the *conveyor theory of communication*. Communication is seen as a conveyor that carries messages from one person to another. No real consideration is given to whether the receiver understands or accepts the communiqué. This type of communication is ineffective. Effective communication consists of four steps: attention, understanding, acceptance, and action.

Attention entails getting the receiver to listen to what is being communicated. Quite often this requires overcoming *message competition,* which occurs when the receiver has other things on his or her mind. For example, the listener, Mr. Jones, may have three pressing problems out on the assembly line. In this case, the manager, Ms. Smith, who is communicating with him faces message competition because she must get Mr. Jones to put aside his problems and listen to her for the moment. If the attention of the receiver is not secured, the communication process can go no further.

Understanding means that the receiver grasps the essentials of the message. Many managers find that their attempts to communicate break down at this stage because the receiver does not really know what he or she is supposed to do. Some executives try to surmount this problem by asking the subordinates *if* they understand the message. Unfortunately, such attempts are generally useless because all the pressure is on the individuals to say "yes." Instead, the manager should ask subordinates *what* they understand. By having individuals repeat the message in their own words, it becomes clear whether or not accurate understanding has been achieved.

Acceptance implies a willingness on the part of the receiver to comply with the message. As noted earlier in the discussion of the acceptance theory of authority, feelings and attitudes of subordinates often dictate whether or not something will get done. In this phase of the process it is sometimes necessary for the manager to sell the subordinate on the idea. For example, employees in a particular company may have a habit of taking turns clocking in their fellow workers. Management, upon learning of this, may order the supervisors to halt the practice. However, the lower level managers may be opposed to enforcing the directive, believing it will lead to a confrontation with their people. The department manager may have to point out that the practice is in violation of company rules. In addition, some of the workers may be arriving late because they know they are being clocked in on time. Once the supervisors realize that management is asking for no more than an equitable solution, they may prove more willing to go along with the directive.

The *action* phase entails implementation of the communication. The challenge facing the manager in this stage is seeing that things are done in the agreed upon manner. Sometimes unforeseen delays will occur; other times expediency will require a change in the initial agreement. Unless the manager puts aside time to check on the progress, communication may falter at this point. For example, Mr. Brown calls in his expediter and asks him to check on a particular order and see that it is sent out by the end of the day. The expediter traces the order, finds it, has it filled, packaged, stamped, and sent down to the mail room by 4 P.M. However, unless the manager checks, it may occur to no one that the last mail pickup is at 3:30 P.M., and the order will sit in the mail room until the next day. By making themselves available for assistance and ensuring that proper action is taken on directives, managers can help the communiqué reach this fourth and final phase.

Margin notes:

Many managers use the conveyor theory of communication.

Attention involves getting the receiver to listen.

Understanding means that the receiver comprehends the message.

Acceptance requires a willingness to comply.

Action entails implementation of the communiqué.

Since managers spend approximately 70 per cent of their time receiving and transmitting information, it is vital that they be able to communicate effectively. This calls for a knowledge and understanding of the four steps in the communication process.

There are numerous barriers to effective communication. Some managers may be inadequate; some subordinates may be unreceptive. More commonly, however, both groups are competent in their jobs and are trying to communicate with each other. Why then does communication break down? One barrier has already been examined, namely, message competition. Some of the others include perception, language, status, and resistance to change.

COMMON BARRIERS TO EFFECTIVE COMMUNICATION

The overriding cause of most communication problems is *perception,* which can be defined as a person's view of reality. Since no two people have had the same training and experiences in life, no two see things *exactly* alike. The sender's meaning and the receiver's interpretation are not always identical, but it is not necessary that they be so; it is sufficient if the receiver understands the essence of what is being transmitted. In short, from the sender's point of view, the receiver's comprehension must be satisfactory. To some managers this means that subordinates should be "in the ball park," while to others it means "doing it the way I would have done it."

Perception

Perception can be defined as a person's view of reality.

SENSORY AND NORMATIVE REALITY. The differences in perception can be attributed to the differences in one's conception of reality. *Sensory reality* is physical reality. A chair, a horse, and a car all represent physical reality. When managers and subordinates communicate about physical reality there are few communication problems. Both individuals know what is meant by a chair, a horse, and a car. However, there are times when meanings are not definitive and the receiver of the message may have a different interpretation of the communiqué. This is known as *normative* or interpretive reality. Whenever two individuals discuss matters of personal opinion, for example, there is a good chance of communication breakdown.

Sensory reality is physical reality.

Normative reality is interpretive reality.

Sensory and normative reality can be placed on a continuum such as:

Sensory _____ Normative
Reality   Reality

As one moves from sensory to normative reality, interpretations become increasingly relative. There is no longer any *one* right answer but rather a lot of right answers. Figures 11–2 to 11–6 illustrate this idea graphically. Before reading on, look at the five figures and answer the question accompanying each.

Each of the first three figures has one right answer. In the first, as can be verified by placing a piece of paper along the lower line, alternative "a" is correct. In the next two, neither of the lines running across the diagrams bends in or out; they are all parallel. However, the background design makes it appear as if the first is bending out (Figure 11–3) and the second is bending in (Figure 11–4).

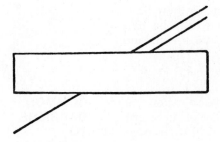

FIGURE 11-2   Using just your eyes, if the line at the bottom of this diagram were drawn through it and emerged at the top, which of these answers would be correct? (a) it would run right into the shorter, lower line at the top; (b) it would run right between the two lines; (c) it would run right into the longer, upper line at the top.

In which of these two diagrams do the two horizontal lines bend in at the ends? In which of the two do the lines bend out at the ends?

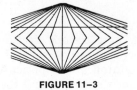

FIGURE 11-3

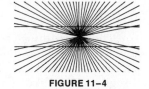

FIGURE 11-4

FIGURE 11-5   What do you see here?

FIGURE 11-6   What do you see here?

The next figure (Figure 11–5) has three common answers. Most people see a bird or a duck with a big beak looking to the left. The second most common response is a body of water surrounded by land with an island in the middle; in the center of the island is a small lake. The "spots" north and south of the island are clouds. The third most frequent response is that it is a picture of a rabbit looking to the right, the bird's beak becoming the rabbit's ears. The author has found that most older people (50 years or more) opt for the lake and the island interpretation. Younger people (20 to 50) see a bird or a duck. Grammar and high school students tend to agree overwhelmingly that it is a rabbit. Naturally, any of these three could be right because the picture is purposefully designed to have more than one possible interpretation.

The final figure (Figure 11–6) receives many different interpretations. Some people see a mask; others believe it is an elephant; still others claim it is burned toast. Another common answer is that it is part of a dock, the ruffles in the upper part representing the rope used in tying up a boat. Still another interpretation is a silhouette of a woman with her hands over her head. Once again, there is no one right answer. Whatever the person sees is what is there. The point to be extracted from this is that some of the messages sent by the manager to the subordinate are similar to these last two figures. What the manager believes he or she said and what the subordinate interprets may be two different things. Too often superiors think their messages fall within the realm of sensory reality, that they are crystal clear. Actually, the messages are interpretive and fall within the realm of normative reality. Figure 11–7 illustrates the different interpretations that are possible from one, supposedly "crystal clear," message.

Language, Logic, and Abstraction

Managers use language as the method of representing their ideas. As such, it is the basis for most communications. Of course, astute managers gear their communiques to the level of their audience through careful word selection and sentence construction. In addition, they employ certain laws of logic such as those advocated by Aristotle. First is the *law of identity* — a house is a house. Second is the *law of the excluded middle* — the object is either a house or it is not a house. Third is the *law of noncontradiction* — something cannot be a house and not a house at the same time. These simple laws of logic relate to communication because they help managers construct and convey messages in a manner that is understandable. Laws of logic reduce confusion.

Aristotelian laws of logic.

Although these laws are helpful, managers still face the problem associated with *abstraction*. Any time something is left out of the message, abstraction occurs. Yet, if managers allowed for no abstraction, they would be spending all their time spelling out their communiqués in detail. This is, of course, impossible. They must assume that if they take care in formulating their message, the subordinates will interpret it the way they want them to. Yet this is not always the case, as seen when the subject of inference is examined.

INFERENCE.   An inference is an assumption made by the listener that may or may not be accurate. Any time a message requires interpretation of the facts, inference enters the picture. The speaker implies and the listener infers. For example, many restaurants have a policy of establishing waiting lists when all their tables are filled. Yet, unknown to many customers, sometimes preferred clientele are moved to the front of the list and seated almost immediately. Professional people such as

An inference is an assumption made by a listener.

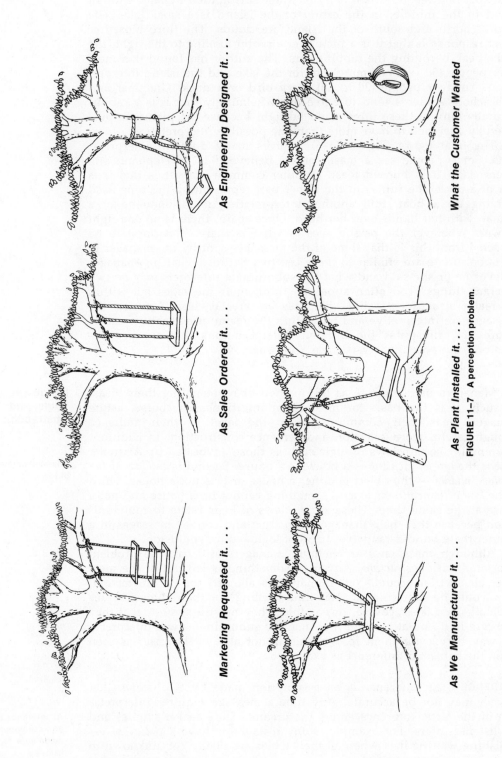

As Engineering Designed it. . . .

What the Customer Wanted

As Sales Ordered it. . . .

As Plant Installed it. . . .

FIGURE 11–7 A perception problem.

Marketing Requested it. . . .

As We Manufactured it. . . .

clergymen and doctors often qualify. Whenever faced with such a waiting list, a colleague of the author makes it a habit not only to use the title "Dr." in front of his name but also asks that he be paged immediately should he receive a call from either neurosurgery or the cardiovascular unit at the nearby hospital. Then he writes his name on a piece of paper along with his license number so the parking lot attendant can bring his car around in a hurry should a call come for him. This gimmick serves to drastically reduce waiting time thanks to the inferences made by the head waiter. It should be noted that although the professor makes several *implications,* he never *states* that he is an M.D. or that he *will* receive a call from the hospital. As a Ph.D., he is entitled to use the term "Dr.," and there is always a chance that the nearby hospital will call him no matter how remote the possibility. The communication problem rests with the head waiter who reads facts into the message. In this case, of course, inference proves helpful because the receiver responds the way the sender wishes him to.

However, inferences are often stumbling blocks to effective communication because the receiver misinterprets the message. For example, a company is having problems in getting its product out and management begins stressing production efficiency. Things go well for the first couple of weeks. Then, suddenly, the production line again starts to have some problems. The general manager calls in one of his trouble shooters, explains the situation, and tells him to go down to the line, find out what is causing the trouble, and get rid of it. The man goes down, finds the automatic control unit is causing the problems, pulls it off, and replaces it. In turn, the general manager calls him in and chews him out for stopping the line to put in a new unit. "You don't pull out perfectly good equipment," he tells the man, "you fix it." What really caused the communication problem? It was inference. The man going down to the line followed the manager's instructions to the letter. He found the trouble and he got rid of it. Unfortunately that was not what the manager had in mind. By "get rid of it" the manager meant to fix the present unit and only pull it out if absolutely necessary. The manager was operating under the conveyer theory of communication and it got him into trouble. He thought his message was clear as a bell, and it was — to him. As communication theorists like to say "what's clear to you is clear — to you."

Albers defines status as "the totality of attributes that rank and relate individuals in an organization."[2] Status affects communication because listeners tend to judge the sender as well as the message. Union representatives may feel directives from management are deliberately designed to undermine or weaken their relationship with the men, and they regard such communiqués as troublesome. On the other hand, complaints from the men are seen as accurate descriptions of problems and firm bases from which to file charges against management. The union representatives and the membership may have high regard for each other but hold the management in low esteem.

Conversely, management often discounts complaints made against its people as "union rhetoric." However, very few managers regard communiqués from higher echelons as anything but authoritative. Furthermore, the higher in the hierarchy the message originates, the more

Status

A person's status will affect the way his or her message is received.

[2]Henry H. Albers, *Principles of Management: A Modern Approach,* 4th edition (New York: John Wiley & Sons, 1974), p. 172.

likely it is to be accepted, because such executives have a great deal of status among the other managers. In short, if a person has status with the listener, he or she is regarded as accurate or credible. If not, the message is discounted accordingly.

Resistance to Change

Basically, people resist change. And the greater the proposed change, the stronger the resistance. For this reason, one of the principles of communication states that the greater the change, the farther in advance must notice be given. A company planning to change work procedures may find it necessary to announce the upcoming changes four weeks prior to their enactment. The same firm planning to move the company plant from Brooklyn to Staten Island may find it necessary to announce the move 18 months beforehand.

Change is inevitable, but so is resistance. There are various techniques people employ in coping with change. For example, consider the case of the company that announces its intentions of hiring the hard-core unemployed. How do the personnel cope with this policy change? One way is *avoidance*, in which they pretend no policy changes have been announced; they simply ignore the directive. A second common approach is *rejection*. "Oh, I know what they said, but that's just talk to improve our community image." The third, and most common, is *distortion*, in which the receiver interprets the message through personal judgment. Those opposing the policy say the company will bring in one or two token employees, but that is all. Those favoring the policy claim that virtually all new hiring will be of the hard-core unemployed.

People cope with change in various ways, including avoidance, rejection and distortion.

The manager's job is to overcome resistance to change. One way of accomplishing this is to explain how new ideas can be beneficial to the subordinates as well as to the management. The difficulty of the task is clearly seen in Table 11–1. Research shows that although superiors believe they communicate information about impending changes, subordinates do not agree. Furthermore, careful scrutinization of the table indicates that this communication breakdown increases as one moves down the hierarchy. The problem is severe between the top staff and foremen, but it is even more severe between the foremen and the workers.

COMMUNICATION CHANNELS

There are two types of communication channels available to the manager, formal and informal. Each can be useful in carrying information to and receiving feedback from other parts of the hierarchy.

TABLE 11–1 Do Superiors Tell Subordinates in Advance About Change?

	Top Staff Say About Themselves	Foremen Say About Top Staff	Foremen Say About Themselves	Men Say About Foremen
Always	70%	27%	40%	22%
Nearly Always	30	36	52	25
More Often than Not		18	2	13
Occasionally		15	5	28
Seldom		4	1	12

Source: Adapted from Rensis Likert, *New Patterns of Management* (New York: McGraw-Hill Book Company, 1961), p. 52.

Formal channels are those established by the organization's structure. An organization chart, as seen in Figure 11–8, provides a simple illustration of what is meant by the expression "going through channels." This is true whether the communication is going down the chain or coming up. The following discussion examines these channels, with major attention devoted to downward and upward communication and the problems associated with each.

Formal Channels

DOWNWARD COMMUNICATION.   Downward communication is used to convey directives from superior to subordinate. The classical theorists placed prime attention on this form of communication and today many organizations continue to do so. Katz and Kahn have identified the five basic purposes of such communication as being: to give specific job instructions; to bring about understanding of the work and its relationship to other organizational tasks; to provide information about procedures and practices; to provide subordinates with feedback on their performance; and to provide a sense of mission by indoctrinating the workers as to organizational goals.[3] A downward orientation also helps link the levels of the hierarchy by coordinating activities among them.

Five basic purposes of downward communication.

There are, however, drawbacks associated with such an orientation. First, it tends to promote an authoritative atmosphere, which can be detrimental to morale. Second, it places a heavy burden on subordinates because much of the information coming down the organizational hierarchy will be expanded, affecting an increasing number of personnel. Third, because of distortion, misinterpretation, or ignorance, information is often lost as it comes down the line. For example, Nichols,

Drawbacks associated with downward orientation.

---

[3]Daniel Katz and Robert L. Kahn, *The Social Psychology of Organizations*, 2nd edition (New York: John Wiley & Sons, 1978), p. 440.

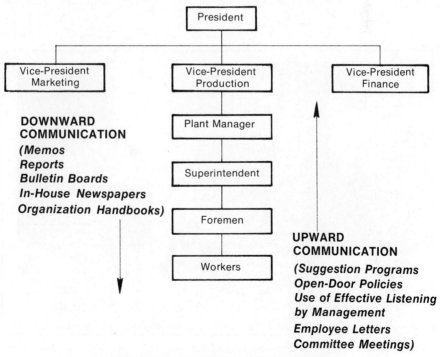

FIGURE 11–8   Formal Channels of Communication

studying communication efficiency in 100 business and industrial firms, recorded the following loss of information among six hierarchical levels:

Level	Percentage of Information Received[4]
Board	100
Vice Presidents	63
General Supervisors	56
Plant Managers	40
General Foremen	30
Workers	20

This communication problem is brought on by the *number of links* in the chain. The greater the number of people involved, the more likely that information loss will occur. One way of overcoming these problems is to supplement downward orientation with an upward emphasis.

UPWARD COMMUNICATION.   The upward communication channel provides subordinates with a route for conveying information to their superiors. However, research indicates that it does not receive adequate attention from management. For example, Likert has reported that when he and his colleagues at the Institute for Social Research asked managers to think of the most important and difficult communication problem they had faced during the previous six months, approximately 80 per cent said it dealt with downward communication. Only 10 per cent indicated that it involved upward communication.[5]

Upward communication channels carry information from subordinates to superiors.

---

[4]Ralph G. Nichols, "Listening is Good Business," *Management of Personnel Quarterly,* Winter 1962, p. 4.
[5]Rensis Likert, *New Patterns of Management* (New York: McGraw-Hill Book Company, 1961), p. 46.

'WHAT COURAGE! THE POOR DEVIL MUST HAVE RIDDEN NON-STOP FOR THREE DAYS CLEAR ACROSS TOWN TO DELIVER THIS!'

PAT OLIPHANT, Copyright 1976, The Washington Star. Reprinted with permission, Los Angeles Times Syndicate.

TABLE 11–2   How Free Do Subordinates Feel to Discuss Important Job Matters With their Superior?

	Top Staff Say About Foremen	Foremen Say About Themselves	Foremen Say About the Men	Men Say About Themselves
Very Free	90%	67%	85%	51%
Fairly Free	10	23	15	29
Not Very Free		10		14
Not Free at All				6

Source: Adapted from Rensis Likert, *New Patterns of Management* (New York: McGraw-Hill Book Company, 1961), p. 47.

In achieving accurate feedback from their subordinates, many managers rely upon techniques such as suggestion boxes and "open door" policies. However, as seen in Table 11–2, research data show that these approaches are often ineffective.

Subordinates do not feel as free to discuss their views as their superiors believe. Furthermore, upward communication is so poor in many firms that studies have consistently revealed managers as incapable of placing themselves in their subordinates' shoes and accurately responding to the question, what do the workers want from their jobs? Table 11–3 clearly illustrates this, showing that upward organizational channels need to receive a great deal more attention from the manager.

In many firms, upward communication is poor.

At present, Figure 11–9 seems to represent accurately the frequency and intensity of superior-subordinate communication.

DOWNWARD COMMUNICATION

UPWARD COMMUNICATION

FIGURE 11–9 Frequency and Intensity of Upward and Downward Communication

TABLE 11–3   What Do Workers Want From Their Jobs?

	Responses, as Ranked by:	
	Supervisors	Workers
Good Wages	1	5
Job Security	2	4
Promotion and Growth With Company	3	7
Good Working Conditions	4	9
Interesting Work	5	6
Management Loyalty to Workers	6	8
Tactful Disciplining	7	10
Full Appreciation for Work Done	8	1
Sympathetic Understanding of Personal Problems	9	3
Feeling "In" on Things	10	2

Reported in Paul Hersey and Kenneth H. Blanchard, *Management of Organizational Behavior: Utilizing Human Resources,* 3rd edition (Englewood Cliffs, N.J.: Prentice-Hall, 1977), p. 47.

LATERAL AND DIAGONAL COMMUNICATION. Lateral or horizontal communication takes place among departments or people on the same level of the hierarchy. Such an interchange of information often serves to coordinate activities. For example, at the upper levels of a manufacturing firm the vice presidents of marketing, production, and finance will coordinate their efforts in arriving at an integrated master plan. Lateral communication also occurs between line and staff departments for the purpose of transmitting technical information necessary to carry out some particular function. As seen earlier, Fayol recommended the use of lateral communication in his famous gangplank theory.

> *Lateral communication occurs among people on the same level of the hierarchy.*

Diagonal communication involves the flow of information among departments or individuals on different levels of the hierarchy. This often occurs in the case of line and staff departments, in which the staff has functional authority. It is also common to find diagonal communication among line departments, again in which one of them has functional authority.

> *Diagonal communication occurs among people not on the same level of the hierarchy.*

Informal Channels

Since formal communication channels represent only a portion of those channels that exist within the structure, much of the communication taking place is informal in nature; it is not planned by superiors. The term most often used to identify these informal channels is "the grapevine."

THE GRAPEVINE. The grapevine can be a source of factual data, although the term carries the connotation of inaccurate information. One reason for this is that anyone can start a rumor or a half-truth circulating through the organization. Since the channel is informal in nature, it is virtually impossible to determine its precise source and thereby authenticate or refute its validity. Nevertheless, the grapevine is very useful in *supplementing* formal channels. Often it is not only a source of factual information; it provides members with an outlet for their imaginations and apprehensions as well. For example, a male supervisor, realizing that he may be beaten out for the upcoming promotion by his female counterpart who has a better production record, may start a rumor that management is putting emphasis on female promotions. This story can be beneficial to the supervisor for two reasons. One, it may cause management to bend over backwards in giving him the promotion, showing that it is not going to promote women on the basis of sex alone. Two, if he does not get the promotion, he can claim blatant discrimination and save face among his peers. It is therefore quite easy to see the importance of informal communication channels to organizational members, although it should be noted that the manager must *not* allow the grapevine to serve as a *substitute* for formal channels.

> *The "grapevine" carries the connotation of inaccurate information.*

CLUSTER CHAINS. Everyone in an organization can participate in the grapevine either by initiating or passing on information given to them by others. For this reason, the channel is very similar to its formal counterpart, carrying messages in four directions: up, down, horizontally, and diagonally. However, since this channel is strictly verbal in nature, it can be formed and disbanded very quickly. This spontaneity prevents it from having permanent membership.

> *The cluster chain is characterized by selective communication.*

Nevertheless, there is a logical pattern to informal channels of communication. There are certain individuals to whom messages will be deliberately passed and there are others who will be deliberately by-passed. This is often known as the *cluster chain* channel and is charac-terized by *selective* communication. For example, George, vice president of finance, has just been called into the president's office where he was informed that the "old man" has decided to announce his retirement at the upcoming Christmas party. Several individuals, including George, have been in the running for some time. The president has determined that George will get the job, but he wishes this to remain a secret until the Christmas party in four weeks. When George leaves the office he is elated. He wants to tell someone the news, but on whom can he rely? Finally, he thinks of his best friend Tom. He tells him, and Tom keeps his secret. George has been highly selective in his informal communica-tion.

There are also times when individuals want to get news around quickly but they want it to appear to be a secret. For example, Frank has decided to quit his job if he cannot get a 15 per cent raise, even though he knows the average for the firm is going to be 9 per cent. Rather than call his boss directly, he decides to go through the informal chain, telling the boss's secretary "in secret." It is not long before his superior comes by to visit with him about his upcoming raise.

The cluster chain is not the only type of chain used in informal communications. Davis has noted that there are three others, as seen in Figure 11–10. There is the *single strand,* in which information is passed through a long line of recipients, for example, from A to Z. There is the *gossip chain,* in which one person tells everyone else, thereby serving as the prime source of information. Finally, there is the *probability chain,* in which information is passed on randomly. The cluster chain, howev-er, is the most predominant, indicating that people are selective in choosing their informal communication channel links.

Other informal communication channels.

THE MANAGER AND INFORMAL CHANNELS. In Chapter 6 it was noted that the manager must attempt to use the informal organization to help attain organizational objectives. The same is true regarding informal channels of communication. One of the greatest advantages of the grape-vine is the rapidity with which it can disseminate information. An-other is its potential for supplementing formal channels. A third is the predictable pattern of informal communication, which Davis has noted

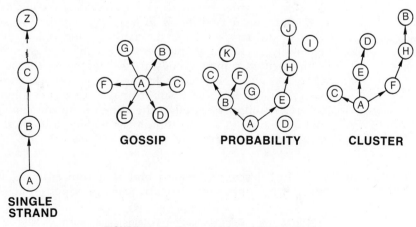

SINGLE STRAND **GOSSIP** **PROBABILITY** **CLUSTER**

FIGURE 11–10 Types of Informal Communication

as being: (1) people talk most when the news is recent; (2) people talk about things that affect their work; (3) people talk about people they know; (4) people working near each other are likely to be on the same grapevine; and (5) people who contact each other in the chain of procedure tend to be on the same grapevine.[6]

Although the informal organization is not controlled by the manager, it can be employed in helping communicate management's point of view. Of course, success will depend to a great degree on the compatibility of the formal with the informal organization. Nevertheless, management must recognize that informal communication networks are an inevitable part of the organization and should endeavor to use them in attaining formal objectives.

COMMUNICATION MEDIA

Media transmission can take the form of words, pictures, or actions. *Words* are the most commonly used, as evidenced by both oral and written communication. It is therefore essential for the manager to employ them effectively. *Pictures* are useful as visual aids. The fact that businesses employ them in posters, charts, and blueprints is clear evidence of their value. *Action* is an important communication medium, as noted by the adage "actions speak louder than words." A grimace, a handshake, a wink, and even silence, have meaning; people will attach significance to them.

Written Communication

Written communication can take a myriad of forms. Some of the more common are memos, reports, posters, bulletin-board items, in-house newspapers, and organization handbooks. There are a number of advantages to be gleaned from written communications. One of these is the relative permanence of the communiqué, which provides a record of what was transmitted. Another is the value associated with rereading and studying the message should it initially be unclear. Moreover, written messages are often more carefully constructed than oral ones because there is less opportunity for explanation. In addition, if a message must go through many people, written communication provides protection against continuous reinterpretation. In fact, written communications are often used when a directive contains detailed instructions that are too lengthy to be trusted to oral communication. Still another reason favoring written messages is that they carry a degree of formality not present in their verbal counterparts.

Advantages to written communication.

On the other hand, there are drawbacks to written communication. For example, it is difficult to keep some forms of written communication up to date, i.e., job descriptions and policy manuals. Things are changing so fast that these are often in need of revision. In addition, some written communiqués are so lengthy that superiors refuse to read them. An example is seen in the case of reports coming up the line. It is not uncommon for a subordinate to submit a long report and then spend ten minutes briefing the superior on the content. The latter does not have time to wade through the paper, so he or she has the subordinate condense it verbally.

Drawbacks to written communication.

Oral Communication

Most executives regard oral communication as superior to written since it not only saves time but also provides a basis for achieving bet-

---

[6]Keith Davis, "Communication Within Management," *Personnel*, November 1954, p. 217.

ter understanding. Some of the more common forms are face-to-face verbal orders, telephones, public address systems, speeches, and meetings.

Of these, face-to-face communication is the most effective mode. As with other forms of oral communication, it gives each party an opportunity to respond directly to the other. Disagreement, dissension, fear, tension, and anger can often be eliminated by solving the problem on the spot. This give and take gives each participant a basis for clarifying his or her own position and getting a firsthand view of that held by others. In addition, face-to-face communication provides the sender an opportunity to note body language such as gestures and facial responses, thereby obtaining more complete feedback than is available with any other form of oral communication. How a person says something is often as important as what he or she says.

Face-to-face communication is the most effective.

Unfortunately, effective face-to-face communication cannot occur among large groups. Here the manager must rely on such modes of communication as meetings, speeches, and public addresses. A good understanding can often be achieved with these methods, but there is little opportunity for immediate feedback. If some people do not understand the logic behind a particular statement, they must wait until later. Most managers, if they are able to see the group, can recapitulate or reword part of the message if it becomes evident they are not conveying their ideas properly. They will usually do this only if they feel the majority of the audience is confused. If it seems that almost everyone understands, the managers may well continue, leaving the one or two confused listeners to work out the meaning for themselves. There is also the case in which managers speak from a company-prepared text, a combination of written and oral communication. Many firms require the manager to stay with the text, thereby limiting their freedom and preventing them from clarifying points they feel are nebulous to the audience.

Limitations among large groups.

In summary, there are advantages and disadvantages to both written and oral communication. Managers must be aware of the problems and pitfalls that prevent a message from being properly interpreted by the receivers. Then, by carefully planning all communiqués, they can surmount or sidestep these problems.

TOWARD EFFECTIVE COMMUNICATION

Numerous techniques are available for improving communication. Some of these help managers convey their message; others are designed to provide them with *feedback*. Yet all are important because managers need to know whether the receiver understands, accepts, and is willing to take the required action. Managers must also know how successful the receiver is in carrying out the directive. Following are some of the most useful techniques for obtaining effective communication.

Developing Sensitivity

The foremost way for a manager to improve communication is to be *sensitive* to the needs and feelings of the subordinates. Although most superiors think they are, research shows they are neither as perceptive nor as sensitive as they believe. The data in Tables 11–1 and 11–2 have illustrated this. If managers were made aware of these findings, it would be a start toward sensitizing them.

A second useful approach is that of *two-way communication*. By allowing subordinates to speak openly and freely, managers can assure them-

Two-way communication is important.

selves of a more accurate upward flow of information. However, since most do not like to hear unfavorable reports, subordinates tend to screen their comments. Some executives will try to overcome such resistance by telling their people that they want accurate reporting; bad news as well as good is to be communicated. If managers really mean this, upward communication can become a reality. However, if they become flustered and angry, subordinates will again begin paring their reports and removing all unfavorable information. The further up the hierarchy this occurs, the greater the danger to the organization. For example, failure to encourage feedback was one of Hitler's greatest failings as an administrator. As Langer has noted in his secret wartime report, Hitler burst into rage whenever bad news was conveyed to him:

> It must not be supposed, however, that these rages occur only when he is crossed on major issues. On the contrary, very insignificant matters might call out this reaction. In general they are brought on whenever anyone contradicts him, when there is unpleasant news about which he might feel responsible, when there is any skepticism concerning his judgment, or when a situation arises in which his infallibility might be challenged or belittled. . . . among his staff there is a tacit understanding: "For God's sake don't excite the Fuehrer—which means do not tell him bad news—do not mention things which are not as he conceives them to be."[7]

Such an attitude discourages the free flow of ideas and impedes any development of sensitivity to the feelings of others.

Employing Understandable, Repetitive Language

Understandable repetitive language will improve communication.

Technical terminology and multi-syllable words may be impressive, but they can also be troublesome to the listener, as seen in Figure 11–11. The manager should try to use language that is *understandable*. A foreman talking to production line workers must deliver a communiqué appropriately; so too, of course, must the executive making a report to the board of directors. Effective communication will differ according to the receiver, but it must always be understandable. One way of accomplishing this is to use *repetitive language*. Sometimes a message will not be fully grasped the first time and a rephrasing or recapitulation is in order. Another guideline is to convey information gradually, building the essence of the message as one goes along. This is especially helpful in conveying technical or sophisticated data.

---

[7]Walter C. Langer, *The Mind of Adolf Hitler* (New York: Basic Books, Inc., Publishers, 1972), p. 76.

In Federal Government Bureaucratic Language:
We respectfully petition, request, and entreat that due and adequate provision be made, this day and the date hereinafter subscribed, for the satisfying of these petitioners' nutritional requirements and for the organizing of such methods of allocation and distribution as may be deemed necessary and proper to assure the reception by and for said petitioners of such quantities of baked cereal products as shall, in the judgment of the aforesaid petitioners, constitute a sufficient supply thereof.

In Plain English:
Give us this day our daily bread.

FIGURE 11–11 Federal government English versus plain English. Source: "Turning Federalese into 'Plain English'", *Business Week*, May 9, 1977, p. 58.

One criterion for managerial effectiveness is credibility, or believability. When Mr. Anderson, the manager, communicates with his subordinates, they listen to and obey him because he has demonstrated through his competence, drive, character, and past performance that he is worthy of their trust. However, the astute manager knows that he must not only gain credibility, but he must protect it as well. Every time he communicates an order or issues a directive, there is a chance that his credibility may be damaged. One way of illustrating the problem and a method for successfully coping with it is through the use of what is called *balance theory.*

Consider the following situation. A manager, Ms. Fairlane, just told her subordinate that the company has decided to introduce new work procedures. In this instance there are three relevant relationships: (a) the attitude of the receiver toward the sender; (b) the attitude of the receiver toward the new changes; and (c) the receiver's perception of the sender's own attitude toward the changes. Based on the receiver's perception, either a balanced or unbalanced triad will result. If the receiver has a positive attitude toward both the changes and the sender, and believes the latter also favors the new work procedures, there is a balanced triad, as seen in Figure 11–12. However, what if the situation is unbalanced because the receiver does not like the new procedures? That is:

Protecting Credibility

Relevant relationships in balance theory.

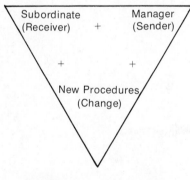

FIGURE 11–12   Balanced Triad

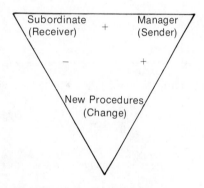

FIGURE 11–13   Unbalanced Triad

How can balance be restored? There are a number of ways, but the important thing to realize is that in the triad there must be all pluses or two minuses and a plus if it is to be balanced.[8]

Thus the manager has three options: (a) tell the subordinate that she also opposes the new procedures (Figure 11–14); (b) allow the subordinate to develop a negative attitude toward her (Figure 11–15); or (c) persuade the subordinate to accept the new changes (Figure 11–16).

Establishing balance and protecting credibility.

Since the manager's job is to communicate and support directives coming down the line, it is vital that she choose alternative (c). This will not only establish balance and protect the manager's credibility with her own subordinates, but it will also prevent alternative (a) from occurring. One way an effective manager will do this is by empathizing with

---

[8]For an excellent discussion of the balance theory and refinement of this statement about pluses and minuses, see Robert Noel Widgery, "Using Balance Theory in Developing Persuasive Strategies," General Motors Institute, February 1972, pp. 1–10.

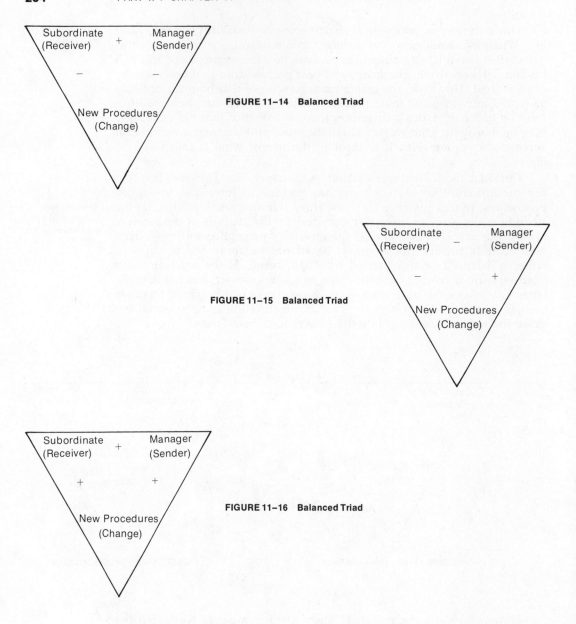

FIGURE 11–14   **Balanced Triad**

FIGURE 11–15   **Balanced Triad**

FIGURE 11–16   **Balanced Triad**

the subordinate and demonstrating that he or she believes and is positively oriented toward many of the same values and ideals held by the subordinate, i.e., good working conditions, a challenging job, a chance for advancement, and recognition. In this way, the manager ensures that the subordinate will continue to rely upon and trust him or her. Then, having protected his or her credibility, the manager can direct attention toward showing the subordinate how the new work procedures will be beneficial in attaining these values and ideals. In turn, this will lead the subordinate to alter his or her perception and view the work changes positively. The result is a balanced triad. By employing balance theory, the effective manager is able to assess communication situations, determine when credibility is threatened, and take necessary steps to protect it.

Avoiding Bad
Listening
Habits

Approximately 70 per cent of the manager's day is spent communicating. One researcher, in breaking down the subfunctions of communication, has estimated that 9 per cent is spent in writing, 16 per cent in reading, 30 per cent in speaking, and 45 per cent in listening.[9] Yet research shows that managers are not good listeners. Nichols has estimated that when people listen to a ten-minute talk, they operate at only 25 per cent efficiency. This is unfortunate, because of all the sources of information a manager has which help him or her to know and accurately evaluate the personalities of the people in the department, listening to the individual employee is one of the most important.

Becoming a more effective listener requires an understanding of the ten most common bad habits of listening. Nichols has defined them as follows:

1. *Calling the subject uninteresting.* Instead of tuning in first and seeing if the speaker has something worthwhile to say, the listener assumes from the start that the topic will be boring.
2. *Tuning the speaker out because of his delivery.* The listener allows delivery to take precedence over content.
3. *Getting overstimulated.* The minute the listener hears something with which he or she disagrees the person stops listening and starts fuming, thereby missing the rest of the message.

Ten most common bad habits
of listening.

4. *Concentrating only on facts, to the exclusion of principles or generalizations.* Facts do not always present the whole picture. Principles and generalizations are often necessary to put everything in its proper perspective.
5. *Trying to outline everything.* Some speakers are less organized than others, and until the individual gets into the presentation, it can be difficult to follow him or her via an outline. Good listeners are flexible in their note taking.
6. *Faking attentiveness.*
7. *Allowing distractions to creep in.*
8. *Tuning out difficult or technical presentations.* This often occurs when managers are listening to financial or quantitatively oriented reports.
9. *Letting emotional words disrupt the listening process.* Any time a word evokes emotion, there is a good chance that listening will be interrupted.
10. *Wasting thought power.* Most people speak at the rate of 125 words per minute. However, the brain is capable of handling almost five times that number. If the speaker goes on for more than a few minutes, it presents a temptation to the listener to wander mentally, returning only periodically to check in and see where the speaker is.[10]

Managers who make a concerted effort to avoid these common pitfalls find that they can improve their level of efficiency far above the 25 per cent average.

Employing
the Commandments
of Good
Communication

Although many guidelines have been put forth to improve communication, one of the most extensive compilations is that constructed by the American Management Association. Often known as the ten commandments of good communication, they are the following:

1. *Clarify ideas before communicating.* By systematically thinking through the message and considering who will be receiving and/or affected by it, the manager overcomes one of the basic pitfalls of communication—failure to properly plan the communiqué.

---

[9]Ralph G. Nichols, "Listening, What Price Inefficiency?" *Office Executive*, April 1959, pp. 15–22.
[10]Adapted from *ibid.*

The more systematically a message is analyzed, the more clearly it can be communicated.

2. *Examine the true purpose of communication.* The manager has to determine what he or she *really* wants to accomplish with the message. Once this objective is identified, the communiqué can be properly designed.

3. *Take the entire environment, physical and human, into consideration.* Questions such as what is said, to whom, and when, will all affect the success of the communication. The physical setting, the social climate, and past communication practices should be examined in adapting the message to the environment.

4. *When valuable, obtain advice from others in planning communiqués.* Consulting with others can be a useful method of obtaining additional insights regarding how to handle the communication. In addition, those who help formulate it usually give it active support.

5. *Be aware of the overtones as well as the basic content of the message.* The listener will be affected by not only what is said but also how it is said. Voice tone, facial expression, and choice of language all influence the listener's reaction to the communiqué.

Ten commandments of good communication.

6. *When possible, convey useful information.* People remember things that are beneficial to them. If the manager wants subordinates to retain the message, he or she should phrase it so that it takes into consideration *their* interests and needs as well the company's.

7. *Follow up on communication.* The manager must solicit feedback in ascertaining whether the subordinate understands the communiqué, is willing to comply with it, and then takes the appropriate action.

8. *Communicate with the future, as well as the present, in mind.* Most communications are designed to meet the demands of the current situation. However, they should be in accord with the long-range goals as well. For example, communiqués designed to improve performance or morale are valuable in handling present problems. Yet they also serve a useful future purpose by promoting long-run organizational efficiency.

9. *Support words with deeds.* When managers contradict themselves by saying one thing and doing another, they undermine their own directives. For example, the executive who issues a notice reminding everyone that they are to be in the building by 8:30 a.m. while he or she continues to show up at 9:15 a.m. should not expect anyone to take the notice seriously. Subordinates are always cognizant of such managerial behavior and quickly discount such directives.

10. *Be a good listener.* By concentrating on the speaker's explicit and implicit meanings, the manager can obtain a much better understanding of what is being said.[11]

SUMMARY

In this chapter interpersonal and organizational communication have been examined. It was noted that the communication process entails four steps: attention, understanding, acceptance, and action. In implementing the process there are two basic kinds of channels, formal and informal. The astute manager uses both to his or her advantage, keeping in mind that there tends to be an overemphasis on downward communication and an underemphasis on upward. This is unfortunate, for without some form of upward communication there is a distinct lack of feedback. Many managers overlook the need for this feedback, tending to follow the old conveyer theory of communication. They send their subordinates a message and expect them to act accordingly. However, communication does not work that way. People do not always interpret messages in the same way. There are many reasons for this, and all constitute barriers to effective communication. Some of the more important are perception, language, abstraction, inference, status, and resistance to change. In order to overcome these barriers, steps must be taken to establish lines of feedback. Some of the more effective tech-

---

[11]Adapted from American Management Association, "Ten Commandments of Good Communication," as reported in Max D. Richards and William A. Nielander, *Readings in Management* (Cincinnati, Ohio: South-Western Publishing, 1958), pp. 141–143.

niques are sensitivity, understandable repetitive language, credibility, the avoidance of bad listening habits, and a general adherence to the commandments of good communication. Although these ideas might appear obvious to many, it is really quite difficult to adhere to them in practice.[12]

In Chapter 12 motivation will be examined. What motivates people? The answer will differ from person to person, but one thing is certain: if the manager cannot communicate with his or her people and get the feedback necessary to understand and empathize with their points of view, he or she has little basis for formulating an intelligent approach to motivating them. Communication helps the manager establish the basis for this activity.

1. What is meant by "the communication process"? Explain.

2. What is the conveyer theory of communication?

3. What are the four steps for implementing effective communication? Describe them.

4. What are some of the common barriers to effective communication?

5. What is meant by the term perception? Give an illustration.

6. What is meant by the term inference? Give an illustration.

7. Why do people resist change? Is it really inevitable?

8. What is meant by "going through channels"?

9. What is meant by "informal communication channels"?

10. What are the advantages of using written communication? Oral communication?

11. How can a manager promote sensitivity? Be complete in your answer.

12. How is balance theory useful to the manager in protecting his or her credibility? Explain.

13. What are some of the most common bad listening habits?

14. How can a manager obtain feedback for effective communication?

Athanassiades, J. C. "The Distortion of Upward Communication in Hierarchical Organizations." *Academy of Management Journal*, June 1973, pp. 207–226.

[12]For an excellent follow-up to the ideas contained in this chapter, the reader is directed to Stewart L. Tubbs and Sylvia Moss, *Human Communication*, 2nd edition, (New York: Random House, 1977).

Berlo, D. D. *The Process of Communication.* New York: Holt, Rinehart and Winston, Inc., 1960.

Davis, K. *Human Behavior at Work,* 5th edition. New York: McGraw-Hill Book Company, 1977, Chapters 21 and 22.

Foltz, R. G. "Communication: Not an Art, a Necessity." *Personnel,* May–June 1972, pp. 60–64.

Greenbaum, H. H. "The Audit of Organizational Communication." *Academy of Management Journal,* December 1974, pp. 739–754.

Hall, J. "Communication Revisited." *California Management Review,* Spring 1973, pp. 56–67.

Luthans, F. *Organizational Behavior,* 2nd edition. New York: McGraw-Hill Book Company, 1977, Chapter 9.

Newman, R. G. "Case of the Questionable Communiqués." *Harvard Business Review,* November–December 1975, pp. 26–28.

Nichols, R. G. "Listening Is Good Business." *Management of Personnel Quarterly,* Winter 1962, pp. 2–9.

Tubbs, S. L., and S. Moss. *Human Communication,* 2nd edition. New York: Random House, 1977.

CASE: GOOD WORK IS EXPECTED

An eastern pharmaceutical company hired an outside management consulting firm to analyze its operations. After five weeks, the consultants made their report to management. One of the areas they had investigated was communication between superiors and subordinates. To its dismay, management learned that there were numerous discrepancies between what superiors said they did and what their subordinates said their superiors did. For example, the consultants conducted a confidential questionnaire survey of 20 per cent of the managers and workers; the responses to the question, "Do you tell your subordinates when they do a good job?" are tabulated in Table 11–4.

Management was quite distraught with the findings. As a result, at its next board of directors meeting the chairman proposed that the firm bring back the consultants to advise and counsel them on how they could deal with this problem. The resolution was passed unanimously.

When the middle and lower level managers learned of the action, they expressed surprise. One of them noted, "Just because the data indicate poor communication is no need to get excited. After all, the men say lots of things that aren't accurate." A fellow colleague explained, "Look, I expect subordinates to do a good job. I only tell them when they are doing a poor one. If I praise them every time they did something right, they'd all have swelled heads. My approach is to say nothing."

TABLE 11–4   Do You Tell Your Subordinates When They Do a Good Job?

	Top Management Says of Itself	Middle Management Says of Top Management	Middle Management Says of Itself	Lower-Level Management Says of Middle Management	Lower-Level Management Says of Itself	Workers Say of Lower-Level Management
Always	93%	82%	95%	63%	98%	39%
Often	7	14	5	15	2	23
Sometimes		4		12		18
Seldom				6		11
Never				4		9

1. What do the data in Table 11–4 show? Explain your findings.

2. What do you think of the comments from the two managers? Are they valid?

3. What types of recommendations would you expect from the consultants? Explain.

CASE: MANAGERS DON'T LISTEN[13]

How important is communication in the modern organization? According to James L. Haynes, president of the American Management Association and former dean of the School of Business Administration at Duquesne University in Pittsburgh, "Perhaps the No. 1 fault with American management is that executives, even in the biggest corporations, don't get out of their offices and listen to what workers have to say." As a result, very few other members of the management team spend time listening to the workers. This leads to all sorts of problems and, as the firm expands, the problems magnify. How do you deal with this? One way is through the use of an open-door policy, which encourages employees to come in and discuss their problems. When asked if he felt every boss should adopt this policy, Mr. Haynes commented:

Yes—if you'll let me make a modification. Any worker ought to feel free to go to his boss at any time and talk about anything that's on his mind. But the open door shouldn't mean that if he can't get satisfaction from his own boss, he can go to the boss's boss. The practice doesn't work.

Also, the basic role of a manager ought to be one of problem prevention rather than problem solving. If the boss sees himself in the position of "the great problem solver," then he's just promoting the idea that the way people get recognition is to create problems and either bring them to him for solution or work them out on their own and get the credit and the recognition.

Speaking in very broad terms, Mr. Haynes claims that company management should not concern itself primarily with motivation, because people basically motivate themselves. The task of the boss should be to create a climate for job satisfaction. Effective listening can play a key role in this process.

Questions

1. Do you think Mr. Haynes is right about managers not listening to the workers?

2. Do you agree with Mr. Haynes' comments on an open-door policy? Why or why not?

---

[13]The data in this case can be found in: "Want to Be a Better Boss? Advice from an Expert," *U.S. News & World Report,* March 21, 1977, pp. 68–70.

3. In addition to Mr. Haynes' comments, what else would you recommend that managers do to improve communication with subordinates?

CASE: A TWO-WAY EXPERIMENT

To emphasize the importance of communication, Mr. Fontane, director of in-house training of a large western retail chain, decided to conduct an experiment during his upcoming session with a group of middle managers. When they were all settled in the room, he began by asking the value of two-way communication. All agreed it was of prime importance for effective management. He then asked them how they went about establishing feedback from subordinates. Although some of the men contributed ideas, it was evident that the group was unsettled by the question. Finally one of the managers, Mr. Clauson, spoke up. "Mr. Fontane, two-way communication is great if you have a problem, but most of us really believe we can achieve our goals with successful downward communication. We really don't have trouble getting our meanings across to the workers."

By the hum in the room, Mr. Fontane realized that the rest of the managers basically agreed. "Do you mean to tell me that you are all such good communicators that your subordinates know exactly what you are talking about without asking questions?

"Well, I'm not saying we're perfect," said Mr. Clauson, "but speaking personally, I can make myself understood if I really have to. When I make the concerted effort, there is no real need for questions. And I'm not kidding or bragging. I've worked at it a long time and I'm just that good."

With that Mr. Fontane asked Mr. Clauson to come to the front of the room and read the piece of paper sitting on the podium. "Gentlemen, while Mr. Clauson is looking at the piece of paper I have left on the podium, I would like the rest of you to get ready to draw. Mr. Clauson is going to describe some diagrams to you. You will note that he is going to tell you how to draw these diagrams. However, you are not to ask any questions, make any noise, or provide him with any kind of feedback indicating whether or not you are able to follow the logic of his directives. Just do exactly what he tells you to."

The diagrams that Mr. Clauson was asked to describe to the group are presented in Figure 11–17. The instructions that accompa-

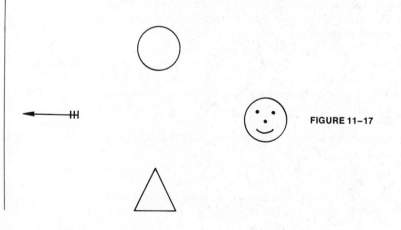

FIGURE 11–17

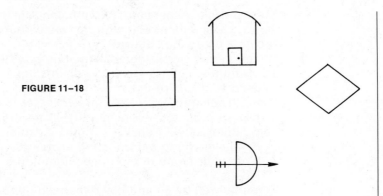

FIGURE 11–18

nied the diagrams told him not to use any geometric terms. Instead, he was to get the other people in the room to draw these figures by merely using lines, dots and geographic directions. In addition, he was to keep his head down throughout the experiment so he would be unable to see the group.

Mr. Clauson began. By the time he finished it was evident to Mr. Fontane that many of the men were unable to follow some of the directions. "All right, let's play show and tell," he said. "How many of you feel you got all four diagrams right?" Four of the twenty-four men raised their hands. Then Mr. Fontane held up the diagrams for all to see. It turned out that everyone had at least one of them right, but no one had all four correct. In fact, only seven of the men had three right.

Mr. Fontane then ran the experiment again, using the diagrams in Figure 11–18. This time he permitted Mr. Clauson to look out on the group and answer any questions they had. In addition, if he felt that he had lost the men at any point, he could go back and repeat the directions. At the end of this experiment everyone in the room had at least two of the diagrams right and twelve of the men had all of them correct. "Well, Mr. Clauson," said Mr. Fontane, "you seem to have improved markedly over your first performance."

"I know," he replied, "but I never really realized how much can be lost if you don't allow people to ask questions. In fact, I was even more surprised regarding how much feedback I was getting just by looking at their faces and their body movements. I guess your point is that there is a tremendous increase in understanding between one- and two-way communication, right?"

Questions

1. Is there really any correlation between this experiment and two-way communication on the job? Explain.

2. What are some of the most effective ways to promote two-way communication? Explain.

CASE: SPEED AND COMPREHENSION

One of the greatest communication problems is that of getting people to increase their reading speed and comprehension. Take out a clean piece of paper before continuing with this case. Then read the following assignment. Each of the twenty-four items requests you to execute a prescribed activity.

The items vary in complexity, but you should be able to cope easily with them all, as this is not an intelligence test. The exercise is designed to measure only how well you read and carry out instructions with accuracy. You have three minutes in which to complete the exercise. So, be sure to time yourself and remain within this constraint. Enter all your answers on the clean piece of paper.

Read everything before doing anything.

1. Write your name in the upper right corner of the clean piece of paper.
2. Multiply 23 by 68 and place the result under your name.
3. Draw a square on the reverse side of the paper.
4. Draw a circle inside the square.
5. Draw a diamond inside the circle.
6. Write the month and date in the upper left corner.
7. Multiply the square root of 9 by the square of 16.
8. Subtract 1462 from 2221 and place the result in the lower left corner.
9. Underline your answer to question #2.
10. If a farmer has 17 pigs, and all but 12 die, how many pigs are left alive?
11. Add 14,421 to 27,969 and place the result in the lower right corner.
12. Now subtract 14,421 from 27,969 and place the answer under the result for #13.
13. Square the number seven and put your answer immediately below.
14. Compute the square root of 169 and add this to the answer you worked out in number 13.
15. Write down the name of the sixteenth President of the U.S.
16. Write Jimmy Carter's middle name on the bottom of the page.
17. If Dr. Joyce Brothers married comedian Dickie Smothers, what would her new name be?
18. Which space project was the one that got America to the moon: Gemini, Apollo, or Mercury?
19. Who won the last National League Pennant?
20. Who won the last American League Pennant?
21. Who won the first Super Bowl?
22. Take a number from 1 to 10. Add 10. Subtract 5. Multiply by 7. Square the number. What is your answer?
23. Write down the year you graduated from grammar school as a four digit number; for example, 1974. Add to this your present age. Then write down how long you have been out of grammar school. Finally, write down the year you were born. Add all four numbers together.
24. Carry out the instructions in item #1 only and ignore all the rest.

Questions

1. What is the purpose of this exercise? What does it relate about communication problems?

2. How can these problems be overcome? Explain.

CHAPTER TWELVE

MODERN MOTIVATION THEORY

One of the greatest challenges facing the manager is that of motivating the workers. In this chapter, modern motivation theory will be examined. The major part of the chapter will deal with what are called **substantive** or *content* theories. These are concerned with *what* it is within the individual or environment that stimulates or sustains behavior; i.e., what are the specific things that motivate people? The last part of the chapter will examine three mechanical or *process* theories, which are concerned with explaining *how* behavior is initiated, directed, sustained, and halted. The goals of this chapter are to acquaint the reader with modern motivation theory and to indicate its relevance to management.

When you are finished reading this chapter you should be able to:

1. Explain the relationship between needs and behavior.
2. Identify and describe the five basic needs in Maslow's need hierarchy.
3. Compare and contrast the tenets of Theory X and Theory Y.
4. Discuss the value of money, status, working conditions, increased responsibility, and challenging work in motivating people.
5. Describe some of the new process theories of motivation that emphasize individual stimulation (rather than mass motivation).

GOALS OF THE CHAPTER

If managers are to be successful in getting workers to attain organizational objectives, they must understand the fundamentals of motivation. However, this is not an easy job, for motivation is an *intervening variable*. It is an internal, psychological process; that is, the manager cannot see motivation, he or she can only assume its presence (or absence) based on observance of worker behavior. If the workers are busy at their tasks, the manager may well infer that they are motivated. If they are standing around talking, he or she may conclude that they are not motivated to work.

NEEDS AND BEHAVIOR
Motivation is an internal, psychological process.

This is only a superficial approach and fails to answer the key question, why do people behave as they do? Although there are various answers, one approach is a *need-satisfaction* explanation. Everyone has needs that require satisfaction. In turn, these needs will cause the person to undertake some form of *goal-oriented behavior*, which, hopefully, will satisfy the need. For example, hunger pains may lead a person to go into a nearby cafe and eat. Using just this information, it is possible to design the following simple diagram of motivation.

One way of examining motivation is through a need-satisfaction approach.

FIGURE 12–1 Simple Motivation Process

Of course, every individual has many needs, but it is the need with the greatest strength that will tend to dictate current behavior.

Once the need has been satisfied, it will decline in importance and another need will become dominant. This "need" theory of motivation has been explained in detail by Abraham Maslow.

MASLOW'S NEED HIERARCHY

According to Maslow, man is a wanting being; there is always some need he wants to satisfy. Once this is accomplished, that particular need no longer motivates him and he turns to another, again seeking satisfaction. These needs can be represented in hierarchical form, with those at the lower levels requiring *basic* satisfaction before the individual can move on to the next level. Figure 12–2 illustrates Maslow's need hierarchy of physiological, safety, social, esteem, and self-actualization needs. However, before discussing these, it should be noted that Maslow *never* contended that a need must be satisfied 100 per cent before the next level becomes important. As he has explained:

> In actual fact, most members of our society who are normal are partially satisfied in all their basic needs and partially unsatisfied in all their basic needs at the same time. A more realistic description of the hierarchy would be in terms of decreasing percentages of satisfaction as we go up the hierarchy of prepotency. For instance, if I may assign arbitrary figures . . . it is as if the average citizen is satisfied perhaps 85 per cent in his physiological needs, 70 per cent in his safety needs, 50 per cent in his love needs, 40 per cent in his self-esteem needs, and 10 per cent in his self-actualization needs.[1]

Physiological Needs

The most basic needs are physiological.

At the base of the hierarchy are *physiological* needs, which are necessary to sustain life. These include food, water, clothing, and shelter. An individual who lacks the basic necessities in life will probably be motivated primarily by physiological needs. As Maslow noted, "A person who is lacking food, safety, love, and esteem would most probably hunger for food more strongly than for anything else."[2] When this is so, Figure 12–3 accurately depicts the need hierarchy.

---

[1]Abraham H. Maslow, "A Theory of Human Motivation," *Psychological Review*, July 1943, pp. 388–389.

[2]Abraham H. Maslow, *Motivation and Personality*, 2nd edition (New York: Harper & Row, Publishers, 1954), p. 37.

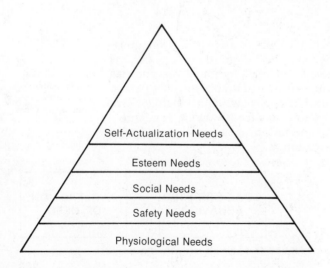

FIGURE 12–2 Maslow's Hierarchy of Needs

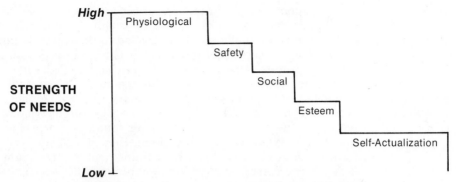

FIGURE 12–3   Need Hierarchy Showing Physiological Needs Dominant

Research indicates that satisfaction of physiological needs is usually associated with money — not money itself, of course, but what it can buy. Although one could look at Figure 12–2 and argue that other needs could also be satisfied with money, it seems clear that the value of this factor diminishes as one goes up the hierarchy. Self-respect, for example, cannot be bought.

When physiological needs are basically fulfilled, *safety* needs begin to manifest themselves. One of the most common is protection from physical dangers such as fire or accident. In an industrial setting, signs such as "No smoking in this area" and "Beyond this point safety glasses must be worn" provide illustrations of how management attempts to satisfy this need.

Safety Needs

Then comes safety, which can take many forms.

A second safety need is economic security. Fringe benefits such as accident, health, and life insurance programs help to fulfill this need.

A third common safety need is the desire for an orderly, predictable environment. This may be difficult to understand until one realizes that people often feel threatened by work changes or are afraid to voice their opinion on a particular matter for fear of losing their job. When these things happen, safety needs are clearly evident.

Research indicates that there are some individuals who place great emphasis on the safety need, for example those whose parents were heavily security-minded. The parents, often having suffered economic crises, regard themselves as victims of the environment and they pass this strong lack of security on to their children. The offspring, in turn, seek secure, nonthreatening positions in, for example, major corporations or federal bureaucracies, where they can carve out a stable, protected niche for themselves.

Another common cause for the security-minded employee is overprotective parents. Continually sheltering their child from disappointment, they paint an unrealistic view of the world. Once the young person goes out and suffers a setback, he or she is thrown for a loss and is unable to cope with the accompanying frustration, tension, and anxiety. Subconscious security motives developed through interaction with the parents have not prepared the person for this new experience. Safety needs become important to the individual and he or she seeks a noncompetitive, sheltered environment.

When physiological and safety needs are basically satisfied, *social* needs become important motivators. The individual wants to receive and

Social Needs

give acceptance, friendship, and affection. People need to feel needed. Medical research has proved that if a child is not held, stroked, and cuddled, it can actually die. This has led to the currently popular concept of "stroking." People seek strokes or pats on the head from others and, in turn, reciprocate. These need not be physical strokes; they can be mental or psychological. For example, George notices Mary's new dress and remarks, "Mary, you look lovely." Mary, in turn, replies, "Thank you, George. You always know how to make a person feel good." Both people pat each other on the head by saying something nice. People need this interaction. When it is refused them, they actually suffer. This accounts for the use by prisons of solitary confinement for maximum punishment. It deprives a person of the fulfillment of his or her social needs, and there is no more serious way to inflict punishment than psychologically. In a manner of speaking, the prisoner is prevented from giving and receiving strokes.

Individuals need to feel needed.

The concept of stroking explains why Schachter has found that people who have similar beliefs tend to group together.[3] They share a common bond and can reinforce each other's feeling and convictions through stroking. This is especially true when things are not going well, for misery does love company.

Esteem Needs

Feelings of self-esteem and self-confidence are important.

When physiological, safety, and social needs are basically satisfied, *esteem* becomes the dominant need. This need is twofold: the person must feel important and must receive recognition from others which supports these feelings. Recognition is invaluable, for without it most people would conclude that they are greatly overrating themselves. When those around them, however, make it clear that they are indeed important, feelings of self-esteem, self-confidence, prestige, and power are all produced. Of course, full satisfaction of the need rests with the individual. For instance, if one believes he is overrated by his peers, nothing they do will be beneficial in convincing him of their sincerity. He may continually feel inferior. However, if he has confidence in himself, respect and support from those around him will serve to justify that confidence.

Research shows that as the United States moves toward becoming a middle-class society, esteem-related needs such as prestige are more evident; people want to keep up with the Joneses and be viewed as important. This was clearly indicated in Packard's book *The Status Seekers*.[4] Joining the right country club, obtaining a reputation as a hard worker, or earning an advanced degree are some ways of securing this prestige. For example, many teachers who hold a Ph.D. like to be called "Doctor" rather than "Professor" or "Sir" because of the prestige the title carries.

Power is another esteem-related need. The power drive actually begins at childhood when the baby realizes that crying influences the parents' behavior. Adler contends that this ability to manipulate others is inherently pleasurable to the child.[5] Of course, during these early years the infant needs this power; he or she is helpless without the parents and must have some method for ensuring their assistance. Later in life, when one can fend for oneself, this motive of power changes to one of winning respect and recognition from others. When this esteem need is basically satisfied, the self-actualization need becomes important.

---

[3]Stanley Schachter, *The Psychology of Affiliation* (Stanford, Calif.: Stanford University Press, 1959).
[4]Vance Packard, *The Status Seekers* (New York: David McKay Company, Inc., 1959).
[5]Alfred Adler, *Social Interest* (London: Faber & Faber Ltd., 1938).

Maslow defined *self-actualization* as the "desire to become more and more what one idiosyncratically is, to become everything that one is capable of becoming."[6] The individual attempts to realize his or her full potential at this level of the hierarchy. The person is interested in self-fulfillment, self-development, and creativity in the broadest sense of the word.

Of all five needs, the least is known about self-actualization. This is because people satisfy the need in so many different ways that it is difficult to pin down and identify. However as Hersey and Blanchard note, competence and achievement are closely related motives, and extensive research has been conducted on them.[7]

White has concluded that human beings desire *competence* because it gives them a form of control over their environment.[8] As they mature, people learn their limitations and capabilities from experience, and they work within these confines. For example, it is rare to find intelligent adults seriously overrating their abilities. They basically know what they can do and will remain within these parameters, choosing an objective that is attainable such as job mastery. The person pits himself or herself against the work as a goal that is challenging but not beyond attainment. This competence desire is related to the self-actualization need identified by Maslow.

Another such related need is *achievement*. Some individuals will accomplish more than others because their need to achieve is greater. McClelland and his associates at Harvard have been studying this need for over 25 years.[9] They have found that high-achievers are neither low nor high risk-takers. Rather, they set moderately difficult but potentially achievable goals for themselves. They like a challenge, but they want some influence over the outcome. They are aggressive realists. In addition, they are motivated more by the accomplishment of a particular objective than by the rewards associated with it. Money, for example, is merely used as a means of measuring or assessing progress. High-achievers also have a strong desire for feedback on how well they are doing. They want to know the score.

Maslow's theory has general application for the manager, but several points merit specific attention. First, the hierarchy must not be viewed as a rigid structure. Levels are *not* clear-cut and tend to overlap. When the intensity of one need is on the decline, the next one may be on the rise as seen in Figure 12–4. When, for instance, the safety need passes the peak of the physiological need, it assumes the dominant role and holds it until the social need rises above it.

Second, some individuals may remain primarily at the lower levels of the hierarchy, continually concerned with physiological and safety needs. This often occurs among people in underdeveloped countries. Conversely, others may spend a great deal of their time at the upper levels of the hierarchy. If middle-class parents have the best chance of producing high-achievers and the United States is a middle-class society, it follows

Self-Actualization Need

The realization of one's full potential is also important.

Competence provides people with a form of control over their environment.

Some individuals have a high need to achieve.

The Individual and the Hierarchy

Hierarchical levels are not clear-cut.

Some people may remain at certain levels of the hierarchy.

[6]Maslow, *op. cit.*, p. 46.
[7]Paul Hersey and Kenneth H. Blanchard, *Management of Organizational Behavior: Utilizing Human Resources.* 3rd edition (Englewood Cliffs, N.J.: Prentice-Hall, 1977), p. 42.
[8]Robert W. White, "Motivation Reconsidered: The Concept of Competence," *Psychological Review*, September 1959, pp. 297–333.
[9]David C. McClelland et al., *The Achievement Motive* (New York: Appleton Century Crofts, Inc., 1953); and David C. McClelland, *The Achieving Society* (Princeton, N.J.: D. Van Nostrand Company, Inc., 1961).

NEED

INTENSITY

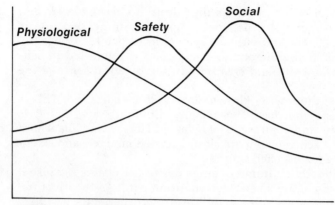

FIGURE 12–4   Changing Needs

that Americans probably spend a good deal of their time trying to satisfy social, esteem, and self-actualization needs.

Third, the specific order of needs suggested by Maslow may not apply to everyone; there is certainly no empirical support that it does. For example, for some people esteem needs may be more basic than safety needs.

Lack of empirical evidence.

Fourth, the same type of behavior from two different people does not necessarily represent the same need. One person may speak in a cocky manner because he is certain of his subject and feels there is no one more qualified to speak on this topic than he. Another person may use the exact same approach to hide her feelings of insecurity. The former may be fullfilling either esteem or self-actualization needs while the latter is fulfilling the safety need.

People respond differently to identical needs.

Maslow's concept is useful for indicating that individuals have needs. However, in order to motivate workers the manager must know which need(s) requires satisfaction. Whatever approach the manager takes, it will be based on *assumptions* about the worker and his need-satisfactions.

McGREG-OR'S AS-SUMP-TIONS

The late Douglas McGregor provided some important insights into the area of managerial assumptions in his book *The Human Side of Enterprise.*[10] It was McGregor's thesis that "the theoretical assumptions management holds about controlling its human resources determine the whole character of the enterprise. They determine also the quality of its successive generations of management."[11] By this he meant that every management has a philosophy or set of assumptions it uses in handling its workers. In essence, McGregor divided these assumptions into two groups: Theory X assumptions and Theory Y assumptions. Theory X assumptions may be placed on one end of a continuum and Theory Y assumptions on the other.

---

[10]Douglas McGregor, *The Human Side of Enterprise* (New York: McGraw-Hill Book Company, 1960).
[11]*Ibid.*, pp. vi–vii.

McGregor found Theory X assumptions implicit in much of the literature about organization and in many of the current management practices. These assumptions are:

1. **People inherently dislike work and, when possible, will avoid it.**
2. **They have little ambition, tend to shun responsibility and prefer to be directed.**
3. **Above all, they want security.**
4. **In order to get them to attain organizational objectives it is necessary to use coercion, control, and threats of punishment.**[12]

Theory X assumptions.

At first glance it might appear that McGregor was constructing a straw man. With this contention, however, he vehemently disagreed, noting that Theory X assumptions are actually subscribed to by many managers in United States industry. Furthermore, he noted, "the principles of organization which comprise the bulk of the literature of management *could only have been derived from assumptions such as those of Theory X.* Other beliefs about human nature would have led inevitably to quite different organizational principles."[13]

The result of these assumptions, according to McGregor, is that many managers are giving prime consideration to the satisfactions of physiological and safety needs. However, it is quite easy to see that these needs cannot be satisfied while one is on the job. Money, for example, which can purchase food, clothing, and shelter, can only be spent when the worker goes home. Likewise, safety needs as reflected in fringe benefits such as vacations, profit-sharing plans, and health and medical coverage yield satisfaction only outside of one's place of work. Nevertheless, many managers seem to feel these low-level physiological need satisfiers are of major importance. Why is this so? In the case of money, one answer is found in the simple fact that managers can manipulate this variable rather easily, so they rely upon it as a motivational tool, giving or withholding financial rewards in an effort to stimulate production. Another reason is the attitude of many managers:

Prime emphasis is placed on satisfying low-level needs.

. . . most . . . are highly achievement-oriented; in the psychologist's terms, they are "high in *n* Ach." We know that such men attach special significance to money rewards. They are strong believers in steeply increasing financial rewards for greater accomplishment. Because they themselves are particularly interested in some concrete measure that will sensitively reflect how well they have done, it is easy and natural for them to mistake this idea for a related one — namely, that the more money you offer someone the harder he will work.[14]

However, as noted earlier, once the employee's physiological and safety needs are taken care of, his attention is focused on higher-level needs, and this is where the problem begins. Management has made no provisions for satisfying these needs, so they offer the workers more physiological and safety rewards. If the workers balk at this, management brings out the threat of punishment, which is in accord with the fourth Theory X tenet above. The use of punishment seems to be a logical method of solving the issue; either the workers do the job or management will get tough. However, the problem rests with the fact that management mistakes causes for effects, the result being a self-fulfilling prophecy. Believing punishment is a necessary tool for effective management, the company introduces it the minute the workers start offering resistance, noting

[12]*Ibid.*, pp. 33–34.
[13]*Ibid.*, p. 35.
[14]David C. McClelland, "Money as a Motivator: Some Research Insights." *In* David R. Hampton, Charles E. Summer, and Ross A. Webber, *Organizational Behavior and the Practice of Management*, (Glenview, Ill.: Scott, Foresman and Company, 1973), p. 641.

"See, it's just like we said. You have to get tough with these people if you want any performance." Yet it is management's fault that the workers are discontent in the first place.

Why do many managers have trouble motivating their workers? The answer is that they hold erroneous assumptions about the nature of man. Management believes they should treat their people like children, providing low-level need-satisfaction rewards if the work is done well and withholding these benefits if the work is done poorly. This concept of motivation is known as the "carrot and stick" theory. It may be useful in getting a donkey to pull a cart, but it seldom works effectively in motivating human beings. A more realistic set of assumptions are those contained in Theory Y.

AN AGE OLD PHENOMENON. Before examining Theory Y, however, it should be realized that the basic assumptions of Theory X have been in existence for years. The reader may remember that the philosophy of the early business managers was very similar to that of modern Theory X advocates. Knowles and Saxburg have identified the assumptions employed by these early managers as:

1. The employee is a "constant" in the production equation. The implication here is that man has a fixed nature.
2. The employee is an inert adjunct of the machine, prone to inefficiency and waste unless properly programmed.
3. The employee is by nature lazy; only managers honor the "hard work" creed of the Protestant Ethic.
4. The employee's main concern is self-interest. At work, this is always expressed in economic values.
5. Given appropriate expression, these values will make man fiercely competitive among his peers as an accumulator of financial rewards.
6. Man (at least the working man) must therefore be tightly controlled and externally motivated in order to overcome his natural desire to avoid work unless the material gains available to him are worth his effort.[15]

A "carrot and stick" approach is used.

Theory X is not new.

---

[15]Henry P. Knowles and Borje O. Saxburg, "Human Relations and the Nature of Man," *Harvard Business Review,* March–April 1967, p. 32.

"What we're really looking for is a not-too-bright young man with no ambition and who is content to stay on the bottom and not louse things up." (Courtesy of Dick Lucas)

Theory X, then, is certainly not a new phenomenon; it has been in existence for years. The only notable change is that management has been able to reduce economic hardship and improve working conditions among the employees since the time of Taylor and his associates. This has all been done, however, without any change in their *fundamental* theory of management.

Human behavior research has provided the basis for a new theory of management, which McGregor called Theory Y. Its assumptions are:

Theory Y

1. Work is a natural phenomenon and if the conditions are favorable people will not only accept responsibility, they will seek it.
2. If people are committed to organizational objectives they will exercise self-direction and self-control.
3. Commitment is a function of the rewards associated with goal attainment.
4. The capacity for creativity in solving organizational problems is widely distributed in the population and the intellectual potentialities of the average human being are only partially utilized.[16]

Theory Y assumptions.

In contrast to Theory X, Theory Y presents a dynamic view of man. The individual is seen as having growth and development capacities, and the problem of motivation is now placed directly in the lap of management. Since the worker has potential, management must decide how to tap it. No longer can management hide behind old Theory X assumptions. Management must re-evaluate its thinking and begin focusing attention on ways of allowing the workers to attain their upper-level needs.

THEORY Y CRITICISM. Many individuals think of Theory X as outmoded and of Theory Y as a modern, superior view of the worker, but Theory Y also has its critics. Some point out that Theory Y is unreasonably idealistic. After all, not everyone is self-directed and self-controlled; many workers seem to like security and shun responsibility. As Fromm has noted, people want freedom, but only within defined limits.[17] Strauss supports this finding, pointing out that individuals who accept complete freedom in certain areas will demand restrictions in many others.[18] Maslow also echoes this sentiment, stating that gratification of basic needs is important, but unrestricted indulgence can lead to irresponsibility, psychopathic personality, and inability to bear stress.[19]

Theory Y may be unreasonably idealistic.

A second criticism is that Theory Y advocates tend to believe that the primary place of need satisfaction is on the job. However, many workers satisfy their needs off the job. This is particularly apparent in light of the trend toward a shorter work week; people are seeking satisfaction during their leisure time. Theory Y may thus overemphasize the importance of satisfying higher-level needs in the work place.

Need satisfaction may not occur on the job.

A third common criticism involves whether or not there is a personality-organization conflict in large-scale mass-production industries. Critics contend that Theory Y assumes that concepts such as work simplification and standardization have reduced job satisfaction. However, this may be only one cause of organization conflict and perhaps is greatly overemphasized by Theory Y advocates.

The individual and organization are not always in conflict.

---

[16]McGregor, *op. cit.*, pp. 47–48.
[17]Erich Fromm, *The Sane Society* (New York: Holt, Rinehart & Winston, Inc., 1955), p. 318.
[18]George Strauss, "Some Notes on Power-Equalization." *In* Harold J. Leavitt, ed., *The Social Science of Organizations* (Englewood Cliffs, N.J.: Prentice-Hall, 1963), p. 50.
[19]A. H. Maslow, *Toward a Psychology of Being* (Princeton, N.J.: D. Van Nostrand Company Inc., 1962), pp. 153–154.

Which of the two theories is correct? The answer will depend on the situation and will always represent some combination of the two. One thing appears certain, however. Most managers tend to underrate the workers, subscribing more heavily to Theory X than to Theory Y. This has been made very clear by Chris Argyris.

ARGYRIS' IMMATURITY-MATURITY THEORY

Argyris, while at Yale University, studied industrial organizations to determine the effect of management practices on individual behavior and personal growth within the organization.[20] According to him, seven changes take place as an individual moves from infancy (immaturity) to adulthood (maturity). First, the passive state of the infant gives way to the increasingly active state of the adult. Second, the child becomes relatively independent as he or she matures. Third, an infant is capable of behaving in only a few ways whereas an adult can behave in many ways. Fourth, a child tends to have casual, shallow interests; an adult develops deep, strong interests. Fifth, a child's time perspective is very short, encompassing only the present; an adult's is longer, encompassing the past and future as well as the present. Sixth, an infant is subordinate to everyone whereas an adult is equal or superior to others. Seventh, children lack an awareness of "self" whereas adults are aware of and able to control "self." These seven stages can be viewed as stages in a continuum:

Seven stages of maturity development.

Immaturity ——————————— Maturity

Organizations keep people in an immature state.

Argyris contends that most organizations keep their people in a state of immaturity. Position descriptions, work assignments, and task specialization lead to routine, unchallenging jobs. They also minimize the amount of control workers have over their environment. This, in turn, encourages them to be passive, dependent, and submissive. Keeping people in this state is one of the formal organization's goals. The management likes to control everything, the workers being viewed as small cogs in a big machine. Of course, this type of thinking is incompatible with the development of a mature personality. The result is a formal organization incongruous with the mature individual. Argyris' findings echo McGregor's Theory X assumptions, indicating that management's view of the worker may be the major stumbling block in the motivation process. Unaware of what *really* motivates people, management is unable to come up with a viable theory of motivation. One individual who has attempted to shed light on this problem by extending Maslow's hierarchical concept and applying it to the job is Frederick Herzberg.

HERZBERG'S TWO-FACTOR THEORY OF MOTIVATION

In the late 1950's, Herzberg and his associates at the Psychological Service of Pittsburgh conducted extensive interviews with two hundred engineers and accountants from eleven industries in the Pittsburgh area.[21]

The individuals were asked to identify the elements of their job that made them happy or unhappy. An analysis of the findings revealed that when people were dissatisfied, their negative feelings were generally

---

[20]Chris Argyris, *Personality and Organization* (New York: Harper & Brothers, Publishers, Inc., 1957); *Interpersonal Competence and Organizational Effectiveness* (Homewood, Ill.: The Dorsey Press, 1962); *Integrating the Individual and the Organization* (New York: John Wiley & Sons, Inc., 1964).

[21]Frederick Herzberg, Bernard Mausner, and Barbara Bloch Snyderman, *The Motivation to Work*, 2nd edition (New York: John Wiley & Sons, Inc., 1959).

associated with the *environment* in which they were working. When people felt good about their jobs, this was generally associated with the *work itself*. Herzberg labeled the factors that prevent dissatisfaction *hygiene factors* and those that bring about satisfaction *motivators*.

The factors that prevent dissatisfaction are called hygiene factors because their effect on the worker resembles that of physical hygiene on the body. Consider, for example, the case of Barney, who slips on an icy path and suffers superficial hand cuts. At home Barney washes his hand and puts iodine on the wound. Two weeks later the hand is back to its normal state. The iodine did not make the hand any better than it was previous to the injury, but it prevented further deterioration such as gangrene and helped the hand return to its original state.

Hygiene Factors

This is what hygiene does. It takes a negative condition (cut hand) and brings it back to its original position (uncut hand). Conversely, if hygiene is denied, things can go from bad to worse. For example, Nancy, who is in excellent health, will not become any healthier by eating food but if she does not eat, she will eventually become sick and die. Likewise, breathing will not make her any healthier but failure to breathe will kill her. Hygiene will not improve health beyond one's original state, but it prevents deterioration by returning the person to his or her original state, which can be called condition zero.

Herzberg found that there are many hygiene factors in the work place. These include money, supervision, status, security, working conditions, policies and administration, and interpersonal relations (see Table 12–1). These factors do not motivate people, they merely prevent dissatisfaction. They produce no growth in worker output, but they prevent loss in performance caused by work restriction. They maintain motivation at *zero-level,* preventing a negative type of motivation from occurring. This is why they are often referred to as *maintenance* factors.

Hygiene factors prevent dissatisfaction.

Herzberg found that factors relating to the job itself can have a *positive effect* on job satisfaction and result in increased output. He called these motivators or satisfiers and identified them as the work itself, recognition, advancement, the possibility of growth, responsibility, and achievement.

Motivators

Motivators have a positive effect on job satisfaction.

Herzberg's two-factor theory presents some interesting ideas, but the reader should also be aware of what the critics say. First, the original study, consisting of accountants and engineers, is attacked as being unrep-

Motivation-Hygiene Under Attack

TABLE 12–1 Hygiene and Motivators

Hygiene Factors (Environment)	Motivators (Work Itself)
Money	Work Itself
Supervision	Recognition
Status	Advancement
Security	Possibility of Growth
Working Conditions	Responsibility
Policies and Administration	Achievement
Interpersonal Relations	

resentative of the work force in general. Second, although Herzberg has cited replication of the results of his study among groups such as manufacturing supervisors, hospital maintenance personnel, nurses, military officers, and professional women,[22] other researchers have uncovered different results.[23] In some cases, hygiene or maintenance factors, such as wages or job security, were found to be viewed as motivators among blue-collar workers. In addition, what one person might call a motivator, another person in the same department might term a hygiene factor. In

Criticism of Herz-
berg's theory.

one study conducted among both managerial and professional workers, Schwab, DeVitt, and Cummings found that Herzberg's hygiene factors were as useful in motivating employees as were his motivators.[24] Third, Vroom contends that Herzberg's findings are debatable because his two-factor conclusion was only one of many that could have been drawn from the research.[25] He argues that people are more likely to assign satisfaction to their own achievements and attribute dissatisfaction to company policies. Thus, the findings are interpretive at best.

The criticism indicates that the two-factor theory is certainly not universally accepted and more research is needed before definitive conclusions about it can be drawn. As Myers noted, "Motivation-maintenance theory, like any theory of management, is at the mercy of its practitioners and will remain intact and find effective utilization only to the extent that it serves as a mechanism for harnessing constructive motives."[26] Nevertheless, Herzberg's theory of job satisfaction has helped extend and apply Maslow's need hierarchy to work motivation.

**The Need
Hierarchy
and
Motivation-
Hygiene**

Herzberg's framework is compatible with Maslow's need hierarchy. Maslow's lower-level needs are analogous to Herzberg's hygiene factors, and his upper-level needs correspond to Herzberg's motivators. The comparison between the two is seen in Figure 12–5. As the figure indicates, Herzberg's hygiene factors encompass Maslow's physiological, safety, social, and, to some degree, esteem needs. The reason for placing status in the hygiene category and advancement and recognition in the motivator group is that status is not always a reflection of personal achievement or earned recognition. For example, an individual could achieve status through family ties such as inheritance or marriage. Conversely, advancement and recognition are more often reflections of personal achievement.

However, it must be realized that Maslow and Herzberg both tend to oversimplify the motivational process. Although Herzberg makes an interesting extension of Maslow's theory, neither of their models provides an adequate link between *individual* need satisfaction and the achievement

---

[22]Frederick Herzberg, *Work and the Nature of Man* (Cleveland, Ohio: The World Publishing Company, 1966); Valerie M. Bockman, "The Herzberg Controversy," *Personnel Psychology,* Summer 1971, pp. 155–189; Benedict S. Grigaliunas and Frederick Herzberg, "Relevancy in the Test of Motivation–Hygiene Theory," *Journal of Applied Psychology,* February 1971, pp. 73–79.

[23]For an interesting summary of some of this work see: Alan C. Filley, Robert J. House, and Steven Kerr, *Managerial Process and Organizational Behavior,* 2nd edition (Glenview, Illinois: Scott, Foresman and Company, 1976), pp. 197–200.

[24]Donald P. Schwab, H. William DeVitt and Larry L. Cummings, "A Test of the Adequacy of the Two-factor Theory as a Predictor of Self-Report Performance Effects," *Personnel Psychology,* Summer 1971, pp. 293–303.

[25]Victor H. Vroom, *Work and Motivation* (New York: John Wiley & Sons, Inc., 1964), pp. 128–129.

[26]M. Scott Myers, "Who Are Your Motivated Workers?" *Harvard Business Review,* January–February 1964, p. 88.

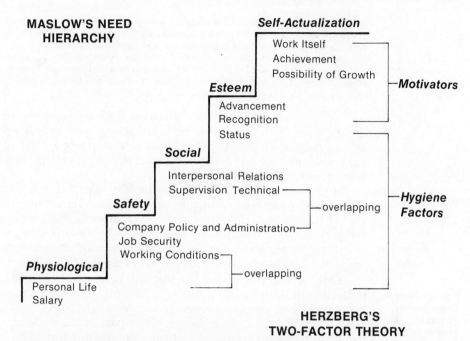

MASLOW'S NEED HIERARCHY

Self-Actualization
- Work Itself
- Achievement
- Possibility of Growth

Esteem
- Advancement
- Recognition
- Status

Social
- Interpersonal Relations
- Supervision Technical

Safety
- Company Policy and Administration
- Job Security
- Working Conditions

Physiological
- Personal Life
- Salary

overlapping

overlapping

Motivators

Hygiene Factors

HERZBERG'S TWO-FACTOR THEORY

FIGURE 12–5   Comparison of Maslow and Herzberg Models (See also Keith Davis, *Human Behavior at Work*, 5th edition, New York, McGraw-Hill Book Company, 1977, p. 53.)

of organizational objectives. Nor does either of their theories really handle the problem of individual differences in motivation. For this one must turn to *process* or mechanical theories.

Before doing this, however, two key concepts of modern motivation theory will be examined: expectancy theory and learned behavior.

EXPECTANCY THEORY AND LEARNED BEHAVIOR

Some of the most important modern process theories rely on what is called *expectancy theory*. In relating this concept to motivation:

. . . expectancy theory predicts that an individual will generally be a high performer when he: (1) sees a high probability that his efforts will lead to high performance, (2) sees a high probability that high performance will lead to outcomes, and (3) views these outcomes to be, on balance, positively attractive to himself.[27]

In comparing Maslow's concept of needs with this idea of expectancy, it becomes evident that there are two ways of studying motivational intensity. One can examine *need deficiencies*, as in Maslow's hierarchy, which promote a particular form of behavior; or one can examine *the goals the individual has chosen*, in which case motivation is seen as a force pulling the person toward the desired objective. Furthermore, in the case of need deprivation, the emphasis is on internal deficiencies; in the case of expectancy, the focus is on external goals that help alleviate these deficiencies. In essence, although the two ideas are different, they are related. However, today motivation researchers tend to favor the expectancy theory approach. Two of these individuals, Lyman Porter and Edward Lawler, cite the following reasons for choosing this approach:

Need-deprivation and expectancy theory approach are related.

Basically, the terminology and concepts involved seem to us to be more applicable to consideration of the complexities of human motivation and behavior, and, therefore, more

[27]L. L. Cummings and Donald P. Schwab, *Performance in Organizations: Determinants and Appraisal* (Glenview, Ill.: Scott, Foresman and Company, 1973), p. 31.

applicable to understanding the attitudes and performance of managers in organizations. The emphasis in expectancy theory on rationality and expectations seems to us to describe best the kinds of conditions that influence managerial performance. . . .

Expectancy theory also greatly facilitates the incorporation of motives like status, achievement, and power into a theory of attitudes and performance. There is a considerable amount of evidence that the central motives for most managers are those for *achievement, self-actualization, power and status,* and *income and advancement.*[28]

In addition, it should be noted that studies employing expectancy theory have been conducted in both private and public organizations, among employees ranging from production-line operators to managerial personnel, and have proved very successful in providing insights into this area of motivation.

If individuals are indeed motivated by expectations, they must have established some relationship between present action and future reward; i.e., if I work hard, I will be promoted. How is this causal relationship formulated? The answer is found in *learned behavior.* Through either direct or indirect experience, individuals learn to establish cause-effect relationships, which dictate how a person will respond in a given situation.

Reinforcement is one of the key factors in learned behavior.

One of the key factors in learned behavior is *reinforcement.* If an individual does something right and the manager wants to reinforce this behavior, he or she must respond in a way which the subordinate finds satisfying, such as giving the person a pat on the back or a raise. This response will help establish a causal relationship and it is likely that the individual will repeat the behavior in the future. Conversely, if the manager wants to extinguish a given behavior, he or she can turn to punishment or negative reinforcement such as a reprimand or a demotion.[29]

When the concept of expectancy theory is combined with that of learned behavior, one has the basis for understanding some of the most important modern motivation theories. One of these is Victor Vroom's expectancy-valence theory.

VROOM'S THEORY

Victor Vroom's motivation theory, despite its complexity, is viewed with great favor. His basic concept can be expressed in the following way:[30]

$$\text{Motivation} = \Sigma \text{ Valence} \times \text{Expectancy}$$

Motivation is equal to the summation of valence times expectancy. To understand Vroom's theory, three concepts must be grasped: instrumentality, valence, and expectancy.

Instrumentality is the relationship an individual perceives between a first- and second-level outcome.

An individual's motivation is a result of the actual or perceived rewards available to him or her for accomplishing some goal. For example, the company wants Roger to be productive. But what is in it for Roger? This will, of course, depend upon his perception of available rewards, but suppose for a moment that he believes there is a direct correlation between productivity and promotion, i.e., promotion depends on productivity. Then, given this assumption, there are two outcomes to consider. There is the "first-level outcome," which is productivity, and there is the

[28]Lyman W. Porter and Edward E. Lawler III, *Managerial Attitudes and Performance* (Homewood, Ill.: Richard D. Irwin, Inc. and the Dorsey Press, 1968), pp. 12–13.
[29]See, for example, Fred Luthans and Robert Kreitner, "The Role of Punishment in Organizational Behavior Modification (O.B. Mod.)," *Public Personnel Management*, May–June 1973, pp. 156–161; and Fred Luthans and Robert Kreitner, *Organizational Behavior Modification* (Glenview, Ill.: Scott, Foresman and Company, 1975).
[30]Vroom, *op. cit.,* Chapter 2.

"second-level outcome," which is promotion. This introduces the first of Vroom's three concepts, namely, instrumentality. *Instrumentality* is the relationship perceived by an individual between a first-level outcome and a second-level outcome.

Next, one has to consider Roger's *valence* or preference for the first-level outcome (productivity). To make it more meaningful, three variations of productivity will be used: high, average, and low. What is Roger's valence for high productivity? This will depend on his desire for promotion. If it is very high, his valence will be positive. If he is indifferent to promotion, it will be zero. If he does not want a promotion, it will be negative. The same logic can be used in determining his valence for average and low productivity. Thus, valence and instrumentality can be brought together in the following way:

> Valence is a person's preference for a particular outcome.

Valence or preference ⟶ Instrumentality ⟶ Second-level
for first-level   *(Perceived relationships*   outcome
outcome   *between first- and second-*   *(Promotion)*
(Productivity)   *level outcomes)*

In grasping Vroom's theory, one must work backward from instrumentality to valence. An individual's preference for a first-level outcome is dictated by the extent to which he or she believes this will lead to the attainment of a second-level outcome.

Vroom's third concept, *expectancy,* is the probability that a specific action will be followed by a particular first-level outcome. For example, what is the probability that if Roger works hard he can attain high productivity? This objective probability will range from zero (no chance) to one (certainty). If Roger is convinced that with hard work he can attain high productivity, his expectancy will be equal to one. These three concepts, instrumentality, valence, and expectancy, are incorporated in Figure 12–6.

> Expectancy is the probability that a specific action will yield a particular first-level outcome.

Motivation is thus equal to the algebraic sum of the products of the valences of all first-level outcomes (the person's preference for each of the first-level outcomes) times the strength of the expectancy that the action will be followed by the attainment of these outcomes (the probability of

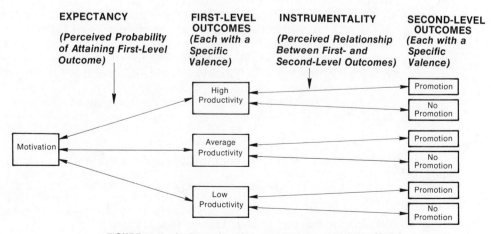

FIGURE 12–6 An Example of Vroom's Expectancy-Valence Model

attaining the respective first-level outcome). This formula helps the manager understand what motivates the *individual* worker.

Of course, Vroom's theory is difficult to comprehend and usually requires rereading. Additionally, because of the complexity of his motivation formula, we shall not attempt to apply it to a specific situation. An understanding of the basic ideas presented above is all the reader really needs. Keep in mind, however, that current researchers have higher regard for Vroom's theory than for most of the other motivation theories. As Hunt and Hill note:

> More work must be done before we can make any statements concerning the overall validity of Vroom's model. But the rigor of his formulation, the relative ease of making the concepts operational, and the model's emphasis on individual differences show considerable promise. We are also encouraged by the results of relatively sophisticated studies testing the theory. We believe it is time for those interested in organizational behavior to take a more thoroughly scientific look at this very complex subject of industrial motivation, and Vroom's model seems a big step in that direction.[31]

PORTER AND LAWLER'S MODEL

Another modern process theory is that proposed by Lyman Porter and Edward Lawler.[32] Porter and Lawler's model, also based on the expectancy theory of motivation, implies that individuals are motivated by future expectations based on previous experiences. In essence, their model contains a number of key variables, including effort, performance, reward, and satisfaction. Figure 12–7 illustrates the relationship among these variables.

It is important to note that Porter and Lawler use a semi-wavy line between *performance* and *intrinsic* rewards to indicate that a direct relationship exists *if* the job has been designed in such a way that when the person has performed well, he can reward himself with, for example, an internally generated payoff such as a feeling of accomplishment. The wavy line between *performance* and *extrinsic* rewards in the figure shows that such rewards are often not directly related to performance; e.g., an externally generated payoff such as a pay increase. The arrow between performance and perceived equitable rewards depicts the fact that a person's performance influences his perception of what he should receive, i.e., if Harry does not get the level of rewards he believes he should, satisfaction will be negatively affected.

Lawler has recently made several refinements of his own, presented in the model in Figure 12–7. In particular, he believes that there are *two* types of expectancies: E→P (effort leads to performance) and P→O (performance leads to a specific outcome).

A person's effort or motivation is influenced by his or her perception of the relationship between effort and performance (if I work hard, will I obtain the desired performance?) and the perception of the relationship between performance and a specific outcome (if I have high performance, will I get a promotion?). Finally, the person's valence for the promotion must be considered. Some people have suggested a simple way of integrating all three ideas into a formula for determining an *effort* or *motivation index*. It is:

$$\frac{E \to P}{(0 \text{ to } 1.0)} \times \frac{P \to O}{(0 \text{ to } 1.0)} \times \frac{\text{Valence}}{(0 \text{ to } 1.0)} = \frac{\text{Effort}}{\text{Index}}$$

[31]J. G. Hunt and J. W. Hill, "The New Look in Motivation Theory for Organizational Research," *Human Organization*, Summer 1969, p. 108.
[32]Porter and Lawler, *op. cit.*

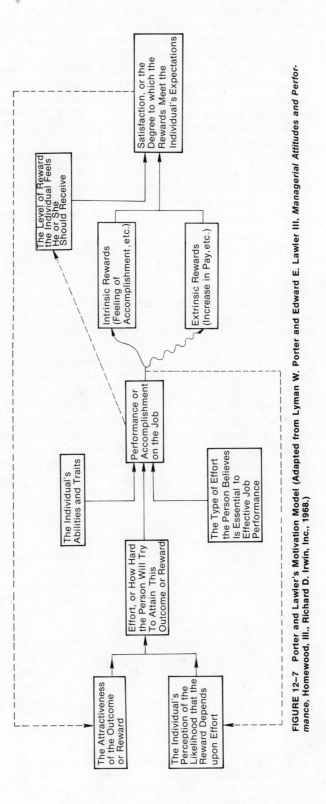

FIGURE 12–7 Porter and Lawler's Motivation Model (Adapted from Lyman W. Porter and Edward E. Lawler III, *Managerial Attitudes and Performance*, Homewood, Ill., Richard D. Irwin, Inc., 1968.)

Employing this formula, consider the case of Steven, who believes that effort is directly related to performance (1.0); that high performance is very likely to bring about the desired outcome of promotion (0.8); and he has a high valence for the promotion (0.9). In this case, Steven's effort or motivation index is: $1.0 \times 0.8 \times 0.9 = 0.72$.

In contrast, consider the case of Ruth, who believes effort is directly related to performance (1.0), but high performance is not likely to bring about a promotion (0.4), although she does have a high valence for the promotion (0.9). In this case Ruth's effort or motivation index is: $1.0 \times 0.4 \times 0.9 = 0.36$. Note that if one of the three factors in the effort index is low, motivation suffers greatly.[33]

Returning to the Vroom model and comparing it with the one in Figure 12–7, it is evident that the latter is more comprehensive. It also proposes the relationship between rewards and performance, concluding that an individual's satisfaction is a function of the rewards received. In turn, these rewards are brought about by performance. Thus:

$$\text{Performance} \xrightarrow{\substack{\text{Leads} \\ \text{To}}} \text{Rewards} \xrightarrow{\substack{\text{Which} \\ \text{Bring} \\ \text{About}}} \text{Satisfaction}$$

This is a rather interesting finding since many managers feel that satisfaction leads to performance; i.e., a happy worker is a productive worker. However, Porter and Lawler report just the opposite; performance causes satisfaction.

Today the performance-satisfaction controversy continues. Which is the cause? Which is the effect? By way of confusing the issue, it should be noted that there are some individuals who contend that both performance and satisfaction are caused by the reward system.[34]

Although research is still being conducted in an attempt to resolve the issue, one fact is indisputable. Rewards are important in the motivation process and the level of these rewards must be commensurate with what the individual believes they should be. This concept is known as equity theory, and although it was treated in Porter and Lawler's model, it will be considered separately now.

The performance-satisfaction controversy still rages.

EQUITY OR SOCIAL COMPARISON THEORY

People compare their rewards with those received by others.

Equity theory is an extension of Barnard's concept about the worker's weighing what he or she is getting from the company against what he or she is giving to the company. However, equity theory goes further, contending that the individual evaluates not only his or her personal position, but that of others as well. People are motivated not only by what they get but also by what they see, or believe, others are getting. They make a social comparison of inputs (education, effort, time spent on the job) and rewards (money, working conditions, recognition) for themselves and others in the organization. For example, Roger feels that he is entitled to a raise of $1000 for the upcoming year. His superior calls him and tells him he is going to get $1750. Roger is elated. However, later in the day he discovers that George, his archrival, has received $2300. Now Roger is

---

[33]For more on this subject see: Richard M. Steers and Lyman W. Porter, *Motivation and Work Behavior* (New York: McGraw Hill Book Company, 1975), Chapter 6.
[34]Charles N. Greene, "The Satisfaction-Performance Controversy," *Business Horizons*, October 1972, pp. 31–41.

angry because he feels he is giving as much to the company as George, but is receiving less. Initially he was happy with the "extra" $750 but now he is not, because social comparison has shown that George is getting a bigger reward than he. Figure 12–8 shows how this social comparison works.

When people feel they are not being properly treated, tension results. In relieving this tension, there are a number of alternatives available. For example, Roger may quit his job. Or he may go to his boss and demand more money, thereby establishing equality with George. Or he may stop comparing himself with George because he cannot hope to keep up, and find a different rival. Or he may do less work. However, the most likely alternative is that he will change his perception of George's input-reward ratio. For example, "George has three kids and I only have one, so my $1750 will go a lot further than his $2300."

It is also interesting to note that some research shows that when a person feels overpaid, at least initially, he or she tends to do more work. In this way the individual justifies the higher salary. However, in time one will usually reevaluate his skills and position, concluding that he is indeed worth the higher salary. Output will then drop back to its former level. This accounts for the belief of some researchers that money is a short-run motivator at best, and only one tool among many that the manager can use in the motivation process. As McClelland has pointed out, money:

. . . is a treacherous tool because it is deceptively concrete, tempting many managers to neglect variables in the work situation and climate that really affect productivity. In the near future, there will be less and less excuse for neglecting these variables, as the behavioral sciences begin to define them and explain to management how they can be manipulated just as one might change a financial compensation plan.[36]

SUMMARY

In this chapter modern motivation theory has been examined. First, the relationship between needs and behavior was shown through the use of Maslow's hierarchy. These ideas were then refined and applied to the work place through Herzberg's model.

Both theories provide important *general* insights into workers' behavior because they stress the importance of examining the *causes* of human activity and help answer the question, *what* specific things motivate people?

However, the manager must also be concerned with explaining *how* behavior is initiated, directed, sustained, or halted. To do this he or she must understand process or mechanical theories. In this chapter three of these theories were examined: Vroom's expectancy-valence theory, Porter and Lawler's motivation model, and equity or social comparison theory. All three place great emphasis on *individual* motivation.

In the past few years, increased attention has been given to these process theories because of their value in applying general motivation

---

[36]McClelland, *op. cit.*, p. 649.

FIGURE 12–8 Social Comparison

| Roger | | George |

Compared with

INPUTS **INPUTS**

REWARDS **REWARDS**

theory to specific situations. Yet, whatever approach the manager uses, one question must remain foremost — what will motivate the worker(s) to attain organizational objectives? Once this is answered, the manager is in a position to examine the area of leadership. Now that the manager knows what will motivate the people, he or she can focus attention on leading them. The topic of leadership will be the subject of the next chapter.

REVIEW AND STUDY QUESTIONS

1. What is the relationship between needs and behavior?

2. What are the five needs in Maslow's hierarchy? What relevance do they have to the study of motivation?

3. What are the assumptions of Theory X? Theory Y?

4. What is Argyris' immaturity-maturity theory? Do you agree or disagree with his findings?

5. What does Herzberg mean by hygiene factors? Identify some of them.

6. What does Herzberg mean by motivators? Identify some of them.

7. What relationship do Herzberg and Maslow's theories bear to one another in general and specifically to motivation? Explain.

8. What does Vroom mean by instrumentality? Valence? Expectancy? Explain.

9. Of what value is Vroom's theory to the practicing manager?

10. How does Porter and Lawler's model expand the ideas presented by Vroom?

11. Of what value is the Porter-Lawler model to the practicing manager?

12. What is meant by equity or social comparison theory? Give an illustration. What is its relevance to motivation theory?

13. In your own words, what are the steps to effective motivation? What should every manager know about the process?

SELECTED REFERENCES

Annas, J. W. "Profiles of Motivation." *Personnel Journal,* March 1973, pp. 205–208.

Bockman, V. M. "The Herzberg Controversy." *Personnel Psychology,* Summer 1971, pp. 155–189.

Davis, K. *Human Behavior at Work,* 5th edition. New York: McGraw-Hill Book Company, 1977, Chapter 3.

Gellerman, S. W. *Management by Motivation.* New York: American Management Association, 1968.

Greene, C. N. "The Satisfaction-Performance Controversy." *Business Horizons,* October 1972, pp. 31–41.

Herzberg, F., B. Mausner, and B. B. Snyderman. *The Motivation to Work.* New York: John Wiley & Sons, Inc., 1959.

Herzberg, F. *Work and the Nature of Man.* Cleveland: The World Publishing Company, 1966.

Hulin, C. L., and P. C. Smith. "An Empirical Investigation of Two Implications of the Two-Factor Theory of Job Satisfaction." *Journal of Applied Psychology,* October 1967, pp. 396–402.

Lindsay, C. A., E. Marks, and L. Gorlow. "The Herzberg Theory: A Critique and Reformulation." *Journal of Applied Psychology,* August 1967, pp. 330–339.

Maslow, A. H. *Motivation and Personality.* New York: Harper & Row Publishers, Inc., 1954.

Maslow, A. H. *Eupsychian Management.* Homewood, Ill.: Richard D. Irwin, Inc., and The Dorsey Press, 1965.

Organ, D. W. "A Reappraisal and Reinterpretation of the Satisfaction-Causes-Performance Hypothesis." *Academy of Management Review,* January 1977, pp. 46–53.

Paul, R. J. "Workers' Compensation — An Adequate Employee Benefit?" *Academy of Management Review,* October 1976, pp. 112–123.

Pinder, C. C. "Concerning the Application of Human Motivation Theories in Organizational Settings." *Academy of Management Review,* July 1977, pp. 384–397.

Porter, L. W., and E. E. Lawler III. *Managerial Attitudes and Performance.* Homewood, Ill.: Richard D. Irwin, Inc., 1968.

Steers, R. M., and L. W. Porter. *Motivation and Work Behavior.* New York: McGraw-Hill Book Company, 1975.

Vroom, V. H. *Work and Motivation.* New York: John Wiley & Sons, 1964.

Weaver, C. N. "Job Preferences of White Collar and Blue Collar Workers." *Academy Of Management Journal,* March 1975, pp. 167–175.

CASE: MONEY AND MOTIVATION[37]

Is money a motivator? Some people say it always is, others believe that it depends on the situation. For example, someone earning $10,000 a year will be more motivated by a raise of $1000 than someone earning $100,000 a year. Still other people believe that every raise must be separated into two parts: that which is given for cost of living (no motivation potential) and that which is given for merit (high motivation potential). James L. Haynes, president of the American Management Association, was recently asked how important pay raises or bonuses are in motivating people to work harder or produce more effectively. He gave the following answer:

Well, they ease the pain, but pay certainly isn't the whole answer. If you have a worker who finds his job distasteful, merely changing his pay level won't keep him satisfied. Unfortunately, the "more pay" approach to job satisfaction is being taken all too often by workers and unions as well as by management.

Actually, a company's wage or salary policy can sometimes foster misunderstanding. Many a boss calls in a worker and says, "You're not doing the job we expect, but we're still going to give you a modest raise."

Nothing should signal a job well done better than a raise. But many companies continuously reward people with pay boosts year after year, then suddenly surprise them by telling them they haven't been doing satisfactory work and they're going to be separated.

Questions

1. How important is money as a motivator? Explain your answer.

2. In addition to money, what else motivates people to work hard? Cite some illustrations.

3. When is money likely to be one of the most important motivators (if not *the* most important) and when is it likely to finish way down the list? Based on

---

[37]The data in this case can be found in: "Want to Be a Better Boss? Advice from an Expert," *U.S. News & World Report,* March 21, 1977, pp. 68–70.

your answer, what conclusions can be drawn regarding the use of money as a motivator?

CASE: WHITE COLLAR STATUS[38]

When Arthur King was laid off from his production job at a textile factory in Kinston, N.C., he found another at an Eaton Corporation plant in nearby Greenville. His new job paid nearly $100 less a week, yet when he was recalled to the textile mill a month later, he decided to stay at Eaton. Why? Arthur found the Eaton Plant to be a lot less regimented than his former organization. The Greenville division is one of 13 Eaton plants in which the company has instituted a new philosophy of labor-management relations. Under the new philosophy, blue-collar workers are treated basically like white-collar employees. They get weekly salaries instead of hourly wages, participate in the corporate pension program, and get paid for sick absences. In addition, the supervisors use loose, as opposed to close, control. The result has been a more meaningful work environment:

The "new philosophy" emphasizes equal treatment of blue-collar and office workers. Thus, informal "dialogues" have replaced formal interviews in the hiring process, probationary periods for new employees have been eliminated, and blue-collar workers no longer have to punch time clocks. No longer, as in the old days, does a foreman recite a long list of disciplinary rules to a new worker. To demonstrate management's "trust" in the worker — a key element of the new approach — no formal system of rules and penalties is applied.

... Under the new system, production workers are allowed to repair their own equipment and to switch work situations as bottlenecks occur. They, or their representatives, are invited to attend weekly staff meetings, production planning sessions, and other discussions.

Eaton officials say the new program aids productivity growth. Hourly product output in the new plants ranged up to 35 per cent higher than at Eaton's older plants ... data indicate that the new plants are also more efficient in other ways: Absenteeism is running at a 0.5 to 3 per cent rate in the new plants, compared with 6 to 12 per cent in the old plants, and turnover as a result of voluntary resignations has been reduced from as high as 60 per cent a year in the old plants to 4 per cent in the new ones.

All of the firm's new plants are located in rural areas of the South and Midwest, which may help account for why none are unionized. However, it is interesting to note that at least six union representation elections have been held at the 13 plants, and the workers, who mostly come from nonunion backgrounds, have voted down the union in each case. A company spokesman insists that the objective of the new philosophy is not to keep out the union, but obviously the new working conditions are playing some role in the election outcomes. Eaton says that it has no intention of forcing the new system on plants that are already unionized, because the union would probably fight it strongly. However, in those plants where it has been established, both the workers and the management intend to keep it.

---

[38]The data in this case can be found in: "Where White-Collar Status Boosts Productivity," *Business Week*, May 23, 1977, pp. 80–85.

1. What particular needs in Maslow's hierarchy does this new philosophy help the workers satisfy?

2. Are these new conditions an illustration of hygiene factors or motivators?

3. Using Porter and Lawler's model of motivation, how can you explain the increases in output in those plants where this new philosophy has been adopted?

CASE: SET YOUR OWN TIME[39]

An increasing number of Americans are deciding for themselves which hours to spend on the job. The term used to describe this adaptable work schedule is "flexitime." The following is a brief primer on flexitime:

What it is: **A system of flexible working hours, often arranged to suit a worker's convenience.**
How it is scheduled: **At both the beginning and end of the workday, employees arrive and leave at times of their own choosing.**
Core time: **A central time period when everybody is expected to be on the job.**
Illustration: **A worker shows up at 8 A.M. and leaves at 4:30 P.M. two days a week. On the other three days, he arrives at 9 A.M. and leaves at 6 P.M. Lunch times can be shifted too — for example, they can be taken at any time between noon and 2 P.M.**

Do the workers like flexitime? Many do. One reason is that they feel they have some control because they are not fitted into a time mold. Another is that those who like to sleep a little later in the morning can do so, while others who peak by mid-afternoon can start earlier in the day and avoid the "late afternoon blahs." Workers in major metropolitan areas can schedule their time to avoid the rush hours, reducing travel time by as much as 50 per cent.

Managers also seem to like the idea. At Northwestern Life, for example, the turnover rate with flexitime has dropped to its lowest level since World War II. Meanwhile a spokesman for General Motors of Canada calls flexitime "an employee benefit that carries no price tag."

Of course, many jobs do not lend themselves to flexitime. However, companies that have adopted it can count on trouble if they try going back to the old schedule. As one employee put it, "If you ask me, flexitime is great. I wouldn't have it any other way."

---

[39]The information in this case can be found in: "The Swelling Ranks of Workers Who Set Their Own Hours," *U.S. News & World Report,* August 1, 1977, pp. 62–63.

Questions

1. Why do workers like flexitime? Explain.

2. According to Herzberg's theory, is flexitime a hygiene factor or a motivator? Give your reasoning.

3. Are there any drawbacks to flexitime? What are they?

CASE: IT'S UP TO THE MANAGER[40]

Historically, the United States has been an achievement-oriented culture. The national archives are bursting with tales of rugged men with a purpose who tamed the frontier, moved mountains so trains could run, and built industrial empires. Yet we know from industry research that not all managers are successful in their efforts to get subordinates to accomplish their goals.

A recent study reveals that there are some marked differences between successful and unsuccessful managers. The former are commonly high achievers while the latter are often low achievers. Those in the middle, meanwhile, are known as average achievers. In contrasting them, one researcher employed the following description:

High Achievers place major emphasis on the actualization, belonging and ego-status needs composing the motivator package, paying only average attention to the hygiene factors. Low Achievers, on the other hand, virtually ignore motivators while stressing the importance of creature comfort and, particularly, safety and security issues having hygiene significance. Average Achievers stress ego-status, giving adequate attention to the actualization needs of their subordinates, essentially promoting motivation seeking among those they manage. As ... expected, managerial achievement is linked to the motivational climate one creates for ... subordinates as well as to personal striving.

Additionally, recent research shows that subordinates' behavior tends to reflect the attitudes of bosses. Low achievers are most interested in hygiene factors and so are their subordinates. High achievers are more interested in self-actualization than in mere comfort, and so are their subordinates. Finally, average achievers tend to place highest concern on belongingness and ego-status and so do their subordinates. In putting this all in perspective, Jay Hall notes:

Thus are motivational prophecies fulfilled. Not only does personal motivation affect a manager's achievement level, so does his perception of the motivational process and his consequent practices in the management of motives. Indeed, in what appears to be causal fashion, a manager's achievement is directly linked to the motivational profile of his subordinates. A sobering thought is inferred: *the needs and quality of motivation characterizing a manager's subordinates may say more about the manager than about his subordinates.*

---

[40]The data in this case can be found in: Jay Hall, "To Achieve or Not: The Manager's Choice," *California Management Review,* Summer 1975, pp. 5–18.

1. Why are high achievement–oriented managers more successful in motivating their people than are low achievement–oriented managers?

2. Exactly what does the above statement "the needs and quality of motivation characterizing a manager's subordinates may say more about the manager than about his subordinates" mean? Explain.

3. How can findings such as those reported in this case help companies motivate their personnel? Explain.

CHAPTER THIRTEEN

LEADERSHIP EFFECTIVENESS

GOALS OF THE CHAPTER

What differentiates the effective leader from the ineffective leader? Perhaps the answer rests in the very definition of management, namely, getting things done through people. In any event, there are some managers who are successful at their jobs and others who are not. The goals of this chapter are to investigate the nature of leadership and to examine some of the current theories of leadership. The central theme will be leadership *effectiveness*.

When you have finished reading this chapter you should be able to:

1. Define the term *leadership*.
2. Discuss the relevance of trait theory to the study of leadership.
3. Explain what is meant by situational theory and why it is so well accepted today.
4. Relate the value of continuum models to the understanding of leadership.
5. Describe the importance of two-dimensional models in the study of leadership.
6. Relate the value of contingency leadership theory to the modern manager, with particular attention to Fiedler's contingency model, Reddin's 3-D theory, Hersey and Blanchard's life cycle theory, and House's path-goal theory.
7. Discuss the importance to the modern manager of adaptive leadership styles.

THE NATURE OF LEADERSHIP

Definitions of leadership.

Leadership, as McFarland notes, is an "elusive" concept.[1] It has been described in many different ways. Koontz and O'Donnell call it "the ability of a manager to induce subordinates to work with confidence and zeal."[2] Haimann, Scott, and Connor see it as a "process by which people are directed, guided, and influenced in choosing and achieving goals."[3] Glueck defines it as "a set of interpersonal behaviors designed to influence employees to cooperate in the achievement of objectives."[4] In synthesizing current views, it is accurate to say that most writers in the field of management feel leadership is a process of *influencing* people to direct their efforts toward the achievement of some particular goal(s). As such, leadership is a part of management. Of course, managers must do more than merely lead, but if they fail to influence people to accomplish assigned goals, they fail as managers.

---

[1]Dalton E. McFarland, *Management: Principles and Practices,* 4th edition (New York: The Macmillan Company, 1974), p. 484.
[2]Harold Koontz and Cyril O'Donnell, *Management: A Systems and Contingency Analysis of Managerial Functions,* 6th edition (New York: McGraw-Hill Book Company, 1976), p. 587.
[3]Theo Haimann, William G. Scott, and Patrick E. Connor, *Managing the Modern Organization,* 3rd edition (Boston: Houghton Mifflin Company, 1978), p. 410.
[4]William F. Glueck, *Management* (Hinsdale, Illinois: The Dryden Press, 1977), p. 183.

Every organization needs leaders, but what is it that distinguishes these individuals from others? For years, many people have sought to answer this question by turning to all sorts of quackery. The analysis of handwriting (graphology), the study of skull shapes (phrenology), and the investigation of the position of the stars and other celestial elements upon human affairs (astrology) have all been employed. However, the two most scientific approaches that have been used are trait theory and situational theory.

Trait Theory

Trait theory examines successful leadership from the standpoint of the individual's personal characteristics; that is, what is it about a person that makes him or her a good leader? In 1940, Charles Byrd examined twenty lists of traits that were attributed to leaders in various surveys but discovered none of the items appearing on all lists.[5] Later in the decade, Jenkins, after reviewing a wide spectrum of studies encompassing such diverse groups as children, and business, professional, and military personnel, categorically stated that, "No single trait or group of characteristics has been isolated which sets off the leader from the members of his group."[6] This undoubtedly accounts for the decline in the importance of trait theory. Clear-cut results have just not been forthcoming, the reason being that the method fails to consider the entire leadership environment. Traits are important, but they are only one part of the picture. The members of the work group and the situation itself (task, technology, goals, structure) are also major variables, for leadership is a function of the *leader*, the *follower*, and the *situation*, i.e., $L = f(l, f, s)$.

Clear-cut findings have not been obtained.

Yet, despite its failures, one must not be too hasty in discarding trait theory, for it has made some contributions toward clarifying the nature of leadership. For example, studies show that there are four traits that appear to be related to successful leadership. Davis identifies these as:

Traits of successful leaders.

Intelligence. **Leaders generally are slightly more intelligent than the average of their followers.**
Social maturity and breadth. **Leaders are emotionally mature, capable of handling extreme situations. They are also able to socialize well with others and have reasonable self-assurance and self-respect.**
Inner motivation and achievement drives. **Leaders have a strong drive to accomplish things.**
Human relations attitudes. **Leaders know they rely on people to get the work done; they therefore try to develop social understanding. They are employee-oriented.**[7]

Yet trait theory tends to be more descriptive than analytical. As such, its value in predicting success has been, at best, very limited. As a result, to a large degree it has been replaced by situational theory.

Situational Theory

Situational theory is now more commonly accepted than is trait theory. According to this theory, there are situational factors or dimensions which are finite in number and vary according to the leader's personality; the requirements of the task; the expectations, needs, and attitudes of the

[5]Charles Byrd, *Social Psychology* (New York: Appleton-Century-Crofts, 1940), p. 378.
[6]William O. Jenkins, "A Review of Leadership Studies with Particular Reference to Military Problems," *Psychological Bulletin*, January 1947, pp. 74–75.
[7]Keith Davis, *Human Behavior At Work*, 4th edition (New York: McGraw-Hill Book Company, 1972), pp. 103–104. For further information on this area see Fred E. Fiedler and Martin M. Chemers, *Leadership and Effective Management* (Glenview, Ill.: Scott, Foresman and Company, 1974), pp. 22–28; 31–34.

followers; and the environment in which all are operating. For example, Filley, House, and Kerr, after conducting a review of the literature, found that the following factors tend to have an impact on leadership effectiveness:

1. History of the organization.
2. Age of the previous incumbent in the leader's position.
3. Age of the leader and his previous experience.
4. Community in which the organization operates.
5. Particular work requirements of the group.
6. Psychological climate of the group being led.
7. Kind of job the leader holds.
8. Size of the group led.
9. Degree to which group-member cooperation is required.
10. Cultural expectations of subordinates.
11. Group-member personalities.
12. Time required and allowed for decision making.[8]

Factors influencing leadership effectiveness.

Unfortunately, these studies all tend to focus on widely differing variables. Although they are not contradictory, neither are they supportive of one another. Nevertheless, they do illustrate that certain types of leadership behavior are effective in certain kinds of situations.

(By permission of John Hart and Field Enterprises, Inc.)

Leadership Behavior

Having discussed the nature of leadership, attention will now be focused on the various types of *leadership behavior*; that is, how does a leader act with his or her group?

A Leadership Continuum

The most common approach is to view leadership behavior on a continuum, such as illustrated in Figure 13–1. As one moves from the left to the right, the manager exercises less authority and the subordinates have greater areas of freedom.

Leadership characteristics.

The manager who stays on the left side of the continuum is known as an *authoritarian leader*. This person is an individual who tends to determine all policy, maintain close control of the subordinates, and tell people only what they need to know to get the work done. Conversely, the manager on the right side of the continuum is known as a *democratic leader*. This person tends to allow the people to have a say in what goes on, use less control, and encourage feedback from the subordinates. The

---

[8]Alan C. Filley, Robert J. House, and Steven Kerr, *Managerial Process and Organizational Behavior*, 2nd edition (Glenview, Ill.: Scott, Foresman and Company, 1976), pp. 241–242. See also Fiedler and Chemers, *op. cit.* pp. 28–31.

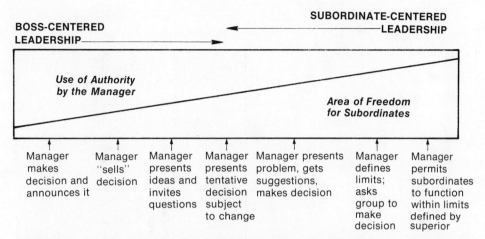

FIGURE 13–1 Continuum of Leadership Behavior (From Robert Tannenbaum and Warren H. Schmidt, "How To Choose a Leadership Pattern," *Harvard Business Review*, March-April 1958, p. 96. Reprinted with permission.)

behavior continuum illustrates that the manager has various options available. Figure 13–1 also indicates that there are two types of leadership style. One emphasizes the work to be done (boss-centered leader) and the other gives attention to the people who are doing this work (employee-centered leader). This basic idea has been developed in greater depth by various researchers such as Rensis Likert.

The basic concept presented in Figure 13–1 has been expanded through the work of Rensis Likert and his associates at the Institute for Social Research of the University of Michigan. After conducting leadership research in literally hundreds of organizations, Likert has discovered four basic styles, which can be depicted on a continuum from System 1 to System 4 as follows:

Likert's Management Systems

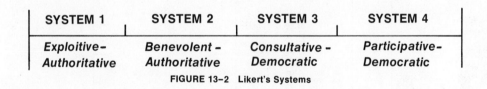

FIGURE 13–2 Likert's Systems

System 1. Management has little confidence in the subordinates as seen by the fact that they are seldom involved in the decision-making process. Management makes most decisions and passes them down the line, employing threats and coercion when necessary to get things done. Superiors and subordinates deal with each other in an atmosphere of distrust. If an informal organization develops, it generally opposes the goals of the formal organization.

System 2. Management acts in a condescending manner toward the subordinates. Although there is some decision making at the lower levels, it occurs within a prescribed framework. Rewards and some actual punishment are used to motivate the workers. In superior-subordinate interaction, the management acts condescendingly and the subordinates appear cautious and fearful. Although an informal organization usually develops, it does not always oppose the goals of the formal organization.

Four basic systems of leadership.

System 3. Management has quite a bit of confidence and trust in the subordinates. Although major important decisions are made at the top, subordinates make specific decisions at the lower levels. Two-way communication is in evidence, and there is some

ORGANIZATIONAL VARIABLE	SYSTEM 1	SYSTEM 2	SYSTEM 3	SYSTEM 4
Leadership Processes Used				
Extent to Which Superiors Have Confidence and Trust in Subordinates	Have no confidence and trust in subordinates	Have condescending confidence and trust, such as master has in servant	Substantial but not complete confidence and trust; still wish to keep control of decisions	Complete confidence and trust in all matters
Character of Motivational Forces				
Underlying Motives Tapped	Physical security, economic needs, and some use of the desire for status	Economic needs and moderate use of ego motives, e.g., desire for status, affiliation and achievement	Economic needs and considerable use of ego and other major motives, e.g., desire for new experiences	Full use of economic, ego, and other major motives such as motivational forces arising from group goals
Character of Communication Process				
Amount of Interaction and Communication Aimed at Achieving Organization's Objectives	Very little	Little	Quite a bit	Much with both individuals and groups

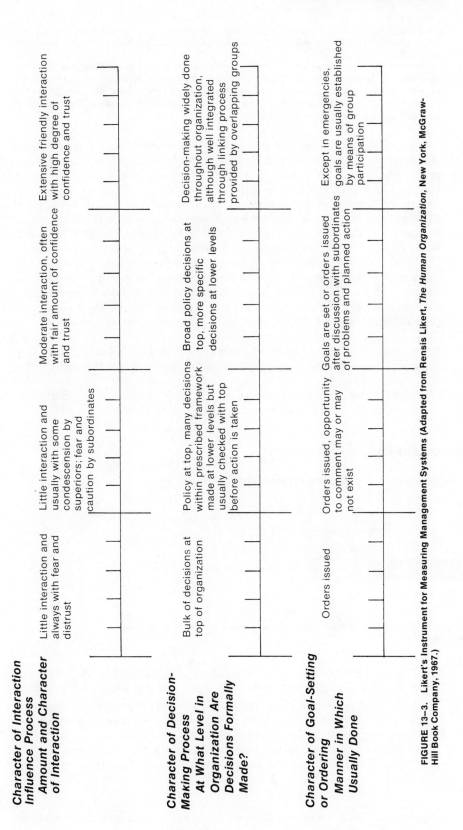

FIGURE 13–3. Likert's Instrument for Measuring Management Systems (Adapted from Rensis Likert, *The Human Organization,* **New York, McGraw-Hill Book Company, 1967.)**

Character of Interaction Influence Process

Amount and Character of Interaction

Little interaction and always with fear and distrust

Little interaction and usually with some condescension by superiors; fear and caution by subordinates

Moderate interaction, often with fair amount of confidence and trust

Extensive friendly interaction with high degree of confidence and trust

Character of Decision-Making Process

At What Level in Organization Are Decisions Formally Made?

Bulk of decisions at top of organization

Policy at top, many decisions within prescribed framework made at lower levels but usually checked with top before action is taken

Broad policy decisions at top, more specific decisions at lower levels

Decision-making widely done throughout organization, although well integrated through linking process provided by overlapping groups

Character of Goal-Setting or Ordering

Manner in Which Usually Done

Orders issued

Orders issued, opportunity to comment may or may not exist

Goals are set or orders issued after discussion with subordinates of problems and planned action

Except in emergencies, goals are usually established by means of group participation

confidence and trust between superiors and subordinates. If an informal organization develops, it will either support or offer only a slight resistance to the goals of the formal organization.

System 4. Management has complete confidence and trust in the subordinates. Decision making is highly decentralized. Communication not only flows up and down the organization but among peers as well. Superior-subordinate interaction takes place in a friendly environment and is characterized by mutual confidence and trust. The formal and informal organizations are often one and the same.[9]

Systems 1 and 4 approximate the Theory X and Theory Y assumptions elaborated upon in Chapter 12. System 1 managers are highly job-centered and authoritarian in nature; System 4 managers are highly employee-centered and democratic in nature.

In evaluating an organization's leadership style, Likert's group has developed a measuring instrument, a sample of which is illustrated in Figure 13–3. There are 51 items encompassing variables related to leadership, motivation, communication, interaction-influence, decision making, goal setting, control, and performance goals. By evaluating a manager in each of these areas, a profile can be compiled. For example, an individual may be basically a System 2 manager, meaning that, in general, the person is a benevolent-authoritative leader (see Figure 13–2). The same type of profile can be constructed for the organization as a whole.

RESEARCH RESULTS AND MANAGEMENT SYSTEMS. Likert reports that most managers feel high-producing departments are on the right of the continuum (System 4) whereas low-producing ones are more on the left (System 1). Some research results seem to support this pattern. For example, a study of clerical supervisors revealed the following:

NUMBER OF SUPERVISORS WHO ARE:

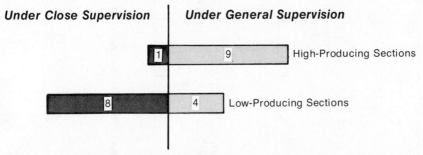

FIGURE 13–4   (Reported in Rensis Likert, *New Patterns of Management,* New York, McGraw-Hill Book Company, 1961, p. 9.)

Those section heads who were closely supervised tended to have lower producing units than those who were under general supervision.

A study of railroad maintenance-of-way crews provided the results in Figure 13–5. Foremen who ignored mistakes or tried to use them as educational experiences in showing their men how to do the job correctly had higher producing sections than their critical-punitive counterparts.

When workers in a service operation were asked how free they felt to

---

[9]Adapted from Rensis Likert, *The Human Organization* (New York: McGraw-Hill Book Company, 1967), pp. 4–10.

FOREMAN'S REACTION TO A POOR JOB
(in the opinion of the men)

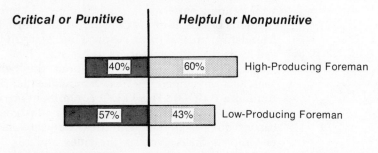

FIGURE 13–5 (Reported in Rensis, Likert, *New Patterns of Management*, McGraw-Hill Book Company, New York, 1961, p. 11.)

set their own pace, the general pattern of responses was similar to that of the previous two studies (see Figure 13–6).

Likert has found that "Supervisors with the best records of performance focus their primary attention on the human aspects of their subordinates' problems and on endeavoring to build effective work groups with high performance goals."[10] In short, they are the employee-centered managers.

An extension of this leadership continuum is found in two-dimensional leadership models as reflected in the work of Ohio State University researchers and Blake and Mouton's managerial grid.

Two-dimensional Leadership

OHIO STATE LEADERSHIP RESEARCH. In 1945, the Bureau of Business Research at Ohio State University began an extensive inquiry into the area of leadership. Eventually, they narrowed down leader behavior into two

---

[10]Rensis Likert, *New Patterns of Management*, (New York: McGraw-Hill Book Company, 1961), p. 7.

PRODUCTIVITY

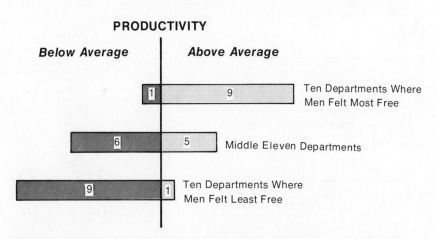

FIGURE 13–6   Relationship Between Freedom to Set Own Pace and Department Productivity (Reported in Rensis Likert, *New Patterns of Management*, New York, McGraw-Hill Book Company, 1961, p. 8.)

dimensions: *initiating structure* and *consideration*. Initiating structure referred to "the leader's behavior in delineating the relationship between himself and members of the work-group and endeavoring to establish well-defined patterns of organization, channels of communication, and methods of procedure." Consideration referred to "behavior indicative of friendship, mutual trust, respect, and warmth in the relationship between the leader and the members of his staff."[11]

In gathering information about the behavior of leaders, the researchers developed the now-famous Leader Behavior Description Questionnaire (LBDQ). The LBDQ contains items relating to both "initiating structure" and "consideration" and is designed to describe *how* a leader carries out his or her activities. Items related to "initiating structure" encompass areas such as the rules and regulations the leader asks the people to follow; the degree to which the leader tells the followers what is expected of them; and the assignment of members to particular tasks. Items relating to "consideration" deal with topics such as the amount of time the leader finds to listen to group members; the willingness to undertake changes; and whether or not he or she is friendly and approachable.

Initiating
Structure ———————————————————————————————— Consideration

FIGURE 13–7 An Initiating Structure-Consideration Continuum

"Initiating structure" and "consideration" are separate dimensions.

From their work, the researchers found that "initiating structure" and "consideration" were *separate* and *distinct* dimensions. A person could rank high on one dimension *without* ranking low on the other. Thus, instead of being on a continuum such as seen in Figure 13–7, the leader could prove to be a *combination* of both dimensions. On the basis of these findings, the researchers were able to develop the following leadership quadrants:

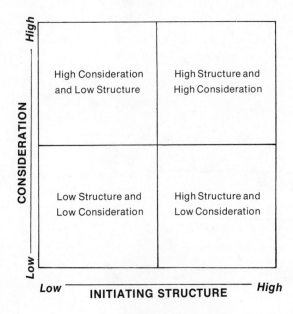

FIGURE 13–8 Ohio State Leadership Quadrants

[11]Andrew W. Halpin, *The Leadership Behavior of School Superintendents* (Chicago: Midwest Administration Center, The University of Chicago, 1959), p. 4.

A leader who is high on "structure" but low on "consideration" is greatly interested in the work side of the job such as planning activities and communicating information necessary to get the tasks done on time. Conversely, a leader who is high on "consideration" but low on "structure" tends to encourage superior-subordinate cooperation and works within an atmosphere of mutual respect and trust. The leader who is high on both dimensions is interested in both the work and the people sides of the job. The leader who is low on both dimensions tends to stand back and let the workers do their jobs without interference or interaction on his or her part. Which of the four is best? The answer is going to vary. In some situations the individual who is high on structure is superior; in other cases the manager who is high on consideration is most effective; other times the leader who is high on both dimensions does the best job; still other times the leader who is low on both dimensions is most desirable.

The quadrant approach to examining leadership behavior is more realistic than a continuum because it permits *simultaneous* consideration of two factors. This undoubtedly accounts for the fact that those who used to view leadership on a continuum are now modifying their views.

MANAGERIAL GRID.   Another two-dimensional approach is the managerial grid developed by Robert R. Blake and Jane S. Mouton. After undertaking research of their own, they rejected the Ohio State four-quadrant paradigm and developed their own now-famous grid.[12] Along the vertical axis they placed the term "concern for people" and along the horizontal axis the term "concern for production." In addition, on each axis they placed a scale, ranging from 1 to 9, for measuring degree of concern.

As can be seen in Figure 13–9, they identified five basic leadership styles. The person who is a 1,1 manager has little concern for either people or production. The 1,9 manager has great concern for people but little concern for production. The 9,1 manager has a great concern for production but little concern for people. The 5,5 manager balances the concern for people and production although it is certainly not a maximum concern. The 9,9 manager demonstrates maximum interest for both people and production.

Five basic leadership styles.

Unlike much of the research done on leadership, the managerial grid has proven to be a useful tool for developing effective managers. Many companies have found such training helpful to their people in terms of redirecting their orientation and getting, for example, a 1,9 manager more interested in the production side of the job or a 9,1 manager more interested in the personal aspect.

SIX PHASE PROGRAM.   Blake and Mouton propose a six-phase program to attain these objectives. The two initial phases involve management development and the last four help the manager work toward more complex goals of organizational development. Briefly outlined, these are:

Phase 1: Laboratory-Seminar Training.   **Conducted by line managers who have already taken the seminar, the purpose of this phase is to introduce the managerial grid concept. During this period managers analyze and assess their own leadership style.**

An implementation program.

Phase 2: Team Development.   **The concepts from Phase 1 are transferred to the job situation, and each work group or department decides its own 9,9 ground rules and relationships.**

---

[12]Robert R. Blake, Jane Srygley Mouton, and Benjamin Fruchter, "A Factor Analysis of Training Group Behavior." *Journal of Social Psychology*, October 1962, pp. 121–130.

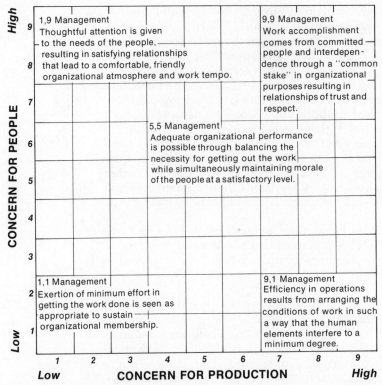

FIGURE 13-9   Managerial Grid (Adapted from Robert R. Blake and Jane S. Mouton, "Managerial Facades," *Advanced Management Journal,* **July 1966, p. 31.)**

Phase 3: Intergroup Development. **Focus is placed on building 9,9 ground rules and norms between groups in the work unit. Tensions between the groups are identified and examined in way of eliminating them.**

Phase 4: Organizational Goal Setting. **Attention is now focused on overall organizational goals. In addition, the identification of broad problems, e.g. cost control, over-all profit improvement, and union-management relations, requiring commitments from all levels, is undertaken.**

Phase 5: Goal Attainment. **The goals and problems identified in Phase 4 are studied in greater depth and appropriate actions formulated and implemented.**

Phase 6: Stabilization. **Changes brought about during the first five phases are evaluated and reinforced to prevent any pressure toward "slipping back."[13]**

Which of the managerial grid styles is best? This will depend on the situation. Based on their seminars, Blake and Mouton report that 99.5 per cent of the participants say that a 9,9 style is the soundest way to manage. Furthermore, after taking a reading two to three years after the grid has been used in a company, they have found many managers still holding to their 9,9 position. The second most popular style is 9,1 and the third is 5,5. Some writers have contended that the grid concept assumes a 9,9 style is best. Actually, it is managers themselves who speak so highly of the 9,9 approach. Blake and Mouton recommend using the style that proves best for the particular work place. This "situational approach" to leadership also permeates the work of Fred Fiedler.

[13]Robert R. Blake, Jane S. Mouton, Louis B. Barnes, and Larry E. Greiner, "Breakthrough in Organization Development," *Harvard Business Review* November–December, 1964, pp. 137–138.

After years of empirical research, Fiedler has developed what is commonly called a *contingency model of leadership effectiveness.*[14]

Fiedler's Contingency Model

The essence of Fiedler's research is that *any* leadership style can be effective, depending on the situation. The manager must therefore be an *adaptive* individual. Employing Blake and Mouton's terminology, sometimes the leader should be a 9,9 manager, other times a 5,5 and still other times a 1,1 manager. According to Fiedler, three major situational variables will determine the leader's effectiveness:

1. *Leader-member relations* — refers to how well the leader is accepted by his subordinates.
2. *Task structure* — refers to the degree to which subordinates' jobs are routine and spelled out in contrast to being vague and undefined.
3. *Position power* — refers to the formal authority provided for in the position the leader occupies.

The major situational variables.

Employing these three dimensions, eight combinations or conditions are possible, as seen in Figure 13–10.

Note that above the eight conditions in the figure there is a schematic representation of the performance of relationship- and task-motivated leaders in different situational conditions. The vertical axis in the figure shows the group's or organization's performance. The horizontal axis indicates the favorableness of the situation, i.e., the degree to which the situation provides the leader with control and influence. The dotted line illustrates the performance of relationship-motivated leaders. It is best when their relations with the subordinates are good but task structure and position power are low. They also perform well when subordinate relations are poor but task structure and position power are high. Both of these are situations of *moderate* favorableness.

---

[14]Fred E. Fiedler, *A Theory of Leadership Effectiveness* (New York: McGraw Hill Book Company, 1967).

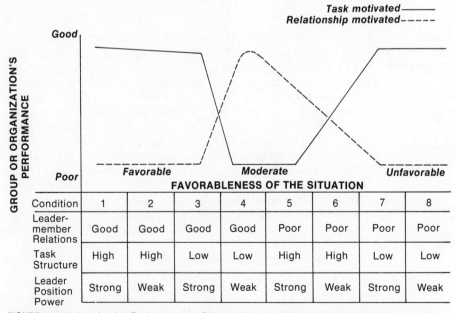

Condition	1	2	3	4	5	6	7	8
Leader-member Relations	Good	Good	Good	Good	Poor	Poor	Poor	Poor
Task Structure	High	High	Low	Low	High	High	Low	Low
Leader Position Power	Strong	Weak	Strong	Weak	Strong	Weak	Strong	Weak

FIGURE 13–10 Leadership Performance in Different Situational Favorableness Conditions (Adapted from Fred E. Fiedler, "The Leadership Game: Matching the Man to the Situation," *Organizational Dynamics*, Winter 1976, p. 11.)

Task-motivated leaders perform best when all three of the factors defining control and influence are either high or low. Thus task-motivated leaders do best in *either highly favorable* or *highly unfavorable* situations. Commenting on the data in the figure, Fiedler has noted that:

> . . . . We can improve group performance either by changing the leader's motivational structure — that is, the basic goals he pursues in life — or else by modifying his leadership situation. While it is possible, of course, to change personality and the motivational structure that is a part of personality, this is clearly a difficult and uncertain process. It is, however, relatively easy to modify the leadership situation. We can select a person for certain kinds of jobs and not others, we can assign him certain tasks, give him more or less responsibility, or we can give him leadership training in order to increase his power and influence.
> . . . . we will be better served by training our leaders in how to change their leadership situations than in how to change their personalities. Our recent studies of contingency model training show that leaders can recognize the situations in which they tend to be most successful and they can modify their situations so that they perform more effectively. We have reason to believe that this approach holds considerable promise for the future of leadership training.[15]

The importance of Fiedler's model.

Fiedler's model is important for three reasons. First, it places prime emphasis on *effectiveness*. Second, it illustrates that no one leadership style is best; the manager must *adapt* to the situation. Third, it encourages management to *match* the leader with the situation. If the situation is very favorable or very unfavorable, appoint a task-oriented manager; otherwise, use an employee-centered manager. Although these findings may appear to conflict with those of Likert, for example, they actually do not. After all, most situations are going to be of intermediate favorableness or unfavorableness, requiring an employee-centered manager. This is why Likert found such good results occurring among groups with employee-centered leaders (systems 3 and 4). The challenge for management is recognizing that effective leadership is contingent upon the three variables described by Fiedler, i.e. leader-member relations, task structure, and position power.

Three-dimensional Leadership

In recent years, William Reddin has combined Blake and Mouton's managerial grid with Fiedler's contingency leadership style theory into a *3-D theory of management.*[16] In essence, Reddin employs the same basic grid as Blake and Mouton but changes "concern for production" to TO, or *task orientation,* and "concern for people" to RO, or *relationships orientation.* Figure 13–11 depicts the four basic styles of his 3-D theory.

The *separated* style is the one with low task orientation and low relationships orientation; it is separated from both TO and RO. The *dedicated* style describes managerial behavior with a high task orientation but low relationships orientation; it is behavior that is dedicated to the job. Conversely, the *related* style describes managerial behavior with high relationships orientation but low task orientation; it is behavior that is related to subordinates. The *integrated* style has high task and relationships orientation. It describes managerial behavior, which combines high TO and high RO.

Reddin has done more than merely redescribe the Blake-Mouton grid

---

[15]Fred E. Fiedler, "The Leadership Game: Matching the Man to the Situation," *Organizational Dynamics,* Winter 1976, pp. 12, 15–16.
[16]William J. Reddin, *Managerial Effectiveness* (New York: McGraw-Hill Book Company, 1970).

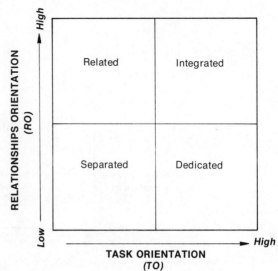

FIGURE 13–11 Reddin's Basic 3-D Management Styles

in his own words. He has also introduced a third element that turns this two-dimensional grid into a three dimensional one. It is *effectiveness,* which he defines as "the extent to which a manager achieves the output requirements of his position."[17] Reddin's theory not only goes one step beyond the Blake-Mouton grid, but also reiterates Fiedler's main theme, namely, effectiveness depends on the situation. Some leadership styles are appropriate to a given situation, others are not. Figure 13–12 depicts Reddin's 3-D model.

Effectiveness is important.

A description of the eight styles in the model is the following:

More Effective Leadership Styles:
Bureaucrat: A manager who uses a low task orientation and low relationships orientation where such behavior is appropriate. This person is primarily interested in rules and procedures for their own sake and is seen as wanting to maintain and control the situation personally. This individual is also very conscientious.

Benevolent Autocrat: A manager who uses a high task orientation and low relationships orientation where such behavior is appropriate. This person knows what he or she wants and knows how to go about getting it without creating resentment.

Developer: A manager who uses a high relationships orientation and a low task orientation where such behavior is appropriate. This individual has implicit trust in people and is concerned with developing them as people.

Executive: A manager who uses a high task orientation and high relationships orientation where such behavior is appropriate. This person is a good motivator who sets high standards, treats everyone somewhat differently and prefers team management.

Less Effective Leadership Styles:
Deserter: A manager who uses a low task orientation and low relationships orientation where such behavior is inappropriate. This individual is uninvolved and passive.

Autocrat: A manager who uses a high task orientation and a low relationships orientation where such behavior is inappropriate. This person has no confidence in others, is unpleasant, and is interested only in the immediate job.

Missionary: A manager who employs a high relationships orientation and a low task orientation where such behavior is inappropriate. This individual is primarily interested in harmony.

Compromiser: A manager who uses a high task orientation and a high relationships orientation in a situation that requires high emphasis on either one or neither. This person is a poor decision maker, and attempts to minimize immediate pressures and problems rather than maximizing long-term production.[18]

[17]*Ibid.,* p. 3.
[18]William J. Reddin, "Managing Organizational Change," *Personnel Journal,* July 1969, p. 503.

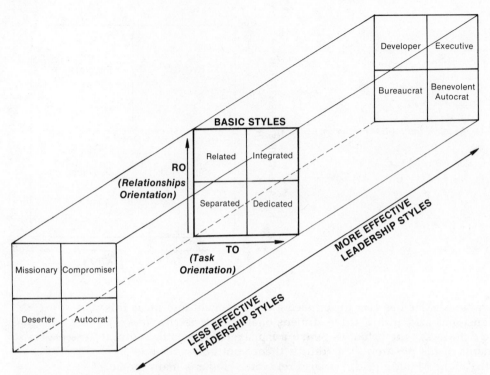

FIGURE 13–12 Reddin's 3-D Leader Effectiveness Model (Adapted from William J. Reddin, *Managerial Effectiveness*, McGraw-Hill Book Company, New York, 1970, p. 230.)

The grid in the center of Figure 13–2, illustrating the four combinations of RO and TO, represents the *basic* styles. If the manager's behavior is appropriate to the situation, he or she will be more effective and their style can be found on the back grid in the figure. For example, if the individual's behavior is high relationships-oriented and high task-oriented, the manager will be adopting the style Reddin calls "executive." Conversely, if the behavior is less effective, the manager's style will be found on the front grid, namely, "compromiser."

There are two main points to be extracted from this three-dimensional theory. First, every manager will employ some combination of TO and RO in dealing with the situation. This behavior will be either appropriate (more effective) or inappropriate (less effective). Second, one must not view effectiveness as an either-or condition. Rather, it is a continuum, ranging from very effective to very ineffective. Effectiveness is a matter of *degree*, and the style that was effective in one situation may not be effective in another.

> **Effectiveness is a matter of degree.**

It can now be seen why the 3-D theory is so useful. First, it brings together the concepts of task and relationship orientation, which are proven dimensions of leadership. Second, it stresses that effective leadership behavior depends on the situation. Third, it encourages leaders to be aware of the fact that no one style is always right and, as with a night club entertainer constantly facing a new audience, an adaptive style is important.

Life Cycle Theory of Leadership

In recent years, Reddin's 3-D leader effectiveness model has been used as the basis for formulating a *life cycle theory of leadership*. This theory was developed at the Center for Leadership Research at Ohio

University.[19] Its basic theme is that as the maturity of the followers increases, appropriate leadership behavior requires *varying degrees* of task and relationship orientation. The following four-stage illustration should make this more clear. When a boy is very young, his parents will initiate all the structure from dressing him to feeding him; their behavior is basically task-oriented. As he gets older, the parents will also begin increasing their relationship behavior by showing trust and respect for him. Now there is a high task and a high relationship orientation. As the boy begins moving into high school and college, however, he starts accepting responsibility for his own behavior. At this point his parents will begin employing low task and high relationship behavior. Finally, when the young man marries and starts his own family, his parents will exercise a minimum of task and relationship orientation with him.

As the individual progresses from a state of immaturity to maturity, he requires different kinds of behavior from his parents. This is also true in a work situation. If the management allows the employee to mature, changing leadership behavior will be needed. This is seen in Figure 13–13, where the four basic leadership styles have been designated with the notations Q1 (Quadrant 1, representing high task, low relationship behavior), Q2 (high task, high relationship behavior), Q3 (high relationship, low task behavior), and Q4 (low task and low relationship behavior). Beneath the grid is a continuum representing the maturity of the followers: M1 is low maturity, M2 is low to moderate maturity, M3 is moderate to high maturity, and M4 is high maturity. Bringing together the quadrants and the maturity of the followers, the Life Cycle Theory or, as it has been recently renamed, the Situational Leadership Theory, contends that:

How mature is the worker?

---

[19]The theory was first published by Paul Hersey and Kenneth H. Blanchard, "Life Cycle Theory of Leadership," *Training and Development Journal*, May, 1969, pp. 26–34.

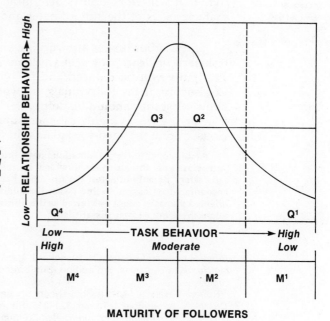

FIGURE 13–13 Life Cycle Theory of Leadership (Adapted from Paul Hersey and Kenneth H. Blanchard, *Management of Organizational Behavior: Utilizing Human Resources*, 3rd edition, Englewood Cliffs, N.J.: Prentice-Hall, Inc. 1977, p. 167.)

. . . in working with people who are low in maturity in terms of accomplishing a specific task, a high task/low relationship style (Q1) has the highest probability of success; in dealing with people who are of low to moderate maturity (M2), a high task/high relationship style (Q2) appears to be most appropriate; in working with people who are of moderate to high maturity (M3) in terms of accomplishing a specific task, a high relationship/low task style (Q3) has the highest probability of success; and a low relationship/low task style (Q4) has the probability of success with people of high task—relevant maturity (M4).[20]

Hersey and Blanchard also postulate probabilities of success or the order of preference the manager should have for each of the maturity levels. It is the following:[21]

If Maturity Level Is	Order of Preference of Leadership Styles Is			
	1st	2nd	3rd	4th
M1	Q1	Q2	Q3	Q4
M2	Q2	Q1	Q3	Q4
M3	Q3	Q2	Q4	Q1
M4	Q4	Q3	Q2	Q1

The life cycle theory complements Blake and Mouton's managerial grid as well as Fiedler's contingency and Reddin's three-dimensional models because it encourages the leader to evaluate the subordinates in determining an effective style.

Path-Goal Theory of Leadership

The leader should reduce roadblocks and increase the chances for personal satisfaction.

A recent contingency theory of leadership, proposed by House and advanced by House and Mitchell, is the *path-goal theory.*[22] This theory is rather simple, holding that the leader's job is: (a) to help the subordinates by increasing their personal satisfactions in work-goal attainment, and (b) to make the path to these satisfactions easier to obtain. Leaders achieve this by clarifying the nature of the work, reducing the road blocks from successful task completion, and increasing the opportunities for the subordinates to obtain personal satisfactions. Subordinate motivation will increase to the degree that the leader succeeds. The specific leadership style that will work best is determined by two situational variables: the characteristics of the subordinates and the task itself.

If the subordinates are working on highly unstructured jobs and their tasks are unclear, they will welcome leader direction. If they receive it, ambiguity will be reduced and individual job satisfaction will increase. Conversely, if the individuals are working on structured tasks and they know what they should be doing, the leader should use less directiveness if he or she wants highly satisfied subordinates. Dessler, who has helped House refine the theory, explains these points:

. . . Ambiguous, uncertain situations have the potential for being frustrating and . . . in such situations the structure provided by the leader will be viewed as legitimate and satisfactory by subordinates. On the other hand, in routine situations, such as might be encountered on assembly-line tasks, the additional structure provided by a production-oriented manager might be viewed as illegitimate and redundant by the subordinates, who might therefore become dissatisfied.[23]

---

[20]Paul Hersey and Kenneth H. Blanchard, *Management of Organizational Behavior: Utilizing Human Resources,* 3rd edition (Englewood Cliffs, N.J.: Prentice-Hall, 1977), p. 168.
[21]*Ibid.*
[22]Robert J. House, "A Path Goal Theory of Leader Effectiveness," *Administrative Science Quarterly,* September 1971, pp. 321–338; Robert J. House and Terence R. Mitchell, "Path Goal Theory of Leadership," *Journal of Contemporary Business,* Autumn 1974.
[23]Gary A. Dessler, *Organization and Management: A Contingency Approach* (Englewood Cliffs, N.J.: Prentice-Hall, 1976), p. 172.

The path-goal theory is actually based on Vroom's theory of motivation which was examined in Chapter 12. Although such terms as instrumentality, valence, and expectancy are not used directly, their meanings are readily evident in the theory.

Currently, there are many leadership researchers who have high regard for the path-goal theory. One reason is that the model does not indicate the "one best way" to lead, but rather suggests that a leader select the style that is most appropriate to the particular situation. Of course, its full value will not be known before more research is conducted.[24] However, it does hold great promise in helping explain leadership effectiveness.

THE ADAPTIVE LEADER

The personal behavior theories examined in this chapter illustrate there is no such thing as "one best leadership style." The effective manager must be an adaptive individual. Some people contend that an employee-centered manager is more effective than a job-centered manager. Likert's research certainly seems to indicate that this is a valid statement, as does the research of other writers. Davis, for example, notes that "Speaking very generally and recognizing many exceptions, high positive, participative, and employee-centered styles are considered desirable."[25]

However, arguments can be made either way. For example, after reviewing a half-dozen experimental studies related to supervisory leadership, Sales found that, in terms of productivity, no one style was consistently superior. Of six studies he reviewed, for which objective production data were available, one reported democratic supervision to be more effective, one reported authoritarian supervision to be more effective, and the other four noted no differences of consequence between the two styles.[26] Thus, because there is so much variation, careful consideration of the concepts contained in the Blake-Mouton grid, Fiedler's contingency theory, Reddin's 3-D theory, Hersey and Blanchard's life cycle theory of leadership, and House's path-goal theory will continue to be of great value to the practicing manager. The leader must evaluate each situation on its own merits.

No one style of leadership is best.

The major problem most managers face is that of sizing up the situation. If a system 4 style were always best, the leader would have no trouble determining effective behavior; the challenge would be one of implementing the style properly. However, the issue is never this easy. Furthermore, since effective behavior in one situation may be ineffective in another, as noted by Reddin, the challenge becomes even greater. Leadership research has provided a wealth of information about effective behavior, and the latest findings all point to the need for a flexible, adaptive style.

[24]Andrew D. Szitagyl and Henry P. Sims, Jr., "An Exploration of Path-Goal Theory of Leadership in a Health Care Environment," *Academy of Management Journal*, December 1974, pp. 622–634; H. Kirk Downey, John E. Sheridan, and John W. Slocum, Jr., "Analysis of Relationships Among Leader Behavior, Subordinate Job Performance and Satisfaction: A Path-Goal Approach," *Academy of Management Journal*, June 1975, pp. 253–262; John E. Stinson and Thomas W. Johnson, "The Path-Goal Theory of Leadership: A Partial Test and Suggested Refinement," *Academy of Management Journal*, June 1975, pp. 242–252; and Thomas C. Mawhinney and Jeffrey D. Ford, "The Path Goal Theory of Leader Effectiveness: An Operant Interpretation," *Academy of Management Review*, July 1977, pp. 398–411.
[25]Davis, *op. cit.*, p. 116.
[26]Stephen M. Sales, "Supervisory Style and Productivity: Review and Theory," *Personnel Psychology*, Autumn 1966, pp. 275–286.

SUMMARY   In this chapter leadership has been defined as the process of influencing people to direct their efforts toward the attainment of some particular goal(s). What makes an individual an effective leader? Some people feel the answer rests with personal traits and, to some degree, they are right. However, today situational theory is more commonly accepted — that is, some leadership styles are more effective than others, depending on the situation.

One way of studying leadership is by placing the elements of leadership on a continuum. Likert's research, for example, shows that an employee-centered manager is more effective than a job-centered manager. In recent years however, scholars and practitioners alike have found a two-dimensional model more realistic since it sidesteps an either-or approach and allows consideration of two factors. The Ohio State leadership research and the Blake-Mouton grid are illustrations of this two-dimensional approach.

Currently, however, the most widely accepted approach is probably that of Fiedler's contingency model, which places prime emphasis on three major situational variables: leader-member relations, task structure, and position power. Fiedler's model is important because it stresses effectiveness, illustrates that no one leadership style is best, and encourages management to match the leader with the situation.

In recent years, Reddin has combined Blake and Mouton's managerial grid with Fiedler's contingency model in arriving at a three-dimensional theory of leadership. Meanwhile, at the Center for Leadership Research at Ohio University, a life cycle theory of leadership has been formulated. More recently, House has postulated the path-goal theory. All three of these emphasize the importance of the adaptive leader who can rise to the demands of the situation. In short, the emphasis today is on a flexible style that achieves results. When there are problems attaining positive results, modern organizations will often turn to human resource development programs. These will be the focus of attention in the next chapter.

REVIEW AND STUDY QUESTIONS

1. Of what relevance is trait theory to the study of leadership?

2. Why is situational theory so well accepted today? Explain, incorporating the word "adaptive" into your discussion.

3. What does Likert mean by systems 1, 2, 3, and 4? Which is the best? Why?

4. How do two-dimensional leadership models differ from leader continuum theories? Which is more accurate? Why?

5. What is the managerial grid? What leadership dimensions does it measure?

6. What leadership style is most effective according to managerial grid advocates? Is this right or wrong? Explain.

7. What is the theme of Fiedler's contingency model of leadership effectiveness?

8. What are the three major situational variables in Fiedler's model? Explain.

9. How does Reddin's three-dimensional leadership theory supplement Fiedler's work?

10. How can the life cycle theory of leadership be of value to the manager?

11. In your view, how valuable is the path-goal theory for the modern manager?

12. What is meant by the "adaptive leader"? Explain.

Barrow, J. C. "The Variables of Leadership: A Review and Conceptual Framework." *Academy of Management Review,* April 1977, pp. 231–251.
Berlew, D. E. "Leadership and Organizational Excitement." *California Management Review,* Winter 1974, pp. 21–30.
Blake, R. R., and J. S. Mouton, "Managerial Façades." *Advanced Management Journal,* July 1966, pp. 30–37.
Davis, K. *Human Behavior at Work,* 5th edition. New York: McGraw-Hill Book Company, 1977, Chapters 7–9.
Fiedler, F. E. *A Theory of Leadership Effectiveness.* New York: McGraw-Hill Book Company, 1967.
Fiedler, F. E., and M. M. Chemers, *Leadership and Effective Management.* Glenview, Ill.: Scott, Foresman and Company, 1974.
Fiedler, F. E. "The Leadership Game: Matching the Man to the Situation." *Organizational Dynamics,* Winter 1976, pp. 6–16.
Filley, A. C., R. J. House, and S. Kerr. *Managerial Process and Organizational Behavior.* 2nd edition. Glenview, Ill.: Scott, Foresman and Company, 1976.
Gellerman, S. W. "Supervision: Substance and Style." *Harvard Business Review,* March–April 1976, pp. 89–99.
Hersey, P., and K. H. Blanchard, *Management Of Organizational Behavior: Utilizing Human Resources,* 3rd edition. Englewood Cliffs, N.J.: Prentice-Hall, 1977.
Hovey, D. E. "The Low-Powered Leader Confronts a Messy Problem: A Test of Fiedler's Theory." *Academy of Management Journal,* June 1974, pp. 358–362.
Justis, R. T. "Leadership Effectiveness: A Contingency Approach." *Academy of Management Journal,* March 1975, pp. 160–167.
Likert, R. *The Human Organization.* New York: McGraw-Hill Book Company, 1967.
Likert, R. *New Patterns of Management.* New York: McGraw-Hill Book Company, 1961.
McClelland, D. C., and D. H. Burnham. "Power Is the Great Motivator." *Harvard Business Review,* March–April 1976, pp. 100–110.
Reddin, W. J. *Managerial Effectiveness.* New York: McGraw-Hill Book Company, 1970.
Skinner, W., and W. Earl Sasser, "Managers with Impact: Versatile and Inconsistent." *Harvard Business Review,* November–December 1977, pp. 140–148.
Tannenbaum, R., and W. H. Schmidt. "How to Choose a Leadership Pattern." *Harvard Business Review,* May–June 1973, pp. 162–175;178–180.
Tosi, H. H. "The Effect of the Interaction of Leader Behavior and Subordinate Authoritarianism." *Personnel Psychology,* Autumn 1973, pp. 339–350.
Vroom, V. H. "Can Leaders Learn to Lead? *Organizational Dynamics,* Winter 1976, pp. 17–28.

CASE: A MATTER OF STYLE

Whisk Insurance, a medium-sized insurance company located in New England, had been taking steps to improve the effectiveness of its management. As a result, it contracted with a private consulting company for some management training. Some of the sessions involved familiarization with and use of the managerial-grid technique. The managers were asked to rate themselves, and their subordinates were given an opportunity to comment on the leadership ability of their superiors. Chuck Hansen, one of the seminar participants, had been rated as a 7,7 manager by his people. Evelyn Edems, another participant, had been rated as a 1,9.

When this phase was complete, the trainers took these basic styles and tried to explain why a 9,9 style was the most desirable by stressing the importance of placing maximum emphasis on both the production and the people aspects of the job. However, both Chuck and Evelyn disagreed with this, and both used the same reasoning. Each had excellent efficiency ratings and had been told that they would be promoted within the next six months. Their argument was that their current style was effective. Why should they worry about becoming 9,9 managers? Their 7,7 and 1,9 styles were apparently good enough. They referred to the 9,9 concept as "pie in the sky."

Questions

1. Is the 9,9 concept "pie in the sky" or does it have value? Explain.

2. What answer would you give to both Chuck and Evelyn if you were the trainer?

3. Is the trainer right or wrong? Explain.

CASE: OLD HABITS

George Chila was known around the company as a "tough cookie." If one had to rate him in terms of Systems 1 to 4, he was definitely a System-1 man. However, he was also a good manager. He seemed to get his work out on time, his men appeared to have respect for him, and he showed promise as a manager. George's superior, Frank Dunbar, decided to send him to a week-long training program entitled "Developing An Effective Leadership Style." Mr. Dunbar believed the training would help improve George's style.

During the program, George was introduced to many different concepts, from Likert's four systems to the Blake-Mouton grid, from Reddin's three-dimensional theory to Fiedler's contingency model. When it was all over George returned to work and began to practice much of what he had learned. If employee-centered managers are often more effective than job-centered managers, maybe I should try to change my style, he reasoned. In line with this thinking George took two steps. First, he called a meeting of the men to discuss work assignments and get their opinions. Second, he told them that from that point on there was going to be less checking on their work. He was going to employ loose control and rely on them to do their jobs correctly.

For the next three months things went along smoothly. At first the workers were puzzled by George's sudden change in style. However, after they realized that he really intended to be more "employee-oriented" than before, they increased their output and began to establish lines of communication with him. George liked the new approach and so did the men. However, as the end of the year approached, the usual stress on increased productivity began to mainfest itself. First, there was a memo from top management which was passed out to all the supervisors. Then Mr. Dunbar called George in to tell him to keep things going at as fast a clip as possible. Slowly, but surely, the pressure began to build up. Overtime work was assigned to the men, and the company went to Saturday and Sunday shifts. George found himself working a 12-hour day and a six-day week.

With the increased pressure, George started making more and more decisions without consulting the men. He assigned jobs as he saw fit and spent more time than usual out on the line checking up on things. By the middle of October, it was evident that he had reverted to his old style. This continued until the beginning of the year when things were finally back to normal. During the first week of January he called the men together:

Listen, Mr. Dunbar has just talked to me and he says we did a real good job during that end-of-the-year rush. Now that we're back on an even keel, let's start talking about job assignments and how we're going to handle things for the next three months. I'd like to show you what Mr. Dunbar wants us to do and perhaps some of you have ideas on how we can handle these things.

It was then that one of the men spoke up.

Hey, George, before we get into that let me ask you a question. Why didn't you ask us to help you draw up some work plans during that big end-of-the-year push?

Well, I don't know. I guess I was just too busy getting things done to think about it. You know how it is when you get pushed. You find yourself going back to your old way of doing things. Well, if you find me doing that again, let me know.

The men promised to do so.

Questions

1. According to his new style, in which would you place George: system 1, 2, 3, or 4? Explain.

2. Why were the men skeptical when George switched from being a work-oriented manager to an employee-oriented manager?

3. How can one keep from slipping back to one's old leadership style? Explain.

CASE: THE FAST GUN

Hank Sidney has been president of his company for seven years, and initially things had gone very well. Sales increased an average of 17 per cent a year, and return on investment during this period had never been lower than 15.3 per cent. However, slowly but surely other firms began to realize the kind of profits that could be attained in the industry and they began moving in. As they did, competition increased and the big profit margins began to shrink. Prices dropped as each company tried to capture and retain large market shares. Within a few years, Hank's firm was barely able to keep its head above water. It was then that the board of directors decided that Hank had to go.

This was not an easy choice for the directors to make. Everyone liked Hank. He was a pleasant, easy going, friendly individual. The management respected him and the workers seemed to hold him in the highest regard. Nevertheless, the board felt that the president was unable to turn the company around, and they would have to get someone who could.

The eventual choice was Fred Whitney, a general manager who worked for one of the company's competitors. Fred told the board that he would take the job only if he were allowed to do things his way. In turn, he promised results. The board agreed.

Within six months of his appointment, Fred had fired over half of the old management team and one third of the workers. In addition, he refused to hire any new personnel. If someone quit or was fired, the others were required to pick up his work. When asked about this, Fred gave the following explanation:

When I came in here the company was going broke. There were too many people in management positions who were doing nothing. I got rid of them. The workers were having a field day. The average guy was putting in a five-hour day. Well, I changed all that by tightening things up. Now everyone around here has to pull his own weight. There's no room for fat when a company is in trouble, so I got rid of it.

It was difficult to argue with Fred in light of the fact that his leadership style seemed to get results. For example, within 18 months of the time he took over, the company had as large a share of the market as ever and return on investment had risen to over 16 per cent.

Some of the directors, however, felt that Fred's style was too rough. They believed that the company was going to get in trouble if it thought a system-1, task-oriented manager could continue to achieve such results in the long-run. These directors acknowledged the fact that Fred had been very successful thus far, but they wondered if there would not be a backlash. Doesn't the task-centered manager run the risk of driving off his best workers and irreparably damaging morale? they asked. One of the directors compared Fred with a fast gun in the old west. "You know," he said, "a fast gun would be brought in to save the town. But once he had done his job the mayor would have to get rid of him because he was bad for the town's reputation. I think Fred falls into this category." The chairman of the board disagreed. "We were elected by the stockholders to protect their interests. When we brought in Fred we told him he could do things his way. Besides, we have to evaluate a man's leadership style by how effective it is. And Fred sure has been effective." On this point no one had anything to say.

Questions

1. Why was Hank ineffective in turning the company around?

2. How do you account for such results? After all, isn't an employee-centered leader superior to a task-centered leader?

3. Do you think Fred should be replaced or retained? Explain.

CASE: CONTINGENCY CHAOS

Jennifer Kendehl, a university administrator of a large eastern state-wide system, had just returned from a week-long training program on leadership styles and techniques. Before going back to her office, she dropped in to visit her superior, Dr. Henry Adams, Ed.D., for a few minutes.

Well, Jenny, how did you like that seminar?

Oh, fine, Dr. Adams, just fine.

I sent you there, Jenny, because I feel you have real potential as a manager. I attended that seminar last year and thought it was great. You know, money for higher education is going to run out. We have to be more efficient with our resources and this means placing a greater stress on effective management. Now tell me, what did you learn?

Well, to be quite frank, Dr. Adams, I'm not really sure.

What do you mean?

Well, we spent an awful lot of time looking at various leadership theories. You know, Likert's management systems, Blake and Mouton's managerial grid, Fiedler's contingency model, and Reddin's three-dimensional theory. Stuff like that.

It sounds like you picked up a great deal of knowledge. What seems to be the problem?

It gets back to implementation, Dr. Adams. I find I'm confused about how to apply this stuff.

In what way?

Well, the trainers seemed to believe that Fiedler's contingency model has a great deal of value for effective leadership. But this contingency idea is what throws me. I mean, if effectiveness depends on the situation, then the manager has to size up each one on its own merits. But I think there must be an easier way. For example, they never really proved to me that a system-4 manager was not better than a system-1 manager. Therefore, why not be a system-4 individual and worry about the exceptions to the rule when they crop up? Why spend so much time worrying about each individual situation? Why not develop an effective style and then deal with the exceptions when they manifest themselves?

That certainly is the way most managers do it. But isn't that approach too general? After all, you're not dealing with the individual situation; you're just playing the odds and assuming that your basic style will help you through any situation.

Sure, but at least I have a basic style to get me through most situations. I think if you try to be too much of a "contingent" manager, you'll never be able to develop any one style effectively. I'd rather try to be a system-4 manager than subscribe to Fiedler's contingency theory, which to me leads to an overly flexible and chaotic style.

Questions

1. Evaluate Jennifer's comments. What do you think?

2. What response should Dr. Adams make? Be explicit in your answer, bringing into your discussion Fiedler's contingency model and Reddin's 3-D theory.

CHAPTER FOURTEEN

HUMAN RESOURCE DEVELOPMENT

GOALS OF THE CHAPTER

The behavioral school adherents believe strongly in the importance of communication, motivation, and leadership. However, they also realize that, at times, communication will break down, motivation will be poor, and leadership will be less than effective. The way to prevent or minimize the negative impact of such factors is to develop the organization's human resources through the use of the latest behavioral techniques.

Human resource development serves as a control loop which feeds back into the original behavioral effort. For example, using just the three behavioral areas of communication, motivation, and leadership, it is possible to tie them together by noting that the manager must first communicate with the subordinates, for this is the basis of effective motivation and leadership. Second, the individual must try to motivate the people toward attaining organizational objectives. Finally, the manager has to adapt the leadership style that will be most effective in each particular situation. In carrying out each of these three functions (communicating, motivating, and leading), the manager must constantly be aware of the fact that the personnel are the organization's most important assets and must be treated appropriately. One way of ensuring that they are is through a human resource development philosophy, which is usually implemented through human resource programs. It is thus possible to develop the following initial conceptual framework for the behaviorial school:

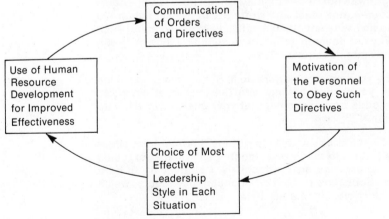

FIGURE 14–1 Behavioral School Functions

The goal of this chapter is to examine some of the tools and techniques that modern organizations are using for this purpose.

When you are finished reading this chapter you should be able to:
1. Discern between manipulation and motivation.
2. Describe what is meant by job enrichment, including arguments both for and against this human resource development tool.

3. Explain the value of sensitivity training for the modern manager.
4. Relate the benefits of transactional analysis in understanding and communicating with subordinates.
5. Explain what behavior modification is all about and how modern organizations are using it to manage their human resources.
6. Relate what human resources accounting is all about and how organizations can go about making periodic evaluations of these assets.

Many chief executives seem to realize that they are not as effective as they could be in handling their people. Some of them, for example, when recently asked to describe the effect they have on their subordinates, replied:

> I believe that a real business leader is incapable of generating a climate where people can grow.
> Hell, none of us would work for people like ourselves!
> A real executive under any one of us would leave because he couldn't stand it.
> We couldn't work for dominant characters such as ourselves. We are leaders.[1]

THE GREAT JACKASS FALLACY

On the other hand, most companies realize that they must take steps to combat the above problems. It is important to note, however, that some managers will adopt the newest approaches for handling their personnel but still fail, because under the guise of motivating their people, they actually attempt to manipulate them. This is what Levinson calls the "great jackass fallacy."[2] Workers know the difference between motivation and manipulation; they are not fooled. As a result, the best technique or tool in the world is useless in the hands of an insincere manager. The ultimate success of the methods discussed in this chapter rests solely with management.

Workers know the difference between motivation and manipulation.

In this chapter we are going to examine a handful of the *human resource development* (HRD) programs used by modern organizations. In recent years these programs have been getting more attention by many firms. Common characteristics of these companies include: (a) many of them are quite large and are well up in Fortune's 500 list; (b) they tend to be conspicuously well-managed and have consistently high past performance and earnings; (c) many have a high proportion of social psychologists, usually trained in organizational development, on HRD staffs and consultant teams; (d) the decision to push an HRD effort tends to be made at the top and work its way down into the organization; and (e) the people who handle this HRD effort are less concerned with traditional personnel and employee relations areas (recruiting, training, compensation, benefits, labor relations) and more concerned with organizing (or reorganizing), designing (or redesigning), structuring (or restructuring) of line functions and the people and machines performing them.[3] Perhaps the best place to start in examining these HRD programs, therefore, is with the work of those at the lowest levels of the organization, and by investigating how modern organizations are attempting to implement job enrichment.

[1]Chris Agyris, "The CEO's Behavior: Key to Organizational Development," *Harvard Business Review*, March–April, 1973, p. 57.
[2]Harry Levinson, "Asinine Attitudes Toward Motivation," *Harvard Business Review*, January–February 1973, pp. 70–76.
[3]Ted Mills, "Human Resources—Why The New Concern?" *Harvard Business Review*, March–April 1975, pp. 124–125.

JOB EN-
RICHMENT

In 1973 a government report entitled *Work in America* revealed what many people had long believed.[4] Most workers were dissatisfied with their jobs:

> The principal sources of worker discontent . . . are to be found in the confines of the individual workplace itself. The central villains of the piece are (1) the process of work breakdown and specialization associated with the pernicious influence of Frederick W. Taylor and his industrial engineer disciples, and (2) the diminished opportunities for work autonomy, resulting from the shift in focus of jobs from self-employment or small scale enterprise to large interpersonal corporate and government bureaucracies.[5]

While these trends have been recognized for many decades, the report found a revolutionary change in attitudes and values among many members of the work force, including youth, minority members, and women. With higher expectations generated by increased educational achievement, these groups (and the majority of workers in general) are placing greater emphasis on the intrinsic aspects of work and less on the strictly material rewards. As an attempt to overcome these problems and increase employee motivation, many firms today are adopting an approach known as *job enrichment*.

Meaningful
Work

Job enrichment is an extension of job enlargement, but instead of just giving the person more work, management provides the opportunity for increased recognition, advancement, growth, and responsibility. The technique is a direct extension of Herzberg's two factor theory of motivation and has been highly popularized by M. Scott Myers, formerly of Texas Instruments (TI), and Robert N. Ford of the American Telephone and Telegraph Company (AT&T).

Job enrichment is an extension of job enlargement.

Enrichment of the job can take many forms. Myers has encouraged making "every employee a manager" in the sense that they help plan their own work and control the pace and quality of output.[6] Within this framework, the individual knows the deadlines he must meet and the standards he must maintain. In some cases he is even given the authority to check the quality of the output. In short, management relies on him to get the job done right. No one looks over his shoulder; he is on his own. Myers has described one of these situations as follows:

> Assemblers on a radar assembly line are given information on customer contract commitments in terms of price, quality specifications, delivery schedules, and company data on material and personnel costs, breakeven performance, and potential profit margins. Assemblers and engineers work together in methods and design improvements. Assemblers inspect, adjust and repair their own work, help test completed units, and receive copies of customer inspection reports.[7]

Positive results have been obtained.

At AT&T, Ford has reported that after job enrichment was installed in the Shareholder Relations Department there was a 27 per cent reduction in the termination rate and, over a twelve-month period, an estimated cost

---

[4]W. E. Upjohn Institute for Employment Research, *Work in America*, Report to the Secretary of Health, Education, and Welfare (Cambridge, Mass.: M.I.T. Press, 1973).

[5]Harold Wool, "What's Wrong with Work in America?" A Review Essay," *Monthly Labor Review*, March 1973, p. 38.

[6]M. Scott Myers, *Every Employee a Manager: More Meaningful Work Through Job Enrichment* (New York: McGraw-Hill Book Company, 1970).

[7]M. Scott Myers, "Every Employee a Manager," *California Management Review*, Spring 1968, p. 10.

saving of $558,000.[8] Other firms are introducing the approach on their assembly line. For example Motorola has workers who put together and test an entire unit by themselves,[9] and Cadillac[10] has abandoned some of its small assembly lines in favor of each worker building one complete part.

Overseas, Volvo, the Swedish automaker, has found that work teams can be more effective than assembly lines. Its Kalmar factory in the south of Sweden is completely different from that found in the United States:

> The design for Kalmar incorporated pleasant, quiet surroundings, arranged for group working, with each group having its own individual rest and meeting areas. The work itself is organized so that each group is responsible for a particular, identifiable portion of the car—electrical systems, interiors, doors, and so on. Individual cars are built up on self-propelling "carriers" that run around the factory following a movable conductive tape on the floor. Computers normally direct the carriers, but manual controls can override the taped route. If someone notices a scratch in the paint on a car, he or she can immediately turn the carrier back to the painting station. Under computer control again, the car will return later to the production process wherever it left off.[11]

Each work group has its own areas for incoming and outgoing carriers so it can pace itself as it wishes and organize work inside its own areas, with the members working individually or in subgroups to suit themselves. Additionally, to gain a sense of identification with the work, each team does its own inspecting.

---

[8]Robert Janson, "Job Enrichment: Challenge of the 70's," *Training and Development Journal,* June 1970, p. 7.
[9]"Motorola Creates a More Demanding Job," *Business Week,* September 4, 1971, p. 32.
[10]"G.M.: The Price of Being 'Responsible'," *Fortune,* January 1972, p. 172.
[11]Pehr G. Gyllenhammar, "How Volvo Adapts Work to People," *Harvard Business Review,* July–August 1977, p. 107.

TABLE 14–1 Characteristics of Traditional and Modern Management Styles

Traditional Style	Modern Style
1. Management dictates the goals and standards to the subordinates.	1. Management and the subordinates participate in setting goals and standards.
2. The manager checks worker performance and evaluates it as either an achievement or a failure.	2. The manager encourages the subordinates to check their own performance and counsels them on how to capitalize on their mistakes.
3. The manager works out all the shortcuts and does all the innovating.	3. The manager encourages the subordinates to develop their own new methods and induces them to innovate.
4. The manager is basically a Theory X individual.	4. The manager is basically a Theory Y individual.

Adapted from William J. Roche and Neil L. MacKinnon, "Motivating People with Meaningful Work," *Harvard Business Review,* May–June 1970, p. 100.

The management at Volvo admits that it costs a little bit more money to build a nontraditional plant. However, they are beginning to show increased productivity. More importantly, perhaps, is the fact that a recent union survey of Kalmar employees revealed that almost all of them were in favor of the new work arrangements. This has led Volvo to increase its focus on working groups at other plants.[12]

Job enrichment research in this country also reveals that it can be a very useful technique in overcoming some of the previously mentioned causes of worker alienation, because it shifts the emphasis from the traditional management style to a more modern one (see Table 14–1). The key, of course, rests with structuring the job correctly.[13] As Ford points out, "When the work is right, employee attitudes are right. That is the job enrichment strategy — get the work right."[14]

Job Enrichment Under Attack

Not everyone, however, has found that job enrichment pays off. Although individuals such as Herzberg, Myers, and Ford[15] sing its praises, others have raised doubts about the technique.[16] Kilbridge, for example, discovered that assembly-line workers in a television plant did not necessarily regard the repetitive work as either frustrating or dissatisfying.[17] In another study, Reif and Schoderbek found that some workers actually liked routine jobs because it gave them time to daydream or socialize without impairing their productivity.[18]

It is not necessary to seek out new companies using the technique if one wishes to uncover shortcomings of job enrichment. Findings at TI and AT&T illustrate that many of the early promises just have not materialized. Fein, for example, has assessed TI's program as follows:

> Texas Instruments' management was probably more dedicated to job enrichment than any other company in the world. They earnestly backed their managing philosophies with millions of dollars of efforts. After 15 years of unrelenting diligence, management announced in its 1968 report to the stockholders its program for "increasing human effectiveness," with the objective: "Our goal is to have approximately 10,000 TI men and women involved in team improvement efforts by the end of 1968 or 1969." Since TI employed 60,000, the program envisioned involving only 16 percent of its work force. The total involved was actually closer to 10 percent.[19]

In the case of AT&T, Ford himself has reported that "Of the nineteen studies, nine were rated 'outstandingly successful,' one was a complete

[12]*Ibid.*, p. 108.

[13]Richard C. Grote, "Implementing Job Enrichment," *California Management Review*, Fall 1972, pp. 16–21.

[14]Robert N. Ford, "Job Enrichment Lessons from AT&T," *Harvard Business Review*, January–February 1973, pp. 106.

[15]William J. Paul, Jr., Keith B. Robertson, and Frederick Herzberg, "Job Enrichment Pays Off," *Harvard Business Review*, March–April 1969, pp. 61–78; M. Scott Myers, "Overcoming Union Opposition to Job Enrichment," *Harvard Business Review*, May–June 1971, pp. 37–49; Robert N. Ford, *Motivation Through the Work Itself*, (New York: American Management Association, 1969).

[16]For an excellent summary of these criticisms see William E. Reif and Fred Luthans, "Does Job Enrichment Really Pay Off?" *California Management Review*, Fall 1972, pp. 30–37; and Fred Luthans and William E. Reif, "Job Enrichment: Long on Theory, Short on Practice," *Organizational Dynamics*, Winter 1974, pp. 30–49.

[17]M. D. Kilbridge, "Do Workers Prefer Larger Jobs?" *Personnel*, September–October 1960, pp. 45–48.

[18]William E. Reif and Peter P. Schoderbek "Job Enlargement: Antidote to Apathy," *Management of Personnel Quarterly*, Spring 1966, pp. 16–23.

[19]Mitchell Fein, "Approaches to Motivation" (Hillsdale, N.J., 1970), p. 20.

'flop,' and the remaining nine were 'moderately successful'."[20] One reason for such cases may well be, as found by a recent study, that firms using job enrichment "seem to have a limited understanding of the concept, are unsure of how or where to apply it, and have only a vague notion of what to expect from it or how to evaluate it."[21]

Job enrichment has shortcomings.

In short, job enrichment has not been an overwhelming success. Why not? Reif and Luthans have proposed three reasons; some workers do not find satisfaction in the work place, so job enrichment has no value for them; some workers prefer boring or unpleasant jobs with good social interaction to enriched jobs that reduce the opportunity for such interaction; and some workers react to the technique with feelings of inadequacy and fears of failure.[22] Additionally, Reif and his associates have found that some workers have great difficulty adjusting to enriched jobs.[23] This is not to say that job enrichment is worthless; there are many benefits to be gained from it. But it must not be viewed as an organizational panacea for managing human assets. There are benefits and drawbacks, and management must be aware of both.

Another approach that has gained in popularity is *management by objectives* (MBO). Filley, House, and Kerr report that it is perhaps the most widely employed organizational dynamics effort.[24] Like job enrichment, MBO gives the subordinate a voice in what goes on. Although first advocated by Drucker,[25] MBO has been made famous by Odiorne, who describes it as:

MANAGE-MENT BY OBJEC-TIVES

...a process whereby the superior and subordinate managers of an organization jointly identify its common goals, define each individual's major areas of responsibility in terms of the results expected of him, and use these measures as guides for operating the unit and assessing the contribution of each of its members.[26]

In essence, the process entails a meeting between superior and subordinate for the purpose of setting goals for the latter that are in line with overall company objectives. The two individuals jointly establish: (a) what the subordinate will do; (b) by what period of time; and (c) how performance will be evaluated. Finally, when the allotted time period is over, they meet again to review the results and set further goals.

The MBO process.

One of the greatest benefits of MBO is the participation it allows the subordinate in the goal-setting process. In addition, the clear statement of what is to be done and how performance will be measured is useful in reducing ambiguity and employee anxiety. Finally, there is the fact that MBO can be used by virtually any organization, public or private.[27]

---

[20]Ford, *Motivation Through the Work Itself, op. cit.,* p. 188.

[21]Luthans and Reif, "Job Enrichment: Long on Theory, Short on Practice," *op. cit.,* p. 33.

[22]Reif and Luthans, "Does Job Enrichment Really Pay Off?" *op. cit.,* p. 36.

[23]William E. Reif, David N. Ferrazi, and Robert J. Evans, Jr., "Job Enrichment: Who Uses It and Why?" *Business Horizons,* February 1974, p. 76.

[24]Alan C. Filley, Robert J. House, and Steven Kerr, *Managerial Process and Organizational Behavior,* 2nd edition (Glenview, Illinois: Scott, Foresman and Company, 1976), pp. 489–503.

[25]Peter F. Drucker, *The Practice of Management* (New York: Harper & Brothers, Publishers, 1954).

[26]George S. Odiorne, *Management by Objectives* (New York: Pitman Publishing Corporation, 1965), pp. 55–56.

[27]See, for example, Rodney H. Brady, "MBO Goes to Work in the Public Sector," *Harvard Business Review,* March–April 1973, pp. 65–74.

Yet, despite all its advantages, MBO can be a complete flop if it is not implemented properly. One of the key factors in implementation is top management support. Research shows that the most successful implementations are those in which the top-level managers explain, coordinate, and guide the program.

In addition, there are many errors that managers make when they sit down with their subordinates to identify and define what they are to do. Kleber has identified some of these as:

1. Setting goals that are too easy to attain.
2. Setting goals that are actually unattainable.
3. Setting goals which conflict with company policies.
4. Holding the subordinate accountable for something beyond his control.
5. Failing to get a commitment from the subordinate as to the agreed upon goals.[28]

Common MBO errors.

If management is aware of these problems, MBO has a much better chance of being implemented successfully.

Perhaps the greatest potential of this technique is that it provides the basis for effective decision making, communication, and control through its emphasis on participative decision making and two-way communication. To date there is little empirical research to validate the effectiveness of MBO as an overall management system, but the technique is widely used and holds a great deal of promise for the future. Another technique which is also used is sensitivity training.

SENSI-TIVITY TRAINING

One of the reasons why many managers handle their workers ineffectively is that they simply do not understand them. Since the late 1940's a technique known as *sensitivity training* has gained acceptance in business organizations as a method for overcoming this deficiency.

The general approach used in this training is that of group discussion. With a leader who is skilled in the technique, the group decides what it wants to talk about or do. Since everything is so unstructured, many of the participants feel frustrated. As Davis notes:

Basically, sensitivity training is small-group interaction under stress in an unstructured encounter group which requires people to become sensitive to one another's feelings in order to develop reasonable group activity. . . .

In this environment they are encouraged to examine their own self-concepts and to become more receptive to what others say and feel. In addition, they begin to perceive how a group interacts, recognize how culture affects it, and develop skills in working with others. In summary, therefore, the goals of sensitivity training are understanding of self, understanding of others, insight into group process, understanding the influence of culture, and developing behavioral skills.[29]

After attending one of these sessions, the participant is supposed to be more open with his or her subordinates, willing to communicate with them, and determined to use a leadership style to which they can respond. In many cases this is precisely what happens, and the manager is better off for having participated in the training or, as it is often called, T-group session. However, not everyone would agree. The technique also has its

---

[28]Thomas P. Kleber, "Forty Common Goal-Setting Errors," *Human Resource Management*, Fall 1972, pp. 10–13.
[29]Keith Davis, *Human Behavior At Work*, 5th edition (New York: McGraw-Hill Book Company, 1977), pp. 183–184.

opponents who argue the other side, claiming that sensitivity training is of little, if any, value. For example, Kearney and Martin sent a mail questionnaire to 300 business firms employing 1000 or more people throughout the United States.[30] Two hundred twenty-five of the questionnaires were returned and used. Of these, 40.4 per cent of the respondents said that their firm believed that sensitivity training had improved the performance of the managers. However, 43.4 per cent said it had not. Additionally, while 26.2 per cent of the respondents said that they would personally recommend to other firms that they emphasize sensitivity training in their management development programs, 48.9 per cent said they would not.

Who is right then, the supporters or the opponents?[31] This is a difficult question to answer. Miner, for example, reports that a considerable amount of research has been directed at finding out whether the T-group approach really does change people. His answer is that it does. "Thus, potentially at least it can alter value structures on a broad basis and pave the way for widespread reorganization. Managers appear to become more sensitive, more open in their communication, more flexible, and more understanding of others."[32] On the other hand, surprisingly, there are many important aspects of sensitivity training on which virtually no research has been conducted. Dunnette and Campbell, for example, after conducting a comprehensive review of the literature, found little research into the effects of sensitivity training on an individual's ability to face up to and resolve personal conflict, analyze information, or implement solutions to organizational problems.[33]

Sensitivity training has great potential value.

Nevertheless, there is currently such enthusiasm and confidence in this technique that it will undoubtedly continue to be a major organizational development tool for a long time to come.

TRANSACTIONAL ANALYSIS

Transactional analysis (TA) is a technique described by Berne in his best seller *Games People Play.*[34] Since then it has been further popularized by Harris[35] and James and Jongeward.[36] In essence, TA helps the manager communicate with and understand his people through an analysis of both their own behavior and that of the subordinates.

Ego States

At the heart of TA is the concept of *ego states*. Everyone has three ego states: the parent, the adult, and the child.

The *parent ego state* contains the attitudes and behavior that a child receives from his or her parents. For better or worse the parents leave an

[30]William J. Kearney and Desmond D. Martin, "Sensitivity Training: An Established Management Development Tool?" *Academy of Management Journal,* December 1974, pp. 755–760.

[31]For further insights into the pros and cons of sensitivity training see: Filley, House, and Kerr, *op. cit.,* pp. 498–503.

[32]John B. Miner, *The Management Process: Theory, Research, and Practice.* 2nd edition. (New York: The Macmillan Company, 1978), p. 346.
The Macmillan Company, 1973), p. 279.

[33]Marvin D. Dunnette and John P. Campbell, "Laboratory Education: Impact on People and Organizations," *Industrial Relations,* October 1968, p. 23.

[34]Eric Berne, *Games People Play* (New York: Grove Press, Inc., 1964).

[35]Thomas A. Harris, *I'm OK — You're OK* (New York: Harper & Row, Publishers, Inc., 1969).

[36]Muriel James and Dorothy Jongeward, *Born to Win* (Reading, Mass.: Addison-Wesley Publishing Co., 1971); and *Winning with People* (Reading, Mass.: Addison-Wesley Publishing Co., 1973).

indelible mark on the child by communicating to the latter their beliefs, their prejudices, and their fears. Any time a person acts in a manner learned from the parents, he or she is said to be in the parent ego state. Generally this occurs when the individual acts officious or assumes a dominant role. (This is the way it is to be done.)

The *adult ego state* is characterized by attention to fact gathering and objective analysis. No matter what prejudices or emotions were communicated by the parents, a person who is in the adult state deals with reality from an objective standpoint and analyzes the situation as dispassionately or realistically as possible. (Let's look at the facts.)

The *child ego state* contains all the impulses learned as an infant. When a person is in this ego state, he or she can be described in terms such as curious, impulsive, sensuous, affectionate, or uncensored. The individual is acting just the way he or she did as a child. A common illustration is people at a football game who are rooting and cheering. They are uncensored and impulsive. (We want a touchdown!)

These three ego states are often described by one-word adjectives. The parent state is referred to as *taught,* the adult state as *thought,* and the child state as *felt.* In addition, for purposes of analysis, the three are often diagrammed as in Figure 14–2.

At the heart of TA is the concept of ego states.

FIGURE 14–2   Simplified Ego State Structure

Types of Transactions

Throughout a normal day people will move from one ego state to another. The manager's job is one of discerning which ego state the person is in and then responding appropriately. To do so requires an understanding of the three basic types of transactions: complementary, crossed, and ulterior.

COMPLEMENTARY TRANSACTIONS.   Berne defines a complementary transaction as one that is "appropriate and expected and follows the natural order of healthy human relationships."[37] Sometimes an employee will ask the manager a simple question (adult ego state) and expect a truthful response (adult ego state), as in Figure 14–3.

It is not necessary, however, that people remain in the adult state at all times. For example, a worker may feel sick and ask to go home. In this

Complementary transactions are appropriate and expected.

---

[37]Berne, *op. cit.,* p. 29.

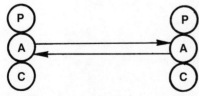

FIGURE 14–3   A Complementary Transaction

Employee:

Will there be any overtime
work this weekend?

Manager:

To the best of my knowledge
there will be.

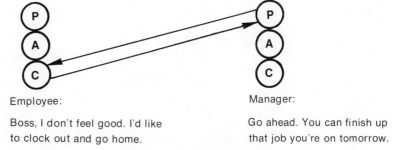

Employee:

Boss, I don't feel good. I'd like
to clock out and go home.

Manager:

Go ahead. You can finish up
that job you're on tomorrow.

FIGURE 14–4   A Complementary Transaction

case the individual acts like a child requesting a favor from the parent
(please, Daddy, may I?). In turn the manager assumes the parent role (you
certainly may). Such a transaction is illustrated in Figure 14–4.

As long as the manager responds appropriately, there is a complementary transaction, and communication and understanding are
achieved.

CROSSED TRANSACTIONS.   Crossed transactions occur when there is *not*
an appropriate or expected response. A diagram of the transaction can
easily reveal this. Figures 14–5 and 14–6 are two examples, the first being
one in which the manager errs, the second being one in which the
subordinate creates the problem.

> Crossed transac-
> tions are inap-
> propriate or un-
> expected.

ULTERIOR TRANSACTIONS.   Ulterior transactions are the most complex
because they *always* involve more than two ego states. Usually the real
message is disguised under a socially acceptable transaction. For example,
the manager wants one of the subordinates to take a job in a branch office,
believing the individual needs this experience in order to succeed with
the firm. However, the manager also believes the subordinate is unwilling
to do so. The manager therefore sends the person two messages, which
can be seen in Figure 14–7. The verbal one is represented by a solid arrow,
the ulterior one by a dotted arrow.

> Ulterior transac-
> tions always in-
> volve more than
> two ego states.

The manager appears to be stating a fact, but he is really appealing to
the subordinate's child state by throwing him a challenge and hoping he
will respond appropriately. If the subordinate says, "You're right, I want
to stay here at the home office," the manager has failed, for the individual
has answered the overt message only and responded on an adult-to-adult

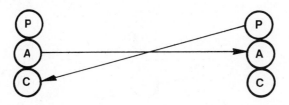

Subordinate:

I was on vacation last week and
didn't get a copy of the new policy
changes. Do you happen to have
an extra copy?

Manager:

What do I look like, the printing
office? If you want one, go up
to personnel and get one.

FIGURE 14–5   A Crossed Transaction

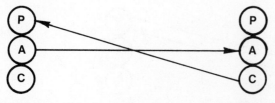

Manager:

Barry, according to the master
schedule it's your turn to stay late
tonight and clean up the work place.

Subordinate:

Oh, c'mon. I have a heavy date
tonight. Why don't you get
someone else, huh?

FIGURE 14–6   A Crossed Transaction

basis. On the other hand, if the manager injures the subordinate's pride
(as he hopes to do), the man might say "I think I can handle the job. I'd
like to try it." In so doing, he responds as a child (I can too do it. Just you
watch!). The point to remember is that when there are disguised messages, the transaction is known as ulterior.

**TA and the
Manager**

TA is currently being used by a number of different firms, including
American Airlines, to help managers understand and deal with their
subordinates. As long as managers realize that both they and their people
have ego states and operate within them, they are in a position to analyze
what is being said and how they should respond. One of the things TA
emphasizes is building a strong adult ego state and encouraging others to
do the same. If the manager can do this, he or she will deal with the
subordinates in a forthright and objective manner. Naturally, there are
times when the subordinates are justified in adopting other ego states. For
example, an employee may begin sulking because he or she has failed to
get a promotion (child state) and the manager offers encouraging words
(parent state). It is important to refrain from using ulterior transactions or
treating subordinates as if they have no place in the decision making
process. If the manager can do this, the people will respond more effectively. In explaining how TA can help managers communicate change,
reduce resistance, and encourage participative decision making, American Airlines offers the following advice:

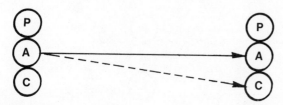

Manager:

Frank, there's been talk about
sending you to the branch office,
but I'm not so sure you're the
right man.

Subordinate:

You're right, I want to stay
here at the home office.

FIGURE 14–7   An Ulterior Transaction

What can you do to minimize your own as well as others' resistance to change and to improve efforts to improve? Remember that resistance to change comes from the Parent or the Child. Sometimes resistance can be reduced by providing or obtaining more data about the change. Involving people in some aspect of the decision-making (thereby requiring the use of their Adult) will help to get them unhooked from their Parent or Child reactions.

The method you use in trying to improve something is also extremely important. Telling people they *should* or *must* (Parent initiated "oughtmanship") improve something will probably hook their Child (and therefore generate resistance.) For example, telling a group of employees, "You *must* improve your customer service and also reduce costs" will likely generate only anger, anxiety, guilt or fear (Child reaction). Similarly, telling people that they should worry (thereby hooking their Child) about this same problem will probably not lead to improvement or change. On the other hand, the more relevant data you give employees about service and cost performance problems, the more likely you will engage their Adults in problem-solving.[38]

Another technique that is currently receiving a great deal of attention is *organizational behavior modification* or, as Luthans calls it, OB Mod.[39] In essence, the technique attempts to modify behavior by rewarding correct conduct and punishing or ignoring incorrect conduct. In this way, the individual learns to do what is expected of him. Quite simply, the technique uses learning theory to train (or retrain) people to do things the way the manager wants them to.

ORGANIZATIONAL BEHAVIOR MODIFICATION

OB Mod employs learning theory.

Behavior modification has been used by many organizations. One area in which it has been very successfully employed is in handling mental patients and autistic children. A common approach has been to give the mental patients tokens for performing certain functions such as work around the hospital. These tokens can then be cashed in as payment for allowing them to engage in activity they like such as watching an hour of television. This "token" approach serves to modify the behavior of the mental patients because it gets them to carry out certain tasks they would not otherwise perform.

Behavior Modification in Practice

Behavior modification, however, is not restricted to hospitals and clinics. This same basic approach has been used in training the hard-core unemployed. In one case, report Beatty and Schneier, the trainer starts off by giving instructions to the recruits prior to the time they actually start the job. In this phase the trainer teaches:

Behavior modification is not confined to hospitals and clinics.

... the skills required on the job by breaking the task into its component behaviors, using verbal instruction to demonstrate correct behaviors, and reinforcing correct behaviors. For example, consider a task requiring the trainee to *procure* materials from the proper place and in the proper amounts, then to *arrange* those materials, then to *feed* them to a machine, then to *place* the finished product on a tray or rack. In such a job, the trainee would be reinforced first for successfully procuring the materials, then reinforced for both procuring the materials correctly and arranging them correctly beside the machine, and finally reinforced for procuring, arranging, feeding, and placing correctly. Eventually, the reinforcement schedule would only reinforce completion of the entire task several times in succession.

By reinforcing each consecutive part of a task, we can "shape" behavior toward correctly performing the entire task.[40]

[38]Lyman Randall, *P–A–C at Work*, American Airlines, 1971, p. 46.

[39]Fred Luthans and Robert Kreitner, *Organizational Behavior Modification* (Glenview, Illinois: Scott, Foresman and Company, 1975), p. 12.

[40]Richard Beatty and Craig E. Schneier, "Training the Hard-Core Unemployed Through Positive Reinforcement," *Human Resource Management*, Winter 1972, p. 13.

As the training continues, the reinforcement (money, praise) can be varied; i.e., the individual is either rewarded only when he or she completes the task correctly five times in a row, or is rewarded on a random basis. This reinforcement schedule will, of course, depend on the individual and the job. However, remember that this positive reinforcement only occurs if the job is done right. If it is done incorrectly, the person is reinstructed on the proper way–for the goal is to train the individual correctly. However, if the person continues to do it wrong, the manager will turn either to punishment (reprimanding or threatening the person with dismissal) or to extinction (ignoring the person). Neither of these two techniques will, by themselves, get the trainee to perform correctly, but they may prevent him or her from doing it incorrectly. The trainer increases the probability that the individual will start seeking positive reinforcement rather than punishment or extinction by doing the job right.

Another objective for which behavior modification is being used is *reducing tardiness.* A hardware company in St. Louis, for example, has set up a lottery system for this purpose. If an individual is on time for work and takes only the allotted period for work breaks, he or she is eligible for a drawing at the end of the month. There is a prize worth about $25 awarded for every 25 eligible employees. Furthermore, at the end of six months, people with perfect attendance are eligible for a color television set drawing. In addition, the names of all winners, as well as those who were eligible, are printed in the company paper. Within 16 months of the program's installation, the firm's sick leave costs dropped by 62 per cent and the number of employees eligible for the monthly drawing rose from 151 (out of 530) in the first month to 219 in the sixteenth month.

The technique can be used for reducing tardiness.

Luthans and Kreitner, meanwhile, have reported a number of successes with OB Mod in changing specific on-the-job behavior. In one case, a particularly disruptive female machine operator was chosen as the subject of an experiment. Her supervisor decided to use a strategy known as *extinction/positive reinforcement.* Every time the woman had satisfactory production or constructive suggestions, the supervisor reinforced her with praise. Whenever she complained, the supervisor ignored her. Within forty-five working days, the manager reduced the woman's complaint frequency from three times daily to less than once daily on the average.

It can also be used in modifying organizational behavior.

In another case, the researchers reported that a supervisor was having little success in reducing the scrap rate among his work group. Posting equipment maintenance rules and frequently reminding the workers about it had little noticeable effect. The supervisor then decided to install a feedback system to inform the group of its scrap rate and to actively solicit suggestions from the workers on how to improve the rate. Within 10 weeks the group scrap rate declined from an average of 50 pieces per day to less than 20.

In a third case, a supervisor decided to use behavior modification to reduce the number of rejects of assembled components by one of his assemblers. He decided that anything over two per hundred was unacceptable:

> Beginning a shaping process at five or less errors, the supervisor contingently praised the assembler for any improved quality. As the reject level began to drop, the reinforcement schedule was gradually stretched. In other words, the worker had to have four, then three, and eventually only two rejects before praise was given by the supervisor. Summarized reject statistics were charted and presented to the assembler as a form of feedback on performance. Discussions of this feedback data between the assembler and the supervisors

provided the opportunity for the supervisor to reinforce desirable behavior and ignore undesirable behavior.[41]

Within two weeks the supervisor had the assembler down to an average of one reject per hundred assembled components.

One argument often made against OB Mod is that it is a manipulative technique. In behavioral terminology, this means that managers offer their subordinates contrived reinforcers that are external to the work environment. For instance, if OB Mod is used to limit tardiness, the manager thinks up "gimmicky" approaches that will induce the workers to show up on time. Although such reinforcers are useful at first, managers have to face the problem of what to offer next, when the initial approach proves ineffective. For this reason, OB Mod adherents attempt to arrange the work environment more efficiently, using reinforcers that are internal to the job such as praising a person for work well done and ignoring a person whose work is poor.[42]

Today the technique of behavior modification is being taken out of clinics and mental institutions and being applied to the management of humans in organizations.[43] Of course, a great deal more needs to be done before its full value for management can be determined. However, it has had a promising start and appears to be an effective technique for helping organizations manage their human assets.[44]

HUMAN RESOURCES ACCOUNTING

The ultimate objective of all the programs and techniques we have discussed thus far is that of obtaining maximum efficiency. When an organization decides to review its effectiveness, it will usually examine its financial statements, such as the balance sheet, in which physical assets (cash, accounts receivable, inventory, and plant) are recorded. However, nowhere in the financial statements of most firms is there any accounting for either the productive capability of the workers or the good will of the customers. In the case of the personnel, for example, there are many variables that can make one firm superior to another, including:

1. Level of intelligence and aptitudes.
2. Level of training.
3. Level of performance goals and motivation to achieve organizational success.
4. Quality of leadership.
5. Capacity to use differences for purposes of innovation and improvement, rather than allowing differences to develop into bitter, irreconcilable, interpersonal conflict.
6. Quality of communicating upward, downward, and laterally.
7. Quality of decision making.
8. Capacity to achieve cooperative teamwork versus competitive striving for personal success at the expense of the organization.
9. Quality of the control processes of the organization and the levels of felt responsibility which exist.
10. Capacity to achieve effective coordination.
11. Capacity to use experience and measurements to guide decisions, improve operations, and introduce innovations.[45]

---

[41]Luthans and Kreitner, *op. cit.*, p. 157.

[42]For more about these on-the-job-rewards see Luthans and Kreitner, *ibid.*, pp. 100–104.

[43]See, for example, Fred Luthans and Donald D. White, Jr., "Behavior Modification: Application to Manpower Management," *Personnel Administration*, July–August, 1971, pp. 41–47.

[44]For an excellent summation of this area see: Craig Eric Schneier, "Behavior Modification In Management: A Review and Critique," *Academy of Management Journal*, September 1974, pp. 528–548.

[45]Rensis Likert, *The Human Organization* (New York: McGraw-Hill Book Company, 1967), p. 148.

Nowhere on the balance sheet are these factors accounted for. In an attempt to overcome this deficiency, an area known as *human resources accounting* has developed. The method has taken two paths: viewing the acquisition and development of personnel as an investment, and obtaining a regular evaluation of these assets by measuring what are called "causal" and "intervening" variables. The following discussion will examine both of these approaches.

Personnel as an Investment

If a company is to be successful, it needs to hire and maintain competent personnel. How much are these people worth to the firm? This is a question human resources accounting attempts to answer. As Likert points out, this term

> ...refers to activity devoted to attaching dollar estimates to the value of a firm's human organization and its customer goodwill. If able, well-trained personnel leave the firm, the human organization is worth less; if they join it, the firm's human assets are increased. If bickering, distrust, and irreconcilable conflict become greater, the human enterprise is worth less; if the capacity to use differences constructively and engage in cooperative teamwork improves, the human organization is a more valuable asset.[46]

One way for the company to decide how much its human assets are worth would be to determine the amount of money it took to hire, train, and retain these people. Offsetting this figure will be factors such as retirement, transfers, separations, and obsolescence (or failure to keep up) on the part of the personnel. (See Figure 14–8) If one wished to include the customer in this analysis, the cost of maintaining good will could be written in and loss of customer orders (ill will) deducted.

---

[46]*Ibid.*, pp. 148–149.

"There's always a place in our organization for a fine, compassionate human being—but he must have the killer instinct, too."

Reprinted by permission of the Wall Street Journal and Bo Brown.

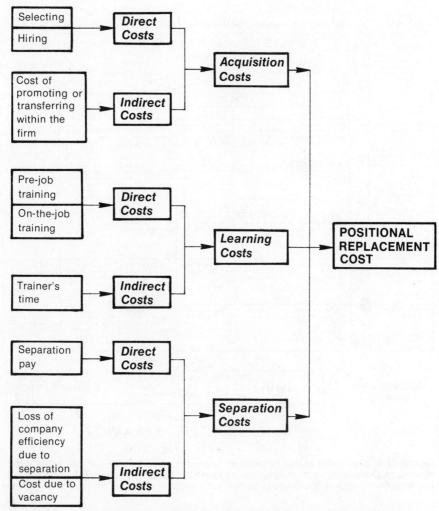

FIGURE 14–8   Determining Human Resource Replacement Costs (Adapted from Eric G. Flam-holtz, "Human Resource Accounting: Measuring Positional Replacement Costs," *Human Resource Management,* **Spring 1973, p. 11.)**

Another method has been proposed by Mirvis and Macy, who developed a model for reflecting member participation in light of attendance at work and performance while on the job. In the former category, factors included absenteeism, turnover, strikes, and tardiness. In the latter, they placed production under standard, quality under standard, grievances, accidents, unscheduled downtime, machine repair, material utilization, and inventory shrinkage. They then analyzed a firm and determined how much each of these factors was affecting the company. Mirvis and Macy found that tardiness was costing the firm $56,920 a year, absenteeism was costing $286,330 annually, and losses owing to quality below standard were estimated at $663,589.[47] Human resources are thus reflected in an organization's financial statements. By managing these resources well, the

A dollar-investment approach is used.

[47]Philip H. Mirvis and Barry M. Macy, "Human Resource Accounting: A Measurement Perspective, "*Academy of Management Review*, April 1976, pp. 76–83.

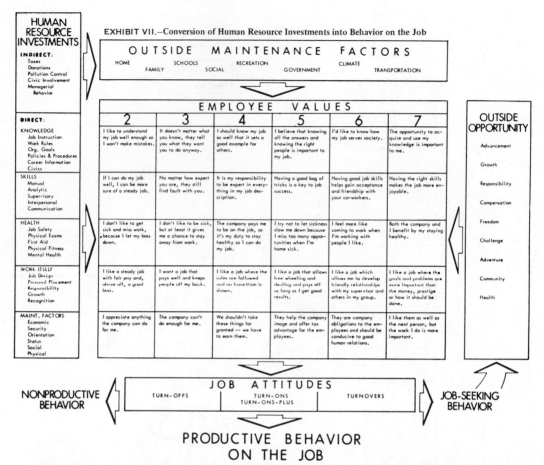

FIGURE 14–9 Conversion of Human Resource Investments into Behavior on the Job (M. Scott Myers and Vincent S. Flowers, "A Framework For Developing Human Assets," Copyright 1974 by the Regents of the University of California. Reprinted from *California Management Review*, volume XVI, number 4, p. 14, by permission of the Regents.)

organization can increase productivity and profits. Figure 14–9 shows how human resources investments can be converted into productive job behavior.

Obviously, converting human assets into dollars in the financial statements is a difficult task because the approach is very subjective. After all, how does one really decide the costs associated with the retention or loss of personnel? No definitive answer will be presented here, because the entire area is still in the developmental stages. It should be noted, however, that some companies are actually trying to reflect human resources in their financial statements.[48] If human resources accounting continues to grow at its current pace, other firms will undoubtedly be doing the same.

---

[48]William C. Pyle "Monitoring Human Resources — On Line," *Michigan Business Review*, July 1970, pp. 19–32; and D. M. C. Jones, "Accounting for Human Assets," *Management Decision*, Summer 1973, pp. 183–194; Geoffrey M. N., Baker, "The Feasibility and Utility of Human Resource Accounting," *California Management Review*, Summer 1974, pp. 17–23.

A second suggested approach is periodic evaluation of the state of the company's human resources. One way of doing this, in the opinion of some human resources accounting people, is to use Likert's four management systems which were discussed in Chapter 13. By determining whether a company is operating under Systems 1, 2, 3, or 4, they believe it is possible to draw conclusions about how the human resources are being managed. Their primary thesis is that the current state of a company's human resources will be reflected in future performance. If today's workers are operating under a System-3 or System-4 manager, future performance should be high. If they are working under a System-1 or System-2 manager, future performance will be lower.

When Likert's management systems are used to measure the current state of the human resources, questions such as those presented earlier in Figure 13–3 are employed. Based on the responses, the researchers approximate a profile of the system under which the company is operating. In addition, three types of variables are examined. These are:

1. *Causal* **(or independent)** *variables,* **which determine the results the company is going to achieve. Management decisions, business strategies, and leadership behavior are all illustrations.**
2. *Intervening variables,* **which reflect the internal state of the organization. Loyalty, attitude, and motivation are all illustrations.**
3. *End-result* **(or dependent)** *variables,* **which reflect the organization's achievements. Earnings, productivity, and costs are all illustrations.**

According to human resources experts, a company's earnings, productivity, and costs (end-result variables) are a result of causal variables such as business strategies and leadership behavior. However, one must do more than merely analyze cause-effect relationships. It is also necessary to examine the transformation process or *intervening variables*. For example, why does a particular leadership behavior result in higher earnings? The answer may well be found in factors such as loyalty, attitude, and motivation.

This particular concept has important implications for management because it indicates that a change in leadership style (causal variable) will result in a change in factors such as costs or earnings (end-result variables) only if there is change in factors such as loyalty, attitude, motivation, and so on (intervening variables). This particular idea is often used by human resources accounting people to illustrate what they call the *liquidation of human assets*. In essence, they believe that a company that wishes to increase its current earnings can do so if it moves toward System 1. Figure 14–10 provides an illustration.

CHANGES IN LEADERSHIP STYLE. As seen in Figure 14–10, by changing its strategy and leadership behavior (causal variables) the company's short-run financial position (end-result variable) improves. Of course, this lasts for only a few years and then deteriorates. However, one point to be noted from Figure 14–10 is that as the firm moves toward System 1, leadership behavior declines; managers become increasingly autocratic and start applying pressure in an attempt to improve earnings. This behavior is followed by a decline in employee attitudes and motivation. During this same period, it is also common to find some of the best workers leaving the firm. The company is thus liquidating its human resources. In a manner of speaking, it is analogous to selling machinery and equipment at a discount. On the positive side, however, the financial picture (earnings) improves and, in the above illustration, remains there for two years before finally dropping below the initial level of zero.

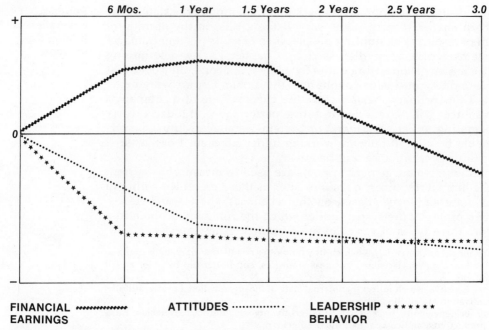

FINANCIAL ·········· ATTITUDES ············· LEADERSHIP ✶✶✶✶✶✶
EARNINGS   BEHAVIOR

FIGURE 14–10   Moving Toward System I (Courtesy of Dr. Tony Hain, General Motors Institute.)

The same basic concepts are used by human resources people to explain what happens when a company moves toward System 4, illustrated in Figure 14–11. First the leadership behavior (causal variable) is changed. This is followed by improvement in attitudes (intervening variable) and then improvement in earnings (end-result variable).

If the management moves toward System 1, it can milk or liquidate its human assets and achieve short-run increases in earnings. However, after a given time period the intervening variables will come into play and these earnings will decrease. Thus, in the short-run, when a critical financial situation develops, it may be advisable to change to System 1, but this approach cannot be maintained indefinitely.

Conversely, moving toward System 4 may not result in any increases in earnings for quite a while. As Likert points out, *"Changes in the causal variables toward System 4 apparently require an appreciable period of time before the impact of the change is fully manifest in corresponding improvement in the end-result variables."*[49] This entails a good deal of faith on the part of the management, for they must be willing to continue moving toward System 4. In the long-run, however, earnings will improve.

Human resources researchers thus believe that the firm's current financial position may not reflect the true status of the causal and intervening variables, for these are lead factors. However, changes in these variables will be reflected in *future* financial statements, and this is why they are so important:

Causal and intervening variables are lead factors.

The measurements of the causal and intervening variables should be obtained for the corporation as a whole and for each profit center or unit in the company.... By using appropriate statistical procedures, relationships can be computed among the causal, interven-

---

[49]Likert, *op. cit.*, pp. 80–81; for more on this topic see; William F. Dowling, "At General Motors: System 4 Builds Performance and Profits,"*Organizational Dynamics*, Winter 1975, pp. 23–38.

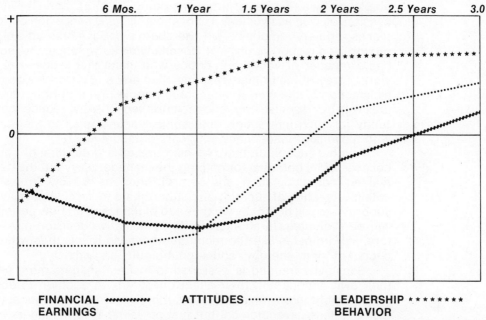

FINANCIAL ~~~~~~~~   ATTITUDES ············   LEADERSHIP ★ ★ ★ ★ ★ ★ ★
EARNINGS   BEHAVIOR

FIGURE 14–11   Moving Toward System 4 (Courtesy of Dr. Tony Hain, General Motors Institute.)

ing, and such end-result variables as costs and earnings. . . . These estimates of probable subsequent productivity, costs, and earnings will reveal the earning power of the human organization *at the time* the causal and intervening variables were measured, even though the level of estimated subsequent earnings may not be achieved until much later. These estimates . . . provide the basis for attaching to any profit center, unit, or total corporation a statement of the present value of its human organization.[50]

The *future* of the firm depends on its ability to manage its human assets *today*.

Before ending this discussion, one point must be noted. Figures 14–10 and 14–11 represent only a general pattern of results as postulated by human resources researchers. As Koontz and O'Donnell note, "To date, only a few experiments have been undertaken to measure the investment costs and losses in human resources. While it is believed that present 'value' of human resources . . . can be reasonably well approached through the use of the Likert measurements, there is still little evidence that this has been done with an acceptable degree of creditability."[51] On an overall basis, then, we will have to withhold judgment on the value of human resources accounting until more research has been conducted in the area.

In this chapter some of the latest tools and techniques for managing the firm's human assets have been examined. One technique, job enrichment, has been getting a lot of attention recently. It is currently being   **SUMMARY**

---

[50]*Ibid., p. 150.*
[51]Harold Koontz and Cyril O'Donnell, *Principles of Management: A Systems and Contingency Analysis of Managerial Functions,* 6th edition (New York: McGraw-Hill Book Company, 1976) p. 715.

employed by a number of firms, including TI, AT&T, and GM's Cadillac division, as well as overseas in Volvo plants. In essence, job enrichment places primary emphasis on Herzberg's motivators: advancement, growth, and responsibility. Yet, despite wide acceptance, the technique has a number of vociferous critics who claim that it does not always work. Three of the primary reasons cited are: some workers do not find satisfaction in the work place; some people prefer boring, unpleasant jobs with good social interaction to enriched jobs that reduce the opportunity for such interaction; and some workers react to the technique with feelings of inadequacy and fears of failure.

Another technique that has also gained a great deal of popularity because of its potential for helping the manager carry out the decision-making, communication, and control functions is MBO. In essence, it entails a meeting of superior and subordinate for deciding: (a) what the subordinate will do; (b) by what period of time; and (c) how performance will be evaluated. In addition to its participative decision-making feature, subordinates like the technique because it tells them what is expected of them, thereby reducing ambiguity and anxiety.

Sensitivity training is designed to make managers more aware of their own actions and their effect on others, in addition to obtaining better insight into what makes the subordinates tick. Another approach, which is less psychological but just as valuable to managers in communicating with their people, is transactional analysis. A number of companies, particularly American Airlines, are using this technique to help their managers communicate more effectively with their subordinates.

Behavior modification is the newest of the techniques discussed in the chapter. In essence, it attempts to get people to do what management wants them to by discouraging incorrect behavior and rewarding correct behavior. Although used most widely by hospitals and clinics, today it is being adopted by business for handling numerous organizational challenges from training the hard-core unemployed to reducing employee tardiness.

The last technique that was examined was human resources accounting. This technique suggests that the company evaluate its personnel and that this evaluation be reflected in the financial statements. After all, well-trained, well-motivated people are an asset. Another approach is to evaluate the personnel on a periodic basis by measuring causal, intervening, and end-result variables. This technique gives management a reading on the kind of performance it can expect from its people in the near future.

REVIEW AND STUDY QUESTIONS

1. What is meant by the "great jackass fallacy"?

2. What is the primary goal of job enrichment? Will we see more of it throughout this current decade? Explain.

3. What are some of the arguments raised against job enrichment?

4. How does management by objectives work?

5. What are some of the problems one must be aware of in using MBO?

6. In what way can sensitivity training be of value to the manager?

7. How does TA help the manager communicate with and understand the subordinates? Bring into your discussion the three basic types of transactions: complementary, crossed, and ulterior.

8. How does behavior modification work? What are the basic steps or ideas in the process?

9. Behavior modification is nothing more than manipulation. Defend or oppose this statement.

10. Why should a company think of its personnel as an investment? Should these people be accounted for in financial statements?

11. What is a causal variable? An intervening variable? An end-result variable? Of what value is this information to management?

12. In general, can a company improve its short-run earnings by switching from a System-4 to a System-1 management? Explain.

13. Why does a company, in moving from a System-1 to a System-4 management, not witness an immediate increase in earnings? Explain.

SELECTED REFERENCES

Baker, G. M. N. "The Feasibility and Utility of Human Resource Accounting." *California Management Review*, Summer 1974, pp. 17–23.

Barton–Dobenin, J., and R. M. Hodgetts. "Management Training Programs: Who Uses Them and Why?" *Training and Development Journal,* March 1975, pp. 34–40.

Berne, E. *Games People Play.* New York: Grove Press, Inc. 1964.

Bowers, D. G. *Systems of Organization: Management of the Human Resource.* Ann Arbor: The University of Michigan Press, 1976.

Bright, W. E. "How One Company Manages its Human Resources." *Harvard Business Review,* January–February 1976, pp. 81–93.

"Business Tries Out 'Transactional Analysis'." *Business Week*, January 12, 1974, pp. 74–75.

Dowling, W. F. "At General Motors: System 4 Builds Performance and Profits." *Organizational Dynamics,* Winter 1975, pp. 23–38.

Drucker, P. F. *The Practice of Management.* New York: Harper & Row Publishers, 1954.

English, J., and A. R. Marchione. "Nine Steps in Management Development." *Business Horizons*, June 1977, pp. 88–94.

Flamholtz, E. G. "Human Resources Accounting: Measuring Positional Replacement Costs." *Human Resource Management,* Spring 1973, pp. 8–16.

Ford, R. N. *Motivation Through the Work Itself.* New York: American Management Association, 1969.

Giblin, E. J., and O. A. Ornati. "Optimizing the Utilization of Human Resources." *Organizational Dynamics,* Autumn 1975, pp. 18–33.

Harris, T. A. *I'm OK — You're OK.* New York: Harper & Row Publishers, 1969.

Heenan, D. A., and C. Reynolds, "RPO's: A Step Toward Global Human Resources Management." *California Management Review.* Fall 1975, pp. 5–9.

Hollingsworth, A. T. "Improving Managerial Decisions That Affect Human Resources." *Personnel Journal,* June 1973, pp. 446–450.

Hollmann, R. W. "Supportive Organizational Climate and Managerial Assessment of MBO Effectiveness." *Academy of Management Journal,* December 1976, pp. 560–576.

Hollmann, R. W., and D. A. Tansik. "A Life Cycle Approach to Management by Objectives." *Academy of Management Review,* October 1977, pp. 678–683.

James, M., and D. Jongeward. *Born to Win.* Reading, Mass.: Addison-Wesley Publishing Co., 1971.

Koontz, H. "Making MBO Effective." *California Management Review,* Fall 1977, pp. 5–13.

Levinson, H. "Asinine Attitudes Toward Motivation." *Harvard Business Review,* January–February 1973, pp. 70–76.

Locke, E. A. "The Myths of Behavior Mod in Organizations." *Academy of Management Review,* October 1977, pp. 543–553.

Luthans, F., and R. Kreitner. "The Role of Punishment in Organizational Behavior Modification (OB Mod)." *Public Personnel Management*, May–June 1973, pp. 156–161.

Mills, Ted. "Human Resources — Why the New Concern?" *Harvard* Business Review, March–April 1975, pp. 120–134.

Mirvis, P. H., and B. A. Macy. "Human Resource Accounting: A Measurement Perspective." *Academy of Management Review,* April 1976, pp. 74–83.

Myers, M. S., and V. S. Flowers. "A Framework for Measuring Human Assets." *California Management Review,* Summer 1974, pp. 5–16.

Nemiroff, P. M., and D. L. Ford, Jr. "Task Effectiveness and Human Fulfillment in Organizations: A Review and Development of a Conceptual Contingency Model." *Academy of Management Review*, October 1976, pp. 69–82.

Puett, J. R., Jr., and D. D. Roman. "Human Resource Valuation." *Academy of Management Journal.* December 1976, pp. 656–662.

Reif, W. E., and F. Luthans. "Does Job Enrichment Really Pay Off?" *California Management Review*, Fall 1972, pp. 30–37.

Schneier, C. E. "Behavior Modification in Management: A Review and Critique." *Academy of Management Journal*, September 1974, pp. 528–548.

Stiner, Jr. F., and R. M. Hodgetts. "The Social Audit and the Unit of Measurement." *Virginia Accountant*, September 1975, pp. 47–51.

Tosi, H., and S. J. Carroll, Jr. "Improving Management by Objectives: A Diagnostic Change Program." *California Management Review*, Fall 1973, pp. 57–66.

Walker, J. W. "Human Resource Planning: Managerial Concerns and Practices." *Business Horizons*, June 1976, pp. 55–59.

CASE: NO LAYOFFS[52]

Believe it or not, IBM has not laid off one employee for economic reasons in over 35 years. Instead, the giant computer firm reassigns and retrains workers no longer needed in one area. Since 1970 it has retrained and physically relocated 5000 employees as part of the most extensive corporate education program in this country. The following is an illustration:

Karyl Nichols worked a routine eight-hour day as a secretary in an office of International Business Machines Corporation in Westchester County, New York. Then she went through a "career bend," as IBM calls it, and became a sales representative in New York City. Today, instead of pounding a typewriter, she sells IBM typewriters and other office equipment. Eager to advance — and to make her sales quota — she voluntarily puts in ten-hour days, or "whatever it takes," and loves it.

The 24 year old Nichols does not go so far as to sing company songs at lunchtime, but her loyalty and hard work are typical of benefits that IBM gets for offering near-total job security to its employees.

IBM believes that if people are not concerned about getting laid off, they are willing to cooperate with the firm in working toward company objectives. This enthusiasm shows results at the bottom of the income statement.

On the other hand, the company is quick to point out that it has no place for nonproducers, particularly sales people and managers. The president has noted that the company is "not running a home for unproductive people. . . . But our business has always recognized the effect that job security can have on the morale of the work force. Very frequently you make a fellow very happy when you move him to a new job, and when you can fill the old job you also make someone else happy." To make room for these moves, the company fires the nonproducers and encourages older employees to choose early retirement by offering incentive plans.

---

[52]The data in this case can be found in: "How IBM Avoids Layoffs Through Retraining," *Business Week*, November 10, 1975, pp. 110, 112.

Is this guaranteed emphasis on job security good for the firm or does it result in a form of paternalism that will eventually backfire? IBM believes that it is a very important step in managing its human assets effectively:

IBM's way of dealing with its employees does not produce a regimented work force. While protective job security can produce stagnation, IBM insists that it enables employees to be more individualistic and willing to try new ideas. "If you operate in high job security without demanding performance . . . there would be a problem. But we demand performance."

A former IBM executive says a fundamental "attitudinal difference" between IBM and other companies helps explain IBM's success. He says: "IBM knows that you don't keep workers happy by puffing the work force up and down as though it didn't matter what happened to the people."

Questions

1. In what way does job security help nurture human assets?

2. In a high technology industry a firm's human assets are its most important resources, so IBM really has no choice — it must treat its people well. Support or oppose this statement.

3. If IBM were to change its philosophy and start treating its people in an autocratic manner, what would happen to employee performance? Explain.

CASE: A CASE OF ELIGIBILITY

Absenteeism at the Pallering Corporation had been staggering. Between January and June of 1977 the average employee was showing up 15 minutes late for work three times a week. The management decided that something had to be done.

The problem was turned over to Jerry Peters of the personnel department. After pondering the situation for a few weeks, Jerry suggested that the management undertake an incentive program. Every worker who was on time during the month of August would be eligible for a cash award of $100. There would be three such awards in all, and the drawing would be held on September 4. Within five days of the time the award was announced, absenteeism declined to a lower level than it had ever been in the history of the firm. Furthermore, throughout the ensuing six months, the company continued to maintain this reward system and absenteeism remained lower than ever. In March of 1978 the firm abandoned the plan and absenteeism soared to an all-time high, but it returned to its former low level in April when the award was reinstituted.

Questions

1. Has the management actually modified behavior? Explain.

2. Why did absenteeism soar when the company abandoned the plan?

3. Why does absenteeism remain so low when the incentive award is made available? After all, isn't money only a temporary motivator?

CASE: A LIQUIDATION OF PEOPLE

When Jim Jackson became vice president of manufacturing at the Walters Corporation in 1976 the firm had been in a downward spiral. Profits had declined from $473,000 in 1970 to just over $250,000 in fiscal 1975: Return on investment during this period had dropped from 9.3 per cent to 4.0 per cent.

Within twenty-four months, however, Mr. Jackson turned the financial picture completely around. The accountant's report for these eight quarters revealed the following:

		Profit	ROI
1977	I	$290,000	4.3
	II	370,000	4.6
	III	420,000	4.9
	IV	550,000	6.1
1978	I	625,000	7.2
	II	750,000	8.1
	III	895,000	9.4
	IV	1,050,000	10.7

Then, to the president's dismay, Mr. Jackson submitted his resignation. He had been offered a job at twice his current salary and had decided to accept it. He would be leaving by the end of the month.

With only four weeks in which to find a replacement, the company quickly put out feelers to see who might fill the position. All reports seemed to indicate that Mr. Paul Robertson, factory manager for a large eastern firm, was the ideal choice. Mr. Robertson was invited in to see the facilities and financial reports. Toward the end of his visit he and the president had a chance to sit down and talk.

Paul, you've been here for three days now. Everyone is immensely impressed with your record and we'd like you to be our new vice president of manufacturing. What do you say?

I appreciate the offer, Mr. Canyon. However, quite frankly, I've decided not to accept. I just don't want to step in and spend the next two years rebuilding the firm.

Rebuilding? Why we have the best books in the industry.

True, on paper you look great. But what about the fact that over the last eighteen months half of your skilled work force has quit? These people are going to have to be replaced.

Sure we've lost some people. But Jim Jackson stepped into a tough position. He had to tighten things up. Before he came we were losing money. He made everyone start to pull his own weight.

And in the process he alienated the best employees. He's milked your human assets. I think you've gotten just about all the earnings you're going to get out of your current work force. The way I see it, you have a major rebuilding program on your hands. The man you think you're grateful to has actually liquidated your most important asset — your people.

Questions

1. If Mr. Robertson is correct in his analysis, how has the vice president of manufacturing liquidated the firm's human assets? Explain.

2. Why did the firm allow this to happen? Why did the president not take corrective action before this time?

3. What must the company do now? Explain.

CASE: PRODUCTIVITY AND JOB SATISFACTION[53]

Most organizations would like to attain both high productivity and high job satisfaction. However, many managers are confused as to how this can be achieved. Recent research offers some strategies for improving both job productivity and satisfaction. Some of these suggestions are:

1. Marked improvements in both satisfaction and performance will not occur until at least several major steps are taken that, in combination, create a qualitatively new and better socio-technical system.

2. The key to having satisfied, productive workers is found in motivation.

3. A human resource development program designed to motivate people must provide benefits, financial and nonfinancial alike, to all the workers one wants to motivate.

4. Job design is one way of attaining desired motivation, provided the new designs take into account the needs of the workers.

5. Another way to give the workers a voice in what goes on is through increased autonomy or self-regulation.

6. Satisfaction with salary is greater when it is clearly tied to performance than when it is not.

Questions

1. Will an organization achieve high productivity if it has high job satisfaction? Give your reasoning.

2. What is meant by statement number one above, regarding the need for at least several major steps to be taken in combination to achieve both satisfaction and performance? Explain.

3. Which three human resource development programs discussed in this chapter do you think would be most beneficial to an organization in attaining high productivity and high job satisfaction? Defend your answer.

COMPREHENSIVE CASE: REWARDS FOR PERFORMANCE: THE NAME OF THE GAME[54]

Whether talking about good communication, high motivation, effective leadership, or any other behavioral area of management,

---

[53]The data in this case can be found in: Raymond A. Katzell and Daniel Yankelovich, "Improving Productivity and Job Satisfaction," *Organizational Dynamics*, Summer 1975, pp. 69–80.

[54]The data in this case can be found in: "The Tightening Squeeze on White Collar Pay," *Business Week*, September 12, 1977, pp. 82–85.

somewhere in the conversation one is going to touch on the subject of rewards and performance. No one works for nothing. Every individual wants to be rewarded in some way.

Unfortunately, in recent years United States industry has found that its merit pay system, which it has used to motivate and reward managers and professionals, is in trouble. In particular, those individuals making over $20,000 and under $200,000 are finding that inflation and the income tax rate are squeezing their pay so hard that in some cases they end up with less money after the raise than before. *Business Week* has reported the effect of taxes and inflation at various levels of adjusted gross income. The data are provided in the table below.

Taxes and Inflation Can Seriously Erode an 8% Raise

Adjusted Gross Income		Aftertax Income		Effective Tax Rate	After-tax Income*	Net Change After Taxes and Inflation
Year 1	Year 2	Year 1	Year 2	Year 2	Year 2	Year 2–Year 1
$15,000	$16,200	$13,339	$14,421	10.98%	$13,541	$ +202
20,000	21,600	17,454	18,759	13.15	17,614	+160
25,000	27,000	21,335	22,833	15.43	21,439	+104
30,000	32,400	24,990	26,744	17.46	25,112	+122
35,000	37,800	28,636	30,531	19.23	28,668	+ 32
40,000	43,200	32,237	34,252	20.71	32,162	− 75
45,000	48,600	35,850	37,743	22.34	35,439	−411
50,000	54,000	38,880	41,022	24.03	38,518	−362
55,000	59,400	41,981	44,813	24.56	42,078	+ 97
60,000	64,800	45,112	46,973	27.51	44,106	−1,006
65,000	70,200	47,382	50,738	27.72	47,641	+259
70,000	75,600	50,579	54,169	28.35	50,863	+284
75,000	81,000	53,731	57,229	29.35	53,736	+ 5

*Assuming a 6.5% inflation in Year 2.

Part of this problem is caused, surprisingly, by a compression of salaries at the top. For example, the chief executive officer (CEO) will freeze his or her salary at some given level, e.g., $250,000. This in turn will mean that all staff members below will either have their salaries frozen or find their increases much smaller than would be the case if the CEO chose a different salary plan. Some people believe that under this approach everyone suffers equally. However, this is untrue since the CEO and some of the top officers of large corporations are usually entitled to bonuses, options, perquisites, and other incentives that are often not available to managers down the line. Thus, the top people may be getting another 30 per cent of their base salary in the form of "other compensation." In fact, a recent *Business Week* survey reports that bonuses have driven up the compensation of top executives to 50 per cent and more of their base salary.

How can American industry deal with this current dilemma? A number of firms are experimenting with new approaches. One of the most common is the use of incentive plans, tied at least to the company's performance, if not to the individual's:

. . . for example, Citicorp introduced a new concept into its staff incentive plans that allows employees to choose "book-value stock" rather than common stock, making them less vulnerable to the whims of the stock market. The new plan enables employees to participate in the bank's

growth if the book value grows, even though the price of the common stock may play dead. Citicorp book-value stock over the past ten years would have returned 13.4 per cent a year, had it been available. . . . And Wang Laboratories, Inc. last year introduced a stock option plan for all employees. Each six months they are granted options equal to 3 per cent of their earnings for that period. The options are completely vested after five years and can be exercised at age 60.

Other firms are allowing their managers to work overtime. For example, at Pitney-Bowes, Inc., executives making as much as $35,000 a year are still eligible for overtime.

Steps such as these certainly help. However, there are still some problems many firms are facing. One is the dilemma of hiring new people when those who have been with the firm for an extended period of time are making less than the market rate for these new personnel. In some cases this can happen within a few years of the time the first individual was hired. For example, in some banks salary is a function of internal policy. A superior college graduate with a fine track record in the bank may receive a 15 per cent salary increase each year only to learn that new graduates are being hired at a salary within $200 of his. In order to prevent internal morale problems, companies are trying to determine merit and cost-of-living increases, with enough "extra" to allow those employees to leapfrog past these newly hired people.

The merit system also poses problems. How much should the firm give to its best managers in the form of merit? Most companies feel that they must give everyone some increase, no matter how small. Average workers must get more than the marginal personnel but less than the superior ones; there has to be a higher percentage for those doing the best job. Atlantic Richfield, regarded by compensation specialists as having a "real" merit system, admits that there is no easy solution to this predicament. Recently, the firm established its lowest increase at 4 per cent, the average at 10, and the top at 15. Other firms are trying to review and reward their personnel at shorter intervals, i.e., every 10 months rather than every year:

Many companies also tend to make exceptions to their own compensation rules in order to reward people they do not want to lose, at whatever level. The traditional bell curve distribution, which gave a few people no increase and a few people large increases (10 to 12 per cent) has been supplemented with another small curve representing star performers, who receive raises of as much as 25 per cent, says McKinsey, a management consultant. "Companies are willing to override the system to keep the better person," he says. "Some are even giving promotional increases to keep them."

One of the big problems facing many companies is that if they give a top performing manager an increase of 15 per cent over each of the next five years, they are raising their fixed expenses even higher. For this reason, the one-shot award is spreading through middle and lower management, especially in the paper, chemical, and packaged goods industries. These are "discretionary" pluses which do not bind the firm for a long time but serve as a goal for those who did, and did not, earn them.

Yet, regardless of whether the company is using an incentive or an award system, the bottom line seems to be performance measurement. Are you getting what you are paying for? This has resulted in firms swinging away from payment systems and toward performance systems:

First Pennsylvania Bank is now instituting a behavior standard scale that breaks the job into skills such as communications, administration, and human relations. Each of these skill categories is further divided into "subsets," such as listening, follow-up and control, and assertiveness. And instead of a scale composed of terms such as "outstanding" or "superior," the rater must choose among descriptions such as "understands and learns new tasks quickly."

One unforeseen result of such a system has been the reduction in lawsuits brought on by disgruntled employees.

On the negative side, managers admit that a performance appraisal system can be difficult because everyone believes that his or her performance is superior. Thus, those who are seen as not even slightly productive by the manager are often prepared to argue vociferously about their performance rating. Another problem is that many managers are unwilling to criticize their employees. One of the hardest things to tell an individual is that he or she is not doing acceptable work.

A final trend, worthy of note, is that of opening the books and letting employees see where they stand in the salary scale. *Business Week* has described it this way:

More openness about salaries, ranges, and even the way the company perceives the employee's potential may be the single most striking change in corporate pay policy in the past few years. Whereas employees once knew little more than what their own salary was, today in many companies they are told not only their range but the next one up. And the increasingly common practice of posting jobs, along with salary, gradually spreads the word even in close-mouthed companies. Aetna publishes a salary manual that lists all job classes and the salary ranges that go with them. One year ago, Crocker began giving employees access to all salary ranges except those at the executive level, "It certainly increases our credibility, because nobody is hiding anything," says [a company spokesman]. "Also, the supervisors now know the employees have access to this information, so this influences the small percentage of supervisors who might want to play games." As Hay Associates general partner Daniel L. Stix says, "You have to clean up your act before you can communicate what you are doing."

Meanwhile, at the Security Pacific National Bank employees are now given wallet-sized cards that spell out their job level and salary range. This is all part of a pilot program that asks employees what jobs they aspire to and then describes that job fully, including the salary range. A spokesman for the bank notes that they are reaching the point at which there will be very few secrets about salaries. The emphasis is going to be on explaining the job and the salary openly.

Yet business people admit that the only real way to solve the pay squeeze on white collar employees is to promote them. At Citibank, where more than one in five people are promoted each year and where promotion increases range to 20 per cent, the statistics reveal that promotion is the way to make the greatest amount of money. At the end of 10 years, two people starting together can be as much as 100 per cent apart, depending on the number of raises each receives (or does not receive). The major question then appears to be whether or not managers can continue to move through their organizations. In firms where promotions are stymied, the chances for keeping up with inflation are reduced accordingly:

As discontent increases over the emptiness of merit raises in a prolonged period of inflation, it is likely to cause trouble in companies that lack the growth to support high ratios of promotions. And companies in areas with high living costs and high local taxes will be even harder pressed to attract and hold employees than they already are. Statistics compiled by McKinsey show that managers making from $25,000 to $100,000 a year must receive annual raises of 8 to 8.7 per cent just to stay even when inflation runs at 7 per cent. But they indicate that in New York City, the manager in those brackets must receive increases of between 9 and 10 per cent to stay even. In short, the companies that already have a problem motivating superior managers will find that problem accentuated.

"The pay problem is going to be less susceptible to a total group approach, less susceptible to a group cure. . . . The problem will require more executive involvement. It's just not a problem the technicians can solve."

Questions

1. When it comes to motivating managerial personnel, how important is money?

2. When money is the main topic, as it was in this case, we are generally talking about motivation of people. However, how can money help an organization meet the other behavioral considerations and challenges such as clear-cut communication, effective leadership and the development of its human resources?

3. Given the data provided in this case, how can business deal with this problem during the decade of the 1980's? Use the information you have gathered in Chapters 11–14 to help you formulate your answer.

SECTION E

THE FUTURE OF MANAGEMENT THEORY

The goal of this final section of Part II, which consists entirely of Chapter 15, is to examine modern management theory in terms of where it is now and where it appears to be headed. Primary consideration will be given to the systems and contingency schools of thought, since both appear to hold an important place in the future of management theory.

The beginning of Chapter 15 is devoted to a discussion of the systems school of thought. This is followed by an examination of both general systems theory and applied systems concepts. Next, attention is focused on the general applicability of the systems approach for the practicing manager. Primary consideration is given to viewing the organization as an open system. Then, the three levels of management in the hierarchy are examined in systems terms. Finally, a review of the current status and future development of management theory is undertaken, with major attention given to a contingency theory of management.

CHAPTER FIFTEEN

MANAGEMENT THEORY: CURRENT STATUS AND FUTURE DIRECTION

Sections B to D of Part II have presented the current major schools of management thought. The question now is, where does management theory go from here? The answer is, no one knows for sure. However, two major lines of thinking are currently popular. The first contends that the three schools will merge into a systems school. One group of authors has summarized the position in this way:

GOALS OF THE CHAPTER

> Although the process, behavioral, and quantitative approaches have been widely adopted, a growing group of practitioners and academicians have felt that another approach — the systems approach — would encompass the subsystems emanating from each of the other approaches.[1]

If this is true, the future development of modern management theory can be represented by the following illustration:

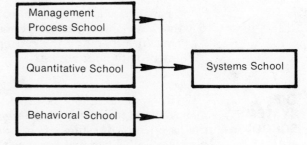

FIGURE 15–1 The Future Direction of Management Theory: One View

There seems to be more support, however, for the second point of view, which holds that there is already a systems school of thought in existence and that the trend is now toward a situational or contingency theory of management. This thinking is represented by the following illustration:

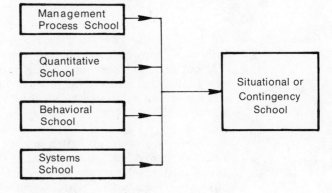

FIGURE 15–2 The Future Direction of Management Theory: A Second View

---

[1]Max S. Wortman, Jr. and Fred Luthans, eds., *Emerging Concepts in Management*, 2nd edition. (New York: The Macmillan Company, 1975), p. 319.

If one keeps in mind that Figures 15–1 and 15–2 represent only two major points of view, and many scholars and practitioners have their own ideas, it should be evident that there is currently much disagreement about the future direction of management theory.

One thing, however, does appear clear. Any examination of the current status and future direction of management theory must consider the subject of *systems*. Questions such as: What is a system? How is the concept of value to management theory? Is there a systems school of thought? all merit consideration. The goal of this chapter is to deal with these questions and, in the process, offer some general guidance about the direction management theory will take in the next decade. Attention will first be focused on what some people call the "systems school," and on the questions, what is the basic philosophy of this school and why has it not been discussed previously? Then the general area of systems, as applied to organizations, will be examined. Finally, management theory in the future will be discussed.

When you have finished reading this chapter you should be able to:

1. Discuss what is meant by the systems school of management.
2. Relate why successful organizations have to function like open systems.
3. Explain the importance of adaptive and maintenance mechanisms in ensuring organizational survival.
4. Describe the three levels of managerial systems and the types of managers who function at each level.
5. Give your opinion of where management theory appears to be heading, incorporating the concept of a contingency theory of management with your answer.

THE SYSTEMS SCHOOL

The systems school is considered by some to be a new school of management thought that emerged sometime in the 1960's. Although this is open to question, there are many computer and systems analyst people who believe that systems theory has now developed to the stage where the formation of a systems school is justified. Whether or not they are right, it is useful for the student of management to have a general idea of what is meant by the term "systems school." In essence, there are two major areas that merit consideration. The first, general systems theory, contains the conceptual and philosophical bases of the systems approach.

General Systems Theory

Perhaps the key word in the vocabulary of this school is *system*. Although many definitions are available, one of the most succinct is that put forth by Kast and Rosenzweig. A system is *an organized, unitary whole composed of two or more interdependent parts, components, or subsystems and delineated by identifiable boundaries from its environmental suprasystem.*[2]

Systems school advocates see all variables in the environment as mutually dependent and interactive. However, before examining the importance of the systems concept to management, some attention should be focused on what is called *general systems theory*. Systems

---

[2]Fremont E. Kast and James E. Rosenzweig, *Organization and Management*, 2nd edition (New York: McGraw-Hill Book Company, 1974), p. 101.

theorists believe that many of the concepts of systems management originated with general systems theory. In addition, an examination of this topic provides a basis for analyzing other important management related areas, including: the movement of individuals into and out of the system; the interaction of individuals with their environment; the interaction of individuals with each other; and the general growth and stability problems of systems.[3]

Many systems management concepts originated with general systems theory.

SYSTEMS LEVELS. Perhaps the most famous article written on systems theory is "Systems Theory — The Skeleton of Science"[4] by Kenneth Boulding. In this article Boulding put forth a classification of the nine hierarchical levels in the universe. He described them as follows:

1. The first level can be called the level of *frameworks* and represents a static structure. Examples include geography and the anatomy of the universe.
2. The next level could be referred to as the level of *clockworks* and is characterized by a simple, dynamic system with predetermined, necessary motions. The solar system is an illustration.
3. Next is the level of the control mechanism or cybernetic system, nicknamed the *thermostat* level. The homeostasis model, so important in physiology, is an illustration.
4. Then comes the open system of the self-maintaining structure, which can be called the level of the *cell*. At this level, life and reproduction enter the scheme.
5. The fifth level is the *genetic-societal level*. This is typified by the plant, which dominates the empirical world of the botanist.
6. Next comes the *animal* kingdom. It is characterized by teleological behavior, increased mobility and self-awareness.
7. Then comes the *human* level. In addition to possessing nearly all the characteristics of animal systems, the individual is also capable of employing language and symbols.
8. The eighth level is that of *social organizations*. At this level, concern is given to the content and meaning of messages, the nature and dimension of value systems, the transcription of images into historical records, the subtle symbolizations of art, music and poetry, and the complex gamut of human emotions.
9. The final level of the structure is *transcendental systems*. These are the ultimates, the absolutes and the inescapable unknowables, which exhibit systematic structure and relationship.[5]

Boulding's system classification scheme.

A cursory review of these levels indicates that the first three are concerned with physical or mechanical systems. As such, they have basic value for people in the physical sciences such as astronomy and physics. The next three levels deal with biological systems. They are thus of interest to biologists, botanists, and zoologists. The last three are concerned with human and social systems and are of importance to the arts, humanities, and, in a more specialized way, modern management.

This classification scheme is important in understanding the systems school because it contains the basic theme of the systems approach: all phenomena, whether in the universe at large or in a business organization, are related in some way.

A second contribution of the article is the emphasis it places on *integration*. One of Boulding's major contentions is that specific disciplines are too narrow in their focus, whereas a general approach lacks substantive content:

Somewhere however between the specific that has no meaning and the general that has no content there must be . . . an optimum degree of generality. It is the contention of

---

[3]Kenneth E. Boulding, "General Systems Theory — The Skeleton of Science," *Management Science*, April 1956, pp. 200–202.
[4]*Ibid.*, pp. 197–208.
[5]*Ibid.*, pp. 202–205.

the General Systems Theorists that this optimum degree of generality in theory is not always reached by the particular sciences.[6]

In order to overcome this deficiency, Boulding recommends an integration of knowledge from many fields. "Because, in a sense, each level incorporates all those below it, much valuable information and insights can be obtained by applying low-level systems to high-level subject matter."[7] The thinking of these systems theorists, however, is not confined to such an esoteric area as general systems theory. They have also put forth some concepts that have practical application.

Applied Concepts

When arguing for a systems school, proponents like to point to useful management tools and techniques that apply the systems concept. Some of these ideas, such as operations research, simulation, PERT, and the critical path method, are directly related to *management decision models*.

Another set of tools and techniques can be placed under the heading of the *systems approach*. These are tools that help the manager choose a course of action by analyzing objectives and comparing costs, risks, and payoffs associated with the alternate strategies. By employing a big picture or systems approach, the manager can evaluate the interrelationships of all factors under consideration. One such approach, discussed in Chapter 7, is zero-base budgeting. Others are systems engineering, which will be examined later in this chapter, and adaptive organization structures, which will be discussed in Chapters 16 and 17.

A third set of systems tools and techniques is in the category of *information systems*. These are systems designed to provide managers with data and knowledge useful in carrying out their jobs, such as computers, information theory, and control systems, topics which were discussed in Chapter 10.

These three main types of tools and techniques all provide illustrations of how the systems concept has proved useful to business. They are classified in Figure 15–3.

Integration of knowledge from many fields is encouraged.

Management decision models.

Systems approach.

Information systems.

---

[6]*Ibid.*, pp. 197–198.
[7]*Ibid.*, p. 207.

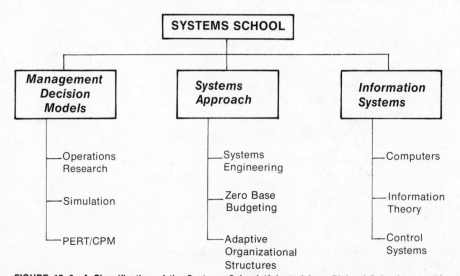

FIGURE 15–3 A Classification of the Systems School (Adapted from Richard Schonberger, "A Taxonomy of Systems Management," *Nebraska Journal of Economics and Business*, Spring, 1973.)

Based on the information so far, it appears that the systems ideas may well be sufficiently different from those of the process, quantitative, and behavioral approaches to justify a fourth school. Critics, however, argue that the systems concept is already being used by the three major schools. For example, many of the ideas in Figure 15–3 have already been examined in the last ten chapters. In addition, process advocates argue that management theory consists of planning, organizing, and controlling processes; each is thus an interrelated subsystem of the overall management system. Behaviorists claim that for years they have been viewing the organization as a group of interrelated formal and informal systems. Quantitative school proponents feel that the systems school is really a part of their own; certainly that was the way it was presented in Chapters 4 and 10. Systems analysts, computer programmers, and so on, were all placed in the quantitative school, and there is a good reason for this. As one researcher has noted:

> Starting in about 1970, the quantitative approach turned away from emphasis on narrow operations research techniques toward a broader perspective of management science. The management science approach incorporates quantitative decision techniques and model building as in the OR approach, but it also incorporates computerized information systems and operations management. This latter emphasis in the quantitative approach marked the return toward a more broadly based management theory.[8]

Is the systems approach, then, sufficiently different to justify a new school or is it really a subsystem of one or more of the current approaches? For the purposes of this text the systems approach will be considered part of the quantitative area.

Yet the systems *concept* itself is too important to be dropped without further elaboration. It contains many useful ideas with which the student of management should be familiar. One of these is that of viewing the organization as an open system.

When the planning process was discussed in Chapter 5, the areas of environmental analysis and forecasting were examined. Likewise, in Chapter 6, when the organizing process was reviewed, common forms of departmentalization were examined. However, when these processes are analyzed from a systems approach, the organization is seen as operating in an *open system*, constantly interacting with its external environment. These open systems are characterized by *flexible equilibrium* as depicted in Figure 15–4. They are continually receiving external inputs, which in turn are being transformed into outputs. Information on the adequacy of the output is fed back into the system for purposes of adjustment and correction. The model can be constructed in this way:

FIGURE 15–4   An open system

One common open system, familiar to all, is the biological system. In the case of fish, for example, the input could be food, which is trans-

---

[8]Fred Luthans, "The Contingency Theory of Management," *Business Horizons*, June 1973, p. 68.

Margin notes

A School or A Subsystem?

Is there a systems school of management?

Systems concept has general value for management.

THE ORGANIZATION AS AN OPEN SYSTEM

Open system constantly interacts with its external environment.

formed into energy and results in a healthy, and perhaps larger fish. If one wishes to go further, changes could be made in the environment. For example, add warm water to the tank and see how the fish adapt to the new surroundings. In both cases, external inputs are introduced into the process and transformed into some kind of outputs.

The same process applies to a business organization. For example, there are a host of economic resources that serve as inputs such as men, money, machines, material, and information, In systems theory thinking, these can be combined in some fashion (organization process) for the purpose of attaining certain output, as seen in Figure 15–5:

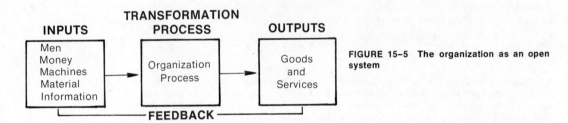

FIGURE 15–5 The organization as an open system

This basic model can be made more sophisticated by breaking down the organizational process into some preliminary design such as marketing, production, and finance departments, as in Figure 15–6. In this illustration, the relationships between each of the departments and (a) the external environment, (b) the other two departments, and (c) the organization at large become clearer.

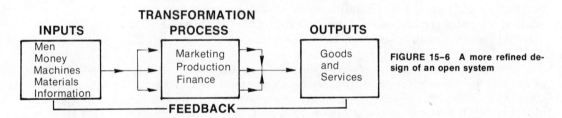

FIGURE 15–6 A more refined design of an open system

Adaptive and Maintenance Mechanisms

Two other important systems concepts useful in analyzing open systems are adaptive and maintenance structures. In an open system, the organization must be able to adapt. At the same time, however, it must maintain a relative state of balance. There are thus two mechanisms in operation. The first, *adaptivity*, encourages response to the external and internal environments. The second, *maintenance*, attempts to stop the system from changing so rapidly that it is thrown out of balance. These two forces may sometimes be in conflict, but both are vital to an organization's survival.

Adaptive forces lead to change.

Adaptive forces lead to change and keep the organization viable. On the other hand, they can create tension and stress. For example, consider the case of a business firm that wishes to hire a junior accountant. The company needs the person to help handle the increase in accounts that has occurred over the last year. It turns out, however, that the starting salary for such an individual is higher than that of some lower-level managers who have been with the firm for three years. The company must hire the accountant if it is to keep up, but to do so may create anxiety among some of the established personnel. Although this may be a natural reaction, it illustrates the problems associated with adapting to environmental conditions.

Maintenance forces are conservative influences that work to prevent disequilibrium. The problem is that they may stunt an organization's growth by encouraging timidity when boldness is needed. In addition, excessive attention to maintenance factors can result in a breakdown of the open system. In Figure 15–6 this could begin to happen if the firm decided not to hire the new accountant. By choosing to maintain present conditions, the company is failing to adapt to its external environment. If it continues to ignore developments in the external arena by concentrating all of its attention on maintaining intracompany equilibrium, the firm will become a closed system. When this occurs, the business faces the danger of entropy.

Maintenance forces are conservative influences.

Entropy and Contrived Adaptivity

One of the characteristics of a closed system is entropy. This is a term that originated in thermodynamics and applies to all physical systems. It refers to the tendency of a closed system to move toward a chaotic, random, or inert state. Webster defines *entropy* as "the ultimate state reached in the degradation of the matter and energy of the universe."[9] All closed physical systems are subject to this force of entropy. Over a period of time the force increases and, ultimately, the system stops. Since it is a closed network with no external inputs, there is really no hope for survival. Eventually, entropy will take its toll.

Closed systems are characterized by entropy.

In open biological and social systems, however, entropy can be arrested and may even be transformed into negative entropy. This is brought about through external inputs. Biological systems, at least in the short-run, provide a good illustration. Drawing upon the resources in their surroundings, organisms are able to survive for a period of time. For most humans, food, clothing, and shelter are the basic resources. As one ages, increased attention is given to medicine. Eventually, however, death occurs, for even biological systems are subject to deterioration.

Social systems, however, are another matter; they are not mechanical or biological, they are *contrived*. Human beings establish them for a particular purpose and although the individuals may die, others can take their place and keep the system alive. As Katz and Kahn note:

Social systems are contrived.

> Social structures are essentially contrived systems. People invent the complex/pattern of behavior that we call social structure, and people create social structure by enacting those patterns of behavior. Many properties of social systems derive from these essential facts. As human inventions, social systems are imperfect. They can come apart at the seams overnight, but they can also outlast by centuries the biological organisms that originally created them. The cement which holds them together is essentially psychological rather than biological. Social systems are anchored in the attitudes, perceptions, beliefs, motivations, habits, and expectations of human beings.[10]

In order for the social system to continue, however, there must be the proper balance between maintenance and adaptive forces. *Mainten-*

[9]*Webster's Third New International Dictionary*, volume 1 (Chicago: Encyclopedia Britannica, Inc., 1966), p. 759.
[10]Daniel Katz and Robert L. Kahn, *The Social Psychology of Organizations.* 2nd edition (New York: John Wiley & Sons, Inc., 1978), p. 37.

ance forces are motivated toward maintaining stability and predictability within the organization. They work to preserve a state of equilibrium. These forces, for example, encourage the organization to make no appreciable shifts in the current pattern of activities. If the company wants to sell more goods and services, it should work toward getting the current customers to buy more. In short, maintenance forces urge the organization to maintain the status quo. On the other hand are *adaptive forces,* which are pushing the organization to respond to external environmental factors such as changes in the market place. Rather than trying to sell more goods and services to the same customers, these forces encourage an expansion of market activities by offering new products and services in new market niches. Adaptive forces encourage the organization to generate appropriate responses to external conditions.[11]

These systems concepts of flexible equilibrium, adaptive mechanisms, maintenance mechanisms, entropy, and contrived adaptivity are all useful in understanding the truly dynamic nature of the modern organization. It is important to realize, however, that an effective organization can also employ these concepts in maintaining a viable, adaptive, on-going organization system.

TOTALLY ADAPTIVE ORGANIZATION SYSTEMS

Adaptive organizations can survive indefinitely.

The organization is a man-made system, capable of indefinite survival if the proper balance between maintenance and adaptive forces can be attained. Figure 15–7 provides an illustration of a totally adaptive business organization system. The figure shows how marketing and production activities can be carried on in the attainment of organizational goals. The finance department and the rest of the enterprise are represented in the boxes entitled "Current State of the Organization," indicating that the decisions made by both marketing and production are going to depend on conditions in the remainder of the organization. There is also a control process built into the model which, in turn, will lead to a redesign of the marketing and/or production systems should disequilibrium manifest itself. The model adapts itself to changing conditions by continuously contrasting internal and external environmental conditions and the effect of both on the goals being pursued.

Total systems design has great promise.

The concept of total systems design is not, of course, restricted to business organizations. It can be applied to such diverse activities as police work and city planning as long as the *total* system is examined. Any attempt to deal with the organization on a micro-level can have disastrous effects because all input factors are not being considered. For example, in police work the objective is to prevent crime. One of the best ways to do this is to concentrate resources on high-crime areas and thereby discourage potential criminals as well as apprehend those who have committed crimes. This can be done by feeding information about people and living conditions in the city into a computer which, in turn, can then analyze the data and provide relevant information to the police regarding how to organize their forces.

The state of California has already used this basic approach in identifying trouble spots within the city of Los Angeles. Employing a team of mathematicians, economists, physicists, political scientists, and sociologists as "idea men," a mathematical model of the city was constructed. Then, after simulating the environment of the metropolis, the computer was called upon to analyze the results. The findings showed that the area of the city most likely to evidence trouble was Watts. Un-

[11]*Ibid.,* Chapter 4.

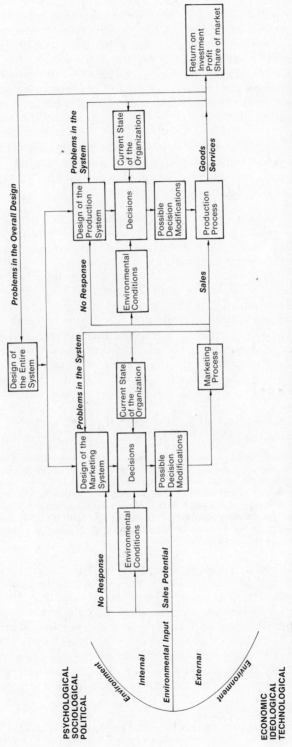

FIGURE 15–7   A Totally Adaptive Organization System (Adapted from Stanley D. Young, "Organization Total System," *Proceedings of the 4th Annual Midwest Management Conference,* Carbondale, Illinois, 1966.)

employment was high and living conditions were very poor in this sector. The analysis proved correct when shortly thereafter the tragic Watts riots occurred.

Another example of the total systems approach to organizing resources has been seen in the construction of new cities such as Columbia, Maryland, located midway between Washington D.C. and Baltimore. It is estimated that by the early 1980's, the 14,000-acre city will have a population in excess of 100,000. In constructing the site, an *ad hoc* systems task force consisting of psychologists, sociologists, religious leaders, and medical personnel worked with architects and planners to determine all the social and institutional needs that would have to be met.

It should now be apparent that systems concepts are very useful in both understanding and relating an organization to its environment. However, the general concept can also be applied within the firm in the examination of managerial systems.

MANAGERI-AL SYS-TEMS

Having viewed the organization as an open, adaptive system, attention will now be focused on *managerial systems*. Parsons has suggested three managerial levels in the hierarchy of complex organizations: technical, organizational,[12] and institutional.

The *technical* level is concerned with the actual production and distribution of products and services. This not only entails turning out physical output but also includes the areas that support this activity, i.e., research and development, operations research, and accounting.

The *organizational* level coordinates and integrates work performance at the technical level. It is concerned with obtaining the continued flow of inputs into the system; maintaining the necessary markets for the outputs from the system; determining the nature of technical tasks; ascertaining the scale of operations; and establishing operating policies.

The *institutional* level is concerned with relating the activities of the organization to the environmental system. As Parson notes:

> . . . not only does . . . an organization . . . have to operate in a social environment which imposes the conditions governing the processes of disposal and procurement, it is also part of a wider social system which is the source of the "meaning," legitimation, or higher level support which makes the implementation of the organization's goals possible. Essentially, this means that just as a technical organization (at a sufficiently high level of the division of labor) is controlled and "serviced" by a managerial organization, so, in turn, is the managerial organization controlled by the "institutional" structure and agencies of the community.[13]

The managerial system spans all three levels by organizing the people, directing the technical work, and relating the organization to its environment. However, before examining the role of the manager in this overall system, a closer view of these three levels is in order. First, it is possible to illustrate them as a composite system, as in Figure 15–8:

Technical level is highly closed system-oriented.

The technical level or core is concerned with turning out a product or service at a profit. In order to do this, it often attempts to set up a boundary between itself and the external environment, thereby forming a closed system. The reasoning is that if the environment is too dynam-

---

[12]Parsons called the second level "the management level," but since there are managers at all three levels, the middle one will be referred to here as the "organizational level."

[13]Talcott Parsons, *Structure and Process in Modern Societies* (New York: The Free Press, 1960), pp. 63–64.

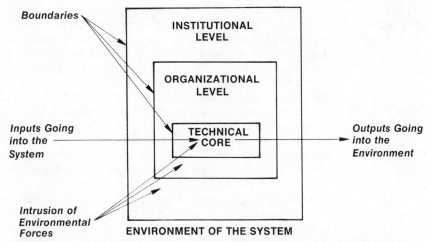

FIGURE 15–8 The Organization as a Composite System (Adapted from Thomas A. Petit, "A Behavioral Theory of Management," *Academy of Management Journal*, December 1967, p. 346.)

ic, people will never get anything done; they will be continually responding to external influences. Modern technology provides an illustration of the intruding environmental force and its effect at this level. For example, many times a company will find that the product it is manufacturing is obsolete even before it leaves the assembly line. However, at some point the design must be frozen and production begun. The technical core is subject to external influences, but it does attempt to minimize them.

Conversely, at the institutional level there is a great degree of uncertainty over environmental conditions, and the organization is unable to set up major boundaries. As a result, management at this level is by nature a very open system, and primary attention is devoted to innovation or adaptation.

Institutional level is very open system-oriented.

The organizational level operates between these two extremes. It coordinates the technical and institutional levels; tries to straighten out irregularities and disturbances occurring in both; and serves as an all-around mediator. In a manner of speaking, it is a buffer between the maintenance forces (technical level) and the adaptive forces (institutional level). Petit has described the three levels in this way:

Organizational level coordinates other two levels.

> The technical level has a boundary that does not seal it off entirely from the firm's environment but does have a high degree of closure. The organizational level has less closure and consequently is more susceptible to the intrusion of external elements. The institutional level has a highly permeable boundary and therefore is strongly affected by uncontrollable and unpredictable elements in the environment.[14]

The three levels are interrelated, constituting subsystems in this overall organizational structure. Each level has individual characteristics, but for effective performance there must be coordination among them. At the same time, however, it is possible to examine the specific requirements of each organizational level in order to classify the managers who work there.

---

[14]Thomas A. Petit, "A Behavioral Theory of Management," *Academy of Management Journal*, December 1967, p. 346.

Types of Managers   In the past, most managers were classified by organizational level (executive, middle manager, first line supervisor) or function (sales manager, production manager, financial manager). Today, however, managers are being classified according to many criteria, including the work itself, time horizon, and decision-making strategy.

Technical managers have engineering viewpoints.   TECHNICAL MANAGERS.   Because technical managers are concerned with producing goods and services as economically as possible, they tend to have an engineering point of view. They are also pragmatic, quick to adopt what will work for them and discard what will not. They like problems with concrete solutions such as what criteria to employ when investing in fixed equipment or the optimal relation that should exist between production and inventory levels. They work best when confronted with quantitative (as opposed to qualitative) issues. They also tend to have a very short-run time horizon, being most interested in the operational aspects of the job.

Institutional managers have philosophical viewpoints.   INSTITUTIONAL MANAGERS.   Institutional managers face the challenge of coping with uncertainty brought on by uncontrollable and unpredictable environmental elements. For them, major concern rests with ensuring the organization's survival. This is done in two ways. First, institutional managers are continually surveying the environment, noting both opportunities and threats. Second, based on the findings, they develop cooperative and competitive strategies for dealing with these elements, thereby reducing uncertainty. In order to conduct this surveillance and construct a viable strategy, they need to have a long-run time perspective. They tend to be philosophical in viewpoint, capable of translating qualitative environmental changes into quantitative estimates of their impact on the organization. This requires wisdom, experience, and good judgment in the formulation of strategy.

Organizational managers are mediators.   ORGANIZATIONAL MANAGERS.   As already noted, the organizational managers coordinate the efforts of the technical and institutional levels. In order to do this, the organizational manager needs to be something

TYPE OF MAN- AGER	TASK	POINT OF VIEW	TECH- NIQUE	TIME PER- SPEC- TIVE	DECISION- MAKING STRAT- EGY
Technical	Technical Rationality	Engineering	Quantitative	Short-run	Computa- tional
Organiza- tional	Coordination	Political	Mediation	Both Short- and Long- run	Comprom- ise
Institu- tional	Deal with Uncertainty and Relate the Organiza- tion to its Environment	Philosophi- cal and Conceptual	Environmental Survey; Strategy Formulation	Long-run	Subjective and Judgmental

FIGURE 15–9   Characteristics of Managers in the Managerial System (Adapted from Thomas A. Petit, "A Behavioral Theory of Management," *Academy of Management Journal*, December 1967, p. 349.)

of a politician, capable of adopting a short- or long-run perspective, depending on the situation, and able to achieve a compromise between the technical and institutional managers:

> Organizational managers use the decision-making strategy of compromise. The best interests of the firm are not served by following either the computational [technical manager] or judgmental [institutional manager] strategies exclusively. The organizational managers attempt to influence the balance between the two according to the nature of the problems facing the firm. Since these problems may be either immediate or in the future, organizational managers have both a short-run and a long-run time horizon.
>
> The viewpoint of the organizational manager is basically political. He must always be concerned with what is possible rather than ideal in mediating between technical and institutional managers.[15]

Figure 15–9 shows the differences among these three types of managers.

The systems point of view suggests that management is continually facing a dynamic environment consisting of forces that are not within its total control. Of course, some organizations have attempted to overcome this problem. The giant trusts of the early 1900's and the major conglomerates of the current day both represent attempts by powerful organizations to obtain major control over their environment. For the most part, however, the organization and the environment still constitute *interacting* forces.

THE SYS-TEMS POINT OF VIEW

The same pattern exists within the organization itself. Managers in all departments and at all levels are *interdependent.* Job descriptions and work assignments, for example, represent only general guidelines regarding what the managers are supposed to be doing. In actuality, as Sayles notes, the:

> . . . systems concept emphasizes that managerial assignments do not have these neat, clearly defined boundaries; rather, the modern manager is placed in a network of mutually dependent relationships. . . . The one enduring objective is the effort to build and maintain a predictable, reciprocating system of relationships, the behavioral patterns of which stay within reasonable physical limits. But this is seeking a moving equilibrium, since the parameters of the system (the division of labor and the controls) are evolving and changing. Thus the manager endeavors to introduce regularity in a world that will never allow him to achieve the ideal. . . . Only managers who can deal with uncertainty, with ambiguity, and with battles that are never won but only fought well can hope to succeed.[16]

This appears to be a very radical change from the organizing process that was discussed in Chapter 6 in very clear, rigid, and easy-to-grasp terms. Now it seems that the process is becoming topsy-turvy. It must be remembered, however, that with this modern-systems view the element of dynamism takes on new dimensions and the heretofore simple concepts of planning, organizing, and controlling are viewed from a much more realistic perspective.

Organizing is a dynamic process.

Having covered the important aspects of systems theory and their relevance for understanding modern management, it is now time to return to the initial question posed at the beginning of the chapter: what will be the future development of management theory?

---

[15]*Ibid.*, p. 348.
[16]Leonard Sayles, *Managerial Behavior* (New York: McGraw-Hill Book Company, 1964), pp. 258–259.

**MANAGE-
MENT THE-
ORY IN
THE FU-
TURE**

At this point, no author can definitively state what will happen in the development of management theory by 1990. However, it appears likely that the three major schools of thought will see attempts to synthesize many of these ideas via a contingency theory of management. This theory contends that there is no approach appropriate to *all* situations. Key variables such as effective organization structure, motivation process, and leadership style are all determined by the situation. One of the leading proponents of this belief writes:

Systems and
contingency
schools are
emerging.

> The beginning of a path called contingency or sometimes situational is just starting to emerge . . . this path may be the one that leads management out of the existing jungle of theories. The pressure leading to a contingency theory has largely come from people who are actually practicing management.[17]

Such thinking has led to the recent formulation of a general contingency theory of management by Fred Luthans and Todd Stewart.

**A General
Contingency
Theory of
Management**

Luthans and Stewart have proposed a *general contingency theory of management,* which could be very useful in integrating process, quantitative, behavioral, and systems schools of thought:

> The systems approach will undoubtedly continue to have a significant integrating effect, but it is not pragmatic enough to serve as a theoretical framework for the understanding, research and practice of management. At the same time there is a growing awareness that the process, quantitative and behavioral advocates have been unable to substantiate their respective claims for universality. Although each construct from the various approaches to management has been effective in particular situations, quantitative advocates have had considerable difficulty accommodating behavioral factors, and behavioral theorists have been only marginally successful in solving management problems more adaptable to quantitative approaches.[18]

A general contingency theory could surmount these problems by providing a theoretical framework for (a) integrating and synthesizing the diverse concepts proposed by the process, quantitative, and behavioral schools into an interrelated theoretical system; (b) incorporating the system's perspective of organization and management; (c) providing a pragmatic basis for analyzing and interpreting current management knowledge; (d) providing a framework for the systematic and coordinated direction of new research in the field; and (e) establishing a mechanism for effectively translating theoretical ideas and empirical research into useful techniques that are relevant to the modern practitioner.[19]

The Luthans–Stewart model, presented in Figure 15–10, contains three dimensions. The *management variables* in the figure include management concepts and application techniques from the process, quantitative, and behavioral schools. The *situational variables* include those that occur when the environment interacts with the organization's resources (people and other physical assets). The *performance criteria variables* are determined by the interaction of the situational and management variables.

The most important contribution of the Luthans-Stewart model is

---

[17]Luthans, *op. cit.,* pp. 69–70.
[18]Fred Luthans and Todd I. Stewart, "A General Contingency Theory of Management," *Academy of Management Review,* April 1977, p. 182.
[19]*Ibid.*

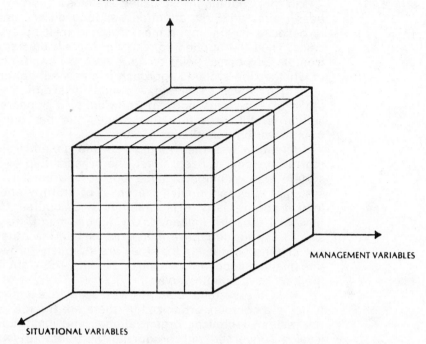

PERFORMANCE CRITERIA VARIABLES

MANAGEMENT VARIABLES

SITUATIONAL VARIABLES

FIGURE 15–10   A General Contingency Matrix for Management (From Fred Luthans and Todd I. Stewart, "A General Contingency Theory of Management," *Academy of Management Review***, April 1977, p. 189. Reprinted with permission.)**

that it provides a *framework* for developing a general contingency theory of management. Having set forth the model, the next step is to test it in various situations to determine whether operational guidelines can be developed.

The empty cells of the matrix indicate specific combinations of situational, management and performance criteria variables for which a functional relationship to system performance has yet to be defined. The framework can also be used to identify contingency functions that require validation by rigorous, empirically based research methodologies. For example, functions that have been derived deductively from case studies are candidates for validation through replication in controlled laboratory or field experiments.[20]

It is still too early to determine the full value of such a general contingency theory of management. However, it is offered as a conceptually pragmatic, research-based framework with considerable potential to alter the future course of management. The framework certainly represents the latest attempt to integrate what is known about management into a composite system. If successful, the design could play a major role in synthesizing the three schools of management thought we have studied in this text.

---

[20]*Ibid.*, p. 190.

SUMMARY

In this chapter the so-called systems school of management has been examined. First, attention was focused on general systems theory because of the importance assigned to it by system school advocates. Then the applied concepts of the systems approach, presented from its advocates' point of view, were reviewed. Finally, the question of whether the systems approach is a new school or a subsystem of a current one was examined. Although it is difficult to deny the existence of a systems body of knowledge, it appears that the systems school is still in its formative stages and has not yet completed its break with the quantitative school.

Attention was then focused on the general value of understanding the systems concept. First, the organization as an open, adaptive system was examined. Since business organizations are contrived systems, they can survive the onset of entropy and, unlike their biological counterparts, exist indefinitely. Of course, this will depend on how well they are managed. On the one hand, they must be responsive to change (adaptive mechanisms); on the other hand, they must not change so quickly that they are seriously thrown out of equilibrium (maintenance mechanisms). Finding the right balance is one of the keys to indefinite survival.

Next the systems concept was used to examine managerial systems. In a complex organization, there are three levels in the managerial system: technical, organizational, and institutional. The technical level is concerned with producing the goods or services. The organizational level coordinates and integrates the technical and institutional level. The institutional level relates the activities of the organization to the environmental system. Within this system there are three types of managers, one for each of the levels. The technical manager is a "nuts and bolts" individual; the organization manager is a political-mediator person; and the institutional manager is a conceptual-philosophical decision maker. Yet, although there are different levels and interests within the structure, all three must combine their talents and energies in the attainment of overall organizational objectives.

In order to do this, managers must plan, organize, and control. They must also make decisions and employ the latest quantitative methods where applicable; and they must understand and utilize the abilities of their subordinates through effective communication, motivation, and leadership. In short, the management process, quantitative, and behavioral schools are all important to modern managers, and today managers are drawing upon the concepts of all three in carrying out their duties. The systems approach encourages this.

The last section of the chapter examined management theory in the future. Whether or not the systems approach is worthy of being considered a school of management thought, a contingency theory of management seems to be emerging which encourages managers to use the concepts of whatever school is necessary in attaining their desired goals. As might be expected, some of the biggest supporters of the contingency approach are practicing managers.

REVIEW
AND STUDY
QUESTIONS

1. Of what value is general systems theory to the systems school of management? Explain.

2. What is meant by an open system?

3. What impact does entropy have on a system?

4. In what way is a business organization a contrived system?

5. What are maintenance mechanisms? What are adaptive mechanisms? How do they affect the organization structure?

6. What is meant by a totally adaptive organization?

7. What are the three managerial levels in the hierarchy of complex organizations? Describe each.

8. How do the tasks and viewpoints of the managers of these three hierarchical levels differ? Explain.

9. Of what value is the systems approach to the practicing manager?

10. Will there ever be a systems school of management? Explain.

11. What is meant by the situational or contingency theory of management? How useful is it to the practicing manager? Explain.

SELECTED REFERENCES

Boulding, K. "General Systems Theory — The Skeleton of Science." *Management Science,* April 1956, pp. 197–208.

Cleland, D. I., and W. R. King. *Management: A Systems Approach,* 2nd edition. New York: McGraw-Hill Book Company, 1975.

Duncan, W. J. "Transferring Management Theory to Practice." *Academy of Management Journal,* December 1974, pp. 724–738.

Greenwood, W. T. "Future Management Theory: A 'Comparative' Evolution to a General Theory." *Academy of Management Journal,* September 1974, pp. 503–513.

Kast, F. E., and J. E. Rosenzweig. *Organization and Management,* 2nd edition. New York: McGraw-Hill Book Company, 1974.

Kast, F. E., and J. E. Rosenzweig. "General Systems Theory: Applications for Organization and Management." *Academy of Management Journal,* December 1972, pp. 447–465.

Luthans, F. "The Contingency Theory of Management." *Business Horizons,* June 1973, pp. 67–72.

Luthans, F., and T. Stewart, "A General Contingency Theory of Management." *Academy of Management Review,* April 1977, pp. 181–195.

Petit, T. A. "A Behavioral Theory of Management." *Academy of Management Journal,* December 1967, pp. 341–350.

Robbins, S. P. "Reconciling Management Theory with Management Practice." *Business Horizons,* February 1977, pp. 38–47.

Von Bertalanffy, L. "The History and Status of General Systems Theory." *Academy of Management Journal,* December 1972, pp. 407–426.

Wooton, L. M. "The Mixed Blessings of Contingency Management." *Academy of Management Review,* July 1977, pp. 431–441.

Wortman, M. S., Jr., and F. Luthans, eds. *Emerging Concepts in Management,* 2nd edition. New York: The Macmillan Company, 1975.

CASE: A GREAT BIG SECRET

Jackson & Jackson, a large west coast manufacturer, instituted an in-house supervisory training program under its new president, William Hopkinson. During the initial phase, 10 per cent of the managers received training related to both the technical and human relations sides of their jobs. Some critics of the program suggested that the training be suspended at this point since it was really of little value to the supervisors. An analysis of the results, however, showed that every manager participating in this initial training phase had been able to attain an increase in his unit's output. The training therefore continued.

Over the next 12 months all the remaining supervisors were put through the program. During this period productivity increased 27 per cent over the previous year. In commenting on the value of the program, the vice president of manufacturing said that he had noticed a number of the supervisors entering the plant earlier than usual in the morning and some staying past the closing whistle.

The results led proponents of the program to call it an unqualified success, but its opponents disagreed. Their arguments took two lines of attack. First, they pointed out that not all supervisors had been able to attain productivity increases. If the training was beneficial, this should have occurred. Second, they argued that the surge in output would be short-lived. One of them put it this way:

What we have here is the old "Hawthorne effect." The supervisors are all excited about being part of this new program, but it won't last long. The training is now complete and the novelty is already beginning to wear thin. Everyone will soon be returning to their old way of doing things. That's the problem with training programs. The initial results are fantastic, but they soon drop off.

Furthermore, there's the old cause-effect identification problem. Look at it this way. We have a new input—the training program. We have a new output—27 per cent increase in productivity. However, what *causes* this increase? Is it really the training program or is it something else? What takes place in the transformation process or the black box? Quite frankly, no one knows, so why attribute it to the training program? Maybe these productivity increases would have occurred in any event. Who knows? It's really all a great big secret.

Questions

1. What is taking place in the transformation process that is causing the 27 per cent productivity increase? Explain, employing the systems concept in your answer.

2. Why does the individual in this case refer to the productivity increase as a "great big secret"?

CASE: INPUT-OUTPUT

The union at MacKelvey Incorporated had been negotiating a new contract with management for over three months, and with only 30 days left, there was still no agreement. The management was willing to give a 3.4 per cent increase in salary and a 3 per cent increase in fringe benefits; the union was asking for 5.2 and 3.9 per cent respectively. However, Mr. Paul Aherne, vice president of industrial relations who had been heading the negotiations all along, reported to the president, George Neffen, that he felt an agreement might be near:

Mr. Neffen, I think the union would settle for a 4.1 per cent salary raise and a 3.3 per cent increase in fringe benefits. We've done quite a bit of negotiating over the past 10 weeks and I'm sure I understand them.

Actually, Paul, the board of directors had hoped that the 3.4 and 3 per cent proposals would lead to a contract.

I see little chance of that, Mr. Neffen. If we maintain our present position we'll either have to hope that the union is willing to work without a contract or face the very real possibility of a strike.

Actually, neither of those alternatives is going to be viewed very favorably by the board, Paul. On the other hand, we certainly don't want to negotiate a contract any higher than we have to.

Mr. Neffen, let me be frank. I think we're almost there now. However, if we force the union to work without a contract or, heaven forbid, strike, we're going to damage one of our most important assets — union-management harmony. We have to think of the men as inputs in the process of management. If we do something to that input we stand the chance of seriously endangering the output, namely, our products and services. I think we should promote the current good will that exists between us.

Questions

1. If you regard the men as an input and the goods and services as an output, how would you describe the transformation process in this case?

2. How does this union contract negotiation fit into a discussion of the systems approach to management?

3. Do you think the company would be wise to follow the advice from the vice president of industrial relations? Explain.

CASE: MODIFICATIONS, MODIFICATIONS

George Chilvers was angry. For the past 12 months he had been in charge of designing a new jet fighter for the United States Navy. After countless days of revising the initial design and incorporating extensive changes, his group was prepared to submit its design for approval. However, just as they were about to do this, George received a call from his boss asking him to come up to the office immediately. The gist of their conversation was as follows:

George, I've called you in because before you submit your plan I want you to know that there's a lot of pressure on us to present the most sophisticated design possible. In addition, if there are any major flaws that result in eventual cost overruns, we're really going to be in trouble. Congress is fed up with paying for contractor mistakes.

Mr. Adkinson, we've designed this craft five times now — I don't think there's a thing we haven't changed for the better at one time or another. I think it will be the finest plane the Navy has ever had.

I'm glad to hear that, George, because the president has really sold the big brass on this one.

Well, believe me, when we submit our design later in the week they'll be impressed.

Actually, George, we want you to wait a month before doing that. We still have a little time before the drawings are due and the president has asked me to have you go over the material once more.

What for?

To see if you can't improve it a little bit. Surely there's something new you can add here and there.

Mr. Adkinson, if you gave me a year I could design an aircraft that's twice as good as this one, but I think there's a point beyond which it's not practical to go. We have a contract and a design that more than fulfills those requirements. At some point you have to quit making changes, freeze the plan, and get on with the production. If we keep delaying, we'll never get to the manufacturing stage.

I understand that, George, but the president wants to be sure that the design is as good as possible. So for the next month I want you and your team to review and make any minor modifications on the material which will improve the overall design.

Questions

1. How would you classify George? Is he a technical, organizational, or institutional manager? Explain.

2. Is Mr. Adkinson a technical, organizational, or institutional manager? Explain. How about the president? Explain.

3. How does George's viewpoint as a manager differ from his superior's? Be specific.

CASE: A SYSTEMS VIEW

Alan Bashion, general manager of a major food chain, met with his people once a month. He liked to regard these meetings as a chance to communicate new ideas and exchange information on any problems that had arisen in the recent month. During one of these meetings he brought up the topic of a systems approach to management. He had recently done some reading on the subject and felt it could be applied to the management of his own stores:

You know, another thing I want all of you to start doing is to think of your department as a system. This is a new idea in management but it's a real good one.

One of the managers asked Mr. Bashion what he meant by a "system."

A system is a host of interrelated items. Each has an effect on and can be influenced by the others. It's like the human body. An attack on any one part can influence the other parts because the body is a system. An organization is the same. If any one part of it has trouble, this can affect the other parts. You people will have to do some reading on this topic. I'll have the secretary send all of you some references on the subject.

With this the meeting broke up and the managers began filing out. Some of them went across the street for lunch. During the meal the following conversation took place:

You know, I'd still like to know how the organization is like a system. That part evaded me completely.

Don't feel bad, I doubt whether anyone understood what he was talking about.

I wonder if he knew.

Well, in any event, if he sends us that material we can read it and find out what it is all about. Sometimes I think Mr. Bashion throws out new ideas before he really understands them himself.

Questions

1. What is meant by the systems approach to management?

2. Does Mr. Bashion really understand the systems concept? Explain.

3. What should a person know if he is truly to understand the systems approach?

PART III
RECENT DEVELOPMENTS IN MANAGEMENT

The goal of Part III is to examine recent developments that are taking place in the field of management. Some of these are direct extensions of work done by quantitative or behavioral people, but primarily they are integrative in nature, and *not* confined to any one of the schools exclusively. In addition, some of the areas, such as social responsibility and international management, do not fit into any particular framework and thus are best discussed in this part of the book.

One of the most significant and enduring developments in the last twenty years has been modern technology, which affects both organization structure and company personnel. The opportunities and challenges presented by technology will be examined in Chapter 16, along with some of the ways organizations attempt to cope with this external force.

In Chapter 17, modern organization structures will be studied. Because of increasing technology and change, business is finding that the old line-staff organizations are no longer sufficient; they are too rigid and inflexible. For this reason, many companies are turning to project, matrix, and free-form organization designs to help them meet the challenge and threat of change.

Next, in Chapter 18, the focus will be shifted from the internal to the external arena with social responsibility as the subject of attention. The modern business firm realizes that it must be responsive to the needs of not only its customers and workers but also the public at large. In this chapter the areas of equal opportunity, ecology, and consumerism will be discussed, with major consideration given to the challenges they present to business.

Continuing this external focus, Chapter 19 will examine the challenges and opportunities facing those firms that decide to expand their operations into the international arena. In particular, attention will be devoted to evaluating the possible advantages and disadvantages associated with going overseas, the various issues in organizing, staffing, and controlling such an undertaking, and the role of the multinational American corporation in the international economic arena.

Finally, in Chapter 20, management in the future will be examined. First, a concise review of past events will be undertaken. Then developments on the horizon, heretofore undiscussed, will be examined, including the trend toward corporate democracy, the challenge of managing executive talent, and the continual trend toward professionalism.

CHAPTER SIXTEEN
TECHNOLOGY, MANAGEMENT, AND THE ORGANIZATION

GOALS OF THE CHAPTER

Much of mankind's progress can be accounted for by technological advances. Such progress in agriculture, transportation, and communication, for example, has allowed us to live more leisurely lives, while breakthroughs in the medical arena are providing us with a greater amount of time in which to enjoy these new things. Technology is also having its impact on business.

The first goal of this chapter is to examine some modern technological advances, such as communication technology and power production, that are providing both opportunities and challenges to modern business. The second objective is to explore the area of technological forecasting with particular attention devoted to nontechnical factors and their role in such a forecast. The final goal is to examine the impact of technology on both the organization's personnel and its structure.

When you have finished reading this chapter you should be able to:

1. Describe the various stages of technological growth from prior to the Industrial Revolution to the modern day.
2. Explain some of the modern technological advances that can be expected in the next three decades in the areas of communication technology and power production.
3. Differentiate between an exploratory and a normative forecast.
4. Discuss how a Delphi forecast is conducted.
5. Relate the problems involved in evaluating the impact of technical and nontechnical factors on a Delphi forecast.
6. Examine the effect of technology on organizational personnel.
7. Describe the impact of technology on the organizational structure.

TECHNOLOGY: AN HISTORICAL PERSPECTIVE

Technology has two basic components: *knowledge and technique*. Mankind's ability to apply an idea (knowledge) in a particular way (technique) has been the basis for much of its progress. A cursory review of the stages of technology from the time just prior to the Industrial Revolution to the current day will make this clear.

Technology consists of knowledge and technique.

First there was the era of *handicraft technology*, typified by craftsmen who made things with their hands. Cobblering, tailoring, and carpentering are all examples. The domestic and putting-out systems were also part of this stage. The eighteenth century, however, saw an end to most of this handicraft technology.

Stages of Technology.

In its place came *mechanized technology*, characterized by power-driven machinery. This was the beginning of the factory system, and for the next two hundred years mankind remained in this era, prospering from a host of inventions from the flying shuttle to the steam engine to the cotton gin.

The next stage was that of *mechanistic technology*, which began around the turn of this century. This stage was characterized by the assembly line, such as that used by Ford to build his Model T, and standardized, interchangeable parts, such as those employed by Whitney a full century earlier in the production of muskets and clocks.[1]

Since then, the assembly line has been developed to the stage where machines are now linked together and integrated in such a fashion that they are performing many functions automatically. These developments represent *automated technology* or, as some people have contended, the second industrial revolution.

Currently, a fifth stage, *cybernated technology*, is beginning. Cybernetics refers to automatic control, and with today's cybernated technology, machines are running and controlling other machines, thereby freeing people for other tasks.

Naturally, it is impossible to say where one stage of technology ended and another began because the time periods have actually overlapped. Now, for example, some business firms are in the automated technology stage whereas others are in the cybernated technology stage. Nevertheless, the entire area presents tremendous opportunities and challenges to management. A closer look at modern technological advances will highlight this.

---

[1]Alex Groner et al., *American Business and Industry* (New York: American Heritage Publishing Co., Inc., 1972), pp. 63–64.

Larry Barton—The (Toledo) Blade

'*But we don't know enough about it. Does it have side effects? Is it physically or psychologically addictive? Can it cause mutant genes?...*' (Reprinted from the (Toledo) Blade with permission.)

Ninety per cent of all the scientists who ever lived are still alive today, and half of all the knowledge acquired by mankind has been accumulated within the last decade. Much of this knowledge has been gained through the large amounts of research and development (R&D) conducted by industry and government. For example, in 1976 alone the top 10 corporate R&D spenders (including General Motors, IBM, Ford Motor, AT&T, and General Electric) invested over $4 billion in R&D, and the entire business community spent more than $16 billion on R&D. Most of these funds went toward product development, resulting in many practical innovations. In addition, not only is the number of these inventions and techniques increasing, but the amount of time between their discovery and their application is decreasing, as illustrated in Table 16–1.

Wolfbein reports that some of the more important areas in which technological advances are having the greatest impact include agriculture, improved machinery and materials handling, advances in transportation, communication technology, and power production. Space prohibits a discussion of all of these, but attention will be focused on the last two by highlighting the opportunities and challenges that technology holds in store for business.

MODERN TECHNOLOGICAL ADVANCES: OPPORTUNITIES AND CHALLENGES

What does the future hold for business in regard to communication technology? Some of the things people have been promised include the ability to:

1. Talk face-to-face with associates regardless of distance.
2. Participate in nationwide (and worldwide) meetings without leaving their office buildings.
3. Perform a large amount of executive functions from their homes.
4. Have access to unlimited computer resources.
5. Own and operate private telecommunications facilities.[2]

Communication Technology: An Opportunity

The future promises great progress in communication technology.

[2]E. Bryan Carne, "Telecommunications: Its Impact on Business," *Harvard Business Review*, July–August 1972, p. 125.

TABLE 16–1   From Discovery to Application

Innovation	Year of Discovery	Year of Application
Electric motor	1821	1886
Vacuum tube	1882	1915
Radio broadcasting	1887	1922
X-ray tubes	1895	1913
Nuclear reactor	1932	1942
Radar	1935	1940
Atomic bomb	1938	1945
Transistor	1948	1951
Solar battery	1953	1955
Stereospecific rubbers and plastics	1955	1958

Source: Seymour Wolfbein, "The Pace of Technological Change and the Factors Affecting It," *Manpower Implications of Automation*, Papers presented by U.S. Department of Labor at the O.E.C.D. North American Regional Conference on Manpower Implications of Automation (Washington, D.C., December 8–10, 1964), p. 19.

Some of this new communication technology will be used for conveying person-to-person information via voice or videotelephone. The rest will be employed for carrying data to and from, or between, computers. Carne has noted that:

> Projections of future telecommunications growth show that the domestic network will almost double in size by the mid-1980's. By this period, we will have over 200 million telephones, including 3 million videotelephones. Some 250,000 computers will have been installed; 200,000 of these computers will be connected to approximately 10 million terminals.
>
> Furthermore, nearly 60% of the United States will be connected to cable systems that provide limited return capabilities. Overhead, a few (perhaps 4) privately owned satellites will provide long-haul connections between important traffic centers in the 50 states. On the ground, several (perhaps 10) companies will compete with existing carriers to provide specialized services.[3]

Thus, communication technology will help the business manager convey information, store data, and utilize the power of the computer as never before. However, not all of this new technology will make life easier; some of it will merely stop things from getting worse. The area of power production provides an illustration.

Power Production: A Challenge

The United States is currently facing an energy shortage. What is causing the problem? There are numerous answers, but they all point to one overriding fact: America consumes more energy resources than she generates. As a result, the country is now importing almost eight million barrels of oil a day (over 40 per cent of her needs). This has led to hurried efforts at developing (or redeveloping) other energy sources, including coal and gas, and the Alaskan pipeline should help relieve some of the demand for overseas oil. All of these steps will help but, because of the nation's ravenous energy needs, they will probably not be enough. This has led some individuals to suggest raising the price of energy, an option favored by President Carter. However, this too will be insufficient, if past experience is any indication, since people tend to be more influenced by the cost of equipment or appliances than by the price of the energy they consume. As a result the most logical answer appears to rest with improved technology.

EFFICIENT USE OF ENERGY.   One method being given serious consideration is that of using energy more efficiently. For example, although modern auto engines are designed to create less environmental pollution, many also get fewer miles to the gallon than they would without all this extra equipment. To help rectify this situation, automakers are now switching to lighter materials. For example, the typical General Motors car, which weighs 3900 pounds today, will be down to 3100 pounds in 1985. Additionally, the V–8 engine will become extinct:

> By 1985, the V–8 engine, which today goes into 77 per cent of all GM cars, will be dead; the last one will go into 1983 Corvettes. Only one third of GM's 1985 cars will even have six-cylinder engines; two thirds will have four-cylinder power plants. Diesel engines will drive 25 per cent of the company's fleet, at least if the regulations on how much nitrogen oxide they can pour into the air are not tightened further. Diesels are noisy, smoky and heavier than gasoline engines, but they burn less fuel.[4]

---

[3]*Ibid.*, p. 131.

[4]"Look at the Cars of 1985," *Time*, May 16, 1977, p. 61.

Another development is *improved building insulation*, which can cut down on heat loss. Currently, "building standards required for Federal Housing Administration insurance have been raised to levels that reduce heat loss by 40 per cent."[5] Such insulation can also result in fuel savings for air conditioning. Netschert reports that "a further opportunity for air-conditioning savings lies in a method now being investigated under a National Science Foundation grant — namely, to store the 'cold' overnight and thus to reduce the load on the air-conditioning equipment during the day."[6]

Energy conservation is now under way.

Another area under consideration is *electricity generation and transmission*. Even the most modern plants operate at only 40 per cent efficiency. New approaches are therefore being examined. One is magneto-hydrodynamics (MHD), which is:

. . . a method of generating electricity directly, with no moving parts, from the flow of a plasma through a magnetic field. MHD, with possible efficiency levels of 50 per cent to 60 per cent, carries with it the additional attractive advantage of totally eliminating fly ash and sulfur and nitrogen oxides. Moreover, if an MHD unit is operated in conjunction with a gas turbine (rather than steam), there is no need for cooling water.[7]

ALTERNATIVE POWER SOURCES.   Scientists are also seeking alternative power sources such as the *earth's heat*. For example, the Pacific Gas & Electric Company has the nation's only geothermal plant. Using drilled wells and natural vents in the earth's surface, engineers capture sulfurous, superheated steam and use it to drive the utility's turbine engines. Along these same lines, the Los Alamos National Laboratory is trying to exploit the dry, hot (600°F) granite underneath most of the earth. By sinking two 15,000-foot wells beneath the surface and pumping cold water down one, scientists hope to get hot steam to flow up the other. If successful, this dry-rock system could provide all the electricity the United States will need for the next thirty centuries.

Alternative power sources are being sought.

And the ideas go on and on. Some scientists are working on a *fusion process*. "The ideal solution is to reproduce the sun's own process of joining atomic nuclei to produce clean, safe energy. The process, which also powered the hydrogen bomb . . . could fill the world's electricity needs for millions of years."[8] Others are seeking to collect *sunshine* and transform it into power, and a Congressional study recently reported that by 1980 solar energy will be the cheapest way to warm homes and heat water.[9] Other scientists are investigating possibilities such as harnessing the ocean's tides, combining animal manure and carbon dioxide under heat and pressure to produce oil, and burning garbage as a low-grade fuel.

Can the United States meet the current energy challenge? If its past record is any indication, the answer is undoubtedly "yes." As one analyst has noted, ". . . of 50 major industrial innovations of the twentieth century, 32 were initiated wholly or partly in the United States and 38 were brought wholly or partly to final commercial application in

[5]Bruce C. Netschert, "Energy vs. Environment," *Harvard Business Review*, January–February 1973, p. 138.
[6]*Ibid.*
[7]*Ibid.*
[8]"Energy Crisis: Are We Running Out? *Time*, June 12, 1972, p. 55; also see: "The Great Nuclear Fusion Race," *Time*, June 6, 1977, pp. 80–81.
[9]"Solar Energy Will Be Cheaper Than Oil, Gas by '80, Study Says," *The Miami Herald*, March 13, 1977, p. 23–A.

this country."[10] Thus, the United States has great potential for solving technological problems. The major question for the manager, however, is how will these new developments affect my company? The answer can be found through technological forecasting.

TECHNO-LOGICAL FORECAST-ING

Today, more than ever before, management needs to evaluate and assess the impact of technology on organizational strategy and survival. This requires an examination of the firm's operations with a view toward answering questions such as:

1. Is the company operating in a technologically sensitive environment?
2. Is the firm a leader or a follower in its operational environment?
3. Are operations sufficiently large to justify technological forecasting activities?
4. How much of a commitment will have to be made in terms of people, budget, and facilities?
5. Does management want occasional, informal technological forecasts or periodic, formal ones?[11]

Types of Technological Forecasting

If management decides to undertake technological forecasting, there are two fundamental approaches: exploratory and normative.

Exploratory forecasting begins with the current knowledge and predicts the future based on logical technological progress. As such, it is a rather passive process. Forecasters using this method tend to assume that current technological progress will continue at the same rate and that this advance will not be affected by external conditions. Then, later, they can speculate on how the forecast might be affected by the nontechnical environment.

[10]Harvey Brooks, "What's Happening to the U.S. Lead in Technology?" *Harvard Business Review*, May–June 1972, p. 113.
[11]Adapted from Daniel D. Roman, "Technological Forecasting in the Decision Process," *Academy of Management*, June 1970, p. 136.

Electronics development provides an illustration of how this method could be used. Immediately after World War II, transistors were expensive and qualitatively unpredictable. Since then, however, their price has declined, their quality has improved, and their application has become widespread. If a business firm had decided to conduct an exploratory forecast right after World War II, it would have been possible to predict these events.

Industrial firms in particular have found great value in this type of forecasting because it is not very difficult to do. In turn, the results can help the company in its search for clues as to market entry, potential competition, and ease of expansion into related product areas.

Normative forecasting begins with an identification of some future technological objective, such as the development of a space shuttle by 1991, and works back to the present, identifying the obstacles that will have to be surmounted along the way. Attention is devoted not only to technical factors but to nontechnical factors as well. For example, when will the technical know-how for a space shuttle be available and how will this time estimate be affected by governmental allocations, i.e., will the government put a lot of money into the project and develop it quickly or will it take a longer time because of reluctance or lack of enthusiasm on Washington's part? In contrast to exploratory forecasting, normative forecasting is a much more dynamic process.

Whichever of the two methods is used, technological forecasting presents a challenge. Fortunately, there are many techniques available to the forecaster. These range in nature from highly intuitive to ultra-sophisticated and include such catchword approaches as morphological analysis, scenario writing, and envelope forecasting.[12]

Currently, however, the most popular technological forecasting approach, developed by the Rand Corporation, is the Delphi technique. At present, between 50 and 100 major corporations are using it. In essence, the approach pools the opinions of experts and calls for:

1. **An anonymous prediction of important events in the area in question, from each expert in a group, in the form of brief statements.**
2. **A clarification of these statements by the investigator.**
3. **The successive, individual requestioning of each of the experts, combined with feedback supplied from the other experts *via* the investigator.[13]**

In the first round of questioning each expert might be asked to list, for example, the developments he or she believes will occur in his or her field within the next 20 years that will have a significant effect on the company. Each may also be asked to comment on the desirability, feasibility, and timing of these developments. Figure 16–1 provides an illustration of the format that might be used.

Then, in round two, each expert receives from the investigator a composite of the predictions made by the others, and is given the opportunity to modify his or her original estimates. This is usually followed by still further rounds, often a total of five. The result is generally a consensus among the participants regarding the most significant events that will affect the company (events A, E, H, and I), the likeli-

Exploratory forecasting projects the future according to logical technological progress.

Normative forecasting works from the future back to the present.

The Delphi Technique

---

[12]For descriptions of these see John P. Dory and Robert J. Lord, "Does TF Really Work?" *Harvard Business Review*, November–December 1970, p. 20.
[13]"The Basic Delphi Method," *Harvard Business Review*, May–June 1969, p. 81.

hood of their eventual development (90 per cent, 70 per cent, 60 per cent, and 40 per cent), and the time period in which they can be expected to occur (1982, 1985, 1987, and 1990). Table 16–2 illustrates the results of some Delphi forecasts.

Delphi allows the participants to revise their estimates.

Despite its apparent lack of scientific rigor, Delphi has proved very successful. In fact, the Rand Corporation has validated the technique through controlled experimentation. However, its use has not been confined exclusively to technological forecasting. It has also been successfully employed, for example, to help participants formulate responses to questions whose answers are already known. For example, how many votes were cast for Lincoln in 1860, or how many oil wells were there in Texas in 1960? In most cases, after a few rounds of questioning, the consensus has moved close to the actual answer. It can thus be seen why Delphi is so popular.[14]

Technical and Nontechnical Factors

The major problem confronting the forecaster is that of evaluating technical and nontechnical factors. In the technical area, for example, a pharmaceutical company might estimate that there will be chemical

[14]For an in-depth review of this area see: Richard M. Hodgetts *The Business Enterprise: Social Challenge, Social Response* (Philadelphia, Pa.: W. B. Saunders, 1977), pp. 295–318.

TABLE 16–2   Examples of Delphi Forecasts

Description of Event	Year Selected by Respondents as Date of Probable Occurrence		
	25%	50%	75%
There will be a single national building code.	1975	1977	1980
Polymers will be created by molecular tailoring, with service temperature ranges in excess of 1000°F.	1971	1976	2000
SST aircraft will be in regular service over land areas.	1980	1982	1985
Hydrocarbon/air fuel cell will be commercially available.	1974	1983	1990
A source of transplant organs for humans will be developed through selective breeding of animals that are tissue compatible.	1990	2015	2015

Source: First two examples from "McGraw-Hill Survey of Technological Breakthroughs and Widespread Applications of Significant Technical Developments," Department of Economics, McGraw-Hill Book Company, Inc., 1968; third example from "Delphi Studies as an Aid to Corporate Planning," Industrial Management Center, Austin, Texas, 1970; fourth from James R. Bright, ed., *Technological Forecasting for Industry and Government*, particularly, "The Delphi Method—an Illustration"; last example, T. J. Gordon and Robert H. Ament, "Forecasts of Some Technological and Scientific Developments and Their Societal Consequences," Report No. 6, The Institute for the Future, in Alan R. Fusfeld and Richard N. Foster, "The Delphi Technique: Survey and Comment," *Business Horizons, June 1971, p. 65.*

DESIRABILITY			FEASIBILITY			TIMING (YEAR BY WHICH PROBABLE EVENT WILL HAVE OCCURRED)		
High	*Average*	*Low*	*High*	*Likely*	*Unlikely*	*10% Probability*	*50% Probability*	*90% Probability*

FIGURE 16–1 Delphi Technique, Round One

Technical factors such as chance occurrence can undermine a forecast.

Nontechnical factors such as lack of public acceptance can also undermine a forecast.

control of hereditary defects through molecular engineering by 1995. However, what if by *chance occurrence* someone stumbles onto a discovery and makes a major breakthrough in this field in 1988? How can one forecast such developments?

Meanwhile, on the nontechnical side, there is the problem of lack of *public acceptance*. The American supersonic transport (SST) is an illustration. In 1963, when the United States learned that the British and French were going to combine their efforts to build an SST, the Concorde, President Kennedy urged the Congress to allocate funds for a feasibility study. By 1970, the plane was already in the mock-up stage, but by this time the entire project had become a political issue. The Nixon Administration stood squarely behind the development and production of the craft, but the public apparently did not, as reflected in the vote of the Congress. One reason was undoubtedly research, such as that conducted by a Ph.D. candidate at Columbia University, which showed that the government and the contractors stood to lose large sums of money if the plane was built. People were just not going to pay the extra money to get, for example, from New York to London a few hours earlier. Nontechnical factors (lack of demand for the aircraft, lack of profit for all parties involved) proved to be more important than the technical ones.[15]

The forecaster must thus evaluate technical progress and nontechnical constraints. These two concepts can be brought together, as seen in Figure 16–2, which illustrates the process of technical innovation. Since the forecast must incorporate changes in the social, political, and economic environment as well as in the technical environment, it is evident that formal forecasting techniques are incomplete. The manager must also employ an informal scanning process, asking the question, is

---

[15]For more on the application of the Delphi technique see: Richard J. Tersine and Walter E. Riggs, "The Delphi Technique: A Long-Range Planning Tool," *Business Horizons*, April 1976, pp. 51–56; and Richard M. Hodgetts, "Applying the Delphi Technique to Management Gaming," *Simulation*, July 1977, pp. 209–212.

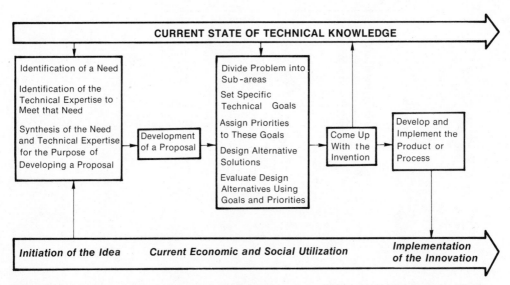

FIGURE 16–2   Process of Technical Knowledge (Adapted from James M. Utterback, "The Process of Technological Innovation Within the Firm," *Academy of Management Journal,* **March 1971, p. 78.)**

there anything else that we have not yet considered that might affect our forecast? Sometimes the answer is so obvious that it is overlooked. Consider the following case of a technology manager in a large company:

> Several years ago he initiated a technological forecasting effort on one-shot basis, using a morphological technique with some Delphi inputs. Over 100 fields of technology were selected for study, with the objective of identifying broad areas of expertise where the company should develop or maintain a capability in the future. After an extensive forecasting procedure, 12 areas of potential importance were selected and recommended to the planning committee. Yet, as the manager of technology later noted, even after this rigorous search, one of the most significant areas — environmental control — was not identified.[16]

The technological forecast will have an impact on the organization's goals since the goals will be reflections of the forecast. However, the impact of technology extends beyond this, affecting the human dimensions as well.

TECHNOLOGY AND THE PERSONNEL

Bringing people and technology together can cause tension. There is, for example, a relationship between effectiveness and tension, as illustrated in Figure 16–3. Up to a point (B), some degree of pressure, accountability, responsibility, pride, and obligation is necessary. However, if tension is increased beyond this point (to C, for example), effectiveness can decline.[17]

The same is true in the case of technological capability and effectiveness, as seen in Figure 16–4. To the left of Point E there is insufficient technological capability for getting the job done, whereas to the right of this point there is too much.

Technology, Tension, and Effectiveness

Technology can cause tension and impair personnel effectiveness.

---

[16]Dory and Lord, *op. cit.*, p. 22.

[17]The data in this section can be found in Henry M. Boettinger, "Technology in the Manager's Future," *Harvard Business Review*, November–December 1970, pp. 4–14, 165.

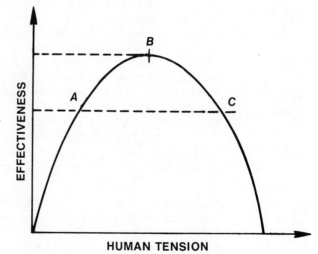

FIGURE 16–3 Relationship Between Effectiveness and Tension

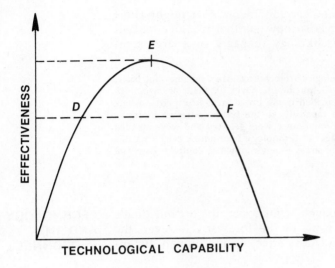

FIGURE 16–4 Relationship Between Effectiveness and Technological Capability

Figures 16–3 and 16–4 can be brought together and overlapped in three-dimensional style. As Boettinger notes:

> . . . if a brilliant technologist makes optimal provision of tools (Point E) to an inept manager who operates at Points A or C, he has wasted his time. If an ideal manager, carrying his people to Point B, has been furnished the wrong processes of equipment (points D or F), his people cannot catch rivals who have skilled technologists looking after their interests.
>
> One can compensate for bad technology, to some extent, with greater leadership, and for poor leadership with superb technology. But peak performance can never be achieved without peaks in *both* domains—the human and the technical.[18]

The challenge is thus one of introducing neither too much nor too little tension or technology, and this is not an easy task.

Effect on the People

At the worker level, for example, technology can affect the social relationships among the people by bringing about changes in elements, such as the size and composition of the work group or the frequency of contact with other workers. This was seen in Chapter 3 when Trist's longwall coal-getting study was discussed. It will be remembered that the miners initially worked in small, independent, cohesive groups. However, new advances in technology and equipment led to changes in the composition of these work groups. The result was a decline in productivity. Only when the management restored many of the social and small group relationships did output again increase.[19] Technological advance may also lead to the abolition of jobs or the reduction of tasks to simplistic levels. All these changes brought about by technology will affect the psycho-social system.

Technology can affect the psycho-social system.

In order to prevent too great an upheaval, it is necessary for management to consider the human as well as the technical needs of the organization. One of the most important studies in this area was con-

[18]*Ibid.*, p. 14.
[19]E. L. Trist and K. W. Bamforth, "Some Social and Psychological Consequences of the Longwall Method of Coal-getting," *Human Relations*, February 1951, pp. 3–38.

ducted by Mann and his associates at the Institute for Social Research.[20] After analyzing the effect on the personnel of a changeover to electronic data processing equipment in a major utility over a five-year period they found:

> One of the most pressing problems during this period was the maintenance of a high level of group morale and individual job satisfaction. Every attempt was made to arrive at solutions that would be satisfactory to each individual. While the general policy of reassignment served as guidelines, many unique solutions had to be invented in individual cases. The old problem remained of devising a solution that would meet the employee's personal needs, the company objectives, and still be perceived as appropriate publicly.[21]

Unless the impact of technology on the worker is considered, organizational effectiveness and efficiency will suffer.

Technology also affects the managerial staff. Today, managers are more specialized than ever before, as seen through the ever-growing number of public relations people, operations researchers, and other staff personnel in the organization. Whereas primary consideration was previously given to breaking jobs into their component parts, the emphasis today is on integrating the work of the managers. This is especially true in industries in which technology plays a major role.

Burns and Stalker, for example, undertook a study of a number of British and Scottish firms. These companies were operating in stable technologies and environments, but they were trying to move into the electronics field, which is characterized by rapidly changing technology.[22] The researchers found that in making this transition, these companies underwent significant changes in their management systems. Initially they were *mechanistic*, characterized by formal job descriptions and a rigid organization structure. Everyone knew what he was doing and to whom he reported. In the new environment, however, an *organic* managerial system developed. (See Table 16–3 for a comparison of some of the key dimensions of mechanistic and organic organization structures.) Management had to adapt to changing conditions and the old, mechanistic structure gave way to a more flexible one. Managers found themselves interacting more with each other and placing greater emphasis on lateral rather than vertical communication. In order to survive in this new dynamic environment, the managers began to restructure the old line-staff relationships and devise more modern, flexible ones. Technology thus affects not only the people but the structure itself.

Technology can also lead to the replacement of mechanistic structures by organic ones.

One of the most significant studies evaluating the impact of technology on structure was conducted by Joan Woodward.[23] Her research, encompassing 100 firms in a London suburb, sought to determine how structural variables affected economic success. She found the answer by

TECHNOLOGY AND STRUCTURE

---

[20]Floyd C. Mann and Lawrence K. Williams, "Observations on the Dynamics of a Change to Electronic Data-Processing Equipment," *Administrative Science Quarterly*, September 1960, pp. 217–256.

[21]*Ibid.*, pp. 244–245.

[22]Tom Burns and G. M. Stalker, *The Management of Innovation* (London: Tavistock Publications, 1961).

[23]Joan Woodward, *Industrial Organization: Theory and Practice* (London: Oxford University Press, 1965).

TABLE 16–3   A Comparison of Some of the Key Dimensions of Mechanistic and Organic Organization Structures

Systems and Their Key Dimensions	Characteristics of Organization Systems	
	Closed/Stable/ Mechanistic	Open/Adaptive/ Organic
Environmental Suprasystem		
General nature	Peaceful	Turbulent
Predictability	High certainty	High uncertainty
Technology	Stable	Dynamic
Degree of environmental influence on organization	Low	High
Overall Organizational System		
Emphasis of organization	On performance	On problem solving
Predictability of actions	Relatively certain	Relatively uncertain
Decision-making process	Programmable	Nonprogrammable
Goals and Values		
Overall values	Efficiency, predictability, security, risk averting	Effectiveness, adaptability, responsiveness, risk taking
Involvement in setting objectives	Primarily from the top down	Wide participation, including people from the bottom as well as from the top
Technical System		
Knowledge	Highly specialized	Highly generalized
Time perspective	Short-term	Long-term
Interdependency of tasks	Low	High

(Table 16–3 continued on opposite page.)

analyzing the types of technology the firms were employing. There were three types in all:

1. *Mass and large batch production.* This type of technology is used for mass-production items. Automobiles and television sets are illustrations.
2. *Continuous process production.* This type of technology is employed in producing continuous-flow production items. The manufacture of chemicals or the processing of oils are illustrations.
3. *Unit and small batch production.* This type of technology is used for "one-of-a-kind" products or those built to customer specifications. Lunar modules and locomotives are illustrations.

The appropriateness of the organizational structure, she found, was dependent on the type of technology the firm used. If the company employed mass-production techniques, a mechanistic structure seemed to work best. Conversely, if the firm used continuous-process or unit production, in which technology plays a more significant role, an organic structure seemed to work best. These findings are illustrated in Table 16–4.

In addition, Woodward found that the organic structures tended to be more human relations oriented than the mechanistic ones.

**TABLE 16–3   A Comparison of Some of the Key Dimensions of
Mechanistic and Organic Organization Structures—Continued**

Systems and Their Key Dimensions	Characteristics of Organization Systems	
	Closed/Stable/ Mechanistic	*Open/Adaptive/ Organic*
Structural System		
Procedures and rules	Many, often formal and written	Few, often informal and unwritten
Levels of the hierarchy	Many	Few
Source of authority	Position in organization	Knowledge of individual
Responsibility	Attached to position	Assumed by individual
Psycho-social System		
Interpersonal relationships	Formal	Informal
Personal involvement	Low	High
Motivation factors	Emphasis on low-level needs (Theory X)	Emphasis on upper-level needs (Theory Y)
Leadership Style	Autocratic	Democratic
Managerial System		
Content of communications	Decisions and instructions	Advice and information
Control process	Impersonal use of devices such as rules and regulations	Interpersonal contacts, persuasion, and suggestions
Means of resolving conflict	Superior uses the "book" in handling the matter	Group resolves issue with situational ethics

Adapted from Fremont E. Kast and James E. Rosenzweig, *Contingency Views of Organization and Management* (Chicago: Science Research Associates, Inc., 1973), pp. 315–318.

Since Woodward's initial study, other researchers have also attempted to evaluate the importance of technology on the organization. Perhaps the most widely known of these is Zwerman, who, using 55 firms from the Minneapolis area, replicated Woodward's research in the United States.[24] In essence, he corroborated her basic findings,[25] concluding that the "type of production technology was most closely and

Follow-Up Research

---

[24]William L. Zwerman, *New Perspectives on Organization Theory* (Westport, Conn.: Greenwood Publishing Corporation, 1970).
[25]Because of a lack of firms in continuous-process operations, however, he was unable to make any inferences about this particular group.

TABLE 16–4   Woodward's Research Findings

Mechanistic	**Organic**
Mass production	Continuous process Unit production

consistently related to variations in the organizational characteristics of the firms. . . ."[26]

Numerous research studies have been conducted on the effect of technology on structure.

In a related study, Lawrence and Lorsch[27] posed the question, what form of management is best under which conditions? Employing a sample of 10 industrial organizations, they grouped them by degree of market and technological change. The six in the plastics industry were categorized as operating in a highly dynamic environment; the two in the consumer foods industry were seen as being in an environment with an "intermediate" degree of change; the two in the standardized container industry were identified as being in a relatively stable environment. The researchers found that to be successful, those in the dynamic environment needed a flexible structure, whereas those in the stable environment were most effective with a mechanistic management system, and those in the intermediate environment needed to operate somewhere between the two extremes.

Meyer, studying the impact of automation on the formal structure, investigated 254 state and local government departments of finance.[28] He found that automation creates interdependency in the organization, and nonhierarchical (organic) structures are better able to deal with the situation than are rigid, hierarchical (mechanical) ones.

Although other research can be cited to substantiate further these findings,[29] the general pattern is already clear: technology has a definite impact on organizational structure (see Table 16–5). It is thus possible to extend Chandler's thesis of "from strategy to structure"[30] by incorporating the technological factor in Figure 16–5:

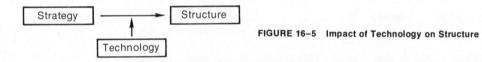

FIGURE 16–5   Impact of Technology on Structure

One final point merits attention. Technology is not the *only* factor affecting structure, nor is it always the most critical. (In fact, Hickson found it to be of significant importance only for small organizations.[31]) Where it does play a role, it is the effect on such variables as the span of control and manager-manager and manager-subordinate relationships that is important. As Woodward has noted:

> Among the organizational characteristics showing a direct relationship with technical advance were: the length of the line of command; the span of control of the chief executive; the percentage of total turnover allocated to the payment of wages and salaries; and the ratios of managers to total personnel, of clerical and administrative staff to manual workers, of direct to indirect labour, and of graduate to non-graduate supervision in production departments.[32]

[26]Zwerman, *op. cit.*, p. 148.

[27]Paul R. Lawrence and Jay W. Lorsch, *Organization and Environment* (Boston: Harvard Graduate School of Business Administration, 1967).

[28]Marshall W. Meyer, "Automation and Bureaucratic Structure," *American Journal of Sociology*, November 1968, pp. 256–264.

[29]For example, see Edward Harvey, "Technology and the Structure of Organizations," *American Sociological Review*, April 1968, pp. 247–259.

[30]Alfred D. Chandler, Jr., *Strategy and Structure* (Garden City, New York: Anchor Books, Doubleday & Company, Inc., 1966).

[31]David J. Hickson, D. S. Pugh, and Diana C. Pheysey, "Operations Technology and Organization Structure: An Empirical Reappraisal," *Administrative Science Quarterly*, September 1969, pp. 378–397.

[32]Woodward, *op. cit.*, p. 51.

TABLE 16–5 Research Findings Relating Technology and Organization Structure

| Researcher | Organization Structure | | |
	Mechanistic	*Intermediate*	*Organic*
Woodward	Mass production		Continuous process Unit production
Zwerman	Mass production		Unit production
Lawrence and Lorsch	Stable environment	Intermediate degree of stability	Dynamic environment
Meyer	Low degree of interdependency		High degree of interdependency

Adapted from Robert T. Keller, "A Look at the Sociotechnical System," *California Management Review*, Fall 1972, p. 89.

SUMMARY

This chapter has examined technology and its impact on the business firm. Many changes have occurred in the modern world because of technological advances. However, the major question for the business is, what impact will technology have on the company? One way of answering this query is through technological forecasting.

There are two types of technological forecasts: exploratory and normative. An *exploratory* forecast is one that starts with the current state of knowledge and predicts the future based on logical technological progress. Forecasters who use this method tend to play down the nontechnical environment. A *normative* forecast is one that identifies a particular technological objective and estimates at what point in the future it will be attained. Instead of working from the present to the future, however, the normative forecaster works backward, from the time he or she believes the breakthrough will occur to the present. In addition, the normative forecaster gives high consideration to the nontechnical environment.

A variety of techniques are available for conducting a technological forecast, from morphological analysis to scenario writing to envelope forecasting. The most popular method at present is the Delphi technique, which pools the opinions of experts, each predicting when a particular future event will occur. These estimates are then recorded and each individual is given a composite of all the forecasts. A second round is then conducted and each expert is given a chance to revise his or her estimates. This process will often continue for a total of five rounds and generally results in a consensus of opinion among the experts. Although Delphi may appear to lack scientific rigor, the Rand Corporation has validated the approach through controlled experimentation.

Regardless of the technique employed, these forecasts must evaluate both technical and nontechnical factors. On the technical side there is not only the rate of progress to be considered but also the likelihood of a major accidental breakthrough that will throw all forecasts awry. On the nontechnical side there is the issue of public acceptance.

Many companies are well aware of the impact of technology on strategy and profit. However, technological advances also affect the organizational personnel from the workers right up to the managers. At the worker level, technology affects social relationships as well as job content. At the managerial level, it encourages greater integration of effort.

Technology also affects the organization structure by causing changes in factors such as the length of the line of command, the span of control of the chief executive, and the ratio of managers to total personnel. In addition, mechanistic designs tend to give way to organic ones. This has been seen in the research of Woodward, Zwerman, Lawrence and Lorsch, and Meyer, to name but a few.

What do these new organic structures look like? How do they work? When, specifically, are they used? These questions will be answered in Chapter 17, in which modern organization structures are examined.

REVIEW AND STUDY QUESTIONS

1. Technology consists of two important components: knowledge and technique. Explain this statement.

2. In your own words, briefly outline the changes that have occurred as mankind progressed from handicraft technology to cybernated technology.

3. Why is the amount of time between the discovery of inventions and their application decreasing?

4. What are some of the changes that can be expected during the next decade in the area of communication technology? How will these affect the manager?

5. Why is the United States facing an energy crisis? What are some of the technological approaches being considered? Explain.

6. How does a manager conduct an exploratory technological forecast? A normative technological forecast?

7. How can a manager use the Delphi technique in making a technological forecast? Explain by discussing the steps in the process.

8. Why are nontechnological factors so important in a technological forecast?

9. What impact can technology have on workers? On managers?

10. What is a mechanistic organization structure? Give an example.

11. What is an organic organization structure? Give an example.

12. Based on recent research, what effect does technology have on organization structure? Include in your answer the research conducted by Joan Woodward.

SELECTED REFERENCES

Boettinger, H. M. "Technology in the Manager's Future." *Harvard Business Review,* November–December 1970, pp. 4–14, 165.

Burns, T., and G. M. Stalker. *The Management of Innovation.* London: Tavistock Publications, 1961.

Carne, E. B. "Telecommunications: Its Impact on Business." *Harvard Business Review,* July–August 1972, pp. 125–132.

"Detroit's Response to the Energy Problem." *Business Week,* May 23, 1977, pp. 100, 102.

Gross, A. C., and W. W. Ware. "Energy Prospects to 1990." *Business Horizons,* June 1975, pp. 5–18.

Hickson, D. J., D. S. Pugh, and D. C. Pheysey. "Operations Technology and Organization Structure: An Empirical Reappraisal." *Administrative Science Quarterly,* September 1969, pp. 378–397.

Hodgetts, R. "Applying the Delphi Technique to Management Gaming." *Simulation,* July 1977, pp. 209–212.

Hunt, R. G. "Technology and Organization." *Academy of Management Journal,* September 1970, pp. 235–252.

Jelinek, M. "Technology, Organizations, and Contingency." *Academy of Management Review,* January 1977, pp. 17–26.

Lawrence, P. R., and J. W. Lorsch. *Organization and Environment.* Boston: Harvard Graduate School of Business Administration, 1967.

Roman, D. D. "Technological Forecasting in the Decision Process." *Academy of Management Journal,* June 1970, pp. 127–138.

"Solar Energy Will Be Cheaper than Oil, Gas by '80, Study Says." *Miami Herald,* March 13, 1977, p. 23–A.

Swager, W. L. "Technological Forecasting in Planning: A Method of Using Relevance Trees." *Business Horizons,* February 1973, pp. 37–44.

"Technology Changes the Office Telephone." *Business Week,* January 19, 1976, pp. 42–44.

Tersine, R. J., and W. E. Riggs, "The Delphi Technique: A Long-Range Planning Tool." *Business Horizons,* April 1976, pp. 51–56.

Utterback, J. M. "The Process of Technological Innovation Within the Firm." *Academy of Management Journal,* March 1971, pp. 75–88.

Woodward, J. *Industrial Organization: Theory and Practice.* London: Oxford University Press, 1965.

Zwerman, W. L. *New Perspectives on Organization Theory.* Westport, Conn.: Greenwood Publishing Corporation, 1970.

CASE: FASTER THAN A SPEEDING BULLET[33]

Technology is increasing at a tremendously rapid rate. In the field of transportation, for example, the fastest means of travel available to man in 6000 B.C. was the camel caravan, which averaged around eight miles per hour. By 1600 B.C., when the chariot was invented, the maximum speed rose to 20 miles per hour. It was not until the 1880's, with the help of the advanced steam engine, that man was able to reach speeds of 100 miles per hour. It had taken a million years to attain this goal, but now the pace picked up. Within the next 60 years, thanks to the invention of the airplane, man was moving at 400 miles per hour. Twenty years later that speed had doubled. And in the 1960's, rocket planes were approaching speeds of 4000 miles per hour, and astronauts and cosmonauts were circling the earth in space capsules at 18,000 miles per hour. If progress in the field of transportation during the last generation were plotted on a graph, the line would run off the page.

The same general acceleration can be seen in many areas, because the amount of time between a product's invention and its fruition is decreasing. For example, it was 2000 years from the time Appollonius of Perga discovered conic sections until they were applied to engineering problems. More recently, the same pattern still existed. In 1836, using technology over 20 years old, a machine capable of mowing, threshing, tying straw into sheaves, and pouring grain into sacks was invented. It was not until the 1930's, however, that such a product was actually marketed. Likewise, the first typewriter patent was issued in 1714, but over 150 years passed before these machines became commercially available. And it was a full century between the time Nicholas Appert discovered how to can food and the time canning became important in the food industry.

In the twentieth century this gap has decreased dramatically. Robert Young of the Stanford Research Institute has found that for a group of appliances introduced before 1920, including the refrigerator, the vacuum cleaner, and the electric range, approximately 34 years passed between introduction and peak production. For a group introduced between 1939 to 1969, including television, the electric frying pan, and the washer-dryer combination, however, the time span was only eight years. In Young's words "The post-war group demonstrated vividly the rapidly accelerating nature of the modern cycle."

---

[33]The data in this case can be found in Alvin Toffler, *Future Shock* (New York: Bantam Books, Inc., 1971).

When one examines the above facts, it becomes evident that technology, fueled by ever-increasing scientific knowledge, is bringing about fantastic changes at an ever-increasing rate. With it, however, comes the possibility that man will be unable to cope with these new conditions; it is too much, too fast. This has led Toffler to conclude:

Our first and most pressing need, therefore, before we can begin to gently build a humane future, is to halt the runaway acceleration that is subjecting multitudes to the threat of future shock while, at the very same moment, intensifying all the problems they must deal with — war, ecological incursions, racism, the obscene contrast between rich and poor, the revolt of the young, and the rise of a potentially deadly mass irrationalism.

Questions

1. How can man learn to live in such a technologically accelerative environment?

2. Is business today facing a situation similar to that described in this case? Explain.

3. What changes can be expected in business organization structures because of technology?

4. What impact will technology have on the organization's personnel? Explain.

CASE: THE NEXT BEST THING TO BEING THERE[34]

Today, thanks to modern technology, companies in the communication industry are reporting the advent of many different types of telephone gadgets and "extras." For example, some firms are having taped music installed on the "hold" line so callers will hear music while waiting to be connected with their party. Another available service is an automatic switchboard which is rigged to give a "beep" on the busy line. Then, if the person being called does not put the first party on hold and answer the second call, the switchboard automatically rings a nearby phone. A third service is a small plugless or cordless PBX which is much easier to manage, thereby freeing the receptionist for other tasks. A fourth is a priority override system enabling executives to break into busy lines when necessary.

Yet the communication industry is doing more than just designing telephone gadgetry. Many companies are developing communication satellites:

Lofted into stationary orbit 22,000 mi. above the equator, a communications satellite acts as a single microwave relay station. But instead of

---

[34]The data in this case can be found in "The Revolution in the Phone Business," *Business Week,* November 6, 1971, pp. 66–69, 72–74.

having a limited range, it can bounce anything, from television pictures to telegraph channels, from Hawaii to Maine and any points in between at equal cost.

The cost benefits are significant, compared to ground-based systems. For a minimum investment of about $46 million, a satellite system can blanket the whole continent with long-distance communication links. In the U.S., which is already wired with cable and microwave from coast to coast, satellite communications will provide economical, extra capacity.

Some of the firms that had applications pending before the Federal Communication Commission included AT&T, Fairchild Hiller, RCA, Western Union, Comsat, and Hughes Aircraft. The payback period on these communication satellites was expected to be around three to four years.

Questions

1. How important is improved telephone service for business?

2. Do you think these new technological advances will mean higher costs? Explain.

3. What further new developments affecting business do you think there will be by the 1980s? Explain.

CASE: 1985: AN EARLY LOOK[35]

What do the 1980s hold in store for business? In an attempt to answer this question, four large corporations, Lever Brothers, Monsanto, Scott Paper, and Du Pont, have given financial backing to an undertaking called Project Aware, a unique attempt to predict the economic, technological, and social environment these firms will face during the 1980s. Using the Delphi technique, the Institute for the Future, which is conducting the analysis, released its first results in August 1973. Some of the predictions were the following:

1. **Quality of life — in all likelihood it will decline. Although economic standards will rise, expectations of citizens will outrun the nation's ability to fulfill them.**
2. **Energy crisis — Will probably be resolved by such market forces as rising prices and the development of new energy sources.**
3. **Worker discontent — Changes in manufacturing methods and the use of job enrichment could increase productivity by as much as 50 per cent but worker discontent will increase throughout the decade.**
4. **Business procedures — Will probably not change much although after about 1985 the costs of computer entry, storage, and access will fall beneath the cost of paper files.**

In addition to the above, the Institute for the Future predicted the probability of the following events occurring by 1985:

---

[35]The data in this case can be found in "A Think Tank That Helps Companies Plan," *Business Week,* August 25, 1973, pp. 70–71.

Event	Per cent Probability
Many chemical pesticides phased out	95
National health insurance enacted	90
Spending on environmental quality exceeds 6% of GNP	90
Insect hormones widely used as pesticides	80
Community review of factory locations	80
Substantial understanding of baldness and skin wrinkling	40
A modest (3%) value-added tax passed	40
Wide use of computers in elementary schools	25
Development of cold vaccines	20
Autos banned in central areas of at least seven cities	20
Breeder reactors banned for safety reasons	20

Are such predictions useful to companies in formulating long-range plans? *Business Week* reports that a number of businesses are incorporating Delphi methods into their corporate planning. Of course, the results of such predictions may be inaccurate, but as one manager put it, "a Delphi study tells you what ballpark you're playing in."

Questions

1. What did the above manager mean by his statement about Delphi telling you "what ballpark you're playing in"?

2. What kinds of questions can the Delphi technique answer that would be of value to business?

3. If, as reported in this case, worker discontent will increase in the 1980s, what impact do you see this having on organization structures? Explain, incorporating into your discussion the concepts of mechanistic and organic organization designs.

CASE: MORE ORDER, NOT LESS

When Nebbing Incorporated started business in 1947, its three founders stated the firm's basic mission as one of "inventing and manufacturing sophisticated telecommunication equipment." Over the next 25 years the company prospered, thanks to the high degree of technical expertise possessed by the owners and the staff they hired. In 1978, however, the three men decided that they had had enough. They wished to retire and spend the rest of their years in leisure. They therefore sold Nebbing to a large national conglomerate for $40 million. This was the conglomerate's first venture into the communication industry; its initial success had come in manufacturing. Nevertheless, the board of directors liked Nebbing's profitability picture and felt that their company would be making an excellent acquisition.

Soon after the takeover, the Nebbing personnel were told that there would be no radical changes; it was to be "business as usual." The only change the conglomerate intended to institute was that of reorganizing the structure, as the new owners wanted to install a line-staff organization. When asked about this, the president of the firm said, "We feel Nebbing is too disorganized. We want to create more formal lines of communication and authority-responsibility relationships. This way everyone will know what they are supposed to be doing and to whom they should report. At present, this is not the case."

Within six months after the reorganization, however, Nebbing's financial statements indicated that something was wrong. Instead of obtaining high profitability, the newly acquired company was reporting its first loss in years. The president and his advisors were unable to explain why. One of the board members put it this way. "We tried to straighten out the firm's chaotic nature by introducing some order into the structure. But instead of becoming more profitable, they're now losing money. The president has talked it over with us and decided to call in a management consulting firm. Perhaps we need more of a formalized structure than we initially thought. In any event, something has to be done."

Questions

1. Why is the new organization structure not working? Explain.

2. What do you think of the president's comment about Nebbing being too disorganized?

3. What recommendations would you make to this firm? Explain, bringing into your discussion the topics of mechanistic and organic structures.

CHAPTER SEVENTEEN
MODERN ORGANIZATION STRUCTURES

One of the greatest challenges facing the modern manager is that of coping with change. Some of this change is brought on by conditions in the external environment and some of it is internally generated. In either case, the organization must be capable of meeting the demands of the situation. One way in which this is being done is through the use of modern organization structures. Organizations are finding that with these new adaptive, flexible designs they are better able to interact with their external environment. At the same time, these structures encourage the use of modern motivation and leadership techniques. Theory X assumptions are replaced by Theory Y assumptions, and fixed ideas about leadership give way to a contingency approach. The goals of this chapter are to examine some of the modern organization structures being used by today's manager and to study what is meant by the term *contingency organization design.*

GOALS OF THE CHAPTER

When you have completed this chapter you should be able to;
1. Define the characteristics of an ideal bureaucracy.
2. Explain why bureaucratic structures are declining in importance.
3. Describe what a project organization is and how it functions.
4. Compare and contrast the project and the matrix structure.
5. Relate how a free-form organization differs from a bureaucratic design.
6. Explain what is meant by the term contingency organization design.
7. Identify and describe those forces that help determine the "best" organization structure.

FIGURE 17-1 An Organization Structure Continuum

Bureaucratic Structures ———————————— Adaptive Structures

In the extreme, there are two types of organization designs: bureaucratic and adaptive. If placed on a continuum, they would appear as in Figure 17-1.

The bureaucracy is a highly structured organization. In its *ideal* form, this structure has five main characteristics. Max Weber, the German sociologist who made one of the earliest and best known studies of this organizational design, identified these characteristics as:

THE DECLINE OF BUREAUCRATIC STRUCTURES

1. A clear-cut division of labor resulting in a host of specialized experts in each position.
2. A hierarchy of offices, with each lower one being controlled and supervised by a higher one.
3. A consistent system of abstract rules and standards which assures uniformity in the performance of all duties and the coordination of various tasks.
4. A spirit of formalistic impersonality in which officials carry out the duties of their office.
5. Employment based on technical qualifications and protected from arbitrary dismissal.[1]

Characteristics of an ideal bureaucracy.

---

[1]Peter M. Blau, *Bureaucracy in Modern Society* (New York: Random House Inc., 1956), pp. 28–33.

Of course, no organization employs the bureaucracy in its ideal form; however, many use some version of it. The problem with these total organization structures is that, to a large degree, they are proving to be unworkable. Quite simply, they lack the ability to cope with the stress, change, and tension brought on by today's complex environment. One reason for this is that they are too closed-systems oriented. A second reason is that they attempt to regiment their personnel with detailed rules and procedures.

Evolving in their place are modern structures capable of dealing with a dynamic environment and a complex employee. These new structures incorporate much of the latest thinking contained in earlier chapters, especially those related to communication, motivation, leadership, human resource development, and the systems concept (Chapters 11 to 15). Furthermore, as McFarland points out, these new structures "are not merely variations or improvements in the bureaucratic model; they represent extensive departures from the underlying assumptions, theories, structures, and aims of the bureaucratic model."[2] One of these new designs is known as the project organization.

THE PROJECT ORGANIZATION

The use of the project organization has increased throughout the last decade. It is currently being employed in numerous and diverse undertakings from building dams and weapon systems to conducting research and development, choosing distribution center sites, and redesigning bank credit-card systems. Although the project organization can take various forms, there is one overriding characteristic which distinguishes it from the usual line and staff departments: once the project has been completed, the organization is phased out. This is made clear by its very definition. Project management is "the gathering of the best available talent to accomplish a specific and complex undertaking within time, cost and/or quality parameters, followed by the disbanding of the team upon completion of the undertaking."[3] In a manner of speaking, the project manager and the personnel work themselves out of a job. The group members then go on to another project, are given jobs elsewhere in the organization, or, in some cases, are phased out entirely.

The major advantage of the project form of organization is that it allows a project manager and his or her team to concentrate their attention on one specific undertaking. The manager makes sure that the project does not get lost in the shuffle of organizational activities. In short, the project managers act as focal points for their project activities.[4]

Criteria for using a project structure.

Although the structure has many advantages, its application is limited. For example, one writer has recommended the following criteria for the use of a project structure: (1) definable in terms of a specific goal; (2) somewhat unique and unfamiliar to the existing organization; (3) complex with respect to interdependence of activities necessary to accomplishment; (4) critical with respect to possible gain or loss; and (5) temporary with respect to duration of need.[5]

[2]Dalton E. McFarland, *Management: Principles and Practices*, 4th edition (New York: The Macmillan Company, 1974), p. 154.
[3]Richard M. Hodgetts, "An Interindustry Analysis of Certain Aspects of Project Management" (Ph.D. diss., University of Oklahoma, 1968), p. 7.
[4]David I. Cleland and William R. King, *Systems Analysis and Project Management* 2nd edition (New York: McGraw-Hill Book Company, 1975), p. 184.
[5]John M. Stewart, "Making Project Management Work," *Business Horizons*, Fall 1965, pp. 54–68.

Once it has been determined that a project organization will be used, the objectives must be set, the personnel obtained, the structure formulated, and a control system designed for obtaining feedback. Although the organization will be more fluid than its conventional line-staff counterpart, there will still be the assignment of authority and responsibility. The structure will therefore be formalized to some degree. A project manager will be appointed to oversee the proceedings and personnel will be assigned to him or her. Some of them will remain through the duration of the project while others may be involved for only a short period of time. The duties of the project personnel are thus going to vary with the objectives and the organizational structure. In the development and production of a ballistic missile, for example, many people would be assigned to the project. Collectively, they would have responsibility for the following activities:

Planning The Project

1. Ascertaining the overall organizational strategic plan.
2. Determining both the technical specifications of the missile and the desires of the customers, i.e., the federal government.
3. Building, testing, and evaluating the prototype.
4. Establishing reliability, maintainability, and supportability requirements of the project.
5. Determining supply sources for the project items that must be purchased.
6. Negotiating and managing all contracts associated with the project.
7. Developing and maintaining all schedules designed to produce the missile on time.
8. Seeing that technical manuals and reports required for the project are drawn up and distributed.
9. Planning, installing, operating, and maintaining the completed project.
10. Providing supportability for the missile after it is produced, i.e., spare parts, support equipment, and trained personnel.
11. Continually monitoring all costs associated with the project.
12. Establishing project design and performance characteristics.
13. Providing the most up to date technology within time and cost parameters.
14. Identifying and developing the personnel skills that will be required in using the product.[6]

---

[6]Adapted from Cleland and King, *op. cit.*, pp. 243–244.

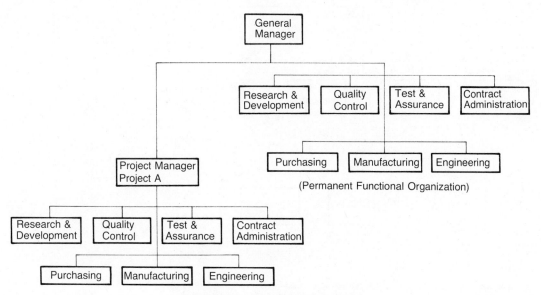

(Permanent Functional Organization)

FIGURE 17–2 Pure Project Organization

Designing The Project Structure

Once the objectives have been ascertained, the project structure can be designed, which may take numerous forms from simple to very complex. In the simple structure, seen in Figure 17–2, the project manager is put in charge of an undertaking and given direct authority over the team members. The project manager has all the resources needed for getting the job done, and the departments under his or her control are exact duplicates of the permanent functional organization. This type of design is often referred to as a *pure* or *aggregate project structure*. However, since it is also one of the most expensive ways to organize a project because of its duplication of facilities, its use is generally reserved for very large undertakings. More common is the structure in which a project manager occupies the role of advisor to the general manager, who in turn administers the entire project within a functional organization hierarchy (see Figure 17–3). A third variation, and most common of all, is the matrix structure.

Pure project structure is reserved for large undertakings.

THE MATRIX STRUC- TURE

A *matrix structure* is a hybrid form of organization containing characteristics of both project and functional structures. Nevertheless, it is common to find the terms "matrix organization" and "project organization" used interchangeably, although there are very distinct differences between the two. The major difference is that in contrast to the project organization, personnel in the matrix structure are only *loaned* to the project manager for a specific undertaking. There is thus a dual responsibility on the part of these team members. First, they are responsible to the head of their functional department, who has assigned them to the project. The functional department head is their line superior and will continue to be so. Second, they must be responsive to the project manager for whom they are working, and who exercises what is called "project" authority.

Matrix structure is functional and project organization hybrid.

Figure 17–4 illustrates three project managers, each with project au-

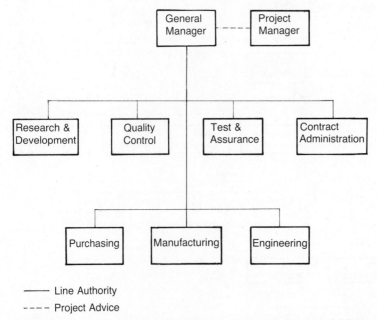

— Line Authority

– – – – Project Advice

FIGURE 17–3   Functional Organization With Project Manager Serving in Advisory Capacity

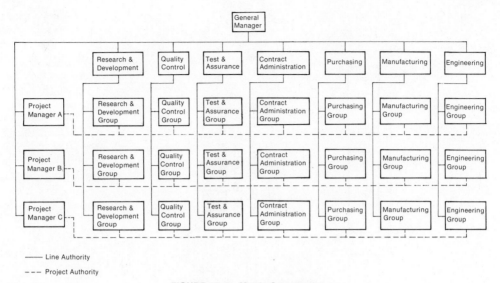

— Line Authority

--- Project Authority

FIGURE 17–4   Matrix Organization

thority over personnel from departments supporting their respective undertakings.

When the concepts of functional and project authority are brought together, the result is a vertical and horizontal organization structure. The vertical pattern is brought about by the typical line authority flowing down from superior to subordinate. The horizontal authority flow is caused by the fact that both the scalar principle and unity of command principle are violated, and in their place comes the need for close cooperation between the project manager and the respective functional managers (see Figure 17–5). This is more clearly seen if the concept of project authority is examined in detail.

Projects authority flows horizontally.

Project authority has been identified and described by one researcher who has written:

Project Authority

> One major problem has been cited consistently in studies made of the project [matrix] organization: while the functional managers have line or direct authority over their subordinates, the project managers must work through the respective functional managers, who supply the team personnel, in running their projects. The project managers have an "authority-gap" because they do not possess authority to reward or promote their personnel. They lack complete authority over the team and thus possess what is called "project authority." Because their responsibility outweighs their authority, the project managers must find ways of increasing their authority and thus minimizing their "authority-gap."[7]

Project authority defined.

This lack of complete authority means that the project manager cannot rely exclusively upon conventional line authority. Instead, he or she must work with the functional managers, convincing them that they should support the project by giving him or her the assistance needed to finish the undertaking within the assigned time, cost, and quality parameters. This calls for a horizontal relationship in which one manager coordinates his or her activities with another. Legal authority such

---

[7]Richard M. Hodgetts, "Leadership Techniques in the Project Organization," *Academy of Management Journal*, June 1968, p. 211.

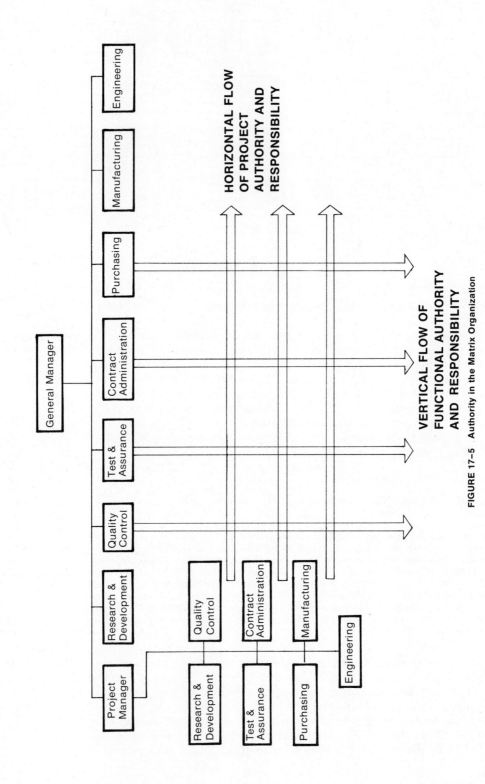

FIGURE 17-5   Authority in the Matrix Organization

as the hierarchical flow, position descriptions, and policy documents are of little value to most project managers. Instead, they must rely upon "reality" authority such as negotiation with their peers, the building of alliances with the functional managers, and the effective use of the informal organization. (See Table 17–1, which compares the functional and project organizations in detail.)

In investigating leadership techniques used by project managers to supplement their project authority and overcome their "authority-gap," the author discovered a general pattern. All project managers in the study indicated that personality and persuasive ability were important. In addition, some of them relied upon negotiation, competence, and reciprocal favors. The use of these approaches illustrates the importance that project managers assign to reality authority.

Of course, each project manager's need for these techniques is going to vary. On those projects where he or she is given little formal authority, the horizontal relationships will be of great importance. Conversely, in those cases where a great deal of authority has been delegated to the manager, the structure is less a matrix organization and more a pure project organization. Research shows that smaller projects (those with less dollar size) tend to be more common than do larger ones, and their project managers tend to have less formal authority than do those who are overseeing larger undertakings.[8] This means that they have to rely more on a human relations than on a formal authority approach. For example, in 41 of the firms surveyed, the author found that there was a continuum ranging from small project organizations to large ones. As one progresses across the continuum, project authority declines in importance and formal authority replaces it. Informal leadership techniques such as negotiation, personality, persuasive ability, competence, and reciprocal favors are not as useful to the manager of a large project as they are to the manager of a small one. One project manager, involved in a multibillion dollar undertaking, explained this phenomenon in the following way:

> . . . it would appear to be vital . . . that the organizational environment, into which the project manager is placed, be such that he need not depend entirely on negotiating ability, a dynamic personality, etc., to perform his most important job. For this reason the organization of a project, in a manner to give the project manager the control he needs over the area of budgeting, planning, and scheduling becomes a basic consideration. The organization must be so designed that the project manager indeed does control the people assigned to the project, in the sense they are responsible to him. Thus, the organization gives the project manager his authority so he can divide more of his time to obtaining the schedule, cost, and technical performance goals of the project.[9]

Thus the project manager's challenge is often related to the amount of delegated formal authority.

Although the manager of a matrix organization faces many challenges, there are also numerous advantages to employing such a structure. Cleland and King identify these as being:

Advantages of Matrix Organizations

1. The project is emphasized by designating one individual as the focal point for all matters pertaining to it.
2. Utilization of manpower can be flexible because a reservoir of specialists is maintained in functional organizations.
3. Specialized knowledge is available to all programs on an equal basis; knowledge and experience can be transferred from one project to another.

---

[8]*Ibid.*, pp. 211–219.
[9]*Ibid.*, p. 218.

TABLE 17–1 Comparison of the Functional and the Project Viewpoints

Phenomena	Project Viewpoint	Functional Viewpoint
Line-staff organizational dichotomy	Vestiges of the hierarchical model remain, but line functions are placed in a support position. A web of authority and responsibility relationships exists.	Line functions have direct responsibility for accomplishing the objectives: line commands, staff advises.
Scalar principle	Elements of the vertical chain exist, but prime emphasis is placed on horizontal and diagonal work flow. Important business is conducted as the legitimacy of the task requires.	The chain of authority relationships is from superior to subordinate throughout the organization. Central, crucial, and important business is conducted up and down the vertical hierarchy.
Superior-subordinate relationship	Peer to peer, manager to technical expert, associate to associate relationships are used to conduct much of the salient business.	This is the most important relationship; if kept healthy, success will follow. All important business is conducted through a pyramiding structure of superiors-subordinates.
Organizational objectives	Management of a project becomes a joint venture of many relatively independent organizations. Thus, the objective becomes multilateral.	Organizational objectives are sought by the parent unit (an assembly of suborganizations) working within its environment. The objective is unilateral.
Unity of direction	The project manager manages across functional and organizational lines to accomplish a common interorganizational objective.	The general manager acts as the head for a group of activities having the same plan.
Parity of authority and responsibility	Considerable opportunity exists for the project manager's responsibility to exceed his or her authority. Support people are often responsible to other managers (functional) for pay, performance reports, promotions, and so forth.	Consistent with functional management, the integrity of the superior-subordinate relationship is maintained through functional authority and advisory staff services.
Time duration	The project (and hence the organization) is finite in duration.	Tends to perpetuate itself to provide continuing facilitative support

Source: David I. Cleland, "Understanding Project Authority," *Business Horizons,* Spring 1966, p. 66. Copyright, 1966, by the Foundation for the School of Business at Indiana University. Reprinted by permission.

4. Project people have a functional home when they are no longer needed on a given project.

5. Responsiveness to project needs and customer desires is generally faster because lines of communication are established and decision points are *centralized*.

6. Management consistency between projects can be maintained through the deliberate conflict operating in the project-functional environment.

7. A better balance between time, cost and performance can be obtained through the built-in checks and balances (the deliberate conflict) and the continuous negotiations carried on between the project and the functional organizations. [10]

Benefits associated with using a matrix structure.

Both the matrix and project organizations represent modern structures for effective organizing. Another such design that is being employed by more and more firms is the free-form or organic organization structure.

FREE-FORM ORGANIZATIONS

The *free-form organization structure* has proved very useful in large-scale organizations, which suffer most severely from the negative effects of bureaucratization. In essence, this structure can take any form, but the objective is always the same: the design must assist the executive in managing change. For this reason, firms using a free-form structure tend to play down the organizational hierarchy with its emphasis on departmentalization and job descriptions. Instead, all attempts are made to free the workers from petty controls. In fact, some individuals have even suggested doing away with the traditional worker-boss relationship.

Free-form structure discourages petty controls.

With rigid bureaucratic rules discarded, the manager is given the freedom he or she needs to get the job done. Many times the only controls top management employs are those related to profits or the allocation of scarce resources. In turn, it is common to find managers in these free-form organizations handling their subordinates in the same way. Reliance on consensus plays a major role and two-way communication is encouraged. The organization operates more as a team, as opposed to a department with a structured superior-subordinate relationship. Many of the theories of McGregor, Likert, and Argyris are put into practice.

Synergism and Strategic Planning

Another common characteristic of free-form structures is the emphasis on getting all departments, units, and subsidiaries to work together. Although some organizational forms such as the holding company will have many separate, unrelated, semiautonomous firms operating under one banner, free-form companies tend to have fewer such holdings, and they try to blend them in harmonious fashion. As a result of this cooperative action, or synergism, the total effect is greater than the sum of the individual parts working independently. This is accomplished to a great degree at the top level of the organization.

Cooperative action is attained via strategic planning.

The central management will draw up a strategic plan designed to obtain the greatest synergistic effect from its units. Resources are then allocated on the basis of this potential synergism. Although the units are encouraged to plan, the final decision on all strategic plans is made by top management. In this way, the master plan for each division can be revised in light of *overall* enterprise commitments and objectives.

The main synergistic ingredient is centralized control with decentralized operation. There is also strong emphasis on organizing along

[10]Cleland and King, *op. cit.*, pp. 251–252.

the lines of profit centers. In addition, managers are urged to take risks and operate their unit more from a human-behavior standpoint than ever before. Perhaps this the reason why firms using free-form structures tend to stress the need for young, dynamic managers unshackled by Theory X assumptions. It also accounts for why free-form organizations are most widely used by firms whose operations are "highly adaptive to products or services on the frontier of public use (e.g., air pollution devices) and those meeting an essential and high-demand industrial, consumer, or military need (e.g., electronic devices, lenses and frames, space-age hardware)."[11] Still another characteristic of these structures is their use of computerized performance evaluations, which determine if a division or department is contributing to overall profitability. If not, it is likely that the unit will be pruned from the organization.

Emphasis is given to decentralized operation with centralized control.

Free-Form Organizations in Action

Polaroid uses sun-satellite systems.

Numerous firms have employed free-form structures. One of these is the Polaroid Corporation, which uses it within the formal organizational pattern. Company managers have dubbed it a "sun-satellite system:"

> Every individual in the overall structure . . . plays two roles. On the primary job assigned to him, he is literally the sun of his own solar system. He is the expert. He is the boss. He is *it*. In this role, he is surrounded by satellites. These satellites serve him. They feed him ideas, back him up, listen to him when he needs listening to, do chores and perform feats for him.[12]

Polaroid's management contends that there are a number of advantages to this free-form structure. First, the individual is secure as a "sun" in his or her own system. The person, therefore, feels no risk in freely helping out others. Second, in handling new or difficult tasks, it is possible to form task groups quickly. Naturally, the structure requires rapid communication and calls for a considerable degree of self-discipline on the part of all. However, these are, as indicated earlier, prerequisites for the effective use of any free-form structure.

IMC employs "cross-hatching."

Another company using this structure is the International Minerals & Chemical Corporation (IMC), which has done pioneering work in the industrial marketing of chemicals, fertilizers, and food additives. In the mid-sixties, IMC established a new function — organization planning — and brought in a former consultant to direct the activity. A specialist in free-form management, his job became one of suggesting change. Soon thereafter the firm started using a concept called "cross-hatching." Teams literally flowed in and out of the organizational structure in much the same way as Polaroid's sun satellites were superimposed on the formal structure. Managers began talking more and more in terms of teamwork. In reference to the new structure, the director of organization planning pointed out that the unity of command concept was inaccurate and that "a man has as many bosses as there are demands upon him, as in life."[13] In short, the structure was designed to fit the job and not vice versa.

A third firm that has turned to the free-form structure is the Insurance Company of North America (INA). In an industry that had

---

[11]John H. Pascucci, "The Emergence of Free-form Management," *Personnel Administration*, September–October 1968, pp. 37–38.

[12]Jack B. Weiner, "The New Art of Free-Form Management," *Dun's Review and Modern Industry*, December 1964, p. 32.

[13]*Ibid.*, p. 54.

seen companies increase their fields of specialization from fire to property, casuality, and life insurance, structures mushroomed haphazardly. Corporations consisted of many small companies with no overall direction. It was commonplace to find managerial duplication, organizational overlap, and inefficiency throughout the structure. INA faced a similar situation. Underwriting was fragmented by the major line of insurance. Field service and production activities serving primary customers contained areas of overlapping activities. Leadership was divided. Policy holder services were handled by separate management so that functions such as audit, inspection, and claims were all going their separate ways. To rectify the situation, INA reorganized according to a free-form structure. The old authoritarian concept of management based on strict obedience was scrapped in order to tap the full potential of each individual. The result, in the president's own words, was that, "Each member of management joins with all the others in an united effort to achieve the objectives sought. And each member of management reaches up to share with his superior or superiors their responsibilities and their objectives."[14]

INA reorganized, using a free-form structure.

In addition to Polaroid, IMC, and INA, other organizations that employ free-form structures include IBM, Litton Industries, American Standard, Xerox, and Textron. Textron, for example, following the free-form concept of evaluating performance and terminating unprofitable units, has given up its textiles mills while adding metal products, precision machines, and other consumer and industrial products to its manufacturing lines. Free-form structures, however, are not without their drawbacks or challenges.

The major challenge of the free-form structure is that it discards or de-emphasizes management principles such as unity of command and the scalar chain. In their place is a form of situational management in which individuals are encouraged to interact and work with other members of the organization. Operating within the profit-center concept, they are encouraged to carry out their strategic plans in an environment designed to deal with change. Although new technology may alter the nature of their work, the organizational structure is able to take advantage of these changes. For the dynamic, mature manager the new environment is a welcome relief; for the average manager it is a nightmare. Tension, anxiety, and fear may result. The lack of rigidity disrupts the average individual's orientation, and many managers are unable to adapt to the new system.

The Challenges of Free-Form Structures

Management principles are de-emphasized.

Second, free-form structures are designed to incorporate change. This is why they are found in firms operating in highly technical industries. All organizations, however, do not operate in this kind of environment. Thus, the structure can have limited value for some firms.

Structures help manage change.

Third, free-form structures encourage excellence. The managers are on their own and allowed to use the approach they feel works best in attaining the objective:

Free-form design encourages excellence.

But if free-form management can bestow such benefits, why don't more companies adopt it? Perhaps the major reason is that time-worn management methods and structures are also protective devices for assigning responsibility for failure. The point is sharply emphasized by Robert H. Schaffer:. . . . "The easiest place to camouflage failures in obtaining goals," insists Schaffer, "is the well-fractioned organization where, as any vet-

---

[14]*Ibid.,* p. 56.

eran can testify, stalled performance almost always is attributable to 'the system,' to other departments or to forces that lie outside the control of any department."[15]

The use of free-form structures appears to be increasing for various reasons. First, managers are demanding more flexible organizations to meet the changes and challenges of the eighties. Second, managers are more competent than ever before, so they can effectively utilize these new organizational structures. Third, new technological developments are putting pressure on companies to modernize their organizational designs. Fourth, bureaucratic super-structures will no longer do the job; too much dependence on organization charts and job descriptions merely shunts the growth of the enterprise. For many, free-form structures will prove to be the answer.

CONTINGENCY ORGANIZATION DESIGN

The right organization structure will depend on the situation.

The key word currently characterizing organization design is *contingency*. Earlier, Fiedler's research was examined and it was noted that the *right* leadership style will depend on the situation. The same is true of organization structure. Today, the development of structures in which there is minimum attention given to the formal division of duties is resulting in increasingly flexible designs. Mechanistic structures are, in many cases, being replaced by organic ones. Of course, each company will have to evaluate its own situation, but, as Lorsch and Lawrence note, there does seem to be a distinct trend toward contingency organization design:

> During the past few years there has been evident a new trend in the study of organizational phenomena. Underlying this new approach is the idea that the internal functioning of organizations must be consistent with the demands of the organization task, technology, or external environment, and the needs of its members if the organization is to be effective. Rather than searching for the panacea of the one best way to organize under all conditions, investigators have more and more tended to examine the functioning of organizations in relation to the needs of their particular members and the external pressures facing them. Basically, this approach seems to be leading to the development of a "contingency" theory of organization with the appropriate internal states and processes of the organization contingent upon external requirements and member needs.[16]

Glueck, after conducting a review of the literature, has offered the following guidelines for contingency organization design:

1. When low cost and efficiency are the keys to successful goal achievement, the effective organization should use functional departmentalization.
2. When the environment is complex and the critical variable is exact meshing of output times, matrix structuring is effective.
3. If it is large and operates in a stable technological and market environment, an enterprise will tend to formalize its organization structure.
4. The greater the intensity of competition, the greater the degree of decentralization.
5. The greater the volatility of the environment, the more decentralized and flexible the organization is likely to be.
6. Organizations that implement the organizational style appropriate to their strategy will be more effective than those that use an inappropriate style.[17]

Influencing Forces

Shetty and Carlisle echo these sentiments about the need for contingency design, noting that the best organization structure will vary according to situation. In essence, it is going to be a function of forces

---

[15]*Ibid.*

[16]Jay W. Lorsch and Paul R. Lawrence, *Studies in Organization Design* (Homewood, Ill: Richard D. Irwin and The Dorsey Press, 1970), p. 1.

[17]William F. Glueck, *Management*, (Hinsdale, Illinois: Dryden Press, 1977), Chapters 15 and 16. For more on this topic see: John Child, "What Determines Organization: The Universals vs. the It-All-Depends," *Organizational Dynamics*, Summer 1974, pp. 2–18.

in the managers, the subordinates, the task, and the environment.[18] *Forces in the managers* are readily evident. If a superior feels that the people are basically lazy, he or she will design a structure that reflects these views and will refuse to delegate much authority. Conversely, if the person is a Theory Y manager, he or she will be more prone to use a design that facilitates decentralization and delegation of authority. *Forces in the subordinates* are motives such as a desire for autonomy and an opportunity to participate in decision making. If these factors are present, they will have an impact on the structure. *Forces in the task* often reflect themselves in technology. "Technology may determine the extent to which the job may be programmed, that is, employee behaviors may be precisely specified. The kind of organization required in a low task structure is not the same as that required in a high task structure."[19] *Forces in the environment* include the availability of resources, nature of the competition, predictability of demand, and the type of products or services being provided by the company.

These four interacting factors influence the type of organizational design that will evolve, as seen in Figure 17–6. By employing this framework, a company can identify the conditions enhancing or impeding a particular structure. Sometimes it needs a more flexible design, other times a more structured one:

> The organization appropriate in one market-technology environment may be irrelevant or even dysfunctional in another environment. A firm producing a standardized product sold in a stable market may require a pattern of organization altogether different from a company manufacturing a highly technical product for a more dynamic market. There is no one pattern of organization style that is universally appropriate.[20]

In essence, then, management must look for the right "fit" among the personnel, the organizational characteristics, and the task requirement. Morse and Lorsch illustrated this when they made an analysis of four business firms, two highly effective and two less effective. One of the highly effective firms was an Akron container manufacturing plant in which formal relationships were highly structured, rules were specific and comprehensive, and the time orientation was short-term. The other was a Stockton research lab where formal relations were less well defined, rules were minimal and flexible, and the time orientation was

Forces in the managers, subordinates, task, and environment will all help determine the best structure.

A Matter of "Fit"

[18]Y. K. Shetty and Howard M. Carlisle, "A Contingency Model of Organization Design," *California Management Review*, Fall 1972, pp. 38–45.
[19]*Ibid.*, p. 42.
[20]*Ibid.*, p. 44.

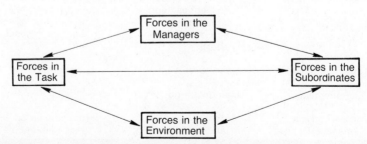

FIGURE 17–6 Forces Affecting Organization Structure (Adapted from Y. K. Shetty and Howard M. Carlisle, "A Contingency Model of Organization Design," *California Management Review*, Fall 1972, p. 44.)

long-term (see Table 17–2). Both firms, despite these differences, were successful because their structures brought the task and the people together in the right way. Conversely, in the two less effective plants they studied, the researchers found that the formal and informal organizational characteristics did not fit the task requirements as well as in their successful counterparts. It is thus important that there be a correct task-organization-people fit:

> In arguing for an approach which emphasizes the fit among task, organization, and people, we are putting to rest the question of which organizational approach — the classical or the participative — is best. In its place we are raising a new question: What organizational approach is most appropriate given the task and the people involved?
>
> For many enterprises, given the new needs of younger employees for more autonomy, and the rapid rates of social and technological change, it may well be that the more participative approach is the most appropriate. But there will still be many situations in which the more controlled and formalized organization is desirable. Such an organization need not be coercive or punitive. If it makes sense to the individuals involved, given their needs and their jobs, they will find it rewarding and motivating.[21]

---

[21]John J. Morse and Jay W. Lorsch, "Beyond Theory Y," *Harvard Business Review,* May–June 1970, p. 68.

TABLE 17–2   Differences in "Climate" Characteristics in High-Performing Organizations

Characteristics	Akron	Stockton
1. Structural orientation	Perceptions of tightly controlled behavior and a high degree of structure	Perceptions of a low degree of structure
2. Distribution of influence	Perceptions of low total influence, concentrated at upper levels in the organization	Perceptions of high total influence, more evenly spread out among all levels
3. Character of superior-subordinate relations	Low freedom vis-à-vis superiors to choose and handle jobs, directive type of supervision	High freedom vis-à-vis superiors to choose and handle projects, participatory type of supervision
4. Character of colleague relations	Perceptions of many similarities among colleagues, high degree of coordination of colleague effort	Perceptions of many differences among colleagues, relatively low degree of coordination of colleague effort
5. Time orientation	Short-term	Long-term
6. Goal orientation	Manufacturing	Scientific
7. Top executive's "managerial style"	More concerned with task than people	More concerned with task than people

Source: John J. Morse and Jay W. Lorsch, "Beyond Theory Y." *Harvard Business Review,* May–June 1970, p. 66. Reprinted with permission.

SUMMARY

In this chapter it was noted that the use of bureaucratic structures is beginning to decline. One reason is that the inherent assumptions upon which these designs are based are unrealistic. The organization cannot function as a highly closed system, and mechanical rules and regulations have limited value in motivating and leading the modern worker.

In overcoming these bureaucratic deficiencies, many firms are turning to adaptive organization structures. These new designs are based on a number of assumptions. One is that the organization is an open system operating in a dynamic environment. A second is that Theory Y assumptions represent the modern employee more accurately than do Theory X assumptions. Modern organization structures employ these ideas in interrelating the personnel, the task, and the environment. In this chapter a number of these modern designs have been examined.

Project organization was discussed first. It was noted that this form entails "the gathering of the best available talent to accomplish a specific and complex undertaking within time, cost and/or quality parameters, followed by the disbanding of the team upon completion of the undertaking." Project organization has been widely employed in numerous and diverse ways, from building dams and weapon systems to conducting research and development and designing bank credit-card systems. The major advantage of this organizational form is that it allows the project manager and his or her team to concentrate their attention on one specific undertaking.

The matrix structure is a hybrid form of organization, containing characteristics of both the project and functional structures. In a matrix design, personnel are only loaned to the project manager. There is thus a dual responsibility on the part of team members— to the line manager who loaned them to the project and to the project manager for whom they are working. The result is a vertical and horizontal flow of authority. Since the project manager has only "project" authority, he or she must rely on human relations techniques such as negotiation, personality, persuasive ability, competence, and reciprocal favors.

Another modern organization design is the free-form or organic structure. This design can take any shape, but it always has the characteristics of playing down rigid bureaucratic rules and emphasizing self-regulation. A number of conglomerates have adopted this organization form, including Polaroid, International Minerals & Chemical Corporation, Insurance Company of North America, IBM, Litton Industries, American Standard, Xerox, and Textron. Perhaps the greatest advantage of a free-form structure is its value to the manager in coping with change.

What kind of structure is best? There is no right answer to this question; it depends on the situation. This is why the area of contingency organization design is currently so important. Some firms need a mechanistic structure, others work better with an organic one. The answer will depend on the forces in the managers, the subordinates, the task, and the environment.

This chapter has examined how organizations are redesigning their structures in order to adapt to their environments more effectively. However, there is one facet of this environment we have not yet examined, namely that of social responsibility. For over a decade, business has been aware of the ever-growing public demand that it become more socially responsible. The result has been a re-evaluation, on the part of many firms, of the role they should play in the society at large. This will be the topic of Chapter 18.

REVIEW AND STUDY QUESTIONS

1. What are the characteristics of an ideal bureaucracy?

2. Why is the bureaucratic form of organization declining today?

3. What is a project organization?

4. When can a project organization be used effectively? Explain.

5. A matrix structure is a hybrid form of organization, containing characteristics of both project and functional structures. Explain this statement.

6. What is "project" authority?

7. How is the free-form organization useful to large-scale organizations?

8. How do free-form organizations employ synergy in their strategic planning?

9. What is meant by "contingency organization design"?

10. What are some contingency organization design guidelines? Explain.

11. Shetty and Carlisle have noted that the best organization structure is going to be a function of four forces. Identify and explain all four.

12. What do Morse and Lorsch mean by the need for a task-organization-people fit? Explain.

SELECTED REFERENCES

Butler, A. G., Jr. "Project Management: A Study in Organizational Conflict." *Academy of Management Journal,* March 1973, pp. 84–101.

Child, J. "Predicting and Understanding Organization Structure." *Administrative Science Quarterly,* June 1973, pp. 168–185.

Cleland, D. I. "Understanding Project Authority." *Business Horizons,* Spring, 1967, pp. 63–70.

Cleland, D. I., and W. R. King. *Systems Analysis and Project Management,* 2nd Edition. New York: McGraw-Hill Book Company, 1975.

Hodgetts, R. M. "Leadership Techniques in the Project Organization." *Academy of Management Journal,* June 1968, pp. 211–219.

Kast, F. E., and J. E. Rosenzweig. *Contingency Views of Organization and Management.* Chicago: Science Research Associates, Inc. 1973.

Kast, F. E., and J. E. Rosenzweig. *Organization and Management: A Systems Approach,* 2nd edition. New York: McGraw-Hill Book Company, 1974, Chapter 9.

Likert, R. *The Human Organization.* New York: McGraw-Hill Book Company, 1967.

Morse, J. J., and J. W. Lorsch. "Beyond Theory Y." *Harvard Business Review,* May–June 1970, pp. 61–68.

Shetty, Y. K., and H. M. Carlisle. "A Contingency Model of Organization Design." *California Management Review,* Fall 1972, pp. 38–45.

Toren, N. "Bureaucracy and Professional Professionalism: A Reconsideration of Weber's Thesis." *Academy of Management Review,* July 1976, pp. 36–46.

CASE: NEW TIMES, NEW STRUCTURES

Bureaucratic structures employ calculable rules and operate with little, if any, regard for people. Although there is precision and speed in much of what they do, there is also strict subordination of the individual interest to that of the organization. In summarizing some of the current criticisms of bureaucracies, Warren Bennis has compiled the following list of deficiencies:

1. **Bureaucracy does not adequately allow for personal growth and the development of mature personalities.**
2. **It develops conformity and "group think."**
3. **It does not take into account the "informal organization" and the emergent and unanticipated problems.**
4. **Its systems of control and authority are hopelessly outdated.**
5. **It has no adequate juridical process.**
6. **It does not possess adequate means for resolving differences and conflicts between ranks, and most particularly, between functional groups.**
7. **Communication (and innovative ideas) are thwarted or distorted due to hierarchical divisions.**
8. **The full human resources of bureaucracy are not being utilized due to mistrust, fear of reprisals, etc.**
9. **It cannot assimilate the influx of new technology or scientists entering the organization.**
10. **It modifies personality structure so that people become and reflect the dull, gray, conditioned "organization man."**[22]

These problems are reason enough for business firms to begin thinking about designing more humanistic structures. A further impetus is being provided by our changing environment. Kast and Rosenzweig, for example, have listed the following changes as some that will be affecting organizations during the current decade:

1. **Organizations will be operating in a continually changing environment.**
2. **The size and complexity of organizations is going to increase.**
3. **Organizations are going to have major problems in gathering and using knowledge; as a result, intellectual activities are going to be heavily stressed.**
4. **Greater emphasis is going to be placed on suggestion and persuasion and less on coercion and the use of authoritarian power.**
5. **Participants at all levels of the organization are going to have influence on company matters, not just the people at the top.**
6. **New methods for attaining interorganizational coordination will be developed to deal with problem interfaces with other organizations.**
7. **Computerized information decision systems will have an increasing impact on organizations.**
8. **The number and influence of scientists and professionals in the organization will increase.**
9. **There will be a decline in the number of independent professionals in the organization and an increase in the number of salaried professionals.**
10. **The goals of complex organizations will expand and emphasis will be given to satisficing a number of them rather than maximizing any one in particular.**[23]

As a result, in many firms there will be a movement away from the mechanistic-bureaucratic structure and toward a flexible organic system.

---

[22]Warren Bennis, "Beyond Bureaucracy," *Trans-Action,* July–August 1965, p. 32.
[23]Adapted from Fremont E. Kast and James E. Rosenzweig, *Organization and Management: A Systems Approach,* 2nd edition (New York: McGraw-Hill Book Company, 1974), pp. 617–618.

Questions

1. Do you think that organizations are beginning to move toward more flexible-organic systems? Explain.

2. In addition to the reasons cited in the case, why else might business firms be abandoning their old bureaucratic structures?

3. In what industries would you expect to find organic structures widely used? In what industries would you expect to find firms staying with a basically mechanistic-bureaucratic structure? Explain.

CASE: THE GLORIFIED COORDINATOR

Bill Lesikar, a graduate student at State University, was writing a paper on modern organization structures. As part of his research he interviewed project, matrix, and free-form organization managers in 10 major corporations throughout the city. One of the managers worked in a consumer products firm. He explained his job as follows:

I'm responsible for developing a consumer product. In order to get the job done, I've had people assigned to me from the various functional departments: research, design, manufacturing, and test. Of course, these people will stay within their own departments, but when I need them, they will work for me.

Most of last week was spent figuring out exactly when I'd need these people. I'm going to need the research and design personnel starting next week. Then, when they're finished with the project, I'll have it manufactured and tested. This will come in about two months. This reason I know the schedule so well is that this week I have to go around to the functional managers and ask them to assign people to me for the project. They'll want to see the time schedule and then they'll figure out whom they can let me have. Of course, these people will continue to report to their functional boss, but they'll be working on my project. Nevertheless, I suppose you'd be right if you called me a glorified project coordinator or expediter. After all, my only goal is to get everyone together and make sure the product is manufactured on time. Then it will be tested in various sections of the country and if it catches on, the company will set up a new product department to handle it. Meanwhile, I'll go on to another project.

Questions

1. What kind of authority does the project manager have over the project personnel in this case?

2. Is this a project, matrix, or free-form organization? Give your reasoning.

CASE: FLY ME TO THE MOON

In his second State of the Union address to the Congress in May 1961, President Kennedy stated, "I believe that this nation should commit itself to achieving the goal, before this decade is out, of landing a man on the moon and returning him safely to earth." The race to the moon was on!

The United States undertook three distinct projects: Mercury, Gemini, and Apollo. Mercury's primary objectives included investigating man's capabilities in the space environment and developing manned space flight technology. Gemini's primary goals entailed subjecting two men and supporting equipment to long duration flights, effecting rendezvous and docking maneuvers with other orbiting vehicles, and perfecting methods of re-entry and landing. Apollo's primary goals, quite simply, were to put two men on the moon, allow them to carry out limited exploration, and then return them safely to earth.

To achieve Apollo's goals, the United States needed a spacecraft to get the astronauts into and out of the moon's orbit and a lunar excursion module (LEM) to take them down to the moon's surface and return them to the spacecraft. In order to build these two pieces of equipment, the National Aeronautics and Space Administration (NASA) solicited contracts. The award for the spacecraft was given to North American Aviation while Grumman Aircraft received the LEM contract. In addition, NASA set up a project organization, known as the Apollo Spacecraft Program Office (ASPO), to monitor the contractors and see that the hardware was built on time and within cost and quality parameters. As the contractors built the spacecraft and the LEM, ASPO personnel would check to see that everything was going according to schedule. If there was a problem, for example, and the contractor wanted to change the design of the hardware, it had to be cleared through ASPO. In short, the Apollo program people were charged with seeing that the contractor did the job correctly. Although ASPO headquarters were located in Houston, the personnel were continually flying out to see the contractors and having reports sent to them so they could ascertain the progress that was being made.

Questions

1. What kind of authority did the ASPO have over the contractors? Explain.

2. Is the ASPO a project, matrix, or free-form organization? Give your reasoning.

CASE: A TEAM APPROACH[24]

There are many possible approaches to organizing a work force. One of these, currently being explored by General Electric, is that of worker teams. *Business Week* described the process as follows:

The idea is to identify a task and then assign a group of 5 to 15 people to handle it. The key is to give the group as much responsibility as possible. [Herbert] Meyer [a GE personnel research executive] cites a group of

---

[24]The data in this case can be found in "Management Itself Holds the Key," *Business Week*, September 9, 1972, pp. 143, 146.

welders in a fabricating plant where the team approach was tried. The welders were given responsibility for scheduling and planning their work load. They determined, for example, how much time it would take to meet specifications on any items requiring special welding techniques, a job formerly done by a methods-and-standards engineer.

The 12 welders were experienced enough to decide which one of them would do a specific job and the time it would take, Meyer says. "The responsibility meant the men had a bigger say in how they did their jobs, and we found that they all became more committed to work as team members," says Meyer. Methods engineers are now freed to work on new product models while the welders decide how the daily work is going to be done. The efficiency and quality of work, Meyer adds, has improved significantly, because the team has a real stake in the outcome.

Questions

1. How would you describe this type of organization structure? Explain.

2. What are the critical factors that account for its success? Explain.

CHAPTER EIGHTEEN

SOCIAL RESPONSIBILITY: A CONTINUING CHALLENGE

Consideration of social responsibility has been a continuing challenge to business in the past decade. Specifically, firms are learning that they must be aware of, and responsive to, three social issues: equal opportunity, ecology, and consumerism. The goal of this chapter is to examine each of these issues by studying what they are and the types of responses business is making toward them.

When you have finished reading this chapter you should be able to:

1. Define what is meant by the doctrine of enlightened self-interest.
2. Describe the major provisions of the Equal Pay Act of 1963 and the Civil Rights Act of 1964.
3. Relate how business is helping ensure equal opportunity for the hard-core unemployed and minority capitalists.
4. Explain the current status of women in business and what is being done to ensure equal opportunity for them.
5. Describe the major ecological challenges facing business and what is being done about them, with primary consideration given to air pollution, water pollution, and noise pollution.
6. Outline some of the major provisions of the Environmental Policy Act of 1969 and the Air Quality Standards Act of 1970.
7. Describe what consumerism is all about and how business firms are attempting to meet the problems associated with product safety.
8. Discuss whether social responsibility is a fad or an enduring challenge for business.

By the 1960s, America was the most affluent nation the world had ever known. With this affluence, however, came a social awakening. People started questioning conditions in America and began demanding corrective action in areas such as equal opportunity, ecology, and consumerism. Feeling that the business community had the resources and the know-how to handle these problems, and convinced that many companies had helped contribute to them, the public insisted that business become involved in social issues.

Such action was not in direct accord with many of business' objectives, i.e., profit, survival, and growth. However, it was related by way of the doctrine of *enlightened self-interest*, which holds that by helping out the community, business is actually serving its own long-run interests. For example, since 1935, when the Internal Revenue Code permitted corporations to deduct up to 5 per cent of pretax income for charitable contributions, business firms have been extremely active in their support of various charities. Of course, not everyone has agreed with this action. Some stockholders have brought suits against their companies, contending that the contributions are in no way related to the running of the business. The courts, however, have consistently ruled for the firms, holding that such donations do indeed serve the interest of the company even though they provide no direct benefits. In addition, business can contribute to higher education. This issue was settled in 1953 by the New Jersey Superior Court when it ruled that a manufacturing firm could donate funds to Princeton University. The court held that giving financial support was not only a right but a duty, because by helping society the company was actually helping itself. In other words:

By helping society, business serves its own long-run interests.

> By the same logic, expenditures to help improve community educational, health, and cultural facilities can be justified by the corporation's interest in attracting the skilled people it needs who would not move into a substandard community. Similarly, a corporation whose operations must inevitably take place in urban areas may well be justified in investing in the rehabilitation of ghetto housing and contributing to the improvement of ghetto educational, recreational, and other facilities. . . .
>
> Indeed, the corporate interest broadly defined by management can support involvement in helping to solve virtually any social problem, because people who have a good environment, education, and opportunity make better employees, customers and neighbors for business than those who are poor, ignorant, and oppressed.[1]

The doctrine of enlightened self-interest extends further than merely pointing out the benefits of involvement. It is also based on the proposition that failure to assume social responsibility can jeopardize the organization's welfare. If business does not voluntarily do its share, the government will pass legislation and force it to become involved.

Statistics show that since the mid-1960's business has not only been aware of this social awakening in America but has also responded with positive action. What has accounted for this? Some say it has been newly enacted legislation. Others contend that the business community is merely trying to protect its image. Still others say that business people today are more socially responsible than their predecessors. There is undoubtedly truth in all these statements. Yet, whatever the specific reason, many businesses have been developing programs to cope with the three most important social issues of the day: equal opportunity, ecology, and consumerism.[2] The remainder of the chapter will be devoted to an examination of these three areas.

EQUAL OPPORTUNITY

There are a number of important areas of equal opportunity currently providing a major challenge to business. In particular, these are legislation, hiring of the hard-core unemployed, minority capitalism, and discrimination against females.

Legislation

One of the main reasons for business' attention to the area of equal opportunity has been legislation. The two most important laws enacted thus far have been the Equal Pay Act of 1963 and the Civil Rights Act of 1964.

The *Equal Pay Act* was signed on June 10, 1963. Its purpose is to correct "the existence in industries engaged in commerce, or in the production of goods for commerce, of wage differentials based on sex."[3] Specifically, the act forbids "discrimination on the basis of sex for doing equal work on jobs requiring equal skill, effort and responsibility which are performed under similar working conditions."[4]

---

[1] *Social Responsibilities of Business Corporations*, A Statement on National Policy by the Research and Policy Committee of the Committee for Economic Development, June 1971, pp. 27–28.

[2] Fred Luthans and Richard M. Hodgetts, *Social Issues in Business*, 2nd edition (New York: The Macmillan Company, 1976).

[3] *Information on the Equal Pay Act of 1963*, pamphlet distributed by the Department of Labor, p. 1.

[4] *Ibid*, p. 2.

The *Civil Rights Act* was signed on July 2, 1964. Of its eleven major sections, Title VII is most important to business because it forbids discrimination on the basis of race, color, religion, sex, or national origin. In addition, the Act established an Equal Employment Opportunity Commission (EEOC) composed of five members appointed by the President and approved by the Senate. Their job is to investigate complaints, seek to end violations through conciliation, and ask the Attorney General to bring suit if such conciliation is unsuccessful.

The law forbids discrimination in employment.

These laws have been very helpful in providing equal employment, basically because people have not hesitated to use them. For example, in the first 18 months of its existence, the EEOC received 14,000 complaints. In addition, minority group organizations such as the NAACP and CORE have been relatively active in using them to bring suit against firms for discriminatory practices. Equal employment, however, has proved to be more than a legal issue. Many firms have voluntarily responded to the challenge by eliminating or reducing their barriers for employment, thanks to a business program known as the National Alliance of Businessmen (NAB), which has just recently dropped the "men" in its title.

The NAB was formed in January, 1968 with Henry Ford II as chairman. It immediately established a program called JOBS (Job Opportunities in the Business Sector) and set out to find employment for 100,000 hard-core unemployed men and women by June 1969. Using a "community chest" type of drive, it established quotas for cities around the country and then canvassed each city, calling on business to pledge a specific number of jobs. In particular, it asked companies to review and modify their hiring policies so they could take on large numbers of these needy applicants. By the end of its first year of operation, the NAB had reached its goal and began setting even more challenging objectives. Today the organization reports that it has found jobs for over two million people. Its latest annual goal calls for securing employment for 400,000 more individuals.

Hiring of the Hard-Core Unemployed

Of course, not everything has been easy for the association since its inception. For example, the NAB has found it difficult to convince some companies, especially small ones, to adopt its philosophy of "hire now, train later." These companies feel that they are not sufficiently financed to participate in the program. In addition, many participating firms have found that hard-core employees need special handling. Previously unable to keep a job, many hard-core employees really do not know what "work begins at 8 A.M." means. Some firms have tried to overcome this deficiency by assigning them a "buddy" or veteran employee who makes sure they get to work on time. Furthermore, there is the problem of training the hard-core, which in many cases averages around $3000 per person. The government, through the Department of Labor, has tried to help solve this dilemma by awarding subsidy contracts to firms willing to undertake such training, but most companies have not been interested, preferring to do it themselves when at all possible.

Business has helped hire the hard-core unemployed.

How successful has this voluntary business venture been? Despite the many problems encountered, the NAB has been quite effective:

An overall assessment would have to conclude that the NAB has made good progress and that the large firms in particular have been successful in their hiring and training efforts. The auto firms have found that they have been able to retain 40 to 50 per cent of the hard-core they hire. Bank of America has been able to retain over 60 per cent of the 800 disadvantaged people they have trained over the last three years . . . in recent years over 60 per cent of all new employees at G.M. have come from minority groups. In New York City about half of

Consolidated Edison's new employees are black or Puerto Rican. . . . In total, the NAB has served to stimulate business involvement in problems of poverty and equal rights.[5]

**Minority Cap-
italism**

In addition to hiring the hard-core unemployed, business has been focusing attention on the promotion of minority-owned enterprises. This program has taken two directions: helping set up new businesses and providing assistance to established ones.

In 1970, it was estimated that there were 150,000 minority-owned businesses in the United States, accounting for 1 per cent of all receipts.[6] In order to stimulate more of these enterprises, many firms· have begun providing assistance in obtaining that crucial initial capital. At this stage there is also great emphasis placed on realism. Those who only think they want to start a business are screened out from the rest. The Colorado Economic Development Association (CEDA) does this by putting would-be minority entrepreneurs through a five-week business program that covers accounting, marketing, advertising, taxes, and other related matters. By the end of the program, half of the people have dropped out. The rest usually reformulate their ideas, emerging with a much clearer picture of the type of business they want to establish. With these new ideas and CEDA's help in planning the business and the loan proposal, they are in a better position to approach banks for money. If they are successful in getting this initial capital, CEDA stays with them, providing managerial experience and helping them get off the ground. The results thus far reveal that only 10 per cent of these new businesses default on their loans. The success rests with the initial training and the emphasis on realistic proposals.[7]

*Minority enter-
prise is en-
couraged.*

Other firms have also provided similar assistance. For example, Western Electric helps to sponsor fairs at which minority businesses present their wares and get advice from the company's purchasing agents. General Motors maintains a list of items it is willing to buy from black suppliers. Other companies make it a practice to maintain deposits in black-owned banks.

What will the future hold for minority enterprise development? A G.E. study has drawn the following conclusions about black-owned businesses:

> Despite some very obvious differences, the drive for 'black power' seems likely to follow some historical parallels with the emergence as a social force of other minority groups in an urban environment. On the economic front, the use of cooperatives to protect group interests and the growth of 'black capitalism' are interesting indicators that history may repeat itself, as group identity and cohesion assert themselves, before assimilation into the mainstream of American life.[8]

Perhaps the same general pattern will also emerge among other minorities during the decade. In any event, business is planning an active role in stimulating these enterprises.

**Female Dis-
crimination**

Although they are often overlooked in discussions of equal employment, many women in the work force suffer discrimination. This is particularly true in the areas of salary and management promotions.

---

[5]Luthans and Hodgetts, *op. cit.*, p. 150.
[6]James M. Roche, "Making Free Enterprise Free," a talk delivered at the National Conference on Minority Enterprise, January 22, 1970.
[7]"Aid for Minority Businesses," *Business Week*, May 20, 1972, p. 102.
[8]Ian Wilson, "How Our Values Are Changing." *The Futurist*, February 1970, p. 6.

SALARY INEQUITIES.   Women at all levels of business organizations, according to the latest reports, tend to make less money on the average than do their male counterparts. What accounts for this difference? The answer is often found in the interpretation of the "equal pay for equal work" doctrine of the Equal Pay Act. Many employers have contended that women do not perform equal work, so they cannot receive equal salaries. Working women recently have begun complaining, however, and the U.S. Labor Department has started filing suits. The most important decision came in 1970, when the U.S. Circuit Court upheld a decision against the Wheaton Glass Company of Milville, New Jersey. In its ruling, the court said that the jobs did *not* have to be identical; if they were "substantially equal" the equal pay law applied. This meant that Wheaton had to pay its female inspector-packers over $900,000 in back pay. Since then several firms have also lost equal-pay suits, some of the best known including RCA, American Can, and Pacific Telephone & Telegraph. Despite such legal action, however, salary discrimination against women continues, and it is still premature to predict that such inequities will be rectified in the near future.

Women are not being paid as much as men.

MANAGEMENT PROMOTIONS.   At the managerial level, women face the problems of obtaining both equitable salaries and promotions. Commenting on women in management, one writer painted the following picture:

> It is bright if one considers that the number of women in professional, managerial, technical, and administrative positions has increased over the past decade from 4.4 million in 1965 to 7 million in 1975, according to the Department of Labor. One out of six young women today plans a career in business or a professional field as opposed to the one in 16 of 10 years ago. In the same period, the percentage of accountants who are women rose by 5 per cent (19.2 to 24.6) and the percentage of personnel and labor relations professionals who are women by 12 per cent (30 to 42.6).
>
> At the same time the picture is bleak. Women nationwide are still being paid much less than their male counterparts, the average salary of women administrators being *58 percent less* than that of males in the same category. It must be argued that this is still because most women are in lower- or entry-level jobs, but that only illustrates another discouraging fact — there are still few women at the top.[9]

Additionally, Hennig and Jardim report that in 1977 women made up 39 per cent of the work force; yet of the 471,000 managers whose annual salaries were $25,000 or above, only 11,000 (2.3 per cent) were women.[10]

Why are women having such a difficult time securing promotions? Some of the answers can be found in the myths that exist about women managers, including: (a) women are more emotional and sensitive to the feelings of others, while men are more rational and coolly objective in their relationships with others; (b) women are uncomfortable in a man's world; (c) women work as a hobby or for luxuries and, as a result, lack the ambition, aggressiveness, and dedication necessary to excel in business; and (d) women have higher rates of sickness and absenteeism.[11] In addition, one must consider the fact that most organizations are not prepared to handle this situation. They simply do not know how to identify, train, and develop their best female managers. McCord has suggested that the following seven factors hamper women in most organizations:

Myths about women managers.

[9]Roger Morris, "Women at the Top," *Training and Development Journal*, May 1977, pp. 39–40.

[10]Margaret Hennig and Anne Jardim, *The Managerial Woman*, (New York: Anchor Press/Doubleday, 1977), pp. 64–65.

[11]William E. Reif, John W. Newstrom, and Robert M. Monczka, "Exploding Some Myths about Women Managers," *California Management Review*, Summer, 1975, p. 72.

1. The occupations that offer prestige and power are not open to women.
2. There may be more confusion over the differences between the sexes and lack of understanding over the causes of sex-role stereotypes than there is actual discrimination.
3. Women generally do not receive the same education for business that men do.
4. Most companies know little about the identification and selection of women who are high-need achievers and have long-range career commitments.
5. Most women are hired into specific positions rather than into training programs or positions leading to general management.
6. Progression into higher levels of management is based on continuity of employment.
7. Whether single or married, women in business are hampered by the male-oriented corporate life style.[12]

Businesses hurt themselves by their failure to provide more opportunities for women. Reif and his associates, after conducting a survey designed to examine the managerial differences between women and men, and the ability of women managers to contribute to the achievement of organizational objectives, reported that:

> In conclusion, there is considerable research evidence to support the fact that women managers psychologically are not significantly different from their male counterparts and that they may possess even superior attributes and skills in some areas related to managerial effectiveness. From a social psychological standpoint — that is, how they view themselves as a part of the environment within which they operate — this study has shown that women managers have much in common with men. Differences do exist, but mostly in ways that would serve to *increase* the probability of women functioning well as managers. It is recommended, therefore, that organizations begin treating women as equals, not because of moral obligations or pressures from outside interest groups to improve female-male ratios, but because they would effectively utilize valuable human resources.[13]

In responding to recommendations such as these, some firms are trying to improve the situation, and in most cases the impetus is coming from the top. First, high-level executives are making it clear that women are to be considered for positions of responsibility. Second, recruiting practices are being modified to overcome traditional hiring barriers. Third, training programs are being established for those with supervisory potential but no prior business training. Fourth, there is a concerted effort being made to evaluate and promote both sexes on the same basis, whereas previously women were most frequently advanced on the basis of technical competence and men were often promoted on the basis of peer relations and anticipated long-range development. Of course, only time will tell whether business is *really* going to promote women through management ranks, but it is definitely in the organization's best interest to take advantage of this virtually untapped human resource, and all signs indicate that management intends to do so.

Steps being taken by business.

ECOLOGY

In order to grasp fully the importance of the ecological challenge facing business, the reader should understand what is meant by the word ecology. Webster defines *ecology* as "a branch of science concerned with the interrelationship of organisms and their environments especially as manifested by natural cycles and rhythms, community development and structure, interaction between different kinds of organisms, geographic distributions, and population alterations."[14] The key to understanding ecology rests with the word *interrelationship*. All organisms must relate

The key word is interrelationship.

---

[12]Bird McCord, "Identifying and Developing Women for Management Positions," *Training and Development Journal*, November 1971, p. 2.
[13]Reif *et al., op. cit.*, p. 79.
[14]*Webster's Third New Intercollegiate Dictionary*, volume 1 (Chicago: Encyclopaedia Britannica, 1966) p. 720.

in some way to their environment. If they cannot co-exist with it, change occurs; the environment is altered or the organism dies. When such changes occur in nature's ecological balance, there can be side effects in other areas. As Ehrlich notes:

> If we do something to an ecological system in one place, the whole system is affected. We must learn to look at the whole world and the people in it as a single interlocking system. It's impossible to do something somewhere that has no effect anywhere else.[15]

The entire world can thus be viewed as consisting of interlocking and interrelated ecosystems. If people start making changes in these systems, havoc can result.

This section will review some of the ecological challenges facing business today. In particular, pesticides and pollution will be examined, since both serve to upset nature's ecological balance and thereby present a potential threat to mankind. Some of the current ecological legislation will then be reviewed.

Ecological concern is not new to America. For years, the nation has been aware of the need to conserve natural resources and protect endangered species. However, in the last two decades ecology has witnessed a popular rebirth, and business has now become one of its prime targets. The issue that started it all was the use of pesticides.

Pesticides

Farmers have used chemical pesticides for years. In the early 1960's Rachel Carson wrote *Silent Spring*,[16] in which she charged that chemicals such as DDT do not decompose in the soil. Rather, they remain stable and dangerous for extended periods of time, posing grave danger to animals and humans alike. She further contended that these chemicals were being used with little or no investigation of their harmful effects; and there are many of them.

In Alamogordo, New Mexico, for example, a hog was accidentally fed seed that had been treated with a highly toxic mercury fungicide compound. The hog was subsequently slaughtered for consumption. Its meat was eaten by three children who thereupon suffered serious brain damage. In another instance, scientists on the West Coast have discovered that pelicans eating fish with high residue levels of DDT lay eggs with extremely thin shells. The result is a premature cracking of the egg. Unless something is done, the pelican in this area faces extinction. Meanwhile, at Miami University, researchers have found a large percentage of terminal cancer patients with high concentrations of pesticide residues in their liver and brain tissues.[17]

Pesticides can be harmful.

Spurred on by such dangers, in mid-1972 William D. Ruckelshaus, head of the Environmental Protection Agency, banned nearly all uses of DDT in the United States. His decision was based on the finding that the pesticide was uncontrollable and capable of persisting in the soil for up to 17 years. However, the issue has certainly not been settled. Defenders of DDT warn that the insect killer is not only important in preventing world starvation, but substitutes such as ethyl and methyl parathion are highly toxic and could prove even more dangerous. Thus the pesticide issue continues to be a major ecological issue facing business. In recent years,

---

[15]"Playboy Interview: Dr. Paul Ehrlich," *Playboy Magazine*, August 1970, p. 56.
[16]Rachel Carson, *Silent Spring* (Boston: Houghton Mifflin Company, 1962).
[17]Frank Graham, Jr., *Since Silent Spring* (Boston: Houghton Mifflin Company, 1970), p. 148.

other pesticides have come under close scrutiny. Legislation is currently being proposed for control of some of them.[18]

Air Pollution

John Lindsay, former mayor of New York, once commented that he liked the city's air because he enjoyed seeing what he was breathing. There is no doubt that air pollution has increased dramatically over the past few decades, especially in a megalopolis such as New York. Two of the primary pollutants have been automobiles and industrial smoke-stacks.

AUTOMOBILES. The major cause of air pollution in America is the auto-mobile. For some time now, the auto makers have been trying to control the three main automotive emissions: carbon monoxide, hydrocarbons, and nitrogen oxides. The basic approach has been engine modification. For example, in attempting to limit hydrocarbons and carbon monoxide, the major auto makers have turned to higher coolant temperatures and altered valve and retarded-spark timing. For limiting nitrogen oxides, they have given major attention to reducing peak combustion tempera-tures through water injection or exhaust-gas recirculation and the use of a reducing-type of catalyst for treating exhaust.

> *The automobile is the major cause of air pol-lution.*

Another approach has been to reduce auto weight, thereby decreas-

---

[18]Bill Richards, "Battle Brews Over Pesticide EPA Says Is Cancer Threat," *Miami Herald*, September 21, 1977, Section G, p. 1.

You drive it backward so it will turn hydrocarbons into pure gasoline.

From *Keystone Motorist*, June, 1972.

ing fuel consumption and the accompanying exhaust pollution. (Table 18–1 contrasts the average weight of a 1970 vs. a 1980 auto.) A third way is through the development of new auto fuels that give better mileage and lower emissions of harmful gases. A fourth, which is being given renewed consideration, is the use of electric cars. Regardless of what is done, however, the United States should witness a reduction in auto air pollution, at least through the 1990's. (See Figure 18–1.) A Chrysler executive has summarized the development this way:

1. Auto emissions climbed to their peak in the atmosphere about 1968 and have been going downhill since then.
2. Emissions will continue to go down each year, even though the car population will rise and vehicle miles driven will go up. That means that the air is already cleaner today than last year or the year before. It will be cleaner year by year through the 1970's and the 1980's.
3. By the early 1980's, we will have air quality — from an automotive standpoint — nearly comparable to the 1940's. Normally, it takes between 10 to 15 years to replace the older, high-emission cars in the vehicle population. Putting it another way, if there were no other vehicles on the road today, except the latest models, we would, overnight, breathe the same clean air we had in the 40's as far as the automobile contribution is concerned. Even if we achieved the impossible by inventing and building zero-emission vehicles today, it still would take up to 15 years to replace the car population.
4. After emissions hit the low point in the air somewhere in the 1990's, they will start going up gradually as more cars keep being added to the population.[19]

INDUSTRIAL SMOKESTACKS. If one drives into a big city on a cold winter day, smokestack pollution can be seen hanging over the metropolis. Among the worst of the industrial air polluters are the utilities, many of them hurling tons of sulphur dioxides into the air daily. Today experts estimate the amount of air pollutants at hundreds of millions of tons annually, with utilities accounting for a significant percentage of this. Smelting and refining firms are also major contributors.

Utilities and refineries are also big air polluters.

In an effort to decrease pollutant emission, these firms are beginning to rely on technological advances such as power plant scrubbers and cyclonic burners. Many of the power plant scrubbers used today employ pulverized limestone for removing sulfur. In this process, a slurry of rock and water is sprayed into the dirty gas as it moves from the boiler to the scrubber. The limestone combines with the sulfur in the gas to form a liquid, which settles out as sludge waste. The remaining "scrubbed" gas then continues up the smokestack.

Another smokestack antipollution process is the cyclonic burner, which is being used by the lumber industry to dispose of waste products while simultaneously preserving clean air:

The cyclonic burner is able to achieve near total combustion of solid mill wastes by "grinding them up and suspending the particles on blasts of air in the fire box. The generated heat provides a handy and economical source of energy." Because the system is virtually closed-loop, exhausts are fed back into the smokestack. Two of these systems already in operation illustrate that the heat from the burner can be used to fire kilns in the mill. As a result, it is possible for a mill cutting one million board feet a year to save $115,000 in carting costs and $85,000 on fuel previously needed to fire the kilns.[20]

Technological advances such as these are helping to reduce smokestack pollution. However, a great deal more remains to be done.

---

[19]Text of a speech delivered by C. M. Heinen, Executive Engineer — Material Engineering, Chrysler Corporation, before the Society of Industrial Realtors of the National Association of Real Estate Boards, Miami Beach, Florida, November 13, 1971, pp. 3–4.
[20]Luthans and Hodgetts, *op. cit.*, p. 278.

TABLE 18–1   Auto Weight

	1970 Auto (Average Weight: 3600 Pounds)	1980 Auto (Average Weight: 2900 Pounds)
Steel	2681 lbs.	1989 lbs.
Rubber	186	182
Plastics	113	167
Glass	105	90
Zinc die castings	96	25
Aluminum	70	154
Copper, copper alloys	43	17
Adhesives, sealants	42	52
Paperboard	30	10
Coatings (dry weight)	19	24
Textiles (including tie cord)	18	19

Source: "What the 1980 Auto Will Be Like," *Business Week,* June 2, 1973, p. 52E.

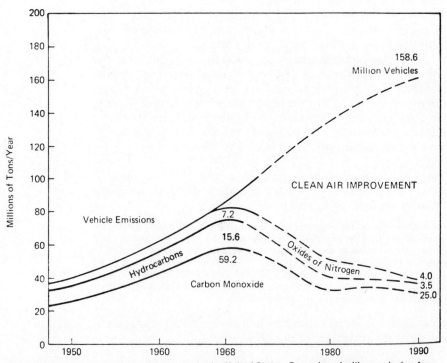

FIGURE 18–1   Atmospheric Improvements in the United States. Reproduced with permission from the Chrysler Corporation.

Many firms have used nearby lakes or streams as drainpipes for carrying off their production wastes. As a result, some bodies of water, such as the Great Lakes, are said to be polluted beyond salvation. In other cases, companies have pumped liquid wastes into underground dumps. Unfortunately, sometimes these dumps have leaked, polluting both underground and surface water.

There is also the case of thermal, or warm-water, pollution, often brought about by hydroelectric plants. In order to generate electricity, the utility brings in cool water from a nearby lake or river. This is converted into steam to turn the plant's turbine engines. The steam is then passed through a condenser, cooled and turned back into water, and then returned to the lake or river. The problem is that often this water is returned at 5 or 10 degrees above its original temperature. The ultimate effect can be a change in the basic ecosystem of the water. The aquatic life, unaccustomed to the warmer environment, may die.

Currently, there is a great deal of pressure on business to cease any activity that may cause water pollution. This is all part of the national goal of cleaning America's waterways by 1985. However, one should be aware that "zero discharge" will undoubtedly *not* become a reality because of the economics involved. As *Business Week* has reported:

**Zero discharge is
not a reality.**

> Like industry, the Administration fears the high cost of strict effluent limits. Russell Train, head of the Council on Environmental Quality, points out that cleanup costs rise exponentially with the degree of cleanliness sought. "The last 1 per cent of treatment costs as much as the first 99 per cent," he says. Preliminary CEQ data estimate the current water program, aimed at reducing pollution by about 85 per cent, would eventually cost $60.8 billion. To achieve a 95 to 99 per cent reduction would nearly double the tab to $118 billion. And to go the last effortful step to zero discharge would escalate the cost incredibly to $316 billion — or some $21 billion a year between now and 1985.[21]

Some of the major steps business has already taken to fight water pollution include the recycling of water through waste treatment systems and the reduction of thermal pollution. General Motors provides a good illustration of the former:

> Water from a foundry is pumped into a large lagoon or settling basin in which the foundry solids gradually settle to the bottom. The clean water is then pumped back into the foundry for use in operations. At the present time General Motors is also looking into a new technique for purifying water to a degree suitable for reuse in any plant process. In essence the purifying process involves passing water through sand filters to remove suspended solids, through activated carbon towers to remove organics, and finally, through reverse osmosis units to reduce dissolved solids.[22]

Meanwhile, in the area of thermal pollution, there is currently a great deal of interest in floating nuclear stations which can be placed three miles out in the ocean, thus reducing warm-water pollution. Another recent development is the installation of special cooling towers, which lower the temperature of heated water by 20 degrees before recirculating it to the condensers. This in turn keeps thermal pollution at a minimum.

**Noise
Pollution**

The amount of noise to which the average urban resident is subjected can be quite extreme. Car horns blast, pedestrians shout, and overhead aircraft roar. In the past, little was done about all of this. Today, however, steps are being taken to reduce "noise pollution." One major cause of concern is medical research, which has established that people who are exposed to prolonged periods of noise at 85 decibels can suffer hearing

**Excessive noise
can damage
hearing.**

[21]"The Stormy Debate over 'Zero Discharge'," *Business Week*, February 5, 1972, p. 71.
[22]Luthans and Hodgetts, *op. cit.*, pp. 278–279.

damage. How loud is 85 decibels? The following should provide a framework for answering this question:

Sound	Decibels
Whispering	30
Moderate conversation	35
Light auto traffic from 100 feet	50
Freeway from 50 feet	70
Heavy truck traffic from 50 feet	90
Power mower	95
Riveter	110
Siren	115
Commercial jet takeoff from 200 feet	120
Rocket launch	180

Today the government has established 90 decibels as an acceptable noise level for people in organized work places, although there is pressure from numerous groups, including unions, to reduce this to 85 decibels. The *Wall Street Journal* reported on the effect of noise pollution on hearing:

> It has long been suspected that as many as 10 million workers may hear poorly due to excessive noise. Now some research links noise to such diverse ills as mental distress and heart disease. In Germany, a recent study of workers found that those subject to the most noise on the job suffered a higher incidence of heart disorders, circulatory problems and equilibrium disturbances. A number of medical men are certain that job noise is a factor in some neurotic and psychotic illnesses.[23]

Noise can also be a source of psychological distress.

Other research indicates that noise can prove to be a source of psychological distress contributing to symptoms such as instability, headaches, nausea, general anxiety, and sexual impotency.[24]

Business has been taking two approaches in meeting the challenge of noise pollution. First, companies are investigating their environments to find and silence sources of noise. At some automotive plants, for example, noise suppressors are being used to reduce the noise level to 80 decibels. At these plants, ceilings and walls are covered with sound-absorbing materials, and over and around particularly noisy departments there are draft curtains — rigid, wall-like panels stuffed with noise-reducing fiber glass. Meanwhile, in factory areas where power tools are used, firms have attached hoses to the machinery to carry the noise out of the building; and to quiet conveyor systems, plants have slowed down the machines. Other types of manufacturers have used similar approaches, employing shields and padding to stifle plant noise and supplying protective ear devices to workers in areas where the noise level is over 90 decibels.

Second, machine manufacturers are redesigning their equipment so that it makes less noise. For example, the hammer-type riveter is being replaced by an orbital and spin riveter. Now, instead of the riveter head being slammed into the ground, the tool compresses the riveter head with an orbital or revolving motion. Attempts are also being made to stifle noise pollution from turbofan or jet engines. The most common method so far has been to redesign the engine by placing sound-absorbing materials on the walls on the inlet duct of the turbofan as well as in the exhaust duct. With these and similar developments, factory and machinery noise is being significantly reduced.

---

[23]Danforth W. Austin, "Factory Workers Grow Increasingly Rebellious Over Noise Pollution," *Wall Street Journal*, June 14, 1972, p. 1.
[24]*Ibid.*

Of course, it is impossible to eliminate all noise pollution. However, a cutback of 10 decibels translates into a 50 per cent decrease in a person's awareness of the noise. Thus, over the next decade, America should become a quieter place in which to work and live.

Thus far in this section the ecological issues facing business have been examined. Some of these problems are being met by voluntary action on the part of the business community. There are also many federal and state regulations that have been enacted in recent years that have called for specific compliance. The two most important have been the Environmental Policy Act of 1969 and the Air Quality Standards Act of 1970.

Ecological Legislation

The *Environmental Policy Act of 1969* established the Council on Environmental Quality. The council's basic duties are to assist the President in developing an annual environmental quality report, gather data on environmental trends, and develop recommendations to promote environmental quality. In addition, the Act established the Environmental Protection Agency (EPA). The purpose of the agency is to coordinate all major federal pollution control programs for the purpose of achieving environmental quality.

A number of ecological laws directly affecting business have been passed.

The *National Air Quality Standards Act of 1970* represents one of the stiffest antipollution bills ever enacted. Some of its provisions are: (1) all new factories must have the latest pollution control equipment; (2) auto manufacturers must drastically reduce exhaust and nitrogen oxide emis-

**TABLE 18–2 Expenditures For Pollution Abatement
(in millions of dollars)**

Industry	1975 Actual	1976 Actual	1977 Planned	1975 vs 1977
Electric Utilities	1650	1990	2348	+42%
Petroleum	1239	1275	1262	+ 2
Paper	489	511	567	+16
Electrical Machinery	136	148	120	−12
Transportation Equipment	116	125	198	+71
Textiles	31	37	36	+16
Chemicals	684	765	749	+10
Rubber	41	37	38	− 7
Mining	73	86	130	+78
Primary Metals	1012	923	1072	+59
Food and Beverages	175	175	204	+17
Air Transportation	11	12	14	+27
Other Transportation	41	38	40	− 2
All Business	6549	6762	7512	+15

Source: Frank W. Segel and Betsy C. Dunlop, "Capital Expenditures by Business for Pollution Abatement: 1976 and 1977," *Survey of Current Business*, June 1977, p. 13.

sions;[25] and (3) the federal government can set emission standards for 10 major pollutants, from soot to sulfur dioxide. In addition, each state is given the authority to set factory-emission tolerances in accord with federal standards, and if they do not, the EPA, after thirty-days' notice to the respective state, can do so itself. Furthermore, the EPA can sue polluters directly, and if it is lax in this task, individual citizens have a right to sue both the agency and the polluter. Finally, violators of the act are subject to maximum fines of $25,000 per day or one year in jail.

These are only a few of the many environmental control acts now in existence. What does the future hold? From a dollars and cents standpoint, business is going to spend increasing sums for pollution abatement (see Table 18–2). In addition, Davis and Blomstrom predict:

1. Tax incentives for pollution control equipment (such as faster depreciation or tax credits).
2. Matching grants or subsidies for installation of pollution control equipment.
3. Denial of government contracts and other privileges to violators (or perhaps privileges to nonpolluters, similar to veterans' preference in government employment).
4. Research grants for development of new control methods, and demonstration grants to test them in service.
5. Effluent charges for pollution emissions (such as a certain number of dollars for each ton of noxious fumes from a smokestack or each gallon of a chemical waste dumped into a river), an approach effective in reducing pollution of certain European rivers.[26]

CONSUMERISM

Since the late 1960s, consumerism has proved to be a major social issue facing business. Kotler has defined consumerism as *a social movement seeking to augment the rights and power of buyers in relation to sellers.*[27] This augmentation is taking two major forms: (a) buyers are demanding more information about the products and services they are purchasing; and (b) buyers are insisting on safer products.

Consumer Information and Assistance

It is no surprise that research reveals that many people, when they lack knowledge about a product, tend to equate price with quality. After all, how does one go about deciding which of five brands of aspirin is *really* the best buy?

LEGISLATIVE PROTECTION.   In recent years, legislation designed to educate the consumer has been enacted. One of these laws is the *Truth in Packaging Act*, which sets forth the following mandatory labeling provisions:

The Truth in Packaging Act sets forth mandatory labeling provisions

1. The identity of the commodity shall be specified on the label.
2. The net quantity of contents shall be stated in a uniform and prominent location on the package.
3. The net quantity of contents shall be clearly expressed in ounces [only] and, if applicable, pounds [only] or in the case of liquid measures in the largest whole unit of quarts or pints.
4. The net quantity of a "serving" must be stated if the package bears a representation concerning servings.[28]

---

[25]The original act called for a reduction of exhaust emissions of 90 per cent by 1975 and a decline in nitrogen oxides of 90 per cent by 1976. However, recent legislation has modified this timetable.

[26]Keith Davis and Robert L. Blomstrom, *Business and Society: Environment and Responsibility*, 3rd edition (New York: McGraw-Hill Book Company, 1975), p. 452.

[27]Phillip Kotler, "What Consumerism Means for Marketers," *Harvard Business Review*, May-June 1972, p. 49.

[28]Stewart H. Rewoldt, James D. Scott, and Martin R. Warshaw, *Introduction to Marketing Management*, revised edition (Homewood, Ill.: Richard D. Irwin, Inc., 1973), p. 270.

In addition, there is the *Truth in Lending Act.* This bill regulates the extension of credit to individuals and is primarily concerned with ensuring that the person knows the charges, direct and indirect, associated with the loan. On open-end accounts such as revolving charges, for example, the individual must be provided with the following information on his or her monthly statement:

1. The amount owed at the beginning of the period.
2. The amount and date of new purchases.
3. Any payments made.
4. The finance charge in dollars and cents.
5. The annual percentage rate.
6. The balance upon which the finance charge is calculated.
7. The closing date of billing and the accompanying unpaid balance.[29]

BUSINESS ASSISTANCE. The business community is taking action of its own to make the consumer more knowledgeable. For example, General Foods and Lever Brothers have sponsored consumer clinics in which customers are taught how to use the firm's product. If something should go wrong, many firms have established departments or offices to expedite the matter. For example, Whirlpool offers its customers a 24-hour "cool line." If the individual has a complaint or a question about service, he or she can call this number toll free, anytime, from anywhere in the country. Other companies have established consumer complaint departments which assign a problem to a specific individual, who stays with it until the customer is satisfied. Corning Glass has extended this idea and appointed a manager of consumer interests, whose job it is to represent the consumer and make sure the complaint does not get lost. In this way, the customer has an in-house agent.

Consumer complaint departments have been established.

Another major issue in consumerism is that of product safety. Two areas currently receiving major attention are auto safety and general product safety.

Product Safety

AUTO SAFETY. Ever since Ralph Nader wrote *Unsafe At Any Speed,*[30] auto safety has been an issue of concern. The last decade has seen a dramatic increase in auto safety legislation. In all fairness to the manufacturers, however, it must be noted that prior to this public outcry, sales indicated that people were not willing to pay for safety features. Now, of course, much of that has changed.

Some of the new features being installed on autos include seat belts, shoulder belts, energy-absorbing steering columns, padded dash boards, and bumpers capable of withstanding minor collisions. In addition, there is still serious consideration being given to the air bag.

Many new auto safety features are being added.

GENERAL PRODUCT SAFETY. Many firms, spurred on by government legislation and the possibility of costly lawsuits, are placing great emphasis on product safety. Some are establishing product safety committees to evaluate current products. Others are providing safety tips, pointing out certain short-cuts that are potentially dangerous and should be avoided. For example, the Hoover Company makes it a practice to tell the operator *not* to pick up puddles of water with the vacuum.

---

[29]"What You Must Tell Your Customers," *Nation's Business*, June 1969, pp. 42–44.
[30]Ralph Nader, *Unsafe At Any Speed* (New York: Grossman Publishers, 1965).

LEGAL ASPECTS. In recent years, liability laws have undergone drastic changes. Two areas of particular importance for business have been *negligence* and *strict liability*.

Privity of contract has been pushed aside.

Under old English law, businesses were liable for negligence only to the person who bought the good. This is known as *privity of contract*. Today the courts have pushed aside this doctrine and an individual does not have to prove a direct contractual relationship. A person who buys a defective car need not sue the dealer; he or she can sue the auto maker directly. This means that manufacturers are now much more prone to suit than before.

Most states have strict liability laws.

Strict liability means that a manufacturer can be held responsible for products that injure the buyer or user; direct negligence need not be proved. If a company places a product on the market, it must take responsibility for it. Today most states have enacted strict liability laws, and it is likely that by 1985 all will have them.

SAFETY CHECKLIST. With the courts making it easier to sue manufacturers for damages, many firms are finding it necessary to review the entire area of product safety. Carl Clark, Chief of The National Commission Task Group on Industry Self-Regulation, has suggested that manufacturers use the following safety checklist:

A manufacturer's safety checklist

1. Review working conditions and competence of key personnel.
2. Predict ways in which the product will fail and the consequences of these failures at the design stage.
3. Select raw materials that are either pretested or certified as flawless.
4. Make use of trade association research and analyses concerning product safety.
5. Insist that product safety factors be tested by an independent laboratory.
6. Document any production changes that might later affect safety problems.
7. Encourage the product safety staff to review advertising or safety aspects.
8. Inform salesmen of the product's safety features and under what conditions they will fail.
9. Provide information to the consumer on product performance.
10. Investigate every consumer complaint.[31]

This list can be valuable to manufacturers in light of the fact that more consumers are now suing *and* winning product liability suits. The percentage of juries ruling in favor of the plaintiff and the amounts of the awards are on the rise.

THE FUTURE OF SOCIAL RESPONSIBILITY

Is the concern for social responsibility a passing fad or it is here to stay? In this chapter, strong arguments have been made which indicate that this interest will endure, and those in business seem to agree. For example, when a group of executives was recently asked about ecological concern, one of the primary social issues, only 3.6 per cent of them said the area was a passing fad in contrast to the 87.6 per cent who felt that it was an enduring issue.[32] Additionally, as seen in Table 18–3, executives report that their firms are greatly interested in the entire concept of social responsibility. The data in Table 18–3 were gathered from people in a diverse number of industries. Why are businesses so concerned with social responsibility? Research shows five of the major reasons to be: (a) enhanced corporate reputation and goodwill; (b) a strengthening of the social system in which the corporation functions; (c) a strengthening of the economic system in

---

[31]"Consumerism: The Mood Turns Mean," *Sales Management*, July 15, 1969, p. 40.
[32]James S. Bowman, "Business and the Environment: Corporate Attitudes and Actions in Energy Rich States," *MSU Business Topics*, Winter 1977, p. 39

TABLE 18-3   Corporate Interest In Social Responsibility

Area of Social Effort	Oil, Gas, & Mining (n = 16)	Manu- facturing (n = 91)	Transpor- tation, Commun- ication, & Utilities (n = 19)	Whole- sale & Retail (n = 12)	Finance, Insur- ance, & Real Estate (n = 51)
Assistance to charities, welfare, health funds, etc.	56.2	67.0	78.9	83.4	90.2
Recruitment and managerial development of racial or ethnic minorities	56.3	56.0	73.7	66.7	58.8
Pollution abatement	100.0	58.2	42.1	0.00	2.0
Recruitment and managerial development of females	31.2	36.3	36.8	75.0	43.1
Upgrading the quality of working life of employees	37.5	31.9	10.5	16.6	29.4
Conservation of resources (including energy) and/or plant and animal life	81.3	23.0	36.8	16.6	7.8
Hiring and training of the hard-core unemployed	6.3	20.9	31.6	25.0	19.8
Assistance to minority enterprises	6.2	17.6	0.00	8.3	37.2
Urban renewal and development	0.0	11.0	0.00	0.00	47.1
Consumer protection	12.5	22.0	5.3	50.0	5.8

Adapted from: Sandra L. Holmes, "Corporate Social Performance: Past and Present Areas of Commitment," *Academy of Management Journal*, September 1977, p. 437.

which the corporation functions; (d) greater job satisfaction among all employees; and (e) avoidance of government regulation.[33]

Will this social philosophy orientation last? Once again, the answer seems to be "yes." For example, in an effort to uncover trends in attitudes toward the social role of the corporation, a large sample of business respondents was recently asked to consider five statements about social responsibility and to select the one that they believed best described their own opinions in 1970, in 1975, and then the one which they believed would be closest to their own in 1980. The results are reported in Table 18–4.

In conclusion, it appears that social responsibility will be a definite factor in future business strategy. Of course, the *specific* area of concern for each company may differ. For example, mining firms are more concerned with pollution abatement, conservation of resources and other ecologically oriented issues, while wholesale and retail firms report heavy interest in the recruitment and managerial development of females. In the aggregate, however, social responsibility is a challenge to which business today is both aware and responsive.

---

[33]Sandra L. Holmes, "Executive Perceptions of Corporate Social Responsibility," *Business Horizons*, June 1976, p. 38.

**TABLE 18–4 Executives' Opinions About the Social Responsibility
of Business: 1970, 1975, and 1980**

	Per Cent of Executives Who Selected the Statement to Describe Their Opinion		
	1970	*1975*	*1980**
Business is responsible for making a profit and abiding by legal restrictions	13.2	.1	.6
Business is responsible for making a profit and helping to solve social problems that business may directly create (such as pollution)	23.1	16.1	9.6
In addition to making a profit, business ought to help solve social problems whether or not it helped create them:			
(a) as long as there is at least some short-run or long-run profit potential	24.2	23.5	21.9
(b) even if there is probably no short- or long-run profit potential	31.3	46.4	46.6
(c) even though doing so may reduce short-run profits and no long-run profit returns are possible	8.2	13.9	21.3

*Predicted opinion.
Source: Sandra L. Holmes, "Executive Perceptions of Corporate Social Responsibility," *Business Horizons,* June 1976, p. 36.

SUMMARY

Social responsibility is a continuing challenge to modern business. Realizing that by aiding the community, business is actually serving its own long-run interests, many firms today are actively meeting the three major social challenges of the day: equal opportunity, ecology, and consumerism.

Both the Equal Pay Act of 1963 and the Civil Rights Act of 1964 were landmarks in helping ensure equal opportunity in the work place. However, the National Alliance of Business has also played a key role in helping find work for the hard-core unemployed, and many firms have also helped minority capitalists by providing them with both technical assistance and business contracts.

Yet in the area of female discrimination, there is still a great deal more to be done. Many women today do not receive equal pay for equal work, nor are their chances for management promotion as good as those of their male counterparts. Fortunately, many companies are aware of these conditions and are taking steps to rectify them.

The second major area of consideration in this chapter was ecology. This concern ranges from pesticides and air pollution to water and noise pollution. In each instance there are demands on business firms and, in every case, there have been attempts to respond positively to the challenge.

Finally, there is the area of consumerism. Today's customers want to know what they are buying and what they are getting for their dollar.

Legislation such as the Truth in Packaging Act and the Truth in Lending Act has helped provide consumers with some of this important information. Yet the consumerism movement is more than just a need for more data. Consumers also want product safety, and when it is overlooked by manufacturers lawsuits are likely. As a result, in recent years more and more companies have begun paying close attention to liability laws and the development of safety check lists that help ensure the requisite quality in their products.

In the last part of this chapter, the future of the notion of social responsibility was discussed. Recent evidence indicates that this challenge is going to be here indefinitely and all signs indicate that business is both willing and able to respond to it.

1. What is meant by the doctrine of enlightened self-interest?

2. In what way has the Equal Pay Act of 1963 been of value in promoting equal opportunity?

3. In what way has the Civil Rights Act of 1964 been of value in promoting equal opportunity?

4. What role has the National Alliance of Business played in the social arena? What contribution has it made?

5. How has the business community helped promote minority capitalism? Give two examples.

6. What are the two most common forms of female discrimination? Explain each.

7. What can business do to ensure equal opportunity for women in the work place?

8. What is meant by the word "ecology"?

9. What is the major cause of air pollution in America and what is business doing about it?

10. Why is "zero discharge" considered unrealistic? Explain.

11. What effect can noise pollution have on people? Give an example.

12. What are the major provisions of the Environmental Policy Act of 1969?

13. What are the major provisions of the National Air Quality Standards Act of 1970?

14. What is meant by the term "consumerism"?

15. What are the major provisions of the Truth in Packaging Act?

16. What are the major provisions of the Truth in Lending Act?

17. What new changes are occurring in liability laws and what effect are they having on business? Explain.

18. Is social responsibility a fad or is it here to stay? Explain.

REVIEW AND STUDY QUESTIONS

SELECTED REFERENCES

Andreason, A. R., and A. Best. "Consumers Complain — Does Business Respond?" *Harvard Business Review,* July-August 1977, pp. 93–101.

Bauer, R. A., and Dan H. Fenn, Jr. "What *Is* a Corporate Social Audit?" *Harvard Business Review,* January-February 1973, pp. 37–48.

Bowman, E. H., and M. Haire. "A Strategic Posture Toward Corporate Social Responsibility." *California Management Review,* pp. 49–58.

Buehler, V. M., and Y. K. Shetty. "Managerial Response to Social Responsibility Challenge." *Academy of Management Journal,* March 1976, pp. 66–78.

Burke, R. J., and T. Weir. "Readying the Sexes for Women in Management." *Business Horizons,* June 1977, pp. 30–35.

Carroll, A. B., and W. B. George. "Landmarks in the Evolution of the Social Audit." *Academy of Management Journal,* September 1975, pp. 589–599.

Carson, R. *Silent Spring.* Boston: Houghton Mifflin, 1962.

Davis, K. "Five Propositions for Social Responsibility." *Business Horizons,* June 1975, pp. 19–24.

Edmunds, S. W. "Unifying Concepts in Social Responsibility." *Academy of Management Review,* January 1977, pp. 38–45.

Fitch, H. G. "Achieving Corporate Responsibility." *Academy of Management Review,* January 1976, pp. 38–46.

Fretz, C. F., and J. Hayman. "Progress for Women — Men Are Still More Equal." *Harvard Business Review,* September-October 1973, pp. 133–142.

Graham, E. "Many Seminars Are Held to Aid Women in Firms: Then What Happens?" *Wall Street Journal,* April 26, 1973, pp. 1, 10.

Graham, Jr. F., *Since Silent Spring.* Boston: Houghton Mifflin, 1970.

Hay, R. D. "Social Auditing: An Experimental Approach." *Academy of Management Journal,* December 1975, pp. 871–876.

Hay, R., and E. Gray. "Social Responsibilities of Business Managers." *Academy of Management Journal,* March 1974, pp. 135–143.

Hennig, M., and A. Jardim. *The Managerial Woman.* Garden City, New York: Anchor Press/Doubleday, 1977.

Holmes, S. L. "Corporate Social Performance: Past and Present Areas of Commitment." *Academy of Management Journal,* September 1977, pp. 433–438.

Kanter, R. M. *Men and Women of the Corporation.* New York: Basic Books, 1977.

Luthans, F., and R. M. Hodgetts. *Social Issues in Business,* 2nd edition. New York: The Macmillan Company, 1976.

Luthans, F., and R. M. Hodgetts. "Government and Business: Partners in Social Action." *Labor Law Journal,* December 1969, pp. 763–770.

Murray, Jr., E. A. "The Social Response Process in Commercial Banks: An Empirical Investigation." *Academy of Management Review,* July 1976, pp. 5–15.

Nader, R. *Unsafe at Any Speed.* New York: Grossman Publishers, 1965.

Ostlund, L. E. "Attitudes of Managers Toward Corporate Social Responsibility." *California Management Review,* Summer 1977, pp. 35–49.

Strother, G. "The Moral Codes of Executives: A Watergate-inspired Look at Barnard's Theory of Executive Responsibility." *Academy of Management Review,* April 1976, pp. 13–22.

Sturdivant, F. D., and J. L. Ginter. "Corporate Social Responsiveness: Management Attitudes and Economic Performance." *California Management Review,* Spring 1977, pp. 30–39.

Veiga, J. F., and J. N. Yanouzas. "What Women in Management Want: The Ideal vs. the Real." *Academy of Management Journal,* March 1976, pp. 137–143.

Winter, R. E. "Reserve Mining Project Illustrates the Dilemma of Jobs vs. Ecology." *Wall Street Journal,* November 15, 1977, pp. 1, 29.

CASE: IT'S INEVITABLE[34]

Is concern for social responsibility a fad, or will it be a fundamental and lasting impetus in American business? Many people tend to believe the latter. They feel that decades ago there was only a slight difference between business's lifestyle and society's lifestyle. Today, however, the incongruity is quite obvious.

Financial income and security used to dominate American life-

[34]The data in this case can be found in: Keith Davis, "Social Responsibility Is Inevitable," *California Management Review,* Fall 1976, pp. 14–20.

style. Business, as an economic institution, helped meet these needs and, in spite of cyclical rises and declines in public favor, its goals were compatible with those of the average person. Modern America, however, has seen a shift toward more socially oriented desires, making the pure economic mission of business now out of step with societal values:

The incongruence between business's lifestyle and society's lifestyle requires intelligent, creative actions to dispel differences and reduce tensions. From a practical point of view it may be assumed that the social environment is the independent variable and business is the dependent variable. The major burden for adaptation, therefore, is upon business. Eventually it must change to meet society's expectations, and not the other way around. There may be minor adaptations by society as it comes to understand business better, but the major change surely will be required of business.

Finally, advocates of social responsibility argue that there is only a limited number of options available to business. First, it can withdraw and refuse to face the issue. Second, it can take a legal approach by dragging its feet and fighting long, expensive legal battles against social progress. Third, it can bargain or negotiate with those pressure groups making claims on it. Fourth, and finally, it can solve the problem by making a genuine study of society's and business's values and needs and attempt to reconcile them in constructive ways. The latter, in the view of social responsibility advocates, is the most viable strategy.

Questions

1. Is there really a growing incongruence between the lifestyles of business and society in this country? Explain.

2. Is the social responsibility factor really here to stay? Cite some illustrations to support your answer.

3. If business does choose the fourth alternative above, namely problem solving, what are some steps it should take? Be specific in your answer.

CASE: EQUAL CREDIT

Many women used to find that, because of their sex, they were denied credit at department stores and banks. For example, a working husband could obtain a $1000 loan on his signature, but the working wife who wanted a similar loan had to get her husband to co-sign. Additionally, if the two divorced, it was likely that she would lose her credit rating while his would be unaffected.

The Equal Credit Opportunity Act has now outlawed such practices, requiring that a creditor apply the same standards of "creditworthiness" to all applicants. This is not to say that a creditor cannot stall a woman on an application for credit. However, she must be notified within 30 days of any action taken on her account. If credit is denied, the notice has to be in writing and must either cite specific reasons for the denial or indicate that such an explanation can be requested. The same right applies if a credit account is closed. Some of the most important rules of this act, as outlined by the federal government, include the following:

1. **You cannot be refused credit just because you are a woman.**
2. **You cannot be refused credit just because you are single, married, separated, divorced, or widowed.**
3. **You cannot be refused credit because a creditor decides you are of childrearing age and, as a result, will not count your income.**
4. **You cannot be refused credit because a creditor will not count income you receive regularly from alimony or child support.**
5. **You can have credit in your name if creditworthy.**
6. **When you apply for your own credit and rely on your own income, information about your spouse or his co-signature can be required only under certain circumstances.**
7. **You can keep your own accounts and your own credit history if your marital status changes.**
8. **You can build up your own credit record because now accounts must be carried in the names of husband and wife if both use the account or are liable on it.**
9. **If you are denied credit, you can find out why.**

Questions

1. Which one of the above rules provides women the greatest protection against credit discrimination? Explain.

2. In addition to those on the list, are there any other rules that you think need to be added to ensure that women are given the same credit opportunities as men?

3. How much effect will this new law have on ensuring equal credit opportunities? Explain.

CASE: QUIET IN THE HOME[35]

Conversations about noise pollution usually center around the more noticeable offenders, such as airplanes, locomotives, buses, and heavy machinery. However, a quick look around the average home is likely to uncover many other polluters, including dishwashers, blenders, garbage disposals, and vacuum cleaners. Most of the noise from these household items goes unnoticed by the average person, although recent government studies show that 16 million Americans suffer from some degree of hearing loss caused directly by noise. Since most people spend a large percentage of their time at home, noisy appliances quite possibly are causal factors in poor hearing.

One reason why many people are unconcerned about noise pollution from appliances is that they equate noise with power. If a machine makes a lot of noise, it is getting the job done. If it is too quiet, it is not very effective. Joseph C. Frantz, executive secretary of the Vacuum Cleaner Manufacturers Association, reports that in the early 1960's a quiet vacuum cleaner was introduced into the marketplace. It promptly flopped because consumers thought it lacked power. Similarly, when

[35]The data in this case can be found in: "The EPA's Next Target: Noisy Appliances," *Business Week*, October 10, 1977, pp. 100, 102

engineers at another vacuum manufacturer were bothered by a clicking sound in one of their vacuums, a consumer survey found that the noise did not disturb the users. They felt it indicated that the vacuum was working.

Nevertheless, the Environmental Protection Agency (EPA) is now planning to crack down on noise from these home appliances. One of its proposals is to require manufacturers to label household appliances to show how much noise they emit. Another is to use a color-coding or numbering system to allow comparison shoppers to compare noise levels of competing appliances and decide which is best for them.

EPA administrators admit that it will cost more to make appliances quieter and implementation will be gradual. Despite such problems, however, noise labeling is meeting with very little industry resistance.

Questions

1. What kinds of home appliances can you identify that make sufficient noise to qualify them as polluters? List six.

2. Why do people associate appliance noise with appliance power?

3. What difficulties do you see the EPA confronting as it attempts to reduce noise in appliances? Explain.

CASE: IT'S GOOD BUSINESS[36]

Not every business firm is responding to consumer pressure. For example, the Pacific Gas and Electric Company of San Francisco, which supplies energy to three million households in the west, refuses to meet with consumer representatives as a matter of policy. They say that talking to consumer representatives is a waste of time, since any agreements have to be approved by the Public Utilities Commission anyway. However, consumer professionals believe that this type of attitude helps account for the results of a recent Harris poll, which revealed that 46 per cent of the respondents felt that most manufacturers do not really care about giving customers a fair deal, and 59 per cent said that companies are too concerned about profits to care about quality.

However, in many firms this is not the case. Consumerism has prompted numerous organizations to set up consumer affairs departments to respond to the customers. A *Business Week* survery reveals that more and more firms are listening to their customers, believing that it pays off on the income statement. Illustrations include the following:

At Pennsylvania Power and Light Company in Allentown, a consumer and community-affairs department sponsored the country's first utility-consumer conference and is planning regular mettings between all PP&L divisions and consumer panels.

---

[36]The data in this case can be found in: "Corporate Clout for Consumers." *Business Week,* September 12, 1977, pp. 144, 148.

Shell Oil Company in Houston has circulated 225 million booklets on driving and car-care tips in a "Come to Shell for Answers" campaign that has generated more than 200,000 letters from users. To reassure the letter writers that they are communicating with people, not computers, Shell often answers in verse.

Whirlpool Corporation, Benton Harbor, Michigan, spends $500,000 annually operating a nationwide toll-free complaint line and regards the cost as a bargain. "We see it coming back in repeat business," says Stephen E. Upton, vice president for consumer affairs. The company is so sold on this principle that it even replies to letters by phone and, if nobody answers the phone, sends Mailgrams.

When asked the reason behind such consumer orientation, business officials admit that they must either deal with the dissatisfied customer or risk losing repeat sales. A contented customer is a repeat customer. Therefore, responding to this social challenge is good business.

Questions

1. Do you agree or disagree with the consumerism philosophy of Pacific Gas and Electric? Explain.

2. Are business firms responding to the consumerism movement because of a social responsibility obligation or a concern for profit?

3. Is government action in the consumerism area any longer necessary? Will not firms respond to the customers' needs if only out of a desire to survive and make profit? Explain.

CHAPTER NINETEEN

INTERNATIONAL MANAGEMENT: CHALLENGES AND OPPORTUNITIES

The United States is the most important nation in the international arena. This is true for two reasons. First, it does more exporting and importing than any other country in the world; there is virtually no nation with which it does not have at least some trade (see Table 19–1). Second, many of its largest business firms, including General Motors, Ford, Exxon, Mobil Oil, IBM, and ITT, earn a substantial percentage of their annual sales in the overseas market. The modern business executive is thus concerned not only with domestic management but international management as well.

GOALS OF THE CHAPTER

The first goal of this chapter is to examine the possible advantages and disadvantages of "going international." The second objective is to analyze the methods used in organizing, controlling, and staffing these overseas operations. The third goal is to scrutinize the role of the multinational corporation in the international economic arena.

TABLE 19–1   U.S. Foreign Trade with Leading Countries and Regions of the World (Millions of Dollars)

	Imports			Exports		
	1973	1974	1975	1973	1974	1975
Canada	15,073	19,932	21,759	17,670	22,282	21,747
France	2,263	2,942	3,031	1,717	2,305	2,137
Germany	3,756	4,986	5,194	5,318	6,428	5,382
Italy	2,119	2,752	2,867	1,989	2,593	2,397
United Kingdom	3,563	4,574	4,525	3,642	4,021	3,784
Iran	771	1,734	3,242	340	2,132	1,400
Saudi Arabia	442	835	1,502	507	1,671	2,625
Israel	961	1,206	1,551	265	282	313
Japan	8,312	10,679	9,565	9,645	12,455	11,268
Philippines	495	747	882	663	1,091	754
19 American Republics	8,921	14,504	15,670	17,670	22,282	4,747

Source: *World Almanac and Book of Facts* (New York: Newspaper Enterprises Association, Inc., 1977), p. 148.

When you have finished reading this chapter you should be able to:

1. Explain why an American business firm will consider entering a foreign market.
2. Discuss the possible advantages and disadvantages of going overseas.
3. Relate how a joint venture works.
4. Describe the various forms of organization structure used in foreign operations.
5. Define the degrees of control that a parent company can exercise over a subsidiary.
6. Explain how a business firm will attempt to staff its overseas operations.
7. Discuss some of the incentives used in motivating personnel to accept overseas assignments.
8. Relate the economic power and international responsibility of the multinational corporation.

ENTERING FOREIGN MARKETS

Why do American businesses enter foreign markets? There are numerous answers, including: (a) a high-level executive pushes for it; (b) an outside group approaches the firm with a proposal such as an overseas joint venture; (c) domestic competitors are expanding into certain areas abroad and the firm decides to join the bandwagon; and (d) strong domestic competition makes foreign expansion desirable.

Identifying the Firm's Basic Mission

What business is the firm in?

Regardless of the reason, the first step a firm must take is to examine its operations. What kind of company is it? What is its real business? These are the same types of questions that were raised in Chapter 5 when strategic planning was examined. This time, however, the focus is on international expansion. In answering the question, how do you define your mission?, Jacques G. Maisonrouge, Chairman of the Board of IBM World Trade, has stated:

> We want to be in the problem-solving business — this is our mission. Our business is not to make computers. It is to help solve administrative, scientific, and even human problems. If your mission is broad enough, you do not find one day that a competitor's new product has outmoded all your equipment.[1]

Meanwhile, Fred J. Borch, former Chairman of the General Electric Corporation, has answered the question this way:

> We no longer define it as energy, electricity, and so on. That is a limiting factor. Rather, it is those areas of opportunity where our talents (whether they are technological, manufacturing, or marketing) can make a contribution that fits both our societal objectives and our growth objectives—those we give serious consideration to. There is no limit to where our talents can take us.[2]

Both responses indicate that the firms see their mission as global in nature. Problem-solving (IBM) and societal and growth objectives (GE) are not restricted to national boundaries. If a firm feels foreign expansion is within the scope of its basic mission, it can begin evaluating the possible advantages and disadvantages of going overseas.

---

[1]Gene E. Bradley and Edward C. Bursk, "Multinationalism and the 29th Day," *Harvard Business Review*, January–February 1972, p. 45.
[2]*Ibid.*

Expansion into a foreign market can have many advantages, some of which are profit, stability, and a foothold in the Common Market or some similar economic union.

Evaluating the Possible Advantages

PROFIT.   One of the biggest attractions in going international is the possibility of increased *profit*. McKinsey and Company, the world-famous consulting firm, found that among 100 major American firms they examined, more than half had doubled their overseas profits during the decade of the fifties, and their ROI was higher in the foreign than in the domestic market. And during the sixties, although the returns were somewhat lower, they were still considered quite good.[3] During the seventies, with American dollar devaluation and an increasing demand for goods and services by the general population in foreign countries, many overseas ventures have produced very high returns. A second profit feature is the favorable tax rate, in contrast to that of the United States, imposed by certain foreign countries. A third is the lower wages paid overseas.

Profit is important.

STABILITY.   A second major advantage of foreign expansion is *stability*. Many firms are capable of manufacturing far more units than they can sell domestically, and a foreign market provides a source of demand for the goods. This can be done through direct export to an agent abroad or through an overseas branch or subsidiary. A third common approach,

A foreign source of demand.

---

[3]See "Foreign Ventures Fetch More Profit for Firms Based in United States," *Wall Street Journal*, November 1, 1973, p. 1.

"I finally taught my son the value of a dollar.
Now he wants his weekly allowance in
Swiss francs."

Reprinted by permission of the Wall Street Journal.

brought on by rising nationalism, is to set up operations abroad and attempt to stabilize sales and production by working directly in both the foreign and domestic markets.

COMMON MARKET AND OTHER ECONOMIC UNIONS. Foreign production, especially in countries such as France, West Germany, Italy, Holland, Belgium, and Luxembourg, can be beneficial also because it gives the company a foothold in the *Common Market*. In 1957, these six countries created the European Economic Community (EEC), or the Common Market as it is often called. The goal of the EEC is to reduce trade barriers among the members. By 1967, duties charged on industrial goods circulating within the Common Market were 20 per cent of what they had been. By mid-1968, they were eliminated entirely. During the current decade, Great Britain, Ireland, and Denmark have been granted membership in the group.

The EEC has helped its member countries improve their standards of living, although the last decade did not witness much progress in countries like England, Ireland, and Italy. Nevertheless, on an overall basis, the Common Market has been a success. In addition to eliminating interior barriers, the EEC put a tariff wall around its members to protect them from outsiders. The result should be a united European market that can compete successfully with American firms. By entering the Common Market, however, U.S. firms can take advantage of these developments. Servan-Schreiber points out that American companies are not only doing this, but they are also getting Europeans to help them. In his famous book, *The American Challenge,* he put it this way:

> During 1965 the Americans invested $4 billion in Europe. This is where the money came from:
> 1. Loans from the European capital market (Euro-issues) and direct credits from European countries — 55 per cent;
> 2. Subsidies from European governments and internal financing from local earnings — 35 per cent;
> 3. Direct dollar transfers from the United States — 10 per cent.
> Thus, nine tenths of American investment in Europe is financed from European sources. In other words, *we pay them to buy us.*[4]

This basic idea of economic competition is not limited to the Common Market. Other economic unions have been formed for similar reasons, including the European Free Trade Association (Austria, Finland, Iceland, Norway, Portugal, and Switzerland), the Central American Common Market (Costa Rica, Guatemala, Nicaragua, Honduras, and El Salvador), and the Latin American Free Trade Association (most of the South American countries and Mexico). American firms doing business in these countries can profit from such unions.

Evaluating the Possible Disadvantages   There are also possible disadvantages associated with going international. Some of these include: (a) lower than anticipated profits; (b) need to understand foreign customs and culture; (c) company-government relations and red tape; and (d) risk, expropriation, and the pressure, especially in underdeveloped countries, to bring in foreign partners.

LOWER THAN ANTICIPATED PROFITS. The primary disadvantage in expanding abroad is the possibility that the expected market will not materi-

---

[4] J.-J. Servan-Schreiber, *The American Challenge* (New York: Atheneum House, Inc., 1968), p. 14.

alize, either because raw materials or personnel are not available in the necessary quantities or the price for the good cannot be obtained. In either case, the result is *lower than anticipated profits:*

Profits may not materialize.

> During the 1960's, Latin America was an ideal illustration, with return on investment by American firms averaging around 13 per cent, far less than in Asia and Africa. Today, however, this may be changing as Latin countries are starting to again encourage foreign investment.[5]

CUSTOMS AND CULTURE. Another disadvantage may be the new market itself. Precisely what does the company know about the country and its people? Does it understand the *customs* and the *culture*? What are the religious beliefs of the people? How do these affect their moral and ethical standards? What about the family — is it basically a matriarchal or patriarchal society? Are the people well educated or virtually illiterate? What are the social relationships and the value systems to which these people subscribe? If the company can answer these questions, it has a basic idea of how to interact with the people.

Customs and culture may be major stumbling blocks.

Yet as Fayerweather, an expert in international marketing, points out, there are still other attitudes among each population that are not covered by these questions:

> Notable . . . are the artistic tastes of the people, which are important factors. . . . That these tastes differ among societies is readily apparent to anyone comparing the dance, painting, music, and other art forms found in various countries. Likewise there are temperamental differences among peoples: the Latins are given to acting on impulse, while the Germans are more solid and rational. There are also a host of specific elements in the life of each country that are significant in some way — white is for mourning in China, a cow is sacred in India, and so on.[6]

In short, if a company is going to set up a business in a foreign country, it needs to familiarize itself with the culture. This can be a time-consuming problem, especially if the firm is in a hurry. The last thing the manager wants to do is violate social custom, but he or she does want to get action. In a country like Japan, where negotiations often move very slowly, American businesspeople may find themselves extremely frustrated. In fact, some companies have cancelled their plans to expand into overseas markets because they found themselves unable to adapt to the norms and customs of doing business in the foreign country.

COMPANY-GOVERNMENT RELATIONS. In many countries, especially those that are in the process of developing themselves industrially, the company must show the government that its proposed business venture will be beneficial to both parties. However, if the government has a master plan (and many do) and there is another business firm already manufacturing the good or providing the proposed service, the company may not be allowed to start up. This can be true even if the firm that is already licensed by the government is less efficient than the one seeking entry into the market.

Furthermore, even if the initial proposal appears feasible, the company must often begin fighting its way through a mass of red tape. The finance minister wants to know how much money the firm will bring into the country and how operations will affect the nation's balance of payments. The minister of power wants to know how much electricity will be-

Government red tape may be too great.

---

[5]See "Reversal of Policy: Latin American Opens the Door to Foreign Investment Again," *Business Week,* August 9, 1976, pp. 34–38.
[6]John Fayerweather, *International Marketing,* 2nd edition (Englewood Cliffs, N.J.: Prentice-Hall, 1970), p. 26.

needed by the proposed plant. Bringing all of these government officials together and obtaining final permissions for the proposed project may take so much time that the company will simply abandon the undertaking.

RISK, EXPROPRIATION, AND FOREIGN PARTNERS.   If it does proceed, the company may find that the government has the authority to set the price of the good and adjust it as it sees fit, allowing the firm a "reasonable" return but no more. Many companies often dislike this idea because they feel the return does not justify the risk associated with the investment and the possibility of expropriation. There are numerous illustrations of rising nationalism leading to a takeover of American business.

In the years 1960 to 1976, there were 292 expropriations of United States investments. Bradley has found that the greatest percentage of these occurred among firms with assets of less than $10 million or more than $100 million. Additionally, when examined on a regional basis, he discovered that:

> As expected, the Latin American countries are the greatest offenders, responsible for 49 per cent of all expropriations since 1960. Over the same decade and a half, the Arab countries of North Africa and the Middle East, plus Israel, were responsible for 27 per cent of the nationalizations, the black African states and Rhodesia for 13 per cent, and the remaining Asian nations for 11 per cent.
>
> The absolute numbers, however, are deceiving. Given the total number of U.S. investments in each region, the rate of expropriation has been considerably lower in Latin America than in the Arab states or in black Africa. In fact, only Asia appears to be a better risk than Latin America for the American investor. Since the overthrow of the procommunist Sukarno government of Indonesia in 1966, there has been only one recorded expropriation among the noncommunist countries of Southeast Asia.[7]

To reduce the possibility of expropriation, many firms take in native partners and operate the business as a joint venture. In some countries the government actually requires such action. On the positive side, the nationals can be useful in helping cut red tape. In addition, their awareness of local customs and marketing channels can be a great advantage. On the negative side, however, most businesses dislike turning over substantial (and possibly controlling) interest to an outside party.

Nevertheless, today most firms must be willing to establish some kind of balance between their own success and the welfare of the country if they hope to succeed in an overseas market. As Cateora points out:

> Unless the multinational investor... concerns himself with the host country's local economy, the growing animosity to U.S. dollars throughout the world will continue to show itself in government-initiated domestication and expropriation of U.S. investments. In order to avoid the economic pitfalls of these two policies, global investment strategies will have to include a social awareness of local needs and wants. The investment must be aimed toward becoming a fully-integrated part of the domestic economy. Such predetermined domestication seems to be the most workable policy for the coming years in light of the evolving hostile political atmosphere found in many countries around the world.[8]

One way of attaining this goal is through a joint venture.

Understanding the Joint Venture

When a firm establishes a *joint venture*, it takes in local partners who provide money and/or managerial talent. In foreign countries, nationalistic pressure, coupled with the desire of local capitalists who are eager to

---

[7]David G. Bradley, "Managing Against Expropriation," *Harvard Business Review*, July–August 1977, p. 78.
[8]Philip R. Cateora, "The Multinational Enterprise and Nationalism," *MSU Business Topics*, Spring 1971, p. 55.

profit from industrial growth, has led to an increase in the use of this organizational form.

On the positive side, the joint venture combines American technical expertise with foreign understanding of how to cut government red tape and market the product. Many companies have used this approach, including Du Pont, which holds a 49 per cent interest in a Mexican chemical plant, and Merck, which has a 50 per cent interest in an Indian pharmaceutical operation.

Foreign partners can be useful.

On the negative side, however, is the issue of control. Some countries insist that their people hold at least a 51 per cent interest in the venture. This idea is not agreeable to many American firms, including IBM, and there are some very valid reasons for opposing joint ventures. First, the local partners are sometimes more interested in their short-run profit than in the company's long-term gains. Second, the nationals may lack managerial skills but, as controlling partners, make decisions that may prove quite costly to the firm. Third, the partners may have a disagreement over policy. Fourth, custom or culture may dictate that the nationals find jobs for their families in the company. In all these instances, the firm stands to suffer. As a result, many businesses will accept a joint venture only when it is forced upon them. Others simply stay out of countries where this organizational form is required. IBM's strategy, for example, is to enter nations that do not require joint ventures, work closely with government officials, and adopt a very low profile. In so doing, the company virtually blends into the business environment of the host country:

However, loss of control can be dangerous.

. . . IBM has done a fine job of blending into France. The French government has a very active policy aimed at stimulating exports. IBM has brought its practices into line with this policy and is consistently that country's No. 1 or 2 exporter. IBM has done this in very clever ways, and the French government gives it much credit for favorably affecting France's balance of trade. (In Europe, IBM has about 65,000 employees, 10 manufacturing plants, and 4 research centers. The company has conscientiously tried to fit into the business climate in every country it has entered.)[9]

The giant computer firm has thus overcome any charges of exploitation, one of the prime reasons for the rise of joint ventures, while simultaneously refusing to give up any control of its operations.

Despite the disadvantages, American businesses are finding that joint ventures are becoming more common today than ever before. Firms that are thinking of going international must be aware of the potentials and pitfalls involved in this organizational form and, especially in underdeveloped countries, be prepared to accept them.

After evaluating the pros and cons, the company's top-level managers will make the final decision. Naturally, the major criterion is going to be profit, but there are many qualitative judgments that will be reflected in the decision. First, how large is the market? Domestic consumers are very different from foreign ones. In America, a large percentage of the population is middle class. In England, the largest group is the working class, whose incomes would put them in the upper-lower or lower-middle levels in America. In India, most people are at the lowest levels of the income scale (less than $2,000). The question of economic growth and stability is thus an important one.

Making the Final Decision

Size of the market.

Second, is the government stable or are political upheavals more the

[9]James K. Sweeney, "A Small Company Enters the European Market," *Harvard Business Review*, September–October 1970, p. 129.

Political stability.

rule than the exception? It will take time to recoup any investment and the company must forecast such developments in the political arena. Some areas of the world are considered very risky.

Third, if the market and political conditions look favorable, is the company going to export goods to the country or set up facilities there? If it is going to export, marketing channels must be established. If it is going **Marketing chan-** to set up facilities in the foreign country, a plant site must be chosen by **nels.** matching the needs of the firm with the locations available. Perhaps the company needs to be located near a river or a source of raw materials. In any event, one site will be more advantageous than the others, and the company will want to select it as the final choice.

Fourth, and finally, a review of the market investment will be necessary. How much money will this venture entail and how long will it take **Review of market** to reach the break-even point? Also, if there are local partners, will they be **investment.** putting up any of the money or will the venture be financed entirely by the firm? The answers to these questions will determine the ultimate fate of the project, for it will come down to a question of risk versus reward.

If the company decides to go ahead, attention must then be focused on the management of the enterprise. What type of organization structure will be best? What kind of control will the company want to exercise? How should the company go about staffing the operation?

MANAGE-MENT OF FOREIGN OPERA-TIONS

Organizationally speaking, the simplest way for a company to handle its foreign operations is by exporting the goods to agents and distributors abroad. Sometimes, of course, because of strong nationalistic feelings, import restrictions, and foreign exchange problems, the company is forced to become more deeply involved. For those wishing to keep the involvement at a minimum, licensing may be the answer. Under a licens-**Exporting or** ing agreement, a manufacturer will permit a product on which it holds **licensing?** patents or trademarks to be produced in a foreign country. In turn, the licensee will make royalty payments to the company for each unit it manufactures. To ensure that the product is made correctly, many firms will train the licensee in production methods and manufacturing management. There is thus some involvement on the part of the company.

Another approach, which entails still more involvement, is to man-**Overseas assem-** ufacture the goods at home and then ship them overseas for assembling. **bly.** Many firms have used this approach, but in time it is common to find them turning more and more to foreign manufacture. In the final stage, it is likely that the entire product will be manufactured overseas and the firm will begin exporting to nearby countries.

Organization Structure

There are many types of organization structure that can be employed in the management of foreign operations. In essence, the structure will depend on the firm's degree of involvement and its desire for control.

A branch organi- BRANCH ORGANIZATIONS AND SUBSIDIARIES. The simplest form is the **zation is an inte-** *branch organization,* which is an integral part of the company structure. **gral part of the** In essence, a branch is simply an outpost or detachment that is placed in a **company struc-** specific location for the purpose of accomplishing certain goals on a local **ture.** level. It is quite common to find branch offices responsible primarily for selling, and the branch manager acting as a sales manager who supervises salespeople, handles order, and resolves local problems. In the area of control, there is great disparity. Some branch offices are highly autonomous and others are under close supervision of the parent company.

A *subsidiary* differs from a branch in that it is a separate company, organized under the laws of the foreign country for the purpose of carrying out tasks assigned by the parent firm. By definition, a subsidiary is controlled (at least 51 per cent ownership) by the parent, although it may not be completely owned by the parent.

Some subsidiaries are highly dependent on the parent for operating instructions. Subsidiary department heads, for example, might report directly to their functional counterpart in the home office, the plant manager to the vice president of manufacturing, the head of sales to the vice president of marketing. Although those in the home office may not be best equipped to make decisions for the subsidiary a thousand miles away, the organization structure does provide for close coordination of foreign and domestic operations.

On the other hand, many subsidiaries are highly autonomous. Some, for example, have a free hand in conducting small local operations or carrying out narrow functions in a limited market. Others are full-scale companies with a great deal of autonomy across a wide area.

A subsidiary is a separate company.

The key criterion in organizing foreign operations is usually that of control: how closely does the parent wish to monitor overseas activities?

Control

There are three degrees of control a parent firm can exercise: heavy, intermediate, and light. Each has advantages and limitations.

HEAVY CONTROL.   When a subsidiary is required to keep the home office aware of all operations and activities and seek permission before undertaking any important actions, the parent is exercising *heavy control*. On the positive side, such control ensures that the subsidiary is operating in accord with home office policies. In addition, this approach makes it easier for the parent to integrate and coordinate its world-wide operations. If a problem arises, the home office is in a good position to help solve the issue because it understands, through continual monitoring of operations, what is going on.

The parent firm can exercise heavy, intermediate, or light control over the subordinate.

On the negative side, heavy control can be expensive and far less effective than the home office would like. In addition, there may be costly delays while the parent company ponders a decision. Also, the subsidiary manager and the staff may quit or ask to be transferred home, feeling that they are merely rubber stamps who are not allowed to exercise any personal initiative.

INTERMEDIATE CONTROL.   When the subsidiary submits continued reports to the home office but has the freedom to make important decisions without obtaining permission in advance, the parent is exercising *intermediate control*. On the positive side, the reporting system helps the home office monitor activities and provide assistance to the subsidiary. In addition, the freedom to make decisions helps the subsidiary manager and the staff deal quickly with operational problems. This freedom of action can be a great morale booster for the overseas staff.

On the negative side, the manager is expected to be an operating executive and a paperwork specialist, and it may be difficult to find an individual who is qualified to fill both roles. Also, the home office may be setting the goals for the subsidiary while the manager's job is to attain them. There may be difficulty here, however, because the subsidiary is not being allowed sufficient input into the plan.

LIGHT CONTROL.   When a subsidiary is allowed virtually complete freedom, having to provide the home office with only a minimum of information, the parent is exercising *light control.* There are several advantages to this type of control. First, the manager can devote full attention to running the subsidiary and making money for the firm. Second, by reducing all the paperwork, the number of personnel can be cut back and the overhead cost reduced. Third, morale is likely to be high when the overseas people realize that the home office is relying on their judgment to get the job done right.

Light control has its disadvantages. First, it may be difficult to find a manager who is qualified to handle such a demanding job. Second, the home office gives up any chance to fully coordinate and integrate worldwide operations. Third, if a problem arises, the parent company may not learn of it until a great deal of damage already has been done.

Experience shows that heavy control is often too inflexible, whereas light control is too lacking in checks and balances. For this reason, many companies use some variation of intermediate control. The manager makes decisions at the local level but continually reports to the home office on subsidiary operations.

Staffing

In addition to organizing and controlling foreign operations, a company must concern itself with staffing the enterprise. Who should head up the subsidiary? What qualifications will the organizational personnel need to have?

CHOOSING THE RIGHT PEOPLE.   Many of the questions about staffing will be answered when the company decides whether to set up a branch or a subsidiary. Others will be resolved when the issue of control over operations is determined. Of those questions remaining, some can be handled quite easily. For example, if the firm has been exporting to a foreign country and now decides to set up a subsidiary there, the export manager may be the natural choice for subsidiary head. If the company has an operation in Venezuela and decides to open one in Colombia, it may simply transfer personnel. After all, these people probably speak the language and undoubtedly know a great deal about South American culture and custom. Their skills are thus transferable.

Careful staff selection is necessary.

In staffing subsidiaries in underdeveloped countries, many firms have formulated guidelines based on past experience. Many, for example, like to employ bachelors because the man has only his personal adjustment to worry about; a married man would have to consider his wife and children as well. On the other hand, one American oil company operating in the Middle East has found that the best risks are middle-aged men with grown children. Economic conditions of the country and the specific operations of the firm can thus have an effect on who is most suitable for the job. So, too, can the geographic terrain. Companies with desertlike surroundings find that people from Texas or California tend to be better risks than those from New England. By employing such guidelines, the firm can often pick those most suitable for the job.[10]

---

[10]For more on this subject see: Jeffrey L. Blue and Ulric Haynes, Jr., "Preparation for the Overseas Assignment," *Business Horizons*, June, 1977, pp. 61–67.

Not all the personnel, however, are going to be Americans. Many firms realize that unless some nationals are recruited, the company may find the going rough. Not only are there cultural and social problems, but there is also the issue of nationalism. Foreign governments may insist that the company hire local people. For both of these reasons, it is common to find multinational firms attempting to recruit local people with either good business judgment or political connections.

MONETARY INCENTIVES. Once the "right" people have been chosen, there is the problem of getting them to accept overseas assignments. In addition to travel, many firms offer *monetary incentives*. Besides their base salary, these people may be given housing subsidies and basic allowances to keep up with the cost of living overseas. In recent years, these extras have risen dramatically. Table 19–2 shows the high cost of conducting business abroad.

This table helps explain why many firms will hire local managers when possible. Not only can they save on these high expenditures, but the pay scale for foreign managers is often much lower. For example, a French manager running a French subsidiary will receive less than an American doing the same job. Such discrepancies are still a source of dispute with

Foreign managers are paid less.

TABLE 19–2   The High Cost Of Doing Business Abroad

City	Apart-ment	House	Food	Cloth-ing	Automo-bile Opera-tion	Hotel	Even-ing out	Tuition
Brussels	$600	$	$125	$365	$27	$50	$160	$3300
Cairo	1500	1800	50	**	18	45	75	2100
Frankfurt	400	650*	95	269	24.20	58	60	2450
London	1040	577	95	253	29.50	49	57	1287
Madrid	800	–	60	275	22.50	45	60	2430
Mexico City	250	1000*	125	137	11	25	80	1500
Milan	800	–	50	237	32.50	60	100	3280
Moscow	785	–	127	**	30	98	40	1500
Paris	700	–	300	460	60	80	130	2300
Sao Paulo	1460	1375*	140	367	35.50	65	160	3000
Singapore	1500	1500*	100	148	21.50	50	60	2000
Sydney	600	–	70	314	40	40	100	1500
Tokyo	1600	–	200	360	34.35	50	125	2500
Toronto	500	750	70	347	26	50	84	2750

*Rented   **Generally bought outside country.

Definitions:
Apartment: Monthly rent for three-bedroom apartment in good residential neighborhood.
House: Monthly payments, including taxes and insurance, for three-bed-room house in good residential neighborhood.
Food: Weekly food bill for family of four.
Clothing: Cost of good business suit, shirt, tie, and pair of shoes.
Automobile: Ten gallons of gasoline, plus downtown parking for five days.
Hotel: Daily rate for double room in first-class hotel.
Evening out: Drinks, dinner, and nightcap for two couples.
Tuition: Yearly cost in middle grade for one child in private school.

Source: Adapted from: "The High Cost of Living Around the World," *Business Week*, November 15, 1976, p. 174.

many foreign personnel. The situation can become even more difficult if one considers the French student who comes to the United States, receives a degree in business administration, and then takes a job in New York City with a multinational firm. In this capacity he or she will receive an equivalent American salary. However, what will happen if two years later the individual is sent to France to assist the manager in running the subsidiary there? This person will be earning more money than his or her superior. What should the company do?

Currently, the entire area of wages and compensation is under examination. Multinational firms have established various schemes for resolving the matter. However, the answer still seems to depend on an individual analysis of the merits of the particular situation. Quite often, paying a competitive wage seems to be the only satisfactory solution.

Rapid promotion is possible.

UPWARD MOBILITY.   Another advantage in going overseas is *rapid promotion*. Most executives admit that the person overseas can move up the subsidiary ranks much faster than he or she would move up the ranks at home, because although many American personnel will stay overseas for two or three years, most prefer to get back to the home office, having done their job in the field. This opens up opportunities for the lower-level managers to advance. Thus, for the individual who is adaptable to foreign habitats and can deal with the emotional strains of "going international," there is the promise of upward mobility.

THE MULTINATIONAL CORPORATION

Recently, a good deal of attention has focused on the multinational corporation, although there is disagreement on how to apply the term. Some individuals say a multinational company is, quite simply, one that operates in more than one country. Others employ a much larger number of criteria. Maisonrouge of IBM, for example, contends that five basic criteria must be present for a firm to qualify for multinational status:

1. The company must do business in many countries.
2. The foreign subsidiaries must be more than mere sales organizations. There must be some services, such as R&D and manufacturing, carried on.

Criteria for multinationalism.

3. Nationals should be running the local companies since they understand the people and the environment better than anyone else.
4. There must be a multinational headquarters staffed by people from many different countries.
5. The company's stock must be owned by people in many different countries.[11]

Most individuals are inclined to accept far less rigid criteria and would tend to agree with the group of authors who identified a multinational company as *"any firm that has a large portion of its operations devoted to activity that is not limited to one country."*[12] This definition allows for various interpretations while conveying the most widely accepted meaning of the term.

American firms have invested large sums in foreign lands (see Figure 19–1). These investments have made the multinational American firm a power in the international economic arena. Giant U.S. companies have significant economic control everywhere. In fact, over a decade ago, American companies in France already controlled virtually two thirds of the country's farm machinery, telecommunications equipment, and film

U.S. firms have international economic power.

---

[11]Bradley and Bursk, *op. cit.*, p. 39.
[12]Richard D. Hays, Christopher M. Korth and Manucher Roudiani, *International Business: An Introduction to the World of the Multinational Firm* (Englewood Cliffs, N.J.: Prentice-Hall, 1972), p. 260.

```
┌─────────────┐
│Latin America│
│14.675       │
└─────────────┘


┌──────────────────┐
│Canada            │
│27.413            │
└──────────────────┘


┌─────────────────────────────────────┐
│Africa, Oceanic, Mideast, Far East    │
│33.212                                │
└─────────────────────────────────────┘


┌──────────────────────────────────────────────┐
│Europe                                          │
│45.815                                          │
└──────────────────────────────────────────────┘
```

FIGURE 19–1 U.S. Direct Investment Abroad (in billions of dollars). (Source: *Survey of Current Business*, August 1976, p. 41.)

photographic paper production, in addition to 40 per cent of the nation's petroleum market. In Europe they controlled 15 per cent of all consumer goods which were being manufactured, 50 per cent of all semi-conductors, 80 per cent of all computers, and 95 per cent of the integrated circuits market. No wonder Servan-Schreiber predicted that, "Fifteen years from now it is quite possible that the world's third greatest industrial power, just after the United States and Russia, will not be Europe but *American industry in Europe*."[13]

General Electric is a good example of American success abroad. Its total and international sales picture for 1971 through 1976 is shown in Table 19–3. International sales are increasing at a faster rate than domestic sales and, in most cases, this picture is not uncommon for multinational firms.

With economic power comes responsibility. As the multinational corporations grow ever larger, they face the problem of rising nationalism. Is American business trying to dominate foreign countries? Some people seem to think so and believe that the challenge of the next decade will be

Becoming Truly International

---

[13]Servan-Schreiber, *op. cit.*, p. 3.

TABLE 19–3 General Electric Financial Data (in millions)

	Total Sales	International Sales	Net Earnings on International Sales
1976	$15,697	$4,024	$196
1975	14,105	3,745	158
1974	13,918	3,218	174
1973	11,945	2,318	151
1972	10,474	1,830	99
1971	9,557	1,584	86

Source: 1976 Annual Report.

one of integrating nationals into the top ranks of these giant organizations so that management's point of view becomes *international* in focus. Simmonds has stated it this way:

> Ensuring that top corporate management in the international corporation does become truly international requires planned action. There are many ways to start. Noteworthy steps include: international executive development programs that concentrate on top management problems, rotation of younger foreign executives through corporate headquarters, decentralization of staff functions to foreign sites, or adoption of policies that treat all executives as internationalists regardless of origin.[14]

Recent statistics reveal that this is indeed beginning to occur. For example, Pohlman and his associates surveyed a large sample of American firms operating overseas and found the following percentage of the foreign subsidiaries' top personnel to be local born:

Percentage Native Born	Percentage of Firms in Category[15]
0–10	6
11–20	0
21–30	13
31–50	16
51–60	9
61–80	6
81–90	13
91–100	31
"Major"	6

They also found that most firms felt that a recruitment policy of "hiring a maximum number of nationals" was most effective. Some of these companies said that Americans were used initially, but they were eventually replaced by local people. It thus appears that more and more American firms doing business overseas are beginning to become multinational in the true sense of the word. Meanwhile, what about the charges of exploitation and imperialism that are often heard abroad? Perhaps the philosophy of American multinationals is expressed best by the chairman of IBM's World Trade subsidiary for Europe, the Middle East, and Africa:

> It has been our constant desire to grow, and to grow by being present in every feasible market, that has led IBM to where it is today. Wanting growth has nothing to do with imperialistic motives. Rather, it is one of the conditions necessary to remain dynamic, to remain young, and to maintain a sound level of excellence. Through time, I am sure, we will have substantial changes in the structure of the company, but one thing that will remain is our desire to grow, our desire to develop the non-U.S. markets, and to be present, as much as we can, in all the countries of the world.[16]

SUMMARY

In this chapter, international management was examined. American firms account for a significant percentage of all international business. The student of management thus needs a working knowledge of this area.

---

[14]Kenneth Simmonds, "Multinational? Well, Not Quite," *Columbia Journal of World Business,* Fall 1966, p. 122.
[15]Randolph A. Pohlman, James S. Ang, and Syed I. Ali, "Policies of Multinational Firms: A Survey," *Business Horizons,* December 1976, p. 17.
[16]Bradley and Bursk, *op. cit.,* p. 45.

In deciding whether or not to "go international" a firm must evaluate many factors. First and foremost is its basic mission. Precisely what business is it in? If the management decides the international arena is within its sphere of operations, it can begin analyzing the possible advantages and disadvantages associated with such an undertaking. On the positive side are profit, stability, and the possibility of a foothold in an economic union such as the Common Market. On the negative side are financial setbacks, foreign customs and culture, company-government relations, risk, expropriation, and the possibility of having to bring in foreign partners, which, for many businesses, constitutes the biggest drawback. IBM, for one, flatly refuses to enter into a joint venture, although because of rising nationalism, they are becoming a common phenomenon.

If a company decides to go ahead with a foreign operation, it must find an appropriate organization structure. This will, of course, depend on the amount of involvement it is willing to undertake. For some firms a branch organization will do; for others a subsidiary is necessary. The next question will be one of control. Which is best: heavy, intermediate, or light? Most firms opt for intermediate. Then comes staffing, which entails identifying qualified people and offering them sufficient monetary incentive and upward mobility to get them to go abroad.

The last section of this chapter examined the multinational corporation. Most of these firms are American, and they carry a good deal of economic power in the international arena. However, with this power comes responsibility, and the challenge of the next decade will be to continue incorporating foreign nationals into the upper ranks of management, and to see that the interests of the host country, as well as the corporation, are properly served. In so doing, the multinational firms will become truly *international* in nature.

---

1. Why do American businesses enter foreign markets? Explain.

2. What are the advantages of "going international"? What are the disadvantages?

3. What is the Common Market? What are its goals?

4. According to Servan-Schreiber, what is the "American challenge"?

5. How does a joint venture work?

6. How does a branch office differ from a subsidiary?

7. What are the advantages associated with heavy control of foreign subsidiaries? Loose control?

8. Why do most firms use intermediate control with their overseas subsidiaries?

9. What are some of the things a firm should look for in the people it chooses for overseas operations?

10. Is the chance for upward mobility of an individual in a foreign subsidiary better or worse than it would be in the home office?

11. What is a multinational corporation?

REVIEW AND STUDY QUESTIONS

12. How powerful are American multinational corporations in the international economic arena?

13. How international are the top management ranks of multinational corporations? Explain.

SELECTED REFERENCES

Apgar, IV, M. "Succeeding in Saudi Arabia." *Harvard Business Review,* January–February 1977, pp. 14–16.

Blue, J. L., and U. Haynes, Jr. "Preparation for the Overseas Assignment." *Business Horizons,* June 1977, pp. 61–67.

Bradley, D. G. "Managing Against Expropriation." *Harvard Business Review,* July–August 1977, pp. 75–83.

Bradley, G. E., and E. C. Bursk. "Multinationalism and the 29th Day." *Harvard Business Review,* January–February 1972, pp. 37–47.

Cuddy, D. J. "Planning and Control of Foreign Operations." *Managerial Planning,* November–December 1973, pp. 1–5.

Foote, M. R. "Controlling the Cost of International Compensation." *Harvard Business Review,* November–December 1977, pp. 123–132.

Hays, R. D., D. M. Korth, and M. Roudiani. *International Business: An Introduction to the World of the Multinational Firm.* Englewood Cliffs, N.J.: Prentice-Hall, 1972.

Hertzfeld, J. M. "New Directions in East-West Trade." *Harvard Business Review,* May–June 1977, pp. 93–99.

Hutchinson, J. "Evolving Organizational Forms." *Columbia Journal of World Business,* Summer 1976, pp. 48–58.

Kujawa, D. "The Labor Relations of U.S. Multinationals Abroad: Comparative and Prospective Views." Paper presented at the Conference on Contemporary International Labor Problems, Madison, Wisconsin, December 1–2, 1977.

Oh, T. K. "Japanese Management — A Critical Review." *Academy of Management Review,* January 1976, pp. 14–25.

Perlmutter, H. V., and D. A. Heenan. "How Multinational Should Your Top Managers Be?" *Harvard Business Review,* November–December 1974, pp. 121–132.

"Reversal Of Policy: Latin America Opens the Door to Foreign Investment Again." *Business Week,* August 9, 1976, pp. 34–38.

Robinson, R. D. *International Business Management: A Guide to Decision Making,* 2nd edition. New York: Dryden Press, 1978.

Schollhammer, H. "Organization Structures of Multinational Corporations." *Academy of Management Journal,* September 1971, pp. 345–365.

Searby, D. M. "Doing Business in the Mideast: The Game Is Rigged." *Harvard Business Review,* January–February 1976, pp. 56–64.

Servan-Schreiber, J. J. *The American Challenge.* New York: Atheneum House, Inc., 1968.

Spencer, W. I. "Who Controls MNC's?" *Harvard Business Review,* November–December 1975, pp. 97–108.

Sweeney, J. K. "A Small Company Enters the European Market." *Harvard Business Review,* September–October 1970, pp. 126–132.

Weigand, R. E. "International Trade Without Money." *Harvard Business Review,* November–December 1977, pp. 28–30.

Widing, J. W., Jr. "Reorganizing Your Worldwide Business." *Harvard Business Review,* May–June 1973, pp. 153–160.

Zeira, Y., and E. Harari. "Managing Third-Country Nationals in Multinational Corporations." *Business Horizons,* October 1977, pp. 83–88.

Zeira, Y. and E. Harari. "Genuine Multinational Staffing Policy: Expectations and Realities." *Academy of Management Journal,* June 1977, pp. 327–333.

CASE: TWENTY QUESTIONS

Before "going international," there are many questions a business should be able to answer. Some of these are:

1. Will our sales force in the new market respond best to straight salary, or to some combination of straight salary and commission?

2. **How will our middleman respond to alternative policies we might employ?**
3. **Will the local partners be interested in long-term capital gain or in current income and prestige?**
4. **Will the government want to give us a maximum of elbow room to operate because they want to show that they welcome foreign investment?**
5. **Or, will the government want to impose controls to assure, for example, that the positive balance of payments effect of the investment is maximized, that the number of foreign nationals in the operation is held down to some minimum, and that at least *x* per cent of the purchases of raw materials, components, and supplies will be from local sources?**

Questions such as these are useful to the firm in developing its alternative strategies, reducing risk and uncertainty, and obtaining the greatest return on its investment.

Questions

1. In addition to the above, what other questions must be answered by a firm that is thinking about going international? Be explicit.

2. How does a firm go about getting answers to these questions?

3. Are there any questions to which the firm will not be able to obtain answers? Explain.

CASE: BE PREPARED[17]

New markets for American goods have begun emerging around the world. As a result, one of the major trends in the past 20 years has been the emergence of the American multinational corporation. As United States businesses participate in developing these overseas markets, however, it is becoming painfully apparent that many of them have failed (and are continuing to fail) in selecting, placing, and preparing managers for these important overseas positions. What most businesses don't realize is that management training for such assignments is a highly complex process.

Some of the most obvious criteria for overseas assignments include independence, self-reliance, physical and emotional health, experience, and adaptability. This last characteristic, in particular, includes the following:
1. An expressed desire for change or new challenge.
2. A variety of supervisory experiences.
3. A knowledge of one or more foreign languages (although fluency is not necessary).
4. Some overseas travel (even holiday travel or military service).
5. Recent immigrant background or heritage.
6. Work experience with cultures different from the employee's own (for example, the urban or rural poor, blacks, Chicanos, or American Indians).
7. A pattern of positive and consistent performance appraisal clearly

---

[17]The data in this case can be found in: Jefferey L. Blue and Ulric Haynes, Jr., "Preparation for the Overseas Assignment," *Business Horizons,* June 1977, pp. 61–67.

identifying the employee's cooperativeness and willingness to collaborate.

American firms wishing to thoroughly prepare their personnel for overseas assignments must be aware of these criteria. In summing up the current status of such personnel, two authors have recently noted that, "Thus far, most American multinational corporations are not realizing their full potential because our overseas managers do not rank among those best equipped to advance the cause of our business interests in foreign lands."

Questions

1. What kind of physical and emotional health would you feel is necessary in personnel assigned to overseas posts?

2. Would an overseas manager need greater independence and self-reliance than his or her counterpart in the United States? Explain.

3. How can business corporations better prepare their people for overseas assignments? Provide some specific suggestions.

CASE: OVERSEAS ASSIGNMENT, ANYBODY?[18]

Just about everybody who works for an American multinational corporation wants an overseas assignment, right? Wrong! In recent years both corporations and personnel have begun rejecting overseas assignments. For the company, the cost of keeping an individual overseas is becoming prohibitive. For example, the United States State Department has released the following cost of living index comparing Washington, D.C. with a dozen foreign cities:

City	Cost of Living Index
Washington, D.C.	100
London	95
Mexico City	98
Milan	107
Sao Paulo	111
Singapore	113
Madrid	116
Cairo	124
Brussels	132
Moscow	136
Frankfurt	148
Tokyo	154
Paris	168

For the personnel, meanwhile, there are problems associated with both living conditions and taxes. One American executive work-

[18]The data in this case can be found in: "The High Cost of Living Around the World," *Business Week,* November 15, 1976, p. 174.

ing in London has remarked, "Your counterpart back home is worrying about buying three cars and you're worried about whether you've got a flush toilet." To compound things, Congress has changed the tax rate affecting overseas compensation. Under a new tax law the exclusion has dropped from between $20,000 and $25,000 (depending on how long one has been overseas) to $15,000; the tax rate on the taxable portion has been increased; and the credit for foreign taxes paid has been reduced to foreign taxes paid on the portion above $15,000.

Questions

1. Given the data on this case, do you think that American multinationals will have trouble recruiting people for overseas assignments? Why or why not?

2. What are some of the advantages of taking such an assignment?

3. How do the data in this case help encourage the trend toward using foreign nationals to manage overseas operations?

CASE: A COUNTERINVASION[19]

Quite a bit has been written about United States multinational corporations. However, unknown to many Americans, foreign firms are staging a counterinvasion. Since 1965, direct foreign investment in this country has risen from $8 billion to over $25 billion. What makes this country such an enviable target? Several factors can be cited.

First, some foreigners are uneasy about the growth rate in their own country. Second, some are concerned about political trends and their impact on business in their country. Third, depreciation of the American dollar has made United States corporations a good buy for foreigners seeking acquisitions. In fact, about half of all foreign investments take the form of acquisitions. For example:

Chemical maker Solvay (a Belgian firm) developed efficient new catalysts for production of high-density polyethylene, a technological edge that it wanted to exploit in the United States. It did so by buying a plant from the Celanese Corporation, which was reorganizing that part of its business.

Union Miniere (another Belgian firm) came into the United States in a deal that started as a sale of advanced refining technology by an affiliate, Mechim, to the New Jersey Zinc Company. When Union Miniere learned that New Jersey Zinc needed capital for expansion, it teamed up in a joint venture to build a new refinery and develop mines in Tennessee. Mechim will do basic engineering for the refinery, United States managers will run it, and Union Miniere is expected to handle the mining operations.

Do these developments worry United States business and labor? According to *Business Week,* they do not. After all, such moves stimulate the economy, creating opportunities for American businesses and jobs for American workers.

---

[19]The data in this case can be found in: "Why Foreign Companies Are Betting on the U.S.," *Business Week,* April 12, 1976, pp. 50–51.

Questions

1. Do you think we will see more foreign investment in the United States during the 1980's? Why or why not?

2. Should Americans be concerned about foreign acquisition of United States companies? Explain.

3. Do you think the problems faced by foreign multinationals doing business here are similar to those of American firms doing business abroad? Explain your answer.

CHAPTER TWENTY

MANAGEMENT IN THE FUTURE

Having discussed past and present developments in the field of management throughout the last 19 chapters, it is now possible to forecast what the future will probably hold. The first goal of this chapter, however, is to synthesize what has already transpired. After all, the future is partially determined by the past. The second goal is to review developments in modern management theory, and the third is to examine developments on the horizon that will continue to gain importance over the next two decades.

GOALS OF THE CHAPTER

When you are finished reading this chapter you should be able to:
1. Review the contribution of early classic management theory.
2. Recapitulate the major concepts contained in each of the three major schools of management thought.
3. Discuss developments currently taking place in modern management theory.
4. Relate some major trends in management today including corporate democracy, the challenge of managing executive talent, and the continuing trend toward professionalism in management.

In management theory, as in history, the past helps determine the events of the future; what has gone before sets the stage for what will follow. In the first section of this book, early management thought was examined. It was noted that scientific management, administrative management, and the human relations movement all made major contributions to the development of modern management theory. Although early classical theorists had their shortcomings, they did help uncover some important principles and theories that are still useful today. Filley and House have concluded that:

THE PAST IS PROLOGUE

> In our review, many critical propositions derived from classical management theory have stood the test of research evaluation rather well. They suffer not so much from what they say as from what they fail to say. For example . . . the principle of unity of command is a pragmatic convenience, not a necessity. Similarly, optimum spans of supervision *do* exist, but their determination depends upon a number of variables which are only now becoming clear.[1]

The classical theorists thus made lasting contributions to management.

There was, however, much more to be learned about the field. As research increased and the boundaries of management knowledge expanded, three distinct schools of thought emerged. The first, representing a continuation and expansion of Fayol's work, is the management process school. Chapters 5, 6, and 7, which examined planning, organizing, and controlling, established the basic framework for this school of thought. The second school, often traced directly to Taylor and his scientific man-

---

[1]Alan C. Filley and Robert J. House, *Managerial Process and Organizational Behavior*, (Glenview, Ill.: Scott, Foresman and Company, 1969), p. 483.

Three distinct
schools of
thought have
emerged.

agement associates, is the quantitative school. Chapters 8, 9, and 10, which examined the fundamentals of decision making and some of the techniques being employed by the modern manager in choosing from among alternatives, and the role of information systems, introduced the basic philosophy of this school. The third school of thought, which is concerned with applying psycho-sociological concepts in the work place, is the behavioral school. Chapters 12 to 15, which examined the areas of communication, motivation, leadership, and human resources development, presented the concepts subscribed to by the advocates of this school. Today, management theory can be represented as in Figure 20–1.

THE FU-TURE OF MODERN MANAGE-MENT THE-ORY

Modern management theory is advancing on a number of fronts.

Systems theory.

Modern management theory is now advancing on a number of fronts, including: (a) continued emphasis on systems theory; (b) the development of modern organization structures; (c) increased research on human behavior in organizations; and (d) greater attention to the management of change.

New developments in *systems theory* were examined in Chapters 10 and 15 to 17. Some individuals believe that this systems area is a school of thought in itself because it is capable of synthesizing the views of all other schools from a pragmatic standpoint. The very description of systems management illustrates this:

> *Systems management* **involves the application of systems concepts to managing organizations. The viewpoint is pragmatic; the method is synthesis (the art of building an organization as a system through the assemblage or combination of parts); and the task is to coordinate operations into an integrative whole. Systems management is vitally concerned with the appropriate design of the organization to achieve maximum operational efficiency as well as enhancing the well-being of human participants.[2]**

At present, however, the systems concept appears to be less a base for a school of thought and more an integrative idea for the manager to employ in carrying out his or her job. Managers today are more likely to view the organization as an open system, subject to developments in the external as well as internal arena. Although the computer is the best known development in the systems area, its impact within the organization has not been as dramatic as many writers had predicted. Rather, external developments such as changing technology and increased competition have had more severe effects, because they have forced many organizations to abandon their mechanistic structures and adopt more organic ones.

The result, as seen in Chapter 17, has been the development of *modern*

---

[2]Richard A. Johnson, Fremont E. Kast, and James E. Rosenzweig, *The Theory and Management of Systems*, 3rd edition (New York: McGraw-Hill Book Company, 1973), p. 504.

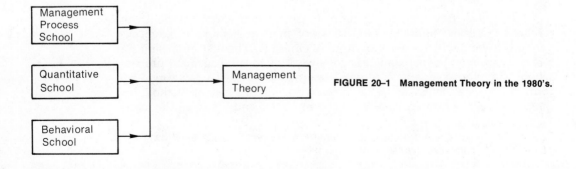

FIGURE 20–1   **Management Theory in the 1980's.**

organization structures. In contrast to their mechanistic-bureaucratic coun- Modern organi-
zation structures. terparts, modern organization structures are less predictable and less orderly. On the other hand, they are very well suited to meet the needs of modern businesses. In predicting what organizations of the future will look like, Kast and Rosenzweig have offered the following descriptions:

1. Organizations will be operating in a turbulent environment where they will have to withstand continual change and adjustment.
2. Organizations will increase in size and complexity.
3. Greater emphasis will be placed upon persuasion rather than coercion in getting employees to participate in organizational functions.
4. The influence of employees at all levels of the organization will increase, thereby resulting in power-equalization.
5. There will be an increase in the number and influence of scientists and professionals within organizations.
6. The goals of complex organizations will increase and emphasis will be given to satisficing a number of them rather than maximizing any one.[3]

Management is also finding that in order to manage its human assets it has to focus increased attention on the demands of the employees for meaningful work and increased responsibility. These demands, as well as their effect on the national and international arenas, were examined in Chapters 14, 18, and 19. Today, the business organization is more than a profit-making institution, and its responsibilities cannot be limited solely to that function. It is a place where individuals come together and, in a give and take process, interact with each other and the organization itself (formal objectives, plans, policies, procedures, and rules) in producing a good or providing a service to some segment of society. In an attempt to achieve the necessary coordination and cooperation of its personnel, management is trying to understand the needs and values of its people through *increased research on human behavior in organizations.* This in- Human behavior
research. cludes techniques such as MBO, job enrichment, TA, and behavior modification. The future will hold more of the same as behaviorists attempt to answer the question, how can the personnel and the organization be brought together in a harmonious, meaningful, and rewarding relationship?

The *management of change* is actually part and parcel of the three areas that have just been described. With the business environment in a continual state of flux, organizations are discovering that they have to live with change on a daily basis. However, as noted earlier in the book, change frightens many people. In overcoming this problem, management is taking a systems approach to bringing together the people and the work. As Kast and Rosenzweig point out:

To ensure the effective coordination of many of the diverse organizational activities, it will be necessary to establish linking departments and individuals such as program or project managers. Emphasis will be placed on horizontal as well as hierarchical relationships. There will be less concern with strict departmentalization of activities and a more free-form fluidity with people assigned to individual programs and projects where their capabilities and knowledge can be utilized.[4]

Management will continue to develop techniques and tools for effectively adapting to, and incorporating, change.

How will management theory integrate all these ideas? Many people feel the answer is to be found in a contingency theory of management, in which the manager draws on functional, quantitative, behavioral, and

---

[3]Fremont E. Kast and James E. Rosenzweig. *Organization and Management*, 2nd edition (New York: McGraw-Hill Book Company, 1974), pp. 617–618.

[4]*Ibid*, p. 618.

systems concepts as needed. Certainly this is the direction in which modern management theory seems to be moving. It should be realized, however, that despite what the contingency theory advocates say about a "new" school of thought, this is really nothing more than the formalization of ancient managerial thinking. After all, did not Machiavelli recommend pragmatism via his four principles of leadership? Is this not contingency theory? In short, the systems and contingency schools may emerge on their own, but the basic thinking is already contained in management theory. Effective administrators are already using *both* systems and contingency concepts in attaining organizational objectives. Thus, a better term for this type of management theory may well be *eclectic.* The manager, having no allegiance to any of the schools, draws the best features from each and employs them pragmatically.

OTHER DEVELOP- MENTS ON THE HORIZON

Although the previous section synthesizes much of what has been said in this book and provides insight into what can be expected to occur over the next few decades, there are three other developments that also merit closer examination. They have been alluded to previously, but have not yet been given sufficient attention. They are: (a) the trend toward corporate democracy; (b) the current challenge of managing executive talent; and (c) the continuing trend toward the professionalism of management.

Corporate Democracy

One of the most pronounced trends in industry today is that of corporate democracy. Employees are indicating that they want some code of fair play enacted.

CURRENT RESEARCH FINDINGS. This has been clearly seen in the results of a recent survey, entitled "What Business Thinks About Employee Rights," conducted under the auspices of the *Harvard Business Review* (HBR). A total of 7000 subscribers of the HBR were polled. Some of the conclusions were:

1. Throughout industry there seems to be a steady broadening of support for methods assuring "due process" to employees who feel they have been wronged by management.
2. Among both top executives and lower management people there is increased willingness to hear employees speak out on controversial issues.
3. Strong majorities of subscribers favor advances in the right of privacy for employees.
4. A majority of HBR subscribers are well ahead of the courts in favoring protection for dissident employees, including "whistle blowers."[5]

Some of these responses were obtained by giving the individual a case situation and then offering alternative solutions. In one case, for example, the survey participants were told that a capable young manager in a financial service company had come back from a month's vacation with a beard and long sideburns. He also started showing up at work in bell-bottom trousers and bright-colored sports shirts. This was a major change in dress habit for the man and in direct contrast to the conservative suits worn by the other managers. How should the situation be handled? The respondents answered as follows:

His superior should sit down with him, tell him that some people object   49 per cent
to his appearance, and that we'd like to have him stay with us but not if he
looks like a hippy.

---

[5]David W. Ewing, "What Business Thinks About Employee Rights," *Harvard Business Review*, September–October, 1977, p. 82.

How he looks is his own business unless it irritates people, in which case I would tell him either to change his ways or begin hunting for another job.   31 per cent

What the kid wears and how he looks is his own business.   19 per cent

He should be dismissed outright. He's worked with us long enough to know better.[6]   1 per cent

In a second case the respondents were told that several top executives of a company in a large city were disturbed by community activist organizations that were protesting the treatment of minority groups. The chief executive had articulated his fears about the activists at local business meetings. However, a young man in the company's personnel department sympathizes with the activists and is spending a great deal of time doing unpaid volunteer work for them. When he is occasionally quoted in the newspaper, he is identified with the employer company. The firm's personnel director is under pressure from several top executives to warn the young man either to stop working for the activists or to resign. What should the personnel director do? The respondents answered as follows:

As long as the person keeps doing a good job, and until there is some concrete factual evidence that the company's public image is being hurt by his association with activists, I shall not interfere.   62 per cent

People in this company and especially this department should be free to express their opinions on public problems. I'll go to bat for the young man as a matter of principle.   19 per cent

I agree it's bad business for the chief executive to be saying one thing and a lesser official to be saying just the opposite. I'll tell the young man he's got to stop.   8 per cent

As long as this person keeps doing a good for the company, I shall not interfere.   6 per cent

This is a question for the chief executive to decide, not you or me.[7]   5 per cent

The above responses provide some interesting insights into the modern manager. The stereotype of the business executive as a conservative and oppressive individual is wide of the mark. Especially in regard to corporate democracy, today's managers indicate that they feel individual liberties and freedoms in the work place are *absolutely necessary*. As expected, younger managers in the study were more liberal and permissive than older ones. However, as the former begin replacing the latter, there will be an even greater trend toward corporate democracy. The above study helped point this out by comparing the responses with those gathered six years earlier in a similar study by the *Harvard Business Review* editors.[8] The later poll showed that managers, on the average, are becoming increasingly concerned with corporate democracy.

SPECIFIC ACTION. If the Harvard survey is accurate and managers are becoming more interested in employee rights, what specific kinds of action are going to have to be undertaken to meet these demands? Hanan sees three necessary developments: an ombudsman's office to handle employee complaints and inquiries; an employee bill of rights; and tenure

---

[6]*Ibid.*, p. 87.
[7]*Ibid.*
[8]David W. Ewing, "Who Wants Corporate Democracy?" *Harvard Business Review*, September–October 1971, pp. 12–28.

agreements tied to middle-management position descriptions.[9] All three are receiving increased attention today.

An *ombudsman* is an individual who handles complaints by investigating problem areas. Some states, for example, have appointed an ombudsman to handle complaints from citizens regarding corruption or inefficiency in state agencies and departments. The individual's job is to cut through red tape and initiate positive action. The same approach is being used in some corporate settings, where the ombudsman listens to complaints and acts as an impartial judge.

> **The ombudsman's domain is developing to include all grievances which adversely affect an individual or a small group of individuals. An ombudsman may function alone as a one-man office. Or he may head an Office of Management Counsel to represent individual interests before the organization. In this enlarged role, the ombudsman's office acts as an impartial tribunal of quasi-judicial review.[10]**

An employee *bill of rights* spells out some of the obligations management has to the workers. This is in direct contrast to the booklet many companies give their new people which relates what the firm expects of them. Some managers, for example, like to comment on the pamphlet they received when they first joined the company, which contained twenty-five pages of duties and obligations and one page of employee rights. As one middle manager stated it, "You learn your responsibilities as soon as you join a company. But you earn the knowledge of your rights one by one over many years. They don't exist anywhere; you have to sense them out. If you sense wrong, or if you sense too much too soon, that's it: you suddenly have another responsibility — to find a new job."[11] The bill of rights (see Chart 20–1) is less a protective device and more a recognition by the company of the freedoms the employees have a right to exercise. Modern organizational personnel feel that corporate life entails some sacrifice of personal liberty, but there is a limit to how much the company may demand.

Tenure agreements for middle managers are, quite simply, employment contracts. They have three very important advantages. First, they acknowledge the individuality of the manager by signifying that, of his or her own volition, the person is willing to perform some service for the corporation and, in turn, will receive some reimbursement. The point to be noted is that the manager chooses to accept the contract; it is not forced upon him or her. Second, this guarantee of employment allows the manager to begin formulating career self-development plans. Third, tenure implies accomplishment and proof of contribution. The manager no longer has to wait for years before being ensured of a permanent place in the organization. He or she is rewarded on the basis of accomplishment, not seniority.

The rise of corporate democracy is actually inevitable. In the late 1950's, Whyte wrote *The Organization Man*, in which he contended that corporate bureaucracies were molding people into company men.[12] The Protestant Ethic, characterized by rugged individualism and thriftiness, was being replaced by a social ethic that put primary emphasis upon conformity to group norms and the need to belong. Today, it appears that

---

[9]Mack Hanan, "Make Way for the New Organization Man," *Harvard Business Review*, July–August 1971, pp. 135–137.

[10]*Ibid.*, p. 135.

[11]*Ibid.*, p. 136.

[12]William H. Whyte, Jr. *The Organization Man* (New York: Doubleday, Anchor Books, 1957).

CHART 20–1   Sample Corporate Bill of Rights

Article 1

Management shall in no way abridge the right of an employee to express his social, economic, political, or religious beliefs within or outside the confines of the organization.

Article 2

The offices, papers, and personal effects of an employee should be secure from unreasonable searches and seizures.

Article 3

No employee shall have to answer for a malfeasance or misfeasance unless management presents to him or her in writing the exact nature and cause of the accusation.

Article 4

If an employee is involved in a dispute, he or she shall be entitled to a public hearing within the organization; have a right to be confronted by those bringing the complaint(s) against him or her; bring in witnesses favorable to his or her position; and be assisted by the company ombudsman or other counsel for his or her defense.

Article 5

No employee shall be dismissed from his or her job without due process of deliberation.

Adapted from Mack Hanan, "Make Way for the New Organization Man," *Harvard Business Review*, July–August 1971, p. 136.

Whyte's fears will not materialize. If anything, industry is putting greater emphasis on individuality. The old organization man is being replaced by a new one who demands freedom of expression as well as personal involvement in organizational affairs.

Managing Executive Talent

During the 1960's and 1970's there was a great demand for young executives, and corporations placed high priority on recruiting this pool of talent. Today, however, this is changing. More and more potential managers are graduating from business schools and the supply is beginning to catch up with the demand. In particular, more people than ever before, including blacks and women, are earning graduate degrees in business:

In 1964, only 6000 graduate degrees were granted in business administration. In 1976, it is estimated that upwards of 30,000 degrees will be awarded, with women receiving some 10 per cent of the total and minority groups receiving 5 per cent. By 1985, it is forecast that the number of graduate degrees in business administration awarded will double this figure, with women making up a whopping 20 per cent of the 60,000 total, or twice the 1964 total.

It is more difficult to judge how minority groups will fare compared to women, but it is generally projected that they will receive less than 5 per cent of the total in 1985. However, this will be almost twice the total number of degrees they received in 1964. Thus not only will the number of highly educated potential business executives increase sharply, but also the effective total — including women and minority groups — will be far greater than might have been projected from reviewing the white, male-dominated past.[13]

---

[13]Arch Patton, "The Coming Flood of Young Executives,": *Harvard Business Review*, September–October 1976, p. 21.

TABLE 20–1 Age Group Trends
1976–1985

1976 Age Group	1976 Total Population (in millions)	Per Cent Increase or Decrease	
		to 1980	to 1985
30–34	13.8	+26	+42
35–39	11.6	+20	+49
40–44	11.1	+ 4	+23
45–49	11.8	− 8	− 3
50–54	11.8	− 3	−10
55–59	10.6	+ 6	+ 3

Source: Arch Patton, "The Coming Flood of Young Executives," *Harvard Business Review*, September–October 1976, p. 21.

The baby boom of the 1940's and 1950's will provide the necessary young management talent for the 1980's (see Table 20–1). Thus, instead of facing a scramble for young executives, business firms will find themselves in a *buyer's* market. However, staffing will get tougher, *not* easier, because the challenge will become one of *managing executive talent*. This situation will have three major consequences for business.

First, young, lower-level executives will not be able to command the large salary increases that they did in recent decades, when demand was greater than supply. To move ahead quickly, young managers will now have to show outstanding performance. This is going to force business into developing a two-track pay system: one for older, experienced executives who are in great demand; and another for new, inexperienced managers who are not in great demand. Patton has described the necessary pay system this way:

> A widening pay spread between the top and bottom of the executive pay scale will make it almost essential during the next decade for companies to formulate a two-track pay system in which tomorrow's relatively few "stars" can receive merit increases at a much faster rate than in the past. This two-track system will be particularly essential if the relatively rapid executive promotion rate of the 1960's slows down perceptibly. In the last decade the pay raise that an outstanding executive received when promoted all too frequently represented the only pay increase differential between his or her increase and the average executive's increase.
>
> The plain fact is that the enormous industrial expansion during the 1950's and 1960's encouraged sloppy salary administration with rapid promotion replacing merit increase as the signal of better-than-average executive performance. When there is less corporate growth, a two-track salary system will provide a normal merit spread for the majority of the executive group but will also allow for a substantially higher top range for the small number of outstanding performers. The upper range of a two-track system, therefore, could be used to offset a decline in the promotion rate if corporate growth slowed moderately.[14]

Second, promotion opportunities for young managers will be fewer. In previous decades, the average company promoted one third of its executives two or more times in a seven year period, one third once during the period, and the last third not at all. In the future, however, it is unlikely that many companies will be able to match this rapid promotion record.

Third, despite these environmental changes, the expectation level of young executives will remain high. In choosing careers and companies, they will be looking for financial opportunities in the form of stock options, bonuses, and other perquisites as well as nonfinancial opportunities in the form of interesting and challenging work. Given such development, management's task during the 1980's will be one of:

---

[14]*Ibid.*, p. 26.

1. Selecting those young executives with the greatest management potential.
2. Motivating these outstanding performers to do their best for the company.
3. Upgrading the importance of all management jobs (especially those at the lower and middle ranks) by forcing decisions down to "where the action is," thereby making the jobs more meaningful.
4. Realizing that the selecting, training and motivating of young executives will require mature managers who are attuned to the company's plans to hire, train and provide incentives for the types of people the business will need during the upcoming decades.[15]

Thus the *future* success of many organizations will depend on their ability to both secure and retain the best available executive talent *today*.

Currently there is a continuing trend toward the professionalization of management. Although many definitions have been given to the word *profession*, the following is one of the most comprehensive:

Continuing Trend Toward Professionalism

A profession is a vocation whose practice is founded upon an understanding of the theoretical structure of some department of learning or science, and upon the abilities accompanying such understanding. This understanding and these abilities are applied to the vital practical affairs of man. The practices of the profession are modified by knowledge of a generalized nature and by the accumulated wisdom and experience of mankind, which serve to correct the errors of specialism. The profession, serving the vital needs of man, considers its first ethical imperative to be altruistic service to the client.[16]

The major criteria for a profession are knowledge, competent application, social responsibility, self-control, and community sanction.[17] Before discussing these it should be noted that management differs from many of the other professions, especially the traditional ones of theology, law, and medicine, in that one cannot rigidly apply a set of conditions. With this in mind, it is possible to show that management is indeed moving toward professionalism.

There are five criteria for a profession.

MANAGEMENT KNOWLEDGE. As seen throughout this book, there has been a tremendous increase in *management knowledge* over the last twenty-five years. As Andrews points out, "No responsible critic . . . will deny that management practice now rests on a developing body of knowledge being systematically extended by valid research methods."[18] Thus, management meets this first criterion.

COMPETENT APPLICATION. Many professions, such as medicine and law, ensure *competent application* by certifying their members for practice. Although this is not the case in management, the surveillance of junior managers by higher-level executives serves the same purpose. Furthermore, ". . . the diversity of business practice, the market mechanism rewarding successful and penalizing unsuccessful entrepreneurship, and the organization means for supervising competence in management all make it impracticable and unnecessary to erect educational requirements in imitation of the formality of law, medicine, and the ministry."[19]

SOCIAL RESPONSIBILITY. This topic was covered in depth in Chapter 18. Today, more than ever before, business is aware of the importance of

---

[15]*Ibid.*, pp. 178, 180.
[16]Cited by Morris L. Cogan in Howard W. Vollmer and Donald L. Mills, *Professionalization* (Englewood Cliffs, N.J.: Prentice-Hall, 1966), p. 10.
[17]Kenneth R. Andrews, "Toward Professionalism in Business Management," *Harvard Business Review*, March–April 1969, pp. 50–51.
[18]*Ibid.*, p. 52.
[19]*Ibid.*, p. 53.

assuming a social role. Although profit is not a dirty word, business is making it increasingly clear that it is pursuing multiple objectives and profit is but one of these.

Other objectives are the provision of goods and services to the customer and the integration of the firm into the everyday life of the community. In this decade many businesses have been formulating *social responsibility* philosophies in way of meeting this criterion.

EMERGENCE OF SELF-CONTROL. Federal and state agencies have been established to regulate business and ensure compliance to prescribed norms. At the national level, for example, are the Federal Drug Administration, Federal Trade Commission, and the Antitrust Division of the Department of Justice. It should be realized, however, that business also exercises degrees of *self-control* as reflected by industry codes of conduct. For example, the National Association of Purchasing Agents has an extensive code, one of its standards being "to buy and sell on the basis of value, recognizing that value represents the combination of quality, service and price which assures greatest ultimate economy to the user." The American Association of Advertising Agencies has an analogous set of standards, one of them being "Advertising shall tell the truth and shall reveal material facts, the concealment of which might mislead the public." Codes such as these will undoubtedly increase in number throughout the ensuing decades. Why? The answer is twofold. First, the public is demanding higher ethical standards. Second, business managers not only believe that ethics are good for business but also feel that an industry code can have many advantages:

> First, it would be a useful aid when businessmen wanted impersonally to refuse an unethical request. Rather than merely turn down an individual, it would be much easier if the executive could point to a code and thus have a nonpersonal basis for refusing. A second advantage would be that a code would help businessmen clearly define the limits of acceptable conduct. Third, it would raise the ethical level of the industry. Fourth, it would, in situations where severe competition existed, reduce cut-throat practices.[20]

There is thus the emergence of self-control.

COMMUNITY SANCTION. The final attribute of a profession, *community sanction*, is also present in management today, even though many groups are not held in esteem by the public. Electricians who are called in to install a new outlet and then charge the home owner $67.50 do little to win community acceptance. Plumbers who fix a sink in five minutes but have a minimum house-call fee of $27.50 leave people angry and disillusioned. Fortunately, however, the management profession does not suffer from such stigmas. "The depression which appears to afflict our society in the presence of . . . rebellious youth, the problems of the cities, and the balance of international payments has not extended to disillusion about the management of our enterprise system."[21] In fact, in many areas such as poverty, housing, and hard-core employment, the public realizes that American management has the technical skill and the organizational expertise to help overcome the problems. If anything, community sanction of management is stronger than ever.

FUTURE DEVELOPMENTS. Of course, management still has a way to go before it will qualify as a profession. However, significant steps have been taken, and this decade will see even greater progress. In particular will be the continuing development of management curricula, including: (a) the

---

[20]Fred Luthans and Richard M. Hodgetts, *Social Issues In Business*, 2nd edition (New York: The Macmillan Company, 1976), p. 53.
[21]Andrews, *op. cit.*, p. 56.

growth of new methods of quantitative analysis associated with the computer; (b) the study of organizational behavior; (c) better concepts for analyzing, understanding, and reacting responsibly to the social, economic, technical, and political environment of business; and (d) the study of policy formulation.[22] This, in turn, will lead to more sophisticated management practices, better self-regulation, and more attention to "people" problems in both the domestic and international arenas.

The purpose of this text has been to identify, define, and place in proper perspective the concepts most important to the modern manager. However, this knowledge alone will not solve all the organization's problems; it will merely provide a basis for formulating intelligent approaches to dealing with each specific situation. From here the manager will have to employ the method which he or she believes will work best. As the late J. Paul Getty, the oil billionaire, has noted:

JUST A BEGINNING

Managerial knowledge is a good beginning.

> . . . to argue that business management is a science, in the sense that chemistry is a science, is to misunderstand the functions of management and to disregard its most significant element: people. Management — the fine art of being boss — is nothing less than the direction of human activities, obtaining results *through* people. Formal business education can only form a basis on which man can build. . . . But no theory in the world holds that a man with one, two or even three degrees in business administration can repair a cracking corporate structure merely because he has a collection of sheepskins hanging on his office wall. Getting results through people is a skill that cannot be learned in a classroom.[23]

When one couples this information with the fact that modern organizations are in a state of flux and the environment promises to become more, not less, dynamic, management may appear to be a profession that should be pursued only by the most daring (or foolhardy). On the other hand, there is much information available to the manager proceeding through the maze of modern organizational problems, and the rewards and challenges promise to make it an exciting career for those who have the potential and the desire.

Management has come a long way since the days of the early classical theorists. It has received contributions from many people in many fields, including psychology, sociology, and anthropology. Thus management thought has not developed in one basic direction. Rather, it has branched out into three schools: management process, quantitative, and behavioral.

SUMMARY

What does the future hold? In one respect it will be more of the same: continued emphasis on systems theory; the development of modern organization structures; increased research on human behavior in organizations; and greater attention to the management of change. There are other developments on the management horizon which also merit mention. These are corporate democracy; the management of executive talent; and the continuing trend toward professionalism.

Managers of the future will need to be aware of these developments. However, this knowledge, in and of itself, is no guarantee of success. The challenges of management are too great to be solved by a simple panacea such as mere knowledge of effective management processes and practices. On the other hand, for those who have the ability and the desire, the opportunities and rewards in the field of management promise to be very great indeed.

---

[22]*Ibid.*, p. 59.
[23]J. Paul Getty, "The Fine Art of Being the Boss," *Playboy*, June 1972, p. 146.

**REVIEW
AND STUDY
QUESTIONS**

1. What contributions did the classical theorists make to management theory?

2. What are the three major schools of management thought? Briefly describe each.

3. What is the contingency school of thought?

4. How are the systems and contingency approaches eclectic in nature?

5. The future will see a continued emphasis on corporate democracy. Explain this statement, incorporating into your answer the results found by the editors of the *Harvard Business Review* in their recent research on this subject.

6. What is a corporate ombudsman? How can this individual be useful to the employees?

7. What is an employee bill of rights? Explain.

8. Why, and how, will the management of executive talent prove to be a challenge to business during the 1980's?

9. What does the term "profession" mean?

10. What are the major criteria for a profession? Explain.

11. Is management a profession? Give your reasoning.

**SELECTED
REFERENCES**

Andrews, K. R. "Toward Professionalism in Business Management." *Harvard Business Review,* March–April, 1969, pp. 49–60.

Boettinger, H. M. "Is Management Really an Art?" *Harvard Business Review,* January–February 1975, pp. 54–64.

Bowman, J. S. "Managerial Ethics in Business and Government." *Business Horizons,* October 1976, pp. 48–54.

Brenner, S. N. A., and E. A. Molander. "Is the Ethics of Business Changing?" *Harvard Business Review,* January–February 1977, pp. 57–71.

Byron, S. J., W. J. "The Meaning of Ethics in Business." *Business Horizons,* December 1977, pp. 31–34.

Drucker, P. F. "New/Old Top Management Aid: The 'Executive Secretariat.' " *Harvard Business Review,* September–October 1973, pp. 6–8.

Duncan, W. J. "Transferring Management Theory to Practice." *Academy of Management Journal,* December 1974, pp. 724–738.

Ewing, D. W. "What Business Thinks About Employee Rights." *Harvard Business Review,* September–October 1977, pp. 81–94.

Ewing, D. W. "Who Wants Corporate Democracy?" *Harvard Business Review,* September–October 1971, pp. 12–28, 146–149.

Ewing, D. W. "Who Wants Employee Rights?" *Harvard Business Review,* November–December 1971, pp. 22–35, 155–160.

Fulmer, R. M. "The Management of Tomorrow." *Business Horizons,* August 1972, pp. 5–13.

Hanan, M. "Make Way for the New Organization Man." *Harvard Business Review,* July–August 1971, pp. 128–138.

House, R. J. "The Quest for Relevance in Management Education: Some Second Thoughts and Undesired Consequences." *Academy of Management Journal,* June 1975, pp. 323–333.

Martin, W. F., and G. C. Lodge. "Our Society in 1985 — Business May Not Like It." *Harvard Business Review,* November–December 1975, pp. 143–152.

Maxwell, S. R. "Corporate Values and the Business School Curriculum." *California Management Review,* Fall 1975, pp. 72–77.

Mee, J. F. "The Manager of the Future." *Business Horizons,* June 1973, pp. 5–14.

Miner, J. B. "Implications of Managerial Talent Projections for Management Education." *Academy of Management Review,* July 1977, pp. 412–420.

Patton, A. "The Coming Flood of Young Executives." *Harvard Business Review,* September–October 1976, pp. 20–22.

Rimler, G. W. "The Death of Management." *Academy of Management Review,* April 1976, pp. 126–128.

Steiner, G. "Invent Your Own Future." *California Management Review,* Fall 1976, pp. 29–33.

Udell, J., G. R. Laczniak, and R. F. Lusch. "The Business Environment of 1985." *Business Horizons,* June 1976, pp. 45–54.

Walters, K. D. "Your Employees' Right to Blow the Whistle." *Harvard Business Review,* July–August 1975, pp. 26–28.

Webber, R. A. "Career Problems of Young Managers." *California Management Review,* Spring 1976, pp. 19–33.

Whyte, Jr., W. H. *The Organization Man.* New York: Doubleday, Anchor Books, 1957.

CASE: A MATTER OF ETHICS[23]

In the last five years, the American public has been shaken by revelations of corporate bribery abroad and illegal campaign donations at home. Are business executives in this country becoming less ethical? This is a difficult question to answer. It is assumed that pressure is on them to compromise their personal ethics, although most say they will not do so. For example, surveys conducted among managers at Pitney-Bowes, world famous manufacturer of business equipment and a leader in the campaign for a code of business ethics, and UniRoyal, the billion dollar rubber and plastics company, revealed the following findings:

	Pitney-Bowes (per cent)	Uniroyal (per cent)
Managers feel pressured to compromise personal ethics to achieve corporate goals.	59	70
Most managers would not refuse orders to market off-standard and possibly dangerous items.	61	54
I personally would refuse to market off-standard and possibly dangerous items.	83	85
Like the junior members of Nixon's re-election committee, young managers automatically go along with superiors to show loyalty.	68	76
I would not give gifts to preferred customers even if other salesmen did.	80	55
Turning in a plausible but incomplete report is unethical.	92	94
Press reports on unethical business practices reveal a valid need for corrective action.	70	unasked
Business ethics are as good as, or better than, ethics in society at large.	90	88

[23]The data in this case can be found in: "The Pressure to Compromise Personal Ethics," *Business Week,* January 31, 1977, p. 107.

Additionally, 90 per cent of the respondents in the two companies supported both a code of ethics for business and the teaching of ethics in business schools. Managers apparently want the leadership to show them what to do, and want to believe that their particular job can be achieved with a high degree of virtue. It is up to the corporate management to confirm this belief.

Questions

1. Based on the survey findings, are ethics considered important by business managers?

2. Do you agree or disagree with the response to the question about whether business ethics are as good as, or better than, ethics in society at large? Defend your answer.

3. How can top business managers provide the leadership necessary to show the rest of the management team that their particular job can be accomplished with a high degree of ethics? Cite some illustrations.

CASE: TELL IT TO THE OMBUDSMAN[24]

Ombudsmen, in one form or another, have been around for 150 years. Usually their goal is to curb abuses of government against individuals. In the early 1970's, corporations began to use ombudsmen also, Xerox and General Electric being two prime examples.

The purpose of the ombudsman is to handle complaints over issues such as salary, job performance appraisals, layoffs, and the scale of employee benefits. Some of these problems can be solved in a few hours; others take weeks. GE ombudsmen, for example, say that they each handle about 150 cases annually. In most instances the procedure is as follows:

The ombudsman goes to an employee's manager to discuss a grievance only if the employee agrees. If the employee, the manager, and the ombudsman cannot work out a settlement that the ombudsman thinks is fair, the GE ombudsman can go to the manager's manager.... But the ombudsmen have no power to overrule managers' decisions.

When the idea of the ombudsman started to become popular in industry, many managers expressed concern over the possibility that the individual would side with the employee to the detriment of management. However, statistics show that this is not what has happened. At Xerox Corporation, for example, one of the ombudsmen relates that his decisions favor the employees about 40 per cent of the time, the management about 30 per cent of the time, and end in compromises the remaining 30 per cent of the time.

One of the most important aspects of the ombudsman's job is to recommend constructive changes in the division producing a multitude of complaints. Of course, companies using ombudsmen admit that they cannot cure everything. However, feedback from this posi-

---

[24]The data in this case can be found in: "Where Ombudsmen Work Out," *Business Week,* May 3, 1976, pp. 114, 116.

tion helps them to recognize the effectiveness of some management policies. As one ombudsman put it, "It's a window through which management can look for a reaction to its style."

Questions

1. In what ways can the ombudsman help ensure corporate democracy?

2. Can ombudsmen really be very effective? After all, are they not merely middlemen trying to work out settlements but possessing no authority to enforce their proposed solutions?

3. Do you think the 1980's will see an increase or decrease in the use of ombudsmen? Explain.

CASE: CAREER PROBLEMS

All young managers face career problems. What should they be doing to ensure themselves upward mobility in the future? How can they be certain that their current career track is the best one for them? Assuming that a manager's goal is to move up the managerial ranks, some of the suggestions that have been offered by various experts include the following:[25]

1. The basic foundation of success is found in good performance that pleases one's superiors. However, since all performance is not easily measured, you must be careful to determine the real criteria by which you are evaluated and be vigorously honest in evaluating your own performance against these criteria.
2. Strive for positions that have high visibility and exposure in which you can be a hero observed by higher officials.
3. Develop relations with a mobile senior executive who can be your sponsor.
4. Learn your job as quickly as possible and train a replacement so you can be available to move.
5. Nominate yourself for other positions. Modesty is not necessarily a virtue.
6. Before taking a position, rigorously assess your strengths and weaknesses, what you like and do not like. Do not accept a promotion if it draws on your weaknesses and entails mainly activities you do not like.
7. Leave at your own convenience but on good terms without practicing criticism of the organization.
8. Do not stay under an immobile superior who is not promoted in three to five years.
9. Accept the fact that responsibility will always exceed authority and organizational politics are inevitable. Establish alliances and fight necessary battles, minimizing upward ones to very important issues.
10. Recognize that you will face ethical dilemmas no matter how moral you try to be. Therefore, from time to time examine your

---

[25]These guidelines can be found in: Ross A. Webber, "Career Problems of Young Managers, *California Management Review,* Summer 1976, p. 29.

personal values and question how much you will sacrifice for the organization.

Questions

1. For the young manager seeking upward mobility, which of the above guidelines is most important? Least important?

2. How likely is it that managers will face ethical dilemmas? How should they handle such problems?

3. In addition to the above, what other recommendations would you make to the young manager seeking upward mobility?

CASE: MANAGEMENT RESEARCH VERSUS MANAGEMENT PRACTICE[26]

Is there a gap between management research and management practice? Many people seem to think so. For example, some management professors claim that their research is ignored by practitioners. One well-known professor has deplored the fact that business executives often fail to use knowledge provided to them by the management sciences. He notes:

> **Some of my graduate students undertook to write to the authors of cases reported in *Operations Research* over the first six years of its publication to determine to what extent the recommendations of the studies had been carried out by management. In no case was there sufficient evidence that the recommendations had been accepted.**

On the other hand, practicing managers complain that there is a big gap between the way scholars say things happen and the way in which they actually occur. One of them put it this way:

> **Most management scientists are still thinking, writing and operating in a world that is far removed from the real world in which most managers operate (and in which I personally have been operating). They often describe nonexistent management problems, tackle relatively minor problems with overkill tools, omit real variables from messy problems and build elegant models comprehensible to only their colleagues. And when managers seem confused or dissatisfied with the results of their activities and reject them, these scientists seem almost to take satisfaction in this confirmation of the crudity and inelegance of the managerial world.**

How can this gap between research and practice be narrowed? One suggestion is the establishment of closer rapport between individual companies and schools of business by having managers work in academia (and vice versa) for short periods of time. Another key suggestion has been:

> **... the founding of a respectable, nonprofit publication designed to evaluate and summarize the best of current research and to report on the status of applications of theory and research. . . . The first year of operations might well cost over $200,000. But as large as that amount is to any uni-**

---

[26]The data in this case can be found in: William G. Ryan, "Management Practice and Research — Poles Apart," *Business Horizons,* June 1977, pp. 23–29.

versity, it would be small for a group of businesses, the organizations to profit most. If this publication were jointly staffed by professors and business executives on loan from their organizations, supported by small professional cadre, the result should be a respected source for both researchers and users.

Questions

1. How much of the research done by professors in business schools do you think is really applied by practicing managers? Explain.

2. In addition to the suggestions given in this case, how else can the gap between theory and practice be reduced?

3. Realistically speaking, how much progress do you believe can be expected between now and 1985? Why?

COMPREHENSIVE CASE: TRENDS AFFECTING MANAGEMENT IN THE 1980's[27]

As the United States enters the 1980's, new trends will be affecting the course of management. One of these is the movement toward a *service economy.* The majority of labor hours in the economic system will be spent in services such as retailing, banking, insurance, and education, as opposed to the production of material goods in fields such as farming, construction, and manufacturing. The United States is the first country to make this move; no nation in history has ever before become a service economy. One of the great challenges presented by such an economy is the need for more managers and supervisors, especially at the lower levels:

Statistics consistently show that for a number of reasons, service work has a smaller span of management than industry or agriculture, so it requires more managers for each 100 workers. This development forecasts a continuing shortage of capable management talent. If the required proportion of managers increases by just one percentage point during the next decade, such as from 10 per cent of the labor force to 11 per cent, about one million new managers and supervisors will be required. Considering the fact that we also have to replace many retiring managers, it is unlikely that we can prepare needed competent managers in the time we have. The result will be a continuing shortage of managers.

A second key development is the shift toward becoming a *knowledge society.* This is a society in which the majority of the work force performs tasks based on knowledge rather than on manual skill. Examples in business organizations include accountants and computer programmers. In society at large, some examples are teachers, lawyers, doctors, and other highly skilled professionals. Here, too, the United States is the first society to reach this plateau, and there are thus few guidelines to rely upon. Yet the effects of this trend will be felt throughout the entire society — in the lifestyles of the people,

---

[27]The data in this case can be found in: Keith Davis, "Some Basic Trends Affecting Management in the 1980s," College and Graduate School of Business Administration, University of Minnesota, Alumni Lecture Series, May 7, 1976.

their motivation, their education, and their business-education experience:

> **The knowledge society also requires a larger proportion of knowledge-oriented, educated citizens. Increasing proportions of people must attend colleges and universities in order to be prepared to assume a useful role in society. No longer are our colleges educating a self-motivated, elite 10 per cent of younger persons. Now they have the upper 50 per cent, many of whom are less motivated and less prepared for intellectual work. Many of these less motivated students feel imprisoned in an educational cycle of 14, 16, or more years before they are ready to enter full-time productive work. . . . A number of approaches have been helpful in reducing this alienation. One is for students to work part-time while finishing advanced education, thereby maintaining a feeling of occupational usefulness. One approach is to introduce more career-oriented educational programs, particularly in community colleges. Another approach is to improve instructional systems in education so that they are more experiential, participative, and self-motivating.**

Another aspect of the knowledge society is the need for employers and educational institutions to enter into closer relationships. Through such collaboration the academic community can better prepare the students for challenging and meaningful business careers.

A third major development is the trend toward a more *socially concerned, humanistic society.* Values are being re-examined and many of them are changing. People are becoming concerned with the broad, complex quality of life instead of mere financial or material gain. This is resulting in a movement *away from* the traditional work ethic and *toward* a less defined social ethic in which social values become *more* central and the work *less* central to people. As a result, employees and customers are "doing their own thing," thereby making it more difficult for companies to establish and maintain employee and customer loyalty. Turnover is increasing in many firms, and those who remain with their companies are insisting on a more participative system in which concern for people ranks as highly as concern for production:

> **A major result of all this concern with quality of life and humanistic values is an emphasis on the *social accountability* of all organizations, public and private. For example, formerly business was viewed as an independent system that could pursue its own interests as long as it obeyed the law. Now business is considered as a system within a larger social system. Business must be concerned about its social inputs as well as its economic outputs. Examples of major areas of concern are equal employment opportunity, urban problems, and ecology.**

At least for the near future, these trends toward social accountability will have obvious consequences. One is value disorientation among those who are unsure of themselves and of their convictions. This will complicate employer-employee relationships. A second result is increased economic costs to businesses and other institutions for restructuring objectives with emphasis on social responsibility. A third is greater government intervention in business and personal life for social, as opposed to purely economic, purposes. Formerly well-defined policies of economic efficiency will be replaced by vague guidelines geared toward social justice, subject to the whims and personal prejudices of those holding government offices.

The fourth major trend, which strongly affects the other three, is that of a *fluctuating, unstable society.* During the 1980's our society will experience a vast amount of change — people will discover themselves under considerable stress resulting from inconsistencies both in family life and job conditions. Some of the predictions made by Alvin Toffler when he spoke of "future shock" will become realities. Families will be uprooted as they change residences every three to four years. Settling in a new locale, friends, acquaintances, educational institutions, and any other roots a family might establish will be temporary at best. People will have to adapt and learn to live in this age of impermanence. So will modern organizations:

Another effect of the unstable society will be more instability in the organizational system. There will be more *ad hoc* **temporary teams, more project organization, and more transfers across organizational lines. Continued emphasis will need to be given to planning for change. Organizational development (OD) programs, which are a way to deal with planned change, are likely to become more common rather than less so.**

Businesses must devise new strategies for coping with modernity. The emphasis of the 1980's will have to be on all the functional areas of management: planning, organizing, controlling, decision making, communicating, motivating, leading, and the development of a social responsibility philosophy. During this decade the environment will be changing dramatically and the modern manager will have to run to keep up. Yet all is not beyond hope. As Davis notes:

Although some managerial stress and disorientation will occur, managers will have an exciting, challenging job. They will work not for perfection (because that is impossible in an uncertain world), but for a high batting average. The best of their intellectual abilities will be required to achieve results that meet human expectations. There will be disappointment, but also successes. THE FUTURE IS AN OPPORTUNITY, NOT A PROBLEM.

Questions

1. Of the four major trends discussed in this case, which will have the greatest impact on organizations of the 1980's? Explain.

2. How should the modern organization go about dealing with the trend you identified above?

3. Outline a plan of action for helping the manager of the 1980's deal with the other three major trends discussed in this case. Integrate your answer with that of number two above.

GLOSSARY OF TERMS

This glossary contains definitions of many of the concepts and terms used in this book. For the most part, the terms correspond to those given in the text and represent ones that the reader is most likely to encounter in the business world. In addition, a few extra definitions not included ·in the book have been added to provide the most comprehensive and useful glossary possible.

Absoluteness of Responsibility — Managers cannot avoid responsibility for the activities of their subordinates. They may delegate authority to their people but they cannot delegate all the responsibility.

Acceptance Theory of Authority — Popularized through the writings of Chester I. Barnard, this theory states that the ultimate source of authority is the subordinate who chooses either to accept or reject orders given to him by his superior.

Activity — An operation required to accomplish a particular event in a PERT network.

Ad Hoc Committee — A committee that is appointed for a specific purpose and, once the job is completed, is disbanded.

Administrative Man — A term used to describe an individual who employs satisficing behavior by looking for a course of action that is satisfactory or good enough, in contrast to an individual who attempts to select the best alternative from among all those available. (See *Economic Man*.)

Aggression — A frustration reaction, it consists of attacking, either physically or symbolically, the barrier(s) preventing goal attainment.

Analog Computer — A measuring machine used principally by engineers in solving job-related problems.

Authority — The right to command.

Automation — The technique of making an apparatus, a process, or a system operate automatically.

Avoidance — A frustration reaction, it entails withdrawing from a situation that is too frustrating to endure.

Balance Theory — A theory used in the study of communication to explain how people react to change. In essence, the theory places primary attention on the consideration of three relationships: (a) the attitude of the receiver toward the sender; (b) the attitude of the receiver toward the new change; and (c) the receiver's perception of the sender's own attitude toward the change.

Basic Socio-Economic Purpose — The reason for an organization's existence.

Behavioral School — A modern school of management thought consisting of those individuals who view management as a psychosociological process. Advocates of this school are very concerned with topics such as needs, drives, motivation, leadership, personality, behavior, work groups, and the management of change.

Benevolent-Authoritative Leadership Style — A basic leadership style in which management acts in a condescending manner toward the subordinates and decision making at the lower levels occurs within a prescribed framework.

Black Box Concept — The inner workings that take place between the input and the output. As applied to human behavior, there may be the introduction of a new wage incentive payment scheme (input) and a 10 per cent increase in productivity (output). The reason for the change may be the wage plan or it may be accounted for by some other cause. The answer is found in the black box or transformation process which occurs between the input and the output.

Branch Organization — Often employed in foreign operations, it is simply an overseas office set up by the parent company.

Break-Even Point — The volume of sales sufficient to cover all fixed and variable expenses but providing no profit.

Budget — A type of plan that specifies anticipated results in numerical terms and serves as a control device for feedback, evaluation, and follow-up.

Carrying Costs — Costs associated with keeping inventory on hand, including sundry expenses such as storage space, taxes, and obsolescence.

Centralization — A system of management in which major decisions are made at the upper levels of the hierarchy.

Certainty Decisions — Decision situations in which the manager knows all the alternatives and the outcomes of each.

Civil Rights Act — Legislation that forbids discrimination based on race, color, religion, sex, or national origin and provides, through the Equal Employment Opportunity Commission, an agency for dealing with complaints or charges of discrimination.

Closed System — A system that does not interact with its external environment.

COBOL — A computer programming language designed especially for business. The word is derived from "common business oriented language."

Common Market — A European economic community formed in 1957 by France, West Germany, Italy, Holland, Belgium, and Luxembourg. Today Great Britain, Denmark, and Ireland are also members.

Communication Process — The conveying of meaning from sender to receiver.

Completed Staff Work — Staff work whose completed recommendation or solution can be either approved or disapproved by a line executive without the need for any further investigation.

Comprehensive Budgeting — A budgeting process that covers all phases of operations.

Comprehensive Planning — Planning that incorporates all levels of the organization: top, middle, and lower.

Compulsory Staff Service — A concept developed centuries ago by the Catholic Church that requires superiors to solicit the advice of their subordinates before making any decision.

Computer Program — A set of instructions that tells the computer what to do.

Consultative-Democratic Leadership Style — A basic leadership style in which management has confidence and trust in the subordinates and a great deal of decision making is carried out at the lower levels.

Contingency Model of Leadership Effectiveness — A leadership model developed by Fred Fiedler which postulates that a leader's effectiveness is determined by three variables: (a) how well the leader is accepted by the subordinates; (b) the degree to which the subordinates' jobs are routine and spelled out in contrast to being vague and undefined; and (c) the formal authority provided for in the position the leader occupies.

Controlling Process — The process of determining that everything is going according to plan. In essence, controlling consists of three steps: (a) the establishment of standards; (b) the comparison of performance against standards; and (c) the correction of deviations that have occurred.

Critical Path — The longest path in a PERT network, beginning with the first event and ending with the last one.

Decentralization — A system of management in which a great deal of decision-making authority rests at the lower levels of the hierarchy.

Decision Making — The process of choosing from among alternatives.

Decision Theory — A term used to describe how managers make decisions under conditions of certainty, risk, and uncertainty.

Decision Tree — An operations research tool that permits: (a) the identification of alternative courses of action in solving a problem; (b) the assignment of probability estimates to the events associated with these alternatives; and (c) the calculation of the payoffs corresponding to each act-event combination.

Delegation of Authority — The process a manager employs in distributing work to the subordinates.

Delphi Technique — A method for forecasting future developments, especially technological discoveries.

Departmentalization — The process of grouping jobs on the basis of some common characteristic, i.e., function, product, territory, customer, process.

Derivative Departments — Departments that are formed when the activities of a major department are subdivided. For example, derivative production departments might include manufacturing and purchasing. (See Figure 6–3 in the text.)

Differential Piece-Rate System — An incentive wage system formulated by Frederick W. Taylor that paid a fixed rate per piece for all production up to standard and a higher rate for all pieces if the standard was met.

Digital Computer — A counting machine which by use of electrical impulses can perform arithmetic calculations far in excess of human capacity. This computer is widely used by business firms.

Discounted Cash Flows — The statement of future cash flows in terms of current dollars.

Division of Work — Breaking down a job into simple routine tasks so that each worker can become a specialist in handling one particular phase of the operation. The result is often increased efficiency.

Domestic System — The basic stage of a materially productive civilization in which individuals, assured of their own survival, begin specializing in an area (such as fabricating textiles) and then sell the goods at the local fair for whatever they will bring. This system was predominant in England in the early eighteenth century.

Economic Man — A term used to identify a person who makes decisions that maximize his or her economic objectives.

Econometrics — A mathematical approach used in economic forecasting.

EDP — Electronic data processing.

Enlightened Self-Interest — A doctrine that states that by helping out the community, business is actually serving its own long-run interests.

Entropy — The tendency of a closed system to move toward a chaotic, random, or inert state.

EOQ Formula — An economic order quantity model useful to the manager in determining how many units to reorder when replenishing inventory.

Equal Pay Act — Legislation designed to correct the existence of wage differentials based on sex in industries engaged in commerce or the production of goods for commerce.

Equity or Social Comparison Theory — A theory that contends that people are motivated not only by what they receive but also by what they see, or believe, others are receiving. Individuals compare their rewards with those of others in judging whether or not they are receiving equitable remuneration.

Esprit de Corps — One of Fayol's principles of management, it means that "in union there is strength."

Event — A point in time when an activity is begun or finished. (See *Program Evaluation and Review Technique* and *Activity*.)

Exception Principle — Managers should concern themselves with exceptional cases and not with routine results.

Expectancy — The probability that a specific action will be followed by a particular first-level outcome. (See *First-Level Outcome*.)

Expectancy Theory — A theory of motivation that holds that individuals will be high-performers when they: (1) see a high probability that their efforts will lead to high performance; (2) see a high probability that high performance will lead to specific outcomes; and (3) view these outcomes as personally desirable.

Expectancy-Valence Theory — A motivation theory formulated by Victor Vroom which states that motivation is equal to the summation of valence times expectancy. (See *Instrumentality, Valence* and *Expectancy*.)

Expected Time — A time estimate for each activity in a PERT network calculated by using the following formula:

$$t_E = \frac{t_o + 4t_m + t_p}{6}$$

where t_E = expected time
t_o = optimistic time
t_m = most likely time
t_p = pessimistic time

Exploitive-Authoritative Leadership Style — A basic leadership style in which management has little confidence in the subordinates and decision making tends to be highly centralized.

Exploratory Forecast — A technological forecasting technique which assumes that future technological progress will continue at the present rate. This technique moves from the present to the future and considers technical factors most heavily.

Extrapolation — The simplest form of economic forecast, it consists of merely projecting current trends into the future.

Factory System — The final stage in the evolution of a materially productive civilization (see *Domestic System* and *Putting-Out System*) characterized by the introduction of power-driven machinery. Instead of work being done in the home, the workers now come to one central site where the machinery is located, namely, the factory.

First-Level Outcome — A factor that brings about a second-level outcome. For example, in many companies, productivity (first-level outcome) leads to promotion (second-level outcome).

Fixed Costs — Costs that will remain constant (at least in the short-run) regardless of operations. Property taxes and administrative salaries are illustrations.

Flat Organization Structure — An organization structure in which there is a wide span of control with only a small number of levels in the hierarchy.

Forecasting — A method of projecting future business conditions for the purpose of establishing goals and budgets.

Formal Organization — The officially designated jobs and relationships in an organization as seen on the organization chart and reflected in the job descriptions.

Formal Theory of Authority — A theory that holds that the source of authority is found in the right of private property provided for in the Constitution and flows down the organization structure from the president to the lowest worker. As such, the theory supports the hierarchical structure of the organization. (For a marked contrast, see *Acceptance Theory of Authority*.)

FORTRAN — A computer programming language designed for scientific work. The word is derived from "formula translation."

Free-Form Organization Structure — See *Organic Organization Structure*.

Functional Authority — Authority in a department other than one's own, as seen in the case of the comptroller who can order production personnel to provide him or her with cost per unit data.

Functional Departmentalization — A department organized along the lines of major activities. In a manufacturing firm so organized, it is not uncommon to find marketing, production, and finance departments reporting directly to the president.

Functional Foremanship — A concept developed by Frederick W. Taylor whereby the functions of the foreman were divided into eight separate subfunctions, each one assigned to an individual foreman. In this way, each foreman could concentrate his attention on one aspect of the job, i.e., inspection, repair, discipline, rather than having to carry out all eight. Taylor believed that such a division of work would result in increased efficiency.

Fusion Process — The process by which the individual and the organization, when they come together, tend to influence each other's objectives.

Game Theory — Theory used in operations research to study conflict-of-interest situations.

Gangplank Principle — Developed by Henri Fayol, this principle holds that individuals at the same level of the hierarchy should be allowed to communicate directly, provided they have permission from their superiors to do so and they tell their respective chiefs afterwards what they have agreed to do. The purpose of the principle is to cut red tape while maintaining the integrity of the hierarchy.

Gantt Chart — A chart on which progress on various parts of an undertaking are compared with time.

Grapevine — The informal communication channel in an organization.

Gross National Product (GNP) — The value of goods and services produced in a year.

Hawthorne Effect — The novelty or interest in a new situation which leads, at least initially, to positive results.

Hawthorne Studies — Studies that provided the impetus for the human relations movement. Conducted at the Western Electric plant in Chicago, Illinois, the research had four major phases: (a) illumination experiments; (b) relay assembly test room experiments; (c) massive interviewing program; and (d) the bank wiring observation room study.

Heuristic Programming — An operations research technique that employs both rules of thumb and the use of trial-and-error.

Hierarchy of Objectives — Short-run objectives are related to intermediate-range objectives which, in turn, tie in to long-range objectives. There is thus an interrelated hierarchy of objectives throughout the organization.

Human Resources Accounting — A recent development in management which attempts to: (a) view the acquisition of organizational personnel as an investment and (b) obtain a regular evaluation of these assets.

Human Relations Philosophy — A philosophy that holds that the business organization is a social system and that employees are largely motivated and controlled by the human relationships in that system.

Human Resources Philosophy — A philosophy that holds that individuals do not want merely to be treated well (see *Human Relations Philosophy*); they want an opportunity to contribute creatively to organizational problems (see *Theory Y*).

Hygiene Factors — Identified by Frederick Herzberg in his two-factor theory of motivation, the term refers to factors that will not motivate people by their presence but will cause dissatisfaction by their absence. Some of the hygiene factors he identified include money, security, and working conditions.

Industrial Psychology — A subfield of psychology concerned with applying psychological knowledge to the selection, training, and development of organizational personnel.

Informal Group Norms — Sentiments to which individuals must adhere if they wish to be accepted as members of a group. In the bank wiring observation room, for example, these included: (a) you should not turn out too much work; (b) you should not turn out too little work; (c) you should not tell a superior anything to the detriment of an associate; (d) you should not attempt to maintain social distance or act officious; and (e) you should not be noisy, self-assertive, or anxious for leadership.

Informal Organization — The unofficially designated relationships in an organization not shown on the organization chart and often not reflected in the job descriptions.

Information Design — A process of filtering the number and kinds of reports and other data being sent to managers to prevent their being inundated with irrelevant information.

Institutional Level — Upper level of the organization concerned with relating the overall organization to its environment.

Institutional Managers — Top level managers concerned with surveying the environment and developing cooperative and competitive strategies that will ensure the organization's survival. These managers tend to have a philosophical point of view.

Instrumentality — The relationship an individual perceives between a first- and second-level outcome. (See *First-Level Outcome* and *Second-Level Outcome*.)

Intermediate-Range Planning — The setting of subobjectives and substrategies that are in accord with the long-run objectives and strategies of the overall plan.

Intervening Variables — Internal, unobservable, psychological processes that account for human behavior. These variables cannot be measured directly; they must be inferred. Motivation is an example.

Job Description — Description of the authority and responsibilities that accompany a job.

Job Enlargement — Increasing the number of tasks being performed by an individual in an attempt to make the work more psychologically rewarding.

Job Enrichment — Popularized by M. Scott Myers, this involves building motivators (see *Motivational Factors*) into the job in an effort to allow the worker to satisfy some of his or her higher-level needs.

Joint Venture — An enterprise undertaken by two or more parties. In foreign trade, it often consists of a foreign corporation, such as a U.S. business firm, and a local partner.

Key Area Control — A control technique by which a firm measures its performance in a number of vital areas. At General Electric, for example, these areas include profitability, market position, productivity, product leadership, personnel development, employee attitudes, public responsibility, and integration of short- and long-range objectives.

Lag Indicators — Series of economic indicators which often follow changes in the economic cycle.

Laplace Criterion — A basis for decision making in which the manager applies equal probabilities to all states of nature.

Law of Triviality — Formulated by C. Northcote Parkinson, this law states that the time spent on any agenda item will be in inverse proportion to the monetary sum involved.

Lead Indicators — Series of economic indicators which often precede changes in the economic cycle.

Leadership — A process of influencing people to direct their efforts toward the achievement of some particular goal(s).

Learned Behavior — Behavior based on some form of reinforcement (or lack of it).

Life Cycle Theory of Leadership — A leadership theory developed by Paul Hersey and Kenneth Blanchard that contends that as the maturity of the followers increases, appropriate leadership behavior requires varying degrees of task and relationship orientation.

Line Authority — Direct authority, as in the case of a superior who can give orders directly to a subordinate.

Line Department — A department concerned with attaining the basic objectives of the organization. In a manufacturing firm, production, marketing, and finance would be line departments.

Linear Programming — A mathematical technique for determining optimum answers in cases in which a linear relationship exists among the variables.

Management — The process of getting things done through people.

Management Audit — An evaluation of how well the management has operated the organization. Some criteria often employed in this evaluation include production efficiency, health of earnings, fairness to stockholders, and executive ability.

Management by Objectives — A process in which superior and subordinate jointly identify common goals, define the subordinate's areas of responsibility in terms of expected results, and use these measures as guides in operating the unit and evaluating the subordinate's contribution.

Management Functions — The activities managers perform in carrying out their jobs. The most commonly accepted are planning, organizing, and controlling.

Management Process School — Modern school of management thought whose adherents believe that the way to study management is through a systematic analysis of the managerial functions, i.e., planning, organizing, and controlling.

Management Science — See *Operations Research*.

Management Systems — Basic leadership styles identified by Rensis Likert. In essence, there are four: exploitive-authoritative, benevolent-authoritative, consultative-democratic, and participative-democratic.

Managerial Grid — A two-dimensional leadership model that permits simultaneous consideration of "concern for production" and "concern for people."

Marginal Cost — The costs incurred by selling one more unit of output.

Marginal Physical Product — The extra output obtained by adding one unit of input while all other factors are held constant. For example, the extra output obtained by adding one unit of labor while holding all other inputs constant.

Marginal Revenue — The additional revenue obtained by selling one more unit of output.

Matrix Structure — A hybrid form of organization containing characteristics of both project and functional structures.

Maximax Criterion — A basis for decision making in which the manager determines the greatest payoff for each strategy and then chooses the one that is most favorable. In so doing, he or she maximizes the maximum gain.

Maximin Criterion — A basis for decision making in which the manager determines the most negative payoff for each strategy and then chooses the one that is most favorable. In so doing, he or she maximizes the minimum gain.

Mechanistic Organization Structure — An organization structure that is often effective in a stable environment where technology does not play a significant role.

Microchronometer — A clock with a large sweeping hand capable of recording time to 1/2000 of a minute. Developed by Frank Gilbreth, the clock is still of use today in photographing time and motion patterns.

Milestone Scheduling — A scheduling and controlling procedure that employs bar charts to monitor progress. In essence, it is very similar to a Gantt chart but its use is not restricted to production activities.

MIS — Management information system.

Monte Carlo Technique — An operations research technique that makes use of simulation and random numbers in arriving at optimal solutions.

Mooney and Reiley's Principles of Organization — According to James D. Mooney and Alan C. Reiley, the first principle of organization is coordination, which is implemented through the chain of command (process) and results in the definition of duties for all individuals in the hierarchy (effect). Taking this principle-process-effect concept and employing a framework developed by Lewis F. Anderson in which every principle, process, and effect has its own principle, process, and effect, the two authors were able, via deductive reasoning, to develop a logically complete three-by-three matrix.

Motion Study — The process of analyzing work in order to determine the preferred motions for completing the job most efficiently.

Motivational Factors — Identified by Frederick Herzberg in his two-factor theory of motivation, the term refers to those factors that will build high levels of motivation and job satisfaction. Some of the motivational factors he identified include recognition, advancement, and achievement.

Multinational Corporation — Any firm that has a large percentage of its operations devoted to activities in more than one country.

Need Hierarchy — A widely accepted framework of motivation developed by Abraham H. Maslow. In essence, the theory states that:
1. There are five levels of needs. In order of importance they are: physiological, safety, social, esteem, and self-actualization.
2. Only those needs not yet satisfied influence behavior.
3. When one level of needs has been satisfied, the next higher level emerges as dominant and influential.

Non-Zero-Sum Games — Games in which gains by one side do not automatically result in equal losses to the other side.

Normative Forecasting — A technological forecasting technique that begins with the identification of some future technological objective and works back to the present, identifying problem areas that will have to be surmounted along the way. This approach considers both technological and nontechnological factors.

Normative Reality — Interpretive reality as manifested by personal opinion.

Ombudsman — An individual who handles complaints by making inquiries and investigating problem areas.

Open System — A system that is in constant interaction with its external environment.

Operational Planning — The setting of short-run goals and targets that are in accord with the subobjectives and substrategies of the intermediate-range plan.

Operations Research — The application of mathematical tools and techniques to the decision-making process.

Optimistic Time — See *Expected Time*.

Optimization — The combining of elements in just the right balance, often to secure maximum profit.

Organic Functions — Activities that must be carried out if an organization wishes to remain in existence. In a manufacturing firm, for example, these would include marketing, production, and finance.

Organic Organization Structure — An organization structure that is most effective in a dynamic environment where technology plays a significant role. These structures can take any design and hence are also known as free-form structures.

Organization Chart — A diagram of an organization's departments and their relationships to each other.

Organizational Level — Middle level of a company concerned with coordinating and integrating work performance at the technical level. (See Chapter 15.)

Organizational Managers — Middle managers whose goal is to bring together the technical and institutional levels in some harmonious fashion. These managers tend to have a political or mediating point of view. (See Chapter 15.)

Organizational Behavior Modification — A behavioral technique designed to modify behavior by rewarding correct conduct and punishing or ignoring incorrect conduct.

Organizing Function — The assignment of duties and the coordination of efforts among all organizational personnel to ensure maximum efficiency in the attainment of predetermined objectives.

Participative-Democratic Leadership Style — A basic leadership style in which management has complete confidence and trust in the subordinates and decision making is highly decentralized.

Payback Period — The time it takes for an investment to pay for itself.

Perception — A person's view of reality.

Personal Power — Informal authority that is created or sustained by factors such as experience, drive, association with the right groups, and education.

Pessimistic Time — See *Expected Time.*

Planning Function — The formulation of objectives and the steps that will be employed in attaining them.

Planning Organization — An organization designed specifically to help a company develop a comprehensive and logical approach to planning at all levels of the hierarchy.

Plural Executives — Committees that have the authority to order their recommendations implemented.

Policy — A general guide to thinking and action.

Primacy of Planning Principle — At least initially, planning precedes all the other managerial functions.

Principle-Process-Effect — A framework for analysis developed by Lewis F. Anderson and employed by James D. Mooney and Alan C. Reiley in formulating principles of organization. (See *Mooney and Reiley's Principles of Organization.*)

Principles of Management — General guidelines (although in the case of the classical theorists, these were basically flexible) useful to the manager in carrying out his or her activities.

Principles of Scientific Management — As set forth by Frederick W. Taylor, there were four:
1. Develop a science for each element of a man's work, which replaces the old rule-of-thumb method.
2. Scientifically select and then train, teach, and develop the workman, whereas in the past he chose his own work and trained himself as best he could.
3. Heartily cooperate with the men to ensure that all the work being done is in accordance with the principles of the science that has been developed.
4. There is almost an equal division of work and responsibility between the management and the workmen. The management takes over all work for which it is better fitted than the workmen, whereas in the past almost all of the work and the greater part of the responsibility were thrown upon the men.

Probability — The likelihood that a particular event will occur.

Procedure — A guide to action that relates the chronological steps entailed in attaining some objective, such as allowing a person to return faulty merchandise.

Product Departmentalization — A department that is organized along product lines. General Electric, for example, uses this approach, as seen by its consumer product group. So, too, do General Motors, Ford Motor, Chrysler, and a host of other large organizations.

Productivity — Output/input.

Profession — A vocation whose practice is founded upon an understanding of some department of learning or science, or upon the abilities accompanying such understanding. Major criteria include: (a) knowledge; (b) competent application; (c) social responsibility; (d) self-control; and (e) community sanction.

Profit — The remainder after expenses are deducted from revenues.

Program Evaluation and Review Technique (PERT) — A sophisticated time-event network series that permits a manager to evaluate and control the progress of a complex undertaking. (See *Event* and *Activity*.)

Project Authority — Authority exercised by the project manager over the personnel assigned to him or her for the project. In contrast to functional authority, project authority flows horizontally. (See Chapter 17.)

Projection — A frustration reaction, it involves blaming others for one's own shortcomings.

Psychology — The study of human behavior.

Putting-Out System — The second stage in the evolution of a materially productive civilization (see *Domestic System*) initially characterized by an entrepreneur's agreeing to take all the output an individual (or family) can produce at a fixed price. This eventually progressed to the stage where the entrepreneur provided the workers with the raw materials and paid them on a piece-rate basis for the finished goods.

Quantitative School — A modern school of management thought consisting of those individuals who view management as a system of mathematical models and processes. Advocates of this school are greatly concerned with decision making. This school had its genesis with the scientific management movement.

Queuing Theory — An operations research technique used for balancing waiting lines and service.

Rabble Hypothesis — The belief that the workers are a disorganized group of individuals, each one acting in his or her own self-interest.

Responsibility — The obligation of a subordinate to perform assigned tasks.

Return on Investment — A control technique used to determine how well a firm is managing its assets. In essence, the ROI computation is:

$$\frac{Earnings}{Sales} \times \frac{Sales}{Total \ Investment}$$

Reverie — Daydreaming.

Risk Decisions — Decision situations in which the manager has some information on the outcomes of each alternative and can formulate probability estimates based on this knowledge.

Rule — An inflexible guide to action such as a "No Smoking" edict.

Saddle Point — A term used in game theory to identify an ideal strategy.

Sales Forecast — A method used for projecting future sales. Some of the common techniques used include survey of current sales information, the jury of executive opinion, the grassroots method, and user expectation. (See Chapter 5 for a description of each of these techniques.)

Satisficing — Striving for a level that is satisfactory or good enough.

Scalar Chain — The chain of command that runs from the top of an organization to its lowest ranks.

Scientific Management — A system of management, popularized by Frederick W. Taylor and others in the early twentieth century, that sought to develop: (a) ways of increasing productivity by making work easier to perform and (b) methods for motivating the workers to take advantage of these labor-saving devices and techniques.

Scientific Method — A logical problem-solving process used in identifying the problem, diagnosing the situation, gathering preliminary data, classifying the information, stating a tentative answer to the problem, and testing the answer.

Second-Level Outcome — The effect brought about by a first-level outcome. For example, in many companies productivity (first-level outcome) leads to promotion (second-level outcome).

Sensitivity Training — A form of training designed to make managers more aware of their own feelings and those of others.

Sensory Reality — Physical reality such as a house or a chair.

Simulation — As used in a business setting, these are often mathematical models designed to provide answers to "what if" questions.

Situational Theory — A theory that views leadership as multidimensional, consisting of the leader's personality, the requirements of the task, the expectations, needs, and attitudes of the followers, and the environment in which they are operating.

Slack Time — The time difference between scheduled completion and each of the paths in a PERT network.

Social Responsibility — The obligations business has to society, especially in the areas of equal opportunity, ecology, and consumerism.

Sociology — The study of group behavior.

Soldiering — A term used by scientific managers, especially Frederick W. Taylor, to describe the workers' practice of restricting output.

Span of Control — The number of subordinates who report to a given superior.

Staff Authority — Auxiliary authority as seen in the case of individuals who advise, assist, recommend, or facilitate organizational activities. An example is the company lawyer who advises the president on the legality of contract matters.

Staff Department — A department that provides assistance and support to line departments in attaining basic objectives of the organization. In a manufacturing firm, purchasing and accounting would be staff departments.

Staff Independence — A concept developed centuries ago by the Catholic Church whereby advisors are neither appointed by the person they advise nor removable by him, thereby avoiding the yes-man pitfall.

Status — Attributes that rank and relate individuals in an organization.

Strategic Planning — The determination of an organization's major objectives and the policies and strategies that will govern the acquisition, use, and disposition of resources in achieving these objectives.

Subsidiary — A company owned partially or completely by another.

System — A combination of parts forming a complex or unitary whole.

Tall Organization Structure — An organization structure in which there is a narrow span of control with a large number of levels in the hierarchy. (For a contrast, see *Flat Organization Structure*.)

Task and Bonus System — A payment plan developed by Henry Gantt that guaranteed each worker a day's wage and a bonus if he accomplished the task assigned to him for that day.

Technical Level — Low organizational level concerned primarily with the production and distribution of goods and services.

Technical Managers — Low-level managers concerned with turning out goods and services as economically as possible. These managers tend to have an engineering point of view.

Tenure Agreements — Employment contracts.

Territorial Departmentalization — A department that is organized along the lines of geographic location. An example is found in the company with four major divisions: eastern, midwestern, western, and foreign.

Theory X — A set of assumptions that holds that people: (a) dislike work; (b) have little ambition; (c) want security above all else; and (d) must be coerced, controlled, and threatened with punishment in order for them to attain organizational objectives.

Theory Y — A set of assumptions that holds that: (a) if the conditions are favorable, people will not only accept responsibility, they will seek it; (b) if people are committed to organizational objectives, they will exercise self-direction and self-control; and (c) commitment is a function of the rewards associated with goal attainment.

Therblig — A term used in time and motion study to identify a basic hand motion such as "grasp" or "hold." The word is formed by spelling Gilbreth backwards with the "t" and "h" transposed.

Three-Dimension Leadership Model — A leadership model developed by William J. Reddin that stresses the importance of three factors: (a) task orientation; (b) relationships orientation; and (c) effectiveness.

Time Study — A method of determining the time it takes to perform a particular task. The procedure often involves the use of a stopwatch for timing all the various elements associated with the task, e.g., the time for picking up a piece of material, positioning it, or inserting it into the machine. Time study was widely used by the scientific managers in determining a fair day's work and is still employed in industrial settings today.

Time-Event Analyses — Control techniques that permit the manager to monitor and evaluate elapsed time and attained progress on an undertaking.

Trait Theory — A theory of leadership that attempts to relate success to an individual's personal characteristics or traits.

Transactional Analysis (TA) — A technique designed to help the managers communicate with and understand their people through an analysis of their own behavior as well as that of the subordinates.

Transformation Process — See *Black Box Concept.*

Two-Way Communication — Transmission of information and ideas both up and down the hierarchy.

Uncertainty Decisions — Decision situations in which managers feel they cannot develop probability estimates because they have no way of gauging the likelihood of the various alternatives.

Unity of Command — A management principle that states that a subordinate should report to only one superior.

Unity of Direction — See *Unity of Management.*

Unity of Management — One of Fayol's classical principles, it calls for one manager and one plan for all operations having the same objective. Another term often given to this is unity of direction.

Valence — A person's preference for a first-level outcome. (See *First-Level Outcome.*)

Variable Costs — Costs that change in relation to output. Labor salaries and cost of materials are examples.

Zero-Sum Games — Games in which gains by one side are offset by losses to the other side.

AUTHOR INDEX

SUBJECT INDEX